T0377249

JAZZ AND TOTALITARIANISM

Jazz and Totalitarianism examines jazz in a range of regimes that in significant ways may be described as totalitarian, historically covering the period from the Franco regime in Spain beginning in the 1930s to present-day Iran and China. The book presents an overview of the two central terms and their development since their contemporaneous appearance in cultural and historiographical discourses in the early twentieth century, comprising fifteen essays written by specialists on particular regimes situated in a wide variety of time periods and places. Interdisciplinary in nature, this compelling work will appeal to students from Music and Jazz Studies to Political Science, Sociology, and Cultural Theory.

Bruce Johnson, formerly a professor in English, is now Adjunct Professor, Communications, University of Technology Sydney, Visiting Professor, Music, University of Glasgow, and Docent and Visiting Professor, Cultural History, University of Turku.

Transnational Studies in Jazz
Series Editors: Tony Whyton, University of Salford, UK, and
Nicholas Gebhardt, Birmingham City University, UK

Transnational Studies in Jazz presents cross-disciplinary and global perspectives on the development and history of jazz and explores its many social, political, and cultural meanings.

Jazz Sells: Music, Marketing, and Meaning
Mark Laver

The Cultural Politics of Jazz Collectives: This is Our Music
Edited by Nicholas Gebhardt and Tony Whyton

JAZZ AND TOTALITARIANISM

Edited by Bruce Johnson

WITH ADVISORY EDITORS
PEDRO CRAVINHO AND HELI REIMANN

NEW YORK AND LONDON

First published 2017
by Routledge
711 Third Avenue, New York, NY 10017

and by Routledge
2 Park Square, Milton Park, Abingdon, Oxon, OX14 4RN

Routledge is an imprint of the Taylor & Francis Group, an informa business

© 2017 Taylor & Francis

The right of Bruce Johnson to be identified as the author of the editorial
material, and of the authors for their individual chapters, has been asserted in
accordance with sections 77 and 78 of the Copyright, Designs and Patents Act
1988.

All rights reserved. No part of this book may be reprinted or reproduced or
utilized in any form or by any electronic, mechanical, or other means, now
known or hereafter invented, including photocopying and recording, or in any
information storage or retrieval system, without permission in writing from the
publishers.

Trademark notice: Product or corporate names may be trademarks or registered
trademarks, and are used only for identification and explanation without intent
to infringe.

Library of Congress Cataloging in Publication Data
Names: Johnson, Bruce, 1943– editor.
Title: Jazz and totalitarianism/edited by Bruce Johnson; with advisory editors
Pedro Cravinho and Heli Reimann.
Description: New York, NY; Abingdon, Oxon: Routledge, 2016. |
"2016 | Includes index.
Identifiers: LCCN 2015035489 | ISBN 9781138887817 (hardback) |
ISBN 9781138887824 (paperback) | ISBN 9781315713915 (ebook)
Subjects: LCSH: Jazz—Political aspects—History—20th century. |
Totalitarianism and music. | Jazz—History and criticism.
Classification: LCC ML3918.J39 J38 2016 | DDC 781.6509—dc23
LC record available at http://lccn.loc.gov/2015035489

ISBN: 978-1-138-88781-7 (hbk)
ISBN: 978-1-138-88782-4 (pbk)
ISBN: 978-1-315-71391-5 (ebk)

Typeset in Bembo
by Keystroke, Station Road, Codsall, Wolverhampton

CONTENTS

Series Foreword	*ix*
List of Contributors	*xi*
Preface	*xvii*
Acknowledgements	*xix*

Introduction   1
Bruce Johnson

PART I
Totalitarian Templates   29

1   Jazz and Fascism: Contradictions and Ambivalences
in the Diffusion of Jazz Music under the Italian Fascist
Dictatorship (1925–1935)   31
Marilisa Merolla

2   Jazz in Moscow after Stalinism   50
Rüdiger Ritter

PART II
In the Soviet Shadow   67

3   Four Spaces, Four Meanings: Narrating Jazz in
Late Stalinist Estonia   69
Heli Reimann

vi Contents

4 Jazz in Poland: Totalitarianism, Stalinism, Socialist
Realism   94
Igor Pietraszewski

5 Jazz in Czechoslovakia during the 1950s and 1960s   114
Wolf-Georg Zaddach

6 Trouble with the Neighbours: Jazz, Geopolitics,
and Finland's Totalitarian Shadow   136
Marcus O'Dair

PART III
Iberia – Spain   **155**

7 Performing the 'Anti-Spanish' Body: Jazz and
Biopolitics in the Early Franco Regime (1939–1957)   157
Iván Iglesias

8 'The Purest Essence of Jazz': The Appropriation of
Blues in Spain during Franco's Dictatorship   174
Josep Pedro

PART IV
Iberia – Portugal   **191**

9 Jazz and the Portuguese Dictatorship before and
after the Second World War: From Moral Panic
to Suspicious Acceptance   193
Pedro Roxo

10 A Kind of 'in-between': Jazz and Politics in
Portugal (1958–1974)   218
Pedro Cravinho

PART V
Apartheid South Africa   **239**

11 A Climbing Vine through Concrete: Jazz in 1960s
Apartheid South Africa   241
Jonathan Eato

Contents **vii**

12	'Fanfare for the Warriors': Jazz, Education, and State Control in 1980s South Africa and After *Marc Duby*	268

PART VI
To the East

295

13	From the 'Sultan' to the *Persian Side*: Jazz in Iran and Iranian Jazz since the 1920s *G. J. Breyley*	297
14	On the Marginality of Contemporary Jazz in China: The Case of Beijing *Adiel Portugali*	325
15	Afterword: Conclusions *Bruce Johnson*	344

Index — *355*

SERIES FOREWORD

Transnational Studies in Jazz

Since the 1990s the study of jazz has changed dramatically, as the field continues to open up to a variety of disciplinary perspectives and critical models. Today, as the music's meaning undergoes profound changes, there is a pressing need to situate jazz within an international research context and to develop theories and methods of investigation that open up new ways of understanding its cultural significance and its place within different historical and social settings.

The *Transnational Studies in Jazz* series presents the best research from this important and exciting area of scholarship, and features interdisciplinary and international perspectives on the relationships between jazz, society, politics and culture. The series provides authors with a platform for rethinking the methodologies and concepts used to analyze jazz, and will seek to work across disciplinary boundaries, finding different ways of examining the practices, values and meanings of the music. The series explores the complex cultural and musical exchanges that have shaped the global development and reception of jazz. Contributors will focus on studies of the music that find different ways of telling the story of jazz with or without reference to the United States, and will investigate jazz as a medium for negotiating global identities.

Transnational Studies in Jazz presents cross-disciplinary and global perspectives on the development and history of jazz, and explores its many social, political and cultural meanings.

Tony Whyton
Nicholas Gebhardt
Series Editors

LIST OF CONTRIBUTORS

G. J. Breyley is an Australian Research Council DECRA Fellow in the Sir Zelman Cowen School of Music at Monash University, Melbourne, Australia. Her research project is entitled 'A historical study of modern Iran and its diaspora through the music, career and cultural significance of pop star Googoosh'. With Sasan Fatemi of the University of Tehran, Breyley is co-author of *Iranian Music and Popular Entertainment: From Motrebi to Losanjelesi and Beyond* (Routledge, 2016). Her other publications include articles in the *Journal of Intercultural Studies*, *Musicology Australia*, *New Formations*, *La Trobe Journal*, *Antipodes*, *Life Writing*, *Ethnomusicology Forum*, *Prose Studies*, *Journal of Australian Studies* and *Borderlands*, as well as chapters in Ruth Hellier, ed., *Women Singers in Global Contexts: Music, Biography, Identity* and other edited volumes.

Pedro Cravinho is a musicologist, a Ph.D. student at the University of Aveiro, and a double-bass player. Currently, as a Doctoral Visiting Researcher in the Birmingham Centre for Media and Cultural Research and Jazz Research at Birmingham City University, he is exploring the intersection between jazz and television in Portugal during the Estado Novo regime (1956–1974) under the supervision of Professor Rosário Pestana and Professor Nick Gebhardt, with the support of the Portuguese Foundation for Science and Technology (FCT) and Birmingham City University. Cravinho was a team member of the first Portuguese jazz research project to be financed by FCT – 'Jazz Messengers: The Reception of Jazz and its Promoters in Portugal during the Twentieth Century' – held at the Instituto de Etnomusicologia – Centro de Estudos em Música e Dança and Centre for Jazz Studies at the University of Aveiro. His research areas include Jazz Studies, Media Studies and Ethnomusicology, with particular interest in the political and social history of the jazz diaspora during the twentieth

xii List of Contributors

century. Cravinho collaborates regularly with the Portuguese music magazine *Glosas* and he has published numerous articles on Portuguese jazz.

Marc Duby was born in Cape Town, South Africa, and obtained a Bachelor of Arts (majoring in English) from the University of Cape Town (UCT) in 1975, having begun his professional career as an electric and acoustic bass-player in that city in 1972. He returned from overseas to begin musical studies at UCT in 1980, culminating in the award of South Africa's first master's degree in jazz performance (*cum laude*; University of Natal, 1987), under the supervision of Professor Darius Brubeck. Duby completed his Ph.D. thesis at the University of Pretoria in 2007 on the topic of 'Soundpainting', the framework for live composition developed by the New York composer/saxophonist Walter Thompson. Awarded established researcher status in 2010 by the National Research Foundation, he has presented papers at conferences in Brazil, the UK, Greece, India, Italy, Mexico, and the United States. A prize-winning composer of film music, he remains active as a performer, composer/arranger, and music educator, and currently serves as Research Professor in Musicology in the Department of Art History, Visual Arts and Musicology at the University of South Africa.

Jonathan Eato is a lecturer in music at the University of York, UK. He is a regular collaborator on interdisciplinary performance projects with Hannah Bruce and Company and has written several pieces for the choreographer Jacky Lansley. In 2007–2008 he was a postdoctoral research fellow at Stellenbosch University, studying various aspects of jazz music in South Africa, and in 2013 he contributed to *Keeping Time: 1964–1974: The Photographs and Cape Town Jazz Recordings of Ian Bruce Huntley*. In 2012 he formed JISA Records with South African pianist and composer Tete Mbambisa, and produced *Black Heroes*, Mbambisa's first solo piano release. In 2015 JISA released *African Day*, an album of previously unavailable tracks that Mbambisa recorded for Rashid Vally's As-Shams label in the 1970s.

Iván Iglesias teaches Popular Music at the University of Valladolid and music historiography and research methods at the Valencian International University, Spain. He holds degrees in History and Musicology, and in 2010 received his Ph.D. in Ethnomusicology from the University of Valladolid. He has been a visiting scholar at the City University of New York, Freie Universität Berlin, Cardiff University, Università Roma-La Sapienza, and the University of La Habana. From 2008 to 2014, he was a member of the board of directors of the SIBE-Sociedad de Etnomusicología. His research focuses on jazz history and historiography, popular music and soundscapes during the Spanish Civil War and the Franco regime, the hybridization of jazz and flamenco, and music as cultural diplomacy during the Cold War. He is the author of *El jazz y la España* *de Franco* (Nortesur-Musikeon, forthcoming) and co-editor of *Current Issues of Music Research: Copyright, Power, and Transnational Music Processes* (Colibri, 2012), *Jazz in Spain* (University of Valencia Press, 2016), and the Spanish entries for the *Continuum Encyclopedia of Popular Music of the World*.

Bruce Johnson, formerly a professor in English, is now Adjunct Professor, Communications, University of Technology Sydney, Visiting Professor, Music, University of Glasgow, and Docent and Visiting Professor, Cultural History, University of Turku. His current research focuses on music, acoustic cultural history, and the emergence of modernity. He is also an active jazz musician and his work can be heard on twenty or so albums recorded in Australasia and Europe. He has won two major broadcasting awards, and has founded two specialist jazz labels. He has been a policy adviser to Australian state and federal governments, with his report on the state of live music in New South Wales (*Vanishing Acts*, prepared with Shane Homan) leading to changes in the state's entertainment legislation. He was a prime mover in the establishment of the government-funded Australian Jazz Archive, and co-founder of the International Institute for Popular Culture, Turku. His publications include *The Oxford Companion to Australian Jazz*, *Dark Side of the Tune: Music and Violence* (with Martin Cloonan), *Earogenous Zones: Cinema, Sexuality and Music* (editor), and *They Do Things Differently There: Essays on Cultural History* (edited with Harri Kiiskinen).

Marilisa Merolla is Associate Professor in Contemporary History and Director of the Music Making History Research Unit at Università di Roma-La Sapienza. Her doctoral dissertation was on politics and the Italian mass media. She has taught and made numerous conference presentations on Italian contemporary history, the history of mass communication, and sound as a historical source. Her publications include the monographs *Rock 'n' Roll, Italian Way: Propaganda americana e modernizzazione nell'Italia che cambia al ritmo del rock (1954–1964)* (Coniglio Editore, 2011) and *Italia 1961: I media celebrano il centenario della nazione* (Franco Angeli, 2004). She has also written numerous book chapters and journal articles, including 'Rock 'n' roll, politics, and society during the Italian economic boom' in Karen Dubinsky and Catherine Krull, eds, *New World Coming: The Sixties and the Shaping of Global Consciousness* (Between the Lines, 2009).

Marcus O'Dair is a lecturer in Popular Music at Middlesex University, UK, where he leads modules on writing about music, music entrepreneurship, and performance. He has an eminent performance CV, including work as one half of the highly praised act Grasscut. As a music journalist, he has written for the *Guardian*, the *Independent*, the *Financial Times*, and *Jazzwise*. He has also presented music podcasts for the *Independent* and *Music Week*, and has produced

xiv List of Contributors

programme copy for the London Jazz Festival and the Barbican. In 2013 he was writer in residence at Take Five, a residential week for leading UK jazz musicians. He has presented papers at a number of forums and conferences, including the AHRC Research Networking Project, Liverpool (March 2014), and the Innovation in Music Conference, York (December 2013).

Josep Pedro is a pre-doctoral researcher at Complutense University of Madrid. His dissertation focuses on musical appropriation, dialogue, and hybridization processes in the blues scenes of Austin, Texas, and Madrid. He has a degree in Audiovisual Communication with Extraordinary Prize (University of Valencia) and a Master's Degree in Sociocultural Analysis (Complutense University of Madrid) funded by a La Caixa Grant. He has delivered numerous conference papers in relation to several disciplines, including Communication, Semiotics, Musicology, Jazz, History, and Francoism Studies, as well as keynote addresses at Spanish blues societies. His articles have been published in *IASPM Journal*, *Cuadernos de Información y Comunicación*, *Revista de Estudios Norteamericanos*, *Síneris: Revista de Musicología*, and he has contributed chapters to *The Handbook of Texas Music* (Texas State Historical Association, 2012), *The Cambridge Companion to the Singer–Songwriter* (Cambridge University Press, 2016), and *Talking Back to Globalization: Texts, Practices and Interventions* (Peter Lang, 2016). He has also contributed to national and international magazines, websites, and cultural organizations, such as Ruta 66: Tiempos de Rock & Roll, All About Jazz, and Diverse Arts Culture Works.

Igor Pietraszewski, Ph.D., is an assistant professor at the Institute of Sociology, University of Wrocław, Poland. His main research interest is the sociology of culture, art, music, and memory. He is the author *Jazz in Poland. Improvised Freedom* (Peter Lang, 2014). Pietraszewski is also a saxophonist and a member of the Polish Jazz Association and of the artistic board of the Jazz on the Odra Festival.

Adiel Portugali, Ph.D., is a researcher and lecturer at the Department of East-Asian Studies in Tel Aviv University. His research focuses on historical, cultural and geographical aspects of contemporary jazz and popular music in China. In 2015 he completed his doctoral thesis – 'Marginal Sounds: The Story of Jazz in China' – at the School of Cultural Studies in Tel Aviv University. At present he is interested in the way phenomena related to contemporary Chinese jazz generate notions and practices of creativity and individuality. In 2013 he was affiliated to the Centre for Chinese Studies in Taipei. He is also a performing percussionist and the former drummer of the Israeli punk band Ziknei Tzfat. In 2006–2010 he lived and worked in China as a percussion player and teacher at the Pearl International Percussion and Culture Education Centre, translated and co-edited Rony Holan's notation book *Rhythm for All* (Chinese version,

List of Contributors **xv**

2007), and served as a cultural attaché at the Israeli Embassy in Beijing (2008–2009).

Heli Reimann gained her Ph.D. in 2015, in the Department of Musicology, University of Helsinki. Her thesis titled 'Jazz in Soviet Estonia from 1944 to 1953: meanings, spaces and paradoxes' was an interdisciplinary study providing new perspectives on jazz in Soviet society. She is currently postdoctoral researcher at the Sibelius Academy, University of Arts, Helsinki. She has presented papers at around fifty conferences around the world. Her publications include a chapter in Gertrud Pickhan and Rüdiger Ritter, eds, *Jazz behind the Iron Curtain* (Peter Lang, 2009) and articles in *Popular Music* and the *Jazz Research Journal*. She is an advisory editor for this collection as well as a teacher and saxophonist.

Rüdiger Ritter studied East European history, musicology, and philosophy in Mainz, Dijon, Köln, Wolgograd, and Krakau, and gained his Ph.D. in 2002 for 'Music for the nation: Stanisław Moniuszko in the Polish National Movement'. He has participated in numerous research projects, including 'West–Eastern Images: the German image of Russians and the Russian image of Germans' (Universities of Wuppertal and Köln), 'Collective identity and history in post-socialist discourses: Belarus, Lithuania, Poland, Ukraine' (University of Bremen), 'Americans in Bremerhaven' (Museum of the Fifties, Bremerhaven), 'Opposition by cultural transfer: jazz in the Eastern Bloc' (Freie Universität, Berlin), and 'Discourses on Europe in Polish drugi obieg periodicals' (Forschungsstelle Osteuropa, Bremen). His main research project was 'Productive misunderstandings: the reception of Willis Conover's radio broadcast "Music USA: Jazz Hour" in the former Eastern Bloc'. His current research focuses on connections between music and politics in East and East Central Europe from the beginning of the nineteenth century, the history of jazz and radio, and oppositional movements in the Eastern Bloc. His publications include: *Musik für die Nation. Der Komponist Stanisław Moniuszko (1819–1872) in der polnischen Nationalbewegung des 19. Jahrhunderts* (Lang, 2005), *Politics, History and Collective Memory in East Central Europe* (with Zdzisław Krasnodębski and Stefan Garsztecki; Krämer, 2012), and the article 'Broadcasting jazz into the Eastern Bloc: Cold War weapon or cultural exchange? The example of Willis Conover' for *Jazz Perspectives*.

Pedro Roxo is in the final stages of his doctoral programme on the Indian Hindu–Gujarati diaspora in Mozambique, Portugal, and the UK at the Institute of Ethnomusicology, Faculdade de Ciências Sociais e Humanas, Universidade Nova de Lisboa, where he also teaches Ethnomusicology and Jazz. His recent research has focused on the reception of jazz in colonial Portugal, a subject on which he has published several articles. He is one of the main drivers of the

xvi List of Contributors

research project 'Jazz in Portugal: the legacies of Luís Villas-Boas and the Hot Clube de Portugal', funded by the Portuguese government through the Foundation for Science and Technology. He has also served as a member of the coordination team for the *Encyclopedia of Music in Portugal in the Twentieth Century*, to which he has contributed fifty-four entries. His other publications include two co-editorships – *Musics and Knowledge in Transit and Current Issues in Music Research: Copyright, Power and Transnational Music Processes* (both Edições Colibri, 2012) – and articles and conference papers on music, identity, and diaspora; Portuguese popular music; and copyright. As a double-bass player he has participated in numerous recordings in a wide range of musical styles.

Wolf-Georg Zaddach was born in 1985 in Lübben/Spreewald, East Germany. He studied musicology, arts administration, and history in Weimar and Jena, and music management and jazz guitar in Prague, Czech Republic. After finishing his Magister Artium he worked as an assistant professor at the Department of Musicology, Weimar. Since October 2012 he has worked at the jazz research project of Martin Pfleiderer (http://jazzomat.hfm-weimar.de/) while continuing to teach. In February 2014 he was awarded a scholarship from The German National Academic Foundation (Studienstiftung des deutschen Volkes) for his Ph.D. project about heavy and extreme metal in East Germany in the 1980s. His current research interests include music and youth cultures in state socialism, jazz and jazz theory, rock and heavy metal, and the music industry and management. He frequently performs live and on recordings as a guitarist.

PREFACE

In 1922, US journalist Burnet Hershey, returning from a journey that took him around the world, reported that jazz was now a global phenomenon. In the following year the term 'totalitarianism' was coined by the Italian writer Giovanni Amendola, and was soon happily adopted by Mussolini as a political objective. In the course of their diasporic journeys, these twin-born children of the twentieth century came to represent central tensions in modernity: the push towards individual autonomy and the imperatives of standardization.

The image of the heroic artist waving the flag of personal freedom in the face of grim state suppression of human vitality has become something of a cliché in the general conception of the encounter between jazz and totalitarianism. The dichotomy has been fostered by both sides. An axiom promulgated by the USSR declared that 'Today you play jazz, tomorrow you betray your country', and serious studies in the field continue to assert – incorrectly – that jazz was officially banned throughout Nazi Germany. From the other side, the message of 1960's *We Insist! Max Roach's Freedom Now Suite* exemplifies the kinds of statement that gave impetus to a perennial romanticization of the political potential of jazz, which continues to underpin its mythologies and even much of its historiography.

It is a useful place to start. There is a significant and historically incontrovertible degree of truth in the model, and it would be perverse contrarianism to deny it. There is no question that if we want to begin our map of evolving twentieth-century modernity with the tension between individualism and state control, then the confrontations between jazz and totalitarianism provide a useful point of departure. But it is also deeply misleading as an end-point, as the studies in this collection document. Since the late twentieth century, developments in both jazz historiography and political theory have helped to open the way

xviii Preface

to a more nuanced understanding of the encounter between the two. The 'New Jazz Studies' have, among other developments, challenged the US-centric model of jazz history that has occluded the major role played by diasporic jazz in the development of the music's forms and meanings. Indeed, the image of jazz as the anthem of modernity was created outside its birthplace. Over the same period, new approaches to cultural and political history have disclosed fissures and contradictions in what had hitherto been regarded as totalitarian monoliths. 'Bottom-up' micro-histories have revealed that lives led and music played in the interstices of political structures have been far more complex than the older schematic models would lead us to expect.

Behind the catchy slogans, a close analysis of the relationship between jazz and a range of regimes seeking total regulation of society reveals that oppositional postures are in many cases just that: postures. Clearly, the tendency of both is towards the extreme. In a constraining political economy there is an important gratification for advocates of jazz to see the music as a gesture of freedom; likewise for the political authorities to believe they have achieved total control of the citizenry. There are times and places where the outcome is violent confrontation, and this oppositional model has dominated the discourse. But in everyday practice, these studies identify a relationship that is more often one of infinitely subtle negotiation, sometimes conscious, sometimes simply as the reflex by which all individuals adapt to the quotidian. These negotiations are so flexible that, far from being uniformly suppressed, jazz has not only evolved new localized forms in response to political oppression, but in some ways may even help to stabilize the regime. Elsewhere, and especially beyond the Western horizon, there is barely any confrontation at all: jazz, to the disappointment of sloganizers, does not speak a universal language.

The studies in this collection challenge the heroic but simplistic binary model of jazz in its relations with political oppression. In doing so, they contribute to the continuing and instructive reappraisal not only of the dynamic nature of both the music and totalitarianism, but also of the theorization of cultural diaspora in general.

Bruce Johnson
Sydney, September 2015

ACKNOWLEDGEMENTS

I wish to acknowledge in particular my advisory editors, Pedro Cravinho and Heli Reimann. It was through conversations with them that the idea for this collection emerged, they assisted in establishing contacts with potential contributors, and they provided other forms of assistance in preparing this volume. The following also assisted in various ways for which I wish to express my appreciation: E. Taylor Atkins, Chris Ballantine, Roger Fagge, Nicholas Gebhardt, Liz Giuffre, Michael Kahr, George McKay, Janne Mäkelä, Aleš Opekar, Goffredo Plastino, Michael Pronko, Nishlyn Ramanna, Hannu Salmi, Walter van de Leur, Tim Wall, and Tony Whyton. Many thanks to you all.

INTRODUCTION

Bruce Johnson

The juxtaposition of the totalitarian nightmare with jazz might seem asymmetrical and even bathetic or tasteless. But in fact there are potentially very instructive junctions here. Jazz and totalitarianism were contemporaneous in their appearance as phenomena of modernity in Europe. As early as 1922, in an article published in the *New York Times Book Review and Magazine*, journalist Burnet Hershey reported that in his recent journey around the world he found the 'zump-zump-zump and toodle-oodle-doo' of jazz everywhere (Walser 1999: p. 26). This was only one year prior to the coining of the term 'totalitarianism'. The dissemination of both in their tendencies towards globalisation was decisively benefited by the modern media of radio, sound recordings and film. Goebbels recognised the potential of all three in the attempt to mobilise the masses in the totalitarian enterprise. Totalitarianism has been identified as one of the 'quintessential forces in twentieth century history' (Geyer and Fitzpatrick 2009: p. 26), one of the keys to understanding the power dynamics of modernisation. Likewise, jazz was the quintessential musical embodiment of modernisation. In the circumstances of its emergence, its formal character, its modes of global dissemination, it is the 'test-piece' of music in the process of modernisation, the canary in the mineshaft of modernity. Studies of jazz in the Soviet Union and the Third Reich have already demonstrated that its cultural baggage (perceived as an ambiguous combination of the music of triumphant capitalism and/or of a community oppressed on racial grounds) placed it in a uniquely perplexing relationship for the two archetypal totalitarianisms of the century. Its receptions in its various diasporic destinations made it a litmus test of the impact of modernity, and in the case of Germany and the Soviet Union the encounter was a revelation of some of the deepest contradictions in the process of modernisation. The two

2 Bruce Johnson

phenomena share something else: a protean history. Before we can discuss the potential explanatory power of an enquiry into jazz and totalitarianism, it must be recognised that neither of those two terms can be taken as fixed and given. What each refers to is highly dynamic both diachronically and synchronically. The original meanings of both have undergone such radical transformations that we must first reflect on how they have been understood, and may be understood in the present volume.

Totalitarianism

The word 'totalitarian' was coined by Giovanni Amendola, an opponent of Mussolini, in 1923, but was then adopted by Mussolini himself, who defined it as 'Everything within the state, nothing outside the state, nothing against the state' (cited in Applebaum 2012: p. xxviii). The diffusion and semiosis of the term have since often been traced; for succinct overviews, see Gleason (1995) and Geyer and Fitzpatrick (2009). I don't wish to duplicate their work here, but to provide a sufficient account to contextualise the essays in this collection. The most important aspect of that contextualisation is to establish how problematic the term has been since entering the political lexicon, so much so that both its meaning and its analytical usefulness have been challenged. Regarding a term that was 'contested virtually from the start' (Roberts 2006: p. 3), the co-editors of a study published as recently as 2009 admit that they cannot agree on its most instructive deployment, and even suggest that following perestroika 'nobody knew what the term meant' (Geyer and Fitzpatrick 2009: pp. 2, 12). In the immediate post-Second World War period, the major templates for the model were not Italy under Mussolini – who had embraced the term – but Nazi Germany – which chose to 'eschew' it (Roberts 2006: p. 3) – and Stalinist USSR.

Focusing primarily on these two regimes, early post-war theorisations favoured structural and essentialist models, situating totalitarianism within 'a political science classification scheme . . . a static system, the category fostered reification' (Roberts 2006: p. 7). Two of these 'first-generation master thinkers' (Geyer and Fitzpatrick 2009: p. 4) were Hannah Arendt and Carl J. Friedrich, the latter of whom, with Zbigniew Brzezinski, formulated a list of six (or five, depending on how you count them; see Applebaum 2012: p. xxiv) structural features that define a totalitarian regime. The list, later described as 'infamous' (Geyer and Fitzpatrick 2009: p. 6), is cited by Linz (2000: p. 65) as

> (1) a totalist ideology; (2) a single party committed to this ideology and usually led by one man, the dictator; (3) a fully developed secret police and three kinds of monopoly or more precisely monopolistic control; namely, that of (a) mass communications, (b) operational weapons, and

(c) all organizations including economic ones, thus involving a centrally planned economy

Arendt's analysis also centralised elements of the political structure, including the 'Leader' principle, initially formulated in the 1940s by Sigmund Neumann, among others. For Arendt, if we consider 'the totalitarian state solely as an instrument of power [it] turns out to be an ideally suited instrument for the realization of the so-called Leader principle' (Arendt 1979: p. 404). More prominent in Arendt's analysis, however, was the use of terror and its various mechanisms. Terror was for her the 'very essence' of a totalitarian regime, a proposition she repeated frequently (Arendt 1979: p. 344; see also, for example, pp. 464, 466). The practical implementation of terror, for Arendt, was the network of concentration camps, 'the true central institution of totalitarian organizational power' (Arendt 1979: p. 438). Arendt's influence has been particularly durable in the debates over totalitarianism, and we shall return to her work.

The problem with essentialist definitions, like the definition of man as a 'featherless biped', is of course that someone will always be able to throw the equivalent of a plucked chicken into the debate. In time it became obvious that these quasi-positivist theorisations simply did not work as watertight descriptions of what was actually happening in Stalinist Russia and Nazi Germany. It was found that the theoretical model of totalitarianism was of little use as an analytic tool:

> with its claim of a monolithic, efficient state and of a dogmatically held, mind-altering ideology . . . [it] did not describe, much less explain, historic reality. It appeared as an overly mechanistic model foisted upon them by political scientists . . . [which] proved unhelpful in articulating new research questions and in organising empirical findings.
>
> *(Geyer and Fitzpatrick 2009: p. 8)*

The idea of absolute top-down control has come to appear 'ludicrous' (Appelbaum 2012: p. xxv; see similarly Linz 2000: pp. 132–3); and in the more extreme reactions it was sometimes claimed by post-perestroika historians that, in practice, Stalin's USSR was not a totalitarian state at all (Applebaum 2012: p xxiv).

These developments in the theorisation of totalitarianism have resulted from a range of factors, among which changes in the political complexion in the late twentieth century have been of great practical impact. The 'demobilization of militant and militarized European politics' (Geyer and Fitzpatrick 2009: p. 8) has softened some of the Cold War postures which found a Manichaean confrontation between totalitarian and liberal democratic forms of government so convenient. In addition, these more open environments have made available a great deal more empirical evidence regarding actual conditions

4   Bruce Johnson

within putatively totalitarian societies, and these data have enabled more nuanced and flexible modelling. Over the same period the field has opened up to more multi-disciplinary approaches that have taken the hard edges off the political science theorisations that dominated during the Cold War (Linz 2000: p. 7), and recent challenges to rigid structural political science models of totalitarianism have produced a more flexible analysis.

This broadening was especially apparent in the Harvard Project. Under the leadership of Alex Inkeles, Raymond A. Bauer and Clyde Kluckhohn, the project took an interdisciplinary approach that opened the study up to a broader range of socio-political interests, including the study of everyday life, through theories of modernization. One effect of this was to challenge the 'exceptionalism' of the Soviet model and to problematise the absolute distinction between totalitarian and liberal democratic models – in practical terms, between the Soviet and the US models – which were shown to have become more convergent with modernisation (Geyer and Fitzpatrick 2009: p. 7).

Broader developments in the social sciences also helped to foster these more open approaches to the study of socio-political formations. The work of Clifford Geertz exemplified a shift in the nature of the 'anthropological gaze' – away from the compulsion to impose explanations in the manner of his predecessors Franz Boaz and Margaret Mead. Geertz represented a more self-reflexive receptivity to field data that recognised and sought to ameliorate the impact of the observer in actually 'creating' the field, as had certainly been the case in much of the Western theorisation of Russian culture during the Cold War, as in the Culture and Personality discourses to which Mead and George Kennan were significant contributors (see Mandler 2013). These developments in anthropology were particularly influential in (New) Cultural History, which itself became so important in Russian cultural analysis as to have been 'a compulsory course in higher education, concerned in particular with the Russian identity and often taught by ex-professors of Marx–Leninism who have been converted from an economic interpretation of history to a cultural one' (Burke 2008: p. 2; see also p. 32). The ascendancy of culturalist as opposed to political and economic theorisations has shifted attention to what in the Annalist tradition would be called *mentalités* and micro-histories of everyday life. These draw on quotidian sources such as letters and diaries, known as *Alltagsgeschichte* in German research into the Third Reich (Linz 2000: p. 27), and identify what Inkeles has called 'islands of separation' that are 'incompatible with some of the more simplistic and overdrawn characterizations of totalitarian systems' (Linz 2000: p. 134).

These shifts have disclosed gaps between the older models that focused on the top-down forces and the actualities of daily life as lived in the interstices of the totalitarian regime. The effect has been to extend, and to document, the challenge to the actual effectiveness of the aspiration to total control; indeed, Roberts (2006: p. 7) goes so far as to declare that 'totalitarianism, as it had come to be conceived, was not remotely realized anywhere'. He articulates a distinction that has become central to studies of the field: there has been an 'ever-deeper awareness of the limits of the totalitarian model, based on top-down domination. Perhaps it was necessary simply to distinguish theory, or aspiration, from practice, or realization' (Roberts 2006: p. 15). Arendt 'ended up fastening upon a common unrealistic totalism that proved weaker as an explanatory principle than she seems to have believed' (Roberts 2006: p. 8). What she called the central institutions of the regime, the camps, were not a part of ordinary life, and it was only 'outgroups' (Roberts 2006: p. 9) that were totally dominated. The usefulness of the term 'totalitarian' might best be judged according to the presence of the aspiration; by this measure, the term has far broader and more heterogeneous application. Contemporary totalitarianism studies have largely shifted from the formal political structures in themselves to the point of tension between them and everyday life, the 'analysis of these tensions between the ideal type and the reality it partly describes' (Linz 2000: p. 132).

These tensions grow out of the countervailing forces against the aspiration towards total and international control. These may be pre-existing institutions, as in, for example, the Roman Catholic Church in the Franco and Salazar regimes (Linz 2000: p. 77), or older cultural traditions and personal and family networks, as in the Boyar culture in Stalinist Russia – what Keenan (1986), in a benchmark essay, called the 'deep structures' of tradition. These have recently been the subject of extended analysis that makes nonsense of the classic models of total party control (Getty 2013). Everyday life is traversed by non-ideological regional lines of force, down to micro-localisms in the form of interpersonal dynamics and simple bureaucratic fatigue (Linz 2000: pp. 96–7). The limits to the agenda of global control that can be exercised by a central authority with global ambitions are especially evident across national barriers, as in the case of the chain of authority from the Comintern to the Communist Party of Australia (CPA) and then to its regional youth organisations (in relation to jazz, see Johnson 2003); more generally 'there was always someone arguing that local circumstances in their country made it impossible to follow the Soviet line' (Applebaum 2012: p. 61).

These tendencies in the evolution of the discourse have opened up the model of totalitarianism to admit a wider range of regimes and movements than the rigid definitions based exclusively on formal political structures as supposedly exemplified in Soviet Russia and the Third Reich. One can experience something of the totalitarian dynamic in areas of everyday life without living in what once would have been rigidly identified as the two classic models of a totalitarian political system, as well as the converse. The definitions of totalitarianism in terms of a quasi-positivist, reified model do not explain what actually happens in such regimes. Totalitariansim (like any political system) is not just out there as a free-standing entity, but operates in highly fluid

6 Bruce Johnson

relational terms. That is, it is a system which is going to be experienced very differently depending on the situation of the individuals or groups within it. The nature of the experience of totalitarianism, how it affects one's social practice, will depend on where an individual is situated in society, in terms of sensibility, vocation, profession, and so on. During the worst period of the interwar purges that have been taken to represent the character of totalitarian society, political émigré in the USSR Thomas Sgovio recalled:

> We lived in our own world, subjects of a state within a state. We received free hotel accommodations, generous monthly allowances, and free clothing . . . we were banqueted. There were free theatre parties and amusements. Those *polit-emigrants* who were ill as a result of their sufferings in fascist and capitalist prisons were sent to exclusive hospitals and sanatoriums on the Black Sea. And here again, because of their special, privileged status, Russian girls flocked after the polit-emigrant for material considerations.
>
> *(Cited in Applebaum 2012: p. 54; see similarly, for example, p. 73)*

At the same time, of course, no one knew quite when those privileges might be withdrawn on the leader's whim (Applebaum 2012: p. 55). Nevertheless, the phrase 'a state within a state' is a succinct caution against the image of a completely monolithic oppression. In Eastern Europe, '[t]he lure of an elitist existence, complete with access to privileges and to privileged information, remained an important part of the attraction of communism for decades' (Applebaum 2012: p. 66). For some, the totalitarian framework might be experienced in daily life as no more oppressive than in any democratic society regulated by law, for temperamental reasons, or professional, or a combination of both. If nothing else is clear from what we know of the Third Reich, for example, a great many people prospered and thrived without any evidence of seeming to feel oppressed. It seems strange to say this about a political system based on the idea of 'totalism', but in terms of its effect on individual social practices, the difference from a putative democracy can be said to be uncertain, a matter of degree. If this were not so, then the simple fact of individual spontaneity would mean that, by the ideological logic that in the classic model organises life in a totalitarian regime, everyone would be in the camps; and, conversely, no one in a democracy would be in prison. My point is that in a democracy under a rule of law, certain kinds of individual desires are going to feel oppressed, penalised, censored for forms of conduct deemed to be 'artistic' by some, but antisocial or criminal by others. Conversely, under a totalitarian regime, people remain unpredictably able to survive in the system's cracks, while others for whom the system is congenial will positively prosper.

The foregoing survey traces the replacement of the classic analyses of totalitarianism with more supple and subtle models which recognise that various regimes shift along a spectrum, at the extreme end of which is the unrealisable totalitarian aspiration of the rulers, and at the other end that tangled web of ambiguous lines of force which intersect and define everyday life. But for all the radical problematisations of the concept, and the occasional declaration that it has no explanatory value, the fact remains that the term 'totalitarianism' remains active in both lay and scholarly discourse, prominent in titles of the literature of political theory and history. So what are some of the constants in its shifting discourse? The word itself suggests perhaps the most obdurate of these: 'totalism', whether as an aspiration or in more or less realised forms. It is this imperative which is ubiquitous in the debate in which other structural features slip in and out in relationships now of adjacency, now as subsets of each other, depending on who is talking about which case. From Mussolini through to Arendt's declaration that totalitarianism seeks 'the permanent domination of each single individual in each and every sphere of life' (Arendt 1979: p.326), the term has signified 'the more or less utopian goal of encompassing the whole individual, the whole society' (Linz 2000: p. 79). At the height of the Cold War that representation of consensus the Penguin *Dictionary of Politics* centralised not, say, the Leader principle or terror but 'totalism': 'The term is widely used . . . to describe political systems which aim at, even if they do not achieve, the "totality of the state"' (Elliott and Summerskill 1957: p. 294). It is ultimately a totalism on a global level: 'The struggle for total domination of the total population of the earth, the elimination of every competing nontotalitarian reality, is inherent in the totalitarian regimes themselves' (Arendt 1979: p. 392). The objective of this control takes us to a second thread running through the discourses of totalitarianism: to implement an ideology.

> The aggressiveness of totalitarianism springs not from lust for power, and if it feverishly seeks to expand, it does so neither for expansion's sake nor for profit, but only for ideological reasons: to make the world consistent, to prove that its respective supersense has been right.
>
> *(Arendt 1979: p. 458; see, similarly, pp. 363, 474)*

The determination to realise an ideological programme even trumps the concept of the state: for Hitler, 'The state is only the means to an end. The end is: Conservation of race'; likewise, for Stalin, the 'highest possible development of the power of the State' is reached by 'preparing the conditions for the dying out of the State; that is the Marxist formula' (Arendt 1979: n. 40, pp. 357–8). Arendt's argument has been challenged (Roberts 2006: p. 8), but the recent convergence of religious fundamentalism with terror has reinstated ideology in the understanding of totalitarianism (Geyer and Fitzpatrick 2009: pp. 10–11).

The convergence of these two imperatives, totalism and ideology, reflects a further undisputed feature of totalitarianism: emerging in the early twentieth century, it is a phenomenon of the processes of modernisation. Mussolini declared that 'a party that governs totalitarianly a nation is a new fact in history' (cited in Linz 2000: p. 51). Geyer and Fitzpatrick (2009: p. 10) describe their collection as an attempt 'to make historical sense of the twentieth century'. I do not suggest simplistically that totalitarianism is a product of modernity; it is arguably a component of it, a contributor to it, as well as a response to it. And the nature of the response can be reactionary – a manifestation of conservative resistance (Italian or Spanish fascism) – or revolutionary (the Marxist-based Soviet experiment; and even within that model there are ambiguities; see Roberts 2006: pp. 20–1). This Janus-face emerges in the argument that totalitarian regimes are secular attempts to fulfil a psychic need no longer served by traditional religious practices emptied of meaning in the twentieth century. Thus the historian Marci Shore sees a direct line from 'God is Dead' to 'the belief that Soviet communism would fill the resulting void' (Applebaum 2012: p. 57). Even apparently reactionary responses may thus be seen, in the words of Philip Morgan, as 'an alternative "modernity", not an alternative to "modernity"' (Morgan 2003: p. 192). Morgan's point is far reaching. From the beginning of the twentieth century, most of the world was immersed in modernity, though not in modernism (the distinction is elaborated in Johnson 2000: pp. 31–53). Every social practice touched by modernity was therefore arguably another version of it. Arendt argues that the centrality of ideology as a 'universal explanation' is itself a phenomenon associated with the rise of the modern scientific preoccupation with 'predictability' (Arendt 1979: pp. 468, 346). As such, there are some homologies between ideology and other attempts at mass mobilisation that are distinctive to modernity, such as advertising (Arendt 1979: p. 345).

Totalitarianism may thus be linked with other modern urges towards standardisation and homogenisation in the service of such 'ideologies' as capitalism and Fordism, as much as with overtly political institutions. Clearly, then, the adversary of totalitarianism – as to all social homogenisation – is that which cannot be predicted in human behaviour, that which interferes with the logic of ideology. 'Those who aspire to total domination must liquidate all spontaneity, such as the mere existence of individuality will always engender, and track it down in its most private forms, regardless of how unpolitical and harmless these may seem' (Arendt 1979: p. 456). The camps were the ultimate site of such liquidation, 'eliminating, under scientifically controlled conditions, spontaneity itself as an expression of human behavior' (Arendt 1979: p. 438). And there are certain social practices which are more likely to harbour unpredictability and spontaneity than others, notably those which require intellectual and expressive autonomy. 'Privatized, inner-oriented man is a latent threat, and certainly many forms of aesthetic expression search for that orientation' (Linz 2000: p. 71). This 'latent threat' provides a way into an understanding of a perennial tremor in totalitarian projects: that is, 'the tense relationship between intellectuals and artists and the political authorities' under totalitarianism (Linz 2000: p. 71).

Music in performance, from whistling to symphonic concerts, is essentially in motion and resistant to containment, an art form that is particularly 'evasive', rather than trapped in objects like books, paintings and sculptural works, which can be captured, hidden away, controlled. And it is unnotated, improvised forms of music that are the most unpredictable. The threat to total control is increased if the music carries semiotic luggage about alternative societies, emancipation, individual autonomy, a 'New World'. For the Czech jazz historian Lubomír Dorůžka, his first direct exposure to what he felt was authentic jazz, 'the real thing', was the Australian band led by Graeme Bell in Prague in 1947, between the end of the Second World War and the communist takeover, and it carried an aura 'of freedom and possibility'; for his compatriot, the musician Luboš Zajíček, the sound represented 'freedom', and as soon as he heard it he switched from being a classical violinist to a jazz trumpeter (Johnson 2000: pp. 136, 137). Here is disclosed an example of one of the powerful brakes on the totalitarian project: the unpredictability of the individual, nowhere more evident than in improvised and unnotated music, of which jazz was the twentieth-century archetype. This is not to fall into the romantic mythologisation of jazz simply as a music of resistance, or the defiant cry of an oppressed race. My point here is to identify aspects of this particular expressive (or art) form that cannot but be held under some suspicion as a countervailing tendency to the homogenising forces of modernisation. As such, jazz itself is, to use Morgan's words, 'an alternative modernity'.

As the pre-eminent popular music of modernity, jazz therefore exists in an extremely instructive and complex relationship with totalitarianism. The local permutations of all the factors producing and constituting totalitarianism will inevitably give a distinctive charge to its negotiations with jazz. As musical modernity, jazz was not just a set of musical gestures (which in its earliest manifestations we would often today barely recognise as jazz); it was the bearer of jostling messages about US culture, Negritude, Jewishness, gender, sexuality, urbanisation, anarchy, mass culture and mass mediations (recordings, film, radio). Each of these diasporic components will negotiate in its own way with the history, the moment, the place of the host culture, including various manifestations of totalitarianism. The encounter is infinitely heterogeneous and volatile. There is no single, simple *schema* for either, and certainly none for the encounter. This was nowhere more obvious that in the case of the Third Reich as well as Soviet Russia. In both cases jazz found itself at the muddy interface of ideological imperatives and the appeal of popular culture. Existing studies of jazz under these two regimes make it abundantly clear that the relationship is both more complex and more instructive than a simplistic model of resistance (see further below). Both regimes entered into ambivalent relationships with jazz. The Soviet oscillated, according to the political breezes,

10 Bruce Johnson

between treating jazz as the music of an oppressed community and a product from the centre of capitalism; in Germany it was anathema ideologically, yet Goebbels recognised its propaganda potential in his sponsorship of Charlie and His Orchestra, broadcasting US swing standards with new anti-British and anti-American lyrics (see Bergmeier and Lotz 1997).

Jazz[1]

Jazz has thus been a sensitive weather-vane of shifts in the political winds. And it has itself been even more of a chameleon than totalitarianism. This is especially so in the case of diasporic jazz, and within that category particularly diasporic jazz in the first half of the twentieth century, the period under most frequent review in this collection of essays. As with totalitarianism, then, the practices to which the word refers have been extremely unstable, and we cannot take the term as a given.

Jazz was circulated globally with a rapidity unprecedented by any other musical form. Within two years of its first recordings local musicians performed under its name as far afield as Australia (1918) and Norway (1919) (Johnson 1987: p. 3; Stendahl n.d.: p. 1). The sound of jazz was globally disseminated first by the new medium of sound recordings, but being pre-electric it was not always easy to construe what was being heard and how to reproduce the spirit it represented. Because of this rapidity and the medium of its transmission, the actual musical practices to which it was felt it referred in different places ranged from a particular dance form to musicians donning clown uniforms or banging kitchenware together (see below). Sound technology was both channel and filter, determining which forms and examples of jazz would be disseminated, depending on access to record production, marketing and distribution.

The selectivity of jazz dissemination because of the politics of the mass media set up definitions of the music which became contested only by later revelations. France was broadly representative in that available recordings gave primary exposure to white jazz bands before disclosing the work of their black models (Nettelbeck 2004: p. 37). Paul Whiteman's record sales made him a major influence on the perception of what 'jazz' meant, occluding the New Orleans and classic styles during the 1920s (Kernfeld 1988: vol. I, p. 587). Because of what was available on record, one of the most important figures in early Russian jazz, Leonid Utësov, took the white vaudevillean Ted Lewis as his model. From Russia to black Africa, a major jazz inspiration was Glenn Miller, largely because of the films *Sun Valley Serenade* (1941) and *Orchestra Wives* (1942) (Starr 1983: pp. 147–9; Stites 1992: p. 126; Ballantine 1991: pp. 131–2). Robert Goffin – author of the first, and therefore influential, history of jazz – declared the trumpeter Arthur Briggs, who toured France with Hugh Pollard's band, to be 'one of the most notable American pioneers who taught jazz to the old world' (cited in Goddard 1979: p. 65). Arthur who?

Though now barely recalled, many such musicians were important diasporic influences, often obscuring the diversity of musical and ethnic streams in jazz both in the United States and in diasporic regional accents (see further Johnson 2002b: pp. 38–9). The erratic access to jazz at an international level, at least up to the late 1950s, was thus crucial in its diasporic history.

Each diasporic site presented its own distinctive conditioning features. Post-revolutionary Russia, a society with access to the most extreme measures of cultural engineering, was faced with resolutely unauthorised US-oriented popular tastes, a tension that produced an approved proletarian jazz as well as a decadent bourgeois form (Starr 1983: pp. 79–99). Germany's defeat in the First World War and the African troops in the French army of occupation aggravated a deep ambivalence towards blacks, modulating to antagonism. The hiring of 'coloured' musicians was proscribed in 1932, and after Hitler's accession to power no black musicians were officially heard live until after 1945. The contrast with France underpinned differences in the development of jazz in both countries. A French tradition of 'regarding their own coloured colonials as rightful citizens' (Kater 1992: p. 18) and the country's relaxed immigration laws made for mutually influential contact with black jazz musicians (Kater 1992: pp. 18–23, 30; Goddard 1979: p. 139, Nettelbeck 2004: pp. 71–5). In South Africa the reception of jazz was influenced by the relationship between race and urbanisation (Ballantine 1993: ch. 3; 2003: *passim*)

The erratic circumstances of early diasporic jazz dissemination meant that the sound of the music and the nature of its performance were far more heterogeneous than would be the case in the late twentieth century. An Australian reviewer wrote in 1918:

> The Jass band consists of a pianist who can jump up and down, or slide from one side to the other while he is playing, a 'Saxie' player who can stand on his ear, a drummer whose right hand never knows what his left hand is doing, a banjo (ka)plunker, an E flat clarinet player, or a fiddler who can dance the bearcat.
>
> *(Quoted in Johnson 1987: p. 4)*

This tells us much about the professional profile of local performers as well as about performance practices. Although some art music composers and musicians showed interest in this new genre, because it was so firmly lodged as a popular style its practitioners were drawn primarily from local popular music sectors, jobbing musicians whose continued employment depended on remaining abreast of the latest fashions. In this very early phase, then, there was no pre-existing pool of jazz expertise, and the performers had been apprenticed in a range of demotic entertainments that varied from region to region, including dance, salon, restaurant, brass and circus bands, burlesque, vaudeville and music

12 Bruce Johnson

hall, with the closest approach to jazz training being work in minstrelsy and black-face. These generic influences were also traversed by ethnic traditions embedded in regional folk musics that in some places had provided a living for performers: Latin, Jewish, Teutonic, Nordic, Oriental, Celtic, depending on the place. To a far greater extent than 'art' musicians who performed a written, internationalised repertoire, this pool of musical labour relied for its living on audibly mediating local styles, resulting in forms of jazz so heavily accented as to have been subsequently scorned.

One axis along which these local accents were articulated was in instrumentation. In the quotation above, the optional fiddle is a reminder of the early preponderance, yet increasing displacement, of softer instruments. Violinists were accustomed to leading the melody in salon styles, and the instrument's retention in hot dance bands softened the impact of jazz (Kater 1992: pp. 15–16). Increasing numbers, however, began to adopt the Stroh violin, or to double on saxophone through the 1920s in recognition of the need for both greater volume and a more modern voice in the lead (Johnson 2000: pp. 72, 90). As another instrument brought forward by the new music, the saxophone was a particularly strong diasporic marker of jazz. In Finland, the use of 'saxophone' in the band name established its status as 'jatsi'. In Russia, Valentin Parnakh singled out the saxophone as the instrument of jazz dissonances; and, for the authorities, to ban the instrument was virtually to extirpate the music (Haavisto 1996: p. 10; Konttinen 1987: p. 21; Starr 1983: pp. 46–7, 85, 216). Much of the rising volume associated with jazz was produced by the drummer, so widely regarded as central to a jazz band that the two terms were often interchangeable, as in Prague and Paris (Kater 1992: p. 24; Shepherd *et al.* 2005: vol. VII, p. 22; Goddard 1979: p. 16; Nettelbeck 2004: p. 106). The prominence of percussion complemented the understanding that flamboyant rhythmic effects were definitive to jazz – a 'hurricane of rhythm,' according to Cocteau (cited in Nettelbeck 2004: p. 106)

What was played in the earliest diasporic jazz performances remains unclear in the absence of sound recordings, but it was assumed that performance should incorporate acoustic anarchy, evoking descriptions like 'general noisy effects', 'general din', and in such terms as the 'noise music' of the Italian futurists, and the German 'Lärmjazz', which was exported to other German-influenced regions like Finland (Johnson 2002a: p. 96; Johnson 2002b: p. 43). While some of these descriptions might simply reflect a principled abhorrence of the music, reviews of Australian jazz performances in 1917 mention gunshots, kitchenware, bells, rattles and even the hurling of instruments about the stage. It appears that, for many, these early discordancies simply reflected a local understanding of the practice of improvisation. This was generally recognised as a characteristic of jazz, but few understood its harmonic foundations to the extent evident in the US 'classic' jazz recordings of the 1920s. Outside that orbit, 'improvisation' might range from musical formlessness (especially in the earliest period), through minor melodic embellishments, to a reasonably advanced harmonic logic by the end of the 1920s (Kater 1992: p. 16; Goddard 1979: p. 16; Johnson 1987: p. 4; see further Whiteoak 1999: pp. 168–83).

The gradual assimilation of jazz was affected by the character of the musical traditions it encountered locally. German martial music encouraged a strong stress on the first beat of each bar, and later its version of swing incurred the charge of a rigidity and lack of suppleness (Kater 1992: pp. 14, 59, 116). Jazz could thus be drawn into debates about the preservation and modernisation of local national musics, exemplified in its layering over folk forms and repertoire in Sweden in titles like 'The Troll Jazz' (Fornäs 2003: p. 216). From Estonia to Colombia, regions with folk music traditions that remained active in community life produced sycretisms with jazz (Shepherd *et al.* 2005: vol. VII, p. 4; vol. III, p. 29). Fusions between South Africa's Bantu music and jazz produced mbaqanga, majuba and msakazo, in which the local marabi form and repertoire are conspicuous (Coplan 1985: p. 161). On aural evidence, such distinctive fusions seem to be especially powerful when jazz encountered robust local, and especially non-Anglophone, narrative and musical traditions. The strength of such traditions could present barely penetrable barriers to the early jazz that had, so to speak, almost exhausted itself in its cultural journey.

The social spaces occupied by diasporic jazz often emphasised a transgressiveness against authorised genteel conduct. The libertarian environment of French and Weimar theatre and cabaret stamped jazz as a heedlessly amoral music. A similar association, but with a more politicised inflection, was established in South Africa where illicit drinking and indoor nocturnal recreation circumvented local street curfews on urban blacks (Ballantine 1991: pp. 122, 135–6). Initially the venues for the music embraced theatres (including, in the United States, revues like *Shuffle Along* in 1922), which, like later 'jazz concert' settings, distinguished it from the performance spaces in its city of origin (see further Whiteoak 1999: pp. 170–4). Josephine Baker's Blackbirds and the Southern Syncopated Orchestra in Europe, and the Coloured Idea in Australia, were theatre presentations. In the early 1920s, these were primarily demotic spaces, including vaudeville or the London Hippodrome, where the Original Dixieland Jazz Band first appeared in that city.

However, they appear to have made greater impact when they moved on to dance venues like the Hammersmith Palais de Danse (Goddard 1979: pp. 23, 30). It has been through its association with dancing that, from the beginning, jazz seems to have energised the widest audiences in terms of numbers and socio-economic range. On 19 April 1919, the Sydney newspaper the *World's News* reported that jazz 'induces old men and elderly women to dance. It incites middle-aged men and women to go on dancing; it makes girls and boys never want to stop dancing.'[2] From the early 1920s through to the late 1950s, when it gave way to rock (voluntarily and by default) as the main

14 Bruce Johnson

youth dance music, jazz dance halls were the most significant sites internationally of popular interactivity with jazz. Jazz was central to the global spread of recreational dancing in the early twentieth century in specialised venues like restaurants and dance halls. The significance of this connection is profound. Dancing is among the most democratic and least mediated forms of self-expression. The dancer *is* the dance. In addition, the alienating distance between producer and consumer is all but dissolved in the act of dancing. The dancer is a vigorous and virtually autonomous producer of culture and the global popularity of dance in the early part of this century is a striking manifestation of a spirit of cultural 'mass production'. Furthermore, in its earliest diasporic manifestations, jazz was not simply music made by musicians. 'The jazz is a dance', reported Australian life-style journal *Table Talk* in August 1919. In Russia, Parnakh made the same connection (Starr 1983: p. 44). 'The jazz', 'jazzing', the modern girl 'jazzes': these now slightly confusing grammatical constructions, all common in the 1920s, tell us how thoroughly jazz was imagined and practised as a dance, like 'the foxtrot' or 'the tango'. Jazz was a music of literal and metaphorical movement, in the idea of improvisation as opposed to score and in the often abandoned animation of the performers and audiences. For the incidental music to a new era, this is a notable contrast with the high-art music tradition and ideology of fixity.

As the discussion has already implied, jazz was not simply a sound. It carried dense and complex socio-political semiotic baggage. It is generally agreed that jazz became the music of urban modernity. This was so both demographically (it was primarily a music generated in cities) and semiotically (it 'meant' or signified the city). This fact is in itself a vindication of its diasporic forms, for it was only in its diasporic phase that jazz came to be the international anthem of the new century; in its city of origin it was just local music (Johnson 2002b: pp. 41–2, 50). The alignment between jazz and modernity was a determining force in situating the music. France's international reputation as a centre for modernist experimentation, which included hospitality towards primitivism and exoticism (particularly African models), the iconoclasm of Dada and the reaction against the German concert tradition, made it a 'natural headquarters for a European jazz cult' (Goddard 1979: p. 115; see also Nettelbeck 2004: pp. 96–122). Jazz was treated as a music deserving of respectful as well as ecstatic regard. By contrast, the convict origins of Australia inculcated in the authorities a nervousness about demotic recreations, reflected in an arts establishment that was suspicious of signs of the breakdown of order, as in the onset of an era of mass-disseminated culture. Australia was one of the countries in which jazz therefore found no place of consequence within the art-music landscape. In its earliest manifestations it aligned itself with 'trivial' demotic forms. First performed in vaudeville or music-hall settings, its range was narrowed emotionally to low comedy, and musically to extroverted novelty routines, a music of insouciance, high spirits, 'lots of clowning and mirthmaking'

(Johnson 1987: p. 10; 2004: pp. 7–10; for a complementary if not counter-argument, see Whiteoak 2004: *passim*). This narrow affective range was widely ascribed to jazz of the period, as in the Japanese coinage 'jazuru' (a verb, as in many diasporic sites), meaning 'to make merry, to mess around, to talk rubbish, to be noisy, to live without cares dancing nonsensically, like jazz' (Atkins 2003: p. 102).

For many, jazz was thus a threat to traditions of responsible citizenship. In every way – origins, musical form, aesthetics, the vehicles of diaspora, generic syncretism, performance practices – jazz in its early diasporic forms was seen by friend and foe alike as the musical embodiment of the twentieth century's interrogation of the past, of *modanizumu*, as it was coined in Japan (Atkins 2001: p. 47). Alfred Baresel, a piano teacher at the Leipzig Conservatory, published an instruction manual on jazz improvisation, and in 1928 wrote jazz études for piano. He wrote that jazz was 'the most original of the music arts of our day' (quoted in Kater 1992: pp. 16–17). In 1932, Leipzig's Karl Marx Primary School 'integrated jazz into its curriculum' (Kater 1992: p. 17). In the progressive cohorts of other art forms, jazz proclaimed modernity even more convincingly than the modernist wings of art music such as serialism and atonalism. Mondrian declared in 1927 that jazz and neo-plasticism were 'highly revolutionary' (quoted in Bakriges 2003: p. 104). Bauhaus students formed their own 'Bauhaus Band', a mixture of a sort of Dixieland and something 'partly inspired by' Hindemith. The mothers of Dessau would warn their daughters that they were from the Bauhaus: 'we were the punks of Dessau' (Helasvuo 1987: p. 6; Jalkanen 1989: p. 395; Starr 1983: pp. 45–6; Whitford 1994).

This moral panic discloses the other side of the coin. Cultural power blocs agreed with this coding of jazz, but could read it as threat rather than promise. German writer Friedrich Hussong summarised the sometimes self-contradictory repertoire of codings, discussing 'the death of music in the jazz band, Nigger song and Nigger art, criminals glorified, the cult of the proletariat, rootless pacifism, bloodless intellectuality, proabortion histrionics, armchair communism, black-red-golden representational pomp, futurism, cubism, Dadaism' (quoted in Kater 1992: p. 29). In Germany, the resistance was led by eminent composers through the 1920s, including Hans Pfitzner, Richard Strauss and Richard Wagner's son Siegfried. Particularly offensive to their point of view was the positive valence given to black musicians in, for example, Krenek's opera *Jonny Strikes Up* (*Jonny spielt auf*). George Antheil was an American resident in Berlin, where he became associated with Dada through compositions like *Ballet Mécanique*, and later returned to the United States as a composer of film music. His work came under attack for his use of 'Negro jazz, mechanical pianos, etc.' in his chamber works. Jazz was also attacked for its 'blue note', the sound of the saxophone, and condemned as the 'invention of a nigger in Chicago' (Kater 1992: p. 21).

16 Bruce Johnson

This American-'negroid' association of jazz was (and remains) a powerful authentication. A French musician in the 1920s who joined Benny Peyton's band in Paris had to black up to get the job, and Creole musicians from Surinam found more work opportunities in Holland if they pretended to be black Americans (Goddard 1979: p. 19; Shepherd *et al.* 2005: vol. III, p. 336). This profile related to modernity in ambiguous ways. For friends and enemies it was both American modernity and a signifier of primitivism. The blackness of jazz was thus a repudiation of European civilised Enlightenment traditions. From the Nordic to the Pacific regions jazz embodied something carnal, 'throbbing', 'coarse' (Sweden), the music of 'brutes' (Australia) and those who 'carry their sensibility between their legs (France), 'savage, primal' (Japan) (Fornäs 2003: pp. 210–11; Johnson 2000: p. 60; Goddard 1979: p. 138; Atkins 2001: p. 109). The first occurrence of the word 'jazz' in a Finnish publication in 1919 described it as 'one of the more savage, senseless, and of course uglier forms of jumping that Negro brains have invented' (Haavisto 1996: p. 6). Jazz was a contamination of cultural purity, introducing 'black blood' into European art, and even into Japanese blood and nation (Atkins 2001: pp. 96, 122). The Brazilian Pixinguinha band returned home after visiting Paris in 1922 and came under attack for compromising the authenticity of their native music (Piedade 2003: p. 44). Jazz threatened all the controlling mechanisms of the cultural gatekeepers (see further Johnson 2002b: pp. 41–2).

How that threat articulated itself depended on the local political dynamic. In South Africa, jazz provided musical models for a range of urban black aspirations, from the link between individual musical success and the possibility of escape from the ghetto to the achievement of more radical changes that would abolish the ghetto altogether. Yet this apparently straightforward message of black emancipation was intersected by conflicting lines of force relating to the emergence of a black middle class which disapproved of the jazz milieu (Ballantine 1993: ch. 3; 2003: *passim*). But one of the most widespread complicities between jazz and power relations was expressed in terms of gender. Few associations were so internationally recognised (and feared) as that between jazz and the modern woman. As early as 1917–18 a London poster for the musical show *Going Up* by Otto Harbach and Louis A. Hirsch had presented women piloting an aeroplane, foreshadowing the phenomenon of the jazz flapper as portrayed in the 1920s Australian sheet music for 'Flappers in the Sky', which spoke of how the young modern woman soared aloft, leaving 'man, mere man' in her wake. Jazz of the 1920s abounded with narratives about the liberated young woman enjoying her 'Breakaway' ('It's got the snappiest syncopation'), and amorous initiatives ('I've gotta have some loving . . . I'm burning up for kisses'). The Swedish song 'In Spare Moments' ('På lediga stunder') from 1929 lamented the modern woman's neglect of housekeeping and child-rearing in favour of dancing to jazz (Johnson 2000: p. 119; Fornäs 2003: pp. 218–19). Black US jazz musicians were, for the most part, somewhere else, but women, by contrast, were everywhere, and everywhere induced a nervousness among conservatives of both genders, and even in the young modern male. An illustration of 'Moderne Jugend (Charletonstunde)' from a German study of contemporary 'indulgences' (Genussleben) from 1929 shows a young woman with bobbed hair, tuxedo top and short dress, dancing the Charleston to a record player, while a young man and a grandmotherly figure look on in disdainful disapproval (Moreck 1929: p. 411; similarly p. 405). She is the centre of energy. In South Africa, black women were involved in early jazz groups, thus finding a public space through which they became models of female independence (Ballantine 1991: p. 141; 1993: pp. 46–50).

The emancipative coding of diasporic jazz attracted the attention of partisan political oppositional interests. By 1921, Trondheim in Norway had its Communist Youth Organisation's Jazz Band, and South Africa, Australia and the UK were three of many countries in which the left courted jazz (Stendahl n.d.: p. 1; Ballantine 1993: pp. 50–5; Johnson 1987: pp. 100–1; 2003: pp. 151–68; McKay 2005: pp. 3–86). The relationship with the left, however, was intersected by other forces, particularly those of (post)colonialism. This could work to the benefit of the music, providing reciprocal pathways for musical migrations. In the 1920s, the UK exported numerous jazz musicians to erstwhile colonies like Australia, and scores of Australian jazz musicians worked at the highest professional levels in the UK. Over later decades the UK's jazz culture would be deeply enriched by musicians from such regions as Africa and the Caribbean. In the 1920s Surinamese jazz musicians were already becoming prominent in Holland (Johnson 2000: pp. 141–63; McKay 2005: pp. 131–90; Shepherd *et al.* 2005: vol. III, p. 336). But the colonial connection could also work against jazz. In China, the socialists vigorously opposed jazz as emphasising colonial status through its main point of entry and active centre, the treaty-port Shanghai. As a token of both the colonial presence and cultural globalisation, in this case the left found common cause with the nationalist right. This grievance against jazz would of course gather strength in an increasingly post-colonial global environment. Jazz would be extirpated after the Chinese communist revolution; likewise in Iran, where the term 'jazz' was applied generally to all Western popular music, and banned after the 1979 revolution until 1993 (Jones 2003: pp. 226–8; Shepherd *et al.* 2005: vol. VI, pp. 207–8).

The international development of jazz maps not only the decline of British colonial influence, but the emergence of its successors in international expansionism. As Starr (1983: pp. 79–129) has documented, the relationship between jazz and political dissent in the Soviet Union was a rather more volatile affair, characterised by a perennial paradox of the post-revolutionary regimes: the disparity between what the ideologues defined as proletarian culture and what the proletariat wanted. There was also an inconvenient

18 Bruce Johnson

economic factor that emerged with increasing force over later decades: while jazz might be ideologically unpalatable, it was a valuable commodity. According to the account of one Prague musician, in Sovietised Czechoslovakia during the 1950s jazz officially was barely tolerated, but it did provide a link with Western Europe. All band touring outside the country was monitored and booked by the state, which then pocketed a substantial percentage of the band's income upon its return (Johnson 2000: pp. 138–9). These 'jazz dilemmas' were faced by other totalitarian regimes, too, notably Nazi Germany.

The urge to modernisation was increasingly widespread through the twentieth century, but what that meant depended very much on the specific history and situation of the country in question. Where a European imperialism had impeded local socio-economic development, modernisation could take the form of virulent nationalism and an admiration of the United States as a model of a new alternative. But these could come into conflict, reflected in an ambivalent reception for jazz, as was conspicuously the case with Japan (Atkins 2001: *passim*). Intellectual and material cultures also performed a delicate *pas-de-deux*. Ideological commitment might have to yield to economic benefits. Nor was any region's response homogeneous: the gap between centralised government policies and local grass-roots tastes left room for infinite permutations. Jazz and the United States were about modernity, but also a dialectical tangle of: emancipation yet oppression of black minorities; urban sophistication yet provincial folk culture; individualism yet a new imperialism. A response to jazz was also an elliptical summary of the historical relations with American culture.

By the end of the 1920s, jazz was irrevocably lodged in the global musical imaginary, within a force field that would shape its subsequent history with modifications of emphasis and balance determined by both international and local events. In the late 1920s, several events reverberated internationally to bring the initial phase of jazz as a dominant musical fashion to a close. Prominent among these was the Wall Street Crash of October 1929, heralding the Great Depression, which generally led to a decline in leisure spending and introduced a more conservative and sombre mood to which the jaunty heedlessness of 1920s jazz seemed inappropriate. The cold which the world caught when Wall Street sneezed led anxious communities to withdraw into their pre-modern native traditions. Largely because of the subsequent 'bad press' of the Holocaust revelations, the strength of racism, xenophobia and eugenicism in countries in the Anglo-Euro–US axis has been underplayed in cultural historiography, and this has tended to occlude one of the increasingly significant forces of reaction against jazz-inflected dance music during the 1930s. Apart from, but related to, the impact of the Great Depression, a nervous nationalism intensified suspicion of the national and cultural 'Other', the alien, the disorderly monstrous, and found vindication in various forms of often very virulent racism and eugenicism in England and Australia as well as the obvious case of Germany (Williams 1995:

pp. 142–59; Carey 1992: pp. 13–14). As a music seen to be dominated by blacks and Jews, as well as coded as a sign of internationalised anarchical modernity threatening local cultures, jazz was an inevitable target. Popular music in general frequently reverted to more traditional national narratives and musical structures, from the nostalgic celebration of rural values in Australia to the emergence of samba as Brazil's national music (Johnson 1987: p. 14; 2000: pp. 13–14; Piedade 2003: p. 45). A second development was the introduction of sound movies, which deprived musicians of a major source of employment, and also increased the appeal of film as an inexpensive alternative recreation to live-music events. While these conditions also affected the United States, various local factors produced locally distinctive consequences. In Germany, for example, the foreign musicians who had enriched the jazz culture began to leave as work dried up, their departure accelerated by political developments (see below).

Jazz had become a major component of radio programming in the 1920s, internationally developing and shaping musical tastes and appetites. The promiscuity of radio signals would become a point of incandescent negotiation between jazz and totalitarianisms like fascism and communism. In 1933, Goebbels declared, 'What the press was to the nineteenth century, radio will be to the twentieth' (quoted in Bergmeier and Lotz 1997: p. 6). Radio jazz therefore became politicised in relation to the rise of fascist and other totalitarianisms from the 1930s. It was Germany that most fully exploited the propaganda possibilities of radio, and by 1941 Hitler's voice would reach an estimated fifty million citizens through the new facility of Volksempfänger, the 'people's radio' (Bergmeier and Lotz 1997: pp. 8–9; see also an extended study in Birdsall 2012). The careful stage management of these broadcasts explicitly politicised a paradox that jazz crooners like Bing Crosby had stumbled upon: through the radio voice it was possible to reconcile the mass with the individual, to speak to everyone as though speaking directly to each individual.

As we have seen, discussions about totalitarianism were underpinned by larger debates about modernisation, cultural standardisation and social regimentation. While fascism, communism and commercial US dance music might appear to be an unlikely trio, for many, and especially the young, they were all tropes for the suppression of the individual spirit and cultural impoverishment. Arnold Toynbee identified what he called the 'internal proletariat', sections of society characterised by a sense of 'cultural loss'. It is a model that helps to account for the emergence of a more or less youthful international community for whom jazz was the musical enactment of resistance to all three forces of homogenisation, singly and in various permutations (Johnson 2003: pp. 166–7). The new wave of young jazz enthusiasts that began to appear internationally in the 1930s looked back to the earliest manifestations of jazz, its forms, functions and performance sites, as examples of folk authenticity,

20 Bruce Johnson

purity and the spontaneous expression of the individual within the collective. As such, it was a 'resistance music', not necessarily in a political but in a larger cultural sense. Its enemy was stifling regimentation, musically expressed in the most commercial forms of dance music. Politically, this group was likely to align itself with the left, where the major threat appeared to be fascism, yet there was also a resistance to forms of socialism that were rigidly authoritarian and centralist (Johnson 2003: p. 159; Hobsbawm (writing as Newton) 1989: pp. 252–74; Kater 1992: pp. 17, 82–5). Although jazz was thus implicated in political change, in a Fordist world its meaning was broader, the embodiment of a general humanist 'élan vital' (Skvorecky 1989: p. 83), and a reaction against modern mechanised regimentation. Although they were not back-to-the-roots purists, at least some of this spirit seems to have informed youth groups like the Hamburg Swing Boys (Kater 1992: pp. 109–10). In Prague, during the brief interval between Nazi occupation and the communist takeover, this coding became central to the reception of the visiting Australian Graeme Bell Band, which represented a brief flash of 'freedom' between two totalitarian episodes and in the context of the tepid swing that had been hitherto available (Johnson 2000: pp. 136–7).

The alignment between jazz (especially in the form of swing) and anti-totalitarianism was reinforced in the course of the Second World War. The entry of the United States on the Allied side reinvested the music with an energy that converged with anti-fascism. The association of jazz with contamination that had strengthened the hand of various conservative and nationalist sectors during the 1930s was of course particularly emphasised in Nazi Germany. Because of the origins of the music and the profile of its earliest performers during the heady, libertarian days of the Weimar Republic, jazz was both black American and Jewish. While it was never banned by central decree in the Third Reich, the hostility of senior party members like Goebbels ensured that localised harassment of jazz musicians was never displeasing to the authorities (Kater 1992: pp. 20, 24–6, 29–30, 33, 45). This accelerated the emigration of musicians, at least for as long as the going was good, setting up a new mini-diaspora that benefited its destinations, including Argentina, Australia, Siberia and even the United States itself (Kater 1992: p. 40). Throughout the war, jazz was hobbled by various collateral bans, such as on live performance of American music, and by the closing down of shows, theatres and cabarets following the assassination plot against Hitler in 1944. Nor was the music assisted by various constraints on record production and distribution after Goebbels's 'Aryanisation' of the industry in 1938 (Kater 1992: pp. 139, 164). As official opprobrium grew, an enthusiasm for jazz increasingly became an anti-Nazi gesture by default. An attachment to jazz could be added to charges of sedition, and various youthful jazz communities, including the Hamburg Swingers and the zarzous of Paris, became more conscious of and active in the politics of their musical preferences (Kater 1992: pp. 146–7, 151–60; Nettelbeck 2004:

p. 58). The connection was made explicit by a Gestapo interrogator who declared to a jazz-loving prisoner in 1944, 'Anything that starts with Ellington ends with an assassination attempt on the Führer' (quoted in Kater 1992: p. 194). As a further confirmation of the relationship between jazz and totalitarianism in general, this chimes with the words of a Stalinist poster: 'Today you play jazz, tomorrow you will betray your country' (reported in Watson 1994: p. 284).

Just like Soviet Russia, however, Nazi Germany faced a 'jazz dilemma'. Although deeply disapproved of by the state, jazz was popular and the jazz industry was therefore both an economic and a propaganda resource. Its popularity embraced the full political spectrum in wartime Germany, including the armed services, the Brownshirts and the SS. Jazz and swing were still performed live as part of the attempt to maintain morale, including among the troops by official entertainment musicians (Kater 1992: pp. 69, 111, 120). Knowing that Germans were tuning into foreign jazz broadcasts, Goebbels found it necessary to set up state-controlled swing groups, including the Golden Seven, although these failed to attract any public support (as had also happened with the USSR's parallel efforts). A special band was formed to keep the Luftwaffe from tuning into BBC music programmes, but it was regarded as tepid (Kater 1992: pp. 47, 49, 54, 127, 129). One of the strangest responses to the jazz dilemma was the formation of the broadcasting 'propaganda swing' group, Charlie and His Orchestra, which played US and English music with new propaganda lyrics (Kater 1992: pp. 130–1; Bergmeier and Lotz 1997: pp. 136–77). Although it included some outstanding jazz musicians from Italy and Holland, its arrangements were lacklustre and to anglophone ears the revised lyrics seem risible, at best.

The most widely dispersed influences of the war on jazz came in 1941. In Russia, the opening of Germany's 'second front' in June saw US jazz and swing suddenly enjoy official favour, especially among the armed services, with even the NKVD forming its own jazz bands. This brief sunshine period gave Russians a glimpse on film of Glenn Miller, who accordingly established considerable influence before the resumption of austerity and the 'jazz purges' that accompanied the Zhdanov proclamations after the war (Stites 1992: pp. 104–18; Starr 1983: pp. 181–234). Even in a region as remote from the European and Pacific theatres as South Africa, the war affected the reception and impact of jazz. Ballantine (1993: pp. 54–61) includes wartime inflation and increasingly dense urban black ghettos among the factors that produced a growing 'New Africanism' and associated localised jazz idioms. D-Day was both a military and a musical invasion, reclaiming continental Europe for jazz. Glenn Miller was influential in the establishment of the Allied Expeditionary Forces radio service, which followed the troops eastward and was also picked up by liberated countries as well as retreating and captured German troops (Kater 1992: pp. 171–2). The war continued to activate jazz in its immediate aftermath. Jazz scenes formed around US garrisons in Europe and Japan as part of what has been called 'coerced Americanisation' (Moore 1998: p. 265).

As in the decade following the First World War, the aftermath of the Second witnessed an expansion of US international hegemony, now driven by Cold War strategies and fuelled economically by the rationalisation and coordination of US cultural exports from the mid-1950s (Breen 1997: pp. 143–62). In some ways the Cold War disrupted old migratory channels. Dizzy Gillespie was unable to bring Cuban pianist Bebo Valdés into the United States to join his band because of the latter's supposedly communist associations (Fernández 2003: p. 10). In many Middle Eastern, Asian and Latin American regions, suspicion of US (and Soviet) expansionism reinforced nationalist sentiments that resisted imported musical forms, though this often fostered local music traditions that would later feed into jazz fusions. More generally, however, there was an increasing internationalisation of jazz, driven to some extent by America's understanding of its value as political propaganda – its 'Secret Sonic Weapon', according to the *New York Times* in 1955 – in the face of grim Stalinist totalitarianism (quoted in Atkins 2003: p. xvii). Apart from the general increase in mobility enabled by the expansion of civil aviation, the US State Department sponsored international jazz packages that increased public exposure and transnational collegiality. Radio was also exploited by the United States in its Cold War policies, with tens of millions behind the Iron Curtain tuning into Willis Conover's nightly jazz programme on the Voice of America (Atkins 2003: p. xviii).

Through the second half of the twentieth century, the music came to be internationally understood as a fully coherent musical tradition, and this was reflected in an increasing homogenisation of diasporic jazz. Apart from the LP recording, jazz codifications and canonisations were conducted through books, histories, discographies, memoirs, documentaries, international jazz festivals, specialist radio/TV programmes, and the arrival of Fake Books and standard chord charts, licks lexicons, 'Music minus One' records, jazz theory and formal education programmes. These processes resulted in an international codification of jazz practices (including performance and deportment, lifestyle and image). The traditional-to-bop body of jazz is increasingly regarded as a kind of fully completed *oeuvre*. While it remains closely implicated with cultural politics, there is now very little dispute as to what constitutes the music.

The point of the foregoing review is twofold. First, to emphasise that we cannot easily talk about earlier forms of diasporic jazz as a fully established form of musical practice that we would now view as jazz. What matters is whether its executants, audiences, the general public and the authorities *thought* it was jazz. Which takes us to the second point: if they did, then the music, whatever it sounded like, was implicated in the international, national, regional and local political dynamic. And for the purposes of this collection, where does that dynamic sit on the spectrum of totalitarianism, and what does that position tell us about both?

We are talking here about a form of musical conduct called jazz, with the issue being that this form of music, which in spite of the objections of certain individuals and groups in the community, is allowed and even encouraged within democracies. Under some forms of government, however, jazz activity is liable to experience explicit proscription or very strong discouragement by regimes that have forms of coercion that go beyond the rule of law at their disposal. Noting that the definition of totalitarianism is both protean and mercurial, and the point I made above about its relational specificity, I could perhaps start with something as basic as: when I, as an Australian, play jazz, I know that the state, the authorities, do not regard it as their business, and within the framework of the law (for example, anti-vilification laws or matters of general community standards, as regulated by censorship), I may play jazz whenever, wherever and in whatever form I please. The cases we are considering do not enjoy that privilege. In all the cases here participation by a particular individual or group in jazz activity is watched and monitored, and at base for ideological reasons. Together, jazz and totalitarianism represent the deep structural tensions of modernity, between mass culture and the fetishisation of individualism. Totalitarianism's aspiration to standardisation, to 'Fordist' solutions to various unpalatable kinds of 'difference' or 'Otherness', is a powerful theme in the modernisation process. Especially in its diasporic forms, jazz was regarded as the musical vehicle of spontaneity, unpredictability, post-First World War emancipation. The incandescent convergence of the two created an arc light that illuminates the paradoxes of modernity.

One of the 'most basic' issues in the exploration of totalitarianism

> is the interplay of what we take to be ahistorical or suprahistorical with what we take to be historically specific. The ahistorical encompasses an array of categories from evil and power to careerism and fear that obviously enter the discussion from very different angles. The historically specific, in turn, may be idiosyncratically national or supranational.
>
> *(Roberts 2006: p. 23; see further pp. 23–31)*

Both are needed, and are served more or less respectively in this collection by this general Introduction and the individual case studies. Of course, they must overlap as the supranational converges with the national: so, for example, the instruments and machinery of control in the modern era, such as the mass media and developments in popular culture, are transnational. But these also play distinctive national roles. Jazz itself and its mediations are as instructive examples as any of this convergence: available globally yet appropriated and deployed in ways that are distinctively local.

24 Bruce Johnson

In the past there have been difficulties in deploying the term 'totalitarianism' because of a dearth of detailed documentation of its specific operational profile (Linz 2000: p.135). One route into an understanding of the phenomenon is an aggregation of 'micro-histories' or detailed case studies of the relationship between what we regard as a totalitarian regime and the specific conditions of different communities within it. As in this case: what did totalitarianism mean in terms of jazz activity? This study is thus part of the move away from macro-political approaches that tend to model totalitarian regimes monolithically to micro-studies of the interface with the complex and unpredictable quotidian. These essays are not simply disclosures of a one-way traffic by which jazz was passively influenced by totalitarian regimes. They also disclose the mutualities in that relationship: how jazz as a social practice interacted with the political environment in a messy feedback relationship.

The general view that totalitarian regimes are detestable evokes a point made in the opening of *Anna Karenina* to the effect that all happy families are alike, but each unhappy family is unhappy in its own way. Indeed, but we may still recognise the category of 'unhappy family'. Likewise, while each society underpinned by a totalitarian dynamic is unique, we may nonetheless recognise the category, while each of the individual studies will explore how its case is totalitarian 'in its own way'.

Notes

1 The following account is adapted from sections of my essay 'Jazz outside the US', written for David Horn and John Shepherd, eds, *The Bloomsbury Encyclopedia of Popular Music of the World*, vol. XII: *Genres: International* (Bloomsbury, forthcoming), used with permission.
2 http://trove.nla.gov.au/ndp/del/article/130596669?searchTerm=laughing%20jazz& searchLimits=sortby=dateAsc, accessed 3 March 2016. My thanks to Liz Guiffre for drawing my attention to this source.

References

Applebaum, Anne. 2012. *Iron Curtain: The Crushing of Eastern Europe 1944–56*. London: Penguin
Arendt, Hannah. 1979 [1951]. *The Origins of Totalitarianism*. New edition with added prefaces. San Diego, New York and London: Harvest/Harcourt Brace and Company.
Atkins, E. Taylor. 2001. *Blue Nippon: Authenticating Jazz in Japan*. Durham, NC, and London: Duke University Press.
Atkins, E. Taylor, ed. 2003. *Jazz Planet: Transnational Studies of the 'Sound of Surprise'*. Jackson: University Press of Mississippi.
Bakriges, Christopher G. 2003. 'Musical Transculturation: From African American Avant-Garde Jazz to European Creative Improvisation, 1962–1981'. In E. Taylor Atkins, ed., *Jazz Planet: Transnational Studies of the 'Sound of Surprise'*. Jackson: University Press of Mississippi, 99–114.

Ballantine, Christopher. 1991. 'Concert and Dance: The Foundations of Black Jazz in South Africa between the Twenties and the Early Forties'. *Popular Music* 10(2): 121–45.

Ballantine, Christopher. 1993. *Marabi Nights: Early South African Jazz and Vaudeville.* Johannesburg: Ravan Press.

Ballantine, Christopher. 2003. 'Music and Emancipation: The Social Role of Black Jazz and Vaudeville in South Africa between the 1920s and the Early 1940s'. In E. Taylor Atkins, ed., *Jazz Planet: Transnational Studies of the 'Sound of Surprise'.* Jackson: University Press of Mississippi, 169–89.

Bergmeier, Horst J. B. and Rainer E. Lotz. 1997. *Hitler's Airwaves: The Inside Story of Nazi Radio Broadcasting and Propaganda Swing.* New Haven, CT, London: Yale University Press.

Birdsall, Caroline. 2012. *Nazi Soundscapes: Sound, Technology and Urban Space in Germany, 1933–1945.* Amsterdam: Amsterdam University Press.

Breen, Marcus. 1997. 'Popular Music'. In Stuart Cunningham and Graeme Turner, eds, *The Media in Australia: Industries, Texts, Audiences.* Second edition. St Leonards, NSW: Allen & Unwin, 143–62.

Burke, Peter. 2008. *What is Cultural History?* Second edition. Cambridge: Polity Press.

Carey, John. 1992. *The Intellectuals and the Masses: Pride and Prejudice among the Literary Intelligentsia 1880–1939.* London and Boston, MA: Faber and Faber.

Coplan, David. 1985. *In Township Tonight: South Africa's Black City Music and Theatre.* Johannesburg: Ravan Press.

Elliott, Florence and Michael Summerskill. 1957. *A Dictionary of Politics.* Harmondsworth: Penguin.

Fernández. Raúl A. 2003. '"So No Tiene Swing No Vaya' a la Rumba": Cuban Musicians and Jazz'. In E. Taylor Atkins, ed., *Jazz Planet: Transnational Studies of the 'Sound of Surprise'.* Jackson: University Press of Mississippi, 3–18.

Fornäs, Jonas. 2003. 'Swinging Differences: Reconstructed Identities in the Early Swedish Jazz Age'. In E. Taylor Atkins, ed., *Jazz Planet: Transnational Studies of the 'Sound of Surprise'.* Jackson: University Press of Mississippi, 207–24.

Getty, J. Arch. 2013. *Practising Stalinism: Bolsheviks, Boyars and the Persistence of Tradition.* New Haven, CT: Yale University Press.

Geyer, Michael and Sheila Fitzpatrick, eds. 2009. *Beyond Totalitarianism: Stalinism and Nazism Compared.* Cambridge: Cambridge University Press.

Gleason, Abbott. 1995. *Totalitarianism: The Inner History of the Cold War.* New York: Oxford University Press.

Goddard, Chris. 1979. *Jazz away from Home.* New York and London: Paddington Press, 1979.

Haavisto, Jukka. 1996. *Seven Decades of Finnish Jazz: Jazz in Finland 1919–1969.* Translated Roger Freundlich. Helsinki: Finnish Music Information.

Helasvuo, Veikko. 1987. 'The 1920s: Fresh Breezes from Europe'. Translated William Moore. *Finnish Music Quarterly* 3–4(87): 2–10.

Hobsbawm, E. J. (writing as Francis Newton). 1989. *The Jazz Scene.* London: Weidenfeld & Nicolson (first published London: MacGibbon and Kee, 1959).

Jalkanen, Pekka. 1989. *Alaska, Bombay Ja Billy Boy: Jazzkulttuurin murros Helsingissä 1920–luvulla.* Helsinki: University of Helsinki.

Johnson, Bruce. 1987. *The Oxford Companion to Australian Jazz.* Melbourne: Oxford University Press.

Johnson, Bruce. 2000. *The Inaudible Music: Jazz, Gender and Australian Modernity*. Sydney: Currency Press.

Johnson, Bruce. 2002a. 'Jazz as Cultural Practice'. In Mervyn Cooke and David Horn, eds, *The Cambridge Companion to Jazz*. Cambridge: Cambridge University Press, 96–113.

Johnson, Bruce. 2002b. 'The Jazz Diaspora'. In Mervyn Cooke and David Horn, eds, *The Cambridge Companion to Jazz*. Cambridge: Cambridge University Press, 33–54.

Johnson, Bruce. 2003. 'Naturalizing the Exotic: The Australian Jazz Convention'. In E. Taylor Atkins, ed., *Jazz Planet: Transnational Studies of the 'Sound of Surprise'*. Jackson: University Press of Mississippi, 151–68.

Johnson, Bruce. 2004. 'Tools not of Our Making: Shaping Australian Jazz History'. In Philip Hayward and Glen Hodges, eds, *The History and Future of Jazz in the Asia-Pacific Region: Refereed Proceedings of the Inaugural Asia-Pacific Jazz Conference (September 12th–14th 2003)*. Queensland: Central Queensland University Publishing Unit, 6–17.

Jones, Andrew F. 2003. 'Black Internationale: Notes on the Chinese Jazz Age'. In E. Taylor Atkins, ed., *Jazz Planet: Transnational Studies of the 'Sound of Surprise'*. Jackson: University Press of Mississippi, 225–243.

Kater, Michael H. 1992. *Different Drummers: Jazz in the Culture of Nazi Germany*. New York and Oxford: Oxford University Press.

Keenan, Edward L. 1986. 'Muscovite Political Folkways'. *Russian Review* 45: 115–81.

Kernfeld, Barry, ed. 1988. *The New Grove Dictionary of Jazz*. Two volumes. London: Macmillan.

Konttinen, Matti. 1987. 'The Jazz Invasion'. Translated Susan Sinisalo. *Finnish Music Quarterly* 3–4(87): 20–5.

Linz, Julian J. 2000. *Totalitarian and Authoritarian Regimes*. London and Boulder, CO: Lynne Rienner Publishers.

Mandler, Peter. 2013. *Return from the Natives: How Margaret Mead Won the Second World War and Lost the Cold War*. New Haven, CT: Yale University Press.

McKay, George. 2005. *Circular Breathing: The Cultural Politics of Jazz in Britain*. Durham, NC, and London: Duke University Press.

Moore, Joe B. 1998. 'Studying Jazz in Postwar Japan: Where to Begin?' *Japanese Studies* 18(3): 265–80.

Moreck, Curt. 1929. *Kultur- und Sittengeschichte der neuesten Zeit: Das Genussleben des modernen Menschen*. Dresden: Paul Aretz.

Morgan, Philip. 2003. *Fascism in Europe, 1919–1945*. London: Routledge.

Nettelbeck, Colin. 2004. *Dancing with de Beauvoir: Jazz and the French*. Melbourne: Melbourne University Press.

Piedade, Acácio Tadeu de Camargo. 2003. 'Brazilian and the Friction of Musicalities'. In E. Taylor Atkins, ed., *Jazz Planet: Transnational Studies of the 'Sound of Surprise'*. Jackson: University Press of Mississippi, 41–58.

Pinckney, Warren R. Jr. 2003. 'Jazz in India: Perspectives on Historical Development and Musical Acculturation'. In E. Taylor Atkins, ed., *Jazz Planet: Transnational Studies of the 'Sound of Surprise'*. Jackson: University Press of Mississippi, 59–79.

Roberts, David D. 2006. *The Totalitarian Experiment in Twentieth-Century Europe: Understanding the Poverty of Great Politics*. New York and London: Routledge.

Shepherd, John, David Horn and Dave Laing, eds. 2005. *Continuum Encyclopedia of Popular Music of the World*, vol. III: *Caribbean and Latin America*; vol. IV: *North*

America; vol. V: *Asia and Oceania*; vol. VI: *Africa and the Middle East*; vol. VII: *Europe*. London and New York: Continuum.

Skvorecky, Joseph. 1989. *Talkin' Moscow Blues*. London: Faber & Faber (first published Toronto: Lester & Orpen Dennys Press, 1988).

Starr, S. Frederick. 1983. *Red and Hot: The Fate of Jazz in the Soviet Union 1917–1980*. New York and Oxford: Oxford University Press.

Stendahl, Bjørn. n.d. 'Jazz in Norway 1920–1940'. Available at: http://jazzbasen.no/jazzhistorie_1920_1940_eng.html, accessed 10 May 2007.

Stites, Richard. 1992. *Russian Popular Culture: Entertainment and Society since 1900*. Cambridge: Cambridge University Press, 1992.

Walser, Robert. 1999. *Keeping Time: Readings in Jazz History*. New York and Oxford: Oxford University Press.

Watson, Derek (compiler). 1994. *The Wordsworth Dictionary of Musical Quotations*. Hertfordshire: Wordsworth Editions Ltd.

Whiteoak, John. 1999. *Playing Ad Lib: Improvisatory Music in Australia 1836–1970*. Sydney: Currency Press.

Whiteoak, John, 2004. 'Our Jazz-Making Tools and how We Chose to Use Them'. In Philip Hayward and Glen Hodges, eds, *The History and Future of Jazz in the Asia-Pacific Region: Refereed Proceedings of the Inaugural Asia-Pacific Jazz Conference (September 12th–14th 2003)*. Queensland: Central Queensland University Publishing Unit, 18–28.

Whitford, Frank. 1994. *Bauhaus: The Face of the Twentieth Century*. Video documentary. London: BBC/RM Arts.

Williams, John F. 1995. *Quarantined Culture: Australian Reactions to Modernism 1913–1939*. Cambridge, New York and Melbourne: Cambridge University Press.

PART I

Totalitarian Templates

1

JAZZ AND FASCISM

Contradictions and Ambivalences in the Diffusion of Jazz Music under the Italian Fascist Dictatorship (1925–1935)

Marilisa Merolla

> The introduction of the Jazz Band (originally a Negro orchestra with Negro instruments and Negro musicians) in our ballrooms will certainly mark a significant date in the history of the culture of our century . . ., as dancing still remains infinitely more rapid and immediate and of a universal impact than reading, in order to spread some distinctive rhythmic or aesthetic principles.[1]
>
> *(Sacchi 1922)*

This chapter will focus on the Fascist radio broadcasting of EIAR (Ente Italiano Audizioni Radiofoniche) during the so-called jazz 'diffusion' period in which Mussolini gradually recognized the importance of radio for the construction of a totalitarian state. It will shed light on the use of jazz music in the 'Volgarizziamo la Radio' (Radio to the People) campaign conducted by Mussolini in the late 1920s and early 1930s. In fact, for its seductive and frenzied rhythms, jazz was chosen as the music that could fascinate Italians and attract listeners to the first Fascist radio shows, not realizing at first that the diffusion of jazz music, with its syncopated rhythms and its cultural associations, was received in different ways by different communities, and in many cases came to represent New World values including forms of freedom and individual expressiveness. This ambivalent relationship between jazz and Fascism gave birth to an 'Italian way to jazz', which even if it did not express an explicit rejection of Fascism and its values represented an anomaly in the building of Italian Fascist totalitarianism.

Introduction

It was around 1919 when jazz music arrived in Italy from the United States. The shattering impact of its rhythms seemed to express the anxieties of a country that had just emerged from the Great War (Merolla 2011, 7–8). Two years earlier, a thirteen-year-old Vittorio Spina had first come into contact with some American musicians based in Rome along with the US troops of General Pershing (Mazzoletti 2004, 12). In that year of 1917 Spina started his long career by playing banjo in a US military orchestra led by Sergeant Griffith of the Marine Corps (Mazzoletti 2004, 12–13). It was only with the end of the war, between late 1918 and 1919, that the spread of jazz music increased thanks to the appearance of several new ballrooms and night clubs in Rome, Milan and Turin (Mazzoletti 2004, 22). As the centre of the record industry, Milan quickly gained a pre-eminent position in the Italian jazz scene, with such noted clubs as the Mirador (Cerchiari 2003, 55). It was founded in 1918 by the dancer and drummer Arturo Agazzi, who had worked since 1914 in the London night clubs of Ciro's and the Embassy, as well as the Murray, which he himself founded (Cerchiari 2003, 72). The Mirador's music programming included the foxtrot, tango and jazz. In 1920, it hosted the first live show of Gaetano 'Milietto' Nervetti, one of the first Italian jazz pianists, who by then had created the Ambassador's Jazz Band with Carlo Benzi. Foxtrot and jazz were enthusiastically appreciated by the bourgeois youth of the 'Milano bene' (Milanese upper class), as reported in *Corriere della sera*, which declared that the music 'comes from niggers'. These were 'two ingenious creations of modern choreography', 'two products of mankind's stomach-ache while facing the end of the war' (Frakka 1921). The following year, again according to *Corriere*, the popularity of African-American music among Italian bourgeois youth was one of the results of the accelerated transformation of Western societies at the end of the First World War (Sacchi 1922).

Recently, historians have begun to consider jazz music not only as a historical source in contemporary Italian history, but also as a peculiar 'agent' that is able to influence evolving socio-political processes. The relationship between jazz music and the Fascist radio broadcasting of EIAR (Ente Italiano Audizioni Radiofoniche) is emblematic of the contradictions and ambivalences of the political use of African-American music by the Fascist dictatorship. According to Adriano Mazzoletti (2004) and Luca Cerchiari (2003), there were three main phrases in the relationship between jazz and Fascism: 'indifference' (1919–1925), 'diffusion' (1925–1935) and 'prohibition' (1935–1943). This chapter will focus on the so-called 'diffusion' period, when Mussolini gradually recognized the importance of radio broadcasting for the construction of a totalitarian state.

The chapter will shed light on the use of jazz music in the 'Volgarizziamo la Radio' (Radio to the People) campaign, conducted by Mussolini in the late 1920s and early 1930s. Jazz was identified as music that could fascinate Italians because of its seductive and frenzied rhythms, and the authorities initially hoped that it would attract listeners to the first Fascist radio shows, not realizing that the diffusion of jazz music, with its syncopated rhythms and its cultural associations, would be received in different ways by different communities, and in many cases would come to represent many New World values, including forms of freedom and individual expressiveness (Johnson forthcoming). The scientific debate about the political repercussions of the spreading of jazz under the Fascist dictatorship highlights the ambivalent relationship between jazz and the Italian authorities during the Fascist regime (Martinelli 2013). Between 1925 and 1935, this ambivalence resulted in 'a watered down, "jazzy" version of jazz reduced to ballroom music and canzonetta [which] goes exactly to the core of the fascist attitude towards this music: jazz could, and therefore ought to, be made national and Italian, adapted to the circumstances of a provincial reality dreaming of a far away, modern America' (Dainotto 2008, 287). Nevertheless, this Italian approach to jazz – 'becoming . . . the note between dreams and reality, between traditionalism and modernism, between Italy and the world' (ibid.) – contrasted with the celebration of strength, autarchy and power of the Fascist marches and hymns, and can be considered a sort of double-edged sword for Mussolini's dictatorship, as the sudden censorship of jazz in later years confirmed.

The 'Industrial Model' of Italian Radio Broadcasting during the Rise of the Fascist Regime

In Italy, the crisis following the First World War abruptly interrupted the transition toward democracy that Prime Minister Antonio Giolitti had launched during the first fifteen years of the twentieth century. Among the many and complex factors that provoked the collapse of the liberal state and allowed the Fascist dictatorship to rise, historians point to the inability of the old Italian political class to understand the needs of the new mass society, which, after the radically transformative experience of the Great War, was claiming major representation. According to Giovanni Sabbatucci (1976, 28), the old liberal state had neither the cultural nor the organizational instruments that were needed to face the deep socio-political transformation arising from the war. In addition, Italy's liberal political elite had not recognized the determining role that the new mass-based political parties were going to play in the modern representative democracies. The liberals were not able to transform themselves into an Italian mass-based party. In a related point, Emilio Gentile underlines the inability of liberal governments to promote a national 'political liturgy', composed of the signs, the cults and the symbols that are essential if the masses are to identify themselves in a modern nation-state. As a result, the old liberal state was, according to Giuseppe Mazzini, a 'state without a soul' (Gentile 1982, 6; 1993, 10–12). At the opposite end of the political spectrum, and tragically denying the liberalism and freedom that had enlivened Italian political unification in 1861, Fascism was the first political movement that was able to understand the crucial importance of creating 'the myth of a new state' (Gentile 1982, vii).

34 Marilisa Merolla

With the realization of the 'new state', Mussolini made Italy one of the first Western European countries to experience 'totalitarian modernity' (Gentile 2008, v; see further Griffin 2007; Ben-Ghiat 2001), while offering a civic religion as the vital catalyst for contemporary mass politics (Gentile 1996).

During the *ventennio* (Italy's Fascist era), Mussolini used signs, cults, myths, spectacles and public ceremonies as instruments of propaganda in order to spread a 'national religion' among the masses. This pedagogical cultural–political operation that aimed to integrate Italians into a Fascist consciousness accelerated between 1925 and 1926 with the promulgation of the *leggi fascistissime* (the exceptional decrees), through which the Fascist regime fully expressed itself like a real dictatorship. Moreover, beginning in 1924, Mussolini had at his disposal the new medium of radio broadcasting by which to shape the mentality and customs of a still-emerging nation. From this point of view, the medium of new mass communication would have represented an obvious propaganda instrument to spread a national myth and a common culture to its still largely illiterate populace, which was territorially split into a multitude of dialects and local cultures. Nevertheless, Mussolini's attempt to convert Fascist radio broadcasting into a consensus machine had many limits and ambiguities, and failed for several reasons (Cannistraro 1975; Isola 1990; Monteleone 1992; Monticone 1978; Papa 1978). The primary reason for this was the strength of the 'industrial model' that underpinned the origins of Italian radio (Castronovo 1984, 75–77), a model that was characterized by the dominant influence of the industrial Italian elite on the new medium.

When, on 6 October 1924, the first Italian radio broadcasting society (URI – Unione Radiofonica Italiana) started to broadcast, it was not yet significantly influenced by political propaganda. In fact, initially, the Fascist regime was not fully aware of the great potential of radio broadcasting to construct a political consensus. URI was based in Rome and led by an engineer, Enrico Marchesi, who had been a partner of Giovanni Agnelli since the foundation of the automobile manufacturer Fiat in 1899. A few years later, two more radio stations were created in Milan and Naples.

After his initial ambivalence, Mussolini started to realize the potential of the new medium and began to formulate the idea of a new national broadcasting society controlled by the government. Hence, in 1928, URI was replaced by Ente Italiano Audizioni Radiofoniche (EIAR; Monteleone 1992, 47).[2] Unsurprisingly, the legislative decree that established EIAR also introduced the Superior Committee of Vigilance, which monitored radio programmes and their adherence to the cultural guidelines of the Fascist dictatorship ('Comitato Superiore di Vigilanza per le Radio-audizioni' 1928, 6). Soon the Ministry of Communication enacted another decree, which obligated the EIAR to submit all cultural content for approval prior to broadcasting (Cannistraro 1975, 230).

By the end of 1928, EIAR had at its disposal five radio stations – Rome, Naples, Milan, Bolzano and Genoa – and was broadcasting 6000 hours of entertainment and news per year, or roughly seventeen hours per day (ibid.). However, the number of Italians who had access to radio remained limited. Radio receivers were still luxury items, inaccessible to the masses. Moreover, further limitations were imposed, as EIAR demanded annual (paid) subscriptions from every radio owner. In 1926, there were around 27,000 subscribers; two years later, that figure had risen to more than 61,000. Despite the increasing number of subscriptions, though, very few Italians were able to listen to radio transmissions in 1928; and there was a distinct geographical imbalance in their distribution. The majority of subscribers were concentrated in northern and north-western Italy – Lombardy, Liguria and Piedmont – with the rest in the large cities (Rome and Naples). Southern and eastern Italy had no radio signals at all (ibid.).

This territorial concentration deepened in 1929 with the Società Idrolettrica Piemonte's – SIP's – acquisition of the national radio broadcasting society, resulting in the so-called 'piedmontization' of EIAR (Monteleone 1992, 48; Ortoleva 1993, 448). SIP, one of the most influential economic groups in the country, was based in Turin, the industrial capital of Italy. Hence, many industrialists joined EIAR's board of governors. First among them was Gianni Agnelli, who was also the president of Radiomarelli, the country's main producer of radio equipment (Ortoleva 1993, 449). To no one's surprise, the headquarters of Italian radio broadcasting soon moved from Rome to Turin. As a result, the 'industrial model' of Italian radio broadcasting was born. On the one hand, this form of radio broadcasting adhered to the dictator's cultural and political guidelines, as it remained under the regime's control. On the other hand, it also meant that Italian radio was dominated by the industrialists' attitudes and their desire to promote their own economic interests. Therefore, Mussolini's goal of using broadcasting to help build a Fascist nation was relegated to secondary importance.

We Want 'Gess'! The Role of Jazz in the 'Radio to the People' Campaign (1925–1933)

From the very beginning, radio was the medium that arguably made the most significant contribution to the spreading of jazz music among the Italian people (Cerchiari 2003, 63). According to the official Italian radio magazine *Radiorario*, after fascinating the major European cities, jazz finally made its appearance in Italian broadcasting in 1925 ('Unione Radiofonica Italiana. Stazione di Roma. Lunghezza d'onda m. 425' 1925, 7–10). The radio station in Rome was the first to introduce a show exclusively dedicated to the latest rhythms: 'Jazz Band' aired daily from 5.45 to 8.30 p.m. It was a live show, broadcast from the luxurious Hotel di Russia in Rome, where jazz bands and other Italian orchestras performed (Cerchiari 2003, 63; 'I programmi della stazione di Roma' 1925, 5–7). Around the same time, the Milan radio station

36 Marilisa Merolla

began broadcasting seventy minutes of jazz featuring Maestro S. Ferruzzi's jazz band. This show was on air from 4.35 to 5.45 p.m. every Monday, Wednesday and Friday. One year later, in 1926, both programmes were included in the unified programming of URI. The following year, URI presented jazz among its music programming dedicated to the 'ballabile' genre – ballroom music. Jazz music accounted for around 10 per cent of the total URI schedule, an appreciable amount considering that the news accounted for only around 11 per cent of the station's output (Cerchiari 2003, 64–65).

The prominent position that Italian radio granted to this new ballroom music was a result of the increasing diffusion of the record industry. Not only opera, classical and chamber music but marches, melodic Italian songs, popular songs and many dance tunes now appeared in the catalogues of the main international labels, such as La Voce del Padrone (His Master's Voice (HMV)) and Columbia. Unsurprisingly, after initial resistance, the interests of broadcasting and recording began to overlap and intertwine, and they soon became inseparable (Mazzoletti 2004, 317–318). In 1928, the screening of Alan Crosland's *The Jazz Singer* marked the introduction of sound film into Italian cinema. As a result, the combination of images, music and dialogue started to provoke a variety of new responses among the public, which were enhanced by Italian movies' frequent references to EIAR programming (Valentini 2007, 206–207). The Fascist dictatorship welcomed this synergy between cinema and radio, beginning with the foundation in 1925 of LUCE (L'Unione Cinematografica Educativa), a national film company whose goal was to promote the making of educational films and documentaries in order to shape a Fascist consciousness (Laura 2000, 44; Merolla 2004, 122–123). Three years later, Mussolini founded the Discoteca di Stato, whose purpose was to collect and preserve the voices of Italian patriots, above all combatants from the First World War, for future generations. However, this innovative national sound archive was actually the brainchild of the Futurist playwright Rodolfo de Angelis; Mussolini merely realized de Angelis's idea (Cerchiari 2003, 59). Fascist rhetoric often exploited Futurism's ideology in order to celebrate the rupture from the old liberal state. In painting, music and poetry, the Futurists advocated a radical break with the past, extolling the virtues of movement, technology and industry that marked the mechanical era (Cannistraro 1975, 58–59).

The Futurist movement also influenced the diffusion of jazz music. Beginning in 1909, the 'Manifesto Futurista' singled out 'noise' as the 'acoustic reality of the modern world' (Valentini 2007, 84–85). In December 1924, a new manifesto dedicated to Futurist music – 'La musica futurista' – recognized jazz as

> the practical, though incomplete, implementation of our principles: the individuality of the singing of instruments, bringing together for the first

time sound elements of a different character; the persistence of its rhythms, bold and necessary, form the basis of Futurist music . . . Music is movement . . . music as harmony is colour. The scale of vibrations of the sounds corresponds to the scale of vibration of the colours.

(Casavola quoted in Bianchi 1996, 234–235)

Two years later, Franco Casavola, the author of this manifesto, reiterated: 'The Jazz Band is the typical product of our generation: heroic, violent, arrogant, brutal, optimistic, anti-romantic, anti-sentimental and anti-graceful. Born from war and revolution. Deny it, it denies ourselves!' (Casavola quoted in Cerchiari 2003, p. 13).

This synergy between the record industry, radio, cinema, as well as the influence of Futurism, increased the interest in jazz music around the country. According to Adriano Mazzoletti (2004, 105–106), starting from 1924, the birth of Italian jazz was particularly influenced by the white New York jazz scene, which was prevalent at the time within the US record industry. Stars such as Bix Beiderbecke, Red Nichols, Frank Trumbauer, Joe Venuti, Eddie Lang, Miff Mole, Jimmy Lytell, Adrian Rollini, Frank Signorelli, Arthur Schutt, and Jimmy and Tommy Dorsey all featured in Italian catalogues. Moreover, this influence increased when Italian jazz musicians and orchestras visited expat Italian communities in Brooklyn and Manhattan, where they performed with the likes of Venuti, Lang and Rollini (ibid.). As a result, new Italian jazz bands started to appear in Milan, Turin, Rome and Genoa, while the luckiest Italian followers sometimes participated in the shows of noted US jazz musicians, including Sam Wooding, who performed at Milan's Eden club in 1926 (Mazzoletti 2004, 148).

Of course, the diffusion of this new musical style also affected the tastes of the emerging radio public. In 1926, *Radiorario* discussed URI's many difficulties in trying to satisfy the broadcasting needs and wishes of an Italian population that was so diverse in age, region and social status. Yet, at the same time, the magazine reported that radio itself was a unifying force: young, old, rich and poor all seemed united in their desire to hear the daily radio broadcast of jazz music (Parelli 1926, 2–4). Later that year, the magazine published a cartoon that features a crowd of people demanding various changes to the radio schedules. Prominent among them are those with placards declaring: 'We Want Jazz' and 'Long Live Jazz' ('De programmibus est disputandum' 1926, 7; see Figure 1.1). This support for jazz music among Italian radio listeners contrasted with the official results of a referendum that URI held the following year. According to the referendum, Italian radio subscribers overwhelmingly expressed a preference for Italian classical music and opera when asked: 'Which kind of music and theatre do you prefer?' By contrast, they seemed to deplore jazz music (Natale 1990, 55). These findings, which were diametrically opposed to *Radiorario*'s pro-jazz articles and cartoons at the time, tallied with the Fascist

38 Marilisa Merolla

FIGURE 1.1 De Programmibus Est Disputandum

dictatorship's desire to use the suggestive power of Italian classical music to shape a national consciousness.

It thus comes as no surprise to find the composer Pietro Mascagni – who strongly rejected the musical avant-garde – playing a prominent role in defending the national tradition. During a radio broadcast on 9 March 1926 Mascagni firmly denounced the dangers of jazz music, saying it was an 'indecent music representing a dishonourable current trend'. Moreover, jazz was guilty of reducing 'the current generation to the lowest level of abjection: cocaine, *bal tabarin* [ballrooms] and jazz bands are the things that – in a manner of speaking – go hand in hand and have ruined the present youth' (Mascagni quoted in Isola 1998, 6–8). Mascagni revisited this topic in 1929, this time in his official role as a member of the Comitato Superiore di Vigilanza sulle Radio-diffusioni, a position he attained after publicly announcing his support for Fascism. In an article for *Popolo d'Italia* he accused Italian broadcasters of spreading the disease of jazz among Italian youth: 'Jazz music has recently influenced Italian radio. Its terrible voice excites the listeners and kills that little love for the real music that still remains' (Mascagni 1929).

As powerful as Mascagni's position was, he did not really affect the prevalence of jazz music on Italian radio. In fact, in 1927, a new version of 'Jazz Band' was launched on Italian radio under the direction of Maestro Ferruzzi, who led the resident orchestra, the Jazz Band della Fiaschetteria Toscana (Cerchiari 2003, 66). At this time *Radiorario* did not highlight any of the jazz programmes on Italian radio, as the magazine preferred to adopt a neutral position towards the genre (Mazzoletti 2004, 176). But it was clear that the musical tastes and critical sensibilities of Italy's population were growing more sophisticated as increasing numbers of them were able to hear radio broadcasts; thus, programing became more complex as listeners proved increasingly difficult to please (Restagno 1984, 112–114). Soon the official EIAR magazine felt obliged to report some subscribers' complaints:

> Let's stop the soporific and antiquated music! We are subscribers, and we have a right to protest! After such music all day, at night, with or without headphones, we want our spirits lifted! . . . Pull out some brilliant, modern music. We prefer the mostly off-key jazz band, any tarantella, any song a thousand times [more than] Wagner, Beethoven, Mozart.
>
> *(Alberini 1929, 8)*

In 1929, the broadcasters seemed to heed such demands and launched a new jazz programme entitled 'EIAR-JAZZ' ('Ufficio Propaganda e Sviluppo' 1929, 4).

In fact, the turning point had been reached the previous year with the transformation of URI into EIAR. After 1928, the industrialists' increased role, along with Mussolini's heightened interest in the medium's potential as a state-building tool, resulted in a policy shift for the national broadcaster. EIAR embarked on a series of new strategies to expand its broadcasting capabilities in the big cities while also attempting to reach the countryside for the first time. Moreover, it set out to improve the quality of the programmes in order to increase the number of subscribers. This resulted in Italian radio's transformation from a medium for amateurs to an influential mass communication instrument that was driven by a desire to reach the whole Italian populace (Natale 1990, 59).

The 'Volgarizziamo la Radio' (Radio to the People) campaign was launched in *Radiorario* in 1928, when the magazine featured a cartoon of black Africans listening to a radio broadcast ('Volgarizziamo la Radio' 1928, 10; see Figure 1.2). The campaign had several overlapping goals: increase subscribers; improve programming; and enforce new editorial guidelines. All of this was promoted by the new Propaganda and Development Office, the Ufficio Propaganda

FIGURE 1.2   Volgarizziamo la Radio

e Sviluppo (UPS; 'Ufficio Propaganda e Sviluppo' 1929, 13). In addition, in 1930 'Pioniere' – a local Fascist official – was introduced into many Italian districts in order to promote the diffusion of radio broadcasting at the local level and to offer a reference point for EIAR's listeners and subscribers while also enlarging the territory of the national radio audience. Furthermore, several initiatives were designed to overcome Italians' traditional diffidence in the face of new technology: national expositions celebrated the many futuristic aspects of radio; public competitions encouraged the production of new, cheaper receivers; and radios were sold at lower prices during certain weeks. As a result, the number of subscribers rose dramatically between 1930 and 1934 – from 176,332 to 438,738 (Natale 1990, 61–62).

Even though Mussolini was not yet fully aware of radio's potential as a propaganda device, the broadcasters were now handed the task of building and expanding the Fascist nation, as Enrico Corradini, the Minister of State and founder of the Italian Nationalist Association (Associazione Nazionalista Italiana), openly declared in the pages of *Radiocorriere* (Corradini 1930, 5), which replaced *Radiorario* as the broadcasting industry's official magazine in 1930. The idea was to spread a common spiritual, national experience among the Italian people by broadcasting 'information, education and entertainment'. In order to make the new EIAR more appealing than its predecessor, in 1931 it was decided that music should account for almost half of the station's programming (Cannistraro 1975, 234). Italian opera, as well as classical and chamber music, had of course been an important component of URI's schedule since the 1920s, but now EIAR's director promised to cater for 'a vast range of inclinations, tendencies, [and] tastes' among 'good music lovers' ('Trasmissioni musicali' 1931, 126–127). The previous year, Gigi Michelotti, the new director of *Radiocorriere*, had highlighted the increased role that music would play in EIAR's summer programming and announced a sharp reduction in the number of classical music concerts: 'Some people desire them [classical music concerts], some people tolerate them, other people would like [them] to be abolished' ('Il programma ideale' 1930, 1). Committed to abiding by its cultural responsibilities, and hoping to meet the demands of its audience, EIAR ordered all Italian radio stations to stop filling their evening schedules with classical music. It was thought that this would also encourage orchestras to introduce more variety into their repertoires and persuade them to combine classical with modern genres in order to give their performances a more sophisticated and refined style ('Il programma ideale' 1930, 1–2). As a result, the Italian 'radio-orchestra' was born. These full-time, publicly funded orchestras appeared on EIAR's four main stations and were encouraged to play modern dance music inspired by the American big bands. This adoption and conversion of a foreign style would soon become the 'Italian way'. The orchestras were led by the Italian conductors Pippo Barzizza, Cinico Angelini and Carlo Zeme, among others ('La musica leggera e le radio-orchestre' 1933, 14).

Searching for an Italian Way of Jazz (1933–1935)

Between 1933 and 1935, as the Fascist regime fully established its power, Italian national radio's programming became definitively propagandist and political (Cannistraro 1975, 246; Merolla 2004, 169–170; Monteleone 1992, 91–92; Natale 1990, 71), a true 'Italian way' (Merolla 2011, 97). Initiatives such as the 'Radio per le Scuole' and the 'Ente Radio Rurale' aimed to broadcast to the masses, many of whom had previously taken little interest in radio (Cannistraro 1975, 236–237). Of course, these ambitious projects had many cultural limitations and entailed several risks (Cannistraro 1975, 241–243). First, enlarging the radio network would almost certainly mean sanctioning the pre-eminence of US radio technology, which was more advanced than the domestic alternatives (Angeletti 1929, 39–42). Mussolini refused to accept this, however. In order to resist the invasion of the US radio transmitters – 'Gugliemo Marconi's nation could not remain in second place in bringing radio to the people' – he encouraged and promoted the domestic radio industry ('La Magneti Marelli fabbricherà apparecchi radio. Emancipazione dell'Italia dall'America' 1930, 6). Beginning in 1929, the Radiomarelli Company attempted to manufacture an Italian radio transmitter that was classier and cheaper than any US import ('La Magneti Marelli fabbricherà apparecchi radio. Emancipazione dell'Italia dall'America' 1930, 9). Of course, EIAR strongly supported the company's efforts with an intensive campaign that aimed to persuade radio subscribers of the superiority of Radiomarelli's model ('La Radiomarelli inizia la vendita a rate degli apparecchi radio' 1931, 14). Several other articles in *Radiocorriere* also highlighted the need to protect the Italian radio industry in the wake of the Wall Street Crash (Angeletti 1932, 29). None of these attempts at persuasion worked, though, so in 1931, with domestic radio manufacturers unable to compete against their giant overseas rivals, the Fascist dictatorship introduced a stiff import tariff on US broadcast devices ('Il nuovo regime doganale per gli apparecchi radiofonici' 1931, 10; 'Comunicazioni RadioMarelli. Il decreto 25 settembre' 1931, 17). Nevertheless, the domestic radio manufacturers were still unable to match firms like Telefunken, Philips and RCA, whose products remained more appealing and better priced.

In 1933, in order to nationalize the music industry, the authorities created a public record company known as CETRA (Compagnia Edizioni, Teatro, Registrazioni e Affini). CETRA's principal task was the production of Italian music, as Mussolini was committed to the construction of an official Fascist musical hegemony – a kind of 'caesarism' of Italian music (Cerchiari 2003, 140) – comprising political, patriotic hymns and songs (Pivato 2007, 154–155). However, the invasion of the new American rhythms and the wide dissemination of the most successful hits obliged the company to extend its output far beyond traditional Italian melodies (Cavallo and Iaccio 2003, 28). Italian musicians and bandleaders who had already assimilated the modern African-American rhythms – including Alberto Semprini, Gorni Kramer, Martinasso,

Pippo Barzizza, Franco Ansaldo, Vittorio Giuliani, Eldo Di Lazzaro, Cesare Andrea Bixio, Dino Olivieri, Raimondo, Vittorio Mascheroni and many others – were now encouraged to develop an 'Italian way' of jazz, swing and other modern dance music (Cavallo and Iaccio 2003, 35). This trend in modern music, now revisited with Italian lyrics and more melodic tunes, was also promoted by FONIT (Fonodisco italiano), formerly a private record company located in Milan, the Italian city that was most involved in the diffusion of jazz music (Cerchiari 2003, 55–59).

Meanwhile, the creation of CETRA marked a tighter bond between the record industry and national radio broadcasting (Boscia 1931, 4; Mazzoletti 2004, 227–229). As a result, many new radio-orchestras were founded in order to perform the most popular repertoires – melodic songs as well as jazz, tango and foxtrot – on both EIAR radio stations and CETRA records. However, the advent of the new Italian-style jazz tunes did not mean the disappearance of American performers (including Ellington, the Mills Brothers, Armstrong, Roy) from either the EIAR schedules or the Italian record industry catalogues ('Dischi Parlophon. La Cetra presenta i seguenti ballabili di successo mondiale' 1934, 26). Moreover, the national broadcaster continued to air many of the most famous American composers' shows and concerts, including those of George Gershwin ('Nord-America musicale. Gorge Gershwin, il più popolare autore americano di "jazz"' 1933, 19).

The great popularity of these syncopated tunes caused concern among the leadership of EIAR as they began to scrutinize the characteristics of the genre (Boscia 1931, 4). While African-American music, with its frenzied rhythms, was recognized as the genre that epitomized the contemporary age (Ciampelli 1933, 13), *Radiocorriere* also emphasized that many Italian people still viewed jazz as 'the music of cannibals or a bacchanal of Negroes' ('Musica di jazz' 1932, 3–4). In the early 1930s, two competing viewpoints were evident: jazz music was high art, fully adopted by Italians; or it undermined the Fascist agenda because it was a manifestation of 'primitive societies' and polluted the health and vigour of Italian youth (Cerchiari 2003, 97; Cavallo and Iaccio 2003, 31).

In 1935, Louis Armstrong performed in Turin amid great public enthusiasm (Soria 1935a, 18; Soria 1935b, 22; Mazzoletti 2004, 273–276). This was a further demonstration that the Italian public loved jazz music; even EIAR's official magazine had to admit that African-American music was gaining popularity in Italy ('La posta della direzione' 1935, 6). Nevertheless, Armstrong's tour was both the climax and the last expression of jazz's dissemination in Italy under Fascism. Moreover, it represented the culmination of the ambivalent relationship between jazz and the Fascist state, if we consider that the 'concert in Turin was organized with the full support of the regime, especially of Vittorio Mussolini', Benito Mussolini's son (Dainotto 2008, 285).

In October 1935, at the start of the Italo-Ethiopian War, the Fascist government pushed for a radical Fascistization of radio broadcasts in order to support the myth of the supremacy of the Italian nation ahead of the invasion. Patriotic choruses and Fascist hymns started to appear on the airwaves alongside the more familiar repertoire of melodic dance music, even if – with few exceptions – they never garnered much popularity among radio listeners and consumers (Cerchiari 2003, 69–71). Nevertheless, this was the definitive signal that jazz censorship had arrived, and it would increase until 1938, when Mussolini promulgated racial laws banning jazz from all radio broadcasts, declaring it 'Jewish' and 'Negroid' (Cerchiari 2003, 145–150; Cavallo and Iaccio 2003, 38–50).

Over the next few years, especially after Italy's entry into the Second World War on the side of Nazi Germany in June 1940, the use and abuse of national radio broadcasting as a propaganda weapon made the era of Italian jazz a distant memory (Giuliani 2014). On the other hand, even before the military defeat, the passivity and revulsion of the Italian people towards the war increased as ever more triumphant Fascist hymns and marches were heard on the airwaves. In 1943, with the arrival of Anglo-American troops in southern Italy, swing and jazz tunes started to interrupt the monotonous broadcasts of Mussolini's regime as the invaders gained control of one radio station after another: Radio Sardegna, Radio Palermo, Radio Bari, Radio Napoli and Radio Firenze all fell to them over the next few months (Lanotte 2012). Of course, the music that these radio stations now played was nothing new to the Italian people. Even though the 'Italian way' of jazz that EIAR had promoted before the war had not expressed an explicit rejection of Fascism and its values, the genre's popularity was certainly an anomaly amid Mussolini's attempt to build his vision of Italian totalitarianism.

Notes

1 All translations into English are the author's.
2 EIAR was introduced by the royal decree: R.D.L. 17.11.1927, n. 2207. The decree then became law the following year: Legge 17.5.1928, n. 1350.

References

Authored Books and Journal Articles

Alberini L. 1929. 'La signorina radio . . .'. *Radiorario*, 7–14 July.
Angeletti, G.B. 1929. 'L'industria radio alla Fiera di Milano. Gli aspetti della mostra radio'. *Radiorario*, 21 April.
Angeletti, G.B. 1932. 'Costruzione italiana e costruzione Americana'. *Radiocorriere*, 24 September–1 October.
Arvidsson, Adam. 2003. *Marketing Modernity: Italian Advertising from Fascism to Postmodernity*. London and New York: Routledge.
Barazzetta, Giuseppe. 1960. *Jazz inciso in Italia*. Milano: Messaggerie Musicali.

Barazzetta, Giuseppe. 2007. *Una vita in quattro quarti*. Siena: Quaderni di Siena jazz.

Ben-Ghiat, Ruth. 2001. *Fascist Modernities. Italy, 1922–1945*. Berkeley and Los Angeles: University of California Press.

Bergoglio, Franco. 2008. *Jazz! Appunti e note del secolo breve*. Milano: Costa e Nolan.

Bianchi, Stefano. 1996. *La musica futurista. Ricerche e documenti*. Lucca: Libreria Musicale Italiana.

Borgna, Gianni. 1992. *Storia della canzone italiana*. Milano: Mondadori.

Boscia, C. 1931. 'Radio e fonografo. Musica sinfonica e musica da jazz'. *Radiocorriere*, 5–12 September.

Bragaglia, Anton Giulio. 1929. *Jazz Band*. Milano: Corbaccio.

Cannistraro, Philip V. 1975. *La fabbrica del consenso: fascismo e mass media*. Roma and Bari: Laterza.

Caraceni, Augusto. 1937. *Il jazz dalle origini ad oggi*. Milano: Suvini Zerboni.

Caroli, Menico. 2003. *Proibitissimo: censori e censurati della radiotelevisione italiana*. Milano: Garzanti.

Castronovo, Valerio. 1984. 'Il modello industriale'. In *La radio, storia di sessant'anni (1924–1984)*, 75–78. Torino: RAI–ERI.

Cavallo, Pietro and Iaccio, Pasquale. 2003. *Vincere. Vincere. Vincere. Fascismo e società italiana nelle canzoni e nelle riviste di varietà 1935–1943*. Napoli: Liguori

Cerchiari, Luca. 1999. *Civiltà musicale afro-americana. Alle origini del jazz, del samba e de canti spirituali*. Milano: Mondadori.

Cerchiari, Luca. 2001. *Il Jazz. Una civiltà musicale afro-americana ed europea*. Milano: Bompiani.

Cerchiari, Luca. 2003. *Jazz e Fascismo. Dalla nascita della radio a Gorni Kramer*. Palermo: L'EPOS.

Cerri, Livio. 1958. *Il mondo del jazz*. Pisa: Nistri-Lischi.

Cesari, Maurizio.1978. *La censura nel periodo fascista*. Napoli: Liguori.

Ciampelli, G. M. 1933. 'Il "jazz" e la sua storia'. *Radiocorriere*, 12–19 February.

Colarizi, Simona. 2000a. *L'opinione degli italiani sotto il regime 1929–1943*. Roma and Bari: Laterza.

Colarizi, Simona. 2000b. *Storia del Novecento italiano. Cent'anni di entusiasmo, di paure, di speranze*. Milano: Bur.

Colarizi, Simona. 2010. *Storia del "Corriere della sera" 1900–1925*. Milano: Fondazione Corriere della sera.

Corradini, Enrico. 1930. 'La radiofonia strumento di espansione nazionale'. *Radiocorriere*, 17–23 May.

Dainotto, Roberto. 2008. 'The Saxophone and the Pastoral: Italian Jazz in the Age of Fascist Modernity'. *Italica* 85: 273–294.

De Felice, Renzo. 1991. *Le interpretazioni del fascismo*. Roma and Bari: Laterza.

De Grazia, Victoria. 1985. 'La sfida dello "star system": l'americanismo nella formazione della cultura di massa in Europa (1920–1965)'. *Quaderni Storici* 58: 98–106.

De Luigi, Mario. 2008. *Storia dell'industria fonografica in Italia*. Milano: Musica e Dischi.

De Luna, Giovanni. 2001. *La passione e la ragione: fonti e metodi dello storico contemporaneo*. Milano: La nuova Italia.

Fabbri, Franco and Plastino, Goffredo, eds. 2013. *Made in Italy: Studies in Popular Music*. New York and London: Routledge.

Fasce, Ferdinando. 2012. *Le anime del commercio. Pubblicità e consumi nel secolo americano*. Roma: Carocci.

46 Marilisa Merolla

Forgacs, David. 1992. *L'industrializzazione della cultura italiana*. Bologna: Il Mulino.

'Frakka' [alias Arnaldo Fraccaroli] 1921. 'Sottovoce. Dancings'. *Corriere della sera*, 29 January.

Gabrielli, Gloria. 2006. 'La propaganda anglo-americana alla radio in Italia (1943–1945)'. In Piero Craveri and Gaetano Quagliariello, eds, *La seconda guerra mondiale e la sua memoria*, 29–60. Soveria Mannelli: Rubbettino Editore.

Gentile, Emilio. 1982. *Il mito dello stato nuovo dall'antigiolittismo al fascismo*. Roma and Bari: Laterza

Gentile, Emilio. 1996. *The Sacralization of Politics in Fascist Italy*. Cambridge, MA: Harvard University Press.

Gentile, Emilio. 1999. *Il mito dello stato nuovo: dal radicalismo nazionale al fascismo*. Roma and Bari: Laterza.

Gentile, Emilio. 2003. *Il culto del littorio: la sacralizzazione della politica nell'Italia fascista*. Roma and Bari: Laterza.

Gentile, Emilio. 2006. *Politics as Religion*. Princeton, NJ, and Oxford: Princeton University Press.

Gentile, Emilio, ed. 2008. *Modernità totalitaria*. Roma and Bari: Laterza.

Gervasoni, Marco. 2002. *Le armi di Orfeo. Musica, identità nazionali e religioni politiche nell'Europa del novecento*. Milano: La Nuova Italia, Milano.

Giuliani, Roberto. 2014. 'La musica nella radio italiana della Seconda guerra mondiale: ruoli e funzioni'. In Ida De Benedictis, and Franco Monteleone, eds, *La musica alla radio: 1924–1954. Storia, effetti, contesti in prospettiva europea*, 93–110. Roma: Bulzoni (Biblioteca di cultura).

Giuliani, Roberto, ed. 2011. *La musica nel cinema e nella televisione*. Milano: Guerini Studio.

Griffin, Roger. 2007. *Modernism and Fascism: The Sense of a Beginning under Mussolini and Hitler*. New York: Palgrave Macmillan.

Gundle, Stephen. 2013. *Mussolini's Dream Factory: Film Stardom in Fascist Italy*. New York and Oxford: Berghahn Books.

Hendel, Lorenzo. 1983. *L'organizzazione del consenso nel regime fascista: EIAR come istituzione di controllo sociale*. Perugia: Istituto di etnologia e antropologia culturale della Università degli studi di Perugia.

Hobsbawm, Eric J. (writing as Francis Newton). 1989. *The Jazz Scene*. London: Weidenfeld and Nicolson (first published London: MacGibbon and Kee, 1959).

Isola, Gianni. 1990. *Abbassa la tua radio per favore. Storia dell'ascolto radiofonico nell'Italia fascista*. Firenze: La Nuova Italia.

Isola, Gianni. 1998. *L'ha scritto la radio. Storia e testi della radio durante il fascismo (1924–1944)*. Milano: Mondadori.

Johnson, Bruce. 2002. 'The Jazz Diaspora'. In Mervyn Cooke and David Horn, eds, *The Cambridge Companion to Jazz*, 33–54. Cambridge: Cambridge University Press.

Johnson, Bruce. Forthcoming. 'Jazz outside the US'. In David Horn and John Shepherd, eds, *The Bloomsbury Encyclopedia of Popular Music of the World*, vol. XII: *Genres: International*. London: Bloomsbury.

Kelly, Alan. 1988. *His Master's Voice/La voce del Padrone: The Italian Catalogue*. London: Greenwood Press.

Lanotte, Gioachino. 2012. *Il quarto fronte. Musica e propaganda dell'Italia liberata 1943–1945*. Bologna: Morlacchi.

Laura, Ernesto G. 2000. *Le stagioni dell'Aquila. Storia dell'Istituto Luce*. Roma: Ente dello Spettacolo Editore.

Levi, Ezio, and Testoni, Gian Carlo. 1938. *Introduzione alla vera musica di jazz*. Milano: Magazzino Musicale.

Librando, Diego. 2004. *Il jazz a Napoli. Dal dopoguerra agli anni Sessanta*. Napoli: Guida Editore.

Liperi, Felice. 1999. *Storia della canzone italiana*. Roma: RAI–ERI.

Mammarella, Giuseppe. 2005. *Destini incrociati. Europa e Stati Uniti nel XX secolo*. Roma and Bari: Laterza.

Martinelli, Dario. 2013 'Da Yeah a Ueee senza passare dal MinCulPop – Strategie di coesistenza e resistenza del jazz italiano durante il fascismo'. *California Italian Studies* 4(1): 1–15.

Mascagni, Pietro. 1929. 'L'opera ha fatto il suo tempo'. *Popolo d'Italia*, 3 August.

Mazzoletti, Adriano. 2004. *Il jazz in Italia dalle origini alle grandi orchestre*. Torino: EDT.

Mazzoletti, Adriano. 2010. *Il jazz in Italia dallo swing agli anni Sessanta*. Torino: EDT.

Mazzoletti, Adriano. 2011. *L'Italia del jazz*. Roma: Stefano Mastruzzi editore.

Merolla, Marilisa. 2004. *Italia 1961. I media celebrano il Centenario della nazione*. Milano: FrancoAngeli.

Merolla, Marilisa. 2006. 'Radio italienne et mémoire de la Résistance'. In Christian Delporte and Denis Marchal, eds, *Les médias et la Libération en Europe 1945–2005*, 331–344. Paris: Ina/L'harmattan.

Merolla, Marilisa. 2011. *Rock'n'roll, Italian Way. Propaganda americana e modernizzazione nell'Italia che cambia al ritmo del rock (1954–1964)*. Roma: Coniglio.

Monteleone, Franco. 1976. *La radio in Italia nel periodo fascista. 1924–1944*. Venezia: Marsilio.

Monteleone, Franco. 1992. *Storia della radio e della televisione in Italia. Costume società e politica*. Venezia: Marsilio.

Monticone, Alberto. 1978. *Il fascismo al microfono*. Roma: Edizioni studium.

Natale, A. Lucia. 1990. *Gli anni della radio (1924–1954)*. Napoli: Liguori.

Nicolodi, Fiamma. 1984. *Musica e musicisti nel ventennio fascista*. Fiesole: Discanto.

Onori, Luigi, 1997. 'Per chi suona quel ventennio? A Roma, a Villa Celimontana, una mostra racconta il jazz sotto il fascismo. Non mancano ambiguità ed omissioni'. *Il Manifesto*, 3 July.

Ortoleva, Peppino. 1993. 'Linguaggi culturali via etere'. In Simonetta Soldani and Gabriele Turi, eds, *Fare gli Italiani*, vol. II, 441–489. Bologna: Il Mulino.

Papa, Antonio. 1978. *Storia politica della radio in Italia*. Napoli: Guida.

Parelli A. 1926. 'La tela di Penelope'. *Radiorario*, 7–13 February.

Parola, Luigi, ed. 1999. *E poi venne la radio. Radio Orario 1925–1929*. Roma: Rai–ERI.

Peroni, Marco. 2001. *'Il nostro concerto'. Storia contemporanea tra musica leggera e canzone popolare*. Milano: La Nuova Italia.

Pivato, Stefano. 2002. *La storia leggera. L'uso pubblico della storia nella canzone italiana*. Bologna: Il Mulino.

Pivato, Stefano. 2007. *Bella ciao. Canto e politica nella storia d'Italia*. Roma and Bari: Laterza.

Pivato, Stefano and Tonelli, Anna. 2001. *Italia vagabonda: il tempo libero degli italiani dal melodramma alla pay-TV*. Roma: Carocci.

Prato, Paolo. 1999. *Suoni in scatola. Sociologia della musica registrata: dal fonografo a internet*. Genova: Costa & Nolan.

Prato, Paolo. 2010. *La musica italiana. Una storia sociale dall'Unità a oggi*. Roma: Donzelli.

Prato, Paolo. 2013. *Le macchine della musica. L'orchestra in casa*. Roma: RAI–ERI.

Restagno, Enzo. 1984. 'La musica alla radio'. In *La radio, storia di sessant'anni (1924–1984)*, 112–114. Torino: RAI–ERI.

Romero, Federico. 2005. 'Dalla convergenza alla divaricazione: l'America nell' immaginario dell'Europa occidentale'. In Tiziano Bonazzi, *Quale Occidente, Occidente perché*, 189–202. Soveria Mannelli: Rubbettino.

Rossetti, Roberto. 1990. *La voce della memoria. La Discoteca di Stato 1928–1989*. Roma: Fratelli Palombi Editori.

Sabbatucci, Giovanni. 1976. *La crisi italiana del primo dopoguerra. La storia e la critica*. Roma and Bari: Laterza

Sabbatucci, Giovanni and Vidotto, Vittorio, eds. 1997. *Storia d'Italia*, vol. IV: *Guerre e Fascismo. 1914–1943*. Roma and Bari: Laterza.

Sacchi F. 1922. 'Dancing. Cosmopolitismi'. *Corriere della sera*, 11 February.

Sachs, Harvey. 1988. *Music in Fascist Italy*. New York: Norton.

Scarpellini, Emanuela. 2008. *L'Italia dei consumi: dalla Belle Epoque al nuovo millennio*. Roma and Bari: Laterza.

Soria, M. 1935a. 'Louis Armstrong'. *Radiocorriere*, 20–26 January.

Soria, M. 1935b. 'Bis sulla formula del "jazz hot"'. *Radiocorriere*, 27 January–2 February.

Tonelli, Anna. 1998. *E ballando ballando. La storia d'Italia a passi di danza (1815–1996). Dal valzer borghese alla macarena dei militanti popolari*. Milano: FrancoAngeli.

Tonelli, Anna. 2001. 'La "sana musica italiana". Divieti e censure fasciste contro jazz e fox-trot'. *Storia e problemi contemporanei* 28: 17–32.

Valentini, Paola. 2007. *Presenze sonore. Il passaggio al sonoro in Italia tra cinema e radio*. Firenze: Le Lettere.

Zani, Luciano. 1988. *Fascismo, autarchia, commercio estero. Felice Guarneri: un tecnocrate al servizio dello 'Stato nuovo'*. Bologna: Il Mulino.

Zenni, Stefano. 2012. *Storia del jazz: una prospettiva globale*. Viterbo: Stampa alternativa/ Nuovi equilibri.

Zunino, Piergiorgio. 1985. *L'ideologia del fascismo. Miti, credenze e valori nella stabilizzazione del regime*. Bologna: Il Mulino.

Articles without a Credited Author

'Comitato Superiore di Vigilanza per le Radio-audizioni'. 1928. *Radiorario*, 15–22 January.

'Comunicazioni RadioMarelli. Conversando'. 1930. *Radiocorriere*, 8–15 November.

'Comunicazioni RadioMarelli. Il decreto 25 settembre'. 1931. *Radiocorriere*, 24–31 October.

'De programmibus est disputandum'. 1926. *Radiorario*, 29 August–5 September.

'Dischi Parlophon. La Cetra presenta i seguenti ballabili di successo mondiale'. 1934. *Radiocorriere*, 25 February–4 March.

'I programmi della stazione di Roma'. 1925. *Radiorario*, 14 March.

'Il nuovo regime doganale per gli apparecchi radiofonici'. 1931. *Radiocorriere*, 3–10 October.

'Il programma ideale'. 1930. *Radiocorriere*, 11–18 October.

'Janssen e la musica americana'. 1933. *Radiocorriere*, 15–22 January.

'La Magneti Marelli fabbricherà apparecchi radio. Emancipazione dell'Italia dall' America'. 1930. *Radiocorriere*, 5–12 April.

'La musica leggera e le radio-orchestre'. 1933. *Radiocorriere*, 22–29 January.

'La posta della direzione'. 1935. *Radiocorriere*, 30 December–5 January.

'La Radiomarelli inizia la vendita a rate degli apparecchi radio'. 1931. *Radiocorriere*, 18–25 April.

'Musica di jazz'. 1932. *Radiocorriere*, March 20–27.

'Nord-America musicale. Gorge Gershwin, il più popolare autore americano di "jazz"'. 1933. *Radiocorriere*, 1–24 September.

'Programmi di venerdì 20 gennaio 1933 delle stazioni radiofoniche di Milano – Torino – Genova – Trieste – Firenze, concerto sinfonico diretto dal M° Werner Janssen'. 1933. *Radiocorriere*, 15–22 January.

'Trasmissioni musicali'. 1931. *Annuario EIAR*: 1931.

'Ufficio Propaganda e Sviluppo'. 1929. *Radiorario*, 24 February–3 March.

'Una nuova iniziativa. L'EIAR-JAZZ'. 1929. *Radiorario*, 31 March–7 April.

'Unione Radiofonica Italiana. Stazione di Roma. Lunghezza d'onda m. 425'. 1925. *Radiorario*, 31 January.

'Volgarizziamo la Radio'. 1928. *Radiorario*, 28 October–4 November.

2

JAZZ IN MOSCOW AFTER STALINISM

Rüdiger Ritter

Jazz in the Soviet Union is often described in Cold War terms: jazz, as the vanguard of American, Western culture, finally conquered Soviet youth despite intensive but ultimately unsuccessful efforts by the authorities to contain this influence. This study examines the jazz scene in Moscow from the mid-1950s to the 1970s and challenges this account: jazz activities in Moscow during that period were the result of constant processes of finding compromises between the jazz milieu and the cultural officials. The latter did not simply reject jazz, but undertook considerable efforts to integrate it within the cultural model of the Soviet Union. This was done by installing a discourse on jazz aesthetics, renewing for example the pattern of the 1930s when Soviet cultural officials distinguished between a 'bad' commercialised white and a 'good' vernacular black jazz. Composers' Union congresses made serious efforts to develop a local Soviet jazz as a contrast to American jazz. Soon, professional jazz teaching in universities began, and members of the jazz scene participated in this: some very well-known musicians, such as Aleksandr Tsfasman and Iuriĭ Saulskiĭ, were members of the cultural commissions, and many listeners not only appreciated US jazz but developed forms of this music which came nearer to the ideas of the authorities, merging jazz with the Soviet ėstrada culture. Soviet jazz in the 1960s evolved in a process of constant negotiation between the jazz milieu and the authorities. Cultural officials offered the musicians and listeners public spaces for their concerts, which meant the cultural officials could monitor and control any developments. This was crucial because their primary goal was to redirect the jazz movement in the Soviet Union to the purpose of educating the people in communist ideals. The Moscow jazz festivals of the early 1960s and the famous cafés (such as Kafė Molodëzhnoe and Kafė Aėlita) exemplify this negotiation. The findings of this case study are based on research in Moscow archives (RGALI, GARF, RFGASPI) and on eyewitness material collected in the RCID, Jaroslavl'.

Introduction: 'Jazz' and 'totalitarianism' – the Problem of Essentialist Definitions

As Bruce Johnson put it in the Introduction to this volume, the notion of totalitarianism has a long and complicated history. Whereas some authors, especially early in the discourse, tried to create a list of criteria to be fulfilled for a society to be called totalitarian, subsequently many scholars have focused on societies that are also commonly regarded as totalitarian, but differ dramatically from these criteria. This has led some to question whether it is even possible to deploy the term 'totalitarian' in a meaningful way as an analytic tool (Losurdo 2004). It is not only the differences between various societies but the differences *within* any one society over several time periods that illustrate the problem of an essentialist use of the term. As we know today from the proliferating studies on Soviet society, social conditions within the Soviet Union changed dramatically more than once. So does it really make sense to call Soviet society 'totalitarian' throughout all of these periods simply because it continued to meet the criteria of Hannah Arendt, including one single party and control of public opinion? Although formally these criteria applied in both cases, the differences between, for example, Soviet society under Stalin and Soviet society in the early Gorbachev years are radical. Consequently, scholars tried to address this problem by speaking of a 'post-totalitarian' system, but this caused further methodological problems (Thompson 2002). As a result, other terms have been proposed, such as 'authoritarian' society, 'unfree' society and 'dictatorial' society.

Rather than enter into a long discussion of theory, I wish to engage directly with an empirical study of a case whose status as 'totalitarian' has been regarded as unequivocal. The chosen context, the 1960s in the Soviet Union, offers an opportunity to conduct an intensive discussion of this society and its construction. Soviet rulers never managed to implement their totalitarian goals like the complete politicization of the society, the subordination of citizens to total control, or the formation of a state-loyal Soviet nation that thought uniformly (Fitzpatrick 2000; Litvin and Keep 2005; Hobsbawm 2002). But in the field of cultural politics, from the 1960s onwards there was a contradiction between the mechanisms of governance and the systems of propaganda, on the one hand, and the real enactment of the Soviet project on entire society, on the other. There was a discourse on the necessity of changes following Stalin's rule, beginning with Khrushchëv's[1] so-called 'secret speech' in 1956, which included all fields of society, including jazz and other music. This discourse was led by both official state activists (party members, composers, cultural politicians) and members of the jazz milieu, both musicians and audiences.

What position was occupied by jazz and the jazz milieu? Did jazz become part of the official discourse? What did that mean for the contradiction between jazz and the political authorities, which had been so prominent in the Stalinist period? Often, individuals belonged to both groups, such as the most important composers of jazz in the Soviet Union at that time, including Aleksandr Tsfasman. By identifying the protagonists of this discourse, one of the most common prejudices of jazz in the Soviet Union is critically tested: was there really a sharp distinction between a jazz-suppressing official sphere and an oppositional jazz milieu? Instead of uncritically sustaining such a Manichaean model of Soviet society, this chapter focuses on an empirical base, using Moscow in the 1960s as a case study.

Almost every scholar writing about jazz agrees that it is difficult, if not impossible, to define 'this thing called jazz', as Porter (2002) titled his study. Often, expressions like 'jazz and jazz-related music' are deployed (Dauer 1992, 42–55). These are responses to the fact that, due to its integrative character and its century-long international diffusion, the music called jazz has developed an immense stylistic diversity. This is most evident regarding the diachronic aspect: no one will deny the differences between New Orleans jazz and bebop, but there is still a strong sense of both styles being parts of the jazz universe. For this study, the synchronic aspect is even more important: during the 1960s, in different countries of the world there coexisted different forms of music which were all called jazz by both the musicians themselves and their audiences. The reason for this is the often neglected fact that jazz did not spread globally only from the Swing era onwards,[2] but considerably earlier. In 1922, a band led by Valentin Parnakh, the 'father' of Russian jazz, gave the first jazz concert in the young Soviet Union (Starr 1983, 46; Volkov 2013, 8–10), and jazz appeared around the same time in almost every other European country, too. Very quickly, local nationals not only listened to these foreign jazz groups, but integrated jazz in their cultures. A jazz discourse evolved, with the first monographs on jazz appearing in the 1920s, with vigorous discussions on the pros and cons of the genre, and with local jazz musicians and jazz composers emerging in these countries.

As a consequence, jazz was never simply American music and nothing more, as the master narrative of jazz history – especially in the USA – often implies (Farley 2008). Although the idea of an American element in jazz was used by jazzmen behind the Iron Curtain to express musical opposition to anti-US governments or structures, especially in the Eastern Bloc (Pickhan and Ritter 2010), and although these governments tried to create an anti-US mood by denying the cultural values of jazz, there was also a totally different notion of the genre. Musicians in the Soviet Union (and, at that time, elsewhere in Europe) did more than simply copy the American model; they started to invent their own music, often building upon the foundations of their local traditions and fusing these with elements of the music from America. Yet they continued to call the results jazz.

The 1960s in the Soviet Union were a time when this issue was intensively discussed in the realm of official political culture as well as by members of the jazz scene. This debate offered a dramatic broadening of propagandistic options for the official sphere as well as an equally dramatic broadening of compositional possibilities. As the capital of the Soviet Union, Moscow was one of the places where these discussions were conducted most intensively, but similar discussions took place in Leningrad and indeed in smaller provincial towns, where one might not have expected to find vibrant jazz scenes (Feĭertag 2013, 208–219). Yet the presence of such scenes in cities like Tallinn and Novosibirsk confirms that Soviet jazz life, unlike official culture, was not restricted to the political centres of the country (Belichenko and Kotel'nikov 2005). Nevertheless, Moscow is used as the case study in this chapter because the capital witnessed both an emerging jazz scene and official discussions of the music. The jazz discourse may have been more advanced elsewhere – especially in the Baltic – but the results of the discussions among cultural politicians in Moscow determined official jazz policy throughout the USSR, including on the periphery. The enforced ending of the jazz festival tradition in Tallinn in 1967 as a result of a Moscow decree clearly illustrates this fact.

Three places were instructive sites of the Soviet jazz discourse: first, the discussions at the Composers' Union meeting of 1962; second, the events at the newly established jazz cafés and festivals in Moscow; and third, the system of Soviet musical education. These three places serve as case studies for an exploration of the subject of this chapter.

Jazz in the Composers' Union

The Composers' Union of the Soviet Union was the official organization for all composers, music-makers, and people working in the field (Tomoff 2006). Public activity was possible only through membership of this organization. Similar organizations existed for all fields of culture, with each of them being an integral part of the cultural politics of the Soviet Union (Taruskin 2010). Party and government organizations sought to supervise all activities in the cultural sphere. Communist ideology included the objective of educating the masses in order to make them suitable for the tasks and needs of a socialist society. Artists' unions were to be the links between this cultural model and the individual artists. So, while these unions had an executive function, they were also the places where cultural policies were developed and discussed. Because their proceedings were closed to the general public, the debates were unconstrained and covered controversial issues, in sharp contrast to the sanitized bulletins and newspaper articles that presented the results of the discussions.

From 13 to 28 November 1962, the Composers' Union held its fourth plenum, which was devoted exclusively to 'Soviet song and éstrada music'.[3] This also included a discussion about jazz. The conference was attended by the country's highest-ranking composers, with the introductory paper presented by none other than Dmitriĭ Shostakovich. Among the other forms of music to be considered at the conference, he mentioned jazz, which he identified as a genre of dance music. This was a common classification at the time, and not only among officials in the Soviet Union. Shostakovich, and after him many other speakers, stressed the idea that music, like all arts in the Soviet Union, had to fulfil the needs of the people and educate them. He pointed out that in a situation in which many young people strongly demanded entertaining music, the Composers' Union was challenged to respond to these demands. Thus, the conference was regarded as very important.

Another member of the union named Chernov[4] stated that 'light music' (*legkaia muzyka*) is always propaganda and agitation. With this he had in mind the Soviet idea of persuading the masses and creating identity through the Soviet ideology. This notion of propaganda was primarily directed towards the people in their own country. In contrast to the use of the term 'propaganda' in the US discourse, here it had a uniformly positive connotation (Kenez 1985). There was no contradiction between propaganda and truth, because communist ideology claimed its own position to be the truth simply by definition, and obliged communists to spread this truth among the people. Thus, for Chernov, light music was a legitimate vehicle for communist propaganda.

Several conference members stated that in recent years a great variety of jazz groups had evolved in the country, including students' bands, amateur combos, professional musicians' ensembles and others. But only an estimated 10 per cent of these groups were enrolled in the Composers' Union, so the majority could 'play what they want'.[5] For the conference members, this was a scandalous situation that demanded immediate action. Several speakers[6] advocated measures of control, up to 'operative' (*operativnost*) measures, which in the Soviet language code meant secret service intervention in these music groups − that is, infiltration by individuals connected with the intelligence services − and various other suppression measures.

Some of the conference members deeply disliked jazz and would have preferred to extirpate it altogether. Among this group was the General Secretary of the Composers' Union Tikhon Khrennikov, who described his impression of a Louis Armstrong concert as '*vulgaire*' (*Stenogramma* 1962, 204). But since the death of Stalin times had changed, and such attitudes were now in the minority. Shostakovich mentioned the vigorous quarrels on jazz throughout the country, but he and some other members of the conference, especially the Soviet jazzmen Oleg Lundstrem, Leonid Utësov and Aleksandr Tsfasman, argued for the genre's importance. In 1962 jazzmen in the Soviet Union could present their position with considerable self-confidence. Lundstrem harshly condemned the recent tendency to identify enthusiastic jazz listeners as hooligans, asking why audience enthusiasm was welcomed in classical concerts but depicted as hooliganism at jazz concerts (*Stenogramma* 1962, 202). Trombonist Konstantin Bakholdin demanded a revision of the famous poet Gorkiĭ's prewar depiction of jazz as 'music of the gross' (*Stenogramma* 1962, 33) – a definition that had been extremely prevalent in the Soviet Union and had often been used to justify the jazz scene's suppression (Starr 1983: 89–90).

In 1962 the existence of jazz in the Soviet Union was thus a fact that could not be denied, so all conference members agreed that it was the task of the Composers' Union to steer jazz and the jazz community in an approved direction. Again, the Soviet jazz musicians who were present articulated their needs: Utësov complained that Soviet composers may write a waltz or a mazurka, but not a foxtrot (*Stenogramma* 1962, 33). As M. Bialik from Leningrad put it: for the development of jazz 'we need freedom' (*Stenogramma* 1962, 229). Utësov pointed to his colleague Tsfasman and said: 'Here A. Tsfasman is sitting, who can do extraordinary things in this genre, but he has fear' (*Stenogramma* 1962, 34).

The conference members discussed the kind of music that should be created. Utësov demanded optimistic, joyful music that would help people build socialism (*Stenogramma* 1962, 33). The music had to be based on motives or melodies from Russian musical culture. No one at the conference disagreed with this position, neither the Russian members nor those from the other Soviet republics, such as the Estonian Valter Ojakäär. Officially called 'Soviet light music', forms of Russian light music were propagated. The Soviet song and entertainment music composer Isaac Dunaevskiĭ was presented as a model for the integration of Russian musical elements into new compositions. Chernov offered Michel Legrand[7] as an example of how to write modern music with the help of traditional, national song material. Again we find here a conception of national music dating from the nineteenth century, which had furnished the blueprint for Soviet musical aesthetics. This model was also used in the attempt to create a distinct, Soviet form of jazz. Chernov stated with great confidence: 'During the 19th century Paris and Vienna were the musical centres of Europe, now this role is held by Moscow, as the capital of the most progressive country of the world' (*Stenogramma* 1962, 228).

But one problem remained: the extremely modern forms of jazz, such as the cool style. Conservative participants in the conference like Khrennikov and Zazovskiĭ denied the artistic value of modern jazz in all its forms, asking, 'What is music without melody?' (*Stenogramma* 1962, 118) According to them, only a small minority listened to this music, just as only a small group of people viewed modern abstract art; thus, they felt it was not sufficiently significant to demand their attention. At this point Chernov, who had raised the problem, put the question of why Western music had to be a model for the development of Soviet music (*Stenogramma* 1962, 43).

Here, we have the basic dilemma of Soviet music theorists: on the one hand, they were convinced by the traditional Russian idea of the uniqueness of

56 Rüdiger Ritter

Russian culture (an idea that can be traced back at least to Nikolaĭ Danilevskiĭ) and sought to incorporate this belief within a new Soviet order; but on the other hand they had to recognize the difficulties of competing with the appeal of foreign music. Soviet theorists themselves had created this dilemma: the Stalinist era had proved that condemning jazz as a whole was a fruitless task; but endorsing all forms of music without any mechanism of control was an intolerable contradiction of Soviet ideology. The solution seemed to be the creation of an independent Soviet jazz, so the composers were tasked with determining what specific form this type of jazz should take. Thus, the field for experimentation was opened, but at the same time it was circumscribed: Soviet officials reserved the right to proscribe any form of musical activity that they deemed inappropriate.

Moscow's Jazz Cafés: Experimenting with Jazz and Jazz Life

In 1960/1, Anastas Mikoian, First Deputy Premier under Khrushchëv, visited the German Democratic Republic and familiarized himself with the ideological work with that nation's youth (Kull' 2013a, 140–170). Back in the Soviet Union, officials attempted to implement the lessons learned in the GDR and set about organizing public places where Soviet youth might meet and enjoy their leisure time in a friendly atmosphere in order to distract them from the problems of everyday life in the USSR (Tsipursky n.d.; Fürst *et al.* 2008; Pilkington 1994). Only 'modern music' was mentioned in official documents, not jazz, but since the practical organization of these places was assigned to local Komsomol groups, where plenty of jazz enthusiasts congregated, it was played more than anything else in the new meeting places. Some of the members of the executive groups, including Vladimir Abatuni, later performed as jazz musicians in the cafés they had planned and organized. As a member of the section for agitation and propaganda in the Moscow Komsomol's town committee, Abatuni was responsible for the work in the cafés and later played drums in various jazz groups in the Kafė Molodëzhnoe (Kull' 2013a, 158). This illustrates the fact that the borders between the jazz scene and the official organizers were not always as sharp as is often assumed.

Several cafés were founded in Moscow from 1961 onwards. Four of them soon became centres of the city's jazz scene: the Molodëzhnoe, the Aėlita and, a little later, the Siniaia Ptitsa and the Romantiki (Kull' 2009; Ponomarev 2003; Kozlov n.d.). These cafés, which were soon openly (albeit unofficially) known as 'jazz cafés', were all situated on Gorkiĭ street (today Tverskaia Street). Since the late 1940s and early 1950s, Soviet *stiliagi*[8] had called this street 'Broadway' or abbreviated it to 'Brod'. Now a kind of night life began to evolve. Young jazz enthusiasts visited the cafés, often switching venues when they learned that a new jazz ensemble was performing at one of the others.

As a result, this section of Gorkiĭ Street became very crowded in the evening, at least until 11 p.m., the latest hour that the authorities would tolerate.

The cultural activities in these cafés encompassed a variety of different art forms. Writers like Evgeniĭ Evtushenko, Vasiliĭ Aksënov and Il'ia Suslov, songwriters such as Bulat Okudzhava and the photographers Leonid Bergol'tsev and Viktor Reznikov would all congregate at the Aélita. Jazz musicians and open-minded, mostly young Komsomol members all understood that the cafés represented an opportunity to create a public forum for Soviet jazz. But calling them jazz cafés would almost certainly have provoked a reaction from the conservative elite. Hence, in an article on the opening of the Kafé Molodëzhnoe, Aleksandr Terent'ev, the first chairman of the café soviet, used the word 'jazz' only once, when he explained that it was a form of dance music (cited in Kull' 2013a, 158). However, many Komsomol members knew that the city's youth would be drawn to any venue that offered jazz. In later years, these same Komsomol members helped Soviet jazz musicians to obtain travel permits to perform at important jazz festivals in Prague and Warsaw (Kull' 2013a, 159).

The Aélita opened on 25 November 1961. The previous evening, Anastas Mikoian himself had met with the members of the café soviet. Some musicians and music groups played regularly at the Aélita. The first of these was a band comprising Evgeniĭ Gevorgian (piano), his younger brother Andreĭ Gevorgian (bass) and Vladimir Zhuravskiĭ (drums). Other regular performers were Nikolaĭ Gromin (guitar), together with Michail Tsurichenko (sax), Fred Margulis (sax), Aleksandr Il'in (flute) and Vladislav Grachëv (trumpet). One of the highlights was a concert by the Neva Jazz Band, with Vsevolod Korolëv (trumpet), Gennadiĭ Lachman (clarinet), Aleksandr Morozov (trombone), Boris Erzhov (banjo), Aleksandr Kolpashnikov (bass) and Valentin Kolpashnikov (drums). However, the Aélita closed in 1963 when the building was demolished to facilitate the widening of Sadovaia kol'tsa Street.

The Molodëzhnoe, which opened on 18 October 1961, was planned from the beginning as a restaurant with a 'scene', and it was here that several American jazz greats chose to play. Gerry Mulligan and Charles Lloyd were the most famous guests in 1967, and Earl Hines performed later (von Eschen 2004, 199). Among the local musicians were several who had already gained a reputation in the Moscow jazz scene. The most important of these were Alekseĭ Kozlov, Vadim Sakun, Andreĭ Egorov, Valerij Bulanov, Nikolaĭ Gromin, Georgiĭ Garanian, Alekseĭ Zubov and Konstantin Bakholdin.

The Siniaia Ptitsa opened in 1964, when the Worldwide Forum of Youth was held in Moscow and young people arrived in the city from every communist and pro-communist country. The name, meaning bluebird, evoked the famous Bluebird Inn in Detroit. During the following years the Siniaia Ptitsa became a venue not only for jazz but for meetings of workers' collectives and their social events. As a result, dance music played a major role in the musical repertoire of the café. On the other hand, according to Michail Kull', bop – the most modern form of music to be heard in Moscow at the time – was also played in the Siniaia Ptitsa (Kull' 2013b: 38).

Jazz was also played at the Romantiki, usually an ensemble consisting of Vladimir Kull' (piano), Mark Terlitskiĭ (bass), Aleksandr Salgannik (drums), often accompanied by Alekseĭ Kuznetsov (guitar). The Romantiki was a particularly important venue for so-called 'Soviet authors' songs' – that is, ballads written by local composers such as Okudzhava.

In general, most of the jazz musicians who performed in these cafés were amateurs, and only a few of them had received formal training on their instruments. Almost all of them hailed from the higher-education sector, with many of them holding university qualifications in physics (Alekseĭ Zubov, Valeriĭ Bulanov, Vadim Sakun), architecture (Alekseĭ Kozlov, Mark Terlitskiĭ), electrical engineering (Vladislav Grachëv, Lev Lebedev, Vsevolod Danilochkin) or some other professional discipline.

Like almost all restaurants with scenes in these years, the musicians in the jazz cafés were also integrated into official structures. They usually received very small remuneration from the Moscow Organization of Musical Ensembles (MOMA). One exception was the Siniaia Ptitsa, where the musicians were paid from the money taken during the evening events. Including these musicians in official structures was one method of exercising state control over the scene, and it was regarded as extremely important among cultural politicians. But other methods were employed, too: for instance, the KGB infiltrated the scene in order to gather first-hand information from jazzmen. Its agents ordered Rostislav Vinarov – who helped to organize the musical programmes of the Kafé Molodëzhnoe in its first few years – to inform them of any important events, and it can be assumed that he was not alone.[9]

Jazz Festivals in Moscow

Five jazz festivals were held in Moscow in the 1960s: one in 1962, and the others between 1965 and 1968 (Kull' 2012, 2013b, 2013c). The 1962 festival was the first such event to take place in Moscow, but not the first in the Soviet Union: a similar event had been held in Estonia five years earlier. 'Festival' is perhaps too grand a term for the 1962 event, which comprised five evening concerts in which Moscow's leading jazzmen played in the Molodëzhnoe. As was the case everywhere in the Soviet Union at the time, there was a variety of local jazz groups in Moscow, but no jazz infrastructure. Any communication between the local jazz scenes took place by word-of-mouth.

The 1962 festival was the Moscow jazz scene's first attempt to establish a communication network by organizing a kind of demonstration of the local jazzmen's talents. In May 1962, after a long diplomatic process, Benny Goodman had played in Moscow (von Eschen 2004, 100–104). Even Khrushchëv had joined the standing ovation after Goodman's concert, so

Moscow's jazzmen were encouraged to start organizing their festival. The festival was a success, although the participants had to adhere to official cultural policies. For instance, Komsomol insisted on a competition structure, with a jury judging the bands to determine winners and losers. Here, the organizers were helped by the fact that Moscow's jazzmen had no experience of festivals in other parts of the world, so they were unaware that a festival did not automatically mean a competition (Kozlov n.d.). As a consequence, both sides benefited from the festival: the jazzmen were able to play to large audiences, while the officials kept the event under strict control.

Shortly afterwards, however, the mood towards jazz changed dramatically – not within the jazz scene itself, but at the highest levels of state. At an exhibition of avant-garde art in December 1962, Khrushchëv harshly attacked jazz, denying its value and describing it as 'cacophony' (Kull' 2012: 54). More criticism followed, which seriously damaged the jazz scene in the Soviet Union. The jazz cafés continued to operate, but they hosted fewer jazz performances, and there were no more jazz festivals in Moscow or anywhere else in the Soviet Union for several years.

However, in October 1964 Khrushchëv was ousted, Leonid Brezhnev became General Secretary of the Communist Party, and jazz was allowed to reassert itself. The previous month, Tat'jana Tëss had launched an attack in *Izvestiia* against Boris Midnyĭ and Igor' Berukshtis (Tëss 1964), but before long the radio journalist and jazz expert Arkadiĭ Petrov was able to publish an article titled 'Jazz is a Serious Thing' (Kull' 2012, 54). Plans were soon under way for a new festival, but this time it would be much more professional. Its venue would no longer be the small Molodëzhnoe café, but the great hall of the Hotel Iunost'. The organization was handled by the city's Komsomol committee, with Rostislav Vinarov assuming a central role. He contacted the Composers' Union, which assembled a jury of nineteen key Soviet musical figures, including Andrejĭ Eshpaĭ, the jazz and light music composers Vadim Liudvikovskiĭ and Aleksandr Tsfasman, and Vano Il'ich Muradeli as jury president. With this official stamp of approval, not only the festival but jazz itself was integrated in the musical establishment of the Soviet Union. For the first time, Moscow jazz was released on a two-disc album (Melodiia ZZD-01709-10 and ZZD-017017-18).

The integration of Moscow jazz into the official cultural discourse meant it could now be used to further the aims of official cultural politics. Most of the music played at the festival was composed by Soviet musicians and it had almost no American flavour; only a small fraction was the work of foreign composers. Moreover, most of the featured Soviet composers were members of the Composers' Union. The cultural officials deemed the festival a great success because, having domesticated the jazz scene, they were convinced that the local musicians and their fans were proud to play and listen to jazz in public with official approval. Up to a point, the musicians apparently tailored their compositions to correspond with what the officials desired. But they wanted more. Despite their pride in their compositions, and despite their identification with 'home-grown' Soviet jazz, the members of the jazz milieu as well as the jazz composers still wished to integrate certain American elements in their music. Indeed, they started to demand more direct contact with the US jazz scene. Therefore, although Soviet officials successfully encouraged the creation of native forms of jazz, they conspicuously failed to reduce the appeal of American jazz. The next few festivals illustrated this.

In 1966, the newspapers covered a Moscow jazz festival in depth for the first time, with articles appearing in both *Moskovskiĭ Komsomolets* and *Komsomol'skaia Pravda*. The official state-owned record company Melodia issued an accompanying disc, and there were many more musicians than the previous year. In the meantime, contact with other cities had intensified, and as a consequence several performers appeared at jazz events in Tallinn and Leningrad as well as Moscow that year. The festival was held in the concert hall of the Moscow Institute of Transportation Engineers, a much more prestigious location than the previous year's venue.

Ever since 1962, officials had used the festivals to hand-pick certain musicians for specific roles. For instance, in that year Vadim Sakun's sextet was chosen to perform at the Warsaw Jazz Jamboree; and in 1965 the Garanian–Gromin quartet performed at the Prague festival after impressing the jury in Moscow. The following year, the Kafė Molodëzhnoe quartet was selected to perform in Prague, while Garanian's quartet represented the Soviet jazz scene in Warsaw. It is difficult to say who benefited most here – the jazz musicians or the official organizers. The musicians were proud and gratified that their music was finally officially appreciated, and they were surely excited to travel abroad, which was not an option for most Soviet citizens at that time. On the other hand, the officials were gratified that the festivals gave them a means to cultivate the jazz scene in a controlled fashion.

The next two festivals once again demonstrated both their potential and their limits. The 1967 festival could be seen as the climax of the developments in the Moscow jazz scene after 1962. There were even more press articles than the year before, and almost all of the Soviet jazz greats performed. But much more significant was the fact that several Americans were allowed to travel to Moscow: Willis Conover, the jazz radio moderator of the Voice of America, attended after previously visiting the festivals in Tallinn and Leningrad; and he was accompanied by Charles Lloyd and his group. Moscow's jazz musicians were excited by the arrival of Lloyd, but they viewed Conover's participation as even more important. Almost all of them were familiar with his voice, as they had listened to his programme 'Music USA – Jazz Hour' since its launch in 1955 (Ritter 2013). Aleksei Kozlov described Conover's arrival and the excitement when he announced, 'Time for jazz' – the words the USSR's devoted VOA listeners had heard every night for over a decade.

For Kozlov, this was 'the visualization of a sonic image, like in a fairy tale' (Kozlov n.d.).

The fact that the arrival of a handful of Americans in Moscow was regarded as a 'fairy tale' demonstrates the success of the USSR's isolationist policies at the time. Confronted with Soviet reality, Charles Lloyd described his astonishment at Moscow's impoverished living conditions and restrictions. Whereas contemporary Soviet jazzmen viewed the new Brezhnev era as relatively joyful and liberal, Lloyd felt it was fearful and strange (Romański 2013, 43; Gitler 1967, 15). One detail in particular was significant for Soviet jazz fans: Vano Muradeli was so disturbed by whistling in the audience that he announced he would suspend the festival if it did not stop immediately. However, his more moderate colleagues Eshpaĭ and Fliarkovskiĭ convinced him that whistling was a common sign of approval at jazz festivals, so Muradeli allowed it to continue. This victory of jazz over the regime generated a sense of triumph among Moscow's jazz community. However, for their American visitors, the incident was simply a further demonstration of the Soviet Union's authoritarianism.

The music the artists played also reflects this contrast. On the orders of the Composers' Union, works built on a Soviet musical base predominated. The organizers' committee set out the rules of the festival, which had to follow the ideological line towards music. Each of the participants was asked to prepare one or two compositions based on a Russian folk song or an improvisation on a Soviet composer's song. In addition, a single original composition and a single title by a foreign composer were permitted. However, the musicians soon realized that the jury mainly comprised composers and musicians rather than bureaucrats, so they tried to play more of their own compositions and more US jazz standards. For instance, in 1967, Igor' Bril' and Alekseĭ Kozlov presented five compositions, including two of their own ('Black and White' by Bril' and Kozlov, 'Ballade' by Kozlov) and two by foreign songwriters ('Round about Midnight' by Thelonious Monk and 'Intermission Riff' by Charlie Parker).

The 1967 festival marked the conclusion of this brief flowering of the Moscow jazz scene. After Soviet tanks ended the Prague Spring, the official attitude towards jazz became as repressive as it had been before 1965. The next Moscow jazz festival would not be held until 1978.

Jazz Education in Moscow

Moscow's jazz musicians were divided into two groups: professional and amateur (Kozyrev 1987). The members of the first group had undergone formal instrumental training, not in jazz but in classical music, most notably at the Moscow Conservatory and the Moscow Gnessin Academy of Music. From the second half of the 1950s onwards some of the brightest students from these institutions fell in love with jazz and joined existing ensembles. For

62 Rüdiger Ritter

instance, Boris Rychkov, who graduated in music theory at the Gnessin Academy in 1956, joined the ZDRI orchestra and also became a member of the Eight ensemble, which was the first Moscow combo to experiment with improvisation. A few years later, Nikolaĭ Kapustin, who had been a pupil of the pianist A. B. Gol'denveĭzer at the Conservatory, joined Oleg Lundstrem's orchestra. Meanwhile, Igor' Bril' and Boris Frumkin both graduated from the Central Music School but then devoted themselves to jazz. In 1965, they won awards at the second Moscow jazz festival, and a year later entered two of the country's most famous jazz ensembles, with Frumkin joining Vadim Liudvikovskiĭ's Concert-Estrade-Orchestra and Bril' playing piano in Juriĭ Saul'skiĭ's VIO-66.

It was impossible to study jazz at the Moscow Conservatory at this time, and it remained impossible. But at the end of the 1960s some of the USSR's music schools started to offer jazz tuition. Juriĭ Pavlovich Kozyrev played a crucial role here. He had completed his piano education at the S. S. Prokofiev Music School in 1947, ten years later gained a diploma at the Moscow State Institute of Physics and Engineering, and subsequently became a well-known scientist. However, he never abandoned music. He had started to collect Dixieland recordings while still an undergraduate, and thereafter performed in Moscow clubs and appeared with his ensemble at the 1962 Moscow jazz festival. Five years later, he established a jazz school at his institute and attracted about twenty amateur musicians who wanted to learn improvisation. The teachers were Kozyrev himself (piano and ensemble playing) and German Luk'ianov (trumpet and ensemble playing), and later Alekseĭ Kozlov (saxophone and ensemble playing), Anatoliĭ Sobolev (bass), Viktor Mel'nikov (bass) and Valeriĭ Bulanov (drums). In 1969, the school transferred to the Moskvorech'e cultural house and gained official status as the location for the 'Experimental Study of Stage Music and Jazz Music'. Also important in the professionalization of jazz activities was the establishment of the Moscow Composers' Union's Commission for Instrumental Stage Music under the direction of Nikolaĭ Grigor'evich Minch and Juriĭ Sergeevich Saul'skiĭ. Finally, in 1974, by decree of the Cultural Ministry of RSFSR, jazz departments were opened in twenty-one music schools throughout the Russian Federation.

Conclusion

Jazz activities in Moscow during the 1960s were characterized by the jazz scene's constant attempts to reach some sort of compromise with the cultural officials, and vice versa. The latter did not simply reject jazz, but instead went to great lengths to try to integrate it into the cultural model of the Soviet Union. They did this by initiating a discourse on jazz aesthetics, thus reviving the pattern of the 1930s, when Soviet cultural officials had distinguished between 'bad' commercial white and 'good' vernacular black jazz. Composers'

Union congresses made serious efforts to develop a native Soviet jazz as a contrast to US jazz. Cultural officials offered the musicians and the listening public the venues they required, which allowed authorities to maintain control over jazz's development in the Soviet Union. This was crucial, as the officials' principal aim was to redirect the jazz movement so that it could be used to spread communist ideals.

Consequently, it makes no sense to speak simplistically of a totalitarian system in relation to Soviet jazz in the 1960s. The authorities could not do whatever they wanted, and even the most ardent opponents of jazz had to accept the existence of this form of music in the capital. Hence, the two sides – the cultural officials and the jazz scene – entered into extensive negotiations. This was an ongoing, fluid process, with first one side then the other gaining the upper hand throughout the 1960s. As a result, the climate for jazz could change dramatically within just a few months.

The simple 'us and them' oppositional model of Soviet jazz life was no longer applicable in the 1960s. Some very well-known jazz musicians, such as Aleksandr Tsfasman and Juriĭ Saul'skiĭ, were members of official cultural commissions, while many listeners appreciated not only US jazz but forms of the genre that merged it with Soviet éstrada culture, as promoted by the authorities. Some forms of jazz had been disseminated under the éstrada label in previous years (Uvarova 1981). Jazz was installed as a form of cultural activity within Soviet society as a result of jazz scene members and state officials – who at first glance might have seemed diametrically opposed to each other – displaying a willingness to negotiate and compromise to produce a specifically Soviet version of the genre.

Young people in this period perceived it as a brief golden age not only for jazz but for cultural activities as a whole. For them, cultural activity entailed a search for a new lifestyle. This generation, later called the '*Shestidesiatniki*' (Sixty-ers), developed a unique collective memory (Vajl and Genis 2013; Kochetkova 2009). For them, even though they continued to live under the tight restrictions of everyday socialism, the contrast with the Stalinist situation of ten years earlier was clear. The idea evolved that jazz and Western culture might be integrated into Soviet society without destroying it. In this sense, jazz helped to stabilize the Soviet system, rather than weaken it. Further research is adding more empirical evidence in support of this conclusion (Abesser 2010).

Notes

1 Transliterations of Russian names and words in this paper follow the Library of Congress system. All translations are mine.
2 Using a convention of German-language jazz scholars, the capitalized word 'Swing' means here the period of jazz history, whereas the lower-case 'swing' is the *terminus technicus* for the musical style.

3 *Stenogramma chetvertogo plenuma pravleniia, posviashchennogo sovetskoĭ pesne i ėstradnoĭ muzyke, Moskva 13–18 noiabria 1962 g.*, RGALI, Fond 2490 (Sojuz Kompozitorov SSSR), Opis' 2, ed. chr. Nr. 28: 1–230 [hereafter *Stenogramma* 1962].

4 Possibly F. Chernov, who wrote the article 'Burzhuaznyĭ Kosmopolitizm i ego reakcionnaia rol"' in *Bol'shevik: Theoretical and Political Magazine of the Central Committee of the ACP(B)*, 5/15 March 1949, pp. 30–41.

5 The words of the leader of Moscow's Sokolniki-Park Dance Orchestra, F. Tumarkin (*Stenogramma* 1962, 5).

6 Such as the president of the Orchestra Department of the Leningrad Town House of Artistic Activity (*Stenogramma* 1962, 15).

7 Legrand had performed in Moscow at the International Youth Festival in 1957.

8 *Stiliagi* (commonly translated as style-hunters) were young people in Soviet towns during the 1950s and early 1960s who pursued a Western-oriented lifestyle in order to provoke the establishment (see Dmitrieva 2010: 239–256).

9 There is no research on this subject as yet. I am grateful for this hint from Cyril Moshkov and Igor' Gavrilov, from the Russian Centre of Jazz Research (RCID), Iaroslavl', who gave me privileged access to Vinarov's reports on the Moscow jazz scene of the 1960s.

References

Abesser, Michel. 2010. 'Between Cultural Opening, Nostalgia and Isolation: Soviet Debates on Jazz between 1953 and 1964'. In Gertrud Pickhan and Rüdiger Ritter, eds, *Jazz behind the Iron Curtain*, 99–116, Berlin: Lang.

Belichenko, Sergej and Valeriĭ Kotel'nikov. 2005. *Sinkopy na Obi ili Ocherki dzhaza v Novosibirske*. Novosibirsk: Sibirskoe universitetskoe izdatel'stvo.

Dauer, Alfons M. 1992. 'Don't Call My Music Jazz'. In Helmut Rösing, ed., *Aspekte zur Geschichte populärer Musik*, 42–55. Baden-Baden: CODA.

Dmitrieva, Marina. 2010. 'Jazz and Dress'. In Gertrud Pickhan and Rüdiger Ritter, eds, *Jazz behind the Iron Curtain*, 239–256, Berlin: Lang.

Farley, Jeff. 2008. 'Making America's Music: Jazz History and the Jazz Preservation Act'. Ph.D. dissertation, University of Glasgow.

Feĭertag, Vladimir. 2013. 'Poslevoennoe Pokolenie. Dzhaz v Iaroslavle kak chast' Dzhaza v Rossii'. In Kirill Moshkov and Anna Filip'eva, eds, *Rossiĭskiĭ dzhaz*, vol. 1, 208–219. Sanktpeterburg: Lan'–Planeta Muzyki.

Fitzpatrick, Sheila. 2000. *Stalinism: New Directions*. New York: Routledge.

Fürst, Juliane, Polly Jones and Susan Morrissey. 2008. 'The Relaunch of the Soviet Project, 1945–64: Introduction'. *Slavonic and East European Review* 86.2: 201–207.

Gitler, Ira. 1967. 'Charles Lloyd in Russia: Ovations and Frustrations'. *Down Beat*, 13 July: 15.

Hobsbawm, Eric. 2002. *Interesting Times: A Twentieth-Century Life*. London: Penguin Press.

Kenez, Peter. 1985. *The Birth of the Propaganda State: Soviet Methods of Mass Mobilization, 1917–1929*. Cambridge: Cambridge University Press.

Kochetkova, Inna. 2009. *The Myth of the Russian Intelligentsia: Old Intellectuals in the New Russia*. London: Routledge.

Kozlov, Alekseĭ. n.d. 'Džazist'. Available at: http://alexeykozlov.com/?p=1960, accessed 5 March 2016.

Kozyrev, Iuriĭ. 1987. 'Dzhaz i muzykal'naia pedagogika (Iz opyta raboty moskovskoĭ studii iskusstva muzykal'noj improvisatsii)'. In Aleksandr Medvedev and Ol'ga

Medvedeva, eds, *Sovetskiĭ Dzhaz. Problemy, sobytiia, mastera*, 194–207. Moskva: Sovetskij Kompozitor.

Kull', Michail. 2009. 'Kafė nasheĭ dzhazovoĭ iunosti'. In Michail Kull', *Stupeni voskhozhdenija*. Moscow: Kniga–Sėfer.

Kull', Mikhail. 2012. '1962 god. Pervyj Moskovskiĭ dzhaz–festival' – ėkho cherez 50 let'. *Dzhaz.ru*, 6/7: 54–58.

Kull', Mikhail. 2013a. 'Poslevoennoe pokolenie. Kafė nasheĭ dzhazovoĭ iunosti'. In Kirill Moshkov and Anna Filip'eva, eds, *Rossiĭskiĭ dzhaz*, vol. 1, 140–170. Sanktpeterburg: Lan'–Planeta Muzyki.

Kull', Mikhail. 2013b. 'Sovetskiĭ Dzhaz. Svidetel'stva po delu. Festivali 60kh na Vinile i v fotografii'. *Dzhaz.ru*, 6: 38–47.

Kull', Mikhail. 2013c. 'Sovetskij Dzhaz. Svidetel'stva po delu. Festivali 60kh na Vinile i v fotografii. Chast' 2: "Dzhaz–66" i "Dzhaz–67"'. *Dzhaz.ru*, 7: 12–21.

Litvin, Alter and John Keep. 2005. *Stalinism: Russian and Western Views at the Turn of the Millennium*. London: Routledge.

Losurdo, Domenico. 2004. 'Towards a Critique of the Category of Totalitarianism'. *Historical Materialism*, 12/2: 25–55.

Pickhan, Gertrud and Rüdiger Ritter, eds. 2010. *Jazz behind the Iron Curtain*. Berlin: Lang.

Pilkington, Hilary. 1994. *Russia's Youth and Its Culture: A Nation's Constructors and Constructed*. London: Routledge.

Ponomarev, Valerij. 2003. *Na obratnoj storone zvuka*. Moskva: Agraf.

Porter, Eric. 2002. *What is This Thing Called Jazz? African American Musicians as Artists, Critics, and Activists*. Berkeley: University of California Press.

Ritter, Rüdiger. 2013. 'Broadcasting Jazz into the Eastern Bloc: Cold War Weapon or Cultural Exchange? The Example of Willis Conover'. *Jazz Perspectives*, 7/2: 1–20.

Romański, Marek. 2013. 'Charles Lloyd. Jestem marzycielem'. *Jazz Forum*, 1/20: 40–44.

Starr, S. Frederick. 1983. *Red and Hot: The Fate of Jazz in the Soviet Union 1917–1983*. New York and Oxford: Oxford University Press.

Stenogramma chetvertogo plenuma pravleniia, posviashchennogo sovetskoĭ pesne i ėstradnoĭ muzyke, Moskva 13–18 noiabria 1962 g. [Transcript of the Fourth Directing Plenary on Soviet Song and Music for the Stage, Moscow, 13–18 November 1962], Rossiĭskiĭ Gosudarstvennyĭ Arkhiv Literatury i Iskusstvo [Russian State Archive for Literature and Art], Fond 2490 (Sojuz Kompozitorov SSSR), Opis' 2, ed. chr. Nr. 28: 1–230.

Taruskin, Richard. 2010. *Music in the Late Twentieth Century*. Oxford: Oxford University Press.

Tėss, Tat'jana. 1964. 'Vot kto budet igrat' v ich dzhaze'. *Izvestija*, 10 September.

Thompson, Mark R. 2002. 'Totalitarian and Post-Totalitarian Regimes in Transition and Non-Transition from Communism'. *Totalitarian Movements and Political Religions* 3/1: 79–106.

Tomoff, Kirill. 2006. *Creative Union: The Professional Organization of Soviet Composers, 1939–1953*. New York: Cornell University Press.

Tsipursky, Gleb. n.d. *The Cultural Cold War, 'Westernized' Youth, and Jazz in the Soviet Union, 1945–64*. Available at: www.gwu.edu/~ieresgwu/assets/docs/Tsipursky_cwc.pdf, accessed 15 November 2014.

Uvarova, Iu. A. 1981. *Russkaia sovetskaia ėstrada, 1946–1977: ocherki istorii*. Moskva: Iskusstvo.

Vajl, Petr and Aleksandr Genis. 2013. *60–e. Mir sovetskogo cheloveka*. Moskva: AST.

Volkov, Konstantin. 2013. 'Pervoprokhodets Valentin Parnakh'. In Kirill Moshkov and Anna Filip'eva, eds, *Rossiĭskiĭ dzhaz*, vol. 1, 8–10. Sanktpeterburg: Lan'–Planeta Muzyki.

von Eschen, Penny. 2004. *Satchmo Blows up the World: Jazz Ambassadors Play the Cold War*. Cambridge, MA: Harvard University Press.

PART II

In the Soviet Shadow

3

FOUR SPACES, FOUR MEANINGS

Narrating Jazz in
Late Stalinist Estonia

Heli Reimann

This study of Estonian jazz in the late Stalinist era argues that for a comprehensive overview of jazz in Soviet society a view from multiple perspectives is necessary. I present this view of Soviet Estonian jazz by applying a model of four cultural spaces of action. To introduce how jazz culture functioned at those different levels, and to explore the meanings framing the actions of cultural actors, I examine four locations of jazz exemplified in four case studies. As I demonstrate, the meaning of jazz as it emerged in four distinct cultural spaces varies greatly. The case of Soviet Estonian jazz also tends to confirm the argument that Soviet power never achieved its totalitarian goals. Despite the regime's efforts to silence jazz, the music did not disappear from private realms in Estonian cultural space.

Introduction

I shall introduce my argument by paraphrasing the Estonian jazz historian Valter Ojakäär (2008: 561): jazz was not allowed in the Soviet Union but it was never forbidden either. This rather humorous and paradoxical statement succinctly conveys the contradictory nature of the Soviet era. The internal paradoxes of Soviet society are extensively discussed by the anthropologist Aleksei Yurchak (2006: 10), who tries to 'rehumanize' life under socialism. He argues that Soviet life was a paradoxical mix of negative and positive values, where 'control, coercion, alienation, fear, and moral quandaries were irreducibly mixed with ideals, communal ethics, dignity, creativity, and care for the future'. This 'allowed–forbidden paradigm', however, represents only the perspective from above – the political authorities' tolerance or intolerance toward jazz. In a society where the regulations and directives from above were not necessarily reflected in the lives of ordinary people, inevitable discrepancies existed between public and private realms. Regarding the state of jazz, my argument is that for a comprehensive overview of jazz in Soviet society it is necessary to take into account the views 'from above' *and* those 'from below'. The main goal of my study is to explain how jazz culture functioned as a multi-level phenomenon, and to explore the meanings that framed the cultural actors' actions.

The second stage of my argument will challenge the popular simplification about jazz in the Soviet Union that sees the music as a mode of resistance against the regime.[1] This description represents in the first instance the remnants of simplistic Cold War ideological binaries by which heroic jazz is juxtaposed with the horrifying power of the Soviet state. The historical school of thought in the 1950s and 1960s that argued on the basis of Soviet ideology and high politics that this accurately reflected the everyday conditions of life has been challenged, and it is now agreed that this approach was overly simplistic and lacked scholarly rigour (Edele 2012: 442). Its premise was that the Soviet populace was subjugated to totalitarian power and that the people were, at most, passively resistant to it. The second objective of this paper is therefore to develop a way of overcoming this schematic model to arrive at a more flexible understanding of the force field that framed jazz in the Soviet Union.

Without delving into detailed discussions on the concept of totalitarianism, which can be found in the Introduction to this volume, my argument regarding its application is that in the case of late Stalinist-era Soviet Estonia the more dynamic and processual notion of 'totalitarization' is preferable to the static noun 'totalitarianism'. The dynamic nature of the period from 1944 to 1953, during which Estonian society moved from post-war relative liberalism to the final establishment of Soviet power,[2] leads to the assertion that this era witnessed the application of the totalitarian project in Estonian society rather than the retention of it.

The understanding of jazz in today's academic discourse is moving towards delineating the music as a practice developed through a range of influences and exchange (Whyton 2011: xx). The gradually increasing interest in intercultural dialogue and acceptance of pluralistic views can be seen as a paradigm shift leading to the globalization of the discipline of jazz research (Reimann 2013). One area that traditionally received relatively little scholarly attention was jazz in the former Eastern Bloc, but this started to change somewhat with Warsaw's 'Jazz behind the Iron Curtain' conference in 2008, organized by Gertrud Pickhan and Rüdiger Ritter, and their subsequent anthology based on the presentations (Pickhan and Ritter 2010). That Soviet jazz has attracted little scholarly interest is indicated by the small number of publications on the topic. The only extensive scholarly monograph on jazz in the Soviet Union is S. Frederick Starr's *Red & Hot: The Fate of Jazz in Soviet Union* from 1983.

Other authors include Gaut (1991), Novikova (2003), Lücke (2004, 2010), Minor (1995), Feigin (1985), Beličenko (2006) as well as my own articles on Soviet Estonian jazz (2010a, 2010b, 2011). These have helped to extend the perspectives on jazz in the cultural space of former Soviet Union. Russian authors providing historical overviews on Soviet jazz include Batachev (1972), Konen (1977) and Feiertag (1981, 1999, 2010).

Jazz scholarship has a tendency to focus on empirical research rather than framing the studies with extensive theorizations. Two examples of theoretical perspectives are Bruce Johnson's (2002) use of diasporic theory and Ingrid Monson's (1996) attempt to apply poststructuralist cultural theory, literary criticism, linguistic anthropology and ethnomusicology. My approach to the object of study combines the perspectives originating from post-revisionist thought in Soviet studies synthesizing perspectives 'from above' and 'from below', Ann Swidler's (1986, 2001) theorization of 'culture in action', and Janken Myrdal's (2012) idea of source pluralism. While a post-revisionist-derived way of seeing the society from multiple perspectives helps to exemplify the variety of cultural spaces in Soviet society, Swidler's 'culture in action' theory allows me to place the cultural actors or musicians and their actions at the centre of the study, while source pluralism justifies the usage of a wide range of sources.

In the first section of the chapter, I will introduce the conceptual models and the methodological tools that frame the study. The subsequent sections are based on an examination of four locations of jazz exemplified in four case studies. First I will discuss the public media discourse as represented in jazz-related texts of the Estonian cultural newspaper *Sirp ja Vasar*; next I will look at the way jazz appeared in the public musical space, using the example of the state-sponsored Jazz Orchestra of the Estonian State Philharmonic; then I will study the informal public realm by focusing on the jazz group Mickeys; and finally I will survey the private space of the jazz world through the jazz group Swing Club.

Conceptual and Methodological Background

The two concepts characterizing the historical period under investigation in Estonian history are late Stalinism and Sovietization. To summarize succinctly: late Stalinism[3] was broadly speaking the period framed by the Soviet victory from 1945 to Stalin's death in 1953. Chris Ward (2004: 446) says this period was characterized by

> anxieties about the party's loss of control over the army, the countryside, the managerial elite, local soviets and culture; by fear of the West, by fear of resurgent socialism abroad and at home, by fear of nationalism, by fear of neo-NEP aspirations and a longing for liberalization among the

masses and the intelligentsia; by the persistence of old quarrels among the elite, their fear of a new generation of apparatchiki, and by the absence of a second Great Purge to keep everyone in check.

Sovietization[4] is a term applied to the years 1944–1953 during which the Soviet regime established its power basis within Estonia. In one sense, this included the adoption of Soviet-like institutions, laws, customs, traditions and the Soviet way of life. In another sense, the term is often applied to mental and social changes within the population of the Soviet Union and its satellites with the aim of creating the 'new Soviet man' or *Homo Sovieticus.*

One of the obvious features of Soviet society was the distinction between public and private social spheres. The importance of the public/private divide is noted by Shalpentokh (1989: 3), who states that 'The distinction between the public and private spheres is of crucial importance for understanding Soviet society.' The scholarly tradition which started to investigate Soviet society both 'from below' and 'from above' was 'post-revisionism'. As the third school in Soviet studies, this emerged in the 1990s as a reaction against the earlier revisionist–totalitarian polemic. The main achievement of the post-revisionist school was to shift the focus from social to cultural history. According to Fitzpatrick (2007: 90), it imposed 'new ground rules that required historical work to have an underpinning in cultural theory and that privileged close textual analysis, especially of ego-documents'. The first landmark study in the post-revisionist tradition, Stephen Kotkin's *Magnetic Mountain: Stalinism as a Civilization* (1995) focused solely on the interaction between state power and society, but Timothy Johnston (2011) and Aleksei Yurchak (2006) were more effective in synthesizing different perspectives, arguing for the interaction, overlap or 'inter-penetration' between different aspects of the social whole.

The divide between the public and private social realms characterized not only Soviet society; it was the key issue for all totalitarian states where the existence of the private in the liberal, individual sense was formally inhibited by the logic of totalitarian ideology (Corner 2009: 5). The private sphere nevertheless survived despite the fact that people often found their private lives and thoughts in conflict with the demands of the state-sanctioned ideology (ibid.: 6). As mentioned above, the dualistic public/private divide is a particularly sharp dichotomy in totalitarian societies, but nonetheless it is clearly an oversimplification that is insufficient to disclose the diversity of the society. Nor can jazz as a cultural form be reduced to this dualistic model: as a musical culture it acted simultaneously at many social levels, spreading beyond the boundaries defined by that simplistic divide.

Using a version of the public/private divide as an analytical tool in approaching Estonian jazz culture, I will distinguish between four spaces constituting the jazz world in late Stalinist Estonia. The first two spaces represent the public sector of the culture and are regulated more or less 'from above'. The public media texts in *Sirp ja Vasar* and state-sanctioned professional orchestras both acted in the public sphere and were guided by official Soviet cultural politics. The third space, formed by non-state-sponsored jazz groups performing in informal scenes, such as dance halls, cafes and restaurants, may be referred to as an 'informal public realm', according to Zdravomyslova and Voronkov (2002). Finally, the space accommodating the most private territories of jazz culture existed at the level of interaction between musical individuals or friendship groups, and musical or non-musical activities supporting the development of jazz musicianship and musical identity.[5] Although these are distinct categorizations, I see those realms as not separated from or in opposition to one another, but as existing in interactive tension in the formation of the totality of Soviet Estonian jazz culture.

In pursuing my objective of transcending binary thinking, I shall also draw on a theory that nuances the oppositional nature of the public/private divide: Ann Swidler's (1986, 2001) powerful actor-centred model of culture. Taking up the idea of 'culture in action', Swidler sees culture as a resource from which social actors draw when they are in the process of action. Her model therefore focuses not on the ends to which individuals orient their action, but the means by which they achieve it. People know how to do different things with culture in different situations (Swidler 1986: 277) – they use specific strategies of action as the means to guide their activities. For Swidler, culture is not a one-way process of imposing ideology and hegemony but rather a set of tools with more or less stable but contested social meanings that are used to solve problems of action. Her idea of culture as a toolkit (Swidler 1986) resolves the structure versus agency problem: she proposes a theory that accounts for both – for individual choice and the structuring of behaviour by institutions, semiotic codes and other large-scale societal structures.

The repertoire of my methods is formed by what Myrdal (2012) calls 'source pluralism'. For a study that uses a number of sources, this means that I will combine discrete fragments from different sources in order to form the historical narratives and build and consolidate my arguments. The importance of considering all the available sources and standpoints, and all the possible angles in approaching Estonian history, is articulated by the historian Enn Tarvel (2005). For him, it is the historian's responsibility to convey history in as many-sided and complex a way as possible, as a mosaic of different possibilities and choices, placing them in the context of their era.

The spectrum of source materials for the study consists of both oral and documented records. I will use the unpublished almanac of the Swing Club, public media texts and interviews with musicians as primary sources. In addition, Valter Ojakäär's historical account and other published sources, the personal notes of the musicians and radio programmes are used as secondary sources.

Sirp ja Vasar and the Public Media Discourse of Jazz

Zolkin (2009: 493) defines totalitarian culture as a specific politico-ideological system of state power necessary for the mythologization of the consciousness of individuals and society. He considers totalitarian culture as a tool for emotional mobilization of mass consciousness for the achievement of defined political goals (ibid.). The space that most directly represents this ideologized perspective 'from above' on culture is the public media sphere. Journalistic publications were the main conduits for the orders from the Central Committee to the populace and the most powerful means to spread propaganda. This was why Soviet journalistic discourse as a direct mediator of the party's politics was entirely ideologized and totally controlled by the Soviet apparatus of censorship.

In this section I will briefly discuss the dynamic of changes of jazz discourse in Estonian public media in the post-Stalinist era. The investigation is based on the overview of jazz-related texts published in the Estonian cultural newspaper *Sirp ja Vasar* (Sickle and Hammer).[6] I will call the immediate post-war years in Estonian jazz journalism the period of objective reflections, when the main subjects of articles were concert reviews and announcements of upcoming events. This discourse is an obvious manifestation of the political situation of the time. The post-war years witnessed a comparatively liberal political climate in the Soviet Union: the tensions between two opposing political systems dissipated for a while because of the Allied victory. Jazz, as one of the symbols of the alliance, was actively performed in the Soviet Union during the Second World War and in the immediate post-war years. Yurchak (2006: 106), for example, links the meaning of jazz with the victory over the Nazis: 'With the opening of the British and American second front in 1944 and the meeting of Soviet and American troops in Germany, American jazz became associated with the nearing victory over Nazis.'

The first sign of the change towards 'ideologization' of the discourse occurred in 1946. An article published on 21 September entitled 'Riikliku filharmoonia jazzi kontserdid' (The jazz concerts of the State Philharmonic) condemned the Jazz Orchestra of the Estonian State Philharmonic for the inclusion of inappropriate tunes of American and German origin in its repertoire. The objects of the critic's attack included the US-style arrangements and the generally low artistic level of the performance. Less than a month later, on 19 October, *Sirp ja Vasar* published Serafim Milovski's article entitled 'Jazz muusikast' (About jazz music). This article expressed the author's concern about the music's adaptation to Soviet aesthetic paradigms. 'Soviet jazz musicians must create their own jazz music, which is not for barrelhouse visitors but for Soviet people who listen to music in the theatre and concert hall,'[7] declared Milovski. Thus, the article did not seek to ban jazz but was rather a call to 'Sovietize' the music.

On 24 April 1948, the article 'Kutse tantsule' (Call to dance) appeared in *Sirp ja Vasar*. This piece expressed an intolerance of jazz and Western dance music. However, the attack was largely in accordance with the Soviet dance reform of the late 1940s, when 'bourgeois' modern dances started to decline amid the rise of older ballroom dances of a more neutral character. The following year, on 8 August 1949, Valter Ojakäär's 'Tänapäeva Ameerika džässimuusikast' (On present-day American jazz music) displayed zero tolerance towards jazz. This piece seems to rely on a simplistic 'Soviet-style' construction of jazz history, in which the focus is less on a historical overview of the genre than on anti-US and anti-capitalist propaganda. Following Ojakäär's article, jazz-related articles disappeared from public discourse for a time. As may be expected, extinguishing the word 'jazz' from public debate seems to have distracted the musical audience from the music itself. However, the word reappeared in public discourse on 18 December 1953, where *Sirp ja Vasar* printed Leonid Utesov's 'Laulust ja kergest muusikast' (On singing and light music).

The shift towards the ideologization of the public discourse of jazz is an indication of a changing political situation induced by the onset of the cultural doctrine known as *Zhdanovshchina*. This was a cultural policy involving stricter governmental control of the arts and the promotion of an extreme anti-Western bias during the period from 1946 to 1953. The impact of three Stalinist campaigns – the resolution of the Central Committee against two literary magazines, *Zvezda* and *Leningrad*, to enforce stricter ideological discipline in 1946; the 'Great Friendship' movement against formalism in 1948; and the anti-Semitic, anti-cosmopolitanism campaign of 1949 that was prompted by fear of foreign influence – led to a decline in tolerance for jazz and finally its temporary disappearance from public discourse. This increasing intolerance toward jazz caused a profound paradigm shift within the public discourse: jazz was no longer constructed as a musical practice; instead, it was politicized and declared incompatible with Soviet ideological discourse. Articles focused not on the music but rather on external, non-musical attributes, on authenticity in terms of 'Sovietizing' the music, or on the music's function, depending on the focus of the principal ideological campaign at the time.

The Jazz Orchestra of the Estonian State Philharmonic

The Eesti Riikliku Filharmoonia Džässorkester (Jazz Orchestra of the Estonian State Philharmonic; JOESP) was one of two state jazz orchestras formed after the Soviet Union's reoccupation of Estonia in 1944. While the Jazz Orchestra of Estonian Public Broadcasting was mainly a studio orchestra that performed on live radio shows, JOESP was a touring group that played all over the Soviet Union.[8] As a state-sponsored orchestra, it was part of the Estonian State Philharmonic – the state-owned concert organization in Soviet Estonia.

The institutionalization of musical culture in the form of state-sponsored musical collectives was part of the Soviet cultural project, which considered the arts important to the Soviet system, and viewed artists as the 'engineers of human souls' – indispensable agents of enlightenment and ideological education (Tomoff 2006: 4). What Yurchak (2006: 12) calls the 'Soviet paradox' was the Soviet state's constant anxiety 'about publicly justifying state control of cultural production while simultaneously attempting to promote its independence and experimentation'. Therefore, all the cultural organizations were subject to educational and political organizations, and the entire cultural production had to be fully supervised by the party (ibid.). The Soviet Union's desire to impose control over the entire cultural sphere drew no significant distinction between what are considered 'high' and 'low' musical forms. The main criteria were artistic quality and ideological correctness. On the one hand, the foundation of state jazz orchestras can be seen as part of the process of the Sovietization of Estonian culture – to achieve control over musical production. But on the other hand, the orchestras ensured permanent jobs for musicians and supported the development of musical culture. As Mertelsman (2012: 142) observes in his overview of the Estonian cultural situation after the Second World War, culture and education expanded under Stalinism, and the state invested enormous sums in order to raise the level of people's *kulturnost* ('culturedness').[9]

JOESP was established on the foundations of the Jazz Orchestra of Estonian State Art Ensembles in Yaroslavl toward the end of 1944. The instrumentation of the collective consisted of five saxophones, three trumpets, three trombones, guitar, accordion, piano, double bass, drums and two violins, which represented a typical big band lineup, with added violins (Ojakäär 2008: 170–176). As mentioned above, JOESP was mainly a touring collective. A painstakingly detailed account of its very busy concert schedule can be found in the notes of the conductor of the orchestra, Vladimir Sapozhnin, who recorded all of the performances between March 1945 and November 1948.[10] JOESP spent most of the year touring throughout the Soviet Union, sometimes performing as many as three concerts per day. Sapozhnin's son Oleg, who often joined the orchestra on tour, recalls that the longest one lasted eight months.[11] He recalls:

> The orchestra was travelling from Tallinn to Leningrad and from Moscow to the Urals. Then back to Moscow for a tour to Transcaucasia. We spent countless hours on trains. And it was hard because the travelling conditions were poor. We often had to sleep on the floor of the train station.[12]

On arrival at their destination, the bandsmen were usually billetted in pairs with local families. Since the older member of the orchestra had a tendency towards alcohol abuse, Vladimir Sapozhnin always ensured that his son lodged with the young pianist Gennadi Podelski. Oleg recalls, 'Gennadi did not drink any alcohol . . . but he was a real lady's man. So I got a really good education on how to chase women at the age of fourteen.'[13]

The authorities imposed control over the orchestra by censoring its concert programmes. In fact, JOESP had to undergo two censorship processes: the first compatibility assessment took place at the local level in Tallinn before a special committee consisting of musically incompetent party officials; the second was conducted in Leningrad by higher-level, all-Union censorship officials (Pedusaar 2000: 101). Music enjoyed a somewhat privileged status, however, because its inherently abstract nature made it difficult for politicians and bureaucrats to police the orchestras. Hence, 'Composers and musicians could use their privileged access to the interpretation of this abstract art form to ensure that they always had some manoeuvrability, that they perceived their agency' (Tomoff 2006: 5). A good example of this 'manoeuvring' strategy was the subtle manipulation of the titles of the pieces they played. Oleg Sapozhnin recalls that his father always added some 'bait' to the programme list by including certain pieces with extremely inappropriate titles in the full expectation that the censors would proscribe them. This strategy helped JOESP to retain its desired repertoire. On other occasions 'cosmetic' changes would help to keep pieces in the programme list. For instance, the jazz piece entitled 'Night in a Big City' – an obvious reference to New York – remained in the programme after it was renamed the more politically acceptable 'Night in the Negro Village' (Pedusaar 2000: 102).

While the censors were relatively liberal during the immediate post-war years, in the course of the subsequent ideological 'cleanout', starting in 1946, their grip started to tighten. For instance, a comparison of the programme lists of 1945 and 1948[14] indicates that while the first contained several Benny Goodman pieces, there was no reference to jazz in the later list. Indeed, only three of the twenty-one pieces were orchestral numbers; fourteen were solo performances by Sapozhnin, and there were three dance numbers with orchestral accompaniment. As Ojakäär (2008: 193) points out, JOESP's programme became, in effect, Sapozhnin performing a series of solo pieces, and the word 'jazz' in the orchestra's name lost its relevance. The reference to jazz was also lost because of changes to the orchestra's instrumentation, with the string group enlarged at the expense of wind instruments, so the orchestra ultimately consisted of four violins, guitar, double bass, two accordions, piano, saxophone, clarinet, trombone and drums.[15]

FIGURE 3.1 JOESP Concert in Rakvere, 1945[16]

78 Heli Reimann

JOESP's position among Soviet jazz orchestras is discussed by the publicist and journalist Heino Pedusaar (2000) in his monograph on Vladimir Sapozhnin. He places JOESP among the Soviet musical elite, along with the orchestras of Eddy Rozner, Oleg Lundström and Leonid Utesov (ibid.: 98). The compere and actor Eino Baskin, who worked with Sapozhnin, attributed the orchestra's success primarily to its repertoire. Because a large proportion of this consisted of 'Western sounds', the collective was often deferentially referred to as a European orchestra (ibid.). However, much of its success must also have been due to its charismatic leader, Vladimir Sapozhnin.[17]

To form an idea of the reception for the orchestra's performances in the Soviet musical arena, we may refer to an article that appeared in *Õhtuleht* on 3 October 1945, which quoted a number of newspaper reviews from all over the Soviet Union. For instance, on 27 June *Vetchernaja Moskva* had reported that 'Vladimir Sapozhnin is an artist of high professionalism. He is a master of the violin, concertina, xylophone; he tapdances, whistles and is an excellent conductor.' Meanwhile, *Zvezda*[18] had said: 'The musical pieces such as Fantasy, Dance of the Shadows, Musical Hunt, Red Rose and 17 Bachelors were performed with good rhythmic feeling and melodically. The conductor uses the rhythms of the instrument with good taste. It is a promising collective.' By contrast, the local Tcheljabinsk newspaper[19] had grumbled: 'The winds are too penetrating and the saxophones don't sound equal enough.'

There are several possible explanations for why JOESP disbanded in November 1948. Sapozhnin was certainly frustrated by the persistent alcohol problems within the orchestra, and annoyed that jazz had been banished from its repertoire (Pedusaar 2000: 102). On the other hand, Ojakäär (2008: 194) argues that JOESP disbanded for economic reasons: the directorate of the State Philharmonic considered it too expensive to continue to pay thirteen bandsmen who in effect merely accompanied Sapozhnin. A new orchestra that focused on 'light music', known as the Estrada Orchestra of the State Philharmonic, was assembled three years later, in 1951 (Ojakäär 2008: 415).

Jazz Group Mickeys

The example I present to represent the cultural space of the informal public realm is jazz group Mickeys, an amateur collective whose main performing venues were school dance halls. The group started as a musical union of schoolboys at the First Secondary School of Tallinn (formerly the Gustav Adolph Gymnasium) in 1945. A stable personnel of eight musicians who stayed together for the next ten years was formed in 1946. This 'reduced big band' octet consisted of a standard rhythm section (piano, guitar, bass, drums) and four horns (two woodwinds and two brass). Mickeys may be regarded as the longest-established jazz group in Estonia: although the personnel and the leaders have often changed, the group still gathers from time to time.[20]

FIGURE 3.2 A Mickeys Gig in the Polytechnic Institute, Tallinn, 1947[21]

The group took its name from the Walt Disney cartoon character, Mickey Mouse. However, the Stalinist ideological cleanout forced it to change its name (Ojakäär 2008: 266). The overt Western reference in 'Mickeys' was muted and Estonianized when it was changed to 'Mikid' in 1949. (Incidentally, in a further allusion to Disney characters, the musicians' girlfriends were known as Minnies.[22])

According to the common practice of the Soviet era, non-professional collectives were required to establish institutional affiliations in order to regulate the citizens' leisure activities; at the same time, however, this secured benefits for the amateur practitioners. People took advantage of the responsibilities of the institution to ensure the best possible material conditions for leisure. The official 'anchor' for Mickeys became the institution which Ojakäär (2008: 269) terms 'the institution with the long name': the Kohaliku Tööstuse Kommunaalmajanduse alal Töötajate Ametühingute Vabariiklik Tallinna Klubi (Tallinn Club of the Workers of the Trade Union of the Local Industry and Communal Economy). In addition to a free rehearsal room, the other advantage of affiliation was that Mickeys was able to hire a professional band leader. The latter's task was not just to conduct the rehearsals, but even more importantly to act as musical arranger. Given that there was very limited access to sheet music, the practice of making original arrangements became a necessary part of the group's everyday musical life. The need for original arrangements was necessitated also in this case by the atypical four-horn composition of the group. Mickeys' first arrangements were prepared by Harry Kõlar, Valter Ojakäär and Ülo Raudmäe. Udo Treufeldt calls this trio the 'godfathers of Mickeys'. Besides composing arrangements, they also educated the group musically. 'They taught us how to play swing in a proper way,' recalls Treufeldt. 'To play jazz is the

80   Heli Reimann

same as speaking English – it is written in one way but you need to pronounce it in another way. Kõlar even invented original combinations of syllables for us to master the "language" of swing.'[23] The first salaried leader of Mickeys was Ülo Raudmäe.[24] He became famous for using difficult key signatures of up to seven sharps or flats in each arrangement, justifying the practice by saying that 'human beings are learning as long as they are alive and even longer'.[25] Raudmäe arranged 'Cherokee', 'Undecided', 'In the Mood', 'Two O'Clock Jump' and 'Ain't Misbehavin', among many other tunes, for Mickeys.[26]

The obligations that accompanied the institutional affiliation of amateur collectives included giving free performances for companies and institutions. The schedule was particularly demanding on and around state holidays, such as the anniversary of the Bolshevik Revolution and International Workers' Day (1 May), when performances continued from early morning till late at night for up to four consecutive days. Treufeldt remembers:

> The May and November holidays were especially busy for us, with nightly performances. On those occasions we usually played with reduced personnel of just four to five people. During one performance our bass player Aksel Talpsepp fell asleep. His fingers were still moving but they did not touch the strings any more. And then he fell with his bass onto the saxophone player, who pushed him back to an upright position. Talpsepp woke up and continued playing.[27]

The repertoire for these public concerts differed from the programme that was played in dance halls. Pieces by Soviet composers such as Solovjov-Sedoi and Dunajevski dominated. But probably the most popular songwriter was 'Ivanov' – an anonymous signifier of a Soviet composer that was used to hide inappropriate authorship, or simply because the composer was not known.[28]

In order to regulate dance culture and provide citizens with more appropriate forms of dancing, the Soviet authorities initiated a campaign of dance reform in the late 1940s. Essentially, this involved replacing the 'vulgar' foxtrot and other modern dances with ballroom dances, such as waltzes and pas des quatre. Treufeldt describes the musicians' reaction to this stricter regulation of their activities: 'We took into our repertoire specially arranged ballroom dances. In school parties we had to play this mandatory pas des pagne. Audiences were usually understanding and did not react negatively. After playing this mandatory tune, we could continue with our regular dance repertoire.' As Treufeldt says, even party officials viewed the new directives as mere formalities: 'Comrades who enthusiastically promoted ballroom dances in public eagerly danced the foxtrot in private.'[29]

It was not only Soviet dance reform which was coolly received by the musicians. As Vello Jõesaar indicates, neither the saxophone ban nor the anti-jazz campaigns had much of an impact on the musicians' everyday practices:

We did not abandon our saxophones when this instrument was labelled an inappropriate Western monster. And we did not change our repertoire either. We played the music we liked and listened to the radio. Yes, our repertoire lists were censored . . . but at dances we played the music we wanted to play.[30]

Treufeldt was similarly indifferent towards the political climate, saying, 'Politics was the subject for our discussions as little as possible. We lived our own lives and made music.'[31] He sums up the musicians' political neutrality perfectly: 'C major sounds the same despite the type of political power.'[32]

The Soviet-era regulations obliged every amateur group to present its repertoire for inspection by a special committee at the People's Commissariat for Education. Treufeldt recalls the sometimes farcical consequences of dealing with incompetent officialdom:

The violinist Boris Kuurman took [his ensemble's] list to the Commissariat. The chief comrade Tamarkin was not there so the list was reviewed by two girls. While Valgre and Strauss were regarded as appropriate, the selection from the operetta *Victoria and her Hussar* seemed suspicious. While 'Victoria' was an acceptable name, 'Hussar' was crossed out as something militant. Kuurman, perplexed, wanted to ask where Victoria ended and Hussar began in the piece, but Tamarkin entered the room and confirmed the list by rubber-stamping it. Now Kuurman had a signed and stamped paper which stated that Victoria was allowed while Hussar was forbidden.[33]

Treufeldt recalls a *haltuura*[34] that Mickeys played at the People's House in Mooste, during which the musicians displayed all of their adaptability and ingenuity:

A truck drove us to the concert venue in Mooste. Sitting in the truck was made more comfortable with mattresses. For protection against the wind and the rain, we covered ourselves with a tarpaulin. The People's House in Mooste was in a terrible state. Only one chair was found and we gave it to our pianist, Pedraudse. An accordion case was appropriated for the drummer, and two saxophonists found a bench to sit on. The piano was in the most awful condition. The ivory was worn through and some of the keys had big holes. So we filled the holes with paper and then covered them with candle wax. Pedraudse then had to tune the piano. But the dance hall was full of people who actively participated in the party.[35]

Treufeldt recorded all of Mickeys' dance-hall *haltuuras* and the band's earnings in his notebook. The group was almost the only option for the organizers of school parties in Tallinn in the late 1940s and 1950s, so the schools would arrange their events according to Mickeys' schedule. The earnings from the *haltuuras* were not high, but the 500–600 roubles they brought in each month were nonetheless a great financial help. The average dance *haltuura* would last about three hours, with the whole band receiving about 150 roubles per hour. Treufeldt recalls precisely how far that income went in the 1940s:

> According to the Soviet rules, all radio sets had been confiscated during the first Soviet occupation in 1941. I remember that one of the storage spaces for confiscated radios was in the gym of Reaalkool. We went to see the radios, and they were marvellous if you looked at them from behind, full of beautiful coloured bulbs. People were clever: they handed in just the shell of the radio, with these bulbs inside, not the radio mechanism itself. So the confiscation order did not have much impact on Estonians. However, after the war, new radio sets came on sale and we all wanted one of them. Since the price of a radio was equal to the income we received for one *haltuura*, from time to time one of the musicians would get to keep the whole 450 roubles so they could buy a set. This was how we got our new radio sets.[36]

Around this time, Mickeys played a signature tune at the beginning and end of each gig – 'Heartbreaker' by Morty Berk, Frank Capano and Max C. Freedman.[37] This ritual act came to signify the group's identity and helped the musicians to connect with their audiences. The song was an instructive example of Heldur Karmo's art of 'Estonianizing' English lyrics. Instead of translating directly from the English version, Karmo (1927–1997) created new lyrics that fitted the melody. In the original version of the song, the final lines warn a young lady: 'Be careful what you do / When you break a heart in two, / For that heart may belong to you'.[38] Karmo's changes illustrate how a form of 'double coding' can be an instrument for lighthearted subversion. On the surface, he simply adhered to the directive that Western music should be Estonianized, but at the same time he subtly parodied Soviet sloganeering:

> Avanenud on säravad [The gates of the new bright]
> Uue õnne väravad [Happiness are open]
> Tulevikku sealt näha saab [Our future can be seen there].

Swing Club and the Private Realm

I now turn to a unique phenomenon in Estonian jazz history – the collective known as Swing Club. According to one of its members, Herbert Krutob, this group came together in 1947 'to develop jazz in Soviet Estonia'.[39] Interestingly, the ensemble was never particularly popular with audiences, and it remained relatively unknown at the time in comparison with such groups as Kuldne 7, Mikid and Rütmikud. But Swing Club's founder, Uno Naissoo, never set out to appeal to a wide audience (Ojakäär 2008: 278). Rather, the ensemble was conceived as a 'laboratory of jazz', a testing ground for new musical ideas and a creative association assembled for the purposes of discussing and learning about jazz.[40] In addition, the group made a great contribution to the document-ation of Estonian jazz history by collating an unpublished almanac that serves as a unique testimony to the contradictions and significance of the late 1940s. In what follows I will discuss how Estonian musicians interacted with the practice of jazz in two ways: by forming a friendship group and by learning new techniques.

The event that inspired the formation of Swing Club was a residency of a few weeks at the Kuning restaurant in August 1947.[41] This was the first collab-oration between those who would later form the core membership of Swing Club. As the violinist, arranger and essayist Ustus Agur (1929–1997) recalled, 'I become acquainted with Uno Naissoo, Ülo Vinter, Herbert Krutob and Heldur Karmo. This musical encounter laid the foundation for several years of musical collaboration and personal contacts.'[42] The initiative came from Krutob, who sought 'to form a band of men who were deeply interested in the further development of modern music, a kind of viable orchestra that would act not because of any craving for *haltuuras* but because of pure enthu-siasm'.[43] Pianist Peeter Saul, who joined the collective in 1949, recalled that Swing Club was first and foremost a friendship group of like-minded people whose prime motivation was not financial. As he said, 'Swing Club was a union of young kindred spirits whose goal was to make music for self-delight. We had two orchestras – one large one for performing at dance parties and a quartet who played just for fun.'[44]

The core membership of the group comprised Naissoo, Krutob, Karmo and Ustus Agur, but Naissoo (1928–1980) – a composer, theorist, musician and educator who played a remarkable role in the foundation of the jazz tradition in Estonia – was the undisputed leader.[45] It was his eagerness and passion for jazz which kept the group together and expanded the musical and aesthetic boundaries of the local jazz scene through his musical experiments. As Agur remembered, 'Restoran Kuning was the place where I first met Uno Naissoo. He was the soul of the group from the very first moments. Besides the reper-toire, he brought with him passionate enthusiasm, deep fanaticism and a love for music. His energy and temperament kindled us.'[46] In fact, Naissoo was the only professionally trained musician among the founder members: for instance, Krutob (1927–2009), Swing Club's vocalist, was a civil engineer who ulti-mately worked at the Ministry of the Economy, while Agur was an electrical engineer with an impressive record as a scholar in the field of informatics. Karmo was neither a musician nor a composer, but he played an exceptional role as the group's 'ideologist'. As the group's almanac explains, 'Heldur Karmo is a jazz historian, theorist and writer who joined the band at the very beginning . . . He was introduced to jazz in 1940 and became a jazz enthusiast in 1943. The first writings and song lyrics originate from the same year.'[47] By the end of his life, Karmo was well known in Estonia as the writer or translator of lyrics for more than 3500 popular Estonian songs.

In his unpublished memoirs, Krutob explains that the group was much more than an ensemble of performing musicians:

> Swing Club was not just a dance orchestra. It was first of all the creative union of young Estonian jazz musicians. We often discussed the developments in jazz at every level – at the world level, in the Soviet context and, of course, at the local level – and we planned new steps for the development of jazz in our country.[48]

Agur recalled that scrupulous text records were kept of these debates:

> In those days we often discussed the directions and styles of jazz. We did not just have 'coffee-table' discussions about the problems of jazz; we took it very seriously. We wrote what we called doctoral dissertations – essays that addressed particular problems. Then we read these essays to each other and discussed them. Unfortunately, all of this work was lost. We passed them on to each other and eventually they disappeared. But I remember Karmo had a thick booklet of essay-like material and ideas. I even remember the title: *Between My Feelings and Common Sense.*[49]

The hunger for new knowledge, on the one hand, and the limited access to any articles on jazz, on the other, generated great interest in every available source, as Agur remembered:

> It is easy nowadays – there is a lot of literature available – but it was really peculiar what we did back then. For us, it was a great event when somebody found, for instance, a journal of popular music from 1937 with an article on jazz in it. This was a new opportunity for us to philosophize and discuss the music at length. And it was a great event if somebody heard some new piece or some new artist.[50]

The reasons for their intense desire to theorize about jazz in the circumstances of such limited access to written material on the subject were clearly expressed by Karmo: 'The theoretical basis was missing but we were curious to learn about the music. We "invented" everything ourselves by listening and analysing'.[51]

Uno Loop[52] makes direct reference to the educational aspects of Swing Club's meetings. He equates listening to the group's discussions with a formal musical education and believes that the debates significantly influenced his own pedagogical activity in later years:

> Swing Club was like a conservatory for me. It was Naissoo and Agur who usually conducted our rehearsals and argued about the arrangements. Their main concern was how to achieve good and balanced sound, how to do so with good taste. And the discussions were really professional. I would listen to them in astonishment and with great respect. I got all the knowledge that I used in my own teaching from those informal 'lectures'.[53]

Estonians also learned about music simply by listening to it. Learning by listening and imitating is recognized as the most common way in which jazz musicians acquire their skills. For example, David Ake (2003: 26) notes:

> No pedagogical tool has left as widespread or as long-lasting an impact on jazz skill acquisition as have the various media of sound recording. Recordings, tapes and CDs not only act as the physical 'text' of jazz, they also serve as the pre-eminent 'textbooks' of the music, providing study materials for virtually all players.

But in the absence of direct contact with jazz culture and the scarcity of sound recordings, the primary musical source for post-war Estonians was radio.[54] Agur described the role of radio in their everyday musical life:

> We did not have any literature, no sheet music, no audio LPs, no tapes. The only contact with the outside world was radio. Every serious musician was sitting at the radio late at night when the quality of reception was better and tried to transcribe the music as best they could. No tape recorders were available in those times, so the musicians who were able to transcribe the music fast were held in high esteem.[55]

In his memoirs, Krutob provides some insights into the daily practice of radio listening. He and Karmo were the first members of the group to be able to tune in as Karmo had managed save his radio set from destruction in 1941. As Krutob recalls,

> During the first Soviet occupation in 1941 all the radio receivers owned by citizens were confiscated . . . to prevent people from listening to 'hostile' radio stations. But Heldur Karmo managed to conceal his receiver (a 1937 Philips) in the cellar and after the departure of the Soviet army we could listen to music in his house with our friends.

Krutob first heard jazz on the BBC, but he was not an immediate convert. It was only after several weeks of listening that he started to find the sound palette familiar and comprehensible:

> In spring 1944 we listened to the BBC, whose short-wave broadcast quality was very high on our receiver. Since we knew a little English, we listened very closely, but the music was, for us, quite strange at first. The melodies were appealing and gripping, but we could not accept the arrangements or the mode of performance, which were very different from German-style pieces. However, we decided with Heldur Karmo not to abandon it before we had tried to understand this music. As we discovered later, only two to three hours of listening every day over the course of three weeks was enough to make the music comprehensible. And now our old German favourites seemed like *Saksa magedad* [tasteless music]. Especially interesting for us were the weekly lectures by the British journalist Denis Preston on jazz history. His historical overviews were illustrated with excellent musical examples.[56]

In addition to the main BBC service and AFN (American Forces Network), Krutob, Karmo and their friends could tune into Radio Nord, the BBC's Finnish service, Swedish Radio and Munich Network.

A little later, in the early 1950s, Estonians were finally able to record music, too. For instance, Kalju Terasma, who joined Swing Club around that time, recalls:

> It was in 1953 when I bought my first tape-recorder, a Dnepr 3. It was quite expensive but I could afford it since I was employed. I bought it from a store on Harju Street and it was tremendously big and heavy. Since I was the first one to own a tape-recorder, I would record all the music programmes and then distribute the tapes to the others. It made our life much easier.[57]

The technological limitations forced jazz fans to be inventive. As Terasma recalls:

> We used telephone lines to transfer music to each other. Special relays [electrical switches] were used to turn the telephone handset into a tape recorder or radio set. Everybody in our circle of jazz fans who owned a telephone had a relay. And if somebody were able to record a new piece, he could transmit it to the others by first calling and then connecting the tape recorder to the relay for music transfer. Then someone else whose recorder was connected to the system could record the piece, too. This system was invented by a sound engineer called Ants Brümmel. He provided us with the relays and set up the system.[58]

The group also used their radios as amplifiers, as Terasma explains:

> I used my radio set as a guitar amp. It was high-quality apparatus, called Baltika. Some of the channels did not receive any programmes but they were suitable for amplifying guitars. So I put a small microphone under the strings and connected the mike to the radio. It produced a really high-quality timbre.[59]

Four Spaces, Four Meanings

This group of four case studies has presented four narratives of Soviet Estonian jazz in the late Stalinist period. I developed the model of four cultural spaces of action in order to generate a comprehensive overview of jazz in this context. Instead of simplistic from above/from below or public/private dichotomies, this model proposes a more nuanced assessment of how jazz as a cultural form manifested itself in a number of social realms in Soviet Estonia. The distinction between those realms is based on their agency and location, with particular reference to the territory of actions of the cultural actors and the social spheres of the cultural activity. I will conclude by articulating the meaning of jazz as it emerged through the actions of cultural actors in these four distinct cultural spaces.

Journalistic discourse was the locus for the perspectives from above. As the dynamic of extinguishing jazz from the public arena demonstrated, the music gradually disappeared as the socio-political climate of late Stalinism became more restrictive. Therefore, in public discourse, the Soviet regime used jazz primarily as another tool in its political and ideological struggle against Western influence. While it was ideologized, the discourse detached itself from real musical life and became a kind of abstract phenomenon framed by Soviet rhetoric.

The second cultural space I categorized as public musical space was represented by the Jazz Orchestra of the Estonian State Philharmonic – the state-owned jazz group that performed on public concert stages. The significance of the orchestra extended far beyond the borders of Estonia: it belonged to the Soviet musical elite and spent most of its time touring throughout the Soviet Union. As a state-owned collective, it adhered to regulation from above: the orchestra's repertoire was censored and the ideology-driven paradigm shift of the late 1940s engendered changes in both repertoire and instrumentation. Despite this strict regulation, though, JOESP's musicians were usually able to keep their favourite tunes on the set list.

Musicians' everyday lives were discussed in the section on the Mickeys amateur dance orchestra, representing what I call the informal public cultural space. The Soviet-era imperative of institutional affiliation enabled Mickeys to gain access to free practice rooms, borrow instruments and hire a professional leader–arranger. The group was active in the relatively less regulated cultural sphere – school parties and leisure in general allowed more space for independent decision-making among actors. Mickeys' flexibility towards directives from above can be illustrated by the way in which the musicians responded to dance reform and anti-jazz campaign related shifts, such as the ban on saxophones and constraints on repertoires. While dance reform obliged the group to incorporate some approved ballroom numbers in their repertoire, they simply ignored the directives that attempted to ban saxophones and jazz-related tunes. Instead, they continued to play their favourite music and made no changes to instrumentation. I would term Mickeys' main strategy 'getting by'.[60] The musicians' primary motivations were their shared passion for jazz music and their desire to earn some extra income through *haltuuras*. To keep performing, they needed to be inventive, to retain a sense of humour, and to adapt to the prevailing circumstances, whatever they may be.

The most private area was represented by the Swing Club musical collective. It was their great passion for and deep interest in jazz music that drove these young Estonians to form a friendship group of like-minded people. In a context that was largely inimical to jazz, they established their own nurturing micro-environment to acquire knowledge and develop their skills through debate and practical learning-by-doing during rehearsals. They kept in touch with developments in jazz primarily by listening obsessively to foreign radio stations, such as AFN and the BBC. This radio listening therefore became another important aspect of their jazz education. 'Learning-by-listening' is a common means of developing jazz musicianship, but these Estonian musicians had to be especially creative to pursue their musical goals: for instance, they invented a relay system to disseminate recorded music between themselves and even used radio sets as amplifiers.

In this study I have sought to develop a model for discussing jazz that transcends simplistic dichotomies such as private/public and from below/from above, and without resorting to the popular mythologizations that produce binary thinking. In addition to the nuanced account that is facilitated by my repertoire of cultural spaces of action, Ann Swidler's model of culture helps us to break out of simplistic binaries, to avoid conceiving of Soviet Estonian jazz culture in schematic oppositional terms as a choice between forces 'from above' and forces 'from below'. By centralizing the musicians and their choices, these forces can be seen as more nuanced and even mutually constitutive. When acting within the Soviet regime, musicians selected their 'strategies of action' from a cultural repertoire defined by particular cultural contexts and historical situations. But the origins of their 'tools' – whether they relate to jazz practices, the cultural heritage of Estonia or a Sovietized socio-cultural environment – have less relevance to the processes than the effectiveness and success of the specific selected strategies in fulfilment of their primary goal – to play jazz.

These four individual case studies represent the synchronic aspect of the theory of four 'spaces of action': that is, how the spaces coexist at any moment. But the spaces can also be deployed from a diachronic aspect based on how they evolve in relation to each other. In other words, we can ask a question about the dynamic between the realms in temporal progression in terms of continuity/discontinuity, divergence/overlap or dissent/consent.

As this study has demonstrated, both Mickeys and Swing Club were active throughout the entire period under investigation. This indicates that jazz disappeared neither in the informal public sphere nor in the private sphere. The overlapping of the spaces was most extensive between 1944 and 1946, when there were no official restrictions on jazz. Thereafter, *Zhdanovshchina* had its most significant impact on the public media realm: newspaper and magazine articles first ideologized the jazz life and then stopped mentioning it altogether, leading to the disappearance of the word from the public sphere in 1950. In the public musical realm, as demonstrated by the example of JOESP, serious changes took effect in 1948, resulting in the disbanding of the orchestra.

The dynamic between the cultural spaces refers again to the paradoxical nature of Soviet society, where contradictory entities could coexist – the non-existence of some entity did not rule out the concurrent existence of the same entity. The application of the model of four 'cultural spaces of action' provides one approach to clarify this paradox. To paraphrase Ojakäär again: jazz was neither allowed nor forbidden in the Soviet Union, but it was never silent.

The case of Soviet Estonian jazz also tends to confirm the argument that Soviet power never achieved its totalitarian goals of the total politicization of society, the subordination of the citizens to total control or the formation of a monolithic-thinking and state-loyal Soviet nation. The totalism of Soviet society was disclosed primarily in the mechanisms of governance and the systems of propaganda, not in the implementation of the Soviet project in all social spheres. Despite the regime's best efforts to silence jazz, the music did not disappear from the private realms in Estonian cultural space.

Notes

1 As an example of 'jazz as a resistance' paradigm in scholarly texts, see, for instance, Novikova 2003.
2 For a closer examination of the historical dynamics of the period, see Reimann 2014.
3 On late Stalinism, see, for example, Fürst 2006.
4 On the Sovietization of Estonia during Stalinism, see, for example, Kuuli 2005, Mertelsman 2003, Zubkova 2009.
5 Because of space limitations, the administration of culture in the Soviet Union remains beyond the scope of this chapter. For an overview, see Kreegipuu 2007.
6 For a detailed overview of jazz discourse in *Sirp ja Vasar*, see Reimann 2014.
7 All the translations from Estonian to English are mine.
8 JOESP was almost never recorded, primarily because it was a touring collective (Valter Ojakäär, email message to the author, 21 January 2015). In the only sound

recording of the orchestra they play Eddie Sauter's 'Bennie Rides Again', available on *Eesti jazz 70* (München: Bella Musica, 1995)

9 Literally 'being cultivated'. The concept of 'culturedness' came into common usage in the 1930s as an alternative antonym for lack of culture (Fitzpatrick 1992: 2).

10 The document is preserved in the collection of the Estonian Museum of Theatre and Music.

11 Author's interview with Oleg Sapozhnin, 23 April 2014.

12 Ibid.

13 Ibid.

14 Printed in Ojakäär 2008: 177, 193.

15 This information is based on an article that appeared in *Sirp ja Vasar*, 10 June 1948.

16 Photo from the collection of the Estonian Theatre and Music Museum.

17 Vladimir Sapozhnin (1906–1996) was a violinist, multi-instrumentalist, estrada artist and impersonator. He started to perform at the age of five in circus shows with his parents. Although his primary instrument was the violin, he also played concertina, xylophone, harmonica and chimes. He was also known as an excellent mimic of musical instruments, sounds of nature and other artists. He worked between 1922 and 1940 as an entertainer in Europe and the USA; from 1944 to 1948 he conducted JOESP; from 1944 to 1990 he was a soloist in the Estonian Philharmonic. He worked later in Viru variety theatre and at the Moskva café (Pedusaar 2000).

18 The *Õhtuleht* article gives no further details of this source.

19 The *Õhtuleht* article gives no further details of this source.

20 According to Ojakäär (2008: 275), more than 150 Mickeys recordings are preserved in the archive of Estonian Public Broadcasting.

21 Photo from the personal collection of Udo Treufeldt.

22 Author's interview with Udo Treufeldt, 17 October 2013.

23 Ibid.

24 Ülo Raudmäe was the leader of the group from 1948 to 1950.

25 Treufeldt interview for 'Musical hour – Mickeys 45' radio show, archive of Estonian Public Broadcasting.

26 Author's interview with Udo Treufeldt, 17 October 2013.

27 Ibid.

28 Ibid.

29 Treufeldt interview for 'Musical hour – Mickeys 45' radio show, archive of Estonian Public Broadcasting.

30 Jõesaar interview for 'Musical hour – Mickeys 45' radio show, archive of Estonian Public Broadcasting.

31 Treufeldt interview for 'Musical hour – Mickeys 45' radio show, archive of Estonian Public Broadcasting.

32 Author's interview with Udo Treufeldt, 17 October 2013. The phrase was originally attributed to the Estonian actor Voldemar Panso.

33 Ibid.

34 *Haltuura* is a Russian word meaning slovenly or negligent work. In musicians' slang, it means occasional or additional earnings. It is almost equivalent to the English word 'gig', but it tends to have more negative connotations.

35 Ibid.

36 Ibid.

37 The tune was frst published by Leeds Music Corp in 1948, and first recorded by the vocal trio the Andrews Sisters (Ojakäär 2008: 271)

38 Available at: http://arhiiv.err.ee/vaata/papa-valter-pajatab-papa-valter-pajatab-mickey-s.

39 Krutob's personal notes for *Minu muusikutee* (My way to music).

40 There are no extant recordings of the group.

41 For a more detailed introduction to the story of the formation of Swing Club, see Reimann 2010.
42 Interview for 'Siis kui džäss ja pop olid põlu all' (When jazz and pop were out of favour), 11 August 1990, archive of Estonian Public Broadcasting.
43 Almanac of Swing Club, *Seletuseks*, p. 4.
44 Interview for 'Muusikaline tund: muusikamees Peeter Saul' (Musical hour: musician Peeter Saul), 11 August 1969, archive of Estonian Public Broadcasting.
45 He graduated from Tallinn Conservatory in 1952 as a composer. His jazz suites opened a new era in the development of the Estonian national jazz tradition. His pedagogical activity led him to found the first non-classical educational unit in Estonia – the Estrada Department at the G. Ots Music School, Tallinn, in 1977.
46 Agur interview for 'Siis kui džäss ja pop olid põlu all', 11 August 1990, archive of Estonian Public Broadcasting.
47 Almanac of Swing Club, p.10.
48 Krutob's personal notes for *Minu muusikutee* (My way to music).
49 Agur interview for 'Siis kui džäss ja pop olid põlu all', 11 August 1990, archive of Estonian Public Broadcasting.
50 Ibid.
51 Karmo interview for 'In memoriam – Uno Naissoo', 10 January 1980, archive of Estonian Public Broadcasting.
52 Loop started attending Swing Club's rehearsals in 1949 and became an official member of the group in 1950.
53 Author's interview with Uno Loop, 1 October 2011.
54 On the role of radio in disseminating jazz in state-socialist societies, see Ritter 2010.
55 Agur interview for 'Siis kui džäss ja pop olid põlu all', 11 August 1990, archive of Estonian Public Broadcasting.
56 Krutob's personal notes for *Minu muusikutee* (My way to music).
57 Author's interview with Kalju Terasma, 12 October 2011.
58 Ibid.
59 Ibid.
60 Term used by Johnston (2011).

References

Ake, David. 2003. 'Learning jazz, teaching jazz'. In Mervyn Cooke and David Horn, eds, *The Cambridge Companion to Jazz*, 1–6. London: Cambridge University Press.
Batachev, Alexei. 1972. *Sovetskii dzhaz*. Moskva: Muzyka.
Beličenko, Sergei. 2006. 'Otechestvennyj dzhaz kak institut kultury'. *Observatoria kultury* 3: 47–53.
Corner, Paul. 2009. *Popular Opinion in Totalitarian Regimes: Fascism, Nazism, Communism*. New York: Oxford University Press.
Edele, Mark. 2012. 'Stalinism as a totalitarian society: Geoffrey Hosking's socio-cultural history'. *Kritika: Explorations in Russian and Eurasian History* 13(2): 441–452.
Feiertag, Vladimir. 1981. 'Dzhaz na estrade'. In Jelena Uvarova, ed., *Russkaja sovetskaja Estrada*, 68–92. Moskva: Isskustvo.
Feiertag, Vladimir. 1999. *Dzhaz ot Leningrada do Peterburga*. Sankt-Peterburg: KultInform Press.
Feiertag, Vladimir. 2010. *Istoria dzhazovova ispolnitelstva v Rossii*. Sankt-Peterburg: Skifija.
Feigin, Leo. 1985. *Russian Jazz: New Identity*. New York: Quartet Books.
Fitzpatrick, Sheila. 1992. *The Cultural Front: Power and Culture in Revolutionary Russia*. New York: Cornell University Press.

Fitzpatrick, Sheila. 2007. 'Revisionism in Soviet history'. *History and Theory* 46: 77–91.

Fürst, Julianne, 2006. 'Late Stalinist society: history policies and people'. In Julianne Fürst, ed., *Late Stalinist Russia: Society between Reconstruction and Reinvention*, 4–36. London: Routledge.

Gaut, Greg. 1991. 'Soviet jazz: transforming American music'. In Reginald T. Buckner and Steven Weiland, eds, *Jazz in Mind: Essays on the History and Meaning of Jazz*, 60–82. Detroit, MI: Wayne State University Press.

Johnson, Bruce. 2002. 'The jazz diaspora'. In Mervyn Cooke and David Horn, eds, *The Cambridge Companion to Jazz*, 33–54. London: Cambridge University Press.

Johnston, Timothy. 2011. *Being Soviet: Rumour and Everyday Life under Stalin 1939–1953*. London: Oxford University Press.

Konen, Vera. 1977. *Puti amerikanskoi muzyki*. Moskva: Sovetskii kompozitor.

Kotkin, Stephen. 1995. *Magnetic Mountain: Stalinism as a Civilization*. Los Angeles: University of California Press.

Kreegipuu, Tiiu. 2007. 'Eesti kultuurielu sovetiseerimine: nõukogude kultuuripoliitika eesmärgid ja institutsionaalne raamistik aastatel 1944–1954'. In Tõnu Tannberg, ed., *Eesti NSV aastatel 1940–1953: Sovetiseerimise mehhanismid ja tagajärjed Nõukogude Liidu ja Ida-Euroopa kontekstis*, 352–388. Tartu: Eesti Ajalooarhiiv.

Kuuli, Olaf. 2005. 'Muutuvad parteitekstid (1946–1952)'. In Maie Kalda and Virve Sarapik, eds, *Kohanevad tekstid*, 259–270. Tartu: Eesti Kirjandusmuuseum.

Lücke, Martin. 2004. *Jazz im Totalitarismus: eine komparative Analyse des politisch motivierten Umgangs mit dem Jazz während der Zeit des Nationalsozialismus und des Stalinismus*. Münster: LIT Verlag.

Lücke, Martin. 2010. 'The postwar campaign against jazz in the USSR (1945–1953)'. In Gertrud Pickhan and Rüdiger Ritter, eds, *Jazz behind the Iron Curtain*, 83–98. Frankfurt am Main: Peter Lang.

Mertelsman, Olaf. 2003. *The Sovietization of the Baltic States: 1940–1956*. Tartu: KLEIO ajalookirjanduse sihtasutus.

Mertelsman, Olaf. 2012. *Everyday Life in Stalinist Estonia*. Frankfurt am Main: Peter Lang.

Minor, William. 1995. *Unzipped Souls: A Jazz Journey through the Soviet Union*. Philadelphia, PA: Temple University Press.

Monson, Ingrid. 1996. *Sayin' Something: Jazz Improvisation and Interaction*. Chicago: University of Chicago Press.

Myrdal, Janken. 2012. 'Source pluralism as a method of historical research'. In Susanna Fellmann and Marjatta Rahikainen, eds, *Historical Knowledge: In Quest of Theory, Method and Evidence*, 154–189. Newcastle: Cambridge Scholars Publishing.

Novikova, Irina. 2003. 'Black music, white freedom: times and spaces of jazz countercultures in the USSR'. In Heike Raphael-Hernandez, ed., *Blackening Europe: The African American Presence*, 73–84. New York: Routledge.

Ojakäär, Valter. 2008. *Sirp ja saksofon*. Tallinn: Kirjastus Ilo.

Pedusaar, Heino. 2000. *Boba: mees kui orkester*. Tallinn: Infotrükk.

Pickhan, Gertrud and Rüdiger Ritter, eds. 2010. *Jazz behind the Iron Curtain*. Frankfurt am Main: Peter Lang.

Reimann, Heli. 2010a. 'Lembit Saarsalu: "Music Saved Me". The Study of Jazz Musician's Early Musical Development'. In *Jazz Behind the Iron Curtain*, edited by Gertrud Pickhan and Rüdiger Ritter, 165-182. Frankfurt am Main: Peter Lang.

Reimann, Heli. 2010b. '"Down with bebop – viva swing!" Swing Club and the meaning of jazz in late 1940s Estonia'. *Jazz Research Journal* 4(2): 95–122.

Reimann, Heli. 2011. 'Ideology and the cultural study of Soviet Estonian jazz'. In Janne Mäkelä, ed., *The Jazz Chameleon*, 23–35. Turku: JAPA.

Reimann, Heli. 2013. 'Jazz research and the moments of change'. *Etnomusikologian vuosikirja* 25: 8–33.

Reimann, Heli. 2014. 'Late-Stalinist ideological campaigns and the rupture of jazz: "jazz talk" in the Soviet Estonian cultural newspaper *Sirp ja Vasar*. *Popular Music* 33(3): 509–529.

Ritter, Rüdiger. 2010. 'The radio – a jazz instrument of its own'. In Gertrud Pickhan and Rüdiger Ritter, eds, *Jazz behind the Iron Curtain*, 35–56. Frankfurt am Main: Peter Lang.

Shlapentokh, Vladimir. 1989. *Public and Private Life of the Soviet People: Changing Values in Post-Stalin Russia*. New York and Oxford: Oxford University Press.

Swidler, Ann. 1986. 'Culture in action: symbols and strategies'. *American Sociological Review* 51(4): 273–286.

Swidler, Ann. 2001. *Talk of Love: How Culture Matters*. Chicago: University of Chicago Press.

Tarvel, Enn. 2005. 'Kas ajalugu saab kirjutada objektiivselt?' *Tuna: Ajalookultuuri* 3: 4–9.

Tomoff, Kirill. 2006. *Creative Union: The Professional Organization of Soviet Composers, 1939–1953*. London: Cornell University Press.

Ward, Chris. 2004. 'What is history? The case of late Stalinism'. *Rethinking History: The Journal of Theory and Practice* 8(3): 439–458.

Whyton, Tony. 2011. 'Introduction'. In Tony Whyton, ed., *Jazz*, i–xx. London: Ashgate.

Yurchak, Aleksei. 2006. *Everything was Forever, until It Was No More*. Princeton, NJ: Princeton University Press.

Zdravomyslova, Elena and Voronkov, Vladimir. 2002. 'The informal public in Soviet society: double morality at work'. *Social Research* 69(1): 50–69.

Zolkin, Aleksei. 2009. *Kulturologia*. Moskva: Unity-Dana.

Zubkova, Jelena. 2009. *Baltimaad ja Kreml 1940–1953*. Tallinn: Varrak.

4

JAZZ IN POLAND

Totalitarianism, Stalinism, Socialist Realism

Igor Pietraszewski

> 1948–1949 were breakthrough years, when in both the political and government circles there evolved an idea of cultural planning, and a concept of the art of the new period of building socialism, art of deeply humanist content, art truly for the people, art pervaded by ideas of international brotherhood and real patriotism.[1]
>
> *(Sokorski 1950, 78)*

In Poland (as in other European countries), jazz appeared after American isolationism came to an end during the First World War. The genre developed in free-market economic conditions, with independence and democracy regained after long years of partition. The founding myth that was fundamental for its further presence, significance and development, however, did not come into being until thirty years later, during the Stalin era (1948–1955). Communist totalitarianism in Stalin's time gradually spread into and sought to control all spheres of people's activity, including the artistic realm. The restrictive cultural policy introduced by the authorities called for institutional consent to engage in any form of art. The rapidly growing jazz movement came to halt. In 1948–1949 the Polish Composers' Union declared this artistic genre to be 'formalist jazz rubbish', and its pursuit was regarded as a manifestation of hostile bourgeois ideology. Socialist ideology of the Cold War era halted the process of the institutionalization of jazz. At the same time the founding myth of jazz as the art of opposition formed. Its essence lay in the protest against the imposed ideology and a new genre in art – Socialist Realism. By symbolic abuse, the authorities strove to Sovietize culture. The authorities did not assign any social role to jazz musicians in the communist system, so they were excluded from official recognition. A stereotype of a jazzman developed

– that of an outsider, a nonconformist who is free of the restrictions of the institutional world. Jazz became a synonym for freedom and independence. The forbidden fruit began to attract those who, through involvement in the field of jazz, wanted to manifest the different lifestyle that they chose and their disagreement with socialist propaganda and imposed standards. The situation began to change only after Stalin's death, but the founding myth of 'anti-system jazz' lived on over the next decades, even though the genre was gradually incorporated into the official cultural profile.

Introduction

Scholars who analyse the social phenomena of Central and Eastern Europe present different opinions as to whether 'totalitarianism' prevailed in Poland and the satellite states of the USSR after the Second World War.[2] Even if they agree as to the legitimacy of using the term, they differ in the way in which they define it and in the essential characteristics which they emphasize.[3] For the purposes of this chapter I treat totalitarianism as a syndromic tool[4] and an analytical category, to describe particular aspects of reality as summarized below, without going into defining subtleties. I will use the term 'Stalinism' as a synonym for 'totalitarianism' to define the model of Poland's ideological, political and economic functioning after the Second World War. Elements present in Poland at the time, typical of totalitarian regimes, were as follows: dominance of the party apparatus over the state apparatus; a disproportionately complex coercive apparatus; the use of terror (mass in the years 1944–1947, then common); the powerful idea of 'the enemy' (real or imagined, internal and external); omnipotence of the state manifested in the attempt to control all spheres of human life; censorship; and monopoly on information and propaganda.

We can characterize Stalinism as a near-perfect totalitarian society based on state ownership of the means of production. I use 'totalitarian' in its common sense, meaning a political system in which all bonds have been fully replaced by a state organization, and where all communities and all individuals are thus to function solely for purposes which are both the purposes of the state and defined by the state in this way. In other words, an ideal totalitarian system would consist in the total destruction of the civil society so that the state and its organizational instruments were the sole forms of social life; all types of human activity – economic, cultural, political and intellectual – are permitted and required (and the difference between what is permitted and what is required tends toward disappearing) only to the extent to which they serve the purposes of the state (again, the purposes defined by the state itself). Each individual (including the rulers) is considered to be the property of the state (Kołakowski 1984, 246).

Stalinist totalitarianism aimed at absolute submission of society to the state in which only one power dictated all principles of communal life to its subjects.

The method to achieve this entailed destroying the civil society, which would then consist of isolated individuals who were completely helpless against the apparatus of repression. The destruction of the civil society and social ties leads to the isolation of the individual, about which Hannah Arendt wrote:

> While isolation concerns only the political realm of life, loneliness concerns human life as a whole. Totalitarian government, like all tyrannies, certainly could not exist without destroying the public realm of life, that is, without destroying, by isolating men, their political capacities. But totalitarian domination as a form of government is new in that it is not content with this isolation and destroys private life as well. It bases itself on loneliness, on the experience of not belonging to the world at all, which is among the most radical and desperate experiences of man.
>
> *(Arendt 1985, 173)*

In the political sphere the differences between the Polish and the classic (that is, the Soviet) version of Stalinism were rather slight (Werblan 1991). Stalinism in Poland was weaker; totalitarianism did not have its roots in a genuine revolution of the masses, but was rather the result of electoral fraud and the permanent presence of the Red Army.

There are also variations in research perspectives pertaining to periodization. According to some, totalitarianism prevailed in Poland only during the Stalinist era, whereas others claim it was also present during the subsequent decades until the collapse of the PRL, the Polish People's Republic, and the transformation of the system into a democracy in 1989 (Świda-Ziemba 1997). Its various elements functioned at different points in time. The terror and repression connected with the imposition of the new order began as early as 1944, the nationalization of the economy started in 1946, and the heavy repression of the Stalinist ideology (including the area of the art world that interests us) continued from 1948 until 1954–1956. It was at that time that jazz was deemed dissident, and excluded from the state's care and patronage. It is also on this period that this analysis focuses.

It must, however, be remembered that the process of implementing the new communist authority in Poland, subordinated to the Soviet Union, was visible as early as 1944, when, in consequence of ongoing hostilities in the country, Red Army troops heading for Berlin entered Poland. It was around then that police and judicial repression of political enemies began. From 1945, Poland found itself on the eastern side of the 'Iron Curtain', in the Soviet sphere of influence under Stalin's rule. Norman Davies (1999) described the specific situation of Poland, betrayed by its allies and left to the mercy of Stalin. This had terrible consequences – mass arrests of the members of the wartime resistance movement, civil war with opponents of communism, and a government led by an NKVD officer, Bolesław Bierut, who pretended to be a non-party leader (Davies 1999, 1130).

On the other hand, 1956, which is assumed to be the turning point of this period, witnessed the so-called 'October thaw' after the transformations in the Moscow headquarters following Stalin's death in 1953. During the session of the VIIIth Plenum of the Central Committee of the PZPR, there was a demand for liberalization of the political system. A new executive body was elected; Władysław Gomułka, previously imprisoned, became First Secretary; some other political prisoners and clergy (including the Primate of Poland, Cardinal Stefan Wyszyński) were released; the activities of the repression apparatus were curbed; more advantageous principles of economic cooperation with the USSR were adopted; and the restrictive approach to the collectivization of agriculture was abandoned.

In this context, how did the processes of the instutionalization of jazz, whose essence was widely believed in Poland to lie in the freedom of expression and collective, spontaneous improvisation, occur?[5] 'Institutionalization' is understood here as a two-level process of creating patterns or models of interaction. It is connected with cultural and social production, development and support of behavioural patterns established by active agents in the field, as well as with the emergence of formal structures that organize a given community (Pietraszewski 2014, 37–38).

An outline of the historical context in which jazz had developed and functioned until 1948 will be helpful in understanding how profound the changes were during the immediate post-war years.

A Historical Outline

1918–1945

From the end of American isolationism and the appearance of jazz in Europe during the First World War to Nazi Germany's invasion of Poland on 1 September 1939 (the beginning of the Second World War), the institutionalization of jazz in Poland took place in free-market conditions in a developing, democratic country. Relations between the field of power and the field of art were practically non-existent. Music was not centrally regulated as a cultural policy and jazz was a new entertainment spontaneously entering society as a functional dance music played in elegant eating establishments, cabarets, varieties and revue theatres. Its natural audiences could afford to frequent such places as they belonged to the wealthier sections of society – the artistic, business and clerical elites.

Gradually jazz became increasingly popular thanks to the development of technology, the media and deeper relations with other art fields. Polish pre-war movie theatres showed top Hollywood productions starring an array of leading

US jazz musicians, including *The Singing Fool, The Jazz Singer, Show Boat, The King of Jazz, Alexander's Ragtime Band, Hollywood Hotel* and others. The popularity of these movies led not only to a rise in the number of jazz lovers, but also to an improvement in the competence of both the well-off audience, which influenced public opinion and artistic taste, and the musicians, who tried to master the new musical style and play like the virtuosi they saw on screen. In big cities one could easily buy instruments, sheet music and records, as well as magazines that were dedicated to jazz. Polish Radio, which began broadcasting in 1925, also provided access to jazz.

The interwar period witnessed an intensive process of jazz institutionalization, with the evolution of the genre from fashionable, big-city entertainment – dance music – into a separate, nascent artistic offering. In those days musicians forged international careers in the field of light music. Adi Rosner was called the 'White Louis Armstrong', with many international audiences considering him the world's second-greatest trumpeter; Henryk Wars wrote music for Hollywood movies; Bronisław Kaper wrote many popular pieces;[6] Jerzy Petersburski composed a number of well-known tunes, including the famous 'Tango Milonga' (internationally known as 'Oh, Donna Clara'), which was performed by such artists as Edith Piaf and Al Jolson; Victor Young (born Wiktor Jung) graduated in composition from Warsaw Conservatory in 1918 and made his debut as a violinist with the Warsaw Philharmonic.

However, the cataclysm of the Second World War disrupted the development of jazz in Poland. The freedom of activity in the field was curbed. In addition to the theft of all possible property, the occupying forces, both Germans and Soviets, carried out deliberate campaigns of extermination of elite social groups, who had until then been mainstays of the jazz audience.[7] At a meeting with Governor-General Hans Frank on 2 October 1940, Adolf Hitler said: 'For Poles there can be only one master, and he is German . . . hence all representatives of the Polish intelligentsia are to be killed. It sounds ruthless, but such is the law of life' (Kurek 2009, 20). The losses resulting from the hostilities between 1939 and 1945 were estimated to amount to some US$650–700 billion in 2004 terms.[8] Out of the thirty-eight million Polish citizens in 1938, more than six million had lost their lives by the end of the war.

1945–1948

In the first years after the war the survivors tried to reconstruct the familiar, pre-war models, relations and structures of the social world. Beginning in 1945, hundreds of entertainment establishments were founded in the rubble of ruined cities, often in the basements of half-burned-down buildings. As the press wrote, 'people wanted to dance the war years away' (*Słowo Polskie* (1947) cited in Pietraszewski 2014, 52).[9] Jazz was democratized due to its accessibility. Participation in jazz was no longer conditioned by the thickness of one's wallet or cultural competence – a new type of listener was born, because of the new cultural policy of the communist government, which included new educational policies that favoured working and peasant classes and the marginalization of the pre-war middle and upper classes.

In Poland's ruined cities many establishments were soon offering live music to everyone. The process of the institutionalization of jazz began anew, but in different political and economic conditions. Beginning in 1944, the bottom-up processes of reconstructing the pre-war world were gradually curbed by the growing omnipotence of the state, which was consistently eradicating the private sector.

Stalinism and Socialist Realism

Politics and economics create a framework in which the institutionalization of art can take place. According to Roger Scruton, 'A state is totalitarian if it permits no autonomous institutions, i.e. if the aims, activities and membership of all associations are subject to the control of the state . . . Complete state control of the means of communication is also essential, together with an ideology' (Scruton 1982, 466–467). The processes of institutionalization of the jazz world were inhibited under Stalinism, and the opportunities for association and joint participation in art events were hindered. It happened suddenly: 'The picture changed drastically, almost overnight, in the summer of 1948 . . . All magazines and instruments of social pedagogy began to speak in one style and language, a language universalized, ideologically aggressive, moralizing and pompous in the Stalinist fashion' (Werblan 1991, 26). The ideological attack was aimed at developing 'a new socialist man' and working out new methods of influencing him. And in reality, as Leszek Kołakowski wrote,

> 'Spiritual pyeryekovka', as it was called, consisted in turning man's soul so as to create 'the new man of socialism' – a mentally blank, passive dummy devoid of will, incapable of opposition, of rebellion, of critical thinking, smoothly accepting everything he was supposed to believe at a particular point by the will of the rulers.
>
> *(Kołakowski 2014, 22–23)*

The process of creating the 'leading, militant intelligentsia' involved, among other things, enrolling working-class and peasant youths into universities without entrance examinations, awarding them preferential points for social background, awarding them dormitory accommodation, grants and scholarships that were unavailable to the old intelligentsia (which anyway had been decimated during the war) or to the descendants of the pre-war middle and upper classes. There was a need for a new socialist intelligentsia. 'Guidelines for the production of this new educated class were simple: their education was

100 Igor Pietraszewski

to be as far as possible limited to professional tasks, and their minds trained in servility' (ibid., 24). The remnants of the educated and once affluent pre-war jazz audiences who survived the war were pushed onto the sidelines of social life. The authorities aimed to develop new elites who would be able to reproduce the centrally imposed ideas of a socialist society. There was no room in this new society for the old bourgeoisie and its warped taste. The authorities had the power and the means to realize their new ideas.

Mobilization of the society and the constraints imposed by the ideological framework affected the art world in a particular manner. Moral and political pressure, and a peculiar form of indoctrination in the field of art in Stalinist Poland, found its expression in Socialist Realism imposed from the top down by the communist authorities. It was an ideological programme according to which the entire field of art was to become nationalist in form and socialist in content. It was also to be lucid and accessible to the new audience of workers and peasants. Art became an element of the struggle for a better tomorrow:

> What should be done – asks Comrade Berman[10] – for our artistic creation to go hand in hand with our economic and political achievements? First of all, our ideology must be strengthened in this respect. The awareness of the great role of the writer and the artist in the People's Poland must be increased. So must awareness of the rightness of the way of Socialist Realism . . . To achieve this goal one needs contact with the masses, contact with life.
>
> *(Sokorski 1950, 150–151)*

Although music, and instrumental music in particular, was not as important as, for example, literature in the accomplishment of political objectives (and, consequently, the degree of censorship was lower), it still found a place in the new reality of Socialist Realism. The cultural policy assigned positions and tasks both to entire genres of art and to individual artists. Music became one of the many tools on the ideological front (the socialist newspeak overflowed with military allusions, such as 'front', 'struggle', 'enemy', 'battle' and 'attack'). Art was to be addressed to the 'labouring masses in the cities and the villages', as they were commonly known, who from now on were to participate *en masse* in Poland's cultural life.

The leading 'ideologist on the music front' – another very common phrase in those days – the previously quoted Włodzimierz Sokorski[11] (a deputy member of the Central Committee of the Polish United Workers' Party, Deputy Minister and then Minister of Culture and Art between 1952 and 1956) was the only high-ranking politician to express any opinion about music (see Wieczorek 2014). He held a dominant position and had unquestionable influence on the shaping and implementation of the idea of Socialist Realism in art. He justified the enforced changes in the approach and realization of music as follows:

> Contemporary music does not rouse the right resonance in the listener, it does not appeal to his emotional sensitivity . . . It is, in the first instance, a question of a different perception, another musical sensitivity of the creator and the listener. This otherness of reaction of the artist and his audience to musical phenomena is, in turn, the result of a different inner mental attitude, a different system of aesthetic experiences, which are conditioned by a different process of the development of the creator and the new listener, who usually comes from the workers' world. The key to solving the issue therefore lies not on the plane of whether the music 'is easy or difficult', but on the plane of overcoming the epigonistic music of decadent capitalism, now showing clear traits of formalistic degeneration, and finding realistic artistic expression both in the treatment of the subject matter and in the form.
>
> *(Sokorski 1950, 60–61)*

This call was promptly answered by the Departments of Culture and Art, and particularly by the culture industries' trade unions and artistic associations. Membership of a union or artistic association was a prerequisite for receiving benefits such as an apartment, vacations, trips abroad and the necessary tools to practise one's profession (including musical instruments and writing paper). The leaders of these organizations were invariably appointed, or at least approved, by the party.

The communist regime had an efficient system of subsidies and censorship which allowed the authorities to control the artistic life. The world of art was organized as a system of official institutions, outside of which there was no room for any artistic, spontaneous activity that was not centrally sanctioned. All artistic activity had to be initiated or approved by the authorities, and was required to conform with the Cold War ideology. The Composers' Convention in Łagów Lubuski in 1949 was the moment when new directions for the development of music in the People's Poland were defined, and opposition to jazz was articulated. It was then that jazz was officially declared to be incorrect and to have no place in 'a healthy, socialist society'. The process of the institutionalization of the jazz world suddenly collapsed (paradoxically, with parallel developments of the genre). 'Here in Łagów there's no more beating around the bush. We say, point blank, that jazz is ideologically foreign, socially suspicious, and based on hostile, American patterns' (Łazarewicz 1999, 22).

The assessment of art was now based on political, not only artistic, criteria. Jazz had come from America, so it was, by definition, hostile. It enjoyed increasing popularity with young people, who searched for it on Western radio stations that the authorities tried to block. To what degree this music was jazz, and to what degree it was dance music, was not always clear. In the 1940s, jazz was considered to be the rhythmic music that came from across the Atlantic; it was good for dancing and for partying. The party's recommendations, on the other hand, called for music based on national folk motifs with lyrics that glorified the toil and accomplishments of workers and peasants. The propagandistic influence of jazz was also visible on the other side of the Atlantic. With growing antagonism between the USSR and the USA, the Cold War intensified. In a speech in 1946, Winston Churchill coined the term 'Iron Curtain'. The Cold War ensued between two enemy camps, with the term pertaining to the Western superpowers' attempts to stop Soviet expansion. In 1947, President Truman announced that American aid would soon be arriving in countries threatened with communism, and the Marshall Plan, an initiative to assist Europe, was launched. But in Poland, already a satellite state of the USSR, it was impossible to accept this offer of aid. In the USA, jazz was named a cultural ambassador. In the Eastern Bloc, everything American was considered hostile. In the official propaganda, jazz became synonymous with vile, bourgeois entertainment. The chairman of the Polish Composers' Association presented the main principles of Socialist Realism music as: 'content linked to the people, nonelitist, a national style, simplified language; an increased focus on vocal and programmatic works' (Tompkins 2013, 41).

After approximately thirty years in Poland, jazz was deemed to be formalist junk and it was roundly condemned. The General Assembly of the Polish Composers' Association asserted:

> The chasm separating the composer from the listeners not only because of many composers breaking away from life and universal problems . . . but also resulting from not preparing a great number of listeners to receive any music other than the jazz junk . . . must be filled. In their works composers should first of all endeavour to express thoughts that are optimistic and constructive towards social issues.
>
> *(Cited in Brodacki 1980, 16–17)*

The convention in Łagów was attended by twenty-five leading Polish composers. The authorities were represented by the Deputy Minister of Culture and Art, Włodzimierz Sokorski. Summing up the convention, he wrote:

> In light of the Łagów debates it turned out to be indisputable that the problem of formalism and realism in music cannot be examined either on the plane of juxtaposing the formal content in music with notional content, or on the plane of juxtaposing formal values with thematic values, but only in the perspective of a principal contrast between the anti-humanistic, abstract and formal music of decadent imperialism, and

humanistic, connotatively emotional, expressively suggestive modern music of the socialist era . . . During the last quarter of the century we have observed in intellectuals and creators, still ideologically stuck in the old world, a distinctive helplessness towards the need to capture the objective truth of the new epoch which they face. It is a consequence of the stumbling capitalist system, which had to result in the stumbling of all previous aesthetic notions . . . With the deepening political crisis, the initially still deep and searing pessimism of Stravinsky, Debussy, Ravel or Szymanowski in our country evolves into formalist juggling, into a dodecaphonist grotesque, into snobbish cultivation of disharmonic jazz.

(Sokorski 1950, 168–169)

Attacks on jazz in Poland were nothing new, but before the war they had appeared in a different political context;[12] and back then, the criticism had pertained solely to aesthetics. Jazz was not an element in political and ideological conflict. By 1948, the Stalinist terror had already been under way for several years, and the ideological indoctrination had recently intensified. Given the repression of the Stalinist era, the statements quoted above caused understandable anxiety among jazz musicians.

Music, along with other branches of art, became an instrument of ideological struggle. Its earlier development was described as follows:

Eliminate the emotions of life and curb aesthetic musical feelings . . . that was the task the American and Western European composers set themselves over the last 50 years. That this kind of music had to be at the same time utterly devoid of national and regional character, that it inevitably had to steer towards soulless cosmopolitanism eventually to fall under the influence of musical deformations, was obvious. It is also little wonder that the American imperialism today uses formalist, cosmopolitan, antinational and anti-humanistic music as one of the major means of influencing the human psyche, striving to dull its ethical and aesthetic sensitivity, to destroy folk art and the national music trend, and therefore to incapacitate nations in their struggle for freedom, for social justice, for the new, constructive, clear-cut order of the socialist system. Thus, the subject of formalism and cosmopolitanism in music is of interest to us not only as an artistic or a social phenomenon, but primarily as a political phenomenon, as a specific form of the penetration of political nihilism, the hopelessness of the so-called Pan-American culture, made through music.

(Ibid., 170–171)

The stages of ideological struggle were connected both with the introduction of Socialist Realism in art and with calls for a battle with nationalism and

104 Igor Pietraszewski

cosmopolitanism, drawing on 'the only right' models of Soviet art. Henceforth, literature and art would glorify workers. 'Eminent' Socialist Realist works created by Soviet authors served as points of reference. Anecdotally, it is recalled that people said: 'Good, better, Soviet.' The 'bond between creators and the masses' became the prerequisite of all artistic creation (Fijałkowska 1985, 77, 100–101). In a world where the radio played mainly Soviet songs glorifying the toil of the workers and the leaders of the peasant masses, jazz, which had been a presence in Poland since the First World War, assumed special features. Its founding myth developed – one of music functioning outside of the official system, the art of resistance. It was not active resistance, but opposition to the centrally imposed ideology of Socialist Realism:

> Because the Soviet strategy of cultural domination was based on control and homogenization inside the satellite camp or a nation state (the proper culture was to be the culture that was socialist in content and national in form), the strategy of resistance consisted in the search for connections with the outside (most often Western) world.
>
> *(Kubik 2006, 278)*

The institutionalization of jazz ceased. In a world where the plan of total control was being put into action, with each activity requiring the approval of the relevant organization and each citizen assigned to specific work, jazzmen found themselves outside of the approved political, ideological and institutional system. A stereotype emerged of a non-conformist outsider functioning outside the social roles imposed by the system.

Economy

The authorities started to enter every area of human activity. After 1948, once the party had unified, the economy was further centralized, and restrictive economic rules typical of communist totalitarianism (in contrast to fascism, which encouraged a capitalist economy) were introduced. In the economic dimension of Stalinism,

> Total power implies, above all, complete control of production and exchange, expropriation of the entire population from the means of production, and strict prohibition of private exchange – that is to say, abolition of the market ... Chronic shortages are not a temporary ailment of the communist anti-market economy, but its essential charac-teristic. There are no economic reasons why production should respond to demand; managers are responsible for fulfilling quotas established by their ministries, not for satisfying their customers.
>
> *(Kołakowski 2014, 58)*

The pre-war reality of the free market was replaced by a centralized economy. For musicians, this meant, among other things, difficulties in obtaining instruments, reeds, strings and other accessories. Importing one's tools of the trade from the West was extremely complicated due to restrictions on foreign travel. Moreover, from 20 June 1945, trading in foreign currency and taking it out of the country were punishable by five years in prison and a cash fine of 200,000 zlotys (an enormous sum: the average monthly salary in 1950 was 551 zlotys). From 1950, the state went even further: private individuals faced fifteen years in prison and a fine for merely possessing US dollars. Hence, sheet music, records and magazines were beyond any Polish jazz fan's wildest dreams.

Everyday Life

In the early post-war years, jazz was often promoted in YMCA clubs, which operated in the major cities, but

> In the 40s . . . jazz went underground. 1948, the year in which the party unified, was the turning point, when all red plagues fell upon it. There was to be no room for American music. In Łódź, for example, the YMCA's entire jazz library was burned, just like the Nazis had done earlier. The records were smashed.
>
> *(Szymon Kobyliński cited in Kowal 1995, 54)*

Musicians who lived through those years routinely compare Stalin to Hitler:

> Stalin, like Hitler, prohibited jazz music, and both times were comparable. The authorities regarded this music as an imperialistic product, which was a total nonsense because not a single capitalist had ever been a fan of jazz music, but it was the point, and full stop. It was nothing new, though, and Stalin was not the only one to do it, but also – what do you know! – Hitler. Interestingly enough, they are always people of a similar sort.
>
> *(Pietraszewski 2014, 94–95)*

How, then, could jazz be cultivated? The answer was that it went underground as an expression of opposition against the state's cultural policy; it began to be played in private apartments and so-called 'cellar clubs'. Should the secret police arrive, the private jam sessions would be explained away as birthday parties or celebrations of name days. As one jazz activist said:

> We once organized a rehearsal on the pretext of a name day. Back then playing was prohibited, and they knew very well when and where such events took place. So it was not safe, but the guys from the secret police

106 Igor Pietraszewski

tolerated name days and drinking vodka . . . The band . . . invited young musicians up on the stage and they performed popular standards. There were usually some informers sitting among the audience, so to mislead the enemy we made up lyrics for these standards as we went along that would conform to the ideology.

(Marian Ferster[13] cited in Brodacki 2010, 138)

Composer and saxophonist Jerzy 'Duduś' Matuszkiewicz recalled:

During the catacomb period we used to meet in private apartments. Music was played quite loudly, so after several hours the police would arrive to check out what was going on. Of course, they had no idea what music we were playing, so we usually turned to the 'Happy Birthday' . . . song and assured them that we were just celebrating somebody's name day, and the case was closed. So, it was possible to smuggle through jazz music, play it underground. Not on a stage, though: that was flatly prohibited. Even in clubs it was difficult, to say nothing of the radio, which was totally cut off to this genre of music.[14]

On the one hand, playing jazz was thought to be a form of opposition against social and political reality. On the other, it was a quest for alternative forms of social organization, which when confronted with the impossibility of playing jazz officially resulted in moving this artistic activity from the public to private sphere of social life. As one musician remembered:

jazz musicians gathered at really quiet soirées in private apartments, where they would play, and jam sessions took place in Kraków, in Łódź. In Warsaw, however, the YMCA still functioned, the American organization which had numerous sections in pre-war Poland, and even after the war, in the 1950s – wonders never cease! – they continued somehow. So concerts took place at the YMCA club in Konopnicka Street. They were closed events . . . and as far as I know, all of them were illegal.

(Pietraszewski 2014, 96)

Music was also played at evening dance parties at the Film School, the Academy of Fine Arts and the Medical School. Hence, over the ensuing decades the elite pre-war jazz audience came to be replaced by students:

When we played at the Film School, we tried to play as much jazz as possible, but when the 'district' activists of ZMP[15] came into the room, someone would always warn us, and we quickly switched to folk music and played the polkas, obereks, and kujawiaks as long as they stayed at the ball . . . [When they left] simply jazz was played instead of the official dance music. It could not be kept secret, and one of our most tireless ZMP activists came one evening, saw that half the school was sitting there, and a frantic affair erupted, they wanted to expel us from the university. The matter died down, because we were supported by the entire film-makers' circle, we survived the attack.

(Jerzy Matuszkiewicz cited in Brodacki 2010, 138)

During student parties, the titles of jazz pieces were sometimes replaced with Russian titles to mislead the ZMP officials, who were tasked with controlling student life.

A change in attitude occurred between the imposition of ideology on art from the beginning of the 1940s and the retreat from Socialist Realist assumptions in 1954–1955, after Stalin's death. In March 1950, a magazine article[16] commented that 'the lack of values practised to this day in the repertoire, based primarily on soulless jazz, cannot be tolerated. Therefore, keeping independent jazz bands seems pointless, and even harmful' (cited in Brodacki 2010, 142). Four years later, during a meeting of composers, the problems of light and dance music were discussed:

Light and dance music – this is one of the most urgent problems of our musical output and one of the most neglected areas of this output . . . Does this 'light repertoire' satisfy the needs of society? Obviously not . . . Most disputes and misunderstandings, however, are provoked by the question of dance music of the international type . . . It is true that the jazz performance manner has caught on, that the society has accepted it, and that the society demands jazz today. Not all that aforementioned degenerate dixieland and bebop, of course, but rhythmic and syncopated, tuneful, good music one can dance to. And this need of the society we are not meeting. We are prevented by a number of fears, as the risk is big. The example of degenerate, uncivilized American jazz is indeed scary, but Italians, for example, did manage to create their own, separate jazz musical style, a music that does not renounce any of the contemporary musical means and very jazz, but they did not go in the direction of barbarism and degeneration. One could also take the example of the pleasant, graceful French song and, last but not least, a number of Russian songs which in a sense are an adaptation of jazz means into the native territory. *Nobody wants to fight against jazz music defined in this way.* But we must be clear that jazz as a performance manner, serving good, rhythmical, syncopated, melodious dance or light music drawing on contemporary harmony is the need of the society, that it does not alone carry the threat of barbarism and degeneration, that also in this field it is possible to write valuable pieces, that the Polish composer faces the difficult task set by the society, the task of creating good dance and light music of this type.

(Henryk Czyż[17] cited in Brodacki 1980, 38–40; my emphasis)

The development of the myth of jazz was also influenced by the attitude of the jazzmen, who were perceived as free people. In a system where everything was owned by the state, and all production was planned by the central authorities, each good produced in that way was an allotted good, with the allotment decided by the authorities. An apartment was a particularly precious commodity – in destroyed cities, where several families often cohabited in one apartment, and the allotted space was seven square metres per person, an apartment of one's own was a great luxury. Everything depended on the class of the citizen as determined by the party and the local authorities: those on the waiting list for an apartment would reach the top only if they stood out in terms of their obedience and zealousness in their service to the authorities. The same was true for cars, cheap vacations with good accommodation and other privileges. Jazzmen were not perceived as obedient, so they were pushed to the sidelines; the authorities did not assign them any approved role in the socialist society, and they did not participate in the race for allotted privileges. This aroused respect, interest and admiration among the general population. As one musician remembered, 'The jazzman was a big shot! Jazz attracted the crème de la crème, the avant-garde of intelligent university students, people of science and art. You were not trendy if you were not affiliated with the jazz community' (Pietraszewski 2014, 99).

After Stalin's death, jazz slowly ceased to be a manifestation of a hostile ideology, so it was decided to put it to work on behalf of the institutional system. The fact that its presence was permitted after several years of ostracism did not mean that it could develop outside of state control. In 1954, a Committee for Light Music was established by the Polish Composers' Association. Its task – 'acceding to the calls of the audience masses in accordance with the public demand' – was to sort out the problems connected with creating and performing light music:

> The committee vigorously resolved to eliminate the shortcomings from which light music was suffering. A number of demands and specific assumptions were made. There was talk about a seminar improving the standard of composers, uniform committees that would qualify and assess a piece, establishing bands at theatres and philharmonics. It was seen as necessary to organize a convention of musicians who worked at eating establishments, define artistic postulates to be followed when assessing light works, commission writers only to write lyrics. The tasks were set with an indication that in the field of light music we were finally getting on the right track.
>
> *(Czesław Lewandowski[18] cited in Brodacki 1980, 44)*

Decisions were made, directions set, targets identified, but, as the press noted, no concrete actions followed:

> The subject ceased to be attractive for the Committee for Light Music. The words of the committee, its recommendations and intentions have still not left the desk drawers, have not been reflected in life. As it was in the past, popular creation is the domain of unqualified composers, with the music market swamped with trash that spoils the audience's taste. As it was in the past, the audience is forced, for want of any alternatives, to listen to untrained bands and poor dance ensembles. There are no seminars, no committees, no conventions, nothing has been done to accomplish ambitious plans or tasks. What was it all for, then?
>
> *(Ibid.)*

While the attempts to institutionalize jazz from the centre caused many problems, the jazz audience attended concerts and increasingly frequent jam sessions in large numbers. When the ban on official involvement in jazz activities was lifted, criticism finally started to focus on the quality of the music. Exaggeration in assigning jazz the attributes of an imperialist symbol was also noted:

> In 1946 we began playing Anglo American, Czech and French music. Our orchestra developed, and most of the audience was quite satisfied. But that was right after the war, when people were craving this music. When it was postulated to fight the inundation of American culture, *the fight that, as we know, had its excesses*, no one was able to give a clear directive as to what the dance music should be like, but criticism was plentiful.
>
> *(Jan Cajmer[19] cited in Brodacki 1980, 41; my emphasis)*

Willis Conover's programmes 'Jazz Hour' and 'Music USA', broadcast by the Voice of America, had enormous influence on jazz life in Poland, and on the competence of musicians and audiences alike. They were invaluable treasure troves of knowledge, especially given the lack of records, scores and jazz tutorials. As one musician noted:

> the radio waves tended to fade out . . . Those crackles could be heard, but you could tune in. Musicians listened and simply learned the broadcasts by heart. The most famous is the story told by Ptaszyn [the nickname of the sax player and composer Jan Wróblewski], how they [the Komeda sextet] tried to put the score down while listening: I'm writing down the first two bars, you are trying to pick up the next two, then it's my turn, and now you will try to catch something. In this

way they were learning not only the music itself, but also about jazz, and the English language. Willis Conover spoke really slowly and clearly . . . In such a low vibrating baritone that our hearts would tremble . . . It was English for learners, splendid. He did it intentionally so that his broadcasts would reach the widest audience, and at the climax of its popularity, he was listened to worldwide by some one hundred million people. And at least half of them lived precisely here, behind the Iron Curtain.

(Pietraszewski 2014, 60)

Summary

Jazz was no longer prohibited after the mid-1950s, when the state began to retreat from its imposed cultural policy and the demands of Socialist Realism. When analysing the intricacies of its development from the perspective of its nearly one-hundred-year presence, one can state that the Stalinist era was a unique period, during which the founding myth of jazz being 'the art of resistance' developed. In an oppressive system, some things happen despite, and others against, the imposed system. Ubiquitous political indoctrination and ceaseless 'ideological struggle' also evoked social reactions that were not welcomed by the authorities.[20] In a society deprived of the right to speak, the imposed bans impacted on the attractiveness of jazz, and gave it special symbolism.

Perhaps the most direct and unmediated way to communicate the jazz ambience of the period is simply to present a few opinions of musicians who participated in the events discussed here:

We would play for fun, and were not aware that after a while our passion obtained some features of political activity. People would come to our concerts not necessarily to listen to music, but to show their attitudes, their objection to the system we lived in, and because this was the forbidden fruit that was fought by the regime.

(Jerzy 'Duduś' Matuszkiewicz cited in Pietraszewski 2014, 62)

In the reality of the early 1950s, jazz was the only music triggering all that was missing, all that was forbidden. In any epoch, young people have music that helps to relieve emotions. Jazz is the music of youth. And it was something important to me, an individual who belonged to a generation seeking freedom, democracy. For jazz is the collective music in which individual improvisations require agreement between all the musicians. And young people understood this perfectly . . .

Listening and playing jazz was an expression of people's protest against the imposed standardization or uniformity of life. The beginning of jazz in Poland coincided with the period of rigorous Socialist Realism. However, it should not be claimed that it was a purely political protest. No, it was rather an objection to the bans.[21]

It is difficult to find examples of political repression due to participation in the world of jazz in Poland. However, although the authorities did not issue official decrees prohibiting involvement in jazz activities, there was a sense of threat in the social consciousness connected to being a member of the jazz milieu. As one musician recalled:

> it was an enormous opposition, even though it wasn't so dramatic because I don't belong to the first post-war generation of jazz musicians who risked a little, and – who knows – they may have had to explain themselves at the security office, if they had been caught . . . [J]azz music was such an affirmation of freedom, it was simply the relation: art *contra* communism.
>
> *(Pietraszewski 2014, 95)*

The perceived oppositional quality of jazz persisted throughout the decades that followed, although it gradually became a part of official, approved and subsidized culture. Even though jazz had left the 'grey area', the image of the 'rebel jazzman' became an important element of the habitus of those who were active in the world of jazz. The myth of 'the art of resistance' functioning, as it were, outside of the official system was a part of the discourse that legitimized the field, enhanced the appeal of jazz and attracted people to it. Jazz became an expression of resistance against the Stalinist system, against Socialist Realism imposed in the cultural policy, and against state control of artistic freedom and cultural activity. The imagined 'American freedom' acquired special significance in the grey world of the communist regime. Participation in that world had the flavour of opposition against a double reality – imposed ideology and the obligation to attend May Day marches, party events, rallies. For this reason, in my opinion, jazz in Poland may be viewed as one of the little springs of freedom that eventually undermined the political system.

Notes

1 All translations are by the author.
2 See, e.g., Friszke Andrzej, 'Stopniowanie zniewolenia'. Available at: www.tygodnik. com.pl/friszke.html, accessed October 2014.
3 As Hanna Świda-Ziemba writes: 'I see the source of the differences between my position and the theses presented by my opponents ... not so much in a different assessment of the empirical facts as in a disparate definition of totalitarianism. Some theoreticians adopt other defining criteria that allow a particular system to be defined as totalitarian' (Świda-Ziemba 1997, 51).
4 'A category of notions which not only enumerate (or otherwise define) the constituent elements of its content, but also reflect the nature of empirical relationships between

112 Igor Pietraszewski

phenomena, marked by the particular components of their definiens' (Nowak 2007, 147).

5 '[Willis Conover] described jazz as "structurally parallel to the American political system" and saw its structure as embodying American freedom: jazz musicians agree in advance on what harmonic progression is going to be, in what key, how fast and how long, and within that agreement they are free to play anything they want … Jazz is a cross between total discipline and total anarchy. The musicians agree on tempo, key and a chord structure but beyond this everyone is free to express himself. This is jazz. And this is America. That's what gives this music validity. This is a reflection of the way things happen in America. We're not apt to recognize this over here, but people in other countries can feel this element of freedom' (Van Eschen 2004, 16–17).

6 Such as 'On Green Dolphin Street', which was performed and recorded by the world's greatest jazzmen, including Miles Davis, John Coltrane and Keith Jarrett.

7 For example, Intelligenzaktion, AB aktion and Katyń.

8 'Raport o stratach wojennych Warszawy', Warszawa: Zespół Doradców Prezydenta m.st. Warszawy, 2004. Available at: www.um.warszawa.pl/v_syrenka/ratusz/Raport_o_stratach_wojennych_Warszawy.pdf, accessed October 2014.

9 The title of the 1947 article was 'Trzeba odtańczyć wszystkie lata wojny'.

10 Jakub Berman – one of the leading communist activists and a member of the 'triumvirate of power' who implemeted Stalin's policy in Poland, along with Bolesław Bierut and Hilary Minc (Werblan 1991, 13–14).

11 Very few of the primary sources I cite have been published in English, so I have tended to extend rather than edit key quotations to give the fullest possible sense of the cultural profile of the time.

12 As early as 1922 in an article titled 'Profanation of Art: Adaptations of Chopin by a Jazz Band', *Rytm* 1: 16, cited in Pietraszewski 2014, 40–41.

13 Founder of Krakow Jazz Club.

14 The comment was made during the panel discussion 'There is Only One Jazz, and Tyrmand is its Prophet', featuring Barbara Hoff, Andrzej Roman, Franciszek Walicki and Jan 'Ptaszyn' Wróblewski, with Paweł Brodowski acting as moderator, during the 'Blameless Sorcerers 56/06: Tyrmand Komeda Polański' festival, organized by the Warsaw Uprising Museum at the Centre of Art 'Montownia'.

15 Związek Młodzieży Polskiej, the Union of Polish Youth – an ideological and political organization that emulated the Soviet Union's Komsomol in the years 1948–1957 and became one of the symbols of Polish Stalinism.

16 'Umasowić studenckie zespoły artystyczne' in *Po Prostu*.

17 The title of Czyż's paper was 'Aktualne problemy muzyki rozrywkowej i tanecznej'.

18 From a 1954 article entitled 'I co dalej?' in *Dziś i Jutro*.

19 From a 1954 article entitled 'Muzyka taneczna i jej zagadnienia' in *Muzyka*.

20 Some scholars emphasize the significance of ideological struggle. For instance, Andrzej Walicki, a historian of ideas and emeritus professor at Notre Dame University, writes: 'The totalitarian regime … realizes the ideal of absolute conformism not only external, but also internal, and not passive alone, but active. It does so by means of unceasing and ubiquitous organized moral and political pressure, supported by terror, but based mainly on indoctrination' (cited in Świda-Ziemba 1997, 52).

21 Jerzy Skarżyński interviewed for the film *Jazz: Leaving the Underground*, directed by Jacek Sawicki (December 1995).

References

Arendt, Hannah. 1972. *Totalitarianism*. San Diego, CA: Harcourt.
Brodacki, Krystian. 1980. *Polskie ścieżki do jazzu*. Warszawa: wydane nakładem Sekcji Publicystów Polskiego Stowarzyszenia Jazzowego.

Brodacki, Krystian. 2010. *Historia jazzu w Polsce*. Kraków: PWM.

Davies, Norman. 1999. *Europa. Rozprawa historyka z historią*, translated Elzbieta Tabakowska. Kraków: Wydawnictwo ZNAK.

Fijałkowska, Barbara. 1985. *Polityka i twórcy (1948–1959)*. Warszawa: PWN.

Friszke, Andrzej. 2014. 'Stopniowanie zniewolenia'. Available at: www.tygodnik.com. pl/friszke.html, accessed October 2014.

Kołakowski, Leszek. 1984. *Czy diabeł może być zbawiony i 27 innych kazań*. Londyn: ANEKS.

Kołakowski, Leszek. 2014. 'O totalnej kontroli i jej wewnętrznych sprzecznościach', in *Niepewność epoki demokracji*, translated Mieczysław Godyń. Kraków: Wydawnictwo ZNAK: 21–31.

Kowal, Roman. 1995. *Polski Jazz*, vol. I. Kraków: Akademia Muzyczna.

Kubik, Jan. 2006. 'Teatr awangardowy a socjalizm państwowy – czyli co było globalne przed erą globalizacji (w teatrze Kantora). I co z tego (wynika)?' in *Stawanie się społeczeństwa*. Kraków: Flis Andrzej, Universitas.

Kurek, Krzysztof. 2009. 'Życie mimo wszystko', in *II Wojna Światowa*, vol. XVIII: *Okupacyjna codzienność*. Warszawa: New Media Concept for Wydawnictwo Narodowe: 18–29.

Łazarewicz, Cezary. 1999. 'Był jazz', *Magazyn Gazety Wyborczej*, 10 November: 10–11.

Linz, J.J. 1975. *Handbook of Political Sciences*, vol. III: *Totalitarian and Authoritarian Regimes: Macropolitical Theory*. Reading, MA: Addison-Wesley.

Nowak, Stefan. 2007. *Metodologia badań społecznych*. Warszawa: Wydawnictwo naukowe PWN.

Pietraszewski, Igor. 2014. *Jazz in Poland Improvised Freedom*, translated Lucyna Stetkiewicz. Frankfurt am Main: Peter Lang.

'Raport o stratach wojennych Warszawy'. 2004. Warszawa: Zespół Doradców Prezydenta m.st.Warszawy. Available at: www.um.warszawa.pl/v_syrenka/ratusz/ Raport_o_stratach_wojennych_Warszawy.pdf, accessed October 2014.

Scruton, Roger. 1982. *A Dictionary of Political Thought*, New York: Harper & Row.

Sokorski, Włodzimierz. 1950. *Sztuka w walce o socjalizm*. Warszawa: PiW

Świda-Ziemba, Hanna. 1997. *Człowiek wewnętrznie zniewolony*. Warszawa: Zakład Socjologii Moralności i Aksjologii Ogólnej.

Tompkins, David G. 2013. *Composing the Party Line: Music and Politics in Early Cold War Poland and East Germany*. West Lafayette, IN: Purdue University Press.

von Eschen, Penny. 2004. *Satchmo Blows up the World: Jazz Ambassadors Play the Cold War*. Cambridge, MA: Harvard University Press.

Werblan, Andrzej. 1991. *Stalinizm w Polsce*. Warszawa: Wydawnictwo Fakt.

Wieczorek, Sławomir. 2014. *Na froncie muzyki. Socrealistyczny dyskurs o muzyce w Polsce w latach 1948–1955*. Wrocław: Wydawnictwo Uniwersytetu Wrocławskiego.

5

JAZZ IN CZECHOSLOVAKIA DURING THE 1950s AND 1960s

Wolf-Georg Zaddach

> Jazz is not just music. It is the love of youth which stays firmly anchored in one's soul, forever unalterable.
>
> *(Škvorecký 1979, 25)*

By analyzing the formation of the jazz scene and its surrounding political discourse, this article aims to examine the development of jazz and its relationship to state socialism in Czechoslovakia during the 1950s and 1960s, with a major focus on the period from 1948 to 1968 – the beginning of Sovietization to the Prague Spring. By concentrating on this time span, the article will analyze the particular historical complexity as well as the varied forms of interplay and negotiation between the jazz scene and the young socialist state. It will be shown that jazz in Czechoslovakia – which itself thoroughly changed during this period – cannot only be understood as a complex interplay between the state and the scene but more as a changing and shifting process of mutual incorporation and assimilation. The drastic break of 1968 particularly symbolizes the pervasive political dimension of everyday life in state socialism. The normalization (*normalizace*) following the Prague Spring led to a new and different phase of oppressive state socialism. At this point new protagonists like the Jazz Section appeared (Motyčka 2010), and the political discourse required new forms of negotiation and change, but these lie beyond the scope of this article.

Introduction

In the context of totalitarianism, the history of Czechoslovakia symbolizes both a typical and a unique trajectory for an East–Central European state in the twentieth century. Coincidentally, the establishment of a democracy and the successive totalitarian occupations occurred in 1918, 1938 and 1948, each of which is remembered as symbolically loaded by Czechoslovakians due to them being the eighth year of each decade (Ťáček *et al.* 2008, 7). 1968 then became the next major break in the history of Czechoslovakia. All these events had important implications for cultural and artistic scenes. In this chapter, jazz is understood as a cultural praxis, consisting of musical and social practices within scenes (Johnson 2002, *passim*; Jackson 2002, *passim*; O'Meally *et al.* 2004, *passim*). To examine these historical social practices the chapter focuses on the production of historical artifacts (publications) and forms of social interaction (jazz and radio broadcasts, associations and live entertainment). It is thus based on critical readings of historical primary sources. Here, not only Czech but also German and English publications and contributions of important scene protagonists and witnesses like Lubomír Dorůžka and Antonín Truhlař will be in focus. These will be contrasted with contemporary German and Anglo-American language research such as the recent publications of Berlin-based Gertrud Pickhan and Rüdiger Ritter, which have established a methodologically broader and contemporary framework on jazz scenes behind the Iron Curtain (Pickhan and Ritter 2010; Ritter 2010, 2011). Whereas contemporary research regarding Czechoslovakia focuses mainly on the 1970s and 1980s (Kouřil 2009, 2010b; Motyčka 2010), or has a specific local or informative reference (Kajanová 1999, 2007, 2009, 2010; Kouřil 2010a), this chapter analyzes the jazz scene's social practices in the 1950s and 1960s within the larger context of Czechoslovakian state socialism.

Jazz in Czechoslovakia before 1948

According to Pickhan and Ritter (2010, 8), talking about jazz in the context of state socialism necessitates discussion of political dimensions. The history of jazz in Czechoslovakia and the history of the politicization of jazz in the context of communist ideology began, however, in the 1920s in the Soviet Union (Lücke 2004, *passim*). At that time, avant-garde circles, especially in Prague, and societies like Devětsil, Mánes and Přítomnost (the latter formed around the composer Alois Hába), were open to this new music without any major socio-political agenda. Even contemporary classical composers like Bohuslav Martinů, Ervín Schulhoff and Emil František Burian appreciated and worked with the new idiom. Burian then published *Jazz* in 1928, one of the first European books to appreciate the genre (Jařab 2010; Voříšek 2010; Matzner 2001; Bek 1983; Kotek 1970, all *passim*). The 1920s and 1930s in Czechoslovakia saw the birth of a young generation who devoted themselves to music: the Swing Youth. Well-known authors of this generation including Josef Škvorecký – quoted above – and Milan Kundera identified with the music and lifestyle and defended it against critics (Gabbard 2002, 336–337).

116 Wolf-Georg Zaddach

It is part of history's irony that Swing aficionados first hid from Nazi persecution and then had to hide again from Czechoslovakia's Stalinist regime. Given this, we can understand the specific historical and spatial dimensions of connotations of resistance against political persecution (Kajanová 2010, *passim*; Dorůžka 1994a, 130), but also against the country's older generations, "with its Czech wind music and stone-like conventions, which see the operas of Bedřich Smetana as the apex of art" (Holý 2005, 359).[1] In the jazz-based novels of Škvorecký we then find the complex relationship between jazz and resistance, for instance in *Konec Bulla Máchy* against the Stalinist politics of Czechoslovakian socialism.

The Field of Political Power and Jazz

Jazz in Czechoslovakia experienced a heyday, especially in Prague, between the two totalitarian regimes, from 1945 to 1948. A vital jazz scene flourished in this "nylon age," as Josef Škvorecký described the period to emphasize the influence of, and orientation to, American culture (Kouřil 2010a). For instance, Prague audiences could enjoy high-quality Czechoslovakian bebop in the jazz venue Pygmalion, located in the basement of the Palac Fenix on Václavské naměstí, courtesy of the group Rytmus 47/Rytmus 48. At the same time, the Australian Dixieland band of Graeme Bell fascinated Czechoslovakians on a tour through forty-four towns in Bohemia and Moravia in 1947 (Johnson 2000, 148). The latter in particular inspired a new amateur jazz movement all over the country, even if jazz was not the most popular music genre, as indicated by a 1947 survey (Kouřil 2010a). Eric T. Vogel, a survivor of Terezín and member of the famous Ghetto Swingers, was a member of the scene after the war and commented: 'Jazzwise, Czechoslovakia was far in front of all other European nations, including Sweden' (Vogel 1961, 492).

Sovietization and Stalinism

In February 1948, the Czechoslovakian Communist Party assumed power, installed state socialism on Stalinist principles (Naimak 2010, 187) and placed culture in the context of the Cold War (Vowinkel *et al.* 2012, *passim*). "Culture" in general was understood by the party as a politically controlled acquisition of the material world. Therefore, the artist was seen as a "budovatel" (builder) for the socialist authorities (Boyer 2005, 18; Knapík 2005, 252). Radio stations, theatres, publishing houses and venues – all parts of the cultural infrastructure – were forced to close or fell under full state control (Hoensch 1992, 141–147; Pešek 1998, 83). The Pygmalion, that venue for excellent bebop music, ceased to operate. The jazz scene suffered from such restrictions on live venues and the recording industry: musicians were simply denied work opportunities. Karel Vlach's big band, one of the leading Czechoslovakian bands of the 1940s, became part of the state circus. Their new task was "to accompany shows of drilled elephants," as the Czech musicologist and leading figure of the jazz scene since the 1940s Lubomír Dorůžka laconically commented (Dorůžka 1994a, 132–133). Throughout most of the 1940s, Vlach's band produced at least one recording each year, but between 1949 and 1952 they were prohibited from releasing any new records (Dorůžka and Poledňák 1967, 281–286). When they were allowed to record again after 1952, the annual sessions increased slowly – with a major boost in 1956, the year of Nikita Khrushchev's 'secret speech' in Moscow.

Indulging one's passion in unofficial, private practices was a typical reaction to the Stalinist discourse – though fatal for the scene's continuation. As a typical reaction to the Stalinist discourse, the unofficial practices of the underground, or the "catacombs," became once again, after the time of the Nazi occupation, an important space and habitus for the jazz scene (Dorůžka 1994b, 39). During the Stalinist period (1948–1953) only a restrictive communist model of jazz was accepted. The Soviets demanded that saxophones must be replaced by cellos after 1948 (Starr 1990, 180; Caute 2003, 443–444). In Czechoslovakia, in particular, musicians were required to compose jazz themes based on Moravian or Slovak folk songs (Dorůžka 1994a, 133). One of the few state-supported jazz projects of this time was a band that was supposed to play nothing but the compositions and arrangements of Jaroslav Ježek, the idol of Czechoslovakian jazz, from the 1930s alongside works by Soviet composers such as Aram Khachaturian and Isaak Dunayevsky. The public interest in this band was marginal, and they eventually disbanded (Kouřil 2010a). One of the other important big bands of the 1940s, besides Vlach's group, was that of Gustav Brom. They were based in Brno and were voted one of the top ten orchestras, along with the band of Karel Krautgartner, in a critics' poll that appeared in *Down Beat* magazine in 1966 (Hennessey 1967, 45). During the first of half of the 1950s, Brom's band had suffered as they were denied access to the radio building where their studio and rehearsal rooms were located.

Around this time, the only way to survive was to understand and follow the logic of the totalitarian ideology. For example, the journalist and Dixieland fan Emanuel Uggé defended jazz in the early days of socialist Czechoslovakia. Two years after Graeme Bell's 1947 tour, Uggé argued that "the real jazz" had some essence of revolution as its aim was "to free the creative power of the people from capitalism" (cited in Macek 1997, 55). However, what "the real jazz" might be remained unclear. This reflects, alongside the socialist discourse of true jazz being that of oppressed African Americans, the ambivalence and possible exploitation of socialist cultural policies. Included within the broader discourse were seemingly meaningless flowery phrases such as those that appear in the following 1956 quote from Dušan Havlíček, when he was an employee at the Ministry of the Interior: "To be clear, we're not fighting against jazz, music for brass instruments, entertainment. We fight against crudity, commercialization, sick sentimentality, the degradation of melody, insubstantiality, false emotions" (cited in ibid.).

With the deaths of Stalin and Klement Gottwald – Czechoslovakia's first socialist president and a communist hardliner – in March 1953, state oppression started to decline, albeit only slightly. The resulting power vacuum created uncertainty about the future. Relying on previous experiences of state socialism was one approach to deal with such uncertainty; nevertheless, musicians began to perform jazz in public again. But jazz could not shed its recent politically subversive tag, and nor was it easy to overcome the fear of making political mistakes. When employees of the cement plant in the Moravian town of Hranice formed an amateur jazz band in 1953, the union committee issued the following response:

> We asked some experts for their opinion, and accordingly the continuation of the band is not welcomed. The band cannot contribute anything new in the context of Socialist Realism. In contrast, the band is focused on free improvisation, and therefore cultivates music-pornography. Even though the band plays the music of [Jaroslav] Ježek, it cannot disguise the fact that it is bad, improvised music. Furthermore, those bands in general conceal, under the cloak of black folk music, dishonest purposes, which lack any educational ambition.
>
> *(Cited in Dorůžka and Poledňák 1967, 102–103;*
> *translation by Anna Koubová and the author)*

Clearly, the committee's argument followed the socialist discourse, which suspected jazz of provoking "mental poverty" and "enslavement" (Gorodinski 1953, 79). This example demonstrates, furthermore, the multiple layers of the dominant discursive structures: underlying the ambivalent arguments of the "correct" Socialist Realism are forms of racism, homophobia, and an aesthetic dichotomy of serious and light music, in which written art works were considered real art and improvised musical entertainment. The final argument of the quote refers to one of the most important discursive elements in socialism: youth education (Gienow-Hecht 2010, 404). Surprisingly, Graeme Bell had already benefited from this, when the band visited Prague to play at the World Youth Festival in June 1947, under the sponsorship of the Eureka Youth League, the youth organization of the Communist Party of Australia (Johnson 2000, 147). Back then, the focus on education had helped sustain a jazz movement. During the Stalinist period, however, the political consequences were more extensive, as for the young musicians at the cement plant. As a possible result, just one entry in their personal files could impact on their career trajectories: "They could never hope to go to university or get any higher grade of education" (Dorůžka 1994b, 39).

De-Stalinization and the Thaw

The period of Czechoslovakian de-Stalinization and consequent thaw (Foitzik 2008; Kaplan 2008, both *passim*), which was delayed due to the revolts in East–Central Europe, can be understood as a consolidation of an alternative music culture in the region (Ritter 2011, *passim*). After the "traumas of Stalinism and the ongoing Cold War," as the East German jazz journalist Bert Noglik put it, "jazz stood also for a breakout from the normative circumstances and a tentative search for a new attitude to life" (Noglik 1994, 148). By emphasizing the generally optimistic character of dance music, politicians slowly accepted jazz from about 1956 onwards (Kajanová 2010, 74). Ultimately, categories, key words, and slogans dictated by Soviet cultural politics gradually became indistinct (Macek 1997, 57).

Fundamental for the approaching 1960s was the re-establishment of venues and the cabaret scene by Czechoslovakian artists and intellectuals. With official permission, venues like Semafor, the Divadlo Na zábradlí, and – particularly important for jazz – the Viola, Reduta, and the Spejbel a Hurvínek in Prague, as well as the Večerní Brno in Brno, opened and provided spaces that were free from direct repression. Many of these venues recruited their own house bands and played jazz repertoires. They also served as training schools and therefore had an important influence on the development of modern combo jazz in Czechoslovakia.

The 1960s: The "Golden Age" of Czechoslovakian Jazz

The 1960s are usually viewed as politically liberal. Due to an economic crisis and the increasing differentiation of social structure, political reforms tended toward the development of democratized socialism (Kemp-Welch 2010; Tůma 2008, both *passim*). The younger generations in particular, born during or after the war and mainly socialized under socialism, were not solely interested in the socialist way of life, but also in emerging Western youth cultures (Golan 1970, 4–6). Cultural scenes experienced a veritable renaissance, during which the Czechoslovakian film industry, among others, was held in high regard, even by international critics (Kazarina 2008, *passim*).

The jazz scene began to encounter less resistance from official cultural politics as well. The late 1950s to the late 1960s was a period of growing acceptance and even official political support, and artistic development was finally freed from the restrictions of Socialist Realism (Glanc 2008, 118; Golan 1970, 6–7). In 1960, two new big bands were founded and performed under the auspices of state radio: the Radio Dance Orchestra and the Jazz Orchestra (Tanečni orchestr and Jazzový orchestr Československého rozhlasu). The two bands comprised almost exactly the same musicians and both were led by Karel Krautgartner, a signatory of the *The Two Thousand Words* manifesto who would flee the country in 1968. Krautgartner had the opportunity to work in a wide

120   Wolf-Georg Zaddach

range of jazz styles – from traditional big-band jazz to the remarkable "Third Stream" compositions of Czechoslovakian composer Pavel Blatný. The importance of such consistently funded bands should not be underestimated. When the American jazz drummer Bill Moody spent a few months with Brom's radio big band in Brno in 1967, he was impressed by an "entirely new and alien concept – working with a radio band that was required to record several jazz pieces each month" (Moody 1993, xxii).

Also in 1960, the state record label Supraphon launched a series of jazz recordings with the *Anthology of Jazz in Czechoslovakia 1958–1960*, which received in the year of its release an award as the "Best European Contribution to the Development of Jazz" from the German Jazz Federation (Hennessey 1967, 45). This anthology was followed by a series of annual samplers, *Jazz in Czechoslovakia*, which presented not only Czechoslovakian bands but also mainly original Czechoslovakian compositions, some of which were arrangements of Bohemian and Moravian folk songs (as demanded by the state in the first half of the 1950s).

Though the foundation of state jazz bands in the 1960s can be read as a symbolic concession by the authorities, one can hardly speak of the total disappearance of the previous socialist discourse. The 1953-born Slovak guitarist Karol Ondreička remembers the ambivalent relationship between cultural politics and jazz, which reflected the special role of the nation's youth in state socialism:

> The image of the enemy of the working class was an American with an upturned bottle of Coca-Cola and smoking a cigar, with jazz music playing and people wriggling on the dance floor. All this conveyed erroneous ideas that Coca-Cola was a terrible booze and that jazz was . . . Well, for instance, they wrote that when Benny Goodman, the King of Swing, played, teenagers would wallow on the floor tearing their hair out. This was what the party members believed. I have no idea what they confused jazz with.
>
> *(Cited in Kajanová 2009, 54)*

While politics remained sceptical about the music, Dorůžka has labelled the 1960s the "third golden age of Czechoslovakian jazz," after the 1930s and 1945–1948 (Dorůžka 1994a, 137). In this third golden age, the jazz scene developed and expressed an assertive artistic self-image, as can be read in the liner notes to 1961's *Jazz in Czechoslovakia*:

> Jazz, which originally arose as dance music . . . more recently does not want to be understood just as an accompaniment to dance. Jazz musicians are convinced that their music is able to cause an emotional reaction in the audience and this reaction does not necessarily have to be presented

by dance. Moreover, it is able to provide the audience with an independent aesthetic experience which does not have to be only a part of social dancing and entertainment.

(Dorůžka 1961, 3)

The 1960s jazz scene was flourishing and stylistically multifaceted, with several professional as well as amateur bands and venues throughout the country. But the above-mentioned "drastic break" of 1968 then violently demolished what the Czechoslovaks had built, and not only in the arts (Karner *et al.* 2008, *passim*). The consequences of 1968's Prague Spring included the emigration of many Czechoslovakians, including such important jazz musicians as the young Jan Hammer Jr. and Miroslav Vitouš. The state then characterized the ensuing period as normalization (*normalizace*), but it was actually a time of heavy-handed oppression. Consequently, the jazz scene had to develop different forms of negotiation and adaptation than it had practised in the 1950s and 1960s (Kouřil 2010a; Motyčka 2010). Furthermore, the cultural field and critical focus of the state changed slightly to encompass other, somewhat popular and often oppositional forms of music, such as the underground rock band the Plastic People of the Universe, rather than jazz. In this restrictive period after 1968, Dorůžka (1973, *passim*) remembered the important arguments of education and youth as "survival patterns."

The strategy of "trying to keep jazz out of trouble" (Dorůžka 1994b, 40) became an unspoken motto for the Czechoslovakian jazz scene during the 1950s and 1960s. With this in mind, up to 1968 the jazz scene made enormous progress in terms of institutionalization, productivity, and aesthetic conceptualization and expression, such as the "Third Stream" compositions of Pavel Blatný. Dorůžka's article on "survival patterns" during the period of oppressive normalization seems to emphasize – without stating so directly – the relative political harmlessness of the jazz scene by that time. The fact that he published it bears witness to the difficult and emotionally burdened conditions of Czechoslovakia's normalization.

Jazz as Cultural Praxis under State Socialism

The jazz scene's capacity for alignment, patience, and dedication to aesthetic preferences was a delicate balancing act. Patterns of conformity to earn respect by emphasizing the seriousness and importance of jazz for education and society were not necessarily mere pretence. Rather, they could have been a result of a convergence of conviction, possibly resigned insight, and learned forms of pretence, based on first-hand experience or knowledge of oppression and threat. The resulting habitus, often involving self-censorship, seemed so common behind the Iron Curtain that in East Germany jazz fans established the polemic term "jazz Marxists" (Rudolf 1964, 33–46). The above-mentioned

122 Wolf-Georg Zaddach

focus on education and intermediation would be a reasonable consequence. Education and transfer of knowledge are also essential for the continuity of and participation in a scene generally. From this perspective, the amount and quality of transfer activities within the scene can be read as results of the ongoing process of negotiation and bargaining between the state and the jazz scene. Therefore, it is revealing to examine the scene's publication activities and the role of jazz on the radio.

What follows is an examination of specific forms of scene formation and practice in the 1960s. However, this examination has to remain limited in view of the complexity of the scene and state activity. It will not include, for example, the increasing opportunities to play abroad or state committees' classification and evaluation of musicians.

Publications

The communists' accession to power in 1948 prevented the release of major publications by the various protagonists of the jazz scene; only a few rather critical newspaper articles made it past the censorship system. Indeed, the state encouraged works that defamed jazz, such as the pamphlet *Muzyka duchovnoj niščety* (Mental poverty in music) by the Soviet musicologist Victor Gorodinski, who accused the genre of "mental poverty" and "enslavement" (Gorodinski 1953, 79). This pamphlet, which referenced Maxim Gorki's article "O muzyke tolstych" (About the music of the fat men; 1929) and Andrej Zdahnov's anti-formalist campaign of 1948, was translated multiple times and widely distributed behind the Iron Curtain. Dorůžka and Poledňák (1967, 38) called it the "*kardinální spis*" (magnum opus) of the official attitude towards jazz after the Second World War. Czechoslovakian scholars, most notably Antonín Sychra (1951, *passim*), employed the Socialist Realism discourse enthusiastically.

The fact that publications which defamed jazz continued to be issued well into the 1960s makes it clear that one can hardly speak of the total cessation of the negative discourse surrounding the genre. For instance, Josef Kresánek's *Sociálna funkcia hudby* (The social function of music), published in Bratislava in 1961, treats jazz as a youth culture with links to alcohol abuse and, as a contemporary extension of the discourse, suggests that members of the jazz scene would benefit from psychiatric treatment (Kajanová 2010, 76). By contrast, pro-jazz publications like the American *Down Beat* magazine were officially proscribed, so Czechoslovakian jazz fans could acquire them only through the black market. They did so at great personal risk, as smuggling was harshly prosecuted during the Stalinist era.

The situation changed slowly during the thaw. Whereas *Jazz* – the first dedicated jazz magazine to be published behind the Iron Curtain – appeared in Poland in 1956 (Domurat 2010, *passim*), Czechoslovakian politicians struggled to find the right balance between de-Stalinization policies and citizens' attempts at artistic organization. After a few illegal underground bulletins were published, the first official pro-jazz magazine was planned for 1958, but it was never distributed. In fact, the first issue was seized (Kouřil 2010a, *passim*; Dorůžka and Poledňák 1967, 130) on the orders of the Czechoslovakian President Antonín Novotný (Škvorecký 1979, 10–11). Most likely, this clamp-down was connected to two significant cultural conflicts that occurred around the same time. In the Soviet Union, the scandal of Boris Pasternak's *Doctor Zhivago* provided ammunition for critics of the thaw. Then a similar scandal arose in Czechoslovakia with the publication of Škvorecký's *Zbabělci* (Cowards), a jazz-based novel.

The negotiations about what could be said in the field of culture affected the Czechoslovakian jazz scene immediately. Around 1960, several impressive publications by Czechoslovakians were released officially through cooperation between the jazz scene and state-publishing houses or unions. The leading protagonists of the scene were experienced and knowledgeable jazz fans who were mostly in their thirties or forties by this time, including Lubomír Dorůžka, Ivan Poledňák, Igor Wasserbauer, Antonín Truhlář and Karel Velebný. The latter – a multi-instrumentalist, a leading figure of the Prague jazz scene and "the father of Czech modern jazz" (Truhlář 1996) – published one of the few Czech educational books on jazz, *Jazzová praktika* (Jazz praxis) in 1965. This theoretical and musicological work soon became an important resource for the country's jazz musicians. Two years later, Dorůžka and Poledňák (1967) published their impressive historical study *Československý jazz. Minulost a přítomnost* (Czechoslovakian jazz: past and present), which started in the 1920s and ended with the contemporary scene. Besides their activities as publishers and journalists, Dorůžka and Škvorecký translated English literature and jazz-related fiction, such as *Jazzová inspirace* (Jazz inspirations) in 1966.

However, the most important Czechoslovakian jazz publication was the *Taneční hudba a jazz. Sborník statí a přispěvků k otázkám jazzu a moderní taneční hudby* (Dance music and jazz: anthology and contribution to the questions of jazz and dance music), a yearbook that was published through the Státní Nakladatelství Krásné Literatury, Hudby a Umění (State Publishing House of Fine Literature, Music and Arts) between 1960 and 1969. The contributors included well-informed authors such as Miloš Bergl as well as composers like Jan F. Fischer. Each issue reported on the US scene and on other socialist scenes. Furthermore, the reader could learn jazz theory through transcriptions and musical analysis, read articles by the likes of Pavel Kohout, and enjoy graphic art such as Libor Fáras's "Rytmu" series and Josef Kubičeks's "Blues."

The apex of 1960s liberal politics in Czechoslovakia was reached with the official translation and publication of *The Jazz Book* by the West German journalist Joachim Ernst Berendt. He knew the Czechoslovakian scene well, as he had produced a documentary on the jazz scenes of Poland, Yugoslavia and Czechoslovakia for the West German television station SWR in 1965.

FIGURE 5.1 Cover (left) and back cover (right) of the 1961 Edition of *Taneční Hudba a Jazz*

According to Berendt, Czechoslovakia was the only one of the three states to provide official support during shooting (Heidkamp 1996).

The publications discussed in this section were released first and foremost because members of the jazz scene were prepared to cooperate with or even work within state institutions. Consequently, the publications were socialist products, and thus part of the socialist discourse. The key words and slogans that had been so important – and simultaneously vague – in the 1950s remained important statements of social affiliation in the 1960s, as Kouřil points out: "Since the 50s, the Czech jazz scene had to argue in front of official departments and administrations with phrases of the music of the oppressed black people corresponding to the doctrine of the Soviet pseudo musicologists" (Kouřil 2009, 510–511).

Essentially, the scene did not exist simply in opposition to the totalitarian state. Rather, during the thaw it became part of the state's social practices at publishing houses and on editorial boards, with jazz enthusiasts sitting around tables with party members and censors.

Jazz and Radio Broadcasting

Another important source for music and information was the radio (Ritter 2010, 37–38; Hagen and DeNora 2012, 446–447). Popular music had been include in the schedules ever since the launch of Czechoslovakian radio in the early 1920s. Radio shows featured Czechoslovakian composers and broadcast the jazz compositions of Jaroslav Ježek (Kralová 2009, *passim*), among others.

TABLE 5.1 Important Jazz-Related Czechoslovakian Publications in the 1950s and 1960s

Title	Date of first issue	Author/publisher	Comments
Hudba duševní bídy [Mental poverty in music]	1952	Victor Gorodinski	Translation of the 1950 Soviet edition; harshly critiques and defames jazz
Stranická hudební kritika spolutvůrce nové hudby [A party musical critique of the co-creators of new music]	1952	Antonín Sychra	Refers to Gorodinski and emphasizes the importance of Socialist Realism in music
Pověry a problémy jazzu [Superstition and problems of jazz]	1959	Jan Rychlík	A positive musicological survey of the history of jazz and musical parameters by the composer Rychlík
Jazz 1958	1958 (but not distributed)	Josef Škvorecký and Lubomír Dorůžka	Whole print run of 5000 seized and destroyed
Mladý svět [Young world]	1958/1959	Svaz česke mládeže [Czech youth union]	Regular articles about domestic jazz and the American scene
Tanečni hudba a jazz [Dance music and jazz]	1960–1969	Státní nakladatelství krásné literatury, hudby a uměli [State Publishing House of Fine Literature, Music and Arts]	Yearbook; intense discourse on Czechoslovakian music and culture; broad insights into other jazz scenes; included history and music theory
Melodie [Melody]	1960s		Monthly magazine; the number of articles about jazz increased after Dorůžka became editor in chief in 1964
Kapitolky o jazzu [Chapters on jazz]	1961	Ivan Poledňák	History of jazz; presents jazz as art
Sociálna funkcia hudby [The social function of music]	1961	Josef Kresánek	Discusses jazz as youth culture and links it with alcoholism and mental unbalance

(Continued)

126 Wolf-Georg Zaddach

TABLE 5.1 *(Continued)*

Title	Date of first issue	Author/publisher	Comments
Tvář jazzu. Vzpomínky, documenty, svědectví [The face of jazz: memories, documents, credentials]	1964	Lubomír Dorůžka and Josef Škvorecký	Extensive publication about the history of jazz, in which the genre is presented as a "lifestyle"; refers to numerous historical documents and sources
Jazzová praktika [Jazz praxis]	1965	Karel Velebný	Extensive textbook about modern jazz (instrumentation, harmony, playing techniques, notation and musical arrangement)
Jazzová inspirace [Jazz inspirations]	1966	Lubomír Dorůžka and Josef Škvorecký	Fictional compilation
Co nevíte o jazzu [What you do not know about jazz]	1966	Bohumil Geist	A history of jazz from its origins to the present day, including transcriptions
Jazzový slovník [Jazz dictionary]	1966	Igor Wasserberger *et al.*	Published in Bratislava
Československý jazz. Minulost a přítomnost [Czechoslovakian jazz: past and present]	1967	Lubomír Dorůžka and Ivan Poledňák	Extensive study of the history of jazz in Czechoslovakia
Hrá jazz [It's jazz]	1968	Antonín Matzner and Igor Wasserbauer	Published in Bratislava
Kniha o jazze [The jazz book]	1968	Joachim Ernst Berendt	Translation of the well-known West German jazz history book

After 1948, state-controlled radio reflected the official anti-jazz attitude and rarely featured such music. However, during the thaw, in 1956, Antonín Truhlář started work on a specialist jazz programme (Anonymous 1956, 5), although Truhlář himself (1959, 16) names Jiří Cikhart as the show's director. In fact, Cikhart conducted and organized several jazz-related radio

("Chceš-li hrát jazz, nesmíš lhát; Jazzová hudba v ČSR a v zahraničí") and television programmes ("Jazz"; "Cesta jazzu") until the late 1960s (Bařinková 2014, *passim*). In a 1964 article Truhlář mentions a jazz programme that was broadcast every second Saturday and featured American combos (Truhlář 1964, 132). This may have been "Jazz kaleidoskop," on which Truhlář was assisted by the Prague bass player Luděk Hulan (Truhlář 1962, 36). Another programme was "Vinárna u pavouka" (The spider's wine tavern), also known as "Nealkoholicka vinárna u pavouka" (The non-alcoholic spider's wine tavern). This satire-and-jazz show, which ran from 1965 to 1969, was produced by the famous Czechoslovakian actors and writers Zdeněk Svěrák and Jiří Šebánek, with the assistance of Karel Velebný. The bass player František Uhlíř (born in 1950 in East Bohemia) remembered it as almost his only opportunity to hear jazz on Czechoslovakian radio in the 1960s (Schneller and Schneller 2006, 22). This gives an insight into how difficult it was to hear jazz in Czechoslovakia outside of Prague's flourishing scene. Further research is needed to explore these programme lists and determine precisely what Czechoslovakians could hear and when.

Unsurprisingly, Western radio had an enormous impact on the jazz scenes behind the Iron Curtain. Almost every Czechoslovakian jazz musician and fan mentions Willis Conover's "Music USA: Jazz Hour" on the Voice of America (Schneller and Schneller 2006, 33, 60, 156): "we seemed to be in touch with America" (Kajanová 2009, 54), recalled the Slovak guitarist Karol Ondreička. The programme also functioned as a jazz training school and therefore became an important medium of cultural transfer (Ritter 2010; Lindenberger 2004, both *passim*). When Conover was a guest at the International Jazz Festival in Prague in 1965, he was acclaimed as a star. Besides the Voice of America, Czechoslovakians could sometimes pick up Radio Free Europe and Radio Liberation as well as jazz programmes on the American Forces Network (including "Midnight in Munich"), the BBC, Radio Luxembourg, Switzerland's Radio Scottens and the Austrian Blue Danube Radio (Dorůžka and Poledňák 1967, 88; Dorůžka 1997, 141; Kajanová 2009, 56).

Associations, Clubs, and Live Entertainment

Especially from around 1960, the cultural thaw enabled jazz aficionados to (re)unite in local jazz clubs and organize concerts and lectures or simply share music. New jazz venues opened even in small towns. For instance, in the Bohemian provincial town of Slaný, fans founded a jazz club in 1962, and six years later they launched Slaný Jazz Days, a festival that continues to the present day (Novák 2014). Fans and musicians soon founded an umbrella association in Prague to lobby for local clubs. When Eric T. Vogel visited the association in 1965, he spoke in front of 300 members (Vogel 1965, 223). The association grew into a network of international jazz associations and became part of the European Jazz Federation in 1968, but it was forced to disband during the normalization era.

In the field of live entertainment, members of the scene tried to establish a festival in Brno in 1958, almost certainly encouraged by the success of Poland's Sopot Festival and Jazz Jamboree the previous year. In September, Antonín Truhlář (1958, 18) reported on the festival dates, the line-up, and the "jazz fever" in Brno, but unfortunately no review of the festival has survived, if indeed it took place at all. A few years later, Truhlář (1962, 37) stated that Czechoslvakia did not host a jazz festival before 1960, so perhaps the 1958 was cancelled amid the controversy over Škvorecký's novel and *Jazz 1958*. Either way, several festivals were founded after 1960, starting with Karlovy Vary's in 1962; others included those in České Budějovice, Mladá Boleslav, Olomouc and Plzeň. However, Prague's Mezinárodní jazzový festival (International Jazz Festival), founded by Dorůžka and Stanislav Titzl, soon outshone the rest. It featured such musicians as Paul Bley, Albert Mangelsdorff and many other internationally famous stars. While the first event in 1964 was euphorically subtitled the "festival of fulfilled dreams," 1968 marked an abrupt change of direction, with far fewer Western musicians appearing as a result of the government's policy of normalization (http://jazzfestivalpraha.com/history/). Although the USA's Cultural Presentation Program, also known as the "State Department Tours," had considerable influence on most of the jazz scenes behind the Iron Curtain (von Eschen 2004; Davenport 2009, both *passim*), Charles Lloyd's 1967 visit had little impact on the Czechoslovakians (Monson 2007, 114–128). In fact, the activities of the domestic scene's own members were much more beneficial. They not only organized concerts for foreign groups but facilitated cooperation between them and Czechoslovakian musicians. Venues and night clubs, like the Reduta and Viola in Prague, put on regular concert programmes and organized jam sessions. One famous foreign guest was Louis Armstrong, who performed in several concerts in Prague in March 1965.

Interestingly, the Czechoslovakian Youth Union – which was founded in the late 1950s with the official aim of "preventing the degeneration of the youth's taste" (Liška 1961, 23) – cooperated with, and even actively supported, the jazz scene. The union facilitated the publication of pro-jazz articles and helped to organize regular lectures and concerts, which featured both local and professional bands, such as the Prague-based Studio 5 (Liška 1961, *passim*). By cooperating with this official state organization, the jazz scene demonstrated its flexibility and prudence in negotiating and dealing with the prevailing political circumstances.

State Socialism and the Secret Service

The activities of the Czechoslovakian secret service StB (Státní Bezpečnost) are of special interest. Besides observation and documentation, forms of indirect

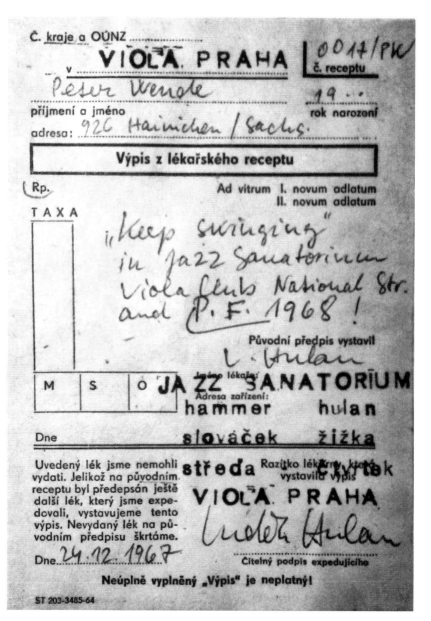

FIGURE 5.2 Admission Ticket for a Concert by Jazz Sanatorium, Led by the Bassist Luděk Hulan, at the Viola, Prague, 21 December 1967. The ticket offers a multi-layered insight into the jazz scene under state socialism. It is based on a general template for all live entertainment venues provided by the authorities, but Hulan's handwritten good wishes for the upcoming new year turned it into a vehicle for international networking within the jazz community, as is evidenced by the fact that the person who purchased the ticket, Peter Wende, from Hainichen in the German Democratic Republic, preserved it after the concert

(Peter Wende Collection, International Archive of Jazz and Popular Music, Eisenach, Germany)

censorship and constraint were constant threats. Musicians who wanted to play concerts in the West were investigated by the StB (Kajanová 2009, 56). According to Dorůžka in a 2005 interview, it was almost impossible to avoid the StB's investigations due to the politicization of jazz under state socialism (Leschtina 2005). In fact, Dorůžka's own case reveals the ambivalence and contingency of everyday life under state socialism: according to the (disputed) Cibulka project (www.cibulka.com), he was an StB agent for some time. Dorůžka, who died in 2013 at the age of eighty-nine, achieved fame due to his dedication to jazz and popular music as a publisher, organizer, and translator. A commentator in the internet magazine *Neviditelný pes* remembered him "as a great propagator of modern jazz and a great music journalist," but also as an "example of inexcusable and inexplicable failure due to his active participation in a totalitarian repressive state" (Perlin 2013). The circumstances of collaboration varied greatly, with individuals often coerced by authorities. In 2005, Dorůžka admitted that during his time at the commercial section of Supraphon his supervisors expected him to sign an agreement with the StB, but he insisted that he refused and never worked for the secret service (Leschtina 2005). The issue of his potential collaboration cannot be resolved without further research, as the existing evidence may be the result of either forgery or blackmail. Equally, Dorůžka may have cooperated simply by offering ambiguous information in the hope that this would reduce the pressure on the jazz scene. Moreover, he was surely not the only member of the jazz scene who may have collaborated with the StB. That being said, the ambivalence and contradictions in the relationship between jazz and totalitarianism are symbolized by such protagonists, who were both leading and ground-breaking figures of the formerly defamed jazz scene and occasionally, under whatever circumstances, unofficial agents of the state's secret service.

Conclusion

This chapter opened with a quote by Škvorecký: "Jazz is not just music. It is the love of youth which stays firmly anchored in one's soul, forever unalterable." Unalterable even by an oppressive totalitarian system like state socialism? By analysing the development of the jazz scene and the political attitude toward jazz, the chapter examined the complexities, negotiations, and changes in the scene in state socialist Czechoslovakia in the 1950s and 1960s. With respect to the supposed unalterability of jazz, this attitude could have been one of several individual options, and was typical especially among Škvorecký's generation (the Swing Youth), who experienced the Nazis' occupation and Second World War. Not only for the case of jazz in the 1950s and 1960s, however, Škvorecký's point of view appears to be an oversimplification.

The history of Czechoslovakian jazz in the 1950s and 1960s is characterized by its complexity as well as by various forms of interplay and negotiation between the jazz scene and the nascent socialist state. This changing and shifting process of incorporation and assimilation from 1948 to 1968 was of the upmost historical significance. The Stalinist era, between 1948 and 1953, was by far the most oppressive period: a vital and growing jazz scene was demolished due to Cold War cultural politics and the official attitude toward jazz in particular. The late Czechoslovakian thaw brought change, and the jazz scene slowly started to flourish again. The 1960s were then a period of liberal politics and widely expanding cultural activities. The jazz scene benefited from official support and fewer restrictions on the main players. Due to these developments, the "golden 60s" witnessed general improvements in the scene's activities, exemplified by the greater number of publications, radio broadcasts, and live concerts. At the same time, the scene partially, and increasingly, cooperated and negotiated in a subtle and flexible way with state institutions, and incorporated key words and slogans of the Socialist discourse. In doing so, it became part of socialist Czechoslovakia and its policies through a process of assimilation. This may, under whatever circumstances, have included cooperation with the secret service. But cooperation and assimilation did not guarantee positive results, as the consequences of the Prague Spring and the politics of normalization once again had a detrimental impact on the scene.

Alignment, opposition, resignation, or loyalty to the system – all of these were possible patterns of behaviour under state socialism. Whereas in the 1950s forms of inner opposition seemed to be typical, in later years cooperation with or even loyalty to the state became more common. In the 1950s and 1960s, the scene did not simply exist as an opponent of the totalitarian state. Rather, after the thaw it became, to some degree, part of the state's social practices. The role of jazz in state socialist Czechoslovakia nevertheless remains a specific expression and *Weltanschauung*, an establishment of a "cultural alternative" (Ritter 2011). As such, jazz was an American-rooted cultural alternative to oppressive, uniform everyday life under state socialism.

Note

1 All translations are by the author unless otherwise stated.

References

Anonymous. 1956. "Jazzaktivität in der CSR." *Westjazz* 9: 5.
Bařinková, Jitka. 2014. "Cikhart, Jiří." In *Český hudební slovník* [Czech music encyclopedia]. Available at: www.ceskyhudebnislovnik.cz/slovnik/index.php?option=com_mdictionary&action=record_detail&id=1002415 (accessed 25 October 2014).
Bek, Josef. 1983. "Die tschechische Musik-Avantgarde." *International Review of the Aesthetics and Sociology of Music* 6: 79–92.

132 Wolf-Georg Zaddach

Boyer, Christoph. 2005. "Der Beitrag der Sozialgeschichte zur Erforschung kommunistischer Systeme." In Christiane Brenner and Peter Heumos, eds, *Sozialgeschichtliche Kommunismusforschung. Tschechoslowakei, Polen, Ungarn und DDR 1948–1965*, 13–32. München: Oldenbourg.

Caute, David. 2003. *The Dancer Defects: The Struggle for Cultural Supremacy during the Cold War*. Oxford: Oxford University Press.

Davenport, Lisa E. 2009. *Jazz Diplomacy: Promoting America in the Cold War Era*. Jackson: University Press of Mississippi.

Domurat, Marta. 2010. "The Jazz Press in the People's Republic of Poland: The Role of Jazz and Jazz Forum in the Past and Today." In Gertrud Pickhan and Rüdiger Ritter, eds, *Jazz behind the Iron Curtain*, 117–128. Frankfurt am Main: Lang.

Dorůžka, Lubomír. 1961. Liner notes to *Jazz in Czechoslovakia 1*. LP. Supraphon SUB 15388.

Dorůžka, Lubomír. 1973. "Am Beispiel Polen – Jazz Survival Pattern." *Jazzforschung/Jazz Research* 5: 132–139.

Dorůžka, Lubomír. 1994a. "Jazz in der Tschechoslowakei." In Wolfram Knauer, ed., *Jazz in Europa*, 129–145. Hofheim: Wolke.

Dorůžka, Lubomír. 1994b. "Jazz under Two Totalitarian Regimes: Problems of East-European Jazz Historiography." In Theo Mäusli, ed., *Jazz und Sozialgeschichte*, 35–46. Zürich: Chronos.

Dorůžka, Lubomír. 1997. *Panoráma paměti* [Panorama of memories]. Prag: Torst.

Dorůžka, Lubomír and Ivan Poledňák. 1967. *Československý jazz. Minulost a přítomnost* [Czechoslovakian jazz: past and present]. Prag: Supraphon.

Foitzik, Jan. 2008. "Entstalinisierungskrise in Ostmitteleuropa. Verlauf, Ursachen und Folgen." In Roger Engelmann *et al.*, eds, *Kommunismus in der Krise. Die Entstalinisierung 1956 und die Folgen*, 35–60. Göttingen: Vandenhoeck & Ruprecht.

Gabbard, Krin. 2002. "Images of Jazz." In Mervyn Cooke and David Horn, eds, *The Cambridge Companion to Jazz*, 332–346. Cambridge: Cambridge University Press.

Gienow-Hecht, Jessica. 2010. "Cold War Culture." In Melvyn P. Leffler and Odd Arne Westad, eds, *The Cambridge History of the Cold War*, vol. I, 398–418. Cambridge: Cambridge University Press.

Glanc, Tomáš. 2008. "'Spaziergang ins Blaue.' Die Kultur der tschechischen 1960er Jahre." *Osteuropa* 7: 109–118.

Golan, Galia. 1970. "Youth and Politics in Czechoslovakia." *Journal of Contemporary History* 1: 3–22.

Gorodinski, Viktor. 1953. *Geistige Armut in der Musik*. Halle: Mitteldeutscher Verlag.

Hagen, Trever and Tia DeNora. 2012. "From Listening to Distribution: Nonofficial Music Practices in Hungary and Czechoslovakia from the 1960s to the 1980s." In Trevor Pinch and Karin Bijsterveld, eds, *The Oxford Handbook of Sound Studies*, 440–458. Oxford: Oxford University Press.

Heidkamp, Konrad. 1996. "Bloß kein Jazz! Ein Gespräch mit Joachim-Ernst Berendt über Musik und Widerstand." *Die Zeit* 1: 14.

Hennessey, Mike. 1967. "Supraphon Comes of Age." *Billboard* 23 September: 45.

Hnátová, Kateřina. 2007. "Jaroslav Jezek: Co-creator of the Czech Inter-war Modern Movement." *Czech Music Quarterly* 1: 26–32.

Hoensch, Jörg K. 1992. *Geschichte der Tschechoslowakei*. Stuttgart: Kohlhammer.

Holý, Jiří. 2005. "Jazz-Inspiration. Erzählungen und Novellen von Josef Škvorecký." In Jiří Holý, ed., *Josef Škvorecký. Das Baßsaxophon. Jazz-Geschichten*, 339–360. München: Deutsche Verlagsanstalt.

Jackson, Travis A. 2002. "Jazz as Musical Practice." In Mervyn Cooke and David Horn, eds, *The Cambridge Companion to Jazz*, 81–95. Cambridge: Cambridge University Press.

Jařab, Josef. 2010. "Marching Regimes and Syncopating Drummers: The Stories of Jazz in Unfree Societies." In Gertrud Pickhan and Rüdiger Ritter, eds, *Jazz behind the Iron Curtain*, 11–24. Frankfurt am Main: Lang.

Johnson, Bruce. 2000. *The Inaudible Music. Jazz, Gender and Australian Modernity*. Sydney: Currency Press.

Johnson, Bruce. 2002. "Jazz as Cultural Practice." In Mervyn Cooke and David Horn, eds, *The Cambridge Companion to Jazz*, 96–113. Cambridge: Cambridge University Press.

Kajanová, Yvetta. 1999. *Slovník Slovenskeho Jazzu* [Encyclopedia of Slovak jazz]. Bratislava: Národné hudobné centrum.

Kajanová, Yvetta. 2007. "The Periodization of Slovak Pop Music and Jazz." *Musicologica Istropolitana* 4: 197–216.

Kajanová, Yvetta. 2009. "Slovak and Czech Jazz Emigrants after 1948." *Jazzforschung/ Jazz Research* 41: 49–64.

Kajanová, Yvetta. 2010. "Denotative Components of Jazz during the Period of Communism as Exemplified in Czech and Slovak Jazz." In Gertrud Pickhan and Rüdiger Ritter, eds, *Jazz behind the Iron Curtain*, 65–81. Frankfurt am Main: Lang.

Kaplan, Karel. 2008. "Die Wurzeln der 1968er Reform." In Stefan Karner *et al.*, eds, *Prager Frühling. Das internationale Krisenjahr*, vol. I, 93–114. Köln: Böhlau.

Karner, Stefan, Günter Bischof, Manfred Wilke and Peter Ruggenthaler. 2008. "Der 'Prager Frühling' und seine Niederwerfung. Der internationale Kontext." In Stefan Karner *et al.*, eds, *Prager Frühling. Das internationale Krisenjahr*, vol. I, 17–80. Köln: Böhlau.

Kazarina, Irina. 2008. "Der tschechoslowakische Film." In Stefan Karner *et al.*, eds, *Prager Frühling. Das internationale Krisenjahr*, vol. I, 141–154. Köln: Böhlau.

Kemp-Welch, Anthony. 2010. "Eastern Europe: Stalinism to Solidarity." In Melvyn P. Leffler and Odd Arne Westad, eds, *The Cambridge History of the Cold War*, vol. II, 219–237. Cambridge: Cambridge University Press.

Knapík, Jiří. 2005. "Arbeiter versus Künstler. Gewerkschaft und neue Elemente in der tschechoslowakischen Kulturpolitik im Jahr 1948." In Christiane Brenner and Peter Heumos, eds, *Sozialgeschichtliche Kommunismusforschung. Tschechoslowakei, Polen, Ungarn und DDR 1948–1965*, 243–262. München: Oldenbourg.

Kotek, Josef. 1970. "Eine Generation im Banne des Jazz. Studie über die Beziehung zwischen ernster Musik und Jazz im Böhmen der zwanziger Jahre." *Jazzforschung/ Jazz Research* 2: 9–23.

Kouřil, Vladimír. 2009. "Jazzová sekce. Co, kdo, proč a jak a co za to/Jazzsektion. Was, wer, warum und wie und was im Gegenzug." In Jürgen Danyel, ed., *Transit 68/89*, 508–519. Berlin: Metropol.

Kouřil, Vladimír. 2010a. "Czech Jazz of the 1950s and 60s." *Czech Music Quarterly* 2: 33–44.

Kouřil, Vladimír. 2010b. "Czech Jazz of the Seventies and Eighties." *Czech Music Quarterly* 3: 37–49.

Kralová, Lenka. 2009. "Radio Days: The Beginnings of Radio Broadcasting in Inter-war Czechoslovakia." *Czech Music Quarterly* 1: 34–38.

Leschtina, Jiří. 2005. "Lubomír Dorůžka. Jsem poník, co umí jen jeden kousek" [Lubomír Dorůžka: I'm a pony who knows only one piece]." *Hospodářské noviny*,

134 Wolf-Georg Zaddach

30 April. Available at: http://archiv.ihned.cz/c1-16063830-lubomir-doruzka-jsem-ponik-co-umi-jen-jeden-kousek (accessed 25 October 2014).

Lindenberger, Thomas. 2004. "Geteilte Welt, geteilter Himmel? Der Kalte Krieg und die Massenmedien in gesellschaftsgeschichtlicher Perspektive." In Klaus Arnold and Christoph Classen, eds, *Zwischen Pop und Propaganda. Radio in der DDR*, 27–46. Berlin: Links.

Liška, Jan. 1961. "Jaz na koncertech 'Hudební mládeže'" [Jazz at the concert series "Music of the Youth"]. *Taneční hudba a jazz 1961*: 23–24.

Lücke, Martin. 2004. *Jazz im Totalitarismus. Eine komparative Analyse des politisch motivierten Umgangs mit dem Jazz während der Zeit des Nationalsozialismus und des Stalinismus.* Münster: LIT.

Macek, Petr. 1997. "Die tschechische Musikpublizistik 1945–1969 im Lichte der semantischen Textanalyse." *Sborník prací filozofické fakulty Brněnské university* 32: 49–58. Available at: http://digilib.phil.muni.cz/bitstream/handle/11222.digilib/112298/H_Musicologica_32-1997-1_7.pdf?sequence=1 (accessed 25 October 2014).

Matzner, Antonín. 2001. "The Beginning of Theoretical Reflections on Jazz in Bohemia 1918–1962." *Musicologica Olomucensia* 4: 179–192.

Monson, Ingrid. 2007. *Freedom Sounds: Civil Rights Call out to Jazz and Africa.* Oxford: Oxford University Press.

Moody, Bill. 1993. *The Jazz Exiles: American Musicians Abroad.* Reno: University of Nevada Press.

Motyčka, Petr. 2010. "The Jazz Section: A Platform of Freedom in Czechoslovakia." In Gertrud Pickhan and Rüdiger Ritter, eds, *Jazz behind the Iron Curtain*, 215–222. Frankfurt am Main: Lang.

Naimak, Norman. 2010. "The Sovietization of Eastern Europe 1944–1953." In Melvyn P. Leffler and Odd Arne Westad, eds, *The Cambridge History of the Cold War*, vol. I, 90–111. Cambridge: Cambridge University Press.

Noglik, Bert. 1994. "Osteuropäischer Jazz im Umbruch der Verhältnisse. Vom Wandel der Sinne im Prozeß gesellschaftlicher Veränderungen." In Wolfram Knauer, ed., *Jazz in Europa*, 147–162. Hofheim: Wolke.

Novák, Jiří. 2014. *Slaný Jazz Days.* Available at: www.pametnaroda.cz/witness/clip/id/2635/clip/8636 (accessed 25 October 2014).

O'Meally, Robert G., Brent Hayes Edwards and Farah Jasmine Griffin. 2004. "Introductory Notes." In Robert G. O'Meally, Brent Hayes Edwards and Farah Jasmine Griffin, eds, *Uptown Conversation: The New Jazz Studies*, 1–8. New York: Columbia University Press.

Perlín, Radim. 2013. "SPOLEČNOST. Lustrace jako nástroj národního sebetrýznění?" *Neviditelný pes*, 21 December. Available at: http://neviditelnypes.lidovky.cz/spolecnost-lustrace-jako-nastroj-narodniho-sebetryzneni-p3m-/p_spolecnost.aspx?c=A131219_201747_p_spolecnost_wag (accessed 28 October 2014).

Pešek, Jiří. 1998. "Kontinuität und Diskontinuität in der tschechischen Kultur 1945–1965." In Gernot Heiss *et al.*, *An der Bruchlinie. Österreich und die Tschechoslowakei nach 1945*, 77–102. Innsbruck: Studienverlag.

Pickhan, Gertrud and Rüdiger Ritter, eds. 2010. *Jazz behind the Iron Curtain.* Frankfurt am Main: Lang.

Riška, J. and M. Jurkovič. 1960. "Mladí a džez v Bratislave [Youth and jazz in Bratislava]." *Taneční hudba a jazz 1960*: 48.

Ritter, Rüdiger. 2010. "The Radio – a Jazz Instrument of its Own." In Gertrud Pickhan and Rüdiger Ritter, eds, *Jazz behind the Iron Curtain*, 35–55. Frankfurt am Main: Lang.

Ritter, Rüdiger. 2011. "Between Cultural Alternative and Protest: On the Social Function of Jazz after 1945 in Central Europe (GDR, Poland, Hungary, CSSR)." *Musicologica* 1: 21–42. Available at: www.musicologica.eu/?p=171&lang=en (accessed 28 October 2014).

Rudolf, Reginald. 1964. *Jazz in der Zone*. Köln: Kiepenheuer & Witsch.

Schneller, Alexander and Ada Schneller. 2006. *That Jazz of Praha*. Prag: Vitalis.

Škvorecký, Josef. 1979. "Red Music." In Josef Škvorecký, ed., *The Bass Saxophone*, 1–30. New York: Knopf.

Starr, S. Frederick. 1990. *Red and Hot: Jazz in Russland 1917–1990*. Wien: Hannibal.

Sychra, Antonín. 1951. *Stranická hudební kritika spolutvůrce nové hudby* [A party musical critique of the co-creators of new music]. Praha: Orbis.

Ţáček, Pavel, Bernd Faulenbach and Ulrich Mählert. 2008. *Die Tschechoslowakei 1945/48 bis 1989. Studien zur Herrschaft und Repression*. Leipzig: Universitätsverlag.

Truhlář, Antonín. 1958. "Tschechoslowakei." *Schlagzeug* 9: 18–19.

Truhlář, Antonín. 1959. "Tschechoslowakei. Auf dem Weg der Anerkennung." *Schlagzeug* 11: 16.

Truhlář, Antonín. 1962. "Lohn der pädagogischen Jazz-Arbeit. Der Durchbruch des Jazz in der CSSR." *Jazz Podium* 2: 36–37.

Truhlář, Antonín. 1964. "Jazz in der CSSR." In Reginald Rudolf, ed., *Jazz in der Zone*, 130–133. Köln: Kiepenheuer & Witsch.

Truhlář, Antonín. 1996. "A Brief Story of Jazz in the Heart of Europe." *Jazz Notes* 8(4). Available at: www.jazzhouse.org/library/index.php3?read=truhlar1 (accessed 25 October 2014).

Tůma, Oldřich. 2008. "Die Dubček-Ära." In Stefan Karner *et al.*, *Prager Frühling. Das internationale Krisenjahr*, vol. I, 81–92. Köln: Böhlau.

Vogel, Eric T. 1961. "Czechoslovakia." In Leonard Feather, ed., *The Encyclopedia of Jazz*, 491–492. London: Horizon Press.

Vogel, Eric T. 1965. "Blick auf Europa." *Jazz Podium* 9: 222–223.

von Eschen, Penny M. 2004. *Satchmo Blows up the World: Jazz Ambassadors Play the Cold War*. Cambridge, MA: Harvard University Press.

Voříšek, Martin. 2010. "Czech Jazz up to 1948." *Czech Music Quarterly* 1: 36–40.

Vowinckel, Annette, Marcus M. Pay and Thomas Lindenberger. 2012. "Introduction." In Annette Vowinckel, Marcus M. Pay and Thomas Lindenberger, eds, *Cold War Cultures: Perspectives on Eastern and Western European Societies*, 1–22. New York: Berghahn Books.

6

TROUBLE WITH THE NEIGHBOURS

Jazz, Geopolitics, and Finland's Totalitarian Shadow

Marcus O'Dair

Although Finnish jazz did not emerge under a totalitarian regime, in return for maintaining its national sovereignty, the country repeatedly deferred to its more powerful neighbour in matters of foreign policy, giving rise to the term 'Finlandization' or 'good neighbourliness'. Is it possible to detect in Finnish jazz a kind of cultural 'good neighbourliness'? It has been argued that until the collapse of the Soviet Union there was a tendency to give a more positive valency to culture coming from the East than from the West. Or, on the contrary, did the musicians attempt to oppose Soviet influence, forming their musical identity in reaction to Russia? This chapter will explore the effects of Soviet totalitarianism on particular Finnish jazz musicians, and also touch on Finland's sometimes uncomfortably close relationship with another totalitarian power, Nazi Germany. Finally, it will explore how more recent Finnish jazz musicians have been affected by the legacy of Soviet totalitarianism.

Finland has never been a totalitarian country. What, then, is a discussion of the country's jazz scene doing in this book? The answer lies in the Finnish experience of the Second World War and its aftermath, and the impact this had on Finnish national identity and culture. To discuss diasporic regional jazz in relation to the United States is relatively common; I will focus instead on the Soviet Union, a more geographically and culturally proximate power bloc. I will ask whether, given its influence over neighbouring Finland, the Soviet Union may be said to have cast a 'shadow' over that nation's jazz scene. I will also touch on Finland's at one point uncomfortably close relationship with another totalitarian power: Nazi Germany. Although my focus will be on the 1960s and 1970s, I will conclude by asking whether a totalitarian 'shadow' has continued to affect more recent Finnish jazz musicians. Of course, no single factor can be regarded as an 'explanation' for the history of Finnish jazz: a range of influences must be considered, including broader anti-authoritarian impulses and a growing interest in American culture. I will focus here, however, on the impact of the 'shadow' of the totalitarian Soviet regime.

Introduction: Finlandization

The popular account has jazz arriving in Finland via the *S/S Andania*, which docked in Helsinki in 1926 and offloaded a number of Finnish-American musicians (Austerlitz 2000, 191; 2005, 124; Kaarresalo-Kasari and Kasari 2010, 11; Konttinen 1987, 21). In fact, Jukka Haavisto suggests (1996, 10–11) that jazz actually arrived in Finland earlier in the decade, while Paul Austerlitz (2005, 125) points out that there were jazz residencies in top Helsinki restaurants as early as 1921.

Scholars sometimes suggest that the first Finnish jazz recording, by trombonist Klaus Salmi and his Ramblers Orchestra, was released in 1932 and that the jazz magazine *Rytmi* followed two years later (Konttinen 1987, 24).[1] At this stage, however, *jatsi* was a generic term for any music featuring drums or, in particular, saxophones (ibid., 21), essentially meaning dance music. Waltzes, tangos and foxtrots were popular (ibid., 24), as was the 'accordion jazz' performed by groups like the Dallapé Orchestra (according to Pekka Gronow (1973, 60), the most important phenomenon in Finnish popular music of the 1930s).

All this, of course, pre-dates a totalitarian influence on the music. Having been a Swedish province until 1809 and a grand duchy under Russia until 1917 (ibid., 53), Finland in these early years of *jatsi* was enjoying the first flush of independence, and the musicians looked west rather than east. The origins of a totalitarian influence on Finnish jazz can be found, instead, in the Second World War. The war had a tremendous psychological impact: Gilmour and Stephenson (2013, 5) suggest it weighs heavily on the Finnish psyche, with a predominant position in the national master narrative.[2] For Finns, forgetting the war has not been an option; instead, 'actively, even obsessively, remembering and commemorating the war has been a central component of Finnish national identity' (ibid., 200).

In fact, Finns tend to regard the conflict as not one but three wars: the Winter War (1939–1940) and the Continuation War (1941–1944), both against the Soviet Union, and the Lapland War (1944–1945) against Germany (Stenius *et al.* 2011, 55). All three, then, were *against* totalitarian powers. At the same time, however, the war(s) left the Finns enduringly and uncomfortably linked to both regimes. They had, after all, been at least co-belligerents with Nazi Germany, since Finnish forces joined the Axis invasion of the Soviet Union in 1941.[3] At the same time, although no Soviet troops 'liberated' Finland at the end of the war, the country remained in the Soviet sphere of influence thereafter – a key point to which I will return.

138 Marcus O'Dair

The Second World War had a direct impact on Finnish jazz, not least by introducing American swing; according to Gronow (1973, 62), it also brought to prominence a new generation of musicians. At the same time, Haavisto (1996, 25) suggests that, since Adolf Hitler considered jazz 'un-Aryan', representatives of the Finnish authorities at times 'deemed it appropriate to forbid the inclusion of jazz in entertainment programmes'. While the influence of Nazi Germany on Finnish culture did not extend beyond the war itself, the influence of another totalitarian power, the Soviet Union, was ongoing. Although not part of the Eastern Bloc, it is often suggested that postwar Finnish neutrality was conditioned by the obligation to be on good terms with the Soviet Union (Stenius *et al.* 2011, 224). By the late 1950s and early 1960s (Singleton 1981, 270), this arrangement was known as 'Finlandization', a term subsequently applied to any country forced into a subservient role by a powerful neighbour. The term, says Allison (1985, 2), refers to a covert, protracted and insidious process leading to the loss of a nation's independence in policy-making; although the Finlandized state may remain outside its powerful neighbour's bloc, it is assumed to lie within the latter's 'soft sphere of influence'. More recent scholars (Meinander 2011, 165; Lavery 2006, 139) have put forward broadly similar definitions.

To many, the term 'Finlandization' is pejorative and 'grossly unfair' (Singleton 1981, 285). To understand such controversy, we must look at the political context in the era in which the notion became prominent. Singleton (ibid., 270) states that the term gained currency at a time when Russo-Finnish relations were undergoing a period of strain, partly because of the internal political situation in Finland but more significantly because of a worsening in Soviet relations with the West. Having been used first by academics such as Professor Richard Loewenthal, Singleton suggests, it soon became common among right-wing journalists and politicians – especially in Germany, where it was primarily used to criticize the *Ostpolitik* of Social Democrat Chancellor Willy Brandt (ibid., 271).[4] This context is important, as it positions the whole notion of Finlandization as a product of the Cold War. The term, Allison makes clear (1985, 3), should be seen within this context, in particular the question of what would happen to a Western Europe bereft of US support. In describing a process that incrementally has led to the loss of Finland's national autonomy, Allison (ibid., 1) suggests the intention was to illustrate, by analogy, a danger posed to Western Europe much more broadly by the Soviet Union in a period of détente.

Urho Kekkonen, Finnish President from 1956 to 1981 and perceived by some as having a 'cosy' relationship with Moscow (Meinander 2011, 165), is synonymous with Finlandization (Lavery 2006, 139). Objecting to a term used to depict Kekkonen as the 'errand boy of the Kremlin', Singleton suggests that Finlandization 'should be removed from the vocabulary of international politics, and be placed where it belongs in the annals of contemporary mythology' (Singleton, 271, 285). Kekkonen himself instead spoke of 'good neighbourliness' (ibid., 278), while others refer to the 'Paasikivi–Kekkonen line', named after Kekkonen and his predecessor as President, J. K. Paasikivi, who also strove to keep Finland neutral and outside the sphere of big-power conflict by adopting 'the prewar attitude of fear, hostility and mistrust of the Soviet Union' (ibid., 283). It is the phrase 'good neighbourliness' that I will use in the rest of this chapter. Whatever term we use, however, the influence of the Soviet Union in Finland in the postwar years was pervasive or even ubiquitous (Gilmour and Stephenson 2013, 142).

To be sure, having been co-belligerents with Germany hardly made the Finns totalitarian in that period; indeed, the country enjoyed what Oula Silvennoinen calls the dubious distinction of being the only democracy to fight on the side of Hitler (cited in ibid., 129). Nor did a postwar policy of deference towards the Soviet Union make the country totalitarian. Somewhat against the odds, Finland remained independent and maintained a multi-party, free-market system (Austerlitz 2005, 138; Allison 1985, 10). Yet, as Bruce Johnson shows in his Introduction to this book, essentialist understandings of totalitarianism have been called into question in the decades since Hannah Arendt,[5] with the dualistic model of confrontation between totalitarian states and liberal democracies replaced by a more nuanced perspective. In terms of jazz, as Rüdiger Ritter points out in Chapter 2 of this volume, it is too simplistic to suggest that the Soviets simply tried and failed to keep out nasty American music as an exemplar of cultural imperialism. But even during the periodic violent crackdowns, totalitarianism was less than total: jazz records remained available on the black market, and musicians and audiences alike refused to be silenced (Starr 1994, 223–224, 332).

It is more than forty years since Dallin and Breslauer (1970, 1; emphasis added) suggested that political terror was the linchpin of totalitarianism, understood as 'the arbitrary use, by organs of political authority, of severe coercion against individuals or groups, *the credible threat of such use*, or the arbitrary extermination of such individuals or groups'. Only from today's vantage point is it clear that the Finns would retain sovereignty; the threat of Soviet force seemed credible enough at the time, and not only during specific crises such as the Night Frost Crisis (1958), the Note Crisis (1961) and the invasion of Czechoslovakia (1968). As Lavery (2006, 140) notes, for instance, many Finns saw the end of the Prague Spring as a possible foreshadowing of a Soviet occupation of Finland. I suggest that totalitarianism might therefore be said to have an *infectious* quality – a quality with the ability to cross borders.[6] As Lavery (ibid., 12) writes, 'since achieving independence in 1917, the shadow of the Russian bear has guided, and in some cases misguided, Finland's foreign policy'. Finland, then, may be seen to represent almost a refracted totalitarianism, one-step-removed totalitarianism; or, in the terminology of this chapter's title, the Soviet Union cast a totalitarian 'shadow' over its democratic neighbour.

140 Marcus O'Dair

One result of this shadow was an attempt to achieve stability based on reducing mistrust between Finland and the Soviet Union (Meinander 2011, 159). For the Finnish media, for instance, Meinander suggests 'good neighbourliness' meant self-censorship, or even 'distortions' (ibid., 185–186). Lavery (2006, 142) points out that, especially during the 1970s, when 'good neighbourliness' was at its peak, Finns would not publish dissident literature such as Alexander Solzhenitsyn's *The Gulag Archipelago*; participation in organizations such as Greenpeace and Amnesty International was discouraged; and, for many, membership of the Finnish–Soviet Friendship Society was a requirement for professional advancement. Lavery also notes that this self-censorship was not necessarily the result of Soviet pressure; instead, 'the Moscow Card' was played for domestic reasons in an era of 'national self-deception'. But it was no less powerful for that.

Though it is an overused term, Finland, strategically poised between East and West (Howell 2006, 265), really does occupy a *liminal* space – and even more so during the Cold War. I have suggested that, although certainly not totalitarian itself, it represented a kind of refracted totalitarianism. It also found itself poised, as Kivimäki (2012) puts it, 'between defeat and victory'. In a sense, the country was even poised between peace and war: we might borrow from Svanibor Pettan the concept of 'a war–peace continuum' (O'Connell and Castelo-Branco 2010, 188). Certainly, the Finns were at the 'peace' end of this spectrum, but the fact that even the war itself was 'cold' is a reminder that the world had moved beyond traditional binaries. This threshold position helped create the conditions for a distinctively Finnish form of jazz.

Towards a Finnish Jazz

Although jazz existed in Finland as early as the 1920s, it was only following the repeal of the wartime ban on dancing in 1948 (Gronow 1973, 62) that it began for the first time to diverge from dance music (Konttinen 1987, 25). Although the American model remained dominant and sales were relatively low (Gronow 1995, 45), some excellent Finnish musicians emerged in the postwar period, among them Olli Häme, Erik Lindström, Valto Laitinen, Herbert Katz, Antero Stenberg and Teuvo Suojärvi. The 1950s also saw the birth of the Scandia label, for jazz and jazz-related recordings (Austerlitz 2005, 139). Most agree, however, that it was not until the 1960s and 1970s that a form of jazz emerged that was fully and distinctively Finnish (Konttinen 1987, 25; Haavisto 1996, 41). Trumpeter Henrik Otto Donner, one of the key musicians to emerge in the era, spoke of a 'paradigm shift' (Austerlitz 2005, 143–144), with Austerlitz agreeing that jazz moved from mere spice in the brew of Finnish dance band music to a music performed by dedicated professionals – and aimed at *listeners*, rather than *dancers* (ibid., 144). Alongside Donner, important musicians of this period included the drummers Anssi

Pethman and Christian Schwindt, the saxophonist Eero Koivistoinen and the saxophonist/flautist Esa Pethman. The momentum towards a national jazz continued to build into the 1970s, spearheaded by another batch of highly talented players: drummer Edward Vesala, reedsmen Juhani Aaltonen and Seppo 'Paroni' Paakkunainen, pianist Heikki Sarmanto, and bass players Pekka Sarmanto and Teppo Hauta-aho.

Such a national jazz is not easy to characterize – the very concept of Finnishness, as Kari Kallioniemi and Kimi Kärki (2009, 62) point out, is 'vague and contradictory', but the following descriptions are useful, apart from anything else, in depicting the most common self-representing stereotypes. Jukka Perko, artistic director of the Viapori Jazz Festival, says Finnish jazz is minimalistic: 'It's similar to our design, with simple lines, perhaps more edgy' (quoted in Chela 2013). Perko also paraphrases a quote from the most famous Finnish classical composer, Jean Sibelius – 'Don't write any unnecessary musical notes!' – and links this minimalist tendency to the Finnish climate: 'Our extreme winter weather conditions have forced us to be accurate when sowing and harvesting the crop. We couldn't afford to lose or waste anything. It was all about precision and hard work, weeding out what was unnecessary – like in our music' (ibid.).

Kaarresalo-Kasari and Kasari (2010, 9) suggest a link between Finland's landscape ('thousands of lakes, vast forests and far-reaching wilderness') and the fact that Finnish jazz tends to be 'calm and peaceful with floating rhythm or static tempo or even with no recognisable tempo at all'. Certainly, the lack of swing was noted as early as the 1950s (Haavisto 1996, 35) and is still remarked upon today (Kaarresalo-Kasari and Kasari 2010, 8). In terms of mood, some say there's a melancholy in Finnish jazz. The journalist Dan McClenaghan (2014), for instance, relates the sombre and introspective characteristics of Aaltonen's music to his nationality: 'perhaps it's a Finnish thing'. Speaking to the Jazz Convention website, the drummer Markku Ounaskari agrees:

> We Finnish people are a mixture of Scandinavian and Slavic, eastern culture. For me this Slavic, very melancholic, but not depressive music is very beautiful. Their simple melodies give us a natural and inspirational base to improvise. And definitely we feel this music very deeply inside us.
>
> *('Finnish Jazz. Interview. Markku Ounaskari' 2011)*

What of totalitarianism's influence on this music? Matti Konttinen (1987, 25) sees Louis Armstrong's 1949 visit to Helsinki as the dividing line between the 'rhythm music' of the early years and the birth of a music we might recognize as jazz today. That visit coincided almost exactly with Finland's Treaty of Friendship, Co-operation and Mutual Assistance with the Soviet Union. Under the terms of the treaty, Finland pledged to defend itself against any attack on

142 Marcus O'Dair

its own territory or on the USSR via Finland 'by Germany or any State allied with the latter', while Finland's desire 'to remain outside the conflicting interests of the Great Powers' was also recognized (Lavery 2006, 137). According to Singleton (1981, 280), the treaty formed the basis of all subsequent Russo-Finnish relations. Is it possible, then, that a policy of 'good neighbourliness' towards the Soviet Union influenced Finnish jazz? Certainly, 'good neighbourliness' refers primarily to foreign rather than domestic policy, but jazz, the sonic secret weapon, was indeed part of the international politics of the Cold War.[7]

The effects of 'good neighbourliness' on jazz are difficult to pin down, in part because the Finnish population was far from homogeneous in its attitude towards the music. Gronow (1973, 63) suggests a split between urban, educated youth, who tended to like jazz and rock, and more conservative, patriotic listeners, who remained loyal, paradoxically enough, to Finnish tango (Austerlitz 2005, 142). The other factor that complicates the effect of 'good neighbourliness' on Finnish jazz is that the history of jazz in the Soviet Union itself is heterogeneous in the extreme, oscillating wildly from censorship and restriction to state sponsorship (Pickhan and Ritter 2010, 83; Lücke 2007, 1).[8] Particularly under Stalin, there were handbrake turns in official policy, with even musicians who had enjoyed considerable support liable to find themselves suddenly in the gulag (Stites 1992, 73–74; Lücke 2007, 2–3; Starr 1994, 79–228). Khrushchev, who became leader after Stalin's death in 1953, was on the whole less hostile towards jazz than his predecessor had been (Pickhan and Ritter 2010, 99; Starr 1994, 261; Stites 1992, 132; Davenport 2009, 33), although there was a backlash between 1962 and the start of the Brezhnev regime in 1964. Richard Stites (1992, 160) suggests it was during the Brezhnev era, which lasted until 1982, that Soviet jazz reached its peak, and it may be no coincidence that there is consensus that a truly distinctive Finnish jazz emerged during the same period (although, even under Brezhnev, the status of the music in the Soviet Union remained uncertain). The liberal interlude that followed his rise to power ended in 1968 with the Soviet invasion of Czechoslovakia (Starr 1994, 275, 290), although the situation was again improving by 1971, when Duke Ellington was invited to tour the Soviet Union, having been refused entry the previous decade (Cohen 2011, 297–300).

Otto Donner has suggested that jazz did not progress in Finland in an orderly historical sequence from swing to bebop and then on to modal and free jazz; for all practical purposes, bebop was skipped over completely (cited in Haavisto 1996, 44). The musician and critic Sami Ahokas agrees:

> When you think of the top musicians of that period, such as Herbert Katz and Teuvo Suojärvi, they in a way just swam through the bebop tidal wave directly to the way of playing we now call mainstream.

> If you want to talk about real bebop, there just simply wasn't any of it in Finland.
>
> *(Quoted in Haavisto 1996, 27)*

It would be easy to assume that a policy of 'good neighbourliness' can explain this apparent failure of bebop to take hold in Finland at that time. Soviet influence certainly seems to have been behind the condemnation of bebop in late 1940s Estonia, for instance (Reimann 2012, 96). To claim too direct or causal a link with 'good neighbourliness' in the case of Finland, however, would be an oversimplification. For one thing, some musicians *did* play bebop, among them the pianist Valto Laitinen (Haavisto 1996, 46) and the saxophonist Antero Stenberg (ibid., 28). And while customs restrictions resulted in a scarcity of imported records until 1956, it was possible to hear bebop in Finland: seamen working on ferries to Sweden would bring back records; musicians would make 'dishwashing' trips to Stockholm to see bebop musicians; and there were radio broadcasts by the BBC and the Voice of America (Haavisto 1996, 27–28). By 1949, there was also a Finnish jazz programme, entitled (oddly, from today's 'jazz as metagenre' perspective) 'From Jazz to Bebop'.

While it may be true that there was relatively little bebop in Finland, this can be explained only partially (at best) by the country's policy of 'good neighbourliness'. Bebop failed to make a significant impact there even when it reached a 'crescendo' in the Soviet Union under Khrushchev (Starr 1994, 243), which suggests it was not only Soviet pressure that prevented it from flourishing in Finland. Instead, the dominant style of the 1950s was cool jazz, as heard on records such as Pentti Ahola's 'Little White Lies', Kalevi Hartti's 'September in the Rain' and Olli Häme's 'Without You' (Haavisto 1996, 35–36). And cool jazz was hardly less American – or more Soviet – than bebop.

Ahokas (cited Haavisto 1996, 27) suggests another, more prosaic, reason for the relative failure of bebop to gain a foothold in Finland: the Finns lacked the technical facility to play it. Haavisto (ibid., 35) offers a number of other possible explanations: a German–Russian musical tradition; Finland's remote geographical location; the almost complete lack of a blues tradition; a general cultural bias against jazz; and, finally, five years of war. The relative lack of bebop might also be explained in part by the fact that Finland was at the time still a predominantly rural country: in 1945, only approximately one-quarter of Finns lived in urban areas, and it was another twenty-five years before the proportion reached 50 per cent (Lavery 2006, 147–148).

Therefore, if there was a relationship between Finnish jazz and the totalitarian 'shadow', it was subtle and complex. It is also contested: the drummer and pianist Jukkis Uotila suggests that, from the 1960s, Finland's leftist movement, under Soviet influence, regarded American jazz as 'something culturally degrading' (quoted in Kaarresalo-Kasari and Kasari 2010, 15). Kaarresalo-Kasari and Kasari (ibid.) suggest that 'anything originating from the west was

144 Marcus O'Dair

negative and anything coming from our eastern neighbour was positive'. Kallioniemi and Kärki (2009, 64) assert that the 'neo-Stalinist atmosphere of the Finlandization era' ensured that all Anglo-American influences were seen as unpatriotic.[9] However, John Coltrane was only one of several prominent American musicians to visit Finland in the early 1960s, while the First Annual Helsinki Jazz Festival, in 1964, featured Miles Davis and Dave Brubeck, among others (Haavisto 1996, 39–40). And evidence of a significant US impact on Finnish music is hard to ignore: Heikki Sarmanto was influenced by Bud Powell; Anssi Pethman by Elvin Jones; Pekka Sarmanto by Paul Chambers and Scott LaFaro; Otto Donner by Miles Davis; Christian Schwindt by Art Blakey and others (Haavisto 1996, 42–43). By the late 1960s, Eero Koivistoinen was performing at international festivals with the American trumpeter Clark Terry (ibid., 50).

Certainly, 'good neighbourliness' was by no means the only influence shaping Finnish jazz in this period. As ever, there were a number of other cultural, social, economic and political aspects; as a reminder that the factors went beyond genre, we might note that it was also in the early 1970s that a distinctly Finnish form of rock came into its own (Meinander 2011, 177–178). One result of 'good neighbourliness', I will suggest, was insularity; but, given the country's geographical position, as well as the lack of immigration in the period (Lavery 2006, 150), it is possible that Finland would have been relatively isolated even without the totalitarian 'shadow' of the Soviet Union. Language barriers may also have contributed to this insularity: Estonian, the closest relative of Finnish, was on the other side of the Iron Curtain. The period from 1950 to 1980 was also the most intensive phase in the creation of the Finnish welfare state (Meinander 2011, 172), something Kaarresalo-Kasari and Kasari (2010, 11) link back to the national jazz scene: 'We are the land of equal rights in many regards. This can also be seen in our bands. They operate without much hierarchy; everyone is equal to each other.'

We can also find other explanations for the artistic success of Finnish jazz from the 1960s onwards. The Finnish Jazz Federation was founded in 1966 – a year that also saw the birth of the Pori Jazz Festival. Having not previously been deemed suitable for monetary stipends or other public cultural support, legislation was introduced to promote the arts from 1967 (Haavisto 1996, 44). Education also played a significant part: following educational camps and workshops in the 1960s, jazz education was formalized with the establishment of the Oulunkylä Pop/Jazz Institute in 1972 (ibid., 53–56). The Sibelius Academy, which had previously regarded jazz 'with a certain degree of disdain', embraced it during the 1970s and officially opened its Department of Jazz Studies in 1983 (ibid., 55–57).

The emergence of a distinctly Finnish jazz in the 1960s and 1970s, then, cannot be explained only in terms of the totalitarian 'shadow'. That said, it may be no coincidence that truly distinctive Finnish jazz emerged when 'good

Jazz and Geopolitics in Finland **145**

neighbourliness' reached its peak (Kivimäki 2012, 493). One key consequence of this policy was insularity. Lavery (2006, 150) suggests that the outcome of the Second World War changed Finns' basic assumptions about their place in the wider world:

> Before the war, Finns struggled to build a national identity in larger, especially European, contexts. After the war they believed that insulating themselves from the outside world best preserved national identity. The Paasikivi–Kekkonen Line encouraged Finns to think that they stood between East and West, really belonging to neither. Finns spoke of Europe as if their country lay on another continent.

This sense of insularity was evident in Finns' retrospective view of their relationship with another previously totalitarian country: Germany. As Silvennoinen (cited Gilmour and Stephenson 2013, 129) notes, many Finns still feel obliged to explain away their nation's partnership with the Nazis, particularly following the 'moral turn' (Stenius *et al.* 2011, 11–16, 25–26) that has emphasized the centrality of the Holocaust and, in the words of Aunesluoma, made Auschwitz the keyhole through which the whole of the Second World War is viewed (cited in Gilmour and Stephenson 2013, 214). The Finnish response has typically been to claim to have fought a 'separate war', distinct from the Second World War and instead simply the latest in a long chain of heroic and lonely defensive wars against Russia (Stenius *et al.* 2011, 60). Although few professional historians still hold this view, it remains remarkably persistent in the general Finnish population today (Gilmour and Stephenson 2013, 202, 215). A similar 'separateness' was evident in Finland's relations with the Soviet Union: the desire 'to remain outside the conflicting interests of the Great Powers' that was recognized in the treaty of 1948.

This sense of separation could not help but affect the country's jazz, especially since it also took the form of geographical isolation. This is in contrast to Denmark and Sweden, both long-time destinations for touring and expatriate US jazz musicians (Nicholson 2005, 206–209; Kaarresalo-Kasari and Kasari 2010, 12). Finland, given its ties to the Soviet Union, was markedly less attractive to these American expats; and Edward Vesala suggested that his country's isolation, the result of Cold War geopolitics, helped keep its music distinct. 'Before I was 21, I didn't even know what the blues was,' he told journalist Phil Johnson (1993).

> I had no record player and no records but sometimes I heard music in a dance-hall in the countryside, when they played tango. That was my first contact; but when I started to play, I started very strong. Famous European players start when they are seven years old and play every day, but now I think that my background was good. I learnt to be in the

146 Marcus O'Dair

country and I didn't even hear people, I heard wind. If you want to copy, to be an American monkey, then it is different.

(Ibid.)

As well as avoiding swing, Finnish jazz of the 1960s and 1970s tended to embrace national folk traditions. For some, this was an ideological decision: there is evidence that the communist youth objected to jazz in the 1950s because of its American associations (Kallioniemi and Kärki 2009, 63) and tried to correct the balance by turning to Finnish folk. Esa Pethman's landmark 1965 album *The Modern Sound of Finland*, for instance, drew on folk and the Finnish classical tradition as well as John Coltrane and Eric Dolphy (Haavisto 1996, 42). This was an album with space for a track entitled 'Finnish Schnapps' as well as one called 'Blues for Duke'. Eero Koivistoinen's debut solo album *Valtakunta*, released later in the decade and featuring lyrics by the Finnish poets Pentti Saarikoski, Jarkko Laine, Tuomas Anhava and Hannu Mäkelä, was a similarly important landmark in terms of Finnish jazz finding its own voice. Finnish jazz musicians' embrace of folk became even more pronounced in the 1970s in the work of the saxophonists Sakari Kukko and Seppo Paakkunainen. Kukko and his band Piirpauke combined jazz with ancient Finnish folk tunes, looking not to western Finnish culture but to that of eastern Finland and Karelia – the northern territories ceded to the Soviet Union and the country's cultural heartland (Gilmour and Stephenson 2013, 131). Such was the symbolic importance of the region that Vesala and Paakkunainen adopted 'Karelia' as the name of the act they formed in 1970, inspired by the folk–rock of Fairport Convention as well as jazz (Austerlitz 2005, 147). Karelia was also closely linked to a Finnish epic, *The Kalevala*, which comprises a number of orally transmitted folk narratives collected and collated by Elias Lönnrot in 1835 (ibid., 122). Vesala adapted *The Kalevala* for the theatre (Nicholson 2005, 208); Kukko played with a band called Kalevala; and Wigwam, a progressive rock group with strong links to jazz, wrote a song, 'Häätö', inspired by the epic (Kallioniemi and Kärki 2009, 63). According to Haavisto (1996, 47), Pethman started working towards a new way of relating to the mythological *Kalevala* landscape as early as 1962: his 'Paimenlaulu' (Shepherd's Song) can be considered the first recorded jazz composition with identifiably Finnish qualities (ibid., 42, 28).

Finnish jazz players' fascination with folk music was not only the result of insularity caused by 'good neighbourliness'; it was also a manifestation of patriotic pride linked to a new self-confidence in relation to the Soviet Union and the Second World War. In the immediate postwar years, Finns tended to see themselves as lacking agency in that conflict (Gilmour and Stephenson 2013, 8), with the dominant metaphor being that of 'driftwood': Finland was an innocent victim of the destructive forces that were unleashed in the autumn of 1939 (Stenius *et al.* 2011, 58). The driftwood concept lost credibility, however, in the 1960s (Gilmour and Stephenson 2013, 211–212). What emerged in its place was the idea that Finland's leaders had deliberately chosen war in 1941. Rather than driftwood, then, the country was a skilfully steered rowing boat (Stenius *et al.* 2011, 59) that towed Finnish jazz in its wake.[10]

It is not my intention to ascribe *every* change in Finnish jazz to the totalitarian 'shadow'; after all, it was not only Finnish jazz that was growing distinct from the American mainstream. Other Nordic musicians were also forging distinctive jazz identities, often by drawing on their own folk traditions (Nicholson 2005, 203), as was often represented on the Munich-based ECM label, for whom Finns including Aaltonen and Vesala also recorded. David Ake (2010, 99) makes the point that ECM was concerned with nostalgia: an imagined home that was both safe and eternal. The fact that musicians from other countries were also searching for such an imagined home is a reminder that we cannot make too simplistic a link between Finnish jazz of the era and the totalitarian 'shadow' cast by the Soviet Union. Yet 'imagined home' could hardly be a more apt description of Karelia, constructed by Finns, according to Outi Fingerroos (2008, 235), as 'a place of memory and utopias'.

Finnish Jazz from the 1980s to the Present

Although this chapter focuses on the influence of Soviet totalitarianism on Finnish jazz of the 1960s and 1970s, I would like to conclude by exploring the influence of the totalitarian 'shadow' on more recent Finnish jazz musicians. After a troubled decade following the invasion of Czechoslovakia, Soviet jazz had regained a measure of stability by the late 1970s, and, according to S. Frederick Starr (1994, 316–317), the music of the 1980s far surpassed that of the 1960s in terms of creative originality.

Soviet officials' acceptance of jazz was, of course, good news for Finnish musicians, even if the same changes, related to a broader culture of *glasnost* and *perestroika*, also reduced the influence of the Soviet Union on Finland in general. Relations between the two countries were relatively warm: Yuri Andropov, the Soviet leader for a brief fifteen months from late 1982, described Soviet–Finnish relations at that time as a 'vivid example of the vital power of peaceful coexistence' (Allison 1985, 108). That process sped up only when Mikhail Gorbachev came to power in 1985 (Meinander 2011, 188). Emboldened by changes across the border, Mauno Koivisto, who succeeded Kekkonen as Finnish President in 1982, tended to be less willing than his predecessor to see Finland as lying in the 'shadow' of Soviet Union.

Lavery (2006, 155) suggests that the easing of East–West tension during the 1980s allowed Finland to remove some of the 'Soviet filter' in its relations with the West. In jazz, international relationships, already pioneered by Vesala and Aaltonen, increased: Teppo Hauta-aho worked with Cecil Taylor and Alexander von Schlippenbach; Koivistoinen with Jack DeJohnette and John

148 Marcus O'Dair

Scofield; Vesala with Reggie Workman. The trumpeters Simo Salminen and Mike Koskinen and the drummer Jukka-Pekka Uotila spent significant periods in the United States. This stronger link to America is perhaps best represented by the guitarist Raoul Björkenheim, who was born in Los Angeles to Finnish parents and has spent approximately half of his life in each country. He is, as the title of one *All about Jazz* article has it, the 'guitarist between two continents' (Shaw, 2005).

All this might suggest that 'good neighbourliness' was no longer a significant influence on Finnish jazz by the 1980s. Yet the influence of Finnish folk remained strong, with musicians such as Heikki Syrjänen of the Ethnoboys utilizing Finnish cowherds' horns in an attempt to escape the stylistic baggage of the saxophone (Austerlitz 2000, 203). Paroni Paakkunainen, meanwhile, joined forces with the Sami writer and musician Nils-Aslak Valkeapää. Kallioniemi and Kärki (2009, 61) suggest that the collapse of the Soviet Union caused rock musicians to embrace the Finnish folk tradition, too: they state, for instance, that it was primarily the generation that came of age after the dissolution of the Soviet Union who turned to *The Kalevala* for inspiration. Finnish jazz, as I have shown, had been there first.

By the time the Soviet Union dissolved at the end of 1991, Finland had reached the end of the 'Paasikivi–Kekkonen Line' (Lavery 2006, 143). Yet, while the collapse of the Soviet Union is an obvious cultural as well as political landmark, it did not lead immediately to a radically different type of Finnish jazz. A boom in Finnish jazz *did* occur, with the appearance of 'nu-jazz' ensembles such as Quintessence, the Five Corners Quintet, Nuspirit Helsinki, U-Street All Stars and Ilmiliekki Quartet, but not until around the turn of the millennium. Far from the brooding Finnish stereotype, this music was closer to acid jazz, building on the work of the pioneering RinneRadio in the 1990s in its incorporation of elements of electronic dance music. It was not melancholic or minimalist, and nor were there bursts of fury; rhythm, a background presence in much previous Finnish jazz, was suddenly prominent.

Though the nu-jazz scene has perhaps already had its day, a number of other leading jazz players are making music that is, at least superficially, a far cry from the tradition that emerged in the 1960s and 1970s. The keyboardist Kari Ikonen plays 'afro-pop-jazz', among other genres (Ikonen, n.d.); the saxophonist Mikko Innanen, associated, like Ikonen, with the Fiasko collective, has been praised for his 'funny' music (Woodard n.d.); Trio Töykeät, led by the pianist Iiro Rantala, are similarly described on their label's website as 'one of the weirdest, *funniest* and most visionary piano trios in international jazz' (ACT n.d.; emphasis added).

It would be easy to assume that this move away from melancholia – or melancholia punctuated by fury – is ubiquitous, and that it can be traced simply and directly to the removal of the Soviet 'shadow'. The reality, of course, is not that simple. Humour was an element in Finnish jazz even under the totalitarian 'shadow'. Equally, an element of fury remains in today's music: Innanen, for instance, makes 'violent skronk' (Langhoff, 2011) with his groups Innkvisitio and Plop. Despite this breadth, and a number of international collaborations, such as those established between Finnish and French musicians by the promoter Charles Gil, much Finnish music is still perceived in Nordic or Scandinavian terms. For instance, Nicholson (2005, 217–218) writes that '[the pianist Alexi] Tuomarila's playing, a rich, expansive vocabulary that is never flaunted but put to compositional ends within the framework of his improvisations, has a very Scandinavian feel to it'. Similarly, reviews of trumpeter Verneri Pohjola, formerly a member of Quintessence and the Ilmiliekki Quartet but now a renowned solo artist, summon up Nordic jazz truisms even as they bat them away: for instance, 'a faintly disconsolate beauty that nonetheless avoids all the usual north-European, windswept-jazz clichés' (Fordham, 2011).

The tendency to locate Finnish jazz within a Nordic context has a certain logic, and no doubt helps Finnish musicians to reach a wider market, but it also distracts and detracts from another, equally important, group of inter-national relationships: those with countries that formerly lay behind the Iron Curtain. The Estonian guitarist Ain Agan, for instance, works with his compatriot Mihkel Mälgand and two Finns: Teemu Viinikainen on guitar and drummer Mika Kallio. Both Björkenheim and Innanen, meanwhile, have worked with Estonian guitarist Jaak Sooäär. The Estonian group Kadri Voorand features Finnish saxophonist Jussi Kannaste. Kari Ikonen's trio includes Armenian bassist Ara Yaralyan. Elena and the Rom Ensemble are a Finnish quintet led by vocalist Elena Mindru, who is of Romanian heritage. Poland's Tomasz Stańko, who previously worked with Vesala, featured two Finns – drummer Olavi Louhivuori and pianist Alexi Tuomarila – on his 2009 ECM album *Dark Eyes*. The list could go on. Such shared sensibility with nations such as Estonia and Poland is a reminder that, as much as it can be seen as a Nordic – and indeed a Western – country, Finland can also be understood as an Eastern European country with Eastern European problems (Gilmour and Stephenson 2013, 133).

For all the collaborations, there is also an enduring separateness to jazz in Finland. This is partly due to geography, of course. Annamaija Saarela, until recently president of the European Jazz Network, has suggested: 'We are far away from pretty much everywhere, so it is always hard to arrange Finnish bands an opportunity to be seen and heard by audiences elsewhere' (quoted in Silas, 2014). But we can also relate it to Finnish history, and the country's ongoing emphasis on having fought a 'separate war'. Did this isolation, *All about Jazz* asked Tuomarila, affect Finnish jazz? 'I believe so,' he replied. 'But I don't know what that characteristic is exactly. Maybe it's something melancholy, some kind of sadness – but in a beautiful way, a good way – a

150 Marcus O'Dair

kind of longing' (quoted in Lindsay, 2013). Again we have an echo of Karelia, and of 'memory and utopias'.

To see the national jazz scene *only* in terms of 'good neighbourliness' would surely be myopic. Even the notion of categorizing jazz by nation can be questioned, particularly in an era of increasing globalization; Finnish jazz musicians, including Rantala (Stenger 2014) and Innanen (Nives 2012), certainly resist it. On the other hand, Biddle and Knights (2007, 1) suggest that the nation – somewhere between the local and the global – remains 'a crucial but ambivalent category for understanding how cultural texts and practices function in the construction of personal and collective identities'. And a powerful neighbour can clearly have a considerable effect on national identity – given that nations are 'imagined communities' (Anderson 2006) – especially when that neighbour is totalitarian and possesses a 'credible threat' of coercion.

I cannot read Finnish, which has left many potential sources beyond my grasp, so I would call for more primary research into the effect of the totalitarian 'shadow' on Finnish jazz before drawing any firm conclusions. Yet, I believe it is safe to say that geopolitical isolation had a significant effect on Finnish cultural life, including jazz, certainly until the collapse of the Soviet Union in 1991 and probably until Finland's entry into the European Union in 1995 (and quite possibly beyond). 'Good neighbourliness' was only one factor in this sense of separateness, but it does provide a useful perspective on the music that is not often discussed, perhaps because the musicians themselves are not even conscious of it. So, while situating Finnish jazz within the totalitarian 'shadow' does not provide a total explanation, I feel it does afford new insights into Finnish musical identity, particularly in relation to Russia, with implications for border countries and relations between East and West more generally, as well as the ways in which jazz mediates identities.

Notes

1 Earlier recordings are sufficiently regarded as jazz to have been included in the Finnish Fazer label's series of historical reissues called *Suomalaista Jazzia* (Finnish Jazz). They include: Markus Rautio with Yrjö's Orchestra, 'Raatikkoon Blues' (the word 'blues' is obviously significant), 1929; and Leo Adamson with the Ramblers, 'Muistan Sua, Elaine' (I remember you, Elaine), 1931 (see Johnson 2002, 53).
2 That the war is the most celebrated and debated moment in Finnish history (Gilmour and Stephenson 2013, 199) is in part explained by its human consequences: over 90,000 Finns died and 400,000 were forced to leave their homes. These are, as Juhana Aunesluoma points out (cited in ibid.), high figures for a population of just four million, if not by the grisly standards of contemporaneous Eastern Europe.
3 The union with Germany was pragmatic: Finns might have had grave reservations about the Nazis, says Silvennoinen (cited in Gilmour and Stephenson 2013, 134), but they also saw Germany as a vital counterweight to increasing Soviet power. It is also worth pointing out that, despite widespread and vocal sympathy for Finland during the previous war (ibid., 135), tangible military help from the Allies had failed to materialize.

4 Allison (1985, 1–2) agrees that the prominence of the term in the late 1960s was related to Brandt's new role as Chancellor of West Germany.
5 See, for instance, Gleason 1995.
6 Finland is not the only country to have bordered the Soviet Union or the Eastern Bloc, yet it was in Finland that this infectiousness was particularly profound. The country's historical relationship with Russia is unique in the region, due to several factors: its former protectorate status under Russia; the fact that, despite the Soviet invasion, Finland, alone in the Baltic sphere, was never Sovietized; and its direct adjacency to Russia. True, Norway also shares a border with Russia but it is very short and in the far north, whereas the Russo-Finnish border is 1300 kilometres long and in part metropolitan.
7 The Americans tended to see jazz as a cultural weapon, so it was employed in Willis Conover's show on Voice of America (von Eschen 2004, 13, 18) and in State Department-endorsed international tours by Dizzy Gillespie, Benny Goodman, Louis Armstrong, Duke Ellington and Dave Brubeck (Crist 2009, 133). In fact, it was depicted as a musical expression of the principles of American democracy (ibid., 138), notwithstanding the paradox that the US government was sending African Americans abroad to perform music that was fundamentally associated with their culture at a time when Jim Crow laws were still in place at home (ibid., 149; Cohen 2011, 305; Pickhan and Ritter 2010, 26; von Eschen 2004, 4; Davenport 2009, 5).
8 If jazz presented a dilemma to all totalitarian states, that dilemma can rarely have been more starkly expressed than in the Soviet Union. The music was indisputably American, but it was the music of *African* Americans, and as such could be seen to represent *both* the corpulent bourgeoisie and the oppressed proletariat. This contradiction resulted, at times, in the division of the music into two camps: a bourgeois salon jazz and an 'authentic' proletarian jazz (Lücke 2007, 4; Starr 1994, 79–99, 103; Pickhan and Ritter 2010, 87).
9 Austerlitz (2005, 143), meanwhile, offers an opposing view – that Finnish musicians defined themselves in opposition to Soviet (rather than American) influence. The cultural baggage carried by jazz – as modern, urban, African American and democratic – might, in other words, have been a key part of its appeal in an era of bureaucratic, hierarchical and regulated cultural politics.
10 Kekkonen began to assert that Finland was pursuing an active policy of neutrality in the late 1960s, with the supreme moment coming in 1975 when he hosted the Conference for Security and Cooperation in Europe and its Final Act in Helsinki. He used this conference to stress that Finland's active neutrality was entirely in accord with the principles of national sovereignty and independence – a point aimed primarily eastwards, since Moscow had been reluctant to recognize Finland as neutral (Meinander 2011, 181–184). Lavery (2006, 142) calls the conference 'Kekkonen's most lasting achievement'. Hosting a prominent international conference might seem to contradict the insularity that I suggest characterized this period, but it could equally be seen as part of Kekkonen's 'balancing act' (Meinander 2011, 167) during this ambiguous and complex era.

References

ACT. N.d. 'Iiro Rantala'. Available at: www.actmusic.com/en/Artists/Iiro-Rantala (accessed 10 November 2014).

Ake, David. 2010. *Jazz Matters: Sound, Place and Time since Bebop*. Berkeley, Los Angeles and London: University of California Press.

Allison, Roy. 1985. *Finland's Relations with the Soviet Union 1944–84*. London and Basingstoke: Macmillan.

152 Marcus O'Dair

Anderson, Benedict. 2006. *Imaged Communities: Reflections on the Origin and Spread of Nationalism*. London and New York: Verso.

Austerlitz, Paul. 2000. 'Birch-Bark Horns and Jazz in the National Imagination: The Finnish Folk Music Vogue in Historical Perspective'. *Ethnomusicology* 44(2): 183–213.

Austerlitz, Paul. 2005. *Jazz Consciousness: Music, Race and Humanity*. Middleton, WI: Wesleyan.

Biddle, Ian and Vanessa Knights. 2007. *Music, National Identity and the Politics of Location*. Farnham and Burlington, VT: Ashgate.

Chela, Carina. 2013. 'Don't Mess with Finnish Jazz'. Available at: http://finland.fi/Public/default.aspx?contentid=277074&nodeid=37598&culture=en-US (accessed 11 February 2015).

Cohen, Harvey. 2011. 'Visions of Freedom: Duke Ellington in the Soviet Union'. *Popular Music* 30: 297–313.

Crist, Stephan. 2009. 'Jazz as Democracy? Dave Brubeck and Cold War Politics'. *Journal of Musicology* 26: 133–174.

Dallin, Alexander and George Breslauer. 1970. *Political Terror in Communist Systems*. Stanford, CA: Stanford University Press. Davenport, Lisa. 2009. *Jazz Diplomacy: Promoting America in the Cold War Era*. Jackson: University Press of Mississippi.

Fingerroos, Outi. 2008. 'Karelia: A Place of Memories and Utopias'. *Oral Tradition* 23(2): 235–254.

'Finnish Jazz. Interview. Markku Ounaskari'. 2011. Jazz Convention, 18 March. Available at: www.jazzconvention.net/index.php?option=com_content&view=article&id=796:finnish-jazz-interview-markku-ounaskari&catid=1:articoli&Itemid=10 (accessed 8 February 2015).

Fordham, John. 2011. 'Verneri Pohjola: Aurora Review'. *Guardian*, 17 February. Available at: www.theguardian.com/music/2011/feb/17/verneri-pohjola-aurora-cd-review (accessed 08 February 2015).

Gilmour, John and Jill Stephenson. 2013. *Hitler's Scandinavian Legacy*. London: Bloomsbury.

Gleason, Abbott. 1995. *Totalitarianism: The Inner History of the Cold War*. New York and Oxford: Oxford University Press.

Gronow, Pekka. 1973. 'Popular Music in Finland: A Preliminary Survey'. *Ethnomusicology* 17: 52–71.

Gronow, Pekka. 1995. 'The Record Industry in Finland 1945–1960'. *Popular Music* 14: 33–53.

Haavisto, Jukka. 1996. *Seven Decades of Finnish Jazz: Jazz in Finland 1919–1969*. Helsinki: Finnish Music Information Centre.

Howell, Tim. 2006. *After Sibelius: Studies in Finnish Music*. Farnham and Burlington, VT: Ashgate.

Ikonen, Kari. N.d. 'Trio Toffa'. Available at: www.kariikonen.com/bandsprojects/trio-toffa/ (accessed 10 November 2014).

Johnson, Bruce. 2002. 'The Jazz Diaspora'. In Mervyn Cooke and David Horn, eds, *The Cambridge Companion to Jazz*. Cambridge: Cambridge University Press: 33–54.

Johnson, Phil. 1993. 'The Cold Dark Knight of the Soul'. *Independent*, 9 November. Available at: www.independent.co.uk/arts-entertainment/jazz—the-cold-dark-knight-of-the-soul-edward-vesala-finlands-jazz-maverick-rages-at-the-world-and-smashes-stereotypes-phil-johnson-ducked-for-cover-1503113.html (accessed 10 November 2014).

Kaarresalo-Kasari, Eila and Heikki Kasari. 2010. 'Finnish Jazz'. *Scandinavian Review* July: 6–18.

Kallioniemi, Kari and Kimi Kärki. 2009. '*The Kalevala*, Popular Music and National Culture'. *Journal of Finnish Studies* 13: 61–72.

Kivimäki, Ville. 2012. 'Between Defeat and Victory: Finnish Memory Culture of the Second World War'. *Scandinavian Journal of History* 37: 482–504.

Konttinen, Matti. 1987. 'The Jazz Invasion' (translated by Susan Sinisalo). *Finnish Music Quarterly* 3–4: 21–26.

Langhoff, Josh. 2011. 'Innanen, Mikko Innanen & Innkvisitio: Clustrophy'. *Pop Matters*. Available at: www.popmatters.com/review/151320-mikko-innanen-innkvisitio-clustrophy (accessed 10 November 2014).

Lavery, Jason. 2006. *The History of Finland*. London and Westport, CT: Greenwood Press.

Lindsay, Bruce. 2013. 'Alexi Tuomarila: From Helsinki to Timbuktu'. *All about Jazz*. Available at: www.allaboutjazz.com/alexi-tuomarila-from-helsinki-to-timbuktu-alexi-tuomarila-by-bruce-lindsay.php?&pg=2#.VE5iVkKGs20 (accessed 10 November 2014).

Lücke, Martin. 2007. 'Vilified, Venerated, Forbidden: Jazz in the Stalinist Era' (translated by Anita Ip). *Music and Politics* 1: 1–9.

McClenaghan, Dan. 2014. 'Juhani Aaltonen: To Future Memories'. *All about Jazz*. Available at: www.allaboutjazz.com/to-future-memories-juhani-aaltonen-tum-records-review-by-dan-mcclenaghan.php#.VE4yAUKGs20 (accessed 10 November 2014).

Mäkelä, Janne. 2012. 'Nordic Jazz: A Historical Overview'. Paper presented at the Nordic Jazz Research Conference, Stockholm, August. Available at: http://carkiv.musikverk.se/www/epublikationer/Online_publ_Jazz_Gender_Authenticity.pdf (accessed 10 November 2014).

Meinander, Henrik. 2011. *A History of Finland*. London: Hurst and Company.

Nicholson, Stuart. 2005. *Is Jazz Dead? Or Has it Moved to a New Address?* New York and London: Routledge.

Nives, Matti. 2012. 'Q&A with Mikko Innanen'. *Music Finland*. Available at: http://musicfinland.fi/en/in-the-spotlight/2012/9/qa-with-mikko-innanen (accessed 10 November 2014).

O'Connell, John and Salwa El-Shawan Castelo-Branco, eds. 2010. *Music and Conflict*. Urbana and Springfield: University of Illinois Press.

Pickhan, Gertrud and Rüdiger Ritter. 2010. *Jazz behind the Iron Curtain*. Frankfurt am Main: Peter Lang.

Reimann, Heli. 2012. 'Down with Bebop – Viva Swing! Swing Club and the Meaning of Jazz in Late 1940s Estonia'. *Jazz Research Journal* 4: 95–121.

Shaw, Anthony. 2005. 'Raoul Björkenheim: Guitarist between Two Continents'. *All about Jazz*. Available at: www.allaboutjazz.com/raoul-bjorkenheim-guitarist-between-two-continents-raoul-bjorkenheim-by-anthony-shaw (accessed 10 November 2014).

Silas, Petri. 2014. 'What's Next for Nordic Jazz?' *Finnish Music Quarterly*. Available at: www.fmq.fi/2014/03/whats-next-for-nordic-jazz/(accessed 10 November 2014).

Singleton, Fred. 1981. 'The Myth of "Finlandisation"'. *International Affairs* 47: 270-285.

Starr, S. Frederick. 1994. *Red and Hot: The Fate of Jazz in the Soviet Union*. New York: Limelight.

Stenger, Wif. 2014. 'Finnish Jazz Opens to Europe and Beyond'. *This Is Finland*. Available at: http://finland.fi/Public/default.aspx?contentid=312298 (accessed 10 November 2014).

Stenius, Henrik, Mirja Österberg and Johan Östling, eds. 2011. *Nordic Narratives of the Second World War*. Lund: Nordic Academic Press.

Stites, Richard. 1992. *Russian Popular Culture: Entertainment and Society since 1900*. Cambridge: Cambridge University Press.

von Eschen, Penny. 2004. *Satchmo Blows up the World*. Cambridge, MA, and London: Harvard University Press.

Woodard, Josef. N.d. 'Quotes'. Available at: www.mikkoinnanen.com/quotes.html (accessed 10 March 2016).

PART III
Iberia – Spain

7

PERFORMING THE 'ANTI-SPANISH' BODY

Jazz and Biopolitics in the Early Franco Regime (1939–1957)

Iván Iglesias

Through the study of censorship, legislation, the press, recordings and photographs, this chapter examines jazz as symbolic reference and musical practice in Franco's Spain and argues that it played a contestatory role during the so-called 'early Francoism' period (1939–1957). The dictatorship that General Franco established after the Spanish Civil War intensively and systematically used culture and music as propaganda to define its image and shape public opinion. By its connotations and active presence, jazz became one of the main negative references of the new regime against which to define Spanish race and music under the precepts of nationalism, Catholicism and fascism.

When the course of the Second World War threatened the authority of the Franco regime and its international position from 1944, the positive references to American music in the media served as examples of the tolerance, renovation and pro-Allies orientation of the dictatorship. As such, it is difficult to find an explicit official condemnation of jazz in Spain after 1945. Nevertheless, jazz dancing continued to be a subversive practice under the Franco regime until the mid-1950s. That subversion was not an intellectual and rational political gesture, but rather a challenge to Francoist biopolitics, the official precepts on morality and the body. Swing and boogie-woogie were directly linked to physical pleasure and corporeal liberation, opposed to the stoicism and restraint promoted by the regime's moral authorities. Consequently, the dictatorship tried to impose continuous constraints on jazz through recreational and fiscal policies, which remained active even after the official discourse about American music changed in the mid-1940s.

Introduction

General Franco's victory in the Spanish Civil War, in April 1939, provided his dictatorship with the legitimacy to tackle the construction of Spanish identity

158 Iván Iglesias

under the precepts of tradition, nationalism, Catholicism and fascism. Germany and Italy's support for the nationalist forces during the conflict and Axis victories in the first years of the Second World War encouraged the dictatorship's identification with fascism. Through the various organizations of the Vicesecretaría de Educación Popular (Vice-Secretariat of Popular Education), administered by the only legal party, Falange, the dictatorship exercised very tight control over the press, radio and theatre. It demanded personal reports, enforced censorship, and sent regular warnings and instructions (Pérez Zalduondo 2011). Music occupied a prominent place in the articulation of the new Spanish identity, as an integral part of the Spanish culture and race and as a means of information and persuasion. By its connotations and active presence, jazz became one of the main negative references of the new regime against which to define Spanish race and music (Iglesias 2010; 2013).

However, at the end of the Second World War, Spain was isolated by the Allies on account of its previous commitment to the Axis powers. This led the Franco regime to cultivate more fluid relations with Western countries, which brought about changes in cultural policy in an attempt to portray Spain as a tolerant, renewed and pro-American country. The media began a propaganda campaign aimed at presenting Franco as a great ally of the West (and especially of the United States) in its new struggle against communism (Viñas 2003). After 1945, the official attitude towards American culture shifted completely, and Franco's cultural authorities and media started permitting and even promoting jazz. The dictatorship also tolerated the reappearance of the Hot Clubs of Barcelona, Valencia and Madrid, permitted jazz-specific publications (such as *Ritmo y melodía*), and even allowed American popular music to become the major topic of the leading music magazine of the time, *Ritmo* (Iglesias 2010; see also Chapter 8, this volume). This was not due to a relaxation of censorship, because, as Elisa Chuliá (2001, 32) has remarked, the implementation phase of the Francoist press did not end until 1948. (See also Chapter 8, this volume; while Pedro's primary focus is on music genre differentiation, my interest here is biopolitics, and in particular jazz dance.)

Jazz is usually seen as an inherently subversive music, positioned against state repression, especially in studies on the Nazi dictatorship (Snowball 2002; Zwerin 1985). However, in the case of the Franco regime, it is difficult to find an explicit official condemnation of jazz after 1945, once the dictatorship had started its process of de-fascistization and launched its pro-American propaganda. Nevertheless, those who lived under the regime remembered dancing to jazz in the 1940s and the 1950s as a dissident practice. Hence, this chapter argues that jazz played an important subversive role in the so-called 'early Francoism' era (1939–1957). However, that rebellion was not an intellectual and rational political gesture, but a challenge to Francoist biopolitics – that is, the regime's official precepts about the body. The dictatorship carried out diverse practices of exclusion, correction, disciplining and normalization of corporeal movements and gestures. This biopolitics was the domain where the Franco regime achieved its most complete form of totalitarianism, and where the main Francoist political 'families' or 'communities of discourse' (the army, the Catholic Church and fascism) converged and agreed. Until the late 1950s, jazz was a form of dance music in Spain; and, by its connotations and practices of consumption, it represented a serious threat to the dictatorship biopolitics.

Defining the Franco Regime

It is extremely difficult to classify the Franco dictatorship as a totalitarian regime, for it never attempted to control the entire economy and all of Spain's social, cultural and religious institutions (see Payne 1987, 626; and Chapter 8, this volume). Moreover, the survival of the Spanish dictatorship for almost forty years and its continuous political adaptations make linking it to a single and unequivocal system of government, such as totalitarianism, problematic. But maybe we are missing the point in trying to accommodate every dictatorship to a theoretical concept that historians specifically apply to Nazism and Stalinism. Within this framework, discussion has been limited to whether or not a regime is indeed totalitarian, or how totalitarian it is.

A second option would be to define the Spanish dictatorship as 'fascist', since the similarities between Mussolini's system and the early Franco regime are undeniable (Payne 1999; Saz 2004; Gallego 2014). However, the long duration and mutability of Francoism are problematic again, because the regime underwent a clear process of de-fascistization between 1943 and 1957. Furthermore, even in its first five years, the Spanish dictatorship lacked much of the political modernism and mobilizing populism that tend to characterize fascist regimes (Gentile 2002; Griffin 2007). Franco did not aspire to any form of social transformation, and he did not associate nation with the people but with its historical institutions: the Church, the army and the monarchy (Saz 2013, 16).

If the Franco regime was neither totalitarian nor fascist, could it be described as authoritarian? Juan José Linz formulated such a theory forty years ago, and since then it has enjoyed a degree of support in many academic circles (Linz 1964; 2000). But this static concept does not define the dictatorship beyond situating it somewhere between totalitarianism and democracy, and therefore assessing it as somewhat 'better' than the former. The same might be said of Javier Tussell's (1988, 88) classification of the Franco regime as a 'non-totalitarian dictatorship'. Additionally, both labels were used by the Francoist authorities themselves (and continue to be invoked by conservatives in Spain) in order to portray the regime as a soft and quasi-paternalistic system.[1] Two radically different Spanish dictatorships – Primo de Rivera's and Franco's – are frequently grouped under the single umbrella of 'authoritarianism', which only serves to highlight the limitations of Linz's theory.

160 Iván Iglesias

References to ideal types, privileged by comparative sociology, can be useful in some contexts, but they tell us little about the specific features of a regime and can even occlude its changes. More than conceptualizing the Spanish dictatorship as a totalitarian, fascist or authoritarian apparatus, I am interested in its dynamics and its effective articulation of power. The Franco regime was a reactionary nationalist dictatorship with deep Catholic roots and a strong element of anti-communism throughout its history. It underwent a period of fascistization in its early stage, but this was gradually reversed during the Cold War out of diplomatic necessity. This particular combination explains the adaptability and durability of the Franco dictatorship, but also many of the music processes I will examine later. On the other hand, it also illuminates some of the reasons for the contradictory reception that the Franco regime accorded to jazz.

Francoism and Biopolitics

The term 'biopolitics' was coined more than a century ago and has been used in different periods with racist, naturalist and ecological connotations (Lemke 2007, 19–46). The specific concept I employ here was developed by Michel Foucault in a series of articles and books published between 1976 and the early 1980s. According to him, the main aim of most Western governments since the late eighteenth century has been the administration and regulation of behaviours, the control of mind and body, in order to achieve the general acceptance of the legal, moral and productive norms imposed by society as a means of ensuring life and coexistence. Biopolitics, which assumes the responsibility and control of the vital processes and bodily discipline, is exerted by diverse official institutions such as the school, the prison, the army and/or the psychiatric hospital (Foucault 1978; 2003).

Recently, numerous thinkers, including Giorgio Agamben (1998), Mitchell Dean (1999), Roberto Esposito (2008), Michael Hardt and Antonio Negri (2000; 2004; 2009), and Nikolas Rose (2007), have paid special attention to biopolitics or, in some cases, have centralized it in their reflections and studies on the relations between state and society. An analysis of biopolitics can bring together social spheres that are usually separated, like race, gender, sexuality and political consciousness. In Spain, the biopolitical approach has been particularly fruitful in its application to the Franco government: Javier Ugarte (2008, 49–78) integrated it in his study of homosexuality during the dictatorship; Salvador Cayuela (2009) used it to explain the political immobilization in the early years of the regime; and Anna Pelka (2014, 23–42) applied it to analyse the concept of femininity in postwar Spain.

Biopolitics has aroused the curiosity of some music scholars in recent times (e.g. Mueller 2014), although it has not yet been extensively deployed in popular music studies. However, this concept can clarify some effects of music that are particularly obscure or difficult to isolate or systematize, such as those that are related to the body in a broad sense. Beyond textual and performative approaches, we lack the tools to help us explain the violent rejection and the deep anxiety generated by various dances in both democratic and authoritarian governments throughout the twentieth century. In this sense, biopolitics can highlight some aspects of the relation between dance and different forms of domination and subversion, as well as the bonds between music, body and memory.

In totalitarian states, claimed Foucault (2003, 221–222), the ancient right to kill and the new disciplinary power over life are combined to create a highly efficient government that completely invades vital processes. In the case of early Francoism, the new regime achieved institutional stability and political hegemony through strict physical and psychological repression (Anderson 2009; Rodrigo 2008; Vega-Sombría 2012). Purges, summary judgements and executions destroyed the last resistance and served as warnings to the people. Along with the memories of war, economic shortages and the difficult living conditions, this policy of terror made any explicit subversion impossible. Moreover, the regime started an acculturation and indoctrination process carried out by various educational and political institutions, and a strict supervision of cultural discourses and practices through censorship. As Francisco Vázquez-García (2009, 16–17) has pointed out, 1939 marked the transition from an interventionist to a totalitarian biopolitics in Spain, characterized by an extremely disciplinary state.

This rigid control was linked, first, to the fascist ideology of the single party, Falange; second, to the military authority and regulation; and, third, to the Catholic precepts and the substantial unity of body and soul supported by the Thomist tradition, the dictatorship's official philosophical doctrine (Heredia-Soriano 1978). When the Spanish Civil War ended, Francoist psychiatry provided biological justifications to 'prove' the strength of Spaniards and some sports programmes to refine the Spanish race (Rodríguez de Alarcón 1940). The official psychiatry also presented 'scientific demonstrations' that communists and Masons were mentally ill and exhibited seditious and anti-Spanish tendencies that justified their violent repression (González-Duro 2008). Black people were also considered inferior, particularly in the context of Spain's North African colonies (Beato-González and Villarino-Ulloa 1944). In this sense, Francoist biopolitics was not too far removed from Nazi thanato-politics, which understood the German people as a sick body in need of the extirpation of those parts that contributed to its racial, moral and spiritual degeneration (Esposito 2008, 128).

The dictatorship focused on this control of the body in youth as the most important stage of life, the phase when ideological and moral values are established. Youth socialization was soon regulated under the influence of the Church, with José Ibáñez Martín serving as Minister of National Education between 1939 and 1951, and Falange, which imitated the mechanisms of the

162 Iván Iglesias

fascist regimes it admired. Three institutions formed the backbone for the instruction of the new generations: the Sección Femenina (Women's Section), which became an official institution in 1937 and was in charge of a compulsory 'social service' for all unmarried woman between seventeen and thirty-five; the Sindicato Español Universitario (University Students Union; 1939), the only legal student organization; and the voluntary Frente de Juventudes (Youth Front; 1940), whose patriotic goal was cultural training and political indoctrination (Payne 1999, 32). Through them, individuals were corrected, guided, and submitted to strict discipline and correct behaviour.

Jazz as Dance and Popular Music in Spain

During its two first decades of government, the Franco regime had to deal with jazz as a set of social dances, due to particular conditions of reception. Jazz had appeared in Spain between late 1919 and early 1920 as an exclusive dance music in the leading hotels and casinos of Madrid, Barcelona and San Sebastián. During Miguel Primo de Rivera's dictatorship (1923–1930), it spread extensively into musical theatre and cinema, helped by the enthusiastic reception for the Charleston and the success of Sam Wooding's, Josephine Baker's and Jack Hylton's performances. The democratic Second Republic (1931–1936) was when jazz established itself in Spain, particularly in Barcelona, where the large and select Hot Club was founded in May 1935, and the prestigious *Jazz Magazine* was published from August 1935 (see Chapters 8 and 9, this volume).

Contrary to what several historians of jazz in Spain have written (García-Martínez 1996, 121; Pujol-Baulenas 2005, 47), jazz did not undergo a particularly significant decline during the Civil War of 1936–1939. It was not suppressed by either side, and its forms and styles were not remarkably altered by the conflict. But the war did transform the spaces and audiences for jazz in Spain: in a context of populist exaltation, a desperate need for entertainment and a severe economic crisis, it was used extensively and strategically by both sides in their competing mass rhetorics. In fact, during the first post-Civil War months, theatres and cinemas presented jazz shows and films to avoid bankruptcy. The Spanish Civil War thus witnessed a quantitative growth of jazz fans in the big cities.

During the 1940s and the 1950s, jazz continued as a popular dance music in Spain, mainly in the forms of swing and boogie-woogie. In the postwar era, most Spaniards still associated jazz with Paul Whiteman, Jack Hylton, Benny Goodman, Duke Ellington and Glenn Miller, but also with Jerome Kern, Cole Porter, Harry Warren and Irving Berlin, and even with actors and dancers such as Fred Astaire, Ginger Rogers, Judy Garland and Dick Powell. This notion of jazz as a physical entertainment, not as an aesthetic contemplation, was also a consequence of the shortage of record players during the Franco regime's first two first decades, which meant that enjoyment of jazz was mostly linked to radio broadcasts and the dance halls.

American cinema became a major vehicle for jazz dissemination after 1943, when Falange's control of the media was progressively relaxed and the authorities abandoned their attempt to exclude Hollywood movies from the domestic film market (Díez-Puertas 2003; León-Aguinaga 2010). The contradictory nature of jazz censorship contributed to this diffusion: on paper, it was radical and inflexible; in practice, its effectiveness depended on many circumstances, as well as the people involved and the participation of various political families in the process (see Chapter 8, this volume). Many of these incongruities were due to the diverse interests of each of the Francoist social pillars, and the difficulties they encountered when trying to decide what to ban. The Church was particularly worried about decorum, whereas Falangists were more concerned about the American origins and racial connotations of jazz (Iglesias 2012).

Only movies with a conventional plot came under the scrutiny of the Junta de Censura (Board of Censorship). Therefore, musical documentaries that contained nothing but a series of jazz performances, such as *Música de hot* (1941), escaped the censors.[2] Sometimes, a film was approved after revision of the plot, the script or the associated songs, but some sections could still be cut from the finished product. And even then each movie was at the mercy of the local critics, who watched it in a private screening and sent their reports to the Vicesecretaría de Educación Popular, the Ministry of Propaganda. Some songs were suppressed because an ecclesiastical member of the Junta de Censura considered them 'indecorous' or 'pornographic'. Even in these cases, however, the cut song could be distributed with a sound recording of the film's music, because record censorship was not systematized until the 1960s. Moreover, it could still be played on the radio, because while both the Cinematographic Department and the Broadcasting Department came under the auspices of Falange, they acted independently and did not maintain direct contact with each other (Iglesias 2012).

In Spain, most people identified one dance with swing music: the lindy hop or jitterbug, an African-American dance that was standardized by 1927 at the Savoy Ballroom in Harlem (Hubbard and Monaghan 2009). In contrast to earlier ragtime dances or the Charleston, swing made use of four beats per measure and accelerated the tempo. Its dancers combined individual and couple formations, continuously moving with their knees bent and their bodies slightly inclined, to facilitate improvisation and frequent spins, jumps and acrobatics. The lindy hop's difficulty and the skills it demanded engendered growing specialization among Spanish dancers, who looked to swing's regular appearances in American films for their inspiration. The most famous dance hall in Spain was the Salon Amaya, opened in Barcelona in April 1943.

Young women, both as performers and as audiences, were fundamental agents for the reception of swing in Spain. The feminine presence was pervasive in the jazz shows and orchestras of the leading cities. There were all-woman orchestras, such as Soro and his Girls, Trudi Bora and Melody Stars, and famous trios, such as the Arveu Sisters and the Russell Sisters. Many singers, including Carmelita Aubert, Elsie Bayron, Rina Celi, Katia Morlands, Mari Merche, Francis Ramírez and Lolita Garrido, even transcended local boundaries to become national stars. The name 'swing girl' or 'hot girl' was applied to women who were defined by their 'modernity' or 'frivolity' and were enthusiastic about American dances, stylish clothing and smoking (Vila San-Juan 1948).

The dance that progressively superseded swing from the late 1940s, boogie-woogie, did not moderate its body language. It was a fast blues style that appeared in the South of the United States in the 1920s and had spread around the world by 1941. Boogie-woogie was first heard in Spain in the 1930s, but the dance did not become popular there until 1944. However, it enjoyed enormous popularity during the second half of the 1940s and the early 1950s, with most jazz orchestras, dance contests and academies adopting it (Iglesias 2010). Boogie-woogie maintained swing's continuous horizontal movement and improvisation, with frequent spins and contortions.

The performances by some American jazz musicians in Spain during the 1950s produced many instances of 'collective hysteria', vividly detailed by the media. The descriptions of these uncategorizable acts, more or less exaggerated, are a good indication of the excitement and sense of liberation that American popular music could engender even before the dissemination of rock and roll. Lionel Hampton was one of the musicians who best illustrated this trend, incorporating swing, boogie-woogie and Latin rhythms in his numerous shows, which combined intensely dedicated performers, large spaces, dance and visual entertainment. On 14 and 15 March 1956, Hampton gave two concerts in Madrid, financed by the US Embassy in an explicit example of American cultural diplomacy (Iglesias 2011). The well-known critic Antonio Fernández-Cid described the show as 'amazing, on the edge of madness, approaching hysteria and epilepsy. The circle of the Carlos III Theatre seemed about to collapse from moment to moment' (Fernández-Cid 1956).[3] Another critic, José Gómez-Figueroa, wrote:

> Yesterday, thousands of spectators kicked the floor as if they were possessed by a sudden madness. They jumped, shouted, uttered real jungle battle-cries. What was happening? Madrid listened to perhaps the best jazz orchestra that performs around the world: Lionel Hampton's. It performed at the Carlos III Theatre yesterday, and the audience filled the hall. Some teenagers pulled up their hair, and more than fifty ladies who were in the front row of the nosebleed section began a tremendous uproar. They leaned so far over the railing that I thought they were going to kill themselves.
>
> (Gómez-Figueroa 1956)

Jazz in the Biopolitics of Early Francoism

In practice, the attitude of the Franco regime towards jazz ranged from condemning it as degenerate music, through toleration once its economic value was appreciated, to its naturalization as mass entertainment, as happened in other dictatorships in the same era (Cerchiari 2003; Kater 1992; Lücke 2004; Starr 1983). However, the Francoist invective against jazz displayed serious concern for the body. The aforementioned connotations of jazz as a somatic experience of African-American origin associated with mass culture turned it into a common enemy for Falange, the army and the Church. By mid-1942, at the height of the enthusiasm for fascism, the Falangist Vice-Secretariat of Popular Education banned the broadcasting of 'so-called black music, swing dances, or any other kind of compositions whose lyrics are in a foreign language, can erode public moral or the most elementary good taste'.[4] Jazz was vilified not only as a genre in itself, but also as a source of hybridization: in August 1942, the National Spectacle Union banned the live performance of works from the classical repertoire by jazz and dance bands, and a month later it extended the prohibition to recordings and movies (Martínez del Fresno 2001). A letter that Falange circulated to all of the radio stations in 1943 pointed out that one of the main worries of the new regime was:

> The development of the so-called 'black music', . . . the arbitrary, antimusical, and anti-human jazz wave with which America has invaded Europe for years. Nothing further from our virile racial characteristics than those dead, cloying, decadent and monotonous melodies, which, like a cry of impotence, soften and feminize the soul, stupefying it in a sickly lassitude. Nothing further from our spiritual dignity than those dislocated and unbalanced dances, in which the human quality of attitude, the selected correctness of gesture, falls to a ridiculous contortionism.[5]

Thus, concerns about the purity of the 'race' coincided with the battle against foreign enemies, joining biopolitical and geopolitical considerations, just as happened in the Nazi Reich (Lemke 2011, 13). On the other hand, the concept of 'Spanish race' also incorporated religion as one of its core elements. Catholicism was conceived as integral to the Spanish nation throughout its history, as a unifying spirit (see also Chapter 8, this volume). Traditionalist musicographers and music critics warned of the dangers of those 'exotic black dances, the products of the American jungles', which were 'collected and exported by Masons and anti-Catholics' and 'should be eliminated without mercy' (quoted in Iglesias 2010, 125–126). The Catholic media said that jazz was a 'savage' and 'pagan' invention that entailed 'a satanic malice', with enthusiasts who were devoted to a perverse hedonism in which 'life was squandered in orgies' (Ruiz-Encina 1944). This worry about jazz was so deep-seated that

FIGURE 7.1 Modern Dances: Youngsters . . . Have Fun in Another Way

ultra-Catholics even distributed posters that condemned modern dances in the 1940s (see Figure 7.1.).

Both swing and boogie-woogie were contrary to the stoicism and restraint promoted by Francoist biopolitics, the official precepts on morals and the body. Many attacks were based on an association between mass culture and women. One of the most influential writers among those attached to the regime, José María Pemán, defined the feminine nature in a book published in 1947. Under the clear inspiration of Mussolini's social precepts, Pemán explained women's qualities as complementary to men's: man is intellectual, analytical and idealistic; woman is instinctive, elementary and materialist; man is creative and rational; woman is prone to mimesis and lacks reasoning ability and abstract thought. Therefore, woman must accept her subordinate condition selflessly (Pemán 1947). Of course, these ideas were not new. As Larry Shiner (2001) has argued, the denial of feminine creativity was part of the configuration of genius and the distinction between art and craft as early as the eighteenth century. The Franco regime merely made this stark binarism official doctrine.

Swing dancing was thought to emasculate men and masculinize women; moreover, women's participation in popular culture was a great nuisance for a dictatorship that wanted to keep them at home as the axis of the Catholic family (Graham 1995). In fact, dancing halls, cabarets and jazz music were all associated with the 'ultra-modern' woman – emblem of the 'anti-feminine' and accused of promoting foreign customs (Pelka 2014, 28). The 'correct' female dances were rhythmic exercises performed to national songs in massive displays, reminiscent of the routines at the Nuremberg rallies. These physical activities were adapted to the Church's axioms to avoid gestural eccentricities and extravagant displays of the female body (Richmond 2003, 25).

The influential idea that, until the end of the 1950s at least, the Franco regime banned black American music but allowed Afro-Cuban and Latin American dances because the latter were supposedly elements of the Hispanic imperial tradition (Labanyi 1995, 210) has some merit, but it is incomplete. The American origins of jazz undoubtedly played an important role in its reception in postwar Spain (Iglesias 2010), and Latin America was one of the main targets of Francoist propaganda (Delgado 1992; Pardo-Sanz 1995). However, this geostrategic explanation is based on the implausible belief that Spanish audiences and the Francoist authorities could distinguish between African–American music and its Latin American counterparts. A simple analysis of scores and recordings reveals that, from 1939 until 1957, US music and Caribbean music were performed by the same ensembles in the same spaces, and they appeared in the same publications and on the same records. Moreover, Spanish songwriters, including Luis Araque, Juan Durán-Alemany, Cástor Vilá, Augusto Algueró and Facundo Rivero, were familiar with such words as 'fox-rumba' and 'son-fox'.

The corporeality of jazz caused the Franco regime to attempt to impose sustained impediments to jazz and modern dancing through both recreational and fiscal policies. The dictatorship established that all of the halls that were dedicated to these dances were linked to luxury consumption and imposed specific fiscal constraints on them from the beginning of the regime. For instance, two legal orders of April 1941 and February 1942 stipulated that the entrance fees for cabarets and dance halls were taxed at 50 per cent; those for movie theatres at 30 per cent; and those for sports events at 15 per cent. By

168 Iván Iglesias

contrast, opera, zarzuela, theatre, variety performances and circus were all tax-exempt.[6] These fiscal restrictions remained in place even after the official discourse about American music changed in the mid-1940s, because they had no detrimental impact on the regime's international relations. In fact, in May 1946, the regime increased the tax on cabarets' and dance halls' entrance fees to 60 per cent. Meanwhile, the theatres and concert halls retained their tax-exempt status.[7]

A similar pattern is evident in the diatribes against jazz dances and their body movements, which persisted in some Catholic publications. As we have seen, jazz was associated during the early Francoist era with physical excitement and even with a transitory mental derangement that threatened public safety. Although, as I have pointed out, the official discourse on jazz changed from the mid-1940s for diplomatic reasons, criticism of modern American dances continued to appear in the leading ecclesiastical magazines, such as *Ecclesia*, until the mid-1950s. The Church's aim was to defend Spanish traditional dances and to anathematize 'Negroid music' as 'orgiastic' and 'obscene' practices that turned respectable people into 'uncontrolled animals' ('Selección de discos' 1949). Applying the same argument, the board of directors of the Palau de la Música, Barcelona, refused to hold 'musical activities that had some relation with jazz music' for many years from the mid-forties onwards (Castellá 1950, 21). Even the proposed visit of such a distinguished performer as the trumpeter Buck Clayton was blocked.

These attitudes gradually changed from 1957, due to a convergence of political, ideological, socio-economic and musical factors. On the one hand, Franco's successive modifications of the government to deal with the political crisis, the nation's near bankruptcy and growing social unrest meant the definitive relegation of the Falangist project and autarky, as well as the undermining of the national-Catholic hegemony, in favour of a conservative technocracy, economic liberalization and moderate cultural *aperturismo* (Molinero and Ysàs 2008, 18–46). At the same time, 'modern' jazz, led by the pianist Tete Montoliu, found ready acceptance in Spain as a set of styles that privileged the intellectual over the sentimental, contemplation over dance, mind over body. This new concept of 'authentic' jazz was constructed in opposition to new music genres such as rock and roll, twist and beat, as well as previous jazz styles. And this conceptualization resulted in a new appraisal of jazz in Spain as an autonomous art, written retrospectively to rid its history of its popular and dance forms (Iglesias forthcoming).

Conclusion

Jazz was an active mediator in the construction and negotiation of the new Spanish identity shaped and promoted by the Franco regime from 1939. Propaganda, economic interests, social demobilization, racism, sexuality and gender questions are essential to understand the discourses and the censorship policies of jazz during early Francoism, but none of them alone can explain the importance of this music as a negative referent for the diverse factions of the dictatorship. In order to explain this reaction we also have to examine an issue that integrates many of these factors as mediations of power: the control of vital processes and the discipline of the body, the sphere in which the Franco regime reached its most definite expression of totalitarianism.

In Spain during the 1940s and 1950s, jazz was still a form of dance music that conveyed the subversion of the corporeal sobriety and gestural correctness claimed by Francoist biopolitics. It was an important means of escapism in a country dominated by the effects of economic autarky, political repression and physical and ideological inhibition. In this sense, it represented a common challenge to the moral, sexual and racial precepts of Falange, the Catholic Church and the army, the main ideological 'families' of the regime. The notion of dance as a liberation of the body was not a creation of rock and roll and late 1950s youth. In fact, swing and boogie-woogie stimulated Francoist discourses and censorship criteria that were later applied to the twist and rock.

By focusing on the body, this article foregrounds the relevance of dance practices to the analysis of cultural politics and the ability of jazz to resist or reinforce somatic norms. The study of modern dances that proliferated in early Francoism sheds light on the consumption and adaptation practices of foreign music genres, body codes, the implicit precepts of censorship and their possible subversion. The biopolitical approach can offer much information about music and dance under dictatorial regimes, as long as we do not separate the musical object from its representation, performance from audience, and discourse from experience.

Acknowledgements

This chapter was written within the framework of the projects 'Música y cultura en España en el siglo XX: discursos sonoros y diálogos con Latinoamérica' (HAR2012-33414) and 'Música durante la guerra civil y el franquismo (1936–1960): culturas populares, vida musical e intercambios hispano-americanos' (HAR2013-48658-C2-1-P), both financed by the Spanish Economic Ministry. I would like to thank Bruce Johnson for his invaluable suggestions with respect to the content.

Notes

1 Linz's article was published for the first time in Spanish towards the end the dictatorship, in a book edited by Manuel Fraga, the Minister for Information and Tourism between 1962 and 1969 (Linz 1974).
2 'Música de hot', November 1941, Board of Censorship, Archivo General de la Administración, Alcalá de Henares, AGA (3) 121 36/04659.

3 All translations are by the author.
4 'Emisiones musicales', 17 September 1942, Circular no. 95, Vice-Secretariat of Popular Education, National Delegation of Propaganda, Broadcasting Section, Archivo General de la Administración, Alcalá de Henares, AGA (3) 49.1 21/701.
5 'Por qué combatimos la música negra', 25 June 1943, Circular no. 79, Vice-Secretariat of Popular Education, National Delegation of Propaganda, Broadcasting Section, Archivo General de la Administración, Alcalá de Henares, AGA (3) 49.1 21/808.
6 Order of 8 April 1941 (*Boletín Oficial del Estado*, 10 April 1941) and Order of 20 February 1942 (*Boletín Oficial del Estado*, 7 March 1942).
7 Order of 14 May 1946 (*Boletín Oficial del Estado*, 17 May 1946).

References

Agamben, Giorgio. 1998 [1995]. *Homo Sacer: Sovereign Power and Bare Life*. Stanford, CA: Stanford University Press.

Anderson, Peter. 2009. *The Francoist Military Trials: Terror and Complicity, 1939–1945*. New York and London: Routledge.

Beato-González, Vicente and Ramón Villarino-Ulloa. 1944. *Capacidad mental del negro*. Madrid: Dirección General de Marruecos y Colonias.

Castellá, José Luis. 1950. 'Concierto frustrado'. *Ritmo* 227: 21.

Cayuela Sánchez, Salvador. 2009. 'El nacimiento de la biopolítica franquista: la invención del "homo patiens"'. *Isegoría. Revista de Filosofía Moral y Política* 40: 273–288.

Cerchiari, Luca. 2003. *Jazz e fascismo: dalla nascita della radio a Gorni Kramer*. Palermo: L'Epos.

Chuliá, Elisa. 2001. *El poder y la palabra. Prensa y poder político en las dictaduras. El régimen de Franco ante la prensa y el periodismo*. Madrid: Biblioteca Nueva.

'Cinco minutos con los campeones del "swing"'. 1944. *Destino* 404 (14 April): 2.

Dean, Mitchell. 1999. *Governmentality: Power and Rule in Modern Society*. London: Sage.

Delgado, Lorenzo. 1992. *Imperio de papel. Acción cultural y política exterior durante el primer franquismo*. Madrid: Consejo Superior de Investigaciones Científicas.

Díez-Puertas, Emeterio. 2003. *Historial social del cine en España*. Madrid: Fundamentos.

Esposito, Roberto. 2008 [2004]. *Bíos: Biopolitics and Philosophy*. Minneapolis: University of Minnessota Press.

Esteve Blanes, Francisco. 1943. *Hacia tu ideal. Unas palabras a una joven*. Barcelona: Pontificia.

Fernández-Cid, Antonio. 1956. 'Presentación de Lionel Hampton y su Orquesta en el Carlos III', *ABC* (Madrid), 15 March: 57.

Foucault, Michel. 1978 [1976]. *The History of Sexuality*, vol. I: *An Introduction*. New York: Vintage.

Foucault, Michel. 2003 [1976]. *Society Must Be Defended*. New York: Picador.

Gallego, Ferrán. 2014. *El evangelio fascista: la formación de la cultura política del franquismo (1930–1950)*. Barcelona: Crítica.

García-Martínez, José María. 1996. *Del fox-trot al jazz flamenco. El jazz en España: 1919–1996*. Madrid: Alianza.

Gentile, Emilio. 2002. *Fascismo: Storia e interpretazione*. Roma: Laterza.

Gómez-Figueroa, José. 1956. '¡Jazz, jazz, jazz! Paroxismo ante el negro Hampton'. *Informaciones*, 15 March: 6.

González-Duro, Enrique. 2008. *Los psiquiatras de Franco. Los rojos no estaban locos*. Barcelona: Península.

Graham, Helen. 1995. 'Gender and the State: Women in the 1940s'. In Helen Graham and Jo Labanyi, eds, *Spanish Cultural Studies: An Introduction: The Struggle for Modernity*, 182–195. Oxford and New York: Oxford University Press.

Griffin, Roger. 2007. *Modernism and Fascism: The Sense of a Beginning under Mussolini and Hitler*. New York: Palgrave-Macmillan.

Hardt, Michael and Antonio Negri. 2000. *Empire: The New World Order*. Cambridge, MA: Harvard University Press.

Hardt, Michael and Antonio Negri. 2004. *Multitude: War and Democracy in the Age of Empire*. New York: Penguin.

Hardt, Michael and Antonio Negri. 2009. *Commonwealth*. Cambridge, MA: Belknap Press of Harvard University Press.

Heredia-Soriano, Antonio. 1978. 'La filosofía en el bachillerato español (1938–1975)'. In Antonio Heredia Soriano, ed., *Actas del I Seminario de Historia de la Filosofía Española*, 83–118. Salamanca: Universidad de Salamanca.

Hubbard, Karen and Terry Monaghan. 2009. 'Negotiating Compromise on a Burnished Wood Floor: Social Dancing at the Savoy'. In Julie Malnig, ed., *Ballroom, Boogie, Shimmy Sham, Shake: A Social and Popular Dance Reader*, 126–145. Urbana: University of Illinois Press.

Iglesias, Iván. 2010. '(Re)construyendo la identidad musical española: el jazz y el discurso cultural del franquismo durante la Segunda Guerra Mundial'. *Historia Actual* 23: 119–136.

Iglesias, Iván. 2011. '"Vehículo de la mejor amistad": El jazz como propaganda norteamericana en la España de los años cincuenta'. *Historia del presente* 17: 41–54.

Iglesias, Iván. 2012. '¿Melodías prohibidas? El jazz en el cine del primer franquismo (1939–1945)'. In Teresa Fraile and Eduardo Viñuela, eds, *La música en el lenguaje audiovisual: aproximaciones multidisciplinares a una comunicación mediática*, 61–73. Sevilla: Arcibel.

Iglesias, Iván. 2013. 'Swinging Modernity: Jazz and Politics in Franco's Spain (1939–1968)'. In Silvia Martínez and Héctor Fouce, ed., *Made in Spain: Studies in Popular Music*, 101–112. New York: Routledge.

Iglesias, Iván. Forthcoming. *El jazz y la España de Franco (1936–1968)*. Barcelona: Nortesur-Musikeon.

Kater, Michael H. 1992. *Different Drummers: Jazz in the Culture of Nazi Germany*. Oxford and New York: Oxford University Press.

Labanyi, Jo. 1995. 'Censorship or the Fear of Mass Culture'. In Helen Graham and Jo Labanyi, eds, *Spanish Cultural Studies: An Introduction: The Struggle for Modernity*, 207–214. Oxford and New York: Oxford University Press.

Lemke, Thomas. 2011. *Biopolitics: An Advanced Introduction*. New York and London: New York University Press.

León-Aguinaga, Pablo. 2010. *Sospechosos habituales: El cine norteamericano, Estados Unidos y la España franquista, 1939–1960*. Madrid: Consejo Superior de Investigaciones Científicas.

Linz, Juan J. 1974. 'Una teoría del régimen autoritario: el caso de España'. In Manuel Fraga, ed., *El Estado y la política: la España de los años 70*, 467–531. Madrid: Moneda y Crédito.

Linz, Juan J. 2000. *Totalitarian and Authoritarian Regimes*. Boulder, CO, and London: Lynne Rienner.

Lücke, Martin. 2004. *Jazz im Totalitarismus: Eine komparative Analyse des politisch motivierten Umgangs mit dem Jazz während der Zeit des Nationalsozialismus und des Stalinismus*. Münster: Lit.

Martínez del Fresno, Beatriz. 2001. 'Realidades y máscaras de la música de posguerra'. In Ignacio Henares Cuéllar *et al.*, eds, *Dos décadas de cultura artística en el franquismo*, vol. II, 31–82. Granada: Universidad de Granada.

Molinero, Carme and Pere Ysàs. 2008. *Anatomía del franquismo. De la supervivencia a la agonía, 1945–1977*. Barcelona: Crítica.

Mueller, Charles. 2014. 'Were British Subcultures the Beginning of Multitude?' In Sheila Whiteley and Jedediah Sklower, eds, *Countercultures and Popular Music*, 65–79. Farnham: Ashgate.

Padín, Francisco. 1943. 'La música de "jazz" y sus estragos'. *Ritmo* 170 (November): 7–8.

Pardo-Sanz, Rosa. 1995. *Con Franco hacia el Imperio. La política exterior española en América Latina, 1939–1945*. Madrid: Universidad Nacional de Educación a Distancia.

Payne, Stanley. 1987. *The Franco Regime, 1936–1975*. Madison: University of Wisconsin Press.

Payne, Stanley. 1999. *Fascism in Spain, 1923–1977*. Madison: University of Wisconsin Press.

Pelka, Anna. 2014. 'Mujer e ideología en la posguerra española: feminidad, cuerpo y vestido'. *Historia social* 79: 23–42.

Pemán, José María. 1947. *De doce cualidades de la mujer*. Madrid: Alcor.

Pérez Zalduondo, Gemma. 2011. 'Música, censura y Falange: el control de la actividad musical desde la Vicesecretaría de Educación Popular (1941–1945)'. *Arbor* 751: 875–886.

Pujol-Baulenas, Jordi. 2005. *Jazz en Barcelona (1920–1965)*. Barcelona: Almendra Music.

Richmond, Kathleen. 2003. *Women and Spanish Fascism: The Women's Section of the Falange, 1934–1959*. New York: Routledge.

Rodrigo, Javier. 2008. *Hasta la raíz: Violencia durante la Guerra Civil y la dictadura franquista*. Madrid: Alianza.

Rodríguez de Alarcón, Justino. 1940. 'Alrededor del deporte: Tesis de mejoramiento racial'. *Destino* 139: 10.

Rose, Nikolas. 2007. *The Politics of Life Itself: Biomedicine, Power, and Subjectivity in the Twentieth-first Century*. Princeton, NJ: Princeton University Press.

Ruiz-Encina, Justo. 1944. 'Concepto "hot" sobre la vida y la muerte'. *El Correo Catalán*, 11 January: 5.

Saz, Ismael. 2004. *Fascismo y franquismo*. Valencia: Universitat de València.

Saz, Ismael. 2013. *Las caras del franquismo*. Granada: Comares.

'Selección de discos'. 1949. *Ecclesia* 432 (22 October): 4.

Shiner, Larry. 2001. *The Invention of Art: A Cultural History*. Chicago: University of Chicago Press.

Snowball, David. 2002. 'Controlling Degenerate Music: Jazz in the Third Reich'. In Michael J. Budds, ed., *Jazz and the Germans*, 149–166. Hillsdale, NY: Pendragon.

Starr, S. Frederick. 1983. *Red and Hot: The Fate of Jazz in the Soviet Union, 1917–1980*. New York and Oxford: Oxford University Press.

Tussell, Javier. 1988. *La dictadura de Franco*. Madrid: Alianza.

Ugarte, Francisco Javier. 2008. 'Las bases ideológicas de la represion'. In Javier Ugarte, ed., *Una discriminación universal: la homosexualidad bajo el franquismo y la Transición*, 49–78. Barcelona/Madrid: Egales.

Vázquez-García, Francisco. 2009. *La invención del racismo. Nacimiento de la biopolítica en España, 1600–1940*. Madrid: Akal.

Vega-Sombría, Santiago. 2012. *La política del miedo. El papel de la represión en el franquismo.* Barcelona: Crítica.

Vila San-Juan, Juan Felipe. 1948. 'Cinematografía. Los estrenos'. *La Vanguardia Española,* 28 March: 11.

Viñas, Ángel. 2003. *En las garras del águila. Los pactos con Estados Unidos, de Francisco Franco a Felipe González.* Barcelona: Crítica.

Zwerin, Michael. 1985. *La Tristesse de Saint Louis: Jazz Under the Nazis.* London and New York: Quartet Books.

8

'THE PUREST ESSENCE OF JAZZ'

The Appropriation of Blues in Spain during Franco's Dictatorship

Josep Pedro

This chapter focuses on the appropriation of blues in Spain during Francoism (1939–1975). It situates the Spanish case within studies about authoritarianism and totalitarianism, and explores the musical evolution and political implications of blues in relation to the more consolidated jazz and rock scenes, which, in their different varieties, serve as frameworks to explore blues' heterogeneous and ambiguous trajectory. In this process, the chapter considers the stigmatization of black music throughout the 1940s; the gradual change of discourse within the 1950s Cold War era, when Spain became an ally of the United States; and the combination of liberalization of cultural policies, diverse musical hybridizations, censorship and political opposition throughout the 1960s and 1970s. As a driving, structuring force of American popular music and its global expansion, blues allowed enthusiasts to develop alternative identities, activities and spaces through intense and partly imagined intercultural dialogues with African-American music, and played an important role in the modernization processes that forged deep and lasting contradictions in Franco's dictatorship before the institution of democracy became possible.

Introduction

General Francisco Franco's dictatorship in Spain (1939–1975) has been considered a peculiar regime within political studies about totalitarianism, authoritarianism and fascism in twentieth-century Europe (Fusi *et al.* 2000; for a complementary perspective, see also Chapter 7, this volume). In 1963, as Francoism increasingly attempted to project Spain internationally as a modern country, Juan Linz initiated an intense scholarly debate about its nature, which remains disputed and unresolved to this day.[1] In his comparative study, the Spanish sociologist and

The Appropriation of Blues in Spain **175**

political scientist (who was based in the United States) made a distinction between totalitarianism and authoritarianism, and defined the Spanish dictatorship as authoritarian. Essentially, totalitarian regimes – exemplified by Germany's Third Reich and Stalin's Soviet Union – were marked by total integration between the state and all areas of society, as well as an unquestionable, guiding leader who was massively reinforced by a cohesive ideology. On the other hand, authoritarian regimes were more interested in preserving power through authoritarian methods, pragmatic policies and depoliticization of the masses, and could eventually evolve into pluralist democracies.

In the following decades, Linz's theory gained considerable publicity and a national and international following to become the 'official' version of the political nature of Francoism. However, the authoritarian interpretation has also drawn significant criticism because of the allegedly unbalanced methodology used in Linz's study and, more importantly, as a result of the political utilization of his theory, which was assumed by both the Spanish dictatorship and US foreign policy-makers throughout the century (Esteban Navarro 1987; Navarro 2013). Focusing on its brutal repression and on his experience as an exiled intellectual, Vicenç Navarro (2011) has argued that the Spanish dictatorship was clearly a totalitarian regime:

> It is surprising that the dictatorship is presented as simply authoritarian and not totalitarian. They should ask the children of the defeated. The constant humiliation and enormous psychological, emotional and totalitarian oppression was totalitarian as it pervaded all aspects of the individual, including his identity.[2]

Other Spanish professors, including Soto Carmona and Martínez Lillo (2011), have also joined this terminological and political discussion in the national mass media, bridging the gaps between scholarly research and public debate. Given its prolonged duration and chameleon shifts, they prefer to talk about different political natures within Francoism: a totalitarian project similar to fascism based on self-sufficient policies (autarchy); and an authoritarian adaptation, which was a forced reaction to the new international context after the Second World War. Throughout an essentially cosmetic evolution, the regime managed to preserve its essence: concentrated political power in the leader figure; widespread repression; and rejection of democracy. Their reasoning and classification coincide with the work of historian Enrique Moradiellos (2000), who distinguishes between a 'frustrated construction of a totalitarian state' in the post-Civil War period (1939–1945) and 'an authoritarian stage of technocratic development (1959–1969)', which followed a period of isolation, national-Catholic ascendancy and gradual reintegration in the Western Bloc (1945–1959).

The aim of this chapter is to articulate a study of blues music in Spain during Franco's changing yet essentially unitary dictatorship – a period that may be

176 Josep Pedro

conceptualized as the origins of a national blues scene.[3] In consonance with Bruce Johnson's Introduction to this volume, I approach the concept of totalitarianism from a heterogeneous perspective that is somewhat sceptical about top-down control, understanding it more as 'theory or aspiration' than as 'practice or realization' (Roberts 2006, 15). In fact, this chapter may be understood as an example of the limits, resistances and alternatives of both total domination and rigid definitions of totalitarianism. Acknowledging blues' original development in the African-American community and prolonging the idea of blues as a dynamic continuum (Jones 2002), I focus on appropriation as a process of active and creative reception undertaken by different actors, who act as selective filters to accept certain elements of a given cultural form while rejecting or 'forgetting' others (Burke 2010). The aim is to search for and analyse blues traces in order to understand how its tradition was appropriated within the Spanish context. I will consider the musical evolution and political implications of blues in relation to the broader and more consolidated jazz and rock scenes, which serve as frameworks to explore blues' heterogeneous and ambiguous trajectory. Therefore, my discussion is about blues not as something distinct from jazz, but as a significant musical practice that largely coalesced with jazz in the discourses of popular music in postwar Spain, and continued to evolve with the development of rock culture throughout the 1960s and 1970s.

I rely on a larger ethnographic and analytical research into blues in Spain, undertaken since October 2011, and focus on the categorization and analysis of popular music recordings, black music historic performances, and media discourses in relation to the changing socio-political context. The chapter is structured into three parts, which correspond approximately to the 1940s, the 1950s, and 1960–1975.

Swingin' the Blues: Boogie-Woogie and Classic Blues in the Silent Spanish Postwar Era

In postwar Spain, as in many native (Jones 2002) and diasporic sites (Wynn 2007), the distinction between blues and jazz was by no means absolute. They were both situated, and often overlapped, on a spectrum of musical practices that could also include dance and symphonic music, gospel, spirituals, folk, rhythm and blues, and rock, which broadly encompassed all modern US popular music.

During the Second World War, Francoism officially stigmatized black American music, defining it in opposition to Spanish culture. As Iván Iglesias has illustrated (2010; 2013b; and Chapter 7, this volume), under the precepts of nationalism, Catholicism and totalitarianism, the dictatorship exerted a firm control over the media and the celebration of public events. The Vice-Secretariat of Popular Education (ruled by the fascist Falange Española)

The Appropriation of Blues in Spain **177**

explicitly battled against black music and distributed reports to radio stations in order to 'banish the arbitrary, anti-musical, and anti-human jazz wave with which America has invaded Europe for decades' (quoted in Iglesias 2013b, 102). Gradually, this vehement discursive opposition would dissipate as Francoism attempted to integrate into the Western Bloc.

In order to understand the multiple meanings of jazz, it is useful to distinguish between two opposing appropriation tendencies: a symphonic approach, more suitable for the European classical music tradition, represented by George Gershwin, Paul Whiteman and, to a lesser extent, Duke Ellington; and a 'purist' approach towards jazz as an African-American tradition, which emphasized the authenticity of traditional and 'uncorrupted' hot jazz, reflecting the emergence of prestige from below (Lipsitz 1990). Discourses about blues would consolidate within the 'purist' minority, but the widespread success of boogie-woogie also situated the genre within the broad scene of Spanish popular bands and dances (on dance, see Chapter 7, this volume).

An African-American style of piano-based blues, boogie-woogie was popularized internationally in the late thirties after John Hammond's 'From Spirituals to Swing' concerts at Carnegie Hall. During the 1940s, a time of 'silence, hunger and misery' (Moradiellos 2000, 81) for Spain, it was often incorporated into the repertoires of bands and orchestras due to its irresistible upbeat appeal, and ultimately instituted 'a new dance culture that was massive and increasingly specialized' (Iglesias 2013b, 103). Musical evidence of Spanish boogie-woogie can be found in the *Postwar Jazz* CD (1941–1956) of *Jazz en Barcelona 1920–1965* (Fresh Sound Records, 2005): 'Ritmo 1944' (Quinteto Murillo, 1944); 'Red Bank Boogie' (José Ribalta y sus Muchachos, 1945); 'Clipper's Bugui' (Los Clippers, 1946); and 'Bugui Azul' (José Valero y su Orquesta, 1947).

National media, still operating under rigid surveillance, produced conflicting discourses about jazz and black music. While the dominant music magazine, *Ritmo*, attacked Americans' 'savage' and 'immoral' folk music, and warned against 'musical prostitution' and contamination of the national spirit (García 2012, 32; Iglesias 2010, 125–127), magazines like *Ritmo y Melodía*, which was launched (and tolerated) after the Second World War, promoted it with considerable depth, while acknowledging the national trends and debate on the subject. Evolving into the only jazz magazine in Spain, *Ritmo y Melodía* featured significant articles discussing boogie-woogie, blues and African-American folklore. Boogie-woogie was generally defined as a new style of jazz or classified 'within the framework of swing interpretation' (Cerri 1947) and described in technical or historical terms, always in relation – and sometimes confrontation – with its swing dance association. In this context, blues was rarely mentioned as a founding genre for boogie-woogie, and was inexactly described as an 'individual creation' of W. C. Handy (P. C. H. 1946).

Apart from its sometimes unrecognized representation in popular culture through boogie-woogie, blues was defined in terms of classic blues – 'the first

178 Josep Pedro

Negro music that appeared in a formal context as entertainment, though it still contained harsh, uncompromising reality of the earlier blues forms' (Jones 2002, 86). Accordingly, *Ritmo y Melodía* focused on classic blues vocalists like Bessie Smith, Ma Rainey, Victoria Spivey and Ethel Waters, and composers such as Handy – dubbed the 'father of blues' for his written compositions. Moreover, it created a valuable section, 'Blues, Old Blues', dedicated to the translation of blues lyrics like 'Good Morning Blues' and 'Lazy Lady Blues', both associated with the singer Jimmy Rushing from the Count Basie Orchestra. Significantly, the magazine introduced blues as the 'source of inspiration of all jazz' (Díaz 1947) and praised its simple and poetic spirit, establishing a connection with several Harlem Renaissance writers. As for classic blues recordings, the aforementioned Fresh Sound Records volume includes a version of the standard 'St Louis Blues' (1947) performed by George Johnson, an African-American jazz musician who moved to Barcelona in 1946. Handy's signature song had been recorded by Bessie Smith ('The Empress of the Blues') and Louis Armstrong in 1925 and clearly disclosed the interpenetration of blues and jazz. *Clamores Jazz, 30 Años* (Pérez Fabián 2012) offers further examples of blues-related recordings, such as 'Georgia on My Mind', translated to 'Georgia de mi pensamiento' (Barcelona Hot Quintet, 1940), and jump blues-inspired songs like 'A lo Calloway' (Antonio Machín, 1944) and 'Hey! Ba-ba-re-bop' (Los Clippers, 1947).

Undoubtedly, the 1940s were the toughest decade for the vast majority of Spanish citizens, who lived under extended mental and physical repression, food rationing, and a political autarchy that led the country to a severe economic depression, which affected 'all orders of Spanish social life' (Moradiellos 2000, 82). Until the mid-1950s, the appropriation of jazz, particularly of the novelty-style dances of swing and boogie-woogie, was intimately tied to escapism, physical pleasure and corporeal liberation, and implicitly opposed to Francoist biopolitics and precepts about attitudes to the body and morality (García 2012, 31–32; Iglesias 2013a; Chapter 7, this volume). Furthermore, the gradual appropriation of blues, generally undertaken by a minority of so-called jazz 'purists', developed a distinctive and more incisive cultural and intellectual focus. While jazz had been more 'contaminated' due to its integration into mainstream pop, Hollywood's happy-ending movies and European classical orchestras, blues was still much less well known to both general and 'jazz' audiences, and cultivated a more exclusive mystique that drove the unstoppable search for authenticity of those who could afford, and were willing, to dig deep into the black American tradition.

The 'Real' Blues Arrives: Associationism and Media Discourses in the 1950s Cold War Context

The distinctive appropriations of blues and jazz became increasingly noticeable throughout the 1950s, as shown in the groundbreaking activities of Barcelona's

The Appropriation of Blues in Spain **179**

Hot Club, an association of upper-middle-class, left-oriented aficionados with a mission of spreading, collecting and enjoying African-American music.[4] Inspired by the original Hot Club de France (see below), Barcelona's Hot Club was responsible for laying the foundations of a specialized music scene, and produced a high-quality selection of unprecedented performances by African-American artists, who generally felt more respected, both artistically and socially, in European settings than in the US. At the same time, it encouraged the creation of similar clubs in Catalan towns and significant cities like Madrid and Valencia.

Blues, boogie-woogie and jazz coexisted in the 'authentic' black music performances presented by Barcelona's Hot Club: Willie 'The Lion' Smith (1950), Bill Coleman (1952), Big Bill Broonzy (1953), Louis Armstrong (1955), Sidney Bechet (1955), Sammy Price (1956), Count Basie (1956), Josh White (1956) and Sister Rosetta Tharpe (1958) all performed there.[5] Broonzy's May 1953 concert at the small Capsa Theatre in Barcelona was a landmark in Spanish blues history, as he is considered the first bluesman to visit the country and is often taken as a starting point (Aznar 2003; Pedro 2012). Aesthetically situated in the transatlantic mid-century folk revival, the concert was the result of a collaboration between Alfredo Papo (Hot Club of Barcelona) and Hugues Panassié (Hot Club de France), who shared an aesthetic and ideological appreciation of black music. (Originally from Milan, Papo grew up in Paris, where he became a jazz enthusiast under the influence of the Hot Club.) Broonzy, who incarnated blues' evolution from rural to urban and subsequent rural comeback ('urban-rural blues'), performed solo with his guitar, and presented a traditional and eclectic repertoire including blues, folk songs and instrumentals and spirituals. Certain songs, such as 'John Henry' (about a legendary black steel worker), 'Just a Dream' (an ironic story blending desire and realist disillusionment) and 'Black, Brown and White' (an overtly political song denouncing racial discrimi-nation), exposed the political implications of blues as socio-political commen-tary within the emerging African-American Civil Rights Movement and its reception in Spain. The original concert brochure (reproduced in Papo 1985, 18–19) reveals that Broonzy's reception as 'the greatest blues singer today' was deeply connected to rural authenticity: 'There's no commercial mystifi-cation, Big Bill restores the atmosphere of blues in its full purity, as sung by the wandering, black troubadours across villages and small towns of the South.' Moreover, the text made an intercultural connection between blues and flamenco, referring to their shared deep folk roots and 'racial' dimension: 'The art of Big Bill Broonzy is similar in many aspects to "cante jondo" because authentic blues [is also] the result of an ancient tradition and a deep racial feeling.'

The arrival of Louis Armstrong, described as 'the liveliest musical phenomenon of our times' (Montsalvatge 1955, 39), disclosed the profound relationship between blues and jazz. Considered the undisputed 'King of Jazz'

180 Josep Pedro

by hot fans, Armstrong was praised for his blues interpretation: 'Nobody has interpreted nor interprets now the blues like him . . . [Blues] is the purest essence of original jazz that we conserve, [and an] immediate derivation of the spiritual chants' (ibid.). This bond was reflected in his Barcelona performances, which included several instrumental and vocal nominally blues numbers, such as 'Basin Street Blues', 'Velma's Blues' and 'St Louis Blues', as well as 'Black and Blue', which reflected upon social marginality and black identity. Moreover, through an essentialist discursive depiction, Armstrong's remarkable musical talents were described as 'direct expressions of his race', and his 'real' jazz as a means to discover 'a race . . . stripped of any artifice' (ibid.). Three years later, the reception for the eclectic singer–guitarist Sister Rosetta Tharpe was also marked by an emphasis on her blues interpretations and her 'mysterious' and 'unnerving' rhythm. By then, based on her representation, black music was being described as a 'direct, schematic and rigorously authentic art form' (Anonymous 1958, 37).

In fact, African–American culture became an important source of inspiration for the developing avant-garde movement in Catalonia. In 1951, Dau al Set, a breakaway artistic group of painters and writers founded in 1948, dedicated one of its monographs to the blues. Directed by Alfredo Papo, the ten-page pamphlet continued the trend of translating blues lyrics into Spanish, as *Ritmo y Melodía* had done. The same year, Papo and the poet José María Fonollosa published an anthology of eighteen Negro spirituals, also translated into Spanish and with accompanying comments about their richness, lyricism and purity. The songs were passionately contextualized in the African–American (and, ultimately, the human) experience: 'the black anguish is that of a man who suffers a terrible martyrdom and shouts his desperation, longing for freedom and triumph not only in true paradise but also in the "paradise" that the earthly world could and should be' (Papo and Fonollosa 1951, 12).

This arrestingly intense cultural production was broadly situated within the new climate of friendly international relations between Spain and the United States, which had encouraged a shift in the official attitude towards black music. After Spain's exclusion from the Marshall Plan (astutely satirized in Berlanga's film *Bienvenido Mr Marshall*, which surprisingly escaped censorship), the détente was publicly manifested in September 1953 (four months after Broonzy's visit) with the signing of three important agreements. Spain accepted the installation of US military bases in exchange for economic and military aid, an operation that ratified the integration of Franco's dictatorship into the Western Bloc of the Cold War, albeit as a 'minor partner, depreciated for its political structure and recent past' (Moradiellos 2000, 101). The military installations led to the arrival of US soldiers, musicians and cultural products (recordings, books, radio shows), and ultimately exerted considerable influence on Spanish society's appropriation of American culture (including black music). Some of the results would become apparent throughout the 1960s, for instance in the arrival of African-American musicians in Madrid and the emergence of Andalusian blues-rock and flamenco-blues (see below).

During the 1950s, the US government – through various institutions, such as the US Embassy in Madrid, the America House and the army – began to sponsor radio programmes and jazz concerts in Spain (see Iglesias 2013b, 105–106). Significantly, these initiatives initially favoured encounters between classical music and symphonic jazz by white musicians or composers, most prominently George Gershwin. After this tentative but successful early stage, celebrated African-American performers were also involved, most notably the cheerful and multifaceted Lionel Hampton, whose 1956 concerts in Madrid were sponsored by the US Embassy. He also recorded the groundbreaking album *Jazz Flamenco* (RCA-Victor, 1956). However, in contrast to these activities, the aforementioned performances by blues and jazz artists in Barcelona were primarily attributable to the accumulated strength and management capacities of the Hot Club.

Comparatively, blues musicians, particularly those associated with rural environments, were deemed less appropriate for propaganda purposes than jazz musicians. Unlike the free and cosmopolitan representation of the United States that even black jazz potentially allowed, blues maintained a stronger association with the shameful, discriminatory statutes of Jim Crow, and was (more) often romanticized as a musical expression of resistance.

Jazz, Rock and Singer–Songwriters: The Heterogeneous Expansion of Blues during Late Francoism

Throughout the 1960s, Franco's political regime – which had vehemently interrupted Spain's economic and social modernization – paradoxically became its new promoter and principal sponsor (Moradiellos 2000, 135). Although resisted by Franco himself, the regime's autarchic policies were finally abandoned and, driven by the technocratic developers, a series of new economic programmes (Stabilization Plan, 1959; Development Plans, 1964–1975) resulted in spectacular economic growth that would 'radically transform the country's social structure' (ibid.). In this process, which was also facilitated by the rise of foreign private investment, European mass tourism and remittances from exiled citizens, Spain evolved from being a predominantly agrarian country to an industrialized one with a diverse service sector. However, while economic development brought short-term legitimacy to the regime, in the long term it generated 'profoundly discordant social and cultural conditions within an increasingly anachronistic political system, maladjusted to its own socio-economic reality' (ibid., 136). The dictatorship also approved several cultural liberalization policies, most notably the 1966 Law of Press and Print (*Ley de Prensa e Imprenta*), which officially abolished preventive censorship (established in 1938) while retaining sanction and control proceedings based on its fundamental (and arbitrary) principles.

182 Josep Pedro

Together, these processes led to increased exposure to Western mass culture and the consumer society, as well as to a deeper and more extended penetration of American and British music in the Spanish soundscape. Within its minority position, blues achieved an unprecedented extension into popular music as it influenced and was present in several music scenes. It was a widely appreciated genre that nurtured the music of some remarkable jazz musicians (Tete Montoliu, Salvador Font 'Mantequilla', Pedro Iturralde *et al.*), and it was featured in the emerging jazz clubs and festivals of cities like Madrid, Barcelona and San Sebastián. The distinguished Whisky Jazz Club (founded in Madrid in 1959) hosted blues performances by Donna Hightower, an African-American singer who grew up in the tradition of gospel, blues and jazz, and developed a successful career in Spanish mainstream pop. Like Bud Powell, Hightower arrived in Madrid from Paris in 1960 to perform at the US military base of Torrejón, which often facilitated intercultural communication. However, she soon became associated with Whisky Jazz, where she sang alongside influential musicians such as Juan Carlos Calderón, and ultimately she made Spain her home in 1969.[6]

Furthermore, in 1960, the promoter Joan Rosselló opened Barcelona's Jamboree, a groundbreaking French-inspired jazz venue described as a 'breath of fresh air within the sad and gray cultural atmosphere' (García-Soler 1999) and as a 'limbo where different social classes got together shamelessly, simply because of the attracting rhythm of jazz' (Jurado 2008). Associated with this liberation role, the club featured such legendary musicians as bluesman Memphis Slim (1963) – who had lived in Paris since 1962 and would repeatedly revisit Spain during this period – Dexter Gordon (1964) and Ornette Coleman (1965, 1968), whose styles were significantly influenced by blues.

The 1961 Madrid Jazz Festival was a landmark in Spain's blues history, as it featured Jimmy Witherspoon (backed by Buck Clayton's orchestra), considered the first bluesman to perform in the Spanish capital.[7] Five years later, Joan Roselló launched the Barcelona Jazz Festival, which soon featured blues-influenced jazz musicians (Illinois Jacquet, Roy Eldridge and Milt Buckner, 1966), impressive blues tour reunions (Big City Blues, 1967; Chicago Blues Festival, 1971) and blues legends (Muddy Waters, 1968; B.B. King, 1973). Furthermore, the San Sebastian Jazz Festival, also initiated in 1966, featured other remarkable bluesmen (John Lee Hooker, 1969; The Aces, 1971; Clarence 'Gatemouth' Brown, 1973). The most significant historic achievement from the viewpoint of blues, as it confirmed a certain genre autonomy, was the organization of two American Folk Blues Festivals. Produced by German promoters Horst Lippmann and Fritz Rau, the festivals were organized by Barcelona's Hot Club in 1965 and 1968, and featured an impressive array of well-known blues musicians, many of whom enjoy legendary status today.[8]

Meanwhile, throughout the 1960s and into the 1970s, blues' unique sounds resonated and became primarily associated with the 'British Invasion' and psychedelic, hippy-era rock bands, many of which exerted a decisive influence

FIGURE 8.1   Extract of the brochure for the American Folk Blues Festival, Barcelona, 1965. Collage by América Sánchez
(Centre de Documentació de l'Orfeó Català)

on Spanish musicians. As modern jazz lost the genre's previous association with dance as well as some of its popular appeal in its attempt to gain legitimacy as (high) art, rock 'n' roll emerged as an increasingly global genre that was similarly stylistically and historically indebted to the blues. Therefore, blues' influence (though invisible to many eyes) was present in the musical structures, forms and sounds of rock and pop songs, as well as in certain lyrics, which were regularly translated into Spanish. A prominent example is 'The House of the Rising Sun', a song of the early folk-blues tradition that became very popular after the Animals released their version in 1964 and was recorded extensively in Spanish as 'La casa del sol naciente', gaining even greater popularity and consolidating an artistic–business model to negotiate transatlantic influences. One of the most popular versions was recorded by Lone Star, a band that developed a more 'purist' appropriation of African-American music than the norm. They also recorded Willie Dixon's 'My Babe' (1963), as well as rhythm and blues and soul compositions by artists like Little Richard, Ray Charles and James Brown, which reflected substantial appreciation of black music. Other significant blues-related bands were: Los Buenos, featuring Rod Mayall (John Mayall's brother), who released versions of modern blues classics, such Albert King's 'Oh Pretty Woman' (1968) and Johnny 'Guitar' Watson's 'Looking Back' (1969); and Smash, a progressive group from Seville that blended rock,

184 Josep Pedro

blues and flamenco (e.g. 'Light Blood, Dark Bleeding' and 'It's Only Nothing', 1970), initiating a significant fusion tendency that was developed by Green Piano, Gong and later Pata Negra. Interestingly, the well-known singer–guitarist Raimundo Amador (a member of Pata Negra), who would take flamenco-blues to its peak in the 1990s, first came into contact with blues and jazz by listening to black soldiers playing at the US military base in Rota, Cádiz, where his father worked (Frías 2004, 149).

Additionally, typical blues forms (e.g. I–IV–V chord progression) and call-and-response patterns were widely reproduced in dance-oriented numbers both of early rock 'n' roll and successive trends like the twist and hully gully, such as *El Rock and Roll de Los Estudiantes* (1959), 'Lolita Twist' (Duo Dinámico, 1963) and 'Hully Gully' (Los Pekenikes, 1964). In contrast, 'Muchacha Bonita' (Los Sirex, 1964) appropriated slow-tempo blues and used it as a way into composition. Another significant sub-category of blues appropriation within rock is formed by recordings that have been associated with rhythm and blues or garage (generally defined in terms of the 1960s British style), such as 'Es la edad' (Los Salvajes, 1966), 'Incomprendidos' (Los No, 1966), 'Corre Corre' (Los Gatos Negros, 1966) and 'He perdido este juego' (Los Cheyenes, 1966).

In contrast to the general dynamic, censorship of rock music intensified in the early 1970s, executed by two offices of the Ministry of Information and Tourism (the General Directorate of Radio and Television and the General Directorate of Popular Culture and Spectacles). Its goal was to protect the country from foreign 'bad taste', generally associated with sexuality, religious and/or political offence or alternative ways of life (e.g. the hippie movement). This control may be related to the 1970 Law on Danger and Social Rehabilitation (*Ley sobre peligrosidad y rehabilitación social*) which replaced the 1933 Law of Slackers and Crooks (*Ley de vagos y maleantes*). It was aimed at citizens whom the regime considered socially and/or morally suspicious. Between 1960 and 1977, 4343 songs were catalogued as 'non-playable', and at least a hundred LP covers were modified by the censors (Valiño 2011, 74–76). Among the examples offered by Valiño are 'Good Vibrations' (a Beach Boys song covered by Hugo Montenegro) and the albums *The Black Man's Burdon* (Eric Burdon and War, 1970), *Sticky Fingers* (the Rolling Stones, 1971), *For Ladies Only* (Steppenwolf, 1971) and *Quadrophenia* (The Who, 1973). As for the above-mentioned Spanish bands, censorship was generally imposed by music industry imperatives and public-sphere limitations, which often amounted to an assumed self-censorship regarding what could or could not be said (Soler García de Oteyza 2012). Nonetheless, these bands embodied musical modernity and often carried messages of personal and generational freedom, which involved 'formal, social, and symbolic innovations that contributed to socio-political and cultural change' (Marc 2013, 115).

Overt political opposition to Francosim was identified with *Nova Cançó*, a countercultural folk-music movement marked by the political use of Catalan (prohibited under Francoism), and associated with well-known singer–songwriters including Lluis Llach, Raimon and Joan Manuel Serrat. In its roots we also find two unique (yet generally unknown) musicians who stand out for their intimate relation to the blues: Guillem D'Efak and Francesc Pi de la Serra. They both recorded groundbreaking blues EPs – *Blues* (1965) and *L'Home Solter* (1964), respectively – which reflected a faithful yet highly personalized appropriation of the genre, showing an updated reincarnation of traditional storytellers, which translated and recomposed the blues in Catalan. Furthermore, D'Efak was originally from Equatorial Guinea. As an educated black singer, poet and actor born to a Spanish father and a Guinean mother, he potentially incarnated the highest degree of artistic and symbolic opposition to Francoism. He founded the legendary La Cova del Drac club (Barcelona, 1965), which became a great supporter of folk artists and writers, as well as an early refuge for developing jazz and blues musicians. However, his blues recordings generally lacked overt political statements: his signature song 'Blues en sol' (1965), later performed by Serrat and Maria del Mar Bonet, revolved around loneliness and desire within affective-sexual relationships, as did 'Febra' (Fever, 1965). A significant exception might be 'Vell Riu Nostre' (1965), an adaptation of 'Ol' Man River' that dealt with the living and working conditions of the 'poor blacks of Mississippi'.

In Madrid, the San Juan Evangelista College Dormitory (founded in 1970) served a similar intellectual and student oppositional function, combining black music, flamenco and singer–songwriter performances with frequent political discussions. The aesthetic connection between folk and blues may be explored through Hilario Camacho, a much-appreciated yet somewhat accursed artist who recorded his debut album, *A pesar de todo* (1972), in London. Produced by the influential French producer Alain Milhaud, who had guided numerous bands throughout the 1960s, it included 'Como todos los días', a veiled protest song focused on the boredom of daily experiences, whose concluding verse reflected social discontent and anticipated the inevitable fall of Francoism, which by then was trapped in a terminal phase of structural crisis:

> You won't take it all your life either, my friend
> Perhaps one day you'll feel that shame is choking you,
> And you'll scream it through the streets . . .
> Yes, perhaps.

Conclusions

This critical exploration and reconstruction of blues history during Francoism has illustrated different appropriations of the blues genre, including its representation in boogie-woogie, classic and folk blues, pop–rock trends, progressive rock and flamenco fusions, rhythm-and-blues-inspired rock and the work

186 Josep Pedro

of singer–songwriters. Being a stylistic and historical common ground between different styles of the hegemonic jazz and rock genres, the foundational musical language of blues provided a unique combination of rhythmic and narrative appeal, form flexibility and exotic socio-cultural mystery, and the genre's minority status and fascinating historical development within Jim Crow racism in the United States guaranteed a distinct authenticity among Spanish aficionados.

Appropriating elements of the Spanish folk tradition, particularly of *copla*, Franco's regime attempted to impose 'national songs of agrarian-related Andalusian imagery, melody and pronunciation' (Vázquez Montalbán 2000, xv–xvi) as the official national soundtrack, projecting its 'idea of nationhood while offering an untroubled escapist vision of life' (Martínez and Fouce 2013, 4). In this situation, jazz and blues were initially stigmatized and persecuted, as they represented a challenge to the normative ideas of national unity, self-sufficiency and Spanish social and 'racial' correctness and particularities. However, 'in practice, the attitude of the dictatorship towards [US black music] was far from unitary and unequivocal, ranging from its condemnation as degenerate music, its tolerance as economic sustenance, and its naturalization as mass entertainment' (Iglesias 2013b, 102). The realignment of international geopolitics after the Second World War, with the emergence of the United States as the leading Western power in the polarized Cold War context, was key in this process insofar as it forced a change of discourse in the Spanish dictatorship, which gradually opened up to external economic contributions and cultural influences, while holding tight to its authoritarian-totalitarian essence.

As a driving, structuring force of American popular music and its global expansion, blues played an important role in the modernization processes that forged deep and lasting contradictions in Franco's dictatorship before the institution of democracy was actually possible (the first democratic elections post-Franco took place in 1977). As part of modern popular music, it allowed enthusiasts to develop alternative identities, activities and spaces through intense and partly imagined intercultural dialogues with foreign cultural expressions (particularly African-American music), which had a liberating, emotional and intellectual impact on their everyday lives. These connections often came through contact with cosmopolitan European capitals such as Paris and London. Until the 1960s, blues was mainly heard and promoted within left-oriented, upper-middle-class, intellectual circles, which, despite regular concerns, the regime did not consider primary threats. Theirs was not an overt political opposition, but a reflection of their need to develop cultural autonomy, involving meaningful musical experiences, constructive economic associations and physical and mental transformations. For the dictatorship, its toleration may have served as an apparent sign of freedom to accompany its chameleonic evolution.

With the international irruption and national appropriation of 1960s and 1970s rock music, and the development of globally oriented cultural

The Appropriation of Blues in Spain **187**

liberalization policies, blues became broadly associated with youth rebellion and student opposition to Francoism, articulated as a whole through a multiplicity of musical references (jazz, rock, flamenco, singer–songwriters and so on). As Joan Ventosa, an experienced cultural activist engaged in the Barcelona Blues Society (2005) and in the production of *Barna Blues. La història del blues a Barcelona* (Bad Music Blues, 2012), expressed in personal conversations with the author on this subject,[9] this kind of musical socialization served as a means to question the official narratives and predicaments, be they social, moral and/ or political, that were constantly imposed upon Spanish citizens. In the 1970s, as social conflicts and censorship intensified, Francoism tried to reaffirm its control but the dictatorship and Franco himself, who continued to be personally identified with it, were exhausted after a (too) long journey of totalitarian direction. The profound dissonance between socio-cultural and political conditions, the manifested desire for change (even within sections of the ruling classes), the oppositional struggle of students and workers, the terrorist attacks (and consequent controversial repression) of FRAP and ETA (who assassinated Franco's designated presidential successor Luis Carrero Blanco in 1973) and, finally, Franco's death in 1975 would precipitate the end of the dictatorship.

Ultimately, this discussion exposes the vitality and associative power of social groups, musicians and scene participants who creatively appropriate cultural expressions from the Other within totalitarian regimes originally based on self-sufficiency. It provides evidence of the limits of top-down control and suggests that, even in situations of widespread repression and censorship, citizens find everyday fissures which, despite being insufficient to change the political system as a whole (perhaps as they are not oriented to it), expose its contradictions, inner struggles and the construction of alternative scenes through dialogues that traverse national, socio-cultural and 'racial' borders.

Acknowledgements

This chapter was supported by the Spanish Ministry of Education, Culture and Sports (Ministerio de Educación, Cultura y Deporte) under the contract FPU (Formación de Profesorado Universitario). I would like to thank Iván Iglesias for his valuable guidance in the early stages of this project. I also wish to express my gratitude to Eugenio Moirón, Ramón del Solo, Javier Rodríguez, Vicente Zúmel and Joan Ventosa for their helpful assistance in my research about the history of blues in Spain.

Notes

1 Linz presented 'Una teoría del régimen autoritario. El caso de España' (A theory of authoritarianism: the case of Spain) at a Sociology Committee symposium in Finland in 1963. Since then, he has republished and reworked his arguments several times, most recently in Linz 2000 and 2009.

188 Josep Pedro

2 All translations are by the author.
3 The origins of blues in Spain are marked by its significant role as an influence on jazz and rock. Following this dialogic evolution, blues would become an autonomous genre in the 1980s scene-crystallization period, once democracy had been reinstalled in 1977. The interest in blues in Europe has produced some valuable publications (such as Wynn 2007), although Spain has generally been overlooked, with the exceptions of Frías (2004), who focused on the relationship between flamenco and blues, and Aznar (2003), who is interested in the construction of a national scene, as am I (Pedro 2012). Moreover, while not addressing the blues directly, recent publications on popular music in Spain, such as Martínez and Fouce (2013) and Mora and Viñuela (2013), have dealt with historical and cultural processes related to its development.
4 The Hot Club of Barcelona was originally founded in the mid-1930s, during the Second Spanish Republic (1931–1939), when it presented shows by the Quintette du Hot Club de France (featuring Django Reinhardt and Stephane Grappelli) and the African-American multi-instrumentalist Benny Carter.
5 The information about Josh White's 1956 performances in Barcelona was provided by the blues musician and alternative journalist Vicente Zúmel in an online interview with the author (October–November 2013). He knew of the concert because of conversations with Alfredo Papo from the Hot Club. The rest of the data were collected from Hot Club documents, and have previously appeared in García Martínez (1996), Pujol Baulenas (2005) and/or Iglesias (2013b).
6 Juan Carlos Calderón, an eclectic composer whose work combined jazz recordings with classical and pop compositions and arrangements, said that he played blues many times with Donna Hightower at Whisky Jazz (www.youtube.com/watch?v=4j2tzgQzIp4, accessed 16 October 2014). Other musicians who might have played blues numbers were Pedro Iturralde and Tete Montoliu, as their styles reflect fondness for the genre.
7 The importance of this event is confirmed and was brought to my attention by the Madrid Blues Society (www.sociedaddebluesdemadrid.com/blues-en-madrid/, accessed 10 March 2016). Additionally, Iglesias (2013b, 107) points out that the two concerts of Buck Clayton's orchestra in Barcelona in 1962 were co-financed by Pepsi-Cola, as part of its rivalry with Coca-Cola, which sponsored jazz concerts in Madrid, Bilbao and Barcelona.
8 The 1965 festival (co-financed by Coca-Cola) featured Roosevelt Sykes, 'Big Mama' Thornton, Buddy Guy, John Lee Hooker, 'Big Walter Shakey' Horton, J.B. Lenoir, 'Doctor Ross', 'Mississippi' Fred McDowell, Eddie Boyd, 'Lonesome' Jimmy Lee and Fred Below. The 1968 festival featured John Lee Hooker, Jimmy Reed, T-Bone Walker, Big Joe Williams, Curtis Jones and Eddie Taylor.
9 These conversations took place during a trip to Barcelona from 30 January to 2 February 2014. I travelled with Madrid blues musicians and made a presentation about the history of blues in Spain, which was organized by the Barcelona Blues Society, Bad Music Blues and the Centre Cultural Collblanc La Torrassa (L'Hospitalet).

Academic References

Aznar, Joan. 2003. 'Blues español'. In Gérard Herzhaft, ed., *La Gran Enciclopedia del Blues*. Barcelona: Ma Non Troppo: 54–56.

Burke, Peter. 2010. *Hibridismo cultural*. Madrid: Akal.

Esteban Navarro, Miguel A. 1987. 'La categorización política del franquismo. Un análisis de las principales aportaciones historiográficas'. *C.I.H. Brocar* 13: 11–26.

Freund Schwartz, Roberta. (2007). *How Britain Got the Blues: The Transmission and Reception of American Blues in the United Kingdom*. Hampshire and Burlington, VT: Ashgate.

Frías, María. 2004. 'Nights of Flamenco and Blues in Spain: From Sorrow Songs to *Soleá* and back'. In Heike Raphael-Hernandez, ed., *Blackening Europe: The African American Presence*. New York: Routledge: 141–156.

Fusi, Juan P., José L. García Delgado, Santos Juliá, Edward Malefakis and Stanley Payne. 2000. *Franquismo. El juicio de la historia*. Madrid: Temas de Hoy. Historia.

García, Jorge. 2012. *Jazz en la BNE. El ruido alegre*. Madrid: Biblioteca Nacional Española.

García Martínez, José María. 1996. *Del frox-trot al jazz flamenco: el jazz en España 1919–1996*. Madrid: Alianza.

Iglesias, Iván. 2010. '(Re)construyendo la identidad musical española: el jazz y el discurso cultural del franquismo durante la Segunda Guerra Mundial'. *Historia Actual* 23: 119–135.

Iglesias, Iván. 2013a. 'Hechicero de las pasiones del alma: el jazz y la subversión de la biopolítica franquista (1939–1959)'. *TRANS* 17: n.p.

Iglesias, Iván. 2013b. 'Swinging Modernity: Jazz and Politics in Franco's Spain (1939–1968)'. In Silvia Martínez and Héctor Fouce, eds, *Made in Spain: Studies in Popular Music*. New York: Routledge: 101–112.

Jones, Leroi (a.k.a Baraka, Amiri). 2002. *Blues People: Negro Music in White America*. New York: Harper Perennial.

Lipsitz, George. 1990. *Time Passages: Collective Memory and American Popular Culture*. Minneapolis: University of Minnesota Press.

Linz, Juan J. 2000. *Totalitarian and Authoritarian Regimes*. London: Rienner.

Linz, Juan J. 2009. *Sistemas totalitarios y regímenes autoritarios*. Madrid: Centro de Estudios Políticos y Constitucionales.

Marc, Isabelle. 2013. 'Submarinos Amarillos: Transcultural Objects in Spanish Popular Music during Late Francoism'. In Silvia Martínez and Héctor Fouce, eds, *Made in Spain: Studies in Popular Music*. New York: Routledge: 115–124.

Martínez, Silvia and Héctor Fouce, eds. 2013. *Made in Spain: Studies in Popular Music*. New York: Routledge.

Mora, Kiko and Eduardo Viñuela, eds. 2013. *Rock around Spain: Historia, industria, escenas y medios de comunicación*. Lleida: Universitat de Lleida.

Moradiellos, Enrique. 2000. *La España de Franco (1939–1975). Política y Sociedad*. Madrid: Síntesis.

Murray, Albert. 1976. *Stomping the Blues*. New York: Da Capo Press.

Papo, Alfredo and José María Fonollosa. 1951. *Antología de los Cantos Espirituales Negros*. Barcelona: Cobalto. For online review and book scans, see: http://librorum.piscolabis. cat/2012/10/cantos-spirituals-negros-1951-dalfredo.html (accessed 4 February 2014).

Pedro, Josep. 2012. 'El Blues en Madrid. Una exploración de la cultura musical en el espacio urbano'. Master's dissertation, Universidad Complutense de Madrid.

Pujol Baulenas, Jordi. 2005. *Jazz en Barcelona 1920–1965*. Barcelona: Almendra Music.

Raphael-Hernandez, Heike, ed. 2004. *Blackening Europe: The African American Presence*. New York and London: Routledge.

Roberts, David D. 2006. *The Totalitarian Experiment in Twentieth-Century Europe: Understanding the Poverty of Great Politics*. New York: Routledge.

Soler García de Oteyza, Guillermo. 2012. *Eco i Distorsió. Els conjunts de música moderna a la Barcelona dels seixanta*. Barcelona: Generalitat de Catalunya.

Vázquez Montalbán, Manuel. 2000. *Cancionero General del Franquismo 1939–1975*. Barcelona: Crítica.

Wynn, Neil, ed. 2007. *Cross the Water Blues: African American Music in Europe*. Jackson: University Press of Mississippi.

Press and Online Articles

Anonymous. 1958. Untitled article. *Destino* 1072, 22 February: 37.

Cerri, Livio. 1947. '¿Qué es el boogie-woogie?' *Ritmo y Melodía*, July: n.p.

Díaz, Carlos. 1947. 'Blues, viejos blues'. *Ritmo y Melodía*, June: n.p.

García-Soler, Jordi. 1999. 'Joan Rosselló, el padre [HH] del Jamboree'. *El País*, 7 April. Available at: http://elpais.com/diario/1999/04/07/catalunya/923447243_850215. html (accessed 11 October 2014).

Jurado, Miquel. 2008. 'Un antes y un después para el jazz'. *El País*, 19 October. Available at: http://elpais.com/diario/2008/10/19/catalunya/1224378450_850215. html (accessed 11 October 2014).

Montsalvatge, Xavier. 1955. 'Louis Armstrong en Barcelona'. *Destino* 957, 10 December: 39.

Navarro, Vicenç. 2011. 'Por cada asesinato que cometió Mussolini, Franco cometió 10.000'. *Nueva Tribuna*, 15 September. Available at: www.nuevatribuna.es/articulo/ sociedad/vicen-navarro-por-cada-asesinato-que-cometi-mussolini-franco-cometi-10-000/20110915180144061735.html (accessed 11 October 2014).

Navarro, Vicenç. 2013. 'La dictadura fue totalitaria, no solo autoritaria: clarificaciones a partir de la muerte de Juan Linz'. *Público*, 14 October. Available at: http://blogs. publico.es/vicenc-navarro/2014/08/25/la-dictadura-fue-totalitaria-no-solo-autoritaria-clarificaciones-a-partir-de-la-muerte-de-juan-linz/ (accessed 11 October 2014).

Papo, Alfredo. 1985. Untitled article. *Solo Blues* 2, Autumn: 18–19.

P. C. H. 1946. 'El "jazz", el "swing" y el "boogie-woogie"'. *Ritmo y Melodía*, January: n.p.

Soto Carmona, Álvaro and Pedro Martínez Lillo. 2011. 'La naturaleza del franquismo'. *El País*, 8 June. Available at: http://elpais.com/diario/2011/06/08/opinion/13074 84011_850215.html (accessed 11 October 2014).

Valiño, Xavier. 2011. 'El Franquismo contra el rock. Tapando culos, tetas, paquetes . . . por vicio'. *Ruta 66* 279, February: 74–76.

Select Discography

Armstrong, Louis and His All Stars. *Historic Barcelona Concerts at the Windsor Palace 1955*. Fresh Sound Records, 2000, Double CD.

D'Efak, Guillem. *Blues*. Concèntric, 1965, EP.

Els 4 Gats. *L'Home Solter*. Ediphone (Edigsa), 1964, EP.

Jazz en Barcelona 1920–1965. Fresh Sound Records, 2005, Triple CD.

Lone Star. *Concierto Teatro Infanta Beatriz. Madrid 1968*. Lone Star Music, 2010, CD.

Smash. *Todas sus grabaciones (1969–1978)*. Rama Lama, 2001, Double CD.

Select Filmography

García Berlanga, Luis (director). *Bienvenido Mr Marshall*. UNINCI, 1953, film.

Martín, José Luis (director). *Barna Blues. La història del blues a Barcelona*. Bad Music Blues, 2012, DVD.

Pérez Fabián, David (director). *Clamores Jazz, 30 Años*. Self-produced, 2012, DVD and CD.

PART IV

Iberia – Portugal

9

JAZZ AND THE PORTUGUESE DICTATORSHIP BEFORE AND AFTER THE SECOND WORLD WAR

From Moral Panic to Suspicious Acceptance

Pedro Roxo

The reception and the practice of jazz in Portugal after the Second World War have, until recently, been understood in academic and jazz promoters' discourses as a cultural form that was seemingly employed in strategies of political resistance to the dictatorship of Estado Novo (New State) (1933–1974). Although this argument must be taken into account, it frequently overshadows other political and social uses of jazz during the Portuguese dictatorship from the 1930s to the mid-1950s. This chapter brings into play the contradictory attitudes of the regime towards jazz, modern dances and American popular music in general. Although these expressive forms were never totally abandoned during the dictatorship, the regime's moral panic during the 1930s, due to a conservative stance and the growing influence of Roman Catholicism, gave way to acceptance, with certain reservations, that was also related to the regime's strategic shift towards the Allies during the second half of the Second World War. The chapter will highlight the way jazz, particularly after the Portuguese participation in the Marshall Plan in 1950, was part of the American popular-culture offensive in Portuguese society. It will also shed light on the role of jazz promoter Luís Villas-Boas in that process and in the dissemination of jazz in Portugal as a serious art music dissociated from commercial dance music products. Through research in archives and jazz collections, and by conducting ethnographic interviews with older-generation jazz promoters, professionals and amateurs, this chapter explores some lesser-known processes in the history of jazz in Portugal.

Introduction

Jazz in its multiple representations has been appropriated and reappropriated by various agendas over the decades. In this process, the narrative that dominates in each period frequently eclipses other possible representations. Until recently, most studies and discourses on jazz in Portugal during the dictatorship headed by António de Oliveira Salazar (1889–1970) have focused on the practice and, especially, consumption of jazz as a metaphor for political resistance against the dictatorship's authoritarian stance. The fact that narratives on jazz music in Portugal were predominantly produced by jazz promoters and jazz critics (some of them also jazz musicians) from the late 1950s until the first years of the last decade has contributed to the perpetuation of this perception throughout the twentieth century and, in some cases, until the present. Most of these jazz promoters, critics and even musicians were opponents of the regime and some of them were even actively involved in oppositional political movements, such as the Portuguese Communist Party (PCP), that were illegal and clandestine.[1] Thus, understandably, the discourses produced by these social agents (who in practice functioned as gatekeepers to the perceptions of jazz in Portugal) perpetuated the meanings attached to jazz that they experienced – jazz as a signifier of political, social and racial emancipation, in addition to being a form of high art. Although such perceptions were common among many jazz aficionados, the perpetuation of this view overshadowed other dynamics of the relationship between Salazar's regime and popular culture, particularly jazz. Furthermore, the 'resistance interpretation' was also reinforced because it seemed to make sense in relation to Estado Novo's propaganda strategy of making use of popular culture – and particularly music – to instil nationalist principles and inculcate in the population values based on a mythical and traditional rural society and corporative[2] Portuguese popular culture (Rosas 2008) that excluded the foreigner and cosmopolitan influences that were viewed as threats to the 'true Portuguese soul'.

Over the last decade, several scholarly studies on jazz in Portugal have addressed the 'jazz as a form of resistance' issue with different approaches and theoretical frameworks, resulting in sometimes contradictory perspectives (e.g. Martins 2006; Cravinho 2011; Santos 2009; Roxo 2009b; Roxo and Castelo-Branco 2016). Of course, at different times and places jazz has indeed been a music of resistance, but it has also been many other things, and has shown great flexibility in its negotiations with the state. This chapter brings into play some of the multiple attitudes to jazz (and American music in general) during the Estado Novo regime before and after the Second World War. Despite the regime's attempt to engineer a top-down model of action and attitude regarding popular culture, the consumption of jazz (and American popular music in general, along with other foreign styles of popular music) was never proscribed, and music groups that also played jazz (or what they perceived as jazz) flourished throughout the 1930s and the 1940s. Perhaps for that reason it is possible to understand the moral panic among sections of the Catholic Church during that period.

In fact, it will also be highlighted how institutions that served Estado Novo's propaganda machine, particularly the state radio Emissora Nacional, never really banned jazz or American music in general from its regular broadcasts – in apparent contradiction of the regime's ideology. This relative tolerance towards jazz was broadened during and after the Second World War, following a closer alignment with the Allies' policies and the growing influence of Britain and the United States in Portugal after 1943, and particularly after Portugal's entry into the Marshall Plan.

The explanation of these processes in this chapter is anchored in specific case studies arising from recent published research (see References), ethnographic materials such as interviews with some of the key players in Portuguese jazz during the period under review, and recent archival research, particularly in the collection of jazz promoter, critic and co-founder of the Hot Clube de Portugal in the late 1940s, Luís Villas-Boas (1924–1999). This collection is in the archives of the Hot Clube de Portugal and it is being catalogued and researched by a team from the Institute of Ethnomusicology of Faculdade de Ciências Sociais e Humanas, Universidade Nova de Lisboa, as part of the project 'Jazz in Portugal: The Legacies of Luís Villas-Boas and the Hot Clube de Portugal' (PTD/EAT-MMU/121834/2010), funded by the Portuguese Foundation for Science and Technology (FCT). As in any research project such as this, no one category of documentation can on its own sustain the arguments, but in aggregate I believe they make the case, provisional on future work that might enjoy the space of a full-length monograph.

The Dictatorship of Estado Novo, Popular Culture and the Regime's Propaganda Machine

The dictatorship of Estado Novo, headed by António de Oliveira Salazar, was implemented following a coup d'état on 28 May 1926, which established a military dictatorship (in 1928 named the 'National Dictatorship') that supposedly sought to end the political and social turmoil that had characterized the First Republic (1910–1926). It can be understood as a political phenomenon framed by the nationalist and authoritarian movements that swept through Europe before the Second World War (Rosas 1996). As stressed by Torgal (2008, 26), the military dictatorship was characterized by the convergence of several heterogeneous groups with a shared desire for a new order and especially a new kind of leader. It included conservative republicans, monarchists, Catholics, supporters of fascism, low-ranking and high-ranking members of the military, former socialists who had turned to a more conservative regime, and modernist artists searching for a new aesthetic and a 'new world'. Besides conservative values, they shared a certain fascination with the new authoritarian European

196 Pedro Roxo

leaders, such as Benito Mussolini. Thus, the first years of Salazar governance were characterized by a search for balance between the different political and ideological factions that supported the dictatorship and the development of ways to secure and centralize power (Torgal 2008, 26; Rosas 2008).

After being installed as head of the government in 1932, Salazar worked for the adoption of a new constitution that would be more consistent with the political and social ideals of Estado Novo. It was in force from April 1933 and envisaged a nationalist and corporative state that would work as a kind of third path against democratic liberalism and communism (Torgal 2008, 27).[3] The political constitution of 1933 represents the institutionalization of Estado Novo's regime that would endure until 25 April 1974 (the democratic revolution), making it Europe's longest dictatorship. During this period, Salazar ruled from 1928 (first as Minister of Finance, then as Prime Minister) to 1968, becoming the longest-ruling Portuguese statesman in the process.

With the support of members from the above-mentioned groups, Salazar encouraged the establishment of a political party, União Nacional (National Union), which would become the only permitted political party in Portugal. In addition, as argued by Rosas (2008), the fascist pressure coming from elsewhere in Europe seemed the only (or at least in the historical context of the time the most reasonable) alternative to liberalism, and the true opponent of communism. This rationale paved the way for the emergence of bottom-up organizations of a fascist type, aimed at the mobilization and ideological indoctrination of the populace. The most significant of these were: the Legião Portuguesa (Portuguese Legion), formed in 1936; the Mocidade Portuguesa (Portuguese Youth), also established in 1936, and somewhat modelled on the Italian Opera Nazionale Balilla and the German Hitler Youth; and the Fundação Nacional para a Alegria no Trabalho (FNAT; National Foundation for Joy at Work), founded in 1935 and based on the Italian Dopolavoro and German Kraft durch Freude, which aimed to educate and fill the leisure time of Portuguese workers, including its cultural activities (see below). The country's ruling elites – conservative, authoritarian, attracted by fascism but not necessarily in favour of its violent aspects – distrusted the officials of these institutions, who displayed aspirations to form fascistic militias and even to achieve a certain level of military autonomy. Nevertheless, they were tolerated initially and may even be said to have facilitated the establishment of Salazar's political strategy as they were part of a series of measures intended to monitor and control all aspects of social life (Rosas 2008).

Other important measures to gain control of society were: the creation of a security service agency in 1933 (the Polícia de Vigilância e Defesa do Estado (State Defence and Surveillance Police); renamed the Polícia Internacional de Defesa do Estado (International and State Defence Police) in 1945); the publishing of corporative legislation which aimed to create institutions to control, supervise and monitor freedom of association, trade unions and freedom of speech (including through the reorganization of censorship); and above all, in

1933, the creation of the Secretariado de Propaganda Nacional (SPN; National Propaganda Bureau), which was tasked with directing and centralizing information from all ministries and public services and developing and spreading the regime's propaganda and cultural policies. The SPN was directly accountable to Salazar, but it was directed by António Ferro (1895–1956), an ex-journalist and writer who was an enthusiastic supporter of both modernism and strong, interventionist states led by charismatic leaders.

In order to try to articulate the propagandistic needs of Estado Novo and modernist ideas and aesthetics, Ferro envisaged a state policy that favoured the arts and culture which he named 'Política do Espírito' (Politics of the Spirit). This was an attempt to promote a kind of aestheticization of politics, designed to reach the spirit of individuals and contribute to raising the cultural standards of society and the creation of a 'new man' imbued with higher standards and nationalist values. In other words, Política do Espírito aimed to construct a Portuguese identity grounded in modernist ideas and in the regime's nationalist ideology. Under this policy, a well-oiled propaganda machine promoted multiple activities, such as the support of (some) arts and artists, the organization of competitions on the aesthetics that were valued by the regime, the establishment of literary prizes, the organization of events related to Estado Novo's views on Portuguese ethnography and folklore (popular art exhibitions, 'typical' village competitions), the promotion of tourism, the support of cinema for propaganda purposes, the organization of national and international colonial exhibitions, and the utilization of radio as a tool for propaganda and educational purposes, including through the promotion of sonic references with nationalist connotations, such as folklore and '*musica ligeira*' (Portuguese light music).

Nery (2010) argues that Política do Espírito was based on a clear conceptual distinction between '*Alta Cultura*' (High Culture) and '*Cultura Popular e Espectáculos*' (Popular Culture and Entertainment). A small group of cultural institutions such as the São Carlos Opera Theatre, Lisbon, ensured the official representation of the state through events directed for a small elite audience. In turn, popular culture was represented by institutions such as the state broadcaster Emissora Nacional (EN) and the above-mentioned FNAT, which promoted regular initiatives aimed at the general population for both entertainment and ideological indoctrination purposes. Thus, as mentioned above, official representations of popular culture by the state during the 1930s and the 1940s were based on the values of a corporative and traditional rural society, and on nationalist renewal (see further Chapter 10, this volume).

Reactions to the Practice and Consumption of Jazz and Modern Dance

In this cultural and political landscape, as argued by Roxo and Lourenço (2013) and Roxo and Castelo-Branco (2016), expressive practices of foreign origin

198 Pedro Roxo

were not always well received, particularly jazz and modern dances of American origin. However, that is not to say that they were wholly absent. In fact, recent studies have shown that musical products of American and African-American origin associated with modern dances, including foxtrot, Charleston, black-bottom and one-step, were consumed in Portugal at least from the 1920s (see Martins 2006; Roxo 2009a; Santos 2009; Ferreira 2012). These music categories were also employed in the marketing strategies of record labels, which often linked a modern dance style to local music styles (for example, fado-foxtrot) in order to appeal to Portuguese consumers at a time when modern dances and dance music were fashionable (Roxo 2009a, 243). The existence of a musical repertoire that combines Portuguese musical traditions with various forms of African-American popular music (e.g. fado-slow, fado-foxtrot, corridinho-one step and marcha-one step) or with other widely disseminated styles of music (e.g. fado-tango) is another indicator of the growing local influence of the emerging phonographic industry. This process can sometimes be conceptualized as producing and promoting hybrid musical products. However, the application of the adjective 'hybrid' to many of these products requires qualification since, in some cases, the mixing of styles was reflected only in the disc label (ibid.). In fact, recent work at the Institute of Ethnomusicology of the Universidade Nova de Lisboa (INET-md FCSH-UNL) on the digitization of old Portuguese 78 r.p.m. recordings from the 1920s and 1930s discloses the circulation of commercial recordings of Portuguese popular music, such as fado, including arrangements with stylized syncopated patterns, accentuating the off-beat, although in most cases without instrumental improvisation (Roxo and Castelo-Branco 2016).

Modern dances and dance music and were also incorporated in '*teatro de revista*' (revue theatre – a kind of Portuguese vaudeville) and practised in popular ballrooms and night-clubs (Roxo 2009a). As a consequence, the number of jazz bands (later known as *jazzes*) increased and their activities were extended to other leisure spaces (restaurants, hotels, casinos, spas) that adopted the new forms of entertainment. Although the repertoires of these bands included multiple musical categories associated with the dance floor (such as the syncopated music styles of the African-American tradition, waltzes, tangos, Latin American music), the term 'jazz', as embodying the spirit of the time (as in the mainstream media, in literary and artistic references), also became the general term to encompass new forms of modern popular music broadcast and marketed globally, based on a new system associated with new technologies of music production and reproduction.

Interestingly, the jazz band as a major signifier of modern times was noted by António Ferro in the early 1920s. As shown by Roxo (2009a), the publication of Ferro's book *A Idade do Jazz Band* (The Jazz-Band Age) in Lisbon in 1924 would substantially define perceptions of jazz in Portugal, probably until the Second World War; it is possible to discern indirect allusions to his work in newspaper articles and also in the discourses of those who were more critical towards jazz, especially representatives of the Catholic Church. Although Ferro's book is not an analytical discourse on jazz, it depicts ways of perceiving modern times through the use of jazz and modern dances as metaphors for social developments, including female emancipation, fashion, consumer society and technological innovations, with references to the artistic and literary avant-garde, Diaghilev's Ballets Russes, cinema and, of course, jazz and modern dances themselves. Moreover, the 'jazz band' concept is employed in his text as a metaphor for modern life through the parallels Ferro establishes between improvisation, spontaneity, artificiality and the prominence of accelerated pace in jazz music with the speed of modern times and modern experience – as a kind of triumph of emotion over reason.

Indeed, allusions to jazz and modern dance signal new perceptions of civilization and the adoption of new poses, conceptual attitudes and relations with the body that challenge the artistic legacy and civilized canons of the nineteenth century and present new models of civilization marked by industrialization and mass consumption.

> Waltz is the sentimental, romantic, dance. Waltz has the rhythm of a love statement . . . In waltz there is still certain shyness. The man holds the women in his arms, like a crystal . . . The bodies are close, close but worried; the bodies are still very soulful . . . In foxtrot, by contrast, there is no romanticism any more; there is no shyness; there is relaxation, happiness, and friendship. The foxtrot is the bohemian dance, crazy, a swinging dance, the dance that does not worry, and the dance that does not think of tomorrow . . . Love born in a waltz is love that ends up in marriage, love for ever. In the foxtrot, it is love that dies, love that lasts for a kiss . . . The one-step is, nevertheless, the most dangerous of dances because it is kidnapping . . . There are women who run in a one-step, like in a car. One woman in a one-step is a woman on a trip . . . Tango is a dance that is a game of patience; an inoffensive dance because it is too geometric . . . Maxixe [Brazilian modern dance] is an alliance of bodies. Finally, the shimmy is a free dance, a dance where arms and legs get together as mates and get drunk on champagne and in the gestures, in the opium of angry eyes, in the metallic electricity of the bodies. The shimmy is the Bolshevik dance, the dance that socializes all parts of the body, making them equal, giving them the same importance, the same function of happiness and abandonment.
>
> *(Ferro 1924: 65–66)*[4]

However, this positive interpretation of modern and African-American expressive practices was not consistent in Ferro's writings. Analysing the reception of jazz in Portugal in the light of Estado Novo's colonial ideology,

Roxo and Castelo-Branco (2016) emphasize the contradictions in relation to African-American expressive practices in Ferro's work as he started to align himself with the regime's policy, and particularly when he insinuated himself with Salazar. The relationship between António Ferro and António Salazar would become particularly intimate after the former published *Salazar – O Homem e a sua Obra* (Salazar – the Man and his Work) in 1933. The book collects a series of interviews between the two men that had appeared in the daily newspaper *Diário de Notícias* the previous year. Soon after its publication, Salazar invited Ferro to be the director of the Secretariado Nacional de Informação (National Information Bureau). In fact, Ferro convinced the Prime Minister of the importance of an effective propaganda machine in order to inform the masses and avoid manipulation of the populace by political rivals (Rosas 2008). As he became a major figure in the cultural politics of Estado Novo, the inconsistency of his discourse reveals the attitude of Salazar's regime towards black Otherness. In point of fact, Estado Novo's colonial ideology emphasized a racialized tripartite society divided into *colonos* (white Portuguese settlers), *creole* or *assimilados* (Creole or black people who adopted Portuguese values and lifestyles, including the Portuguese language and Catholicism) and *indígenas* (the local black population) (Roxo 2009b; Roxo and Castelo-Branco 2016). In light of this, and given the nationalist agenda of Salazar's regime, it is not surprising to see the development of a less favourable attitude towards jazz and modern dances after the institutionalization of Estado Novo.

The Catholic Church's Moral Panic Reactions to Modern Dances and Jazz

The conservative stance of Estado Novo paved the way for increased Catholic influence within Portuguese society. Although the constitution of 1933 retained the principle of separation of Church and state, it did so in a strong spirit of *rapprochement*, which would ultimately facilitate the establishment of the 'Concordata de 1940' between the Catholic Church and Salazar's regime. This agreement would restore a stable and peaceful relationship between the two parties after the hostile attitude towards religion during periods of liberal monarchy and the First Republic. While the Concordata re-established official relations with the Catholic Church, the 1933 constitution had already identified Catholicism as the religion of the Portuguese nation by granting it certain constitutional rights, such as legal status for religious corporations, permission to provide religious education in private schools, and approval of the Estatuto das Missões Católicas (Catholic Missions Statutes; Cruz 1996).

Given the growing influence of Catholicism, which began in the first few years of the national dictatorship, it is not surprising that some religious agents were extremely critical of cultural practices that were considered contrary to

Catholic orthodoxy, such as jazz music and modern dances. Following a series of articles condemning modern dances and balls published in the *Acção Católica* (Catholic Action) archdiocesan newsletter in 1938, the author, Molho de Faria, a priest, expanded his arguments in book form with the publication of *Os Bailes e a Acção Católica* (Dance Events and the Catholic Action) the following year. This volume includes severe criticism of modern dances, reflecting the moral panic that modern dances, jazz and dance music were evoking in Catholic-influenced Portuguese society at the time. A cause of particular concern was the supposed evil influence of modern dances' disordered and lascivious body movements, which were seen as contrary to Catholic decency and a potential threat to appropriate and ordered somatic behaviour. Furthermore, the allegedly democratic access to modern dance events across all social classes was seen as a threat to the social order on the grounds that it promoted contact between different classes and even between different races (Roxo 2009a; Roxo and Castelo-Branco 2016):

> The Episcopal ban on dances is applied to all present or future dances that might include mischief . . . such as schymmi and java, where we can find gross and depraved characteristics; such as the Charleston, foxtrot, black-bottom, Boston, jazz, turkey-trot, camel-trot, cheek-to-cheek, one-step, two-step and other Anglo-American dances, where we can still feel the rationalism and naturalism of [Anglo-American] religion . . . And many other Andalucían dances, all exciting, with constant spiralling and serpentine movements which wake up feelings that are not noble.
>
> *(Faria 1939: 86–87)*

> Is it possible that our people, who think they are civilized, favour these dances? Is it possible that so many [women and men] who are zealous would want to be inferior, descending to the customs of savage peoples, preferring the tango, shimmy, foxtrot, and many other dances. It is clear that these *balls* in which there is no taste, no art, no aesthetics, only lowliness, are absolutely prohibited under any circumstances.
>
> *(Faria 1939: 63; see also Roxo and Castelo-Branco 2016)*

Some of Faria's statements seem to be sermonized reiterations of a 1938 edition of Portuguese Catholic Action's *Regras para a Formação Religiosa e Moral das Dirigentes da Acção Católica Feminina* (Rules for the Religious and Moral Education of the Female Catholic Action Leaders), in which the author warned that:

> The [Portuguese Plenary] Council considers not only dangerous but even entirely evil the dances that have been introduced in recent times (modern dances). It is not lawful to watch them and even less to participate

in them . . . The modern dances are in themselves evil. So, it is not worthy to participate in them. The purposes do not justify the means. The clothing used in these shows is also regrettable – the shapes and the necklines could be said to be objectively immoral . . . It should be noted that dance itself is not evil: even Holy King David danced before the Ark. The modern dances, though, yes, these are evil, immoral, dangerously close to mortal sin – from which everyone should flee as if it were fire itself. It is often said: Enjoy yourselves, but do not sin.

(Nogara 1938, 39–40)

Despite the narrative of crisis in this volume, and regardless of the Catholic Church's and Estado Novo's distrust, modern dances, dance music and jazz all continued to be practised in Portugal throughout the 1930s, although it is difficult to establish how widely they were disseminated. Regardless of the silence or outright condemnation in official documents (reports by the political police, civil government intelligence and religious organizations), numerous newspapers refer to music groups (many of them termed *jazzes*) with different constitutions, describing a varied repertoire of popular music at the time, including modern styles of dance music. Yet, because few recordings have survived, it is difficult to determine if these bands were using improvisation and a musical vocabulary associated with styles currently covered by the jazz canon, as problematized by DeVeaux (1998). From Shipton's (2007) perspective, many of these bands probably played music styles that were unrelated to jazz. However, the use of a modern repertoire of popular music (usually Anglo-Saxon in origin) and modern musical instruments, particularly drums,[5] situated these groups in the modern spirit of which 'jazz' was a main metaphor.

Broadcasting and the Support of Jazz and Modern Music

Further evidence of the continued presence of American popular music (perceived by many as 'jazz') in Portugal, despite the government's suspicion of foreign music, can be found in the changes implemented at the state broadcaster when António Ferro became its director in 1941. Reacting to accusations of excessive airplay of American light music on EN, among other light music styles such as fado (Ferro 1950; Silva 2010), Ferro implemented measures that were designed to refresh radio programming and turn EN into an up-to-date, modern broadcaster with nationalistic values. In this respect, he established a series of measures and departments with the aim of promoting Portuguese music. These included: the institution of annual competitions for music composition covering several genres (opera, chamber music, symphonic music, sacred music, popular music); the Gabinete de Estudos Musicais (Music Studies Bureau), created in 1942 to collect and collate traditional songs, find and catalogue ancient Portuguese music, develop art music, and promote a Portuguese style of popular music; the creation of the Orquestra Típica Portuguesa (Portuguese Typical Orchestra) in 1943 with a remit to perform popular and traditional Portuguese music at *serões para trabalhadores* (workers' evenings) and *serões para soldados* (soldiers' evenings); the founding of the Centro de Preparação de Artistas da Rádio (Centre for the Preparation of Radio Artists) in 1947 in order to train future radio stars, although EN was already actively promoting its performers and vocal music groups by then (e.g. Irmãs Remartinez and Irmãs Meireles). However, once again, this does not mean that jazz and American popular music overall declined on EN in the 1940s. In fact, Nini Remartinez (born 1919) states that she and her sister Fernanda, who performed as Irmãs Remartinez, presented a varied repertoire of Portuguese, Brazilian, Argentinian and Spanish songs, but also many numbers from the American songbook, such as 'Sentimental Journey', 'Paducah' and 'Begin the Beguine' (interview with Remartinez 2007).

It is also significant that other state initiatives – such as EN and FNAT's weekly *serões para trabalhadores* show, which aimed to inculcate nationalistic values – never really proscribed foreign music, including swing and other Anglo-American styles. *Serões para trabalhadores* were variety shows that combined urban popular music with folklore and light classical music. They were organized all over the country, and frequently broadcast live by EN. State-sponsored orchestras from EN's 'orchestra complex'[6] and the station's sponsored and trained individual artists appeared regularly on these shows, but so did modern music groups that had some sort of connection with EN and with the shows' organizers. Such was the case with Os Excêntricos do Ritmo (Rhythm Eccentrics), a group that had a significant impact on jazz practice in Portugal until 1947, when it disbanded.

Os Excêntricos do Ritmo and the Practice of Jazz at Private Events and on State Radio during the 1940s

An interview with Aleixo Fernandes, the last surviving member of Os Excêntricos do Ritmo, and an analysis of EN radio scripts from 1942 reveal that the band performed a varied repertoire, including Portuguese, Brazilian and Cuban popular music as well as jazz. As in virtually all non-US diasporic sites at the time, the understanding of what constituted jazz was flexible, but Os Excêntricos do Ritmo drew on the American popular music repertoire, including swing, which incorporated strong elements of jazz practice, such as modern dances and syncopated rhythms (interview with Fernandes 2014), so in certain contexts they thought of themselves as jazz players.

The band's membership and its performance contexts are good examples of the social networks that developed around the practice of jazz and modern music in the Lisbon area. It consisted of a family of Goan Portuguese origin who had been raised in Mozambique and settled in Lisbon in the 1930s

(Goa and Mozambique were Portuguese colonies in India and East Africa, respectively, at the time). This band was informally founded by the brothers Nereus (piano) and Aleixo Fernandes (guitar), following the family's regular musical soirées at home (a common tradition among many Goan families). They were joined by Fernando Freitas da Silva (guitar) and António Mendonça (double-bass and cello). The Fernandes brothers had no formal musical training; they learned how to play their instruments by listening to radio shows and recordings in the second half of the 1930s (interview with Fernandes 2014). For that reason, they had a very wide repertoire, with special emphasis on the most popular music of the time. The sessions at their home became increasingly popular, attracting many friends, including musicians who were mainly interested in playing jazz. By the early 1940s the band was being invited to play on EN's variety shows (interview with Fernandes 2014), including *serões para trabalhadores* shows, on which they also performed swing. At the same time, the band would participate in jam sessions at the house of Spanish drummer and son of the Spanish Chancellor in Lisbon, Luís Sangareau, where the musicians were most interested in using jazz as a basis for improvisation. These sessions – as well as those at the Fernandes brothers' own home – were attended by Luís Villas-Boas (1924–1999), a jazz aficionado who would become a key figure in the promotion of jazz in Portugal after the war. Roxo and Lourenço (2014) suggest that the network of relationships built around these sessions probably persuaded Villas-Boas that there was sufficient interest in 'real jazz' to start promoting it in earnest in Portugal. Hence he set to work on building the national and international contacts that would eventually lead to the founding of the Hot Clube de Portugal.

The Second World War: A Strategic Shift in the Regime's International Policy and the Consumption of Jazz

If jazz and American popular music in general never totally disappeared in Portugal, even at the height of nationalist and imperialist rhetoric in the second half of the 1930s, during the Second World War the regime's international strategy changed, allowing for a gradual increase in the influence of Anglo-Saxon culture in the country. This change was not accepted by everyone, with opponents from the top to the bottom of Estado Novo's structures. Nevertheless, Salazar retained an apprehensive interest in the outcome of the war. If continued proximity to Spain's Francoist regime was considered strategically useful, given the potential annexationist threat posed by Franco's Falange and the ideological congruence of the two regimes, maintaining cordial relations with the United Kingdom was also helpful, given the latter's control of the Atlantic and therefore the routes to Portugal's overseas territories (Rosas 2008). For these reasons, in 1939 Portugal signed the Treaty of Friendship and Non-Aggression with Spain (Pacto Ibérico; Iberian Pact) a few days before the end of the Spanish

Civil War (Rezola 2008) but also a military cooperation agreement with Britain that reaffirmed the centuries-old Anglo-Portuguese Alliance (Rosas 2008), ensuring Portugal's neutrality in the war. Thus, the prospect of an Allied victory after 1942 and the Allies' request to use Ilha Terceira in the Azores as an air force and naval air base (under the cooperation agreement) in 1943 (Rocha 2009) accentuated the trend that had begun in the late 1930s towards softening the regime's most radical, militaristic and openly pro-fascist organisations (including the above-mentioned Legião Portuguesa and Mocidade Portuguesa). Moreover, special care was taken to avoid any further ideological identification with the Axis powers (Rosas 2008).

The musical impact of the Allied forces on Ilha Terceira during and after the war was felt with the introduction of jazz – including the 'three B's of swing . . . blues, barrelhouse and boogie woogie' (*Atlantic Echo*, 1 December 1944, quoted in Santos and Rubio 2009, 27) – and Anglo-American popular music in general, with concerts by military bands and visiting musicians (including the RAF Quintet and the Stan Kenton Orchestra), concerts promoted by the United Service Organization (Frank Sinatra, Glenn Miller Orchestra, Irving Berlin with Bob Hope), debates on jazz, record listening sessions and jam sessions (Santos and Rubio 2009). The British–American music dynamic on the island impacted on local practices, with the emergence of bands performing swing and other modern styles (ibid.).

In mainland Portugal, the ongoing activities of *jazzbands*, the persistence of jazz and American popular music airplay on EN (including, for example, Irmãs Remartinez's interpretations of the Andrew Sisters' repertoire and Tavares Belo's swing-oriented arrangements; Moreira 2012, 173), and swing and other jazz or American-oriented performances at *serões para trabalhadores* are all indicators of a degree of official permissiveness. Despite Estado Novo's nationalist rhetoric, foreign music continued to be aired on EN, in Ferro's words 'in order not to steal the international imagination from EN listeners' (quoted in Moreira 2012, 164). Furthermore, Portugal's wartime neutrality turned Lisbon into an exit point to the United States, with the consequent arrival in the city of many refugees from multiple parts in Europe. This contributed to an animated nightlife in the Lisbon area (particularly Casino Estoril), with a consequent proliferation of bands and modern music styles, including jazz (interview with Menezes 2001).

The Role of Luís Villas-Boas in the Construction of a Discursive and Performative Arena for Jazz in Portugal

Under this more favourable environment, it is not surprising that Luís Villas-Boas started his EN radio show, 'Hot Club' (co-produced with Augusto Fraga), in November 1945 as a platform for the foundation of the Hot Clube de Portugal (HCP) and the promotion of 'real jazz'. The following month, he wrote to the leading Spanish jazz magazine:

> [On 25 November], I started, along with the well-known journalist Augusto Fraga, at Emissora Nacional, a programme under the name of 'Hot Club', intended to be the voice of HCP and to promote the best values of American and European jazz. For that purpose I have some good French jazz records that are unique in Portugal. They were given to me by a good friend with links to the Hot Club de France. [Portuguese] audience preferences are mostly directed to [the music] of Glenn Miller and Harry James and only a few [listeners] appreciate a good Bix [Beiderbecke] or a good King Oliver. It is also to promote those names that we are starting the 'Hot Club'.
>
> *(Villas-Boas letter to Ritmo y Melodia 1945)*

The 'Hot Club' radio show's shift to Rádio Clube Português (RCP) in January 1946 is often linked to the censorship of jazz at EN (Martins 2006; Santos 2009). However, Roxo and Castelo-Branco (2016) suggest that although the show might have been a target for sabotage by EN staff who were strongly opposed to jazz (Santos 2009), EN's schedule did include other shows that played jazz as well as music from Portugal's African colonies, such as the Cape Verde singer Fernando Quejas's programme in the late 1940s. Despite such music's black origins, and therefore supposed inferior quality, given the regime's colonial and imperialist ideology, it was incorporated into the 'national folklore' repertoire in order to emphasize the unity of Portugal's empire (Roxo and Castelo-Branco 2016). Furthermore, although RCP was a private radio station, it was connected to Salazar's regime, as its founder, Jorge Botelho Moniz, had been a strong supporter of Franco's Falange during the Spanish Civil War (Roxo and Lourenço 2013). Notwithstanding this, RCP's programming was quite open to American and other foreign popular music after the Second World War, which perhaps explains why Villas-Boas was keen to move his radio show there. Moreover, he was probably attracted by RCP's frequent collaborations with Os Excêntricos do Ritmo, with whom Villas-Boas himself had already organized a series of jam sessions to promote 'Hot Club'. Two recordings from these November 1945 events – which also featured Luís Sangareau on drums and the Spanish violin player José Puertas – were recently digitized at INET-md: renditions of the jazz standards 'Lady Be Good' (1924, George and Ira Gershwin) and 'Memories of You' (Eubie Blake, 1930). These are anchored in improvisation, 'with special emphasis on Puertas' sensitive violin playing on *Memories of You*, and the energetic *hot style* improvisation full of technical resources in the performance of *Lady Be Good* (in which piano player Nereus Fernandes also improvises)' (Roxo and Lourenço 2013, 15). The instrumental make-up of the band and the musicians' fondness for 'hot' improvisation, reminiscent of the style of the Hot Club de France's quintet, show that Os Excêntricos do Ritmo and Villas-Boas were clearly inspired by their French counterparts' ideas about jazz. These examples are particularly significant because they represent the start of Villas-Boas's proselytizing in favour of '*la veritable musique de jazz*' (as articulated by Hugues Panassié), as opposed to commercial jazz and other styles of music – an attitude that might have prompted a negative reaction among EN's staff.

Roxo and Lourenço (2013, 2014) have shown that, following the launch of the radio show, Villas-Boas, along with other jazz aficionados, was determined to found HCP and integrate it in the European network of Hot Clubs, headed by the Hot Club de France. To that end, after 1945, he maintained close contact with foreign (especially Spanish) musicians, foreign jazz magazines (e.g. *Ritmo y Melodia*) and members of the Hot Clubs of Barcelona (Alfredo Papo, Antonio Tendes), Madrid (Alberto Urech) and, most of all, France (Panassié and Charles Delaunay) (ibid.; see further Chapters 7 and 8, this volume). Analysis of Villas-Boas's correspondence with these prominent actors in the European jazz scene reveals an exchange of ideas about jazz styles and musicians, discussions on how to promote jazz more effectively, advice on the best ways to manage the clubs, the lending, buying and selling of records, radio show recommendations, and the organization of Portuguese concerts featuring Spanish musicians as well as those from further afield who plied their trade in Spain and France. Above all, though, the letters prove that Villas-Boas modelled his promotion of jazz in Portugal on the strategies that the Hot Club de France had adopted in the early 1930s: launch a radio show; publish pro-jazz articles in the press; organize concerts, festivals and jam sessions; and encourage local musicians to play jazz. Villas-Boas attempted to understand the earlier Hot Clubs' philosophy and then tried to assimilate the doctrines that lay behind the notion of 'hot' jazz as 'true' jazz. However, he was more than a passive, uncritical recipient of French jazz enthusiasts' opinions. He also questioned some of their ideas, as a letter to Panassié from July 1946 indicates:

> I agree with you about the bands (colored bands) playing good jazz. Yes, sometimes Benny Goodman, Gene Krupa, Woody Herman even being jazz what they play, [they] play bad jazz. But I can't agree with you when you say that the so called neo-Dixieland musicians under Eddie Condom [*sic*] (the same musician that played in Chicago 20 years ago the same kind of jazz) play also bad jazz. No, I don't think so, because I heard them play on those Carnegie Hall 'All American Jazz Concerts', and Pee Wee, Brunies, Spanier, Mesirow [*sic*], Bobby Hackett, Ernie Caceres, Gene Schroeder, Art Bernstein, Krupa, Wettling, are great jazz musicians, as great as other colored musicians because they have the jazz feeling that makes a music sound hot and with swing. No, I think you weren't fair about them. Some of them were the ones that played the same kind of jazz with Bix, and Bix even being white, was as great as any colored jazz musician. This is my personal opinion that may be a wrong one. For me

> [it] is good jazz the one that has swing and feeling[. It is] not interesting
> if it is played by negroes or by white man.
>
> *(Villas-Boas letter to Hugues Panassié 1946)*

Besides showing that Villas-Boas was reluctant to categorize jazz in terms of race, this is particularly relevant in the context of Portugal's colonial policies and legislation, because in the late 1940s the tripartite division of Portuguese society into white people, *assimilados* (or *crioulos*) and *indígenas* (black people) was still in place. Indeed, although he initially concurred with Panassié's views on jazz, Villas-Boas eventually moved closer to Charles Delaunay's perspective and embraced modern bebop styles, particularly after the bebop schism of 1947 (Roxo and Lourenço 2014). In any case, Villas-Boas was responsible for creating a discursive and performative arena for jazz in Portugal after 1945, anchored in well-defined aesthetic boundaries and categories of music in general, and jazz in particular.

Anglo-American Influences in Post-War Portugal: Towards a Cautious Openness to Jazz

After the Second World War, in order to avoid international marginalization, Estado Novo 'strategically attempted to combine an approach to Western European democracies and the US without abandoning the (undemocratic) established regime and the long historical–geographical relations with the colonies' (Roxo and Lourenço 2013, 9, citing Pereira 2006). 'Cooperative neutrality' from 1942 onwards and integration within the Atlantic Pact (ensuring US and Western European control of the North Atlantic via the Azores) contributed to Portugal's international acceptance without the need to amend any domestic or colonial policies (ibid.). This was also helped by Portugal's offer of assistance to Europe at the first Paris conference and its support for the Marshall Plan. In order to avoid excessive dependency on the United States Salazar initially declined the offer of financial aid for Portugal in 1948 (Rollo 2007), but he changed his mind amid a financial crisis later that year, and the country finally became eligible for a year of Marshall Plan assistance in 1950 (ibid.).

While British and US propaganda activities were familiar in Portugal during the war (Rendeiro 2013), US influence increased significantly in the post-war period, especially after Portugal's admission to the Marshall Plan. In 1951, Os Excêntricos do Ritmo's guitarist Aleixo Fernandes was one beneficiary of this. After finishing his studies, he was hired as an electrical engineer by RARET (Sociedade Anónima de Rádio Retransmissão, Lda.), a Radio Free Europe (RFE) relay radio station, located seventy kilometres north of Lisbon. Salazar allowed this service to operate under the condition that it would work only as a mirror, meaning that its short-wave transmissions to Eastern Europe could comprise only programmes that had been made in and sent from West Germany (Munich, Holskirshen) for propaganda purposes.[7]

Documents contained within HCP's archives suggest that US influence in Portugal spread through various cultural activities, such as military-band concerts (e.g. the Army Field Band played in Lisbon in 1957), and through the consumption of popular culture, including jazz. American use of music and other cultural activities for propaganda purposes, particularly after the Second World War, is well documented (see, e.g., May 1989; Wagnleitner 1994; von Eschen 2004), but while the dissemination of US popular culture throughout post-war Portugal is well known, systematic research of this phenomenon has been lacking until recently. Now, though, with access to documents relating to the activities of the United States Information Service at the US Embassy, Lisbon, we are learning more about the US government's efforts to disseminate various genres of American music, including jazz. For example, a brochure that gives details of an event in June 1955 includes Duke Ellington under the heading 'jazz and dance music', but also 'chamber music' (Elliot Carter), 'symphonic light music' (George Gershwin, Cole Porter), 'symphonic music' (Purcell, Weber, Beethoven) and 'American folklore' (black spirituals sung by the Wings Over Jordan vocal group). At each such event, the embassy would distribute one of these brochures, which contained biographies of the composers and musicians whose music would be played and/or discussed that evening. These were intended to encourage the audience to build personal files on the 'most famous American composers and performers'. A jazz and dance music event in November 1955 featured ragtime (Wally Rose), blues (Bessie Smith), New Orleans (Louis Armstrong), Chicago (Eddie Condon), New York (Bix Beiderbecke), Dixieland (Phil Napoleon), swing (Duke Ellington, Teddy Wilson and Billie Holiday, Benny Goodman), progressive jazz (Pete Rugolo), New Orleans revival (Turk Murphy) and modern jazz (Dave Brubeck). By 1959, the US Embassy was organizing twice-weekly events on the history of music, again including jazz. (Parallel sessions focused on North American literature and cinema, and Portuguese and American architecture.)

These events proved very popular:

> At that time we [university students] were all pro-American . . . We were interested in American products because of the contrast we felt with the absence of things in our country. There was a notion of progress [in US products] . . . Everything was American: cinema, design, ways of developing publicity . . . Jazz was introduced to Portugal in the American way. They organized several courses and conferences on jazz at the US Embassy's library on Duque de Loulé [Lisbon Street]. These usually comprised a conversation between two people about what jazz was. I used to go with a colleague, and we were also listening to classical music and some jazz records.
>
> *(Interview with Évora 2013)*

FIGURE 9.1 US Armed Forces Big Band (Probably US Naval Forces Europe Band), Hot Clube de Portugal, 1951 or 1952

(FT-68-1-F05-2, Hot Clube de Portugal Archives)

In addition to hosting its own musical educational activities, the US Embassy supported HCP, for instance by lending the club so-called 'V-discs' (interview with Moreira 2012). Moreover, Villas-Boas persuaded bands from the US Navy, the British Royal Navy and cruise ships to perform at the club (see Figure 9.1), US officials would meet there, and imports of US jazz records started to increase – all of which led to significant American influence on HCP's activities. The close relationship with the US Embassy might also explain why the club was initially established on the same street (Duque de Loulé). Furthermore, it may be no coincidence that the government finally granted HCP a licence to operate in March 1950, one month after Portugal had come under the auspices of the Marshall Plan.[8]

However, it is important to question the degree to which the US authorities – in the form of the US Information Service – were actively involved in these developments. Villas-Boas certainly worked closely with the famous American jazz promoter, impresario and musician George Wein from the late 1950s onwards, and particularly in the 1970s, when the two men organized the Cascais Jazz Festival, which was based on Wein's Newport Jazz Festival (Santos 2009; see further Chapter 10, this volume). By then, the State Department was

FIGURE 9.2   Jam Session at the Hot Clube de Portugal, Lisbon, 1951 or 1952, Featuring Fernando Rueda (Drums), Raul Paredes (Double-Bass), Mário Simões (Piano), Art Carneiro (Saxophone) and Mário de Jesus (Trumpet); Luís Villas-Boas Is Standing Second from the Right

(Photo by Augusto Mayer; FT-67-1-F10-10, Hot Clube de Portugal Archives)

collaborating extensively with the private sector (and especially with Wein) in order to identify local jazz enthusiasts and promoters who could stage jazz events in various countries with the ultimate aim of disseminating pro-US propaganda while keeping costs to a minimum (von Eschen 2004, 188–189). However, that was not yet general US policy in the early 1950s.

Either way, HCP became the main performance venue for jazz in Portugal, and so contributed to the development of a community of jazz aficionados and musicians whose affiliation to the club legitimized them as supporters of 'real jazz', as opposed to commercial and/or dance music – although most of the musicians continued to play those styles outside of the club's facilities.

HCP also became a place of contact between Portuguese and foreign musicians, who were now free to meet and communicate through an international musical idiom of US origin. Throughout the 1950s there was exponential growth in Portuguese jazz concerts, particularly in the Lisbon area. Touring jazz musicians would frequently play or jam at HCP, as documents and photographs in the club's archives indicate. Among those who played there were: André Réwéliotty (1955; see further Chapter 10, this volume), Count Basie's (1956) and Quincy Jones's (1960) orchestras, US sax player George Johnson (1952), French singer–guitarist Sacha Distel (1955), piano player Friedrich Gulda (1957), Spanish violinist José Puertas y sus Caballeros (1952), Swiss singer Hazy Osterwald's orchestra (1952), Sam Judel and Gaby Laurent's quintet (1952), Jamaican-British pianist Yorke De Souza (1952), singer Canelina (1953), pianist Jimmy 'Loverman' Davis (1954), the Buddy Bradley Ballet (1955), singer Patsy Parnham with the Colin Beaton Trio (1955), Argentinian clarinetist Panchito Cao (1955), singer Lidia Scotty (1955), Sidney Bechet (1955; see further Chapter 10, this volume), Cuban singer, composer and pianist Pérez Prado (1955), French singer Simone Alma (1956), vibraphone player Paul Lambret (1956), the Fisk Jubilee Singers, accompanied by pianist Anne G. Kennedy (1956), 'Dizzy' Reece (1956), clarinetist and orchestra director Maxim Saury (1957), French pianist Raymond Fol (1957), French singer Anny Fratellini (1957), Brazilian accordion player Sivuca (1958), singers Edith and Joyce Peters (1958), trumpeter Bill Coleman and Gianfranco Mauze (1959), tenor saxophonist Raul 'Bebe' Quesada (unknown date) and Argentinian pianist António Robledo (1960). The huge increase in the number of jazz concerts by foreign musicians throughout the 1950s (particularly in the Lisbon area), alongside HCP's regular activities, suggests that the regime became progressively more open in that decade. In fact, given the the trends towards industrialization and urbanization in the 1950s (Rosas 2008), the boom in these modern practices could even be considered useful to the state.

Nonetheless, jazz was by no means welcomed by every official within Estado Novo's structures. The successful organization of jazz events still often depended on the seemingly arbitrary whims of decision-makers in the Secretariado Nacional de Informação, Polícia Internacional de Defesa do Estado, civil government agents and so on. For instance, HCP received permission to organize the first Lisbon Jazz Festival (1953) only after it agreed to remove the word 'jazz' from posters and flyers and replace it with 'modern music', so the event was officially known as the 'Modern Music Festival' (as was the next edition in 1954). Interestingly, the censors did not interfere with the third edition (held in 1955), so 'jazz' did appear in that festival's title – the 'Session of Cinema and Jazz' (see also Chapter 10, this volume).

HCP tried to comply with the regime's guidelines throughout the 1950s, and its willingness do so probably contributed to its survival to the end of the dictatorship and beyond. However, the club's disregard for the social and political underpinnings that were increasingly associated with jazz around the world led some younger and more politicized enthusiasts to found a rival venue in the late 1950s – the Clube Universitário de Jazz. The genre certainly had a different meaning for this next generation and they used it as a different signifier. (Cravinho explores the formation and development of this club in Chapter 10, this volume.)

Conclusion

Domingos and Pereira (2010) criticize much of the history of Estado Novo for focusing on the decisions and activities of Salazar and Portugal's elite, and consequently neglecting the structures and the rest of society. Accordingly, the traditional perspective tends to be a 'top-down view, where the omnipotent, omniscient power of the leader and the institutional and legal apparatus of the regime will tower over an apathetic and amorphous population' (ibid., 12). Furthermore, these authors highlight that most studies of resistance movements tend to impose a top-down perspective in which individuals exhibit conscious positions towards the authorities as collaborators, resisters, or devoted to passivity (passive or submissive agents), which in practice is synonymous with historical invisibility (ibid.).

This chapter suggests that, despite the regime's political orientation and its leader's will, the reception and practice of jazz in Portugal from the 1930s to the 1950s reveal historical and social processes that are complex, multifaceted and highlight structural contradictions in a regime that cannot be regarded as monolithic and omnipotent (see also Johnson's discussion of totalitarianism in the Introduction, this volume). That is, despite the nationalist, pro-fascist and Catholic orientation of Estado Novo, which censored and felt threatened by jazz and modern dances, these practices were never fully suppressed, even at the height of the regime's fascist orientation during the 1930s. The consumption of popular culture, globally disseminated and associated with modernity, motivated modes of agency and continued practice and consumption among thousands of Portuguese citizens despite and in the face of the regime's directives and surveillance measures, to such an extent that the Catholic Church experienced something akin to moral panic.

On the other hand, changes in the regime's internal dynamics in response to the evolving international context, particularly during and after the Second World War, paved the way for guarded toleration of jazz and British–American popular culture in general. The latter was never particularly at odds with the regime's propaganda apparatus, such as EN, due to the ubiquity of such cultural forces around the world, but also because some decision-makers, including António Ferro, were not totally opposed to jazz. In fact, officials and decision-makers in the regime's various structures displayed significant ambivalence towards the expressive practices that were related to jazz and American popular culture, and sometimes exhibited heterogeneous modes of personal agency that exposed the Estado Novo's inherent contradictions.

The use of jazz as a tool of US cultural propaganda, including the promotion of swing as the music of freedom, along with the European dissemination of discourses and institutions (such as the Hot Club network) that presented jazz as a musical genre with well-defined aesthetic borders (in marked contrast to commercial dance music), led to the emergence of local jazz aficionados, agents and institutions in Portugal. Any analysis of the processes relating to jazz in the post-war Portuguese context must consider the dense and complex interplay between the regime's wary tolerance, the increasing American influence in the country, Villas-Boas and HCP's activities, the rising dissemination of jazz

214 Pedro Roxo

records and radio broadcasts, and the emergence and operation of personal modes of agency. Perceptions of jazz during the Estado Novo era changed and adapted with time. But those changes and adaptations also reveal transformations and reconfigurations in the regime's internal dynamics as a result of domestic (including societal) and international developments. The study of popular culture in general and jazz in particular helps us to unravel these decisive but often veiled processes.

Notes

1 This information is based on interviews I recorded with promoters and musicians, some of whom have since died. Such political sympathies remain a sensitive issue and some of the interviewees requested anonymity.

2 *Corporativismo português* (Portuguese corporativism) during Estado Novo involved state control through various organizations in all areas of social, economic and cultural life. Economically speaking, this placed the Portuguese system in opposition to liberal capitalism, but not entirely. Industry and trade associations (corporations) depended directly on the Secretary of State for the Economy and were supervised and monitored by the National Institute for Work. Hence, Portugal's economy was not self-directed but rather controlled by direct state intervention (through the dictatorship's economic coordination bodies). However, Estado Novo was not wholly opposed to capitalism, as private property, the private sector and the search for profit were all tolerated (Brito 1996). Socially, it meant the promotion of a 'natural order of things' in which each individual should occupy his or her own place in the 'spontaneous and harmonious' hierarchy of society that had been 'established since time immemorial' (Rosas 2008). Culturally, it was organized through the institutions described in the main text.

3 Despite several reviews and revisions over subsequent years, in essence the 1933 constitution would endure until 24 April 1974. Among its major features were: the rejection of democratic liberalism and regimes that are legitimized by civil liberties and popular sovereignty; the consecration of corporative nationalism (subordination to the interests of the nation and the institutionalization of moral and economic corporations in order to frame the citizens' lives); the authoritarian legitimacy of the state; the state's responsibility for coordinating and promoting the economic and social life of the nation; the unification of all of Portugal's colonies in order to create a multi-continental nation, and the application of the idea of a colonial empire (Rosas 1996); and the consolidation of a nationalist ideology supported by strong armed forces.

4 All translations from the Portuguese are by the author.

5 Martins (2006), Roxo (2009a) and Santos (2009) all note that the expressions '*jazz*' and '*jazzband*' were used in Portugal to indicate the use of drums (the instrument of modernity) as well as to describe the groups that played dance music and/or jazz (see also Johnson's Introduction, this volume). This remained common usage at least until the 1960s.

6 According to Moreira (2012), a central component of the state-sponsored music production system established within state radio consisted of the 'orchestra complex' (several orchestras and chamber music ensembles, some of which shared the same musicians, including symphony, light music, and folk music orchestras).

7 A short documentary about RARET, including excerpts from an interview with Aleixo Fernandes, is available at: www.youtube.com/watch?v=fX9s20dhI_c (accessed March 2015).

8 The club first applied for – and failed to receive – government approval in 1947. It then reapplied in 1948. According to Bernardo Moreira (interview 2012), and as revealed in

HCP's file at Lisbon's Civil Government Bureau, 'education' was one of the club's stated goals at that time, so the Ministry of Education had the final say on the application. In February 1950, HCP removed the educational goal from its application, and approval was granted a month later (see Roxo and Castelo-Branco 2016).

References

Brito, José Maria Brandão de. 1996. 'Corporativismo'. In Fernando Rosas and J. M. Brandão de Brito, eds, *Dicionário de História do Estado Novo*. Lisboa: Círculo de Leitores: vol. I, 216–224.

Castelo-Branco, Salwa, Rui Cidra and Pedro Moreira. 2010. 'Música Ligeira'. In Salwa Castelo-Branco, eds, *Enciclopédia da Música em Portugal no Século XX*. Lisboa: Círculo de Leitores: vol. III, 872–875.

Cravinho, Pedro. 2011. '"Gosto de Jazz Porque Gosto da Verdade": O Clube Universitário de Jazz, a Contestação e o Discurso Alternativo ao Meio "Jazzístico" em Portugal, entre 1958–1961'. In *Performa 2011. Encontros de Investigação em Performance*. Aveiro: Universidade de Aveiro: 1–11.

Cruz, Manuel Braga da. 1996. 'Concordata e Acordo Missionário'. In Fernando Rosas and J. M. Brandão de Brito, eds, *Dicionário de História do Estado Novo*. Lisboa: Círculo de Leitores: vol. I, 182–183.

Davenport, Lisa E. 2009. *Jazz Diplomacy: Promoting America in the Cold War Era*. Jackson: University Press of Mississippi.

DeVeaux, Scott. 1998. 'Constructing the Jazz Tradition'. In Robert G. O'Meally, ed., *The Jazz Cadence of American Culture*. New York: Columbia University Press: 483–512.

Domingos, Nuno and Victor Pereira. 2010. 'Introdução'. In Nuno Domingos and Victor Pereira, eds, *O Estado Novo em Questão*. Lisboa: Edições 70: 7–39.

Faria, Molho de. 1939. *Os Bailes e a Acção Católica*. Braga: Tip. da Oficina de S. José.

Ferreira, Manuel Pedro. 2012. 'Ecos do Jazz-Band: Ilustrações Portuguesas (1922–1930)'. In Margarida Acciauoli and Paulo Ferreira de Castro, eds, *A Dança e a Música nas Artes Plásticas do Século XX*. Lisboa: Colibri: 75–105.

Ferro, António. 1924 [1923]. *A Idade do Jazz-Band*. Lisbon: Portugália Editora.

Ferro, António. 1933. *Salazar – O Homem e a sua Obra*. Lisboa: Empresa Nacional De Publicidade.

Ferro, António. 1950. *Problemas da Rádio: 1941–1950*. Lisbon: SNI.

Jackson, Jeffrey H. 2003. *Making Jazz French: Music and Modern Life in Interwar Paris*. Durham, NC: Duke University Press.

Martins, Hélder Bruno. 2006. *Jazz em Portugal (1920–1956)*. Coimbra: Almedina.

May, Lary. 1989. *Recasting America: Culture and Politics in the Age of Cold War*. Chicago: University of Chicago Press.

Moreira, Pedro. 2012. '"Cantando espalharei por toda a parte": Programação, produção musical e o "aportuguesamento" da "música ligeira" na Emissora Nacional de Radiodifusão (1934–1949). Ph.D. dissertation, Universidade Nova de Lisboa.

Nery, Rui Vieira. 2010. 'Políticas Culturais'. In Salwa Castelo-Branco, ed., *Enciclopédia da Música em Portugal no Século XX*. Lisboa: Círculo de Leitores: vol. III, 1017–1030.

Nogara. 1938. *Regras para a Formação Religiosa e Moral das Dirigentes da Acção Católica Feminina*. Lisboa: n.p.

216 Pedro Roxo

Pereira, Pedro Cantinho. 2006. 'Portugal e o Início da Construção Europeia (1947–1953)'. *Nação & Defesa* 115: 235–255.

Rendeiro, Margarida. 2013. '"Britain is not out of date": Actividades de Propaganda Cultural Inglesa em Portugal entre 1939–1945'. In Maria Fernanda Rollo and Ana Paula Pires, eds, *War and Propaganda in the XXth Century*. Lisboa: IHC: 117–121.

Rezola, Maria Inácia. 2008. 'The Franco–Salazar Meetings: Foreign Policy and Iberian Relations during the Dictatorship (1942–1963)'. *eJPH* 6(2): 1–11.

Rocha, Alexandre Luís Morelli. 2009. 'As Pressões dos Aliados e a Evolução da Política Externa Portuguesa entre 1942 e 1943'. *Revista de História* 161: 113–144.

Rollo, Maria Fernanda. 2007. *Portugal e a Reconstrução Económica do Pós-Guerra. O Plano Marshall e a Economia Portuguesa dos Anos 50*. Lisboa: IDMNE.

Rosas, Fernando. 1996. 'Constituição Política de 1933'. In Fernando Rosas and J. M. Brandão de Brito, eds, *Dicionário de História do Estado Novo*. Lisboa: Círculo de Leitores: vol. I, 198–205.

Rosas, Fernando. 2008. 'O Salazarismo e o Homem Novo. Ensaio Sobre o Estado Novo e a Questão do Totalitarismo Nos Anos 30 e 40'. In Luís Reis Torgal and Heloísa Paulo, eds, *Estados Autoritários e Totalitários e suas Representações*. Coimbra: Imprensa da Universidade de Coimbra: 31–48.

Roxo, Pedro. 2009a. 'Modernidade, Transgressão Sexual e Percepções da Alteridade Racial Negra na Recepção do Jazz em Portugal nas Décadas de 1920 e 1930'. In *Arte e Eros*. Lisboa: Faculdade de Belas Artes de Lisboa: 230–272.

Roxo, Pedro. 2009b. 'A Recepção do Jazz no Portugal Colonial e a Produção de Discursos Sobre a Alteridade Racial Negra: Alguns Estudos de Caso'. Paper presented at the Instituto de Ciências Sociais da Universidade de Lisboa, Lisboa, 11 November.

Roxo, Pedro and Salwa Castelo-Branco. 2016. 'Jazz, Race and Politics in Colonial Portugal: Discourses and Representations (1924–1971)'. In Philip Bohlman and Goffredo Plastino, eds, *Jazz Worlds/World Jazz*. Chicago: University of Chicago Press.

Roxo, Pedro and Miguel Lourenço. 2013. 'Jazz Networks in the Iberian Peninsula: The Role of Luís Villas-Boas during the 1940s and the 1950s'. Paper presented at the Congreso Internacional 'El jazz en España', València, 28–30 November.

Roxo, Pedro and Miguel Lourenço. 2014. 'Crossing Mind and Geographic Borders but Fixing Jazz Music Boundaries: The Foundation of Hot Clube de Portugal in the late 1940s'. Paper presented at the 'Rhythm Changes – Jazz beyond Borders' Conference, Amsterdam, 4–7 September.

Santos, João Moreira dos. 2007. *O Jazz Segundo Villas-Boas*. Lisboa: Assírio & Alvim.

Santos, João Moreira dos. 2009. *Jazz em Cascais. Uma História de 80 Anos*. Cascais: Casa Sassetti.

Santos, João Moreira dos and António Rubio. 2009. *Jazz na Terceira: 80 Anos de História*. Praia da Vitória: Bluedições.

Shipton, Alyn. 2007 [2001]. *A New History of Jazz*. London: Continuum.

Silva, Manuel Deniz. 2010. 'Rádio'. In Salwa Castelo-Branco, ed., *Enciclopédia da Música em Portugal no Século XX*. Lisboa: Círculo de Leitores: vol. IV, 1080–1084.

Torgal, Luís Reis. 2008. 'O Fascismo Nunca Existiu . . . Reflexões Sobre as Representações de Salazar'. In Luís Reis Torgal and Heloísa Paulo, eds, *Estados Autoritários e Totalitários e suas Representações*. Coimbra: Imprensa da Universidade de Coimbra: 17–29.

von Eschen, Penny. 2004. *Satchmo Blows up the World: Jazz Ambassadors Play the Cold War*. Cambridge, MA: Harvard University Press.

Wagnleitner, Reinhold. 1994. *The Coca-Colonization and the Cold War: The Cultural Mission of the United States in Austria after the Second World War*. Chapel Hill: University of North Carolina Press.

Interviews

Évora, Elisabeth (university student in the 1950s; architect). 2013. Interview by Pedro Roxo.

Fernandes, Aleixo (guitar player). 2014. Interview by Miguel Lourenço, Pedro Roxo, Inês Cunha and Bernardo Moreira. Transcripted extracts available at: www.hcp.pt/public/uploads/newsletter/HotNews_10._versao_final.pdf (accessed 14 March 2016).

Menezes, Carlos (guitar player). 2001. Interview by Pedro Roxo.

Moreira, Bernardo (double-bass player and director of HCP in the 1990s). 2012. Interview by Pedro Roxo and Miguel Lourenço.

Remartinez, Nini (singer). 2007. Interview by Pedro Roxo.

Archival Sources

Luís Villas-Boas letter to Hugues Panassié [in English], July 1946, PT-HCP-LVB-UI6, Hot Clube de Portugal Archives.

Luís Villas-Boas letter to *Ritmo y Melodia*, 12 December 1945, PT-HCP-LVB-UI20, Hot Clube de Portugal Archives.

10

A KIND OF 'IN-BETWEEN'

Jazz and Politics in Portugal (1958–1974)[1]

Pedro Cravinho

This article will investigate the use of jazz music as: a form of a protest against the Portuguese Estado Novo regime and its colonial policies (1958–1961); and a symbol of freedom to configure new social realities in Portugal (1971–1974).[2] In 1958 Salazar's regime of Estado Novo, in response to international pressure, eased repression and promoted 'free elections' to give the illusion of a free country. In this context, students at the University of Lisbon founded the Clube Universitário de Jazz (CUJ; University Jazz Club). It was closed by the Portuguese police in 1961 after the first signs of the war of independence in Angola. In 1971, during the Caetano administration, Portugal hosted an international jazz festival for the first time. Although state sponsored, it became a space of political resistance for thousands, and led to the arrest of American bass player Charlie Haden. This article will analyse jazz discourses and practices in Portugal during these two important historical moments: 1958 and 1971.

Introduction

In the post-Second World War scenario, in the various European realities, powerful institutions like the armed forces, the Catholic Church, associations and interest groups linked to sectors of the oligarchy became gradually intertwined with another hegemonic power, America's pursuit of political and economic control through policies of modernization and development. As a consequence, *jazz scenes* formed themselves around US garrisons in Europe, as in other parts of the globe, as 'coerced Americanisation', according to Joe Moore's (1998, 2). definition. However, according to Penny von Eschen (2004, 8): 'The official State Department cultural-presentations programs in Western Europe did not include jazz, precisely because jazz was considered

Jazz and Politics in Portugal (1958–1974)   **219**

already established, popular, and commercially viable.' Nevertheless, considering that jazz music was promoted as anti-communist counter-culture in the Eastern Bloc 'to win converts to the *American way of life*' (ibid., 7), what was the collateral impact of these actions in the anti-communist Southern European reality, including Portugal?

The aim of this chapter is to focus on the relationship between jazz and politics during the Portuguese Estado Novo (New State) regime. In particular, it will address questions related to the use of jazz music as: a form of protest against the regime and its colonial policies (1958–1961); and a symbolic embodiment of freedom through which to configure new social realities in Portugal (1971–1974). Using the concepts of 'transformative practice' (Grossberg 1996, 88), and 'ideal human relationships' (Turino 2008, 20), I argue that in Portugal during the Estado Novo era within these particular contexts jazz music was able to propose the configuration of as yet non-existent social realities.[3]

My first case study is the Clube Universitário de Jazz (University Jazz Club), founded in Lisbon in 1958; the second is the Festival Internacional de Jazz de Cascais (International Cascais Jazz Festival), established in 1971 in the village of Cascais. Both of these case studies occurred during the New State regime, but in contrasting periods of its history. The first took place during the administration of António de Oliveira Salazar, known as Salazarism (1933–1968), during a period of political instability which began with the presidential elections of May 1958 and ended with the start of the armed conflict in Angola in March 1961, which in turn led to a colonial war and ultimately independence for the former Portuguese colonies in Africa.[4] The second took place during the administration of Marcello Caetano, who succeeded Salazar as President of the Council of Ministers in September 1968. This period, known as Marcellism (1968–1974), was marked by growing social and political unrest regarding the ongoing colonial war in the Portugal's former colonies in Africa, which led to considerable tension during the final years of the Estado Novo regime.

Salazarism (1933–1968): The Post-War Environment

The broad historical outline and character of the emergence of Salazar's Estado Novo have already been set out in Chapter 9. The nature of the regime may be summarized in its guiding slogan '*Tudo pela Nação, nada contra a Nação*' (All for the nation, nothing against the nation) (Sardica 2008, 48). Salazarism was a dictatorial regime 'based on radical right-wing and anti-liberal social-Catholicism' (Pinto 2003, 26) that survived for several decades with the help of an efficient political secret police. After the end of the Second World War, Salazar managed to survive in the new international Cold War scenario. Although he stated in the 1960s, 'I want this country poor but independent and I do not wish it colonized by American capital' (quoted in Sardica 2008, 67), the regime was unable to block the external influences that the Portuguese population welcomed, directly or indirectly, consciously or unconsciously, in particular from the United States of America. If, on the one hand, other Western nations, and above all the US superpower, felt Salazarism was deficient in democratic values, on the other it provided a very advantageous buffer against communism at the start of the Cold War (ibid., 67). In April 1949, relations with the United States eased further with the international acceptance of Portugal as a founding member of the North Atlantic Treaty Organization (NATO), and some years later, in December 1955, as a full member of the United Nations (UN). These diplomatic affiliations reflect the strategic importance of Portugal's territory in the Cold War context. Salazar's initial refusal of financial aid from the Marshall Plan would only temporarily delay the first effects of the Americanization process that were already under way in several other European countries.

The Emergence of a Lisbon *Jazz Scene* in the Post-War Era

Aspects of the early post-war development of a jazz scene are discussed by Roxo in Chapter 9, primarily with reference to the work of Luís Villas-Boas on Portuguese radio and in the Hot Clube de Portugal. Here I want to address parallel issues, including film music, through which US music styles began to penetrate Portuguese culture. As a consequence, the construction of a musical heritage that started with a very strict and narrow cultural policy and the nationalist values of the Estado Novo regime gradually lost its hermetic nature. According to Jorge de Sá Gouveia (2011), in Portugal during the 1940s and 1950s film music became clearly based on the Hollywood model in which some classical composers often worked on movies. However, this statement may seem contradictory, because, on the one hand, as Sardica (2008, 67) declared, 'Salazar never liked the Americans, and especially the types of civilization and culture the USA stood for', but, on the other hand, according to Gouveia (2011), the film music that was composed for Portuguese cinema over nearly two decades, and funded by the Estado Novo regime, was clearly strongly influenced by Hollywood.

Such US influence helped to pave the way for the emergence of a post-war *jazz scene* in the Lisbon area, supported by practitioners from several different musical sectors, including professional musicians from night-clubs and dance halls, jazz amateurs, classically trained musicians and, sporadically, foreign jazz musicians (Cravinho 2013a). A significant moment occurred in November 1945 when the jazz lover Luís Villas-Boas launched a radio programme named 'Hot Club' (Martins 2006, 126). Thereafter, Villas-Boas's next step was to organize jam sessions over subsequent years in the city of Lisbon. But the decisive step to boost jazz activity in Portugal was his creation of the Hot Clube de Portugal (HCP; Hot Club of Portugal), which he founded with a group of jazz aficionados. On 22 July 1946, a first draft of the HCP's statutes, inspired by the Hot

Club de France, was written. The HCP's organizing committee then submitted this for official approval on 17 January 1947. However, the Conselho Permanente da Acção Educativa (Portuguese Permanent Council of Educational Programmes), part of the Ministério da Educação Nacional (Ministry of National Education), rejected the application because it included a proposal to teach jazz in Portugal (Cravinho 2013b). Three years later, on 6 February 1950, a new application was submitted to the Lisbon Civil Governor, with the educational proposal omitted. Consequently, on 3 March, the Secretary-General of the Ministry of National Education – Manuel Cristiano Marques – informed the Lisbon Civil Governor that the Permanent Council of Educational Programmes no longer had any jurisdiction over HCP's activities. As result, the new HCP statutes were officially approved on 16 March.

Portugal's first jazz festival took place three years later, organized by Villas-Boas's HCP, but under the name 'Modern Music Festival', because the authorities refused to allow 'Jazz Festival' as a designation. It was held at the Cinema Condes on 27 July 1953. Nine months later, on 5 April 1954, HCP and Villas-Boas organized another, also named the 'Modern Music Festival', at the Cinema Capitólio. Then, on 25 July 1955, the third Portuguese jazz festival, again organized by Villas-Boas and the HCP but this time titled the 'Session of Cinema and Jazz', was staged at the Cinema Condes (see Chapter 9, this volume). Perhaps an even more important event for Portuguese jazz aficionados was staged later in the year: a pair of Sidney Bechet and André Réwéliotty Quintet concerts at the Teatro Monumental, Lisbon. Originally just one concert was scheduled for 28 November, but the demand for tickets was so high that Bechet agreed to hold another the next day. Another significant concert took place on 1 October 1956, when the Count Basie Orchestra and the jazz singer Joe Williams appeared at the Cinema Império, Lisbon.

Meanwhile, at the international political level, the world witnessed an increasing movement towards decolonization. Since Portugal's was one of the principal colonial empires in Africa, Asia and Oceania, as a consequence of international pressure Salazar's regime created a kind of 'democratic mirage' in 1958, softening repression and promoting 'free elections' to suggest that it presided over a free country. The participation of the Oposição Democrática (Democratic Opposition Party), led by General Humberto Delgado, was one of the strongest signs of change. On 10 May 1958, at the Café Chave d'Ouro, Lisbon, Delgado promised to dismiss Salazar in response to a question from a France Press correspondent. With this answer, he earned the nickname '*General sem medo*' (General without fear) and managed to unite various sectors of Portuguese society around the notion of establishing a democratic and decolonized society.[5] In this sense the presidential election became a sign of hope for the Portuguese people, both in Portugal itself and in the overseas colonies. However, as a result of extensive electoral fraud, Delgado lost the election (Sardica 2008, 69). Nevertheless, the political framework in Portugal from

1958 – particularly regarding presidential elections – strengthened a desire for change within the Portuguese cultural environment.

This led also to a significant increase in jazz-related activities: for instance, a Portuguese musician participated in the Newport Jazz Festival for the first time, when trumpet player José Magalhães was selected to perform in Marshall Brown's International Youth Jazz Band. Moreover, a new jazz club was formed in Lisbon University's student community; and on 3 November 1958 the fourth Portuguese jazz festival took place in Lisbon. Once again it was organized by HCP and Villas-Boas, but this time the authorities allowed the designation of 'Jazz Festival' (Cravinho 2013b; see also Chapter 9, this volume).

The Clube Universitário de Jazz

It was during this time of high expectations of change regarding the Portuguese presidential election that, as mentioned above, the Clube Universitário de Jazz (University Jazz Club) emerged among Lisbon's academic associations. Its members published the first Portuguese jazz magazine, *JAZZ*, and organized jam sessions, recording sessions, performances and lectures. Despite its short three years of existence, the University Jazz Club provided an alternative to Portugal's traditional jazz scene, which by 1958 had been centred on HCP for almost a decade (Cravinho 2012; see also Chapter 9, this volume). Its activities were coordinated by a core group comprising the founder Raul Calado, Pedro Valente Pereira – editor of the club's magazine – and a handful of other students, such as José Duarte, Raul Vaz Bernardo and Helder Leitão. The club became both a vehicle to promote jazz music among the student community and an agent for spreading political protest against the regime's colonial policies.

Calado was still a student at the University of Lisbon when he founded the club, which he established on the suggestion of a friend, an Angolan by the name of António Escudeiro, who belonged to Lisbon University's Cine Club (interview with Calado 2011). Calado had been an HCP board member,[6] but he resigned in December 1957 when others blocked his proposal to open the club to new members. The inaugural session of Calado's rival club was held at Cinema Roma a few months later, on 2 May 1958.[7] The event had been announced two days earlier in the 'Musical Life' section of *Diário de Lisboa*:

> Next Friday, at 18:30, a jazz music records audition for the University Jazz Club's inauguration will take place at the Cinema Roma, including debate and possibly specialist book and magazine readings.

In order to promote jazz, the new club organized balls, concerts, record sessions and even a *kwela* session for students from Portugal's African colonies. In addition, as mentioned above, it created the first Portuguese journal that was entirely devoted to jazz as the members' official bulletin. It organized itself in a framework that Benedict Anderson (2005, 72) terms a privileged space for the construction of an imagined community. With its associated identity, this imagined community that was formed by the promoters and the readers formally gathered as a body in which jazz music was the common denominator, and the *JAZZ* bulletin was essential to convey its ideals.

Pereira, a member of the club's organizing committee, first submitted a request to publish the magazine to the authorities on 19 July 1958 (NATT: PIDE/DGS). A second application was submitted a week later. The authorities granted their permission for publication on 6 August (NATT: PIDE/DGS), and stated that the magazine would not be subject to any restrictive censorship. The first edition was published later that month (Cravinho 2014a), and thereafter the journal circulated within a young community that was eager to listen to and learn about jazz. A total of ten editions appeared over the next year or so, some of them monthly, others bi-monthly. The monthly editions had between ten and twelve pages, while the bi-monthly issues could run to twenty-four pages. The contents were mainly educational, written to promote a better understanding of jazz music and to generate a better-informed jazz public (ibid.). Moreover, as the magazine was exempt from censorship prior to publication, the writers felt free to lend their support to the Portuguese colonies' civil rights movements. In this sense, the University Jazz Club became a voice for change and helped to mobilize young people who were committed to reform. It exhibited a collective ambition to break free from Portugal's prevailing social and political circumstances, and hoped to use (jazz) music to achieve this goal (Cravinho 2012, 162). Almost five decades later, one of the club's members, Manuel Jorge Veloso, revealed:

> Many of us did phonographic sessions – in cultural associations, students' associations – to promote the music, but at the same time we promoted the music, we promoted the fight of the Negroes. This was associated with colonialism, and therefore, let's say, it was a form of subversion.
>
> *(Quoted in Martins 2006, 169)*

One noteworthy example of such activity appears when we analyse the relationship between the University Jazz Club and the Casa dos Estudantes do Império (Empire Students' House). Salazar's regime established the latter in Lisbon in June 1944 in order to pursue its policy of educating the colonial elite. It was also designed as a means to merge the various associations that had been set up to represent students from Angola, Cape Verde, Macao, India and Mozambique the previous year. The idea of hundreds of young people differentiated by their origins and dispersed among numerous associations did not please the regime, for it ran contrary to the policy of national unity as espoused by Salazar's propaganda. However, the Empire Students' House – which remained active until the political police closed it down in September

224 Pedro Cravinho

1965, at the height of Portugal's colonial wars in Africa – quickly became a place for debate and consciousness-raising, as well as a symbol of transcontinental cultural life in Portugal (Faria 1997, 12). It was obviously an unusual forum for discussion and raising awareness of the Portuguese colonies' independence movements.

It is possible to determine the extent of the Empire Students' House members' political and social awareness through the organization's publications, *Mensagem* and *Boletim*, both of which were published after 1958. The display of political and self-affirmation within this organization became one of the most important models for the independence movements in the colonies (Monteiro 2001). In fact, many of the intellectuals and politicians who led the fight for freedom in the colonies had at one time lived in the Empire Students' House in Lisbon. Among them was Amílcar Cabral, an agronomy student born in Portuguese Guinea and later leader of the Partido Africano da Independência de Guiné e Cabo Verde (PAIGC; African Party for the Independence of Guinea Bissau and Cape Verde Islands). Jazz was a feature of the sessions promoted by this association, as is clear from *Boletim*. By implicating jazz in the fight for civil rights and the African-American struggle for emancipation against white supremacy in the United States, the University Jazz Club's members promoted the same ideals among Lisbon's overseas students, generating collective resistance to colonialism (Cravinho 2012).

Several reports on the record-playing sessions organized by Raul Calado at the Empire Students' House were publicized in its periodicals. In addition, young 'blacks and whites' mingled and danced with each other to jazz music, *merengue*, *kwela*, and other African sounds at many of the balls that were held at the University Jazz Club (interview with Calado 2011). The regime soon became uncomfortable with such activities, especially once the war of independence began in Angola in 1961. Consequently, the University Jazz Club's headquarters were shut down just a few months later. Nevertheless, by then, partly because of the club's activities, jazz was an accepted and recognized part of educated culture in Portugal, particularly under French influence in 'part due to the anti-fascist associations of an anti-racist music' (Hobsbawm 1998, 273), and especially among the student communities of Lisbon and Coimbra (Cravinho 2014a, 2014b).

Marcellism (1968–1974): Renovation in Continuity

When Oliveira Salazar fell seriously ill in September 1968, the Council of State chose Marcello Caetano as his successor.[8] Two months later, Caetano started to make some significant changes to the regime – most notably, in the context of this article, he relinquished any direct influence over the Censorship Bureau.[9] The State Secretariat of National Information, Popular Culture and Tourism (SNI) was abolished, with responsibility for censorship passing to the newly created State Secretariat of Tourism, Information and Popular Culture. The same reformist impulse led to the creation of the Directorate-General of Security (DGS) within the Ministry of the Interior, with its own jurisdiction and responsibilities, and the abolition of the International Police for the Defence of the State (PIDE), resulting in a restructuring of the political police agencies. Caetano presented himself as a 'renovator into continuity' and added some liberal names to his People's National Action party's electoral lists.[10] This period, known as 'Marcello's Spring', became a metaphor for the general hope for change under Caetano's administration in the Portuguese imaginary. And, indeed, there were attempts to liberalize and modernize Portuguese society under his presidency. Nevertheless, the determination to suppress the independence movements and maintain Portugal's colonial wars compromised the regime's attempts to promote itself as reformist. While Caetano claimed the parliamentary elections of 1969 would be a referendum on the regime's colonial policy, and there was relatively free debate during the campaign, voter registration data were rigged in an act of electoral fraud to guarantee victory for the regime, just as Salazar had rigged elections in the past. Hence the wars continued. Over the course of thirteen years, from 1961 to the end of the regime in 1974, 'one in every four' Portuguese young men were conscripted into the armed forces to preserve the integrity of the empire, and as a result more than 'a million Portuguese [did] military service in Africa' (Sardica 2008, 77).

Apart from the social impact of this process, the wars demanded an enormous financial commitment from a small country with limited resources. In the early 1970s, almost 50 per cent of public spending went on the conflicts. Consequently, the last few years of the colonial/independence wars, which were fought mainly by the youngest members of Portuguese society, contributed to rising tension at home. The young – and especially the highly politicized students' movements – became radicalized and diversified into a multiplicity of political groups, with affiliations ranging from communism to Maoism. Mário Mesquita (1996, 20) says of this period:

> Marcellism allowed the introduction of a salutary ambiguity, jeopardizing the dichotomy designs which are predominant in the affirmations against Salazarism. Regime and opposition suddenly appear not as entirely monolithic and coherent blocks, but rather fragmented into tendencies, sensibilities and factions . . . the students' movement lost its unitarian characteristics, inspired by the PCP [the Partido Comunista Português; Portuguese Communist Party], to split into a nebula of leftisms that mostly replaced Soviet references with new interpretations of Marxism.

As Marcellism progressively rejected further liberalization, the regime's opponents became increasingly radicalized and started to engage in ever more extreme resistance activities. The radical left's discourse was now based on a

226 Pedro Cravinho

model of rupture, in which an armed uprising was seen as necessary to overthrow the dictatorship and establish a new, classless Portuguese society (Bebiano 2005).

The International Cascais Jazz Festivals (1971–1973)

It was during this era of social instability that the first of three international jazz festivals took place in Cascais, a small village some thirty kilometres west of Lisbon. Organized by Luís Villas-Boas, Hugo Lourenço and *fado* singer João Braga, the festival was held at the Pavilhão Dramático de Cascais and attracted more than 10,000 people over two nights: 20–21 November (Curvelo 2002; Santos 2009; Veloso *et al.* 2010; Cravinho 2012). The festival enjoyed the official support of the regime through the State Secretariat of Tourism, Information and Popular Culture, which promoted tourism in the region with the slogan 'JAZZ É CULTURA' (Jazz is culture),[11] and it attracted several world-renowned jazz musicians to Portugal for the first time.[12]

The Miles Davis Septet launched the festival on 20 November. Aware of the Portuguese political and social context, and of the expectations generated by the festival itself, Davis demanded the first slot so he could use his 'voice' to inaugurate an event that had already come to symbolize freedom. (He was originally scheduled to go on stage after the Ornette Coleman Quartet.) This episode is important in order to understand the political context surrounding the festival: jazz was being performed on a large scale in Portugal for the first time at an event that was explicitly and symbolically associated with political freedom.

After Davis had completed his set there was a one-hour break for an equipment changeover before Coleman and his band started their performance. During their performance, bass player Charlie Haden dedicated his 'Song for Che' (Guevara) to 'the black people liberation movements of Mozambique, Angola and Guinea'. Extended applause followed, and then Haden played the song while Dewey Redman and Ed Blackwell gave raised-fist salutes. On Amy Goodman's TV programme *Jazz Legend Charlie Haden on His Life, His Music and His Politics*, Haden recalled: 'When I did the dedication there were young people there, students that were in the cheaper seats in front, and they all started cheering so loud that you couldn't hear the music' (Goodman 2006). The censors stopped the Portuguese national press from reporting Haden's dedication and the audience's reaction. However, the Portuguese political police's dossier on the festival (NATT: PIDE/DGS, Procedure no. 690-CI (2), File no. 42) indicates that they knew all about it, and some Portuguese media in exile gave it prominent coverage (NATT: PIDE/DGS). For example, a news report on Algeria's Rádio Portugal Livre (Radio Free Portugal) on 25 November announced:

> The American singer Charles [Haden] . . . at the 'Jazz festival' being held in Cascais dedicated a song to the patriots of Angola, Guinea/Bissau and

Jazz and Politics in Portugal (1958–1974)   **227**

Mozambique. Charles's song . . . was greeted with a standing ovation and mass demonstrations of support and enthusiasm from 5,000 people who attended the festival, an action that turned into a demonstration against the colonial war.

Similarly, in Brazil, *Portugal Democrático* (Democratic Portugal) – a São Paulo newspaper that Silva (2006: 25) describes as the only free publication opposed to the Estado Novo regime – published the following report (NATT: PIDE/DGS):

> At the Cascais Jazz Festival an American musician dedicated a song to the liberation movements of Angola and Mozambique. Although he spoke in English, people who understood him translated his words and the walls of the room almost collapsed with the applause. At the end of the show, he returned to his dressing room, where, as expected, the political police were waiting for him. [They] forced him to leave the country immediately, escorting him to the airport and making him board a flight that same day.[13]

The Portuguese political police actually arrested Haden the following day (21 November), at the airport. He was then taken to police headquarters, where he was interrogated by several agents. In the arrest report (see Figure 10.1), Haden is described as a 'member of the "Hornet Coleman's quartet" [*sic*]' before the interrogation itself is recorded. When 'INVITED TO DECLARE if he had been well received in Portugal and if he had found the environment favourable for his visit', Haden apparently replied in the affirmative. Then the interrogator asked why Haden 'had talked about issues regarding the anti-Portuguese African movements in the colonies during his plane trip and why did he dedicate a song . . . entitled "Song for Che" to the African independence movements during his performance in Cascais'? Haden himself gave more details of his arrest and interrogation on Amy Goodman's programme:

> They took me down a winding staircase to an interrogation room and started pumping questions. They said, 'We're going to transfer you over to PIDE [Portuguese political police] headquarters. And the next thing I know, I'm in a car, and we're travelling to prison. And I'm thrown into a dark room with low lights, and I stay there for I don't know how long – a long, long time . . . And they finally came and got me from the room and took me up to an interrogation room with really, really bright lights. I couldn't see anything. (Goodman 2006)

Prior to deciding to turn his appearance at the festival into a form of political protest, Haden had told Coleman that he didn't want to play there, because he didn't agree with the Portuguese government's policies: 'It was a kind of

FIGURE 10.1 Charles Edward Haden Arrest Report in 'Festival de Jazz em Cascais' Dossier (NATT: PIDE/DGS, Procedure No. 690-CI (2), File No. 42)

sobre gravações suas, entre elas, uma sobre a guerra civil de Espanha, e não abordou assuntos referentes aos movimentos de libertação nos nossos territórios do Ultramar. Que, durante a actuação do conjunto em Cascais ontem à noite, fez realmente uma dedicação da sua canção para o "CHE" aos movimentos de libertação em toda a Africa e nos Estados Unidos, por que o faz sempre que o conjunto actua em qualquer país. Que, antes de começar o festival, os organizadores do mesmo fizeram publicidade das canções e das músicas, razão pela qual a juventude presente já tinha conhecimento que se ia tocar a referida canção e aplaudiu expontâneamente logo que o conjunto começou a tocá-la. Que justifica o ter tocado a "canção para o CHE", porque o tem vindo a fazer em todos os países onde têm actuado, nomeadamente na Inglaterra, França e no Japão, onde já foi várias vezes premiada. Mas que se soubesse que isto lhe ia causar transtornos no seu regresso não teria executado a dita canção nem feito a dedicação, mostrando-se arrependido pelo acto que praticou por desconhecer que afectava o país onde o fazia.- - - - - - - - - - - - - - - - - - CONVIDADO A DECLARAR se deu alguma entrevista a jornais portugueses, ou se contactou com alguém da imprensa diária, declarou: -Que durante a sua estadia em Portugal não contactou com ninguem da imprensa nem deu quaisquer entrevistas, tendo apenas mantido contactos com os organizadores do festival do jaz que são, entre outros, um tal FRANK e o VILLAS-BOAS. - Que os receberam muito Bem convidando-os até a tomarem algumas refeições juntos e pagando por elas. Que, hoje ao chegar ao aeroporto teve conhecimento por intermédio duma tal SIMONE GINEBRE de nacionalidade francesa agente artistica e organizadoras destes festivais em colaboração

FIGURE 10.1 *(Continued)*

DIRECÇÃO-GERAL
DE
SEGURANÇA

com o Secretáriado Portugues da Informação e Turismo, que o festival de jazz que se realizaria hoje à noite foi cancelado devido às reações da parte mais jovem da assistência. - - - - - - - - - - - - - - - - - - -
E mais não declarou. Lidas as suas declarações e devidamente traduzidas pelo intérprete, as achou conforme, ratifica e vai com ele assinar.- - -

E para constar se lavrou o presente auto que vai também ser assinado pelo Excelentíssimo Senhor Inspector-Adjunto e por mim agente servindo de escrivão, que o dactilografei e revi.- - - - - - - - - - - - - - -

FIGURE 10.1 *(Continued)*

fascist government, with colonies in Guinea-Bissau, Angola and Mozambique, and they were systematically wiping out the black race' (ibid.). Coleman had responded: 'Charlie, we've already signed the contract. We've gotta play. It's the last country on the concert tour. Figure out maybe you can do something to protest it, you know?' (ibid.).

Two years later, the third International Cascais Jazz Festival once again took place in a context of protest against Portugal's colonial wars.[14] During Roland Kirk's concert, the audience stood up when the African-American multi-instrumentalist mentioned the 'power of freedom'. This festival was notable for two more subversive acts: the distribution of pamphlets entitled 'NOW, MUSIC IS JAZZ' (a clear protest against the colonial wars); and the hanging of two signs proclaiming, 'FREE GUINEA' and 'DOWN WITH COLONIAL WAR' (Cravinho 2012, 165).

A report of the festival,[15] which was attended by several police agents who saw the signs and collected examples of the pamphlet still exists (General Command of Public Security Police; see Figure 10.2). Below I present two sections from the pamphlet that give a flavour of its content. In the first, jazz's history and roots are explained in a simplistic way to present the music as integral to the struggle of an exploited and oppressed people:

> Jazz was born in the southern United States as a cultural affirmation and a gesture of a people's liberation. People uprooted from Africa, slaves forced to work in the cotton and sugar-cane plantations for the profit of the 'white masters'. Afterwards, large industries, the railway and the mines, compelled the black slaves to spread around North America. And JAZZ travelled with them, following and expressing through time the history of an exploited and oppressed people. And from the United States it invaded the world. And JAZZ, although produced to be sold in this consumer society, is still felt as a contestation gesture of opposition, a cry of revolt, and a roar of liberation.

After this introduction, the pamphlet poses a question that links jazz with Portugal's own problems. This was, after all, its true purpose:

> And what does it concern to us, young people, here in Portugal, in 1973? A GREAT DEAL.
> BECAUSE 10,000 OF US ARE HERE. We are some thousands, but less than the 10,000 young dead, less than the 20,000 cripples and physically diminished, less than the 30,000 wounded, less than the 290,000 defaulters and deserters. BECAUSE THEY WANT TO COMPEL US TO JOIN THE ARMY AND THEY WANT TO SEND US TO AN UNFAIR WAR. BECAUSE OPPRESSORS IN PORTUGAL HAVE BEEN COMMITTED TO THE EXPLOITATION AND DOMINATION

OF THE AFRICAN PEOPLES FOR 500 YEARS …
BUT THEN AGAIN, THERE'S ANOTHER KIND OF MUSIC!!!

That music is mines blowing up, it's bullets whistling, it's the din of mortars, and it's the noise of rockets!!!

FIGURE 10.2 General Command of Public Security Police – Information Services, Ministry of the Interior, Case No. 224.06, SI 573/73, 14 November 1973.

The 'We sing and laugh' of the *Mocidade Portuguesa* is OVER!
Let's play our music! Let's create even more disorder!!!
DOWN WITH THE COLONIAL WAR AND WITH THE
COLONIALIST ARMY.
LONG LIVE THE FIGHT OF THE INDEPENDENT PEOPLES
OF ANGOLA, MOZAMBIQUE AND GUINEA.

As is clear from these passages, at the International Cascais Jazz Festival, jazz
became an instrument through which to oppose the colonial policies and wars
of the Estado Novo regime, a means to motivate thousands of young people
into political resistance.

Conclusion

During the Cold War era, jazz first emerged in Portugal through external
musical influences, including North American and Anglo-Saxon sources. This
was especially apparent after Luís Villas-Boas launched his 'Hot Club' radio
programme in November 1945 and then his Hot Clube de Portugal in March
1950 (Cravinho 2013b; Chapter 9, this volume). Nevertheless, as in other
European countries, the playing and consumption of jazz in Portugal 'as a form
of popularly generated high-art music . . . was confined to a minority, and
remains so confined, although a certain acquaintance with jazz eventually
became an accepted part of educated culture' (Hobsbawm 1998, 273). However,
in early 1958 – as result of a number of national and international political
developments which led the Portuguese regime to generate a 'democratic
mirage', soften its repressive policies and allow (allegedly) democratic elections
in order to give Portugal a veneer of freedom – the University Jazz Club was
founded. This resulted in a gradual change in activities relating to jazz in
Portugal. Aside from being a vehicle to promote jazz itself among the student
community, the University Jazz Club became an agent for the dissemination of
democratic ideals and political protest against the regime's colonial policies. This
was especially true when it joined forces with the Empire Students' House
(Cravinho 2011, 10). Along with the record-playing sessions where they listened
to jazz, the club's members promoted and configured the genre as a 'discourse
of truth' in a period of censorship and repression, using written culture as well
as music to highlight their dissidence. As a consequence of this, through the
club's activities, jazz came to be seen as a 'transformative practice', according
to its social, performative and historical narratives, which had the potential to
facilitate bilateral relationships and change (Grossberg 1993, 8). Using the
association between jazz and the fight for black civil rights and emancipation in
the United States, the club's members disseminated those ideals among Portugal's
overseas students to generate collective resistance against colonialism (Cravinho
2012, 161). As result, a new mentality emerged in Portuguese society that
perceived jazz no longer as 'the music of the Negroes' but, rather, as a musical

vehicle to transmit its own message of freedom. The regime found such views uncomfortable, especially once it had launched the colonial war in Angola (March 1961), and eventually it ordered the closure of the University Jazz Club.

Nevertheless, the dissemination of jazz continued in Portugal throughout the rest of the 1960s. In March 1961, Louis Armstrong's Lisbon concert was received with great enthusiasm. A few years later, on 27 September 1965, Villas-Boas and the Belgian saxophonist Jean Pierre Gebler opened the Louisiana Jazz Club, the first commercial jazz club in the country, in Cascais. The following year the first 'Semanas do Jazz' (Weeks of Jazz) took place in Lisbon, Coimbra and Porto, sponsored by the US Embassy in Lisbon (Cravinho 2014b, 88), and the Duke Ellington Orchestra and Ella Fitzgerald, the Oscar Peterson Trio and the Charles Lloyd Quartet all visited Portugal. Then, in 1967, Coimbra hosted Portugal's first international jazz festival, also sponsored by the US Embassy (Cravinho 2014b, 88).[16]

Notwithstanding all of this official support for – or at least toleration of – jazz in the 1960s, between 1971 and 1973, with the first three editions of the International Cascais Jazz Festival, the Portuguese public (and on some occasions the musicians on stage) transformed jazz into an instrument of resistance against the regime, with thousands of young people persuaded to come out in active opposition to Portugal's colonial wars (Curvelo 2002; Santos 2009; Veloso *et al.* 2010; Cravinho 2012). Jazz became a symbol of freedom (Cravinho 2012, 167), especially after Charlie Haden's protest and subsequent arrest in 1971. Consequently, it came to play a very important role in the fight against colonialism, strengthening the ideals of freedom that were being championed by the independence movements in Portugal's African colonies. First the University Jazz Club's activities, and then the International Cascais Jazz Festival, could also be seen as experiments in the creation of 'ideal human relationships', with jazz becoming a discursive site for the articulation of as yet non-existent, but certainly desirable, social realities (Turino 2008, 20).

As a public event, the arrest of Charlie Haden appears to present a straightforward dichotomy of jazz as a protest against a repressive regime. But such public gestures at the festival, initiated by 'outsiders' (the US musicians), do not reflect the internal complexities of the relationship between Portuguese jazz and the Estado Novo regime. Rather in the way that the 'classic' models of totalitarianism – written from the outside – simplify the actual conditions of life and the political dynamics that frame them under a totalitarian regime, so too in this Portuguese narrative. As the other case studies in this book suggest, the true picture is not so simple, and a range of other lines of force are also active in the way that jazz and the regime negotiated with each other, including the presence of colonial participants, internal local dynamics, ambiguous tensions between the state's political and cultural objectives, and the relationship between foreign musicians who had a reductive view of politics and local conditions that were more multifaceted.

More generally, the events described in this chapter provide useful lessons on the relationship between jazz and totalitarianism, perhaps none more important than the fact that simplistic models that equate the binary 'freedom/repression' with 'jazz/the regime' are of limited value in understanding both terms and their relationship with each other. While totalitarian control might be articulated in the slogan 'All for the nation; nothing against the nation', the realities of life under such a regime allow for considerable tactical flexibility, with the state itself creating spaces in which its own control falters, such as Lisbon's jazz clubs and the Empire Students' House. Recent developments in the modelling of both totalitarianism and jazz provide the foundations for a far more complex understanding of the encounter between the two.

Acknowledgements

This chapter would not have been possible without the support of several people whom I wish to thank: first, Professor Bruce Johnson, who wholeheartedly, despite a very busy academic schedule, read through the text to give it a final English-language brush up (and I also thank him for his excellent editorial work and enthusiasm); second, Professor Susana Sardo, Director of the Centre for Jazz Studies at the Universidade de Aveiro, to whom I am especially indebted for providing all of the necessary support regarding my participation in the 'Research Seminar Series', organized by the Department of Music at the University of York, 16 May 2012; third, to my colleague José Dias, from the Faculdade de Ciências Sociais e Humanas at the Universidade Nova de Lisboa, who promptly reviewed the first draft of this text and provided some invaluable commentary; and finally, Dr Paulo Tremoceiro, Head of the Communication and Access Division at the National Archives of Torre do Tombo, Lisbon, for his careful assistance. To all, my most grateful thanks.

Notes

1 I would like to thank the anonymous referees for suggestions that have strengthened this chapter.
2 An early version of this chapter was presented as a paper in the 'Research Seminar Series' organized by the Department of Music at the University of York on 6 May 2012. I would therefore particularly like to thank Áine Sheil and Catherine Laws, coordinators of the series, as well as my colleague Jonathan Eato for his invitation to participate. The aforementioned paper was condensed and revised for this chapter, and adapted especially in terms of the notes and references. All translations from the Portuguese are by the author.
3 This study is based on archival and fieldwork research, which includes interviews with the founder of the Clube Universitário de Jazz, Raul Calado, as well as other members of the club. It also draws on material held at the National Archives of Torre do Tombo (abbreviated as NATT: PIDE/DGS throughout) and the Archives of the Civil Governor of Lisbon.

236 Pedro Cravinho

4 During February and March 1961, 'conflict broke out in Angola, first with attacks on police stations and prisons in the capital Luanda and then general rioting and massacres of white settlers in the northern provinces' (Sardica 2008, 70).

5 Delgado visited numerous towns and cities throughout the country during the 1958 presidential campaign, walking or driving in a convertible car down the avenues and major streets, sometimes carried on the shoulders of delirious crowds who were willing to brave possible recriminations from the authorities (Rosas 1994, 472).

6 Calado was elected to the HCP board in 1955 (Delegate to the Federation of Societies and Recreation), 1956 (First Secretary of the General Assembly and Delegate to the Federation of Societies and Recreation) and 1957 (Secretary of the Board of Directors).

7 The Clube Universitário de Jazz's headquarters were located at 76 Rua da Alegria, just a few metres from those of the Hot Clube de Portugal, at 39 Praça da Alegria.

8 'Salazar suffered a massive cerebral stroke that rendered him invalid for political power' (Sardica 2008, 75).

9 Decree Law no. 48,686, 15 November 1968.

10 José Pedro Pinto Leite, Francisco Sá Carneiro, João Pedro Miller Guerra, Francisco Pinto Balsemão and João Bosco Soares da Mota Amaral all appeared on the electoral lists. The Popular National Action Party was the new name of the National Union, founded by Salazar in June 1930 as Portugal's sole political party.

11 The State Secretariat of Tourism, Information and Popular Culture, the Costa do Sol Tourism Board and the Cascais Town Hall were the official sponsors of the festival.

12 Miles Davis Septet, with Gary Bartz, Keith Jarrett, Michael Henderson, Don Alias, James Foreman and Leon Chandler; Ornette Coleman Quartet, with Dewey Redman, Charlie Haden and Ed Blackwell; the Giants of Jazz, with Dizzy Gillespie, Thelonius Monk, Art Blakey, Sonny Stitt, Kai Winding and Al Mckibbon; Phil Woods and His European Rhythm Machine, with Gordon Beck, Ron Mathewson and Daniel Humair.

13 *Portugal Democrático*'s sequence of events differs from those described in the police report (see below and Figure 10.1).

14 The second International Cascais Jazz Festival took place in 1972. As far as I have been able to determine, there were no explicit protests against the regime and/or its colonial policies in Africa at that event, so I have not examined it here.

15 General Command of Public Security Police – Information Services, Ministry of the Interior, Case no. 224.06, SI 573/73, 14 November 1973.

16 The information presented here forms part of the author's ongoing doctoral research, which aims to contribute to a better understanding of the use of Portuguese public television as a means to disseminate jazz during the Estado Novo regime (1956–1974).

References

Anderson, Benedict. 2005. *Comunidades Imaginadas*. Lisboa: Edições 70.

Bebiano, Rui. 2005. 'Contestação do regime e tentação de luta armada sob o marcelismo'. *Revista Portuguesa de História* 37: 65–104.

Cravinho, Pedro. 2011. '"Gosto de Jazz porque gosto da verdade": o Clube Universitário de Jazz, a contestação e o discurso alternativo ao meio "jazzístico" em Portugal, entre 1958 e 1961'. In *Atas dos Encontros de Investigação em Performance PERFORMA' 11*, edited by Rosário Pestana and Sara Carvalho, 1–13. Aveiro: Universidade de Aveiro.

Cravinho, Pedro. 2012. '"A MÚSICA AGORA É O JAZZ": O Jazz como palco de resistência em Portugal, entre 1971 e 1973'. In *Música Discurso Poder*, edited by Maria de Rosário Girão Santos and Elissa Maria Lessa, 157–171. Vila Nova de Famalicão: Edições Húmus.

Cravinho, Pedro. 2013a. "Jazz and Television in Portugal: TV Jazz and the Presence of Jazz on the Portuguese Public Television of the 1960s and 70s'. Paper presented at the Rhythm Changes Conference 'Rethinking Jazz Cultures', Media City, Manchester, 11–14 April.

Cravinho, Pedro. 2013b. 'Music, Images and Politics: Jazz and Television in Portugal under the Salazar Dictatorship (1956–1968)'. Paper presented at the First International Jazz Conference, Universitat de Valéncia, 28–30 November.

Cravinho, Pedro. 2014a. '*JAZZ* – a primeira publicação periódica inteiramente dedicada ao jazz em Portugal.' *Glosas* 11: 81–84.

Cravinho, Pedro. 2104b. 'O Clube de Jazz do Orfeon.' *Glosas* 10: 87–89.

Curvelo, António. 2002. 'Notas (muito incompletas) sobre o Jazz em Portugal. Da pré-história aos tempos modernos'. In *Panorana da Cultura Portuguesa no Séc. XX Artes e Letras*, edited by Fernando Peres, vol. II, 48–95. Porto: Afrontamento.

Faria, António. 1997. *Linha estreita de liberdade: a Casa dos Estudantes do Império*. Lisboa: Colibri.

Goodman, Amy. 2006. 'Jazz Legend Charlie Haden on His Life, His Music and His Politics'. Available at: www.democracynow.org/2006/9/1/jazz_legend_charlie_haden_on_his (accessed 16 March 2016).

Gouveia, Jorge de Sá. 2011. 'Sassetti: music is part of the movie's soul'. *Ensaios – novas e velhas tendências no cinema português contemporâneo*. Available at: http://repositorio.ipl.pt/bitstream/10400.21/459/1/sassetti.pdf (accessed 16 March 2016).

Grossberg, Lawrence. 1993. 'Cultural Studies and/in New Worlds.' *Critical Studies in Mass Communication* 10: 1–22.

Grossberg, Lawrence. 1996. 'Identity and Cultural Studies – Is that All There Is?' In *Questions of Cultural Identity*, edited by Stuart Hall and Paul Du Gay, 87–107. London: Sage Publications.

Hobsbawm, Eric. 1998. *Uncommon People: Resistance, Rebellion, and Jazz*. New York: The New Press.

Martins, Hélder Bruno de Jesus Redes. 2006. *O jazz em Portugal (1920–1956) anúncio – emergência – afirmação*. Coimbra: Edições Almedina.

Mesquita, Mário. 1996. *Eduardo Lourenço cultura e política na época marcelista*. Lisboa: Cosmos.

Monteiro, Maria Rosa da Rocha Valente Sil. 2001. *C.E.I. Celeiro de Sonho Geração da 'mensagem'*. Braga: Universidade do Minho.

Moore, Joe. 1998. 'Some Theoretical Reflections on Jazz in Postwar Japan'. CAPI Occasional Paper No. 20. Victoria: Centre for Asia-Pacific Initiatives.

Pinto, António Costa. 2003. 'Twentieth-Century Portugal: An Introduction'. In *Contemporary Portugal: Politics, Society and Culture*, edited by António Costa Pinto, 154. New York: Columbia University Press.

Rosas, Fernando. 1994. 'As mudanças invisíveis do Pós-Guerra'. In *História de Portugal*, vol. VII: *O Estado Novo*, coordinated by Fernando Rosas, 419–431. Lisboa: Editorial Estampa.

Santos, João Moreira dos. 2009. *Jazz em Cascais – uma história de 80 anos (1928–2008)*. Cascais: Casa Sasseti.

Sardica, José Miguel. 2008. *Twentieth-Century Portugal: A Historical Overview*. Lisboa: Universidade Católica.

Silva, Douglas Mansur da. 2006. *A oposição ao Estado Novo no exílio brasileiro, 1954–1974*. Lisboa: Imprensa de Ciências Sociais.

Turino, Thomas. 2008. *Music as Social Life: The Politics of Participation*. Chicago: University of Chicago Press.

Veloso, Manuel Jorge, Carlos Branco Mendes and António Curvelo. 2010. 'Jazz'. In *Enciclopédia da Música em Portugal no Século XX*, coordinated by Salwa Castelo-Branco, vol. CL, 649–659. Lisboa: Círculo de Leitores/Temas e Debates.

von Eschen, Penny. 2004. *Satchmo Blows up the World: Jazz Ambassadors Play the Cold War.* Cambridge, MA: Harvard University Press.

Archival Research

NATT: PIDE/DGS: International and State Defence Police (PIDE)/Directorate-General of Security (DGS), National Archives of Torre do Tombo, Lisbon.

PART V
Apartheid South Africa

11

A CLIMBING VINE THROUGH CONCRETE

Jazz in 1960s Apartheid South Africa

Jonathan Eato[1]

In *Soweto Blues*, Gwen Ansell (2004, 108) states that although the 1960s have been dubbed the 'Silent Time' in South Africa, they were 'far from silent. Like a climbing vine through concrete, music that was deliberately and defiantly assertive pushed through and hung on.' Although the foundations for this oppressive decade in South Africa's history had been laid relentlessly over the preceding years (indeed centuries) of white minority rule, the political concrete of grand apartheid set solid during an era of unprecedented state repression that was tragically announced by the 1960 Sharpeville massacre and shootings in Langa (Horrell 1960). As communities reeled from the devastating imple-mentation of the apartheid regime's infamous Group Areas Act No. 41 of 1950 (Union of South Africa 1950), popular democratic movements were banned (Horrell 1960), a state of emergency was declared (Horrell 1960), the South African Broadcasting Company (SABC) established 'a divisive, ethnically based radio service' (Ballantine 2012, 9) and a steady stream of musicians left for exile in the US and Europe.

In considering the music of this time, John Blacking (1980, 197) concludes that 'Changes in the form and content of music after *King Kong*[2] were not isolated events in the history of South African music. They were the consequence of far-reaching political changes whose impact on music was inevitable.'

While Ansell (2004), Ballantine (2012), Coplan (2007) and others have out-lined the social and political context for jazz music's 'climbing vine', this chapter will consider how the *musical* changes identified by Blacking manifested in jazz as practised by musicians *inside* the country. I am specifically interested in under-standing whether politics can be seen to have affected musical form, harmonic patterns, grooves, voicings, or improvisational language, and why, if a changed music *was* being made, a trope of silence has built up around this period.

Introduction: The South African Context

By way of introduction – and to orientate anyone unfamiliar with South African political history (post-European settlement) and its eventual counterpoint with jazz music – we can observe that the establishment from 7 April 1652 of a victualling station at the Cape by the Vereenigde Oostindische Compagnie (VOC) (Wilson 1969, 187) first paved the way for colonial rule on the southernmost tip of the African continent. Dutch and British imperial governments dominated for the next two and a half centuries, and white minority rule continued after the Union of South Africa was established as a self-governing dominion of the British Empire in 1910. Although significant segregationist legislation was passed before the National Party came to power in the mid-twentieth century, following their 1948 victory a complex series of statutes further enshrined privilege for people classified as 'white' whilst increasingly disenfranchising the majority of the population. Needless to say, the barrage of apartheid legislation, which continued after the formation of the Republic of South Africa in 1961, was not described in these terms by the National Party government, which instead variously justified its actions as beneficial to all by promoting the ideology of apartheid and facilitating separate development of the races. It is abundantly clear therefore that for nearly three and a half centuries, between the initiation of a settlement at the Cape for the VOC and the first democratic elections in 1994, systematic advancement of people thought of as 'white' was pursued at the expense of everybody else. But this is not to say that we should view the beneficiaries of European colonial rule and apartheid (whether reluctant or otherwise) as undifferentiated or unaffected.

Interviewed for *Voëlvry – the Movie* (Ross 2006), singer and writer André Letoit (a.k.a. Koos Kombuis) offered his perspective – arguably as an archetypical *beneficiary* of apartheid – on living in apartheid South Africa. Kombuis, a male Afrikaans-speaker classified as 'white' by the authorities, recalled: 'Ek het grootgeword onder 'n totalitêre politieke stelsel en ek het dit my plig gevoel as jong man om te rebelleer teen hierdie stelsel' (I grew up under a totalitarian political system and I felt it to be my duty as young man to rebel against this system).[3] Kombuis's designation of the apartheid state as 'totalitarian' is instructive as it immediately evokes the totalism Hannah Arendt (1967, 326) described as 'the permanent domination of each single individual in each and every sphere of life' in her seminal work *The Origins of Totalitarianism*. As Bruce Johnson notes in his Introduction to this volume, there is no simple agreement over which conditions should be met for a system of rule to be considered totalitarian, and unsurprisingly there has been some debate over whether apartheid South Africa is most usefully considered in these terms (Baehr 2005, 2342). That said, there has also been a number of formulations in the literature that refer to totalitarian 'powers', 'tendencies' and 'features' whilst stopping short of an outright totalitarian designation: see the International Defence Aid Fund pamphlet

(1969, 1), Mathews (1972, 296), and Hanf *et al.* (1981, 42), who also state that Heribert Adam 'proposed that the concept of totalitarianism be extended, to take account of the realities of the South African political system'.

Writing two years before Sharpeville, Houser (1958, 14) concluded that on balance South Africa could not be considered a totalitarian state, but quoted John Gunther in asserting: 'Not quite. Not yet.' However, one wonders whether the banning of all effective political opposition in 1960 and the appointment of Broederbond head P. J. Meyer to the top position at the SABC the same year (Hayman and Tomaselli 1989, 59–60) might not have tipped the balance of Houser's 'not quite'. Indeed, a consideration of the situation in 1960s South Africa reveals striking concordances with the six traits that Friedrich and Brzezinski (1965, 21) argue are common to all totalitarian dictatorships.[4] And as Charles Hamm (1995, 212; emphasis added) wrote:

> the government of the Republic of South Africa succeeded in having its *entire population, black and white*, listen to its own radio service, theorized and programmed in accordance with state ideology, to the virtual exclusion of other radio programming; and . . . this radio monopoly played a major role in shaping attitudes and relations which still inhibit the formation of a multi-racial society.

But if we are to recognise diversity amongst apartheid's more privileged groups, we must also recognise the diversity of the jazz community in 1960s South Africa and can additionally note that this diversity was mirrored in the various purposes to which the ever-elusive term 'jazz' was put at the time. I do not mean to argue that South Africa is a special case in this regard as I am aware that there is a body of scholarship which addresses the issue from a number of global perspectives (see, for example, Ake *et al.* 2012; DeVeaux 2001–2002; Frith 2007; Gabbard 2002; Horn 2002; Johnson 2002; Merriam and Garner 1998; Nicholson 2005; and Stanbridge 2004). Whilst I do not wish to get embroiled in arguments over what is heard as jazz in different places and at different times, it might be instructive to consider the following as context for the arguments I will go on to make. Charles Hamm (1995, 236, 238) asserts that in the 1940s '"jazz" began to be used as a generic term for a wide range of social dance music' in South Africa, but that by the 1950s 'jive' had gradually replaced 'jazz' as the generic term for 'black South African social dance music descended from marabi'. Furthermore, a group such as The Bogard Brothers provides a good illustration of how convoluted things could get. Hamm (1995, 177, 189) first mentions them as a 'vocal swing' outfit, but also notes that after rock 'n' roll hit South Africa they were recording examples of this 'new music' under titles such as 'Rock by Boogie'. However, on their EP *Street Corner Jazz* (Bogard Brothers n.d.), despite its title, and a cover illustration depicting a *kwela* band, three of the four tracks are twelve-bar blues in classic rock 'n' roll

244 Jonathan Eato

style. We do well to remember that musicians often play a variety of musics (has there ever been a jazz musician who has not at some time played another type of music?) and musicians' choices could be contingent on any number of factors. But how they (or their record companies) decide to describe it to the public may or may not reflect musical decisions. As Hamm (1995, 202) points out, albeit with regards to soul jive, in South Africa 'some record producers simply used the label, even for music having nothing to do with the style'.

That said, the early relationship between jazz and politics in South Africa is detailed by Christopher Ballantine (2012, 8), and in so doing he notes that the late 1940s to the late 1950s represented the apotheosis of a period of astonishing innovation, whilst David Coplan (2007, 204) additionally identifies the 1950s as 'the heyday of passive resistance and anti-pass campaigns'. As many commentators have pointed out, the 1960s represented a time of rapid political change in many parts of the world, and indeed the African continent was no exception, with thirty-three new independent states created. Projecting on from a dual reading of musical and political history in South Africa one might expect the parallel momentum of jazz music and socio-political protest identified by Ballantine and Coplan to yield results in the 1960s. However, for the majority of South Africans the emancipatory zeitgeist of the 1960s remained stalled at the anticipatory stage.

Nevertheless, there were changes in 1960s South Africa, even if they were not the changes most South Africans might have prioritised. Giliomee (2003, 494) shows how, after coming to power in 1948, the Afrikaner-dominated National Party government began removing 'the remaining symbols of the historic British ascendency'. This process culminated in a 'referendum of the enfranchised white population' in October 1960 and led to the formation of the Republic of South Africa (Hayes 1980, 469) in a parody of the independence movements sweeping across the rest of the continent at the time.[5] Giliomee (2003, 539) asserts that economically the new republic 'represented only a symbolic change that did not affect the ties of trade and investment to Britain' and, as former South African president Thabo Mbeki (2004) pointed out, there was certainly no concomitant improvement in political franchise or civil rights for the majority of citizens, in contradistinction to the promise of other independence movements of the 1960s.

Silence ~~is~~ *or* Golden *Castle*[6]

The rejection of British culture by the National Party was not, however, limited to a systematic undoing. The construction (*doing*) of a modern urban landscape for the new republic was, by a curious twist, entrusted to architectural firms from the United States (Chipkin 1998, 251, 254) – the very country that was developing the jazz music which apparently so threatened the apartheid authorities (Jazz Publicity Service 1964). Anyone familiar with 1960s architectural trends in South Africa will appreciate both the role that US architects played in the new urban vision for South Africa and the aptness of Gwen Ansell's simile that I have borrowed for the title of this chapter. South Africa's economic boom of the 1960s ushered in an architectural confidence where the preference for concrete brutalism matched the regime's political intransigence. Clive Chipkin (1998, 251) describes the 'crescendo of roaring compressors and pounding pneumatic drills and the percussion of Kanga hammers and concrete vibrators' that characterised 1960s Johannesburg and caused 'interminable eddies of cement dust from sandblasting of concrete surfaces [to settle] like beach sand on distant pavements'. Clearly, in a very real sense, 1960s South Africa was anything but silent. Similarly, with regards to jazz music in South Africa, Ansell (2010, 1) is clear that describing the 1960s as 'the silent years' misses the mark: 'Nothing could be further from the truth. The top selling album of the period was a jazz album: Winston 'Mankunku' Ngozi's *Yakhal' Inkomo*. It was an era of intense creativity – not silent, but silenced.' So, if Ansell's and Chipkin's analyses are correct, why would cultural historians and commentators describe the 1960s as the 'Silent Time', or evoke silence as a dominant characteristic,[7] especially given the well-established link between music and political protest in South Africa? And exactly how silent was silent? Just a bit silent, or very silent? What might jazz of a Silent Time sound like? How might it be distinct from the bold, showy, African jazz of the 1950s?

It is easy to imagine how the Silent Time trope might have taken hold. South Africa in the 1960s saw a huge rise in silencing of all sorts, most of which were organised by the apartheid state. As has already been noted, the decade began with the most brutal and profound silencing of protesters. The referendum of October 1960 which followed a few months later was open only to voters classified as 'white' (Hayes 1980), meaning that in this and other key elections during the 1960s the majority of the population literally had no voice. In 1963 the Rivonia Trial began, resulting in eight prominent opposition leaders being sentenced to life imprisonment (Coplan 2007, 224), and banned opposition organisations were obliged to operate secretly. As the Emergency Committee of the ANC (1960, 354) instructed: 'DON'T ANSWER QUESTIONS . . . DON'T ASK QUESTIONS,' pointing out that 'the police have long ears . . . We know that most of our people are brave and loyal . . . but some people are too fond of talking.' Inevitably this situation meant that 'many political documents have been lost or destroyed because of fear of political repression' (Drew 1997, 9), thereby extending the reach of the state's silencing to the post-apartheid historical record. But just as the state's grossly repressive actions in the early 1960s required a change of tactic from opposition movements, most crucially the creation of *uMkhonto weSizwe* and the commencement of sabotage campaigns on 16 December 1961 (Drew 1997, 33), it was also necessary for opposition movements to present a united front and

246 Jonathan Eato

effectively silence the voices of members critical of the turn to armed resistance. Whilst this can be partly understood as robust debate within organisations, Scott Couper (2009) argues that in some cases – such as that of the former leader of the ANC, Chief Albert Luthuli – the line between internal debate and silencing was crossed.

Clearly jazz musicians were affected by these events, but we can note that there were also consequences of the political situation that have specifically shaped the *telling* of jazz history in South Africa. Hayman and Tomaselli (1989, 74) have shown how 'the period 1961 to 1971 was marked by the closer alignment of broadcasting and the [apartheid] State', thus a key medium for disseminating jazz music became infected with an ideology that actively discriminated against many of the music's creators. In addition, *Drum* magazine, a key publication for reporting on modern jazz music and liberation politics in South Africa, temporarily stopped appearing as an independent publication in the 1960s and became a fortnightly supplement to *Post* (Chapman 1989, 217). Although *Drum* resumed publishing self-contained issues in 1968 (Chapman 1989) and was therefore available for more time than it was unavailable during the 1960s, the majority of the critical attention paid to the magazine, including its relationship to jazz music, has been concerned with the period Lewis Nkosi (1983, 5) has termed the 'fabulous decade' of the 1950s: see, for example, Chapman (1989), Lorentzon (2007), Pyper (2005), Rabkin (1975) and Titlestad (2005). I would argue, therefore, that this critical bias, the interregnum in *Drum*'s standalone circulation in the 1960s, and analysis concluding that by the 1960s the magazine had 'lost the informing power of its original context' (Chapman 1989, 217) could combine to fuel a perception that jazz music was 'silenced' along with its exposure through, and the efficacy of, *Drum*.

Although Ballantine (2012) and Coplan (2007) both acknowledge that creative spaces for jazz were found and vigorously defended in the 1960s, perhaps inevitably the most striking aspects of their narratives regarding the intersection of politics and jazz for the period concern the banning of popular democratic movements, the SABC's establishment of an apartheid radio service, the steady stream of musicians leaving the country for exile in the US and Europe, and the expulsion of black show business from the city centres. This, in combination with a lack of suitable venues in townships ('Recreational Facilities' 1961, 4), undoubtedly created a dire situation for jazz. As Ballantine (2012, 10) puts it: 'And so the exodus of jazz musicians for Europe and the United States began; most never returned. Those who remained had to find some way of adapting to the new situation; those who couldn't adapt, or wouldn't, simply packed away their instruments.' The lacuna, with regards to 1960s jazz, in Ballantine's and Coplan's important histories is easily explainable: for Ballantine, the decade is largely outside the remit of his study (1920s–1950s); and, for Coplan, who attempts to cover the broad church of 'South African black city music and theatre', other musics came into focus during this

Jazz in 1960s Apartheid South Africa **247**

period. Nevertheless, the danger for South African jazz history is that this narrative lacuna becomes perceived as a musical silence, and any such perception would be reinforced by a consideration of other artistic disciplines. For example, discussing South African literature, Sipho Sepamla (in Seroke *et al.* 1998) characterises the 1960s literary scene in South Africa in terms of demise and vacuum (and therefore absolute silence). And as I have previously argued (Eato 2103a), prior to the recent publication of images by Ian Bruce Huntley (Albertyn 2013), for many years a consideration of South African jazz photography could lead to similar conclusions.

The inaccessibility of much important jazz work from the 1960s compounds the situation, as it is now all but impossible to buy the following recordings: *Dollar Brand Plays Sphere Jazz* (1960); the *Cold Castle National Jazz Festival* (Various Artists, 1962); both of Gideon Nxumalo's pioneering recordings of the 1960s – *Jazz Fantasia* (1962) and *Gideon Plays* (*c.*1968); any of The Malombo Jazz Makers' three albums from the decade (*c.*1966, 1967, 1969) or the EP *Something out of Africa* (Various Artists, 1966b), which features a couple of their tracks; *I Remember Nick* by The Soul Giants (1968); The Soul Jazzmen's *Mankunku Jazz Show* (1968); The Four Sounds' *Jazz from District Six* (1969); *The Indigenous Afro-Jazz Sounds of Phillip Tabane and His Malombo Jazzman* (1969); any number of the 78rpm discs that were still being pressed in South Africa in the 1960s, including those by Gwigwi [Mrwebi] and His Jazz Rascals (1960), Nik Moyake (1960), Dudu Pukwana (*c.*1961a, *c.*1961b), The Jazz Kings (*c.*1961), Philip Tabane and the Pretoria Mellow Crooners (1961), The Hometown Sextet (*c.*1961), and Chris McGregor and His Blue Notes (*c.*1962); and 45rpm singles, such as those by [Wilson] 'King Force' Silgee and His Forces (*c.*1968).[8]

How Silent Was 'the Silence'?

Running some very basic analysis on different collections of recorded South African music enables us to get at least some idea of comparative musical activity across the decades; the first collection of recorded music I considered was my own. Assembled before beginning this project, and with no regard for recording dates, it can be broadly described as an unscientifically chosen selection dating from the 1930s to the present day consisting of 2,951 commercially recorded jazz and popular music tracks with a heavy bias towards jazz, available on CD in retail outlets and online between 2007 and 2014.

As Figure 11.1 indicates, this particular snapshot implies that there was significant recorded activity in the 1960s. Furthermore, even if recorded activity was down on the 1950s and the 1970s, the 1980s were seemingly an even quieter time (at least in terms of the material in my collection).

Looking at the archives of the *Electric Jive* blog (Albertyn *et al.* 2009–present), and concentrating on a narrower time band, Figure 11.2 shows that for a

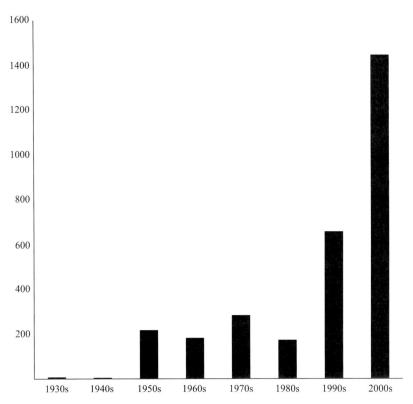

FIGURE 11.1 Author's Recorded Music Collection (Number of Tracks by Decade)

collection of 2,676 tracks recorded from 1950 until 1980, with the focus on jazz, jive and *mbaqanga* recordings on vinyl, 78rpm discs and quarter-inch tape, the 1960s were certainly not silent in terms of this collection either. (I should add that the *Electric Jive* archive has almost no overlap with my collection, because, for the most part, the *Electric Jive* recordings are not currently commercially available in any format.)

It goes without saying that commercial recordings and transcription recordings will only ever give a partial picture, so I have attempted to counter this bias by considering music coverage in the print media as this includes information on both local and national live performances. Clearly this is a vast area, so I concentrated on issues of *Imvo Zabantsundu*, a weekly isiXhosa newspaper (based in King William's Town but covering the whole of what is now known as the Eastern Cape region) for the following periods:

- November 1961–February 1962 inclusive (four months)
- January–September 1963 inclusive (nine months)

- January–December 1965 inclusive (twelve months)
- January–September 1968 inclusive (nine months)

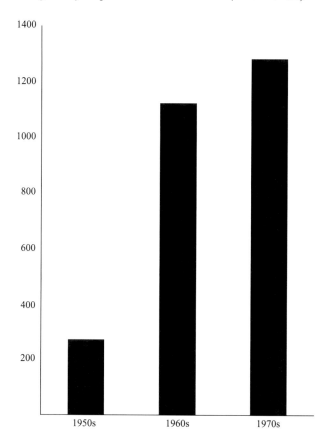

FIGURE 11.2 *Electric Jive* Collection (Number of Tracks by Decade)

This was augmented with issues of the Durban-based *Ilanga Lase Natal*, a weekly isiZulu newspaper, from January 1965 to August 1966 inclusive (twenty months). Finally, the national monthly English-language news, arts and culture magazine *Drum* was searched from January 1960 to April 1965. Although these searches were geographically limited, they did show that jazz coverage remained more or less constant throughout the 1960s (within the constraints of each publication). And evidence from press cuttings and jazz photograph collections alone is that at least 251 musicians/bands sounded what they, or those writing about them, saw fit to identify as jazz during the 1960s in South Africa. It is important to note that there was no television in South Africa during the 1960s, and detailed radio playlists are not available, although the SABC did make a considerable number of transcription recordings during the decade, some of which are discussed below.

250 Jonathan Eato

This continuity of jazz's sounding supports Gwen Ansell's arguments that there was 'intense creativity – not silent, but silenced' (2010, 1) and that music which was 'deliberately and defiantly assertive pushed through and hung on' (2004, 108). Citing the apartheid state's consolidation, and increasingly effective implementation, of its cultural policies, Ansell (2010, 1) argues that the 'effect was to push black creativity to the margins of visibility [as] black urban culture was expelled from the "white" cities'. David Coplan (2010, 7) concurs, although by specifying a link with the United States for this banished musical culture: 'By the 1960s the worldly influence of America had been largely removed from the African stage and studio and had taken refuge in private record collections, shebeens, and house parties in the township.' Given that the state's actions precipitated the separation and isolation of the various constituencies engaged in jazz music, thereby also effectively distancing them from shared mechanisms of historical record, wider public dialogue, and mutual artistic support, we begin to see how important it is that buried within the recording figures from *Electric Jive* cited above are the Ian Bruce Huntley tapes, which are now freely accessible online (Albertyn 2014). Although some of these are undated, it is almost certain that they capture over fifty-six hours of *live* jazz performances from the 1960s.

As is often the case, new sources help us to rethink the past, and in these live recordings we hear musicians establishing their personal improvisational language on a musical syllabus of their own design. Looking to contemporary jazz from the United States as a major inspiration we hear the exploration of a wide range of US jazz standards and certain compositions emerging as favourite vehicles for improvisation, including:

- Miles Davis's 'Milestones'
- Miles Davis's 'Nardis'
- Miles Davis's 'So What'
- Gillespie and Paparelli's 'A Night In Tunisia'
- Kaper and Washington's 'On Green Dolphin Street'
- Thelonious Monk's 'Straight No Chaser'
- Cole Porter's 'Love for Sale'

But whilst US standards dominate, a vernacularised strand also emerges, epitomised by:

- Ronnie Beer's 'Immediately'
- Hugh Masekela's 'Dollar's Moods'
- Tete Mbambisa's 'Leads Dwana'
- Tete Mbambisa's 'Mr Mecca'
- Chris McGregor's 'Vortex Special'

Jazz in 1960s Apartheid South Africa **251**

It is notable that, musically, these local South African standards appear more closely aligned with a modern 1960s US model than with the changed, indigenised modern jazz sound we might expect from Blacking's conclusion, and as exemplified by Eric Nomvete's 'Pondo Blues' (Eric Nomvete's Big Five in Various Artists 1962), Tete Mbambisa's 'uMsenge' (The Jazz Disciples, *c*.1964), or Winston 'Mankunku' Ngozi's 'Ekhaya' (Various Artists 1966a).

1960s Jazz and Government-Controlled Broadcasting

According to Charles Hamm (1991; 1995), if we expect to see a flowering of local, indigenised modern jazz – rather than internationally dominant strains – in 1960s South Africa, we should remember that for many South Africans the situation on the ground was treacherous. Hamm argues that one of the contributing factors was the white minority government's Broadcasting Amendment Act No. 49 of 1960 (Union of South Africa 1960), which established a Bantu Programme Control Board

> charged with expanding the existing Zulu and Xhosa services, establishing new ones in the Northern Sotho, Southern Sotho, Tswana, Venda and Tsonga languages, and arranging for the dissemination of these services to all areas, rural and urban, where these languages were spoken.
>
> *(Hamm 1991, 156)*

These services, collectively known as Radio Bantu, began FM transmission on 1 January 1962 (Hamm 1991, 158) and, according to Hamm, counteracted free creativity in curious ways. For example, whilst South African musicians exiled in Europe and the US in the late 1960s and 1970s became well known for incorporating musical styles that were specifically identified with South Africa in their contemporary jazz – whether folk music or *mbaqanga* – the discourse around jazz *within* South Africa at the time necessitated a delicately balanced ambivalence (see G. R. Naidoo's interview with The Blue Notes (Naidoo *et al.* 1964)).

Hamm states that the SABC's policy, as detailed in the broadcaster's *Annual Report* for 1961, stipulated that 'all music programmed on Radio Bantu should relate in some way to the culture of the "tribal" group at which a given service was aimed' (SABC in Hamm 1991, 160). He then goes on to say that progressive musicians and radical black thinkers both within South Africa and in exile 'rejected commercial, mass-disseminated music in favour of older syncretic genres less contaminated by governmental appropriation' (Hamm 1995, 204). This in turn leads to his theory that, as a direct result of policy, in these circles modern jazz and freedom songs became the order of the day. And Sibongile Khumalo (quoted in Ansell 2004, 112) offers evidence that supports Hamm's point by recalling that certain political and musical classes 'tended to look

252 Jonathan Eato

down at people [who] practiced traditional music as tribalists' implicated in the apartheid regime's agenda for separate development. Hamm (1995, 204) argues that this presented a strange dilemma for musicians and intellectuals alike: 'If they tried to use traditional African culture as a basis for strengthening black social identity and group pride, they risked playing into the government's hands; and they had no access to the media to put forward an alternative view.'

So, whilst the US influence was acknowledged and valued, the desire of earlier South African groups to emulate the sound of their US models precisely (Ballantine 2012, 8) was rejected by The Blue Notes (Naidoo *et al.* 1964). Yet, just as a South African voice was being asserted from within a changed, indigenised, modern jazz, Hamm (1991, 165) states the net result of the SABC's broadcasting policy was that 'true jazz [had] an increasingly limited usefulness to Radio Bantu after 1960', having lost its appeal to the wider uneducated rural black population just at the time when some modern jazz musicians 'chose political stands and actions leading to imprisonment or exile'.

When I first began thinking about 1960s jazz in South Africa, specifically the recordings in the Ian Bruce Huntley archive (Eato 2013a), I thought Hamm's theory linking musical style to the SABC's implementation of the Broadcasting Amendment Act of 1960 explained the situation very neatly. Now, though, I have come to think that his explanation is too neat. Asked by the Junction Avenue Theatre Company about the music people listened to in Sophiatown in the 1950s, Es'kia Mphahlele (1986, 58) recalled:

> It was mainly the educated people like us, who were influenced by American culture and jazz. On Sundays, we would go into Sophiatown and you would always hear a radiogram booming out loud. It was mainly jazz – people took jazz very seriously and we would tune into Miles Davis, Dizzy Gillispie, Thelonius Monk and Charlie Parker. Then 'kwela' took on but that was proletariat music. It was really popular music and it held on. Kwela was more for the kind of people who would go to disco today.

Mbaqanga was for the 1960s what *kwela* was to Mphahlele's 1950s, and when this is weighed up alongside Ballantine's (2012, 99) and Khumalo's evidence regarding class divisions and musical taste, we have to ask whether the 'increasingly limited usefulness' that Hamm (1991, 165) considered modern jazz to have for the SABC after 1960 can be attributed so neatly to political decision-making (as opposed to decision-making by a political broadcaster). Mphahlele doesn't specify whether it was the radio or gramophone aspect of the radiogram that was responsible for blasting US bebop throughout Sophiatown but, although the period he was recalling was before the SABC had set up Radio Bantu in the form that dictated broadcasting policy in the 1960s, he is clear that Rediffusion – an earlier example of state-controlled media – quickly became unpopular (Mphahlele 1986, 58).

There is ample evidence that Radio Bantu *was* heavily compromised by the apartheid regime's agenda (Andersson 1981; Ansell 2004; Ballantine 2012; Coplan 2007; Hamm 1991; Tomaselli *et al.* 1989), yet it was a different beast from Redifussion. Coplan (2007, 251) reasons that because the government required that Radio Bantu should largely fund itself, it was not immune from commercial pressure and therefore needed to strike a balance between serving apartheid's aims and playing what the audience wanted to hear. Radio Bantu was therefore advertised regularly in the newspapers during the 1960s, and the level of advertising remained reasonably constant throughout the decade. The content of listings was variable, but always quite limited: the majority of advertisements in *Imvo Zabantsundu* gave only weekly highlights, whereas *Ilanga Lase Natal* featured adverts for both weekly highlights and, on occasion, a marginally more detailed breakdown. Even where programmes advertised a musical focus it is not always possible to tell what kind of music was being broadcast, although descriptors are sometimes added that give some indication: for example, 'Kubantu abathanda i "Jazz"' (People who love 'Jazz') (Radio Bantu 1968, 8); 'Jazz ngu Jorha' (Jazz with Jorha) (Radio Bantu 1965a, 10); or simply 'Jazz' (Radio Bantu 1965b, 6). Given the very limited information on jazz available from these adverts, the most that can be said is that the proportion of adverts where jazz is specifically mentioned remains fairly constant. But these should not be considered the only possible slots that were available for jazz – even for a date where more complete listings are provided – as a number of other descriptors that may, or may not, indicate the presence of jazz on the radio were also attached to various programmes: for example, 'Ingxubevange' (Variety) or 'Ezimtoti' (Something Sweet) (Radio Bantu 1965c, 5). Radio Bantu was also discussed in the newspapers and a range of views were expressed. A feature-length article by 'Ngumbhaleli wethu – eQonce' (Our Correspondent in King William's Town) in *Imvo Zabantsundu* on 13 July 1963 entitled 'Uza kuqhakaza umsasazo: Kongezwe nabasebenzi' (Broadcasting will shine: additional workers)[9] reported on Radio Bantu's expansion, noted improvements in the station's programming, and generally commended the 'entertainment' that it provided.

But not all the coverage of government broadcasting in *Imvo* was positive. On the eve of Radio Bantu switching to FM transmission an anonymous opinion piece from December 1961, which appeared under the heading 'Bathini na abantu kwaGompo' (What people from Gompo say; 1961, 2), complained of heavy government bias, criticised the one-sided coverage of discussions on apartheid at the United Nations, and implied that 'native' announcers such as Theo Mcinga were government stooges.

Despite this mixed response, and understandable condemnation of the policies and service provided in the literature, David Coplan (2007, 251) makes

254 Jonathan Eato

the point that 'it must be acknowledged that the rich archival resources, programming capacity, and strong institutional development of the nine African language radio stations today, despite changing their names, derive from the Radio Bantu system'. Although Coplan also writes that Radio Bantu's musical programming director Yvonne Huskisson 'campaigned mightily to substitute traditional, or at least neo-traditional, music for her *bête noire*, jazz, which had arrived with its hated linguistic counterpart and medium, American English' (Coplan 2007, 227) jazz music is relatively well represented in the SABC's archive of transcription recordings.[10]

Establishing exactly how much jazz was recorded for Radio Bantu in the 1960s should entail a straightforward catalogue filter by year; however, this is impossible as dates were not entered for the majority of items. Nevertheless, running a search for jazz musicians whom I know were active in the 1960s yielded a body of recordings by fifty artists/bands, and where no date is stated on the recording or in the catalogue, biographical information can be used to try to establish a likely recording year.

Despite the logistical and artistic problems musicians faced in recording for the SABC, such as lack of time on a session for retakes and rehearsal (Mbambisa 2014), and the problems inherent with gatekeepers who were loyal to government ideology, it is interesting to note that when the pianist Noel Stockton (2007, 112) was asked which centres he felt were pivotal in sustaining jazz in apartheid South Africa, he responded: 'I am trying to think of jazz venues [in Johannesburg], but I cannot remember any particular ones where jazz was performed . . . So radio provided an opportunity to perform jazz as such, I cannot remember any particular venues.' Given the apartheid regime's concerted efforts to remove access to live venues for jazz musicians (especially those classified as 'black'), it is not altogether surprising that Stockton struggled to think of venues that played a pivotal role in sustaining the music. And he reminds us that however compromised it may have been, and however limited the competition, the SABC nevertheless provided opportunities of sorts. Writing in 1969, the SABC's Organiser of Bantu Music, Yvonne Huskisson (1969, xi), claimed:

> Radio Bantu has given this JAZZ development every encouragement. During their lean formative years, while Bantu audiences were being initiated into the intricacies of the JAZZ form and the JAZZ disc-market was slowly finding its feet . . . Radio Bantu continuously provided these JAZZ combos with recording facilities and featured them in regular JAZZ programmes, their original JAZZ compositions heard on the air. Today, they are also promoted by their own JAZZ Society operating from Johannesburg.

Exactly what Huskisson, Charles Hamm, the SABC censors or anyone else for that matter heard as jazz music is of course a moot point; as I pointed out above this is as contentious an area for 1960s South Africa as it is for any other country at any other time. Although claims made for certain musical expressions as jazz are of interest regardless of their perceived legitimacy or accuracy inasmuch as they imbue the music with a certain political and cultural cachet in the context of 1960s South Africa (Mphahlele 1986), and in the absence of radio playlists or details of broadcasting royalties (Graeme Gilfillan (in Ansell 2004, 130–131) points out that needle-time payments were abolished in the mid-1960s), it is precisely these descriptions that we have to navigate in order fully to understand the intersection of jazz music and politics in 1960s South Africa.

Suffice it to say that the SABC catalogue does record a classification for each transcription recording in its audio archive, and these include several sub-divisions of jazz ('African Jazz', 'Instrumental Jazz', 'Jazz', 'Jazz (Black)' and 'Soul Jazz'). For the jazz musicians I know to have been working in the 1960s, several other categories also came up ('English Light Vocal', 'Folk Xhosa', 'Folk Zulu', 'Incidental Music (dramas)', 'Instrumental', 'Light Vocal', 'Vocal Group', 'Xhosa Light Vocal', 'Xhosa' and so on). These classifications roughly align to those used by Huskisson in the preface to *The Bantu Composers of Southern Africa* (1969) as she traces the history of the music from 'light instru-mentalists' through to 'jazz'. Huskisson's version of South Africa's jazz history is of interest as it provides insights into the musical views of an SABC official. The first generation she describes as 'light instrumentalists' who 'veered away from the "traditional" and concentrated on mastering the technique of their instruments' (Huskisson 1969, x). These were apparently musicians who focused on 'standard dance band orchestrations', but they were not followed by the musicians Huskisson characterises as the 'second generation'. This latter group, she reports, were 'content to produce a limited "note" range, [and they] returned to the "traditional" and created the so-called BANTU-JAZZ form, restricted melodically but tremendously stimulating rhythmically and basically "traditional" sounding' (Huskisson 1969, x). We might expect Huskisson's jazz sympathies and institutional support to rest here, given Coplan's assertion that she campaigned for jazz to be replaced by traditional or neo-traditional music at the SABC. Similarly, Hamm's (1991, 165) conclusion that, from the early 1960s onwards, a modern jazz sound had 'an increasingly limited usefulness' to an SABC that was attempting simultaneously to reach rural uneducated audiences and to promote the regime's separate development agenda has a resonance with Huskisson's assessment of the 'second generation'. After all, 'music programmed on Radio Bantu [was required to] relate in some way to the culture of the "tribal" group at which a given service was aimed' (Hamm 1991, 160).

However, this seems not to be the case, either empirically or in terms of Huskisson's reading of events. The jazz music she appears to have seen herself supporting was performed by 'a certain number of Bantu musicians, whose skill completely surpassed that of the average instrumentalist' (Huskisson 1969, x). This was the 'Progressive JAZZ' – or more often simply 'JAZZ' – that she considered to have been initiated in South Africa by The Jazz Epistles and which she claimed was the music that Radio Bantu had been nurturing up to her point of writing in 1969; in other words, the type of jazz music exemplified by 'modern' jazz musicians such as The Blue Notes, and indeed they recorded fourteen numbers for the SABC before leaving South Africa for exile in 1964.[11] These were a mixture of originals and compositions by US artists. All were performed in a modern – hard bop – style and all were arranged/composed according to contemporary US modern jazz models. Furthermore, all but one of the numbers – Dudu Pukwana's 'Izithunywa' – have English titles. As 'Izithunywa' translates as 'The Messengers', it is hard not to make the connection to Art Blakey's modern US hard bop group The Jazz Messengers when considered in combination with the musical style of the recordings.

Although there is considerably more work to do regarding the SABC's archive of transcription recordings, initial evidence either directly contradicts Hamm's thesis or counters it in less obvious ways. Huskisson's claims that Radio Bantu nurtured modern jazz – the music Hamm declared was of increasingly limited use to the SABC from the early 1960s onwards – appear to be supported in 1960s transcription recordings made by The Blue Notes, The Soul Giants, The Jazz Disciples, the Early Mabuza Trio, the Nu-African Quavers Rhythm Section, and a number of other key artists, including Masdorph 'Shakes' Mgudlwa, Kippie Moeketsi, Dennis Mpale, Jeanette Tsagane, Count Wellington Judge, Sax-O-Wills Mbali and Johnny Gertze. And these examples of direct contradiction to Hamm are only for those transcription recordings that I can accurately place in the 1960s. There are others with line-ups consistent with groups working in the 1960s but for which I have no definitive proof as yet, and many more examples by artists who were working in the 1960s but whose recordings for the SABC also extend into the 1970s and even the 1980s, making accurate dating difficult.

'uMsenge': A Case Study

A less obvious countering of Hamm's thesis can be seen when different recorded iterations of a specific song are considered, in this case Tete Mbambisa's 'uMsenge'. The original[12] commercially available recording released by The Four Yanks on Gallo in 1962 – see Figure 11.3 – already ticked many of the SABC's ideological requirements, as outlined in the 1961 *Annual Report* (quoted in Hamm 1991): the lyrics are in an indigenous language, in this case isiXhosa; there is an engagement with 'traditional' African culture as *msenge* is the isiXhosa name for a tree, the extract of which is used in traditional medicine; the harmony outlines the repeating whole-step pattern found in much folk music of the amaXhosa (see Dargie 1988, 7); and the unadorned

Jazz in 1960s Apartheid South Africa 257

FIGURE 11.3 The Four Yanks' Recording of 'Msenge' (Tete Mbambisa), 1962

triadic voicings Mbambisa uses to accompany the four vocalists are described by Mbambisa as representing the 'African' side of his harmonic palette (Mbambisa 2012).

Yet, when Mbambisa came to record 'uMsenge' again two years later, this time for the SABC with The Jazz Disciples (1964), his arrangement appeared to fly in the face of Hamm's theorising: the repeating whole-step harmonic pattern remains but the vocals are gone, thereby removing the African-language component; the straight eighth-note feel of the Gallo release is replaced by swung eighths, clearly outlined by the ride cymbal of a modern jazz drum set; and the voicings in both the horn melody (see Figures 11.4 and 11.5) and the piano introduction (see Figure 11.6) explore *both* Mbambisa's 'African' triadic voicings *and* the quartal sonorities redolent of 1960s modern jazz from the United States.

By adding sixths to the basic harmony in his piano voicings, Mbambisa is able to introduce quartal sonorities and relationships in varied ways without the quality of the harmony becoming too far removed from the triadic quality of The Four Yanks' version. Fourths (circled in Figure 11.6) can thereby:

- sound in parts of the harmony other than between the fifth and tonic of a chord;
- outline parallel movement other than the whole-step movement of the main harmony (e.g. of a descending fourth, from Bb second inversion to Fm7 second inversion, b.1–2);

- and create additional harmonic variety by sounding the vacillating whole-step harmonic relationship a sixth above that of the main harmony by implying Gm7 – Fm7 (b.3–4).

The connection between, for example, McCoy Tyner's quartal voicings in John Coltrane's classic quartet of the early 1960s and the way that amaXhosa folk music can be harmonised to feature fourths and fifths[13] is not lost on Mbambisa. Consequently, we need to note the fluidity of this musical signifier; however, Mbambisa (2012) is also clear that in a jazz context he regards upper-structure voicings (whether sounding quartally or otherwise) as representing the contemporary, international, modern jazz side of his harmonic language.

FIGURE 11.4 The Jazz Disciples' Recording of 'uMsenge' (Tete Mbambisa) for the SABC, 1964

FIGURE 11.5 The Jazz Disciples' Recording of 'uMsenge' (Tete Mbambisa) for the SABC, 1964

FIGURE 11.6 The Jazz Disciples' Recording of 'uMsenge' (Tete Mbambisa) for the SABC, 1964

Jazz in 1960s Apartheid South Africa   259

A third opportunity to record 'uMsenge', with a slightly altered and expanded line-up of The Jazz Disciples, presented itself not long after the 1964 SABC recording, but this time for the commercial HMV label (The Jazz Disciples *c.*1964). The unadorned triadic horn voicings of Mbambisa's 'African' harmony at the start of the SABC recording (Figure 11.4) are more or less replicated, along with the rest of the arrangement, in the HMV version (Figure 11.7), and similarly give way to quartal upper-structure voicings that emerge from a unison and triadic set-up (Figure 11.8).

If Mbambisa had felt pressured to adapt his conception of 'uMsenge' for the state broadcaster, it seems almost certain that he would have taken the opportunity to record his preferred version for HMV a few months later. Yet, the close similarities between these two almost contemporaneous recordings are striking. In fact, Mbambisa has stated that the SABC asked him to change something for a recording session only once, and that was regarding the song

FIGURE 11.7   The Jazz Disciples' Recording of 'uMsenge (The Tree Song)' (Tete Mbambisa) for HMV, *c.*1964

FIGURE 11.8   The Jazz Disciples' Recording of 'uMsenge (The Tree Song)' (Tete Mbambisa) for HMV, *c.*1964

'Yehla Nomonde' (Come Down Nomonde), written for the vocal group Masiye Voices (n.d.). Originally titled 'Yehla Moses' (Come Down Moses) in reference to the biblical story, Huskisson insisted the lyrics must be changed before the recording could proceed, telling Mbambisa that he was not to 'jazz the Bible' (Mbambisa 2014). Whilst this was a form of censorship, it was applied to all communities, however defined. The religious sensitivities of the regime had to be observed if official censure and the banning of recordings was to be avoided (see Feldman (1971) for details of the regime's reaction to John Lennon's infamous 'more popular than Jesus' comment).

This brief case study of both commercial and SABC recordings of Tete Mbambisa's 'uMsenge' reminds us that decisions regarding the *musical* content of 1960s jazz in South Africa should not necessarily be assumed to be the result of the apartheid regime's broadcasting policy. For Mbambisa, the musical differences, both within and between tracks, are more to do with his long-standing interest in creatively balancing what he identifies as 'African' and 'modern jazz' signifiers in his music. Indeed, it is this balance that Vuyiswa Ngcwangu (Mbambisa and Ngcwangu 2003) identifies as the chief draw in one of Mbambisa's best-known recordings, *Tete's Big Sound* (Mbambisa 1976). With regards to his commercial recordings, I have previously argued that Mbambisa's 'success, his marketable musical identity, precisely depends on categorical ambiguity' (Eato 2013b, 120–121), and it is clear from the analysis of 'uMsenge' that this modus operandi was not significantly derailed when recording for the SABC in the 1960s.

Concluding Remarks

Clearly the parallel momentum of jazz music and optimistic, overt, socio-political protest of the 1950s did not lead to the emancipatory results anticipated by some in the Republic of South Africa in the 1960s; see, for example, Chief Albert Luthuli ('Freedom in the Air' 1959), Miriam Makeba (in Hirsch 2002) and Mac Maharaj (in Sparks *et al.* n.d.). However, as Gwen Ansell points out, despite the trope of silence that I argue has accumulated across various readings of 1960s South Africa, a jazz momentum *was* maintained under the straitened circumstances that gripped the country. Commercial pressures, combined with the popularity of new styles (*mbaqanga*) and the continuance of established popular styles in 1960s South Africa, played a significant role in the SABC's broadcasting strategies. And, although there is clearly much more work to be done regarding the level of *musical* autonomy possible for artists recording for the SABC, the evidence presented here – of musical styles climbing through the cracks of grand apartheid's concrete without being overwhelmingly compromised or materially altered – could usefully inform our wider understanding of music in 1960s South Africa.

Notes

1 I am indebted to Gwen Ansell for her generosity in discussing ideas for this chapter with me. Also Siemon Allen, Rob Allingham, Christopher Ballantine, Lindelwa Dalamba, Sazi Dlamini, Allison Drew, Francis Gooding, Aryan Kaganof and Stephanus Muller, who have helped me think through some of the implications of this research.

2 *King Kong* was a highly successful and influential South African musical theatre production that premiered on 2 February 1959 (see de Beer 2001 [1960]).

3 I am very grateful to Willem Muller for transcribing Kombuis's Afrikaans and for providing the English translation.

4 'The "syndrome", or pattern of interrelated traits, of the totalitarian dictatorship consists of an ideology, a single party typically led by one man, a terroristic police, a communications monopoly, a weapons monopoly, and a centrally directed economy.'

5 I am grateful to Allison Drew for the idea that South African independence can be considered in terms of parody.

6 From 1961–1964 the Castle Brewery sponsored a series of important national jazz festivals known as the Cold Castle Jazz Festivals. The series was discontinued after violence outside the 1964 event left six dead (Coplan 2007), but, as Francis Gooding (2011) points out, jazz sponsorship continued under the 'Castle Wine and Brandy Company (unconnected to Castle Lager, despite the name) whose promotion of "Golden Castle" involved a "Jazz King of the Year" award, seemingly chosen by a popular vote.'

7 For examples, discussions and refutations of this idea, see Gaylard (2008), Gordimer (2010), Kgalane (1996), Magubane (2006), McClintock (1987), Penfold (2013) and Sepamla (in Seroke *et al.* 1998).

8 I am indebted to Chris Albertyn, Siemon Allen, Olivier Ledure, Nick Lotay and Matt Temple for this discographical information. A small number of tracks from these recordings are currently available on the third volume of *Next Stop . . . Soweto* (Various Artists n.d.b), the recent *Spirit of Malombo* compilation from Strut (Various Artists 1966–1984) and *The History of Township Music* (Various Artists n.d.a), but most remain unavailable. There have been various re-releases of complete albums, all now also out of print, and *Dollar Brand Plays Sphere Jazz* (minus one track) was reissued as part of the compilation *Blues for a Hip King* on Kaz in 1988, but this is currently out of print. Since preparing this text for publication The Soul Jazzmen's 1969 album *Inhlupeko* has been rereleased by Matsuli Music, and Chris McGregor and the Castle Lager Big Band's 1963 recording *Jazz the African Sound* has been rereleased by Jazzman.

9 With thanks to Nontsha Mputhi for translations from isiXhosa to English.

10 I am very grateful to Justice Muthakhi and Cate Jele at the SABC in Auckland Park for facilitating my access to the audio archives and catalogue. Some SABC transcription discs from the 1960s have 'South African Broadcasting Corporation Overseas Transcription Service' printed on the label, raising the question of whether they may have been made as propaganda intended for overseas airplay only. My thanks to Justice Muthakhi (2015) and Rob Allingham (2015) for confirming that, to the best of their knowledge, all SABC transcription recordings were intended for local broadcast (although Allingham notes two examples of SABC transcription recordings being subsequently banned; he attributes this to 'mis-alignment between the production department and the in-house censors').

11 Twelve of these, including two alternate takes, have been released commercially as *Township Bop* (The Blue Notes 1964).

12 Although The Four Yanks's version was the first recorded, 'uMsenge' was originally conceived some time earlier in an instrumental arrangement for Ronnie Beer's group The Swinging City Six (Mbambisa 2010). I have adopted the spelling 'uMsenge' when talking generally about this song (in this isiXhosa title 'u' is the definite article), but when discussing a specific recording I have retained the various published spellings.

13 This is not to say that triadic harmonisations are absent from amaXhosa folk music. For a detailed explanation of how amaXhosa folk music has been variously harmonised, whether for choir music, overtone singing (*umngqokolo*) or bow performances, see Dargie (1988).

References

Ake, David, Charles Hiroshi Garret and Daniel Goldmark, eds. 2012. *Jazz/Not Jazz*. Berkeley: University of California Press.

Albertyn, Chris, ed. 2013. *Keeping Time: 1964–1974 the Photographs and Cape Town Jazz Recordings of Ian Bruce Huntley*. Durban: Chris Albertyn and Associates CC.

Albertyn, Chris. 2014. 'The Huntley Archive: Keeping Time: Photographs and Cape Town Jazz Recordings – 1964–1974'. *Electric Jive*. Accessed 1 May 2014. http://electricjive.blogspot.com/p/ibh-audio-archive-posts.html.

Albertyn, Chris, Siemon Allen, Francis Gooding, Nick Lotay and Matthew Temple. 2009–present. *Electric Jive*. Accessed 20 August 2014. http://electricjive.blogspot.com.

Allingham, Rob. 2015. Email to the author. 11 February.

Andersson, Muff. 1981. *Music in the Mix: The Story of South African Popular Music*. Johannesburg: Ravan Press.

Ansell, Gwen. 2004. *Soweto Blues: Jazz, Popular Music, and Politics in South Africa*. New York: Continuum.

Ansell, Gwen. 2010. 'The Context'. Liner notes for Various Artists, *Next Stop . . . Soweto*, vol. III: *Giants, Ministers and Makers: Jazz in South Africa 1963–1978*. Strut STRUT063CD.

Arendt, Hannah. 1967. *The Origins of Totalitarianism*. 3rd edn. London: George Allen & Unwin.

Baehr, Peter. 2005. 'Totalitarianism'. In *New Dictionary of the History of Ideas*, ed. Maryanne Cline Horowitz. Farmington Hills: Thomson Gale: 2342–2348.

Ballantine, Christopher. 2012. *Marabi Nights: Jazz, 'Race' and Society in Early Apartheid South Africa*. 2nd edn. Pietermaritzburg: University of KwaZulu-Natal Press.

'Bathini na abantu kwaGompo'. 1961. *Imvo Zabantsundu*, 9 December.

Blacking, John. 1980. 'Trends in Black Music of South Africa, 1959–1969'. In *Musics of Many Cultures: An Introduction*, ed. Elizabeth May. Berkeley: University of California Press: 195–215.

Chapman, Michael. 1989. 'More than Telling a Story: *Drum* and Its Significance in Black South African Writing'. In *The Drum Decade: Stories from the 1950s*, ed. Michael Chapman. Pietermaritzburg: University of Natal Press: 183–232.

Chipkin, Clive. 1998. 'The Great Apartheid Building Boom: The Transformation of Johannesburg in the 1960s'. In *Blank: Architecture, Apartheid and After*, ed. Hilton Judin and Ivan Vladislavić. Rotterdam: NAi Publishers: 248–267.

Coplan, David B. 2007. *In Township Tonight! Three Centuries of South African Black City Music and Theatre*. 2nd edn. Auckland Park: Jacana.

Coplan, David B. 2010. 'Johannesburg in the 1960s and '70s Was a Nobody's Baby . . .' Liner notes for Various Artists, *Next Stop . . . Soweto: Township Sounds from the Golden Age of Mbaqanga*. STRUT STRUT054CD.

Couper, Scott Everett. 2009. '"An Embarrassment to the Congresses?" The Silencing of Chief Albert Luthuli and the Production of ANC History'. *Journal of Southern African Studies* 35(2): 331–348.

Dargie, David. 1988. *Xhosa Music: Its Techniques and Instruments, with a Collection of Songs*. Cape Town: David Philip.

de Beer, Mona. 2001 [1960]. *King Kong: A Venture in the Theatre*. Cape Town: Norman Howell.

DeVeaux, Scott. 2001–2002. 'Struggling with Jazz'. *Current Musicology* 71–73: 353–374.

Drew, Allison, ed. 1997. *South Africa's Radical Tradition: A Documentary History*, vol. II: *1943–1964*. Cape Town: Buchu Books/Mayibuye Books/UCT Press.

Eato, Jonathan. 2013a. 'The Ian Bruce Huntley Archive'. In *Keeping Time: 1964–1974 the Photographs and Cape Town Jazz Recordings of Ian Bruce Huntley*, ed. Chris Albertyn. Durban: Chris Albertyn and Associates CC: 23–37.

Eato, Jonathan. 2013b. 'Negotiating Tradition, Modernity, and Cultural Identity in Contemporary South Africa: The Music of Tete Mbabmisa, Louis Moholo-Moholo and Zim Ngqawana'. In *A Collection of Papers Presented at Ethnomusicology Symposium 2013*, ed. Mathayo Ndomondo, Imani Sanga and Mitchel Strumpf. Dar Es Salaam: Department of Fine and Performing Arts, University of Dar Es Salaam: 119–126.

Emergency Committee of the ANC. 1960. 'We Must Learn New Methods of Work'. In *South Africa's Radical Tradition: A Documentary History*, vol. II: *1943–1964*, ed. Allison Drew. Cape Town: Buchu Books/Mayibuye Books/UCT Press: 354–355.

Feldman, Peter. 1971. 'S. African Broadcastmen Lift 4-Year Record Ban on Beatles'. *Billboard*, 27 March.

'Freedom in the Air'. 1959. *Drum*, July.

Friedrich, Carl J. and Zbigniew K. Brzezinski. 1965. *Totalitarian Dictatorship and Autocracy*. 2nd edn. Cambridge, MA: Harvard University Press.

Frith, Simon. 2007. 'Is Jazz Popular Music?' *Jazz Research Journal* 1(1): 7–23.

Gabbard, Krin. 2002. 'The Word Jazz'. In *The Cambridge Companion to Jazz*, ed. Mervyn Cooke and David Horn. Cambridge: Cambridge University Press: 1–6.

Gaylard, Rob. 2008. 'Writing Black: The South African Short Story by Black Writers'. DLitt dissertation, University of Stellenbosch. Accessed 22 December 2014. http://hdl.handle.net/10019.1/1202.

Giliomee, Hermann. 2003. *The Afrikaners: Biography of a People*. Cape Town: Tafelberg.

Gooding, Francis. 2011. 'Jazz Royalty, Swinging Bittersweet'. *Electric Jive*, 19 March. Accessed 5 September 2014. http://electricjive.blogspot.co.uk/2011/03/jazz-royalty-swinging-bittersweet.html.

Gordimer, Nadine. 2010. *Telling Times: Writing and Living 1950–2008*. London: Bloomsbury.

Hamm, Charles. 1991. '"The Constant Companion of Man": Separate Development, Radio Bantu and Music'. *Popular Music* 10(2): 147–173.

Hamm, Charles. 1995. *Putting Popular Music in Its Place*. Cambridge: Cambridge University Press.

Hanf, Theodor, Heribert Weiland and Gerda Vierdag. 1981. *South Africa, the Prospects of Peaceful Change*. Great Britain, South Africa and North America: Rex Collings, David Philip and Indiana University Press.

Hayes, Frank. 1980. 'South Africa's Departure from the Commonwealth, 1960–1961'. *International History Review* 2(3): 453–484.

Hayman, Graham and Ruth Tomaselli. 1989. 'Ideology and Technology in the Growth of South African Broadcasting, 1924–1971'. In *Currents of Power: State Broadcasting in South Africa*, ed. Ruth Tomaselli, Keyan Tomaselli and Johan Muller. Bellville: Anthropos: 23–83.

Hirsch, Lee. 2002. *Amandla! A Revolution in Four-Part Harmony*. DVD. United States and South Africa: Artisan Entertainment.

Horn, David. 2002. 'The Identity of Jazz'. In *The Cambridge Companion to Jazz*, ed. Mervyn Cooke and David Horn. Cambridge: Cambridge University Press: 9–32

Horrell, Muriel. 1960. *Days of Crisis in South Africa: Events up to 15th May 1960*. Johannesburg: SA Institute of Race Relations.

Houser, George M. 1958. 'Mr Louw and the Declaration'. *Africa Today* 5(1): 3–4, 14. Accessed 11 December 2014. www.jstor.org/stable/pdfplus/4183926.pdf?&acceptTC=true&jpdConfirm=true.

Huskisson, Yvonne. 1969. *The Bantu Composers of Southern Africa/Die Bantoe-Komponiste Van Suider-Afrika*. Johannesburg: South African Broadcasting Corporation.

International Defence Aid Fund. 1969. *South Africa: The BOSS Law*. London: Christian Action.

Jazz Publicity Service. 1964. 'Albums by Lena Horne, Randy Weston Banned by South African Government'. Accessed 10 September 2014. www.randyweston.info/randy-weston-resume-pages/randy-weston-uhuru-afrika-banned.html.

Johnson, Bruce. 2002. 'The Jazz Diaspora'. In *The Cambridge Companion to Jazz*, ed. Mervyn Cooke and David Horn. Cambridge: Cambridge University Press: 33–54.

Kgalane, Gloria Vangile. 1996. 'Black South African Women's Poetry (1970–1991): A Critical Survey'. MA dissertation, Rand Afrikaans University. Accessed 11 March 2015. https://ujdigispace.uj.ac.za/handle/10210/6649.

Lorentzon, Leif. 2007. 'Jazz in *Drum*, an Ambiguous Discourse: "Matshikeze" and the Short Stories'. In *Music and Identity: Transformation and Negotiation*, ed. Eric Akrofi, Maria Smit and Stig-Magnus Thorsén. Stellenbosch: Sun Press: 199–214.

Magubane, Bernard. 2006. 'Introduction to the 1970s: The Social and Political Context'. In *The Road to Democracy in South Africa*, vol. II, ed. South African Democracy Education Trust. Pretoria: UNISA: 1–36.

Mathews, Anthony S. 1972. *Law, Order and Liberty in South Africa*. Berkeley: University of California Press.

Mbambisa, Tete. 2010. Interview with the author. 18 August.

Mbambisa, Tete. 2012. Personal communication with the author. 11 April.

Mbambisa, Tete. 2014. Personal communication with the author. 28 September.

Mbambisa, Tete and Vuyiswa Ngcwangu. 2003. 'Tete Mbulelo Mbambisa, Pianist, Composer, Singer, Bandleader'. In *Jazz People of Cape Town*, ed. Lars Rasmussen. København: The Booktrader: 141–152.

Mbeki, Thabo. 2004. 'Foreword'. In *The Road to Democracy in South Africa*, vol. I, ed. South African Democracy Education Trust. Pretoria: UNISA: vii–xiii.

McClintock, Anne. 1987. '"Azikwelwa" (We Will Not Ride): Politics and Value in Black South African Poetry'. *Critical Inquiry* Spring: 597–623. Accessed 11 March 2015. www.jstor.org/stable/1343515.

Merriam, Alan P. and Fradley H. Garner. 1998. 'Jazz – the Word'. In *The Jazz Cadence of American Culture*, ed. Robert G. O'Meally. New York: Columbia University Press: 7–31.

Mphahlele, Es'kia. 1986. 'Es'kia Mphahlele'. In *Sophiatown Speaks*. Johannesburg: Junction Avenue Press: 55–59.

Muthakhi, Justice. 2015. Email to the author. 27 February.

Naidoo, G. R., Johnny Dyani, Mongezi Feza, Chris McGregor, Louis Moholo-Moholo, Nikele Moyake and Dudu Pukwana. 1964. 'A Blow on the Beach'. *Drum*, June.

Ngumbhaleli wethu – eQonce [pseud]. 1963. 'Uza Kuqhakaza Umsasazo: Kongezwe Nabasebenzi'. *Imvo Zabantsundu*, 13 July.

Nicholson, Stuart. 2005. *Is Jazz Dead (or Has It Moved to a New Address)?* New York: Routledge.

Nkosi, Lewis. 1983. *Home and Exile and Other Selections*. London: Longman.

Penfold, Thomas William. 2013. 'Black Consciousness and the Politics of Writing the Nation in South Africa'. Ph.D. dissertation, University of Birmingham.

Pyper, Brett. 2005. '"To Hell with Home and Shame!" Jazz, Gender and Sexuality in the *Drum* Journalism of Todd Matshikiza, 1951–1957'. In *Gender and Sexuality in South African Music*, ed. Chris Walton and Stephanus Muller. Stellenbosch: SUN PReSS: 19–26.

Rabkin, David. 1975. '*Drum* Magazine (1951–1961): And the Works of Black South African Writers Associated with It'. Ph.D. dissertation, University of Leeds. Accessed 6 August 2013. http://etheses.whiterose.ac.uk/id/eprint/2323.

Radio Bantu. 1965a. 'Fm Iintlelo Eziqavile 26 June–2 July'. *Imvo Zabantsundu*, 26 June.

Radio Bantu. 1965b. 'Fm Iintlelo Eziqavile 21–27 August'. *Imvo Zabantsundu*, 21 August.

Radio Bantu. 1965c. 'Uhlelo Lomsakazo'. *Ilanga Lase Natal*, 27 November.

Radio Bantu. 1968. 'Fm Iintlelo Eziqavile January 27–February 2'. *Imvo Zabantsundu*, 27 January.

'Recreational Facilities'. 1961. *Imvo Zabantsundu*, 25 November.

Ross, Lloyd. 2006. *Voëlvry – the Movie*. DVD. South Africa: Shifty Studio.

Seroke, Jaki, Miriam Tlali, Sipho Sepamla and Mothobi Mutloatse. 1998. 'Black Writers in South Africa'. In *Ten Years of Staffrider 1978–1988*, ed. Andries Walter Oliphant and Ivan Vladislavić. Johannesburg: Ravan Press: 303–309.

Sparks, Alistair, Helen Suzman, Eddie Daniels, Dennis Goldberg, Dullah Omar, Nelson Rolihlahla Mandela, Ahmed Kathrada, Joe Matthews, Lungi Sisulu, Mac Maharaj, Amina Cachalia and George Bizos. n.d. 'Mandela: An Audio History. Part Two (1960–1964) the Underground Movement'. *Radio Diaries*. Accessed 13 December 2014. www.mandelahistory.org/stories.php.

Stanbridge, Alan. 2004. 'Burns, Baby, Burns: Jazz History as a Contested Cultural Site'. *The Source* 1: 82–100.

Stockton, Noel Desmond. 2007. 'Noel Desmond Stockton (b. 1930)'. In *Unsung: South African Jazz Musicians under Apartheid*, ed. Chatradari Devroop and Chris Walton. Stellenbosch: SUN PReSS: 105–117.

Titlestad, Michael. 2005. 'Jazz Discourse and Black South African Modernity, with Special Reference to "Matshikese"'. *American Ethnologist* 32(2): 210–221. Accessed 23 November 2014. www.jstor.org/stable/3805279.

Tomaselli, Ruth, Keyan Tomaselli and Johan Muller, eds. 1989. *Currents of Power: State Broadcasting in South Africa*. Bellville: Anthropos.

Union of South Africa. 1950. *Group Areas Act No. 41 of 1950*. Parow: Government Printer.

Union of South Africa. 1960. *Broadcasting Amendment Act No. 49 of 1960*. Parow: Government Printer.

266 Jonathan Eato

Wilson, Monica. 1969. 'White Settlers and the Origin of a New Society, 1652–1778'. In *The Oxford History of South Africa*, vol. I: *South Africa to 1870*, ed. Monica Wilson and Leonard Thompson. Oxford: Oxford University Press: 183–232.

Discography

The Blue Notes. 1964. *Township Bop*. Proper Records PRP CD 013, 2002, compact disc.
The Bogard Brothers. n.d. *Street Corner Jazz*. HMV 7EYJ8, c.1962, 33⅓rpm.
Brand, Dollar. 1960. *Dollar Brand Plays Sphere Jazz*. Continental ZB.8047, 1962, 33⅓rpm.
Brand, Dollar. *Blues for a Hip King*. Kaz KAZ CD104, 1988, compact disc.
The Four Sounds. 1969. *The Four Sounds Play Jazz from District Six*. Trutone TBL-C-1, 1969, 33⅓rpm.
The Four Yanks. 1962. 'Msenge'. Gallotone GB. On Various Artists, *From Marabi to Disco*. Gallo/GMP CDZAC61, 1994, compact disc.
Gwi-Gwi and His Jazz Rascals. 1960. 'Kwa-Obaas/Diepkloof Ekhaya'. USA USA 120, 1960, 78rpm.
The Hometown Sextet. c.1961. *Home Jive/Mamelodi*. Meritone Jazz JZ 62, c.1961, 78rpm.
The Jazz Disciples. c.1964. 'uMsenge (The Tree Song)'. HMV 45JP 887, c.1964, 45rpm.
The Jazz Epistles. 1960. *Jazz Epistle – Verse 1*. Continental CON-T.14, 1960, 33⅓rpm.
The Jazz Kings. c.1961. 'Chapter Two/Falling Leaves'. Meritone Jazz JZ 34, c.1961, 78rpm.
King Force and His Forces. c.1968. 'Vula No.1/Vula No.2'. Tempo KT011, c.1968, 45rpm.
Malombo Jazz Makers. c.1966. *Malompo Jazz*. Gallotone 1464, c.1966, 33⅓rpm.
Malombo Jazz Makers. 1967. *Malombo Jazz Makers Vol. 2*. Continental ZB 8162, 1967, 33⅓rpm.
Malombo Jazz Makers. 1969. *Down Lucky's Way*. Continental SZB 8245, 1969, 33⅓rpm.
Mankunku Quartet. 1968. *Yakhal' Inkomo*. World Record Company ORL 6022, 1968, 33⅓rpm.
Masiye Voices. n.d. 'Yehla Nomonde'. SABC LT10037/8, n.d., 33⅓rpm.
Mbambisa, Tete. 1975. *Tete's Big Sound*. As-Shams GL 1830, 1976, 33⅓rpm.
McGregor, Chris and the Castle Lager Big Band. 1963. *Jazz the African Sound*. Gallo NSL.1100, 1963, 33⅓rpm.
McGregor, Chris and the Castle Lager Big Band. 1963. *Jazz the African Sound*. Jazzman JMANLP 080, 2015, 33⅓rpm.
McGregor, Chris and His Blue Notes. c.1962. 'Ndiyeke Mra/German Luger'. Winner OK.125, c.1962, 78rpm.
Moyake, Nick [Nikele]. 1960. 'Brown Sauce/Shabzaza'. Meritone Big Beat BT 299, 1960, 78rpm.
Nxumalo, Gideon. 1962. *Jazz Fantasia*. Renown NLP 233, 1962, 33⅓rpm.
Nxumalo, Gideon. c.1968. *Gideon Plays*. JAS Pride JLP 02, c.1968, 33⅓rpm.
Phaukwane [Pukwana], Dudu. c.1961a. 'Size 10/Allright Dudu'. Meritone Big Beat BT 354, c.1961, 78rpm.
Phaukwane [Pukwana], Dudu. c.1961b. 'One-Two-Three!/Cape Town Dudu'. Meritone Jazz JZ 24, c.1961, 78rpm.

The Soul Giants. 1968. *I Remember Nick*. Atlantic City AYL 1000, 1968, 33⅓rpm.

The Soul Giants. n.d. "Umsenge". SABC LT10082/3, n.d., 33⅓rpm.

The Soul Jazzmen. 1969. *Inhlupeko*. City Special CYL1000, 1969, 33⅓rpm.

The Soul Jazzmen. 1969. *Inhlupeko*. Matsuli Music MM107, 2015, 33⅓rpm.

The Soul Jazzmen/Jazz Faces Quintet/Lionel Pillay Trio. 1968. *Mankunku Jazz Show: Recorded Live at the 'Y', Orlando*. Jazz Appreciation Society JLP 01, 1968, 33⅓rpm.

Tabane, Philip and the Pretoria Mellow Crooners. 1961. 'Hayiya-Hayiya/Nolizwe'. Drum DR 76, 1961, 78rpm.

Tabane, Phillip [*sic*] and His Malombo Jazzmen. 1969. *The Indigenous Afro-Jazz Sounds of Phillip Tabane and His Malombo Jazzmen*. Atlas City AYC 1004, 1969, 33⅓rpm.

Various Artists. 1962. *Cold Castle National Jazz Festival*. New Sound NSL 1010, 1962, 33⅓rpm.

Various Artists. 1966a. *Selwyn Lissack's Room*. Electric Jive: The Huntley Archive Tape 25, 2014, ¼-inch tape.

Various Artists. 1966b. *Something out of Africa*. Gallotone EP/XYZ 111, 1966, 45rpm.

Various Artists. 1966–1984. *Spirit of Malombo*. Strut STRUT119CD, 2014, compact disc.

Various Artists. n.d.a *The History of Township Music*. Wrasse WRASSE 029, 2001, compact disc.

Various Artists. n.d.b *Next Stop . . .* Soweto, vol. III: *Giants, Ministers and Makers: Jazz in South Africa 1963–1978*. Strut STRUT063CD, 2010, compact disc.

12

'FANFARE FOR THE WARRIORS'

Jazz, Education, and State Control in 1980s South Africa and After

Marc Duby

Before 1994, the apartheid state exercised strict control over the media, banning 'subversive' music and album covers (see Hamm 1991; Devroop and Walton 2007). This was blatant censorship by authorities who were threatened by music's potential to unite and mobilise resistance. Less visible (or audible perhaps) is the role of local music education in mediating jazz, so that the question arises: how did apartheid's repressive ethos influence the implementation of academic jazz education initiatives in the mid-1980s and beyond?

In this chapter I examine aspects of mediation and control in the reception and promotion of South African jazz as well as the role of the post-1994 academy in fostering a somewhat subservient attitude to bebop and 'the great American tradition', examining the changing nature of South African jazz in relation to a dominant ideology of North American jazz aesthetics and education. I argue that this is a very complex historical relationship in which longstanding tensions and contradictions (between 'local' and 'imported' forms of knowledge) continue to abound.

While educational institutions in South Africa seem to promote a somewhat uncritical adherence to African-American models of repertoire and the canon side-by-side with musics that draw from local traditions, I will attempt to illustrate how defining the status of South African jazz remains problematic if these bodies of knowledge are construed as monolithic and oppositional. I maintain that a case exists for understanding these as rather fluid and contested rather than set in stone.

I aim to consider the implications of this question in some detail so as to shed light on the nature of jazz education in South Africa under and after totalitarianism.

Introduction

In fostering the cultural interests of the white minority, the South African apartheid state promoted an ideology of musical culture as 'high art', privileging Western art music as 'serious' and other musics as 'light' or 'traditional', so superimposing the political idea of 'the banality of classification'[1] (Ballantine 2012, 25) onto music education and practice. This represents a form of cultural hegemony made possible by state control of media, education, and culture as aspects of a totalitarian system based on essentialised concepts of 'race'. Given apartheid's policies of separate development and state control of the cultural apparatus to curtail expressions of diversity, how was it possible for educators to introduce jazz studies into the music education landscape of the 1980s, which officially privileged Eurocentric (for which read white) interests as a matter of policy?

This question needs to be understood against the background of a system that was purpose-built to deny black South Africans access to educational opportunities, so maintaining their social status as 'inferior' to whites. One of the official cornerstones of apartheid's educational policy took the form of the Bantu Education Act of 1953, of which Alistair Boddy-Evans (n.d.: original emphasis) writes:

> In 1953 the Apartheid Government enacted The Bantu Education Act, which established a Black Education Department in the Department of Native Affairs. The role of this department was to compile a curriculum that suited the *nature and requirements of the black people*. The author of the legislation, Dr Hendrik Verwoerd (then Minister of Native Affairs, later Prime Minister), stated: '*Natives [blacks] must be taught from an early age that equality with Europeans [whites] is not for them.*' Black people were not to receive an education that would lead them to aspire to positions they wouldn't be allowed to hold in society. Instead they were to receive education designed to provide them with skills to serve their own people in the homelands[2] or to work in laboring jobs under whites.

In this respect, Daniel Chandler (2014) reads the Gramscian concept of hegemony in class terms:

> Gramsci used the term *hegemony* to denote the predominance of one social class over others (e.g. *bourgeois hegemony*). This represents not only political and economic control, but also the ability of the dominant class to project its own way of seeing the world so that those who are subordinated by it accept it as 'common sense' and 'natural'.

270 Marc Duby

In this way, the architects of apartheid theorised the concept of 'race' hegemonically as the basis of 'natural' and 'common-sense' differences between citizens. This concept of difference and its attendant enforcement through increasingly repressive and brutal legislation seem definitive hallmarks of a totalitarian regime. Uppermost in the classification of South African indigenous peoples by the state was 'race' as an ideological and physical means of division, enforced by geographical separation regulating and dictating where people were allowed to live and work, whom they could marry, associate with, play music with, or worship with as aspects of so-called 'petty apartheid' (Beningfield 2006, 310–312).

Beningfield (2006) maps the complex legal framework that enabled total control over the individual's human rights under apartheid, but perhaps the most devastating blow to such rights was dealt by the adoption into law of the Natives Land Act (1913), through which the majority of indigenous people was deprived of land in systematic fashion:

> The Act became law on the 19th of June 1913 limiting African land ownership to 7% which later increased to 13% through the 1936 Native Trust and Land Act of South Africa. The Act restricted black people from buying or occupying land except as employees of a white master. It however gave white people ownership of 87% of land . . . leaving black people to scramble for a mere 13%.
>
> *(Department of Rural Development and Land Reform 2013)*

The Land Act paved the way for the subsequent uprooting of individuals and communities via forced relocation, through which the apartheid state assaulted identities, destroying family relationships and long-term associations with particular places. The dispossession of land for strategic or agricultural advantage was nothing new for South Africa's colonisers, but after 1948 the ruling party enacted a series of laws grounded on the ideology of Afrikaner Christian Nationalism with a concomitant hardening of race-based dogma (Terreblanche 2002, 298–302) and the bedevilment of its inhabitants' daily lives through large-scale state regulation. Facing increasing international isolation through cultural and sports boycotts, the apartheid state (widely construed as a pariah regime by the 1980s) invoked two threats at the citadel gates in the form of '*die rooi gevaar*' (the red danger) and '*die swart gevaar*' (the black danger), playing on white fears of a communist takeover or the collective paranoia of a revolutionary advent of black majority rule, so justifying the rationale for the ideology of difference.

In this chapter I explore the historical trajectory of jazz studies in tertiary education in South Africa from its beginnings during the 1980s against the background of the totalitarian apartheid state and the role of jazz education in the subsequent formation of present-day communities of practice. Reading

Ballantine (2012, 29) in this regard is revealing, especially his notion of genre rebellion:

> For the same reason that the struggle for freedom and power is likely also to be a struggle against categories and classifications, so too is genre rebellion, within a particular socio-historical formation, very likely to be linked to rebellion elsewhere within the formation. That, to be sure, was the case with South African music in the climactic, final years of the anti-apartheid struggle.

Ballantine (ibid.) cites examples of South African bands (Sakhile, Bayete, Sabenza, and Johnny Clegg's Savuka) whose genre rebellions, as transgressions and integrations of ostensibly rigid musical boundaries, proclaimed their resistance to apartheid's 'banal classifications' and in so doing pointed the way to a hoped-for future dispensation, where such classifications might no longer hold sway. On the cover of *Universal Men* (the 1979 debut album by Savuka's predecessor Juluka), for instance, Clegg 'scandalized the White establishment by appearing on the cover of . . . dressed in full Zulu costume next to Mchunu', according to Leon Jackson (n.d.). I would suggest that this purported scandal was not simply the result of a white man explicitly identifying with Zulu culture, but that Clegg, by posing in such costume with Sipho Mchunu, was explicitly challenging the unequal status of black and white musicians (and implicitly the status of black and white people in general under apartheid) with the album's title underscoring this stance. This was, to be sure, a courageous statement in 1979,[3] a mere three years after government forces had brutally repressed the Soweto student uprising.[4]

I begin by invoking Pierre Bourdieu's notion (Bourdieu and Johnson 1993) of 'the cultural field' as a theoretical lens through which to understand the South African cultural climate of the 1980s. Turning next to examine aspects of state-controlled regulation of this cultural field, I argue that these operated within a broadly totalitarian framework, in the sense that the aesthetic discourse classified various musical practices in a hierarchy of value, so limiting the potential cultural capital of popular music practitioners, who operated outside the prevailing norms of Western art music.

This discussion has a bearing on the subsequent section, which examines aspects of jazz practice in relation to a wider global theme of diasporic currents to shed light on a conception of jazz as 'invader culture' (Devroop 2013, 8), a characterisation that I construe as problematic for reasons to be elucidated below. In the fourth section I examine the apparent paradox of jazz education establishing itself despite apartheid's educational and cultural restrictions, concluding by considering aspects of contemporary South African jazz practice and its relationship to the world of work.

272 Marc Duby

'Signs of the Times': Totalitarianism and the Cultural Field in 1980s South Africa

Jen Webb and her colleagues (2002, 23) note that 'Bourdieu understands the concept of cultural field to refer to fluid and dynamic, rather than static, entities. Cultural fields, that is, are made up not simply of institutions and rules, but of the interactions between institutions, rules and practices.' This aspect of 'interactions between institutions, rules and practices' forms a central focus in examining how jazz education took root in the 1980s and how the field of musical practice has changed since then.

I return to the point mentioned above regarding the apartheid state's tendency to privilege Western European art music over other forms of musical practice, understood as a form of cultural totalitarianism. Various mechanisms were put in place to reinforce this privileging of so-called European musical culture: first, through the operations of the former Provincial Arts Councils; second, through an extensive censorship apparatus which policed airplay and censored inappropriate album covers; and, finally, through state-controlled media promoting the ideology of separate development by broadcasting material deemed suitable for maintaining the isolation of cultural groupings on racial and linguistic grounds.

An official network of National Arts Boards visibly (and audibly) proclaimed a one-sided view of culture as European, white, and elitist. At provincial level, these organisations, which were named after the four provinces of the time – the Performing Arts Council of the Transvaal (PACT), the Cape Performing Arts Board (CAPAB), the Natal Performing Arts Council (NAPAC), and the Performing Arts Council of the Orange Free State (PACOFS) – arranged various schools tours and travelling productions encompassing theatre, music, ballet, and opera, but as cultural centres they catered mainly for patrons with their own means of transport, effectively excluding the vast majority of those township[5] dwellers who lacked both the means and the mobility to participate in such productions.

The State Theatre in Pretoria[6] represented the ultimate triumph of high culture over indigenous forms. Opening its doors in the early 1980s – a decisive decade for the establishment of jazz education – this venue accommodated an orchestra, a ballet company, and other visible (and costly) tributes to Eurocentric 'high art' cultural values, such as carefully selected artworks, sculptures, and tapestries.

> Designed by Hans and Roelf Botha, the theatre was completed in 1981. Situated on the corner of Church and Prinsloo Streets, the theatre covers the eastern portion of the block. Housing five theatres, it was at one time the largest theatre of its kind in the southern hemisphere.

> (*'State Theatre'* 2012)

The musical repertoire of venues like the State Theatre and its sister venue the Natal Playhouse in Durban tended to reinforce the official separation between so-called 'serious' and 'light' music, as did organisations like SAMRO (the South African Music Rights Organisation) and the various university music education departments, at least until jazz studies and African traditional musics joined the mainstream of educational offerings. Western art music of the common practice period, and to a lesser extent musicals, certainly dominated the bill of fare at the Playhouse when I worked there (1987–1992), with occasionally more adventurous lunch-hour performances and a late-night weekend jazz gig at the aptly named 'Cellar' in the basement of the theatre – ironic proof of jazz's official sanction as long as it was relegated to the bowels of the building. Less formal jazz gigs usually took place on the beachfront, in the surrounding townships, or in clubs such as the Rainbow Restaurant in Pinetown, just outside Durban.[7]

Censorship of musical and visual content reinforced the state's ideology of separate development. When the Equals (a mixed-race British group) planned to tour South Africa in the 1960s, the government intervened by refusing to grant them entry visas; and after John Lennon's remark that the Beatles were more popular than Jesus, the authorities banned the band's music from the airwaves. While these cases apply to the popular music of the time, government interventions also extended to televised jazz performances, where performers of colour had to use neutral pseudonyms to mask their ethnic origins, so the Indian pianist Lionel Pillay became Lionel Martin (Devroop and Walton 2007). It was unthinkable to the regime that a person of colour could demonstrate a high level of musical competence.

In similar fashion, the state-controlled media established ethnically separate radio stations divided along racial, linguistic, and musical lines. Their objective was to foster the ideology of separate development by entrenching tribal divisions.[8] As Charles Hamm (1991, 169) describes it:

> By the mid-1980s, the grand media strategy theorised in 1960[9] was finally in full operation. All of South Africa, and Namibia as well, was blanketed by a complex radio network ensuring that each person would have easy access to a state-controlled radio service in his/her own language, dedicated to 'mould[ing] his intellect and his way of life' by stressing the distinctiveness and separateness of 'his' cultural/ethnic heritage – in other words, to promoting the mythology of Separate Development. The majority of programme time was given over to music, selected for its appeal to the largest possible number of listeners within that particular ethnic group, functioning to attract an audience to a radio service whose most important business was selling ideology.

Sekibakiba Peter Lekgoathi (2011, 117–133) demonstrates how the apartheid state policed the boundaries of radio by censoring announcers and regulating

274 Marc Duby

musical content so as to maintain the state's emphasis on ethnic, racial, and linguistic differences (as opposed to potential commonalities) in support of the ideology of separate development. This ideology of difference was grounded in state-implemented bureaucratic oppression of its citizens so that in broad sociological terms totalitarian processes operated hegemonically to impose thoroughgoing structural control; in other words, to enforce the hegemony of structure over individual agency.[10]

For many persons of colour in apartheid South Africa, their everyday lives were restricted in accordance with their 'preordained' role in society, mostly as servants to the ruling class, so limiting access to resources for generating social, cultural, and literal capital alike. This is not to suggest that white South African citizens were immune from state repression; for instance, military service was compulsory for white males under apartheid. This state of affairs forced many into self-imposed exile.[11]

Significantly for this discussion, apartheid's discriminatory policies further regulated admission into universities on the basis of colour.[12] While the totalitarian structures of apartheid were put in place to enforce control over the minutiae of daily life (systematically restricting freedom of both movement and association along racial lines),[13] my purpose in this section is chiefly to consider aspects of such control in the cultural and educational fields. I now turn to deconstructing Chats Devroop's (2013) notion of jazz as 'invader culture' with the aim of developing a more nuanced account of jazz's reception history in South Africa and the complexities of musical interactions between the United States and South Africa against the background of diasporic currents and flows.

Diasporic Currents and Flows

> Jazz musicians in South Africa first had to master the musical material and the dynamics of the language of the invader culture and then try to find leeway or elbow room within it. There is an aspect in which jazz was at first a 'mission school' way of expressing oneself, as if through a ventriloquist.
>
> *(Devroop 2013, 8)*

At the heart of this epigraph lies a conception of jazz culture as a colonising invader: monolithic, unyielding, erasing opportunities for agency in its transubstantiation onto African soil. To my mind, there are a number of problems with this view. First, it proposes a straightforward binary opposition between local and foreign cultures. Second, it essentialises North American jazz without due regard for its rich and complex variety of forms of expression. This seems historically questionable. Finally, it proposes a model of local (in this case South African) musicians as passive recipients of imported culture, which seems patently untrue. I will address these concerns in turn.

To attend to the problem of the implicit binary opposition between local and foreign culture, I refer to Bruce Johnson's (2003b, 39) emphasis on the aspect of negotiation that takes place within the cultural field of jazz, and his argument that jazz was responsive to local conditions within a broad diasporic framework:

> The jazz diaspora is thus a case-study of the negotiation between local cultural practices and global cultural processes, between culture and mass mediations. In such negotiations, diaspora is the condition of the music's existence and character. Jazz was not 'invented' and then exported. It was invented in the process of being disseminated. As both idea and practice, jazz came into being through negotiation with the vehicles of its dissemination, and with conditions it encountered in any given location.

As I understand it, Johnson's interpretation of diasporic practice leaves room for its practitioners to adapt jazz to suit local circumstances. By linking the invention of jazz to its dissemination, his argument connects microsociological cultural practices (understood perhaps as local 'scenes') to the mediation of 'global cultural practices' at the macrosociological level. By placing the emphasis on negotiation and adaptability to local conditions, Johnson accounts for the possibility of musical agencies transforming the status quo.

Certainly for a time North American – especially Hollywood – culture was the dominant model for some members of an aspirant South African black bourgeoisie, but this model (as well as associated musical 'exports' such as blues and jazz) was not universally embraced by a mesmerised populace, as the invader culture argument implies. It is true that film, radio, and *Drum* magazine all played significant roles in propagating a particular 'American' cultural imagery during the 1950s. As Ballantine (1991, 131) explains, film proved a particularly important source of ideas for a range of performers:

> Despite controls and strict censorship, the movies had an impact which it is difficult to overestimate. For jazz and vaudeville artists, films were an apparently infinite source of things to be emulated or developed: ideas, melodies, songs, routines, dance steps, styles of presentation, ways of dressing, ways of playing; and of course they also provided ways of estimating local achievement.

In the context of 'concert and dance'[14] practice in South Africa, however, emulating Hollywood did not preclude South African jazz musicians from drawing on a rich repertoire of local practice to forge an 'authentic' style, as Ballantine (1991, 133) argues:

> American – and primarily black American – culture provided the greatest source for the Concert and Dance repertoire. But at the same time – and

surely more significantly for the development of an authentic South African jazz – the troupes and the bands made use of styles and elements whose origins lay on their very doorstep.

South African musicians drew on local resources, early on exhibiting a syncretic approach which integrated elements of jazz improvisation with a wide range of materials: in the case of Abdullah Ibrahim's 1970s music, for instance, Christine Lucia (2002, 127; original emphasis) lists '*marabi*,[15] swing, dance music, carnival, blues, hymns, gospel and spirituals' as constituent elements. She highlights in this case how a prominent South African musician's palette of sounds incorporated a wide range of material adapted to suit his particular musical approach. In similar fashion, but in a different musical context, Denis-Constant Martin (2013, 47; emphasis added) describes the ambivalence of Jamaican reggae practitioners toward 'cultural models' emanating from the United States:

> Contrary to many other interpretations of reggae that have been suggested, it did not signify a blunt rejection of and antagonism towards the United States, but delineated *a field within which identification with the United States and an assertion of Jamaicanness could coexist in unstable combinations*. It therefore supported interpretations in terms of rebelliousness, independence and solidarity with the world anti-imperialist forces, as well as in terms of conformism and adhesion [*sic*] to American cultural models.

Taken together, these arguments characterise such apparently hegemonic cultural relationships and their mediation as unstable and ambivalent, pointing to Bourdieu's notion of a given cultural field as fluid rather than static. One might argue by analogy that similar relationships play out in defining notions of 'South Africanness' and jazz.

The second problem is specifying which aspect of the broad field of North American jazz Devroop has in mind as an 'invader' language. To claim that there is one definitive version of jazz is to essentialise the genre, and this lack of specificity about the exact character of invader culture employs too wide a theoretical lens, to my mind. As in South Africa (Muller 2008), within the borders of the United States exists a wide range of regional musical styles, and within the sub-field of jazz (understood as Afro-American improvised music) there exist further sub-categories, including New Orleans, bebop, fusion, cool, and so on. While such broad stylistic categories are neither exhaustive nor non-porous, it seems to me that this characterisation of jazz is insufficiently specific to critique this purported invader culture.

John Szwed (2005, 202; emphasis added) proposes that 'South Africa's best musicians were also *compelled to reverse years of imitating Americans* by finding

Jazz and State Control in South Africa **277**

new strength in their own folk traditions, even when it seemed artistic suicide to attempt this in a country controlled by a mythology that defined culture as race.' Both of these lines of argument postulate a slavish imitation of a purported dominant culture, and neither fully takes into account various discourses which argue for a more sophisticated understanding of South African jazz as responding to, rather than merely parroting or mimicking, the North American model and its wide variety of sub-genres. Johnson's (2003a, 96) account of early jazz highlights the transitory shapes jazz has reflected within a matrix of shifting power relations, thereby underscoring its fluid and mutating nature:

> Since jazz emerged from its geographical origins it has travelled back and forth across the disputed terrain between high and low culture, variously located as folk, popular, art music and permutations. Its shifting position makes it a particularly instructive vehicle through which to study the matrix of cultural politics, the balances of power that determine which cultural forms carry authority. The migrations of jazz within musical politics and aesthetics depend upon negotiations between text (the particular jazz performance) and context (the physical and cultural space within which it is situated).

From the 1980s onwards, the ECM label had begun to release a catalogue of music that provided Euro-jazz as an alternative concept to its North American counterpart. For the most part, the ECM sound was moody and contemplative, akin to chamber music and eschewing swing as a constituent element. A small number of jazz musicians in South Africa explored this style and others, such as jazz-rock fusion, by way of Chick Corea, Weather Report, and Miles Davis. Intercultural experiments between Indian classical musicians and their jazz counterparts took place especially in the port city of Durban (such as collaborations between Darius Brubeck and the *bansuri* virtuoso Deepak Ram) and within the crossover group Mosaic (Ramanna 1998). The point is that jazz practice in South Africa has encompassed many so-called sub-cultures side-by-side with a mainstream tradition based on standards, the great American songbook, to this day a *lingua franca* for informal jam sessions.

The take-up of a wide variety of approaches by jazz practitioners in South Africa over time suggests that there was a wider range of responses to different aspects of the jazz canon than Steve Biko's (2004, 101) humorous stereotype of 'irresponsible people from Coca-cola and hamburger cultural backgrounds'. An alternative interpretation of 'culture as mimicry' is possible and necessary to arrive at a more nuanced reading of such cultural interactions: namely, as exchanges within a field of social action instead of mere instances of cultural conquest and annexation. While valuing the musical contributions of North American jazz icons such as Duke Ellington and Charlie Parker, local musicians drew from their own traditions, so creating value for themselves within their

278 Marc Duby

own cultural fields. As Bourdieu (Bourdieu and Johnson 1993, 164; original emphasis) defines these terms,

> The artistic field is a *universe of belief*. Cultural production distinguishes itself from the production of the most common objects in that it must produce not only the object in its materiality, but also the value of this object that is the recognition of artistic legitimacy. This is inseparable from the production of the artist or the writer as artist or writer, in other words, as a creator of value.

It follows from this that the 'universe of belief' of many local jazz musicians was profoundly at odds with mainstream apartheid culture, which sought to confine black citizens within specific, preordained social roles. By acquiring and demonstrating expertise in jazz performance, many South African jazz musicians seemed to challenge the foreordained roles the ruling party wished them to inhabit. Within this particular universe of belief, Bourdieu describes how agents in a particular field assign value and thereby legitimise artistic (or musical or literary) products, defining this field (Bourdieu and Johnson 1993, 163–164) as 'a veritable social universe where, in accordance with its particular laws, there accumulates a particular form of capital where relations of force of a particular type are exerted'. I want to draw from Bourdieu's concept of relations of force (while acknowledging as before their default condition of inequality) to propose envisaging mediated exchanges of information as taking place within a metaphorical magnetic field, in accordance with the analogue technology of the time (cassettes, films, vinyl recordings, but first and foremost the ubiquitous transistor radio).

The 'diasporic channels' of which Johnson (2003b, 34) speaks and their attendant migrations of audiences and musicians were facilitated by the circulation of magnetically encoded media, so that by recasting Johnson's idea as 'diasporic currents' it becomes feasible to understand the later mediation of jazz in magnetic formats. Recalling that the period under discussion for the most part antedates the advent of digital technologies such as MP3 files and the internet, analogue media such as vinyl LPs and cassettes were the de facto means of distributing music-related information. Within this field of action musical processes of exchange are mediated as product, literally and figuratively, as both hardware and ideology. Hardware is understood in this case as a medium of delivery, the means by which Bourdieu's value-creations are brought to their audience. However, because Bourdieu conceives of the field as in a state of flux, he acknowledges that conflict and resistance to the status quo emerge from the efforts of the dominated to make themselves seen and heard in the struggle for legitimation.

Read as the product of diasporic encounters between slaves and their masters in the United States and elsewhere (the Caribbean and Brazil come to mind), the musics that emerged from these interactions perforce contain various strands of cultural DNA originating from specific sites on the African continent. This wide range of African elements is downplayed in slogans such as the Smithsonian Institution's 'Jazz: made in America, enjoyed worldwide' (National Museum of American History 2014), which neglects to mention the interactive nature of these meetings. Granted, these took place on territory which often violently enforced unequal power relations, but omitting Africans' contribution to jazz is both historically inaccurate and morally dubious.

In speaking of the reception history of early jazz, Johnson (2003a, 97) highlights its fundamentally pluralistic character:

> Early responses to jazz thus ranged through bewilderment, outrage, fascination and respect, and depended on which version of the music was heard, in what conditions, and of course on the predispositions of the listener. These responses foreshadowed all the positions over subsequent decades, positions that both reflected and affected the range of jazz practices and venues. For its part, jazz obligingly provided exemplifications of whatever its partisans or opponents required of it, since its rapid diaspora was accompanied by a bewildering formal and functional pluralisation unique among musics.

Louis Armstrong's encounters with the African continent (beginning with his first trip to Ghana in 1956) and the Art Ensemble of Chicago's cultural work in later times are two examples of how some US musicians purposefully identified with Africa in general and the African diaspora in particular. Monson (2007, 129) describes Armstrong's encounter with Ghana's traditional music of the time:

> Seated outside underneath umbrellas to protect him from the sun, Armstrong listened to a wide selection of traditional music from Ghana's many ethnic groups. The delegation of chiefs presented him with a specially designed talking drum to commemorate his visit to Ghana, and Armstrong later remarked that 'every time I listened to those cats beat it out on them tribal drums I kept saying to myself, "Satch, you're hearing the real stuff."'

Armstrong's rapturous reception by the people of Accra in Ghana (then known as the Gold Coast) in May 1956 and his performances there for vast numbers of fans speak to his experience of the occasion as a homecoming, whereby he experienced 'a new-found sense of membership in an African diaspora' (ibid., 129). Armstrong's sense of return was deeply personal. Monson (ibid.) describes how '[a]n Ewe woman dancing before him reminded him strongly of his mother', and he is quoted as saying, 'After all, my ancestors came from here, and I still have African blood in me' (von Eschen 2004, 61). Armstrong's performance of Fats Waller's 'What Did I Do (to be so Black and Blue)?' is said to have moved Kwame Nkrumah to tears. As von Eschen (ibid., 63) describes it: 'Among the scenes captured by the film crew was a shot of Nkrumah as Armstrong sang "Black and Blue". The prime minister had tears in his eyes.' *Pace* Devroop, Armstrong, for one, seems an unlikely example of a conquering invader.

It is important to note that Armstrong's moment of epiphany, when he recognised his own 'Africanness', took place on the eve of Ghanaian independence from Britain, on the threshold of the country's liberation from colonialism. Africans across the continent were beginning to take control of their own lives as independent agents as the former colonial order was gradually dismantled. Armstrong returned to Africa in 1960 on a second tour, which included concerts in Ghana, Nigeria, Congo, and Uganda. Richard Long (1994, 87; emphasis added) asserts that 'Many of the Africans who enthusiastically greeted Armstrong were probably not aware of his historical role, but they responded positively to his performance and his personality. He was for them a successful, talented, and gregarious son *returning from a distant land.*'

It seems clear from this account of Armstrong's reception in Africa that the sense of kinship that he had experienced during his first visit to the Gold Coast was reciprocated by his audience, and in April 1966 (a decade after his first trip to the continent) the Senegalese president Leopold Sedar Senghor named him a laureate at the First World Festival of Negro Arts. Long (ibid.) explains Senghor's motivation for honouring Armstrong by highlighting the respect the poet-president accorded to jazz 'as a major cultural expression of the African spirit'.

Armstrong's experiences point to a real or imagined Africa as a place of homecoming for many black musicians from the United States. Randy Weston and Ornette Coleman, among many others, visited the continent to imbibe local culture and collaborate with musicians there. In their embrace of what George Lewis (2009, 449) calls 'a broadly internationalist, Afrodiasporic reading of the black music tradition', members of the Art Ensemble of Chicago explicitly and visibly proclaimed their spiritual links to Africa through dress codes and musical practices (see also ibid., 212–213).

The heart of my objection to Devroop's argument rests on its denial of the capacity of local jazz practitioners to enact agency and adaptability through music-making. This fails to take account of the fluid evolution of culture over time in which human agents play a central role. While there is no denying that power relations between the United States and Africa have always been unequal, it is inadmissible, to my mind, to assume that South African jazz musicians merely imitated their North American counterparts.

'Thieves in the Temple': Jazz and Resistance

> You would be amazed at the bands in those years. Those bands we played in *kept the hopes and dreams of the masses alive.*
>
> *(Johnny Mekoa quoted in Devroop and Walton 2007,*
> *18–19; emphasis added)*

How jazz became wedded to the South African liberation struggle in the 1980s needs to be understood in the broader context of cultural resistance to the apartheid state during this period, which was accompanied by the enforcement of martial law (two states of emergency were declared in the 1980s) and spiralling cycles of violence and state repression. As Mekoa asserts, live performances united the masses and acted as visible demonstrations of the totalitarian mythology of blacks as inferior. Bhekizizwe Peterson (2006, 170) understands performance as central in forging links of solidarity between artists and their wider communities in resistance:

> The centrality of visual, aural and sensory qualities in performance, coupled with its participatory nature, meant that it could foster the ideals of creating unity, awakening consciousness and mobilising artists, audiences and communities. These attributes led to its increasing presence and prominence at political rallies and at funerals.

While challenges to the regime also came from popular music (Durbach 2015) and the mostly white Afrikaner *Voëlvry* movement (Grundlingh 2012), as well as from the fields of the visual arts, literature, and theatre (von Kotze 1988), photography (Nunn 2011), and journalism (Newbury 2009), local jazz variants often accompanied anti-apartheid political rallies at home and abroad and played a large role in cementing a sense of solidarity in the pre-democratic period. For example, through the activities of Cape Town-based musicians like Basil Coetzee and Robbie Jansen,[16] who performed at anti-government rallies, Abdullah Ibrahim's 'Mannenberg'[17] took on the status of an unofficial second national anthem (Mason 2007; 2008).

In practice, black musicians and cultural workers found ways of pushing back against oppression: they were able to assert and define their identity by their creative negotiation with, rather than passive imitation of, a hegemonic model of the music. They enjoyed the paradoxical freedom of the oppressed to work relatively unnoticed in marginal spaces, to call into question 'banal classifications'; second, they had access to a very rich repertoire of indigenous musical traditions and as jazz musicians were free to improvise, unlike their art music counterparts. Jazz provides this space for individual expression because of its crucial improvisatory component. Ironically, it is therefore partly by virtue of being excluded from the 'upper rooms' of culture (e.g. fully notated art music) and consigned to 'low art' that local musicians were able to find the space to express themselves.

282 Marc Duby

It is also noteworthy how jazz was informally shared among township dwellers – geographically cut off from urban cultural centres and therefore excluded on the basis of colour – through the institution of jazz societies[18] and less formally as 'public audio'. By this I mean the kind of scenario the bassist Lex Futshane describes (in Ramanna 2013, 162):

> We grew up listening to jazz: jazz was like what Kwaito[19] is today; popular, popular. It's like you didn't really need to buy records because (whether consciously or unconsciously) there was a communal listening thing in New Brighton.[20] A guy would be cutting grass at his home; he would take out the speaker, put it outside, and play jazz (the Blue Note label was very, very popular).

While music education in the townships mainly depended on a time-honoured apprentice–master model, as in New Brighton in the Eastern Cape (Thram 2013), within an aurally disseminated jazz culture, formal jazz education in the higher education sector took root in four centres during the 1980s: the University of Natal (1983), Technikon Pretoria (1983), Technikon Natal (1987),[21] and the University of Cape Town (1989) (Duby 2014b).[22]

With regard to the introduction of new music courses in ethnomusicology and jazz studies at the former University of Natal, Nishlyn Ramanna (2013, 161) notes, 'Although this was not the music department's primary intention, its decision to include ethnomusicology and jazz in its curriculum in the early 1980s had a similar effect': that is, admitting persons of colour in an attempt 'to challenge the racial status quo by exploiting fissures in the apartheid edifice'. Chris Ballantine, a leader and prime mover in the establishment of new initiatives at this institution, explains (quoted in ibid.) how these innovations were not designed to improve student numbers, but to start taking account of hitherto excluded local cultures:

> We were considered to be out on a limb [because] of things that we were doing here: introducing a degree in ethnomusicology; appointing the first black lecturer in a South African music department; introducing jazz. It was framed not in terms of a recruiting ploy, because in those days [when] black students came to study here permission had to be sought. Of course if you were offering something that was not on offer somewhere else, that was the only ground on which exemption would be granted. So it did work as a recruiting thing. But it was more that we needed to start taking seriously the local cultures.

Mike Campbell (2010) talked of the difficulties of bringing his North American music education experience to bear under the very different circumstances of late 1980s Cape Town:

I'd spent 4 years getting a degree from North Texas State University in the early 80s, so the experience was still quite fresh, and I thought to bring some of that to this new project at the college if I got the job. During the first couple of years, it became clear that the NTSU experience was far from what could be realistically shared in Cape Town, where not much music education was happening in schools, and what there was existed in a narrow bandwidth of classical music. It was also confined to the relatively few wealthy schools which had music programs, attended by mostly white kids at that point in time.

As Campbell describes it, the available 'narrow bandwidth' of potential music students was a direct consequence of an entrenched emphasis on the superior status of 'classical' music and limited access to expensive resources for black participants. He notes that the vast majority of students pursuing courses in jazz education in the 1980s were white, with the totalitarian, race-based tendencies of the regime making such a skewed demographic virtually inevitable. This state of affairs tended to disadvantage those with limited reading and music literacy skills, who often had to enrol for introductory modules as their only means of admission to such offerings.

Significantly, the administrators of the first jazz education departments (Darius Brubeck, Louis Drummond van Rensburg, and Mike Campbell) either grew up with or were later exposed to music education opportunities in the United States, and both of the South Africans (Campbell and van Rensburg) studied at dedicated jazz institutions (NTSU and Berklee, respectively). However, their first-hand experience of this system could not unproblematically be transplanted onto South African soil, because such music education as existed was available only to an elite. As Campbell (ibid.) notes,

> In the US, big concert or marching bands are very much part of the school experience, so there is a solid foundation in instrumental music that many students have had by the time they enter first year college. That tradition is really just beginning here, with the powers that be slowly awakening to the value of it, though still in view of the hegemony of sport in schools.

Since the establishment of jazz education in the 1980s, various music higher education institutions in South Africa have formalised programmes that draw in some instances from a 'more mainstream American pedagogical model, using bebop as its centrepiece' (Whyton 2010, 157). While Whyton is referring to the circumstances of jazz education in the United States, tensions between local and global concerns inevitably arise when institutions in South Africa attempt to take account of local and regional musical styles and preferences and their legacy of politicised meaning.

284 Marc Duby

The situation in South African music education in the 1980s was different from comparable institutional histories abroad because jazz and popular music became explicitly aligned with the liberation struggle over time, so that the practice and performance of local music took on a political role as a marker of resistance. Such tensions between local and global articulations were not 'merely academic', because they were grounded in the problem of widening access to jazz education for many musicians who did not have easy access to study materials and began their musical careers playing by ear. The North American jazz educator Jamey Aebersold (2010, 5), while noting the value of an informal, playing-by-ear approach for fledgling improvisers, argues that this can be problematic for those who lack a foundation in the theoretical aspects of scales and chords:

> [Playing by ear] is a hit-or-miss process that most jazz players (before 1965) had to use to learn their trade. However, this method strengthens the player's ear and is extremely valuable. Everyone should spend time each day playing by ear. The sooner you train your ears to discern, the sooner they can HELP YOU in making music. By using your ear, and knowledge of the needed scales and chords, you will feel much more comfortable with beginning improvisation.

Aebersold goes on to explicate this theoretical foundation in some detail, based on chord scale theory. Based on deploying principles of consonance and dissonance, this pedagogical approach is designed to equip the improviser with a method for choosing appropriate notes for playing 'inside' or 'outside' a given harmonic progression:

> In jazz improvisation theory, the concept of the chord scale defines a set of relationships between vertical (harmonic) structures and horizontal (melodic) ones. This concept allows the improviser the choice of playing inside the changes, where the available notes are made up of chord tones, using harmonic tensions (which may or may not be resolved), or playing outside (where the improviser makes use of chromatic approach notes which are neither chord tones nor harmonic tensions). These note choices range by definition from wholly consonant ('inside') to mildly dissonant (harmonic tensions) to highly dissonant, in the case of chromatic approach notes.
>
> *(Duby 2007, 4–32)*

The late jazz trumpeter Alex van Heerden (Eato and van Heerden 2008) pointed out a potential problem with this approach as applied to *ghoema*, an indigenous Cape musical style. Speaking of Robbie Jansen's playing, van Heerden noted that 'he doesn't phrase like an American jazz musician, and I've heard people playing American jazz lines over a ghoema beat, which I find uneasy'. This uneasiness has to do with the extent to which note choices and phrasing fit the idiomatic demands of this particular style, so that while van Heerden is speaking primarily about stylistic friction, this cannot be construed as independent of the residual political tensions through which a specifically Eurocentric musical culture had been promoted as the supreme ideology.

As van Heerden implied, deploying bebop-derived chromatic lines is not an appropriate approach to *ghoema*, so lines that work for 'Giant Steps' or 'Scrapple from the Apple' will not sound 'correct' in a different (local) context. A 'learned' approach designed for a standard or bebop tune with labyrinthine changes does not translate well into a vamp situation. With a large proportion of the local repertoire built on a specific cyclic progression,[23] this chromaticism will sound out of place in this context as equally might a blues-based or diatonic approach over a complex harmonic progression.

The 'Triple Entente' between jazz, politics, and education which played out in the days before liberation, a formative relationship in those times, may well be seen to be due for reappraisal in the task of articulating or rethinking the inbuilt assumptions of jazz cultures. If choosing and performing a particular repertoire presents an opportunity for displaying musical identities, one might well examine its public manifestations as performances. Whether consciously or otherwise, choice of repertoire is a statement of intent in defining one's musical self. Within the boundaries of institutional legitimation (for example, in the context of performance examinations), musicians may well be assessed as exhibiting a solid (or for that matter superficial) grasp of a particular style. This begs the question of how a given curriculum responds to processes of canon-formation within a cultural field as both dynamic and driven by shifting power relations along the lines of Bourdieu's thinking on these topics.

Conclusion: 'This Is Not America'

Jazz education began in a critical period in South African history – the stormy and violent 1980s. South Africans were beginning to see (if not accept) that change was inevitable, and pressures from within the country and abroad to isolate the regime led to a gradual relaxation of petty apartheid's laws. This tendency, however, needs to be seen against the declaration of two states of emergency in the mid-1980s and escalating levels of violence in the body politic.

For Chris Ballantine, speaking in 2003 (quoted in Ramanna, 2013: 160–162), opening up the field at the University of Natal was a political act; for Mike Campbell at UCT (Duby 2014b), this happened similarly 'under the radar'; and for Louis Drummond van Rensburg at Technikon Pretoria, this was achieved by avoiding the term 'jazz' since the original programme offered a diploma in so-called 'Light Music'. Leaving aside for the moment the implicit essentialism of such terms, these strategies were responsive at least in part to

286 Marc Duby

local conditions in accordance with the regional and political circumstances of the time.

Nonetheless, these educational institutions operated under a prevailing ethos with Western art music as the dominant paradigm, so admitting jazz studies (the music of the 'Other') to the educational field was in itself a sign of resistance to the status quo. Each institution at the time presented a different palette of offerings, incorporating options in arranging and composition, research, and performance, with Technikon Pretoria taking the most overtly 'vocational' path by offering 'Jingle Writing' and 'Film Music' as integral to the degree, the rationale being that this would offer graduates access to other employment opportunities beside the small and highly competitive field of jazz performance.

When Henry Louis Gates Jr. (1991, 98) defines the canon as 'the commonplace book of our shared culture', this suggests that to share a culture implies some measure of equality, and the commonplace book of which he speaks can be accessible to all only if there is some common understanding of what culture means in the first place. In apartheid South Africa, the totalitarian state used the notion of culture as a means of isolating its citizens from one another in service to the ideology of separate development, with people enslaved, displaced, and persecuted on the basis of 'race' and ethnicity. To speak of the unifying potential of South African culture as Johnny Mekoa does necessitates exposing the bare wires of the power relations underpinning apartheid's defunct grand narrative of culture as separate development and of an era in which sharing a bandstand with 'Other' musicians might well have invited various legal sanctions.[24]

The question of what constitutes a 'uniquely South African' (in short, a 'local') sound or approach is then seen to have practical consequences for jazz education as local musicians increasingly gain entrance to the international arena. Additionally, post-apartheid collaborations (that is, after South Africa's transition to majority rule in 1994) between local musicians and those from elsewhere have become more common following South Africa's re-entry into various international music scenes.

With these thoughts in mind, putting one's finger on what is 'distinctly South African' (Muller 2012) about jazz practice is at the same time elusive and necessary as a process of understanding how local musicians strive to comprehend themselves and others. Jazz practice, understood as marshalling a sense of identity in apartheid's heyday, is now firmly institutionalised in South African higher education institutions, providing new avenues of access for those whose interests were not served by the previous regime's emphasis on high culture and Western art music.

Since those turbulent times, jazz education and practice have continued to flourish through educational initiatives such as the Standard Bank National Youth Jazz Festival (held annually in Grahamstown since its foundation in

Jazz and State Control in South Africa **287**

1992) and a steady growth in opportunities for South African musicians to perform abroad and for international musicians to visit South Africa (such as at the Cape Town International Jazz Festival). These possibilities for musical exchanges are testimony to the staying power of jazz studies and the value of widening access to music education in recognising 'Other' musics within the academy.

Acknowledgements

My thanks go to Thomas Pooley and Tony Whyton, who commented on an earlier draft of this chapter, to Bruce Johnson for his editorial guidance and support, and to the anonymous reviewers for their thoughtful suggestions. 'Fanfare for the warriors' in the chapter title refers to the eponymous recording (Atlantic SD 1651, 1974) by the Art Ensemble of Chicago, while the conclusion's title 'This is not America' refers to David Bowie's eponymous song on the soundtrack of *The Falcon and the Snowman* by Pat Metheny Group (EMI America EA 190, 1985). This material is based upon work supported financially by the National Research Foundation of South Africa. Any opinions, findings, and conclusions or recommendations expressed in this material are those of the author and therefore the NRF does not accept any liability thereto.

Notes

1 Ballantine (2012, 30) notes how 'Our new social order is vested in fixed, or molluscan, identities (ironically, exactly the same "race"-based identities that underpinned apartheid), and unreflective, taken-for-granted, often primordial ways of naming, categorising and classifying the world.' It strikes me, though, that these 'ways of naming' operate in a somewhat different ideological climate, one in which critiquing such a situation is at least less likely to lead to incarceration, banning, or worse (the conventional methods employed by the apartheid state to stifle dissidence).

2

> The Bantustans (also known as 'homelands') were a cornerstone of the 'grand apartheid' policy of the 1960s and 1970s, justified by the apartheid government as benevolent 'separate development'. The Bantustans were created by the Promotion of Bantu Self-Government Act of 1959, which abolished indirect representation of blacks in Pretoria and divided Africans into ten ethnically discrete groups, each assigned a traditional 'homeland'. Established on the territorial foundations imposed by the Land Act of 1913 (amended in 1936), the homelands constituted only 13% of the land – for approximately 75% of the population.
>
> *(Overcoming Apartheid n.d.).*

The Overcoming Apartheid website provides access to maps which graphically depict the destructive effects of the Land Act.

3 Given the state's monopoly of broadcast media, Clegg ran the risk of having the album banned from airplay.

4

> On 16 June 1976 Soweto erupted into violence, irrevocably changing the South African political landscape. Early in 1976 the government had stipulated that certain subjects in African schools should be taught in Afrikaans [a Dutch-derived

288 Marc Duby

language spoken by some whites and a large proportion of coloureds, especially in the Western Cape], despite the fact that there weren't enough teachers to teach in Afrikaans. This was the direct cause of an illegal march by thousands of school children in Soweto that ended in a bloody confrontation with police. Disturbances broke out throughout the country, which continued sporadically until 1980.

(Terreblanche 2002, 351–352)

While Terreblanche notes that this was not the only contributory factor, with the post-1974 economic downturn adding to the general malaise, the rejection of this government stipulation by learners was decisive and forthright. While the most immediate cause of this uprising was indignation at the government decree that black students should be taught in Afrikaans, it is important to note that inequalities in the education system had been deliberately and systematically designed to limit educational opportunities for black pupils.

Though Bantu Education was designed to deprive Africans and isolate them from 'subversive' ideas, indignation at being given such 'gutter' education became a major focus for resistance, most notably in the 1976 Soweto uprising. In the wake of this effective and clear protest, some reform attempts were made, but it was a case of too little, too late. Major disparities in racially separate education provision continued into the 1990s.

('Youth and the National Liberation Struggle: The June 16 Soweto Youth Uprising' 2015)

June 16 is commemorated annually as Youth Day in South Africa.

5

Until the early 1990s, when South Africa became an inclusive democracy, nonwhite [*sic*] workers were forced to live outside cities in residential areas known as townships. The systematic segregation dates back to the colonial era: in the late 19th and early 20th centuries, the British colonial government resettled racial groups under the pretense of responding to disease epidemics in overcrowded neighborhoods.

(Findley and Ogbu 2011)

By siting townships some distance away from city centres and white suburbs, the regime sought to enforce geographical separation between whites and blacks but also to divide groups along ethnic and linguistic lines.

6 As Brett Pyper (2008, 237) writes: 'In the maelstrom of cultural debate that attended South Africa's transition to non-racial democracy in the early 1990s, few institutions were more vocally held to symbolise the apartheid cultural apparatus, at least as far as the performing arts were concerned, than Pretoria's State Theatre.'

7 The Rainbow Restaurant (which still exists today) is a jazz venue linked to struggle politics during the 1980s (Duby 2013).

8

Radio broadcasting in apartheid South Africa was monopolised by the state and used as the ruling party's propaganda tool, just like in many other independent African countries (e.g. Kenya, Zambia and Nigeria). However, unlike its usage in post-colonial Africa as a tool for nation building, vernacular radio was used to reinforce ethnic separatism in apartheid South Africa.

(Lekgoathi 2011, 118)

9 1960 marked the founding of Radio Bantu (Lekgoathi 2011, 117–133), an essential component in the 'grand apartheid' strategy of which Hamm speaks.

10 By law, black citizens were required to carry passes, a means of state control restricting freedom of movement:

These laws evolved from regulations imposed by the Dutch and British in the 18th and 19th-century slave economy of the Cape Colony. In the 19th century, new pass laws were enacted for the purpose of ensuring a reliable supply of cheap, docile African labor for the gold and diamond mines. In 1952, the government enacted an even more rigid law that required all African males over the age of 16 to carry a reference book (replacing the previous passbook) containing personal information and employment history.

(Overcoming Apartheid n.d.)

These laws and their arbitrary enforcement sparked successive waves of resistance and protest from the establishment of National Party rule in 1948 until their repeal in 1986.

11 It lies beyond the scope of this chapter to discuss the concept of exile in detail, but following the Sharpeville massacre (21 March 1960) and increasing race-based restrictions as to who was allowed to perform with whom, many South African musicians chose (or were forced) to leave the country to live and work abroad. Some case studies on the topic of musical exile include Dalamba (2012), with regard to the musicians of the musical *King Kong*, Dlamini (2009), on The Blue Notes, and Muller and Benjamin (2011) on Sathima Bea Benjamin.

12

The Extension of University Education Act, Act 45 of 1959, put an end to black students attending white universities (mainly the universities of Cape Town and Witwatersrand). Separating tertiary institutions according to race, this Act set up separate 'tribal colleges' for black university students. The so-called 'bush' Universities such as Fort Hare, Vista, Venda, Western Cape were formed. Blacks could no longer freely attend white universities. Again, there were strong protests.

('Youth and the National Liberation Struggle:
The June 16 Soweto Youth Uprising' 2015)

13 In 1960s Cape Town, for example, 'petty apartheid' regulations were enforced to prevent musicians from different races from performing together, leading to the closure of the non-racial Vortex jazz venue, which was 'closed by the authorities for breaking the apartheid laws', in the words of Lars Rasmussen (2001, 71).

14 Ballantine (1991, 122) defines 'Concert and Dance' as 'characteristically a vaudeville entertainment from 8 p.m. to midnight, followed immediately by a dance which ended at 4 a.m.' These seemingly odd opening hours avoided curfews and the enforcement of the pass laws.

15 David Coplan (2007, 441) defines this local *marabi* genre as 'A pan-ethnic urban African working-class style of music developed in Johannesburg during the 1920s and 1930s.'

16 Robbie Jansen (1949–2010) was a Cape Town-based saxophonist and activist and one of the founding figures of the Cape Jazz movement (Duby 2014a).

17 Ibrahim's 1974 recording 'Mannenberg (Is Where It's Happening)' is named after Manenberg, a township in Cape Town.

18 See Pyper (2013) for an account of informal jazz societies devoted to sessions of listening to recorded jazz, often international and avant-garde rather than local.

19 Coplan (2007, 441) defines Kwaito as 'a South Africanised blend of hip-hop with American dance music, especially house and techno, and pop'.

20 New Brighton is a township near Port Elizabeth where a thriving informal musical culture formed a fertile breeding ground for many musicians (but also see Victoria Butete's (2013) account of gender inequality in that particular local jazz scene).

21 Technikons were rebranded as 'universities of technology' in the early 2000s.

22 Ramanna's calculation of actual teaching staff employed at the beginning of the 1990s in jazz education seems not to factor in the two technikons, which at the time were

classified as vocational rather than research-focused institutions and, by implication, of lower academic status than universities.

23 Gerhard Kubik (2013, 14) defines what he terms the *marabi* cycle thus: 'The most prominent harmonic cycle in South African popular music from *marabi* to *kwela* to *s'manje-manje* is usually described by observers as a progression from I − IV − I (in fourth/sixth inversion) −V.'

24 During the 1980s and into the post-democratic era, ostensibly non-racial performance venues such as the Black Sun and Jameson's in Johannesburg sprang up. In general, the authorities tended to turn a blind eye to these developments, given perhaps that overt violent defiance to the order of the day was a more pressing issue at the time.

References

Aebersold, Jamey. 2010. *The Jazz Handbook*. New Albany, IN: Jamey Aebersold Jazz.

Ballantine, Christopher. 1991. 'Concert and Dance: The Foundations of Black Jazz in South Africa between the Twenties and the Early Forties'. *Popular Music* 10 (2): 121–145.

Ballantine, Christopher. 2012. 'Music, the Word and the World; or the Banality of (South African) Classification'. In *Situating Popular Musics: IASPM 16th International Conference Proceedings*, edited by Ed Montano and Carlo Nardi, 25–32.

Beningfield, Jennifer. 2006. *The Frightened Land: Land, Landscape and Politics in South Africa in the Twentieth Century*. Abingdon: Routledge.

Biko, Steve. 2004. *I Write What I Like: A Selection of His Writings*. Johannesburg: Picador Africa.

Boddy-Evans, Alistair. 2015. 'Soweto Student Uprising − 16 June, 1976'. Accessed January 30, 2015. http://africanhistory.about.com/od/apartheid/a/Soweto-Uprising-Pt1.htm.

Bourdieu, Pierre and Randal Johnson. 1993. *The Field of Cultural Production: Essays on Art and Literature*. New York: Columbia University Press.

Butete, Victoria Blessing. 2013. 'Music Performance in Retrospect: Memories of New Brighton Female Vocalists' Apartheid Experiences'. *Muziki* 10 (supp. 1): 60–71.

Campbell, Mike. 2010. 'The Growth of Jazz Education in Cape Town: A Personal Perspective'. Paper delivered at S.A. Jazz Educator's Conference, Cape Town.

Chandler, Daniel. 2014. 'Marxist Media Theory'. Accessed March 17, 2015. www.aber.ac.uk/media/Documents/marxism/marxism10.html.

Coplan, David B. 2007. *In Township Tonight! Three Centuries of South African Black City Music and Theatre*, 2nd edition. Auckland Park: Jacana.

Dalamba, Lindelwa. 2012. 'Popular Music, Folk Music, African Music: *King Kong* in South Africa and London'. In *IASPM 16th International Conference Proceedings*, edited by Ed Montano and Carlo Nardi, 95–101.

Department of Rural Development and Land Reform. 2013. 'Building the Legacy: 20 Years of Freedom'. Accessed March 17, 2015. www.ruraldevelopment.gov.za/component/content/category/269-1913-documents.

Devroop, Chats. 2013. '"Chasing the Canon"'. *SAMUS: South African Music Studies* 33: 5–10.

Devroop, Chats and Chris Walton, eds. 2007. *Unsung: South African Jazz Musicians under Apartheid*. Stellenbosch: Sun Press.

Dlamini, Sazi Stephen. 2009. 'The South African Blue Notes: Bebop, Mbaqanga, Apartheid and the Exiling of a Musical Imagination'. Unpublished Ph.D. thesis, University of Kwazulu-Natal.

Duby, Marc. 2007. 'Soundpainting as a System for the Collaborative Creation of Music in Performance'. Unpublished Ph.D. thesis, University of Pretoria.

Duby, Marc. 2013. '"Reminiscing in Tempo": The Rainbow and Resistance in 1980s South Africa'. *South African Music Studies* 33: 81–100.

Duby, Marc. 2014a. 'Alweer "Die Alibama"? Reclaiming Indigenous Knowledge through a Cape Jazz Lens'. *Muziki: Journal of Music Research in Africa* 11 (1): 99–117.

Duby, Marc. 2014b. 'Interview with Professor Mike Campbell'.

Durbach, David. 2015. 'A Study of the Linkages between Popular Music and Politics in South Africa in the 1980s'. Unpublished MA thesis, University of South Africa.

Eato, Jonathan and Alex van Heerden. 2008. 'Alex van Heerden (23 November 1974– 7 January 2009)'. Accessed March 17, 2015. http://ev2.co.uk/jisa/musicians_statements/alex_van-heerden.html.

Findley, Lisa and Liz Ogbu. 2011. 'South Africa after Apartheid: From Township to Town'. Accessed March 17, 2015. https://placesjournal.org/article/south-africa-from-township-to-town/.

Gates, Henry Louis Jr. 1991. 'The Master's Pieces: On Canon Formation and the African-American Tradition'. In *The Politics of Liberal Education*, edited by Darryl J. Smith Gless and Barbara Herrnstein, 95–117. Durham, NC: Duke University Press.

Grundlingh, Albert. 2012. '"Rocking the Boat" in South Africa? Voëlvry Music and Anti-Apartheid Social Protest in the 1980s'. In *Music and Protest*, edited by Ian Peddie, 293–324. Farnham: Ashgate.

Hamm, Charles. 1991. '"The Constant Companion of Man": Separate Development, Radio Bantu and Music'. *Popular Music* 10 (2): 147–73.

Jackson, Leon. n.d. 'Juluka: Artist Biography'. Accessed March 17, 2015. www.allmusic.com/artist/juluka-mn0000302191/biography.

Johnson, Bruce. 2003a. 'Jazz as Cultural Practice'. In *The Cambridge Companion to Jazz*, edited by Mervyn Cooke and David Horn, 96–113. Cambridge: Cambridge University Press.

Johnson, Bruce. 2003b. 'The Jazz Diaspora'. In *The Cambridge Companion to Jazz*, edited by Mervyn Cooke and David Horn, 33–54. Cambridge: Cambridge University Press.

Kubik, Gerhard. 2013. 'Generations of Jazz'. In *Generations of Jazz at the Red Location Museum*, edited by Diane Thram, 10–16. Grahamstown: ILAM.

Lekgoathi, Sekibakiba Peter. 2011. 'Bantustan Identity, Censorship and Subversion on Northern Sotho Radio under Apartheid, 1960s–80s'. In *Radio in Africa: Publics, Cultures, Communities*, edited by Liz Gunner, Dumisani Moyo, and Dina Ligaga, 117–33. Johannesburg: Wits University Press.

Lewis, George. 2009. *A Power Stronger than Itself: The AACM and American Experimental Music*. Chicago: University of Chicago Press.

Long, Richard A. 1994. 'Louis Armstrong and African-American Culture'. In *Louis Armstrong: A Cultural Legacy*, edited by Marc A. Miller, 67–93. New York: Queens Museum of Art, in association with the University of Washington Press.

Lucia, Christine. 2002. 'Abdullah Ibrahim and the Uses of Memory'. *British Journal of Ethnomusicology* 11 (2): 125–43.

Martin, Denis-Constant. 2013. *Sounding the Cape: Music, Identity and Politics in South Africa*. Somerset West: African Minds.

Mason, John Edwin. 2007. '"Mannenberg": Notes on the Making of an Icon and Anthem'. *African Studies Quarterly* 9 (4): 25–46.

Mason, John Edwin. 2008. *The Making of Mannenberg*. Vlaeberg, Cape Town: Chimurenga.

Monson, Ingrid. 2007. *Freedom Sounds: Civil Rights Call out to Jazz and Africa*. Oxford: Oxford University Press.

Muller, Carol. 2008. *Focus: Music of South Africa. Focus on World Music*, 2nd edition. Abingdon: Routledge.

Muller, Carol. 2012. 'Sounding a New African Diaspora: A South African Story (1958–1978)'. *Safundi* 13 (3–4): 277–94.

Muller, Carol and Sathima Bea Benjamin. 2011. *Musical Echoes: South African Women Thinking in Jazz*. Durham, NC: Duke University Press.

National Museum of American History, Kenneth E. Behring Center. 2014. 'JAM: Jazz Appreciation Month'. Accessed March 17, 2015. http://smithsonianjazz.org/index.php?option=com_content&view=article&id=11&Itemid=22.

Newbury, Darren. 2009. *Defiant Images: Photography and Apartheid South Africa*. Pretoria: Unisa Press.

Nunn, Cedric. 2011. *Call and Response*. Johannesburg: Fourthwall Books.

Overcoming Apartheid. n.d. Accessed February 2, 2015. http://overcomingapartheid.msu.edu/multimedia.php?id=65-259-7.

Peterson, Bhekizizwe. 2006. 'Culture, Resistance and Representation'. In *The Road to Democracy in South Africa*, edited by South African Democracy Education Trust, vol. II: 161–185. Pretoria: Unisa Press.

Pyper, Brett. 2008. 'State of Contention: Recomposing Apartheid at the State Theatre, 1990–1994: A Personal Recollection'. In *Composing Apartheid: Music for and against Apartheid*, 311. Johannesburg: Wits University Press.

Pyper, Brett. 2013. 'On Jazz, Sociability and Symbolic Mobility in South Africa: Thinking across Some Post-Apartheid Fault Lines'. *SAMUS: South African Music Studies* 33: 137–157.

Ramanna, Nishlyn. 1998. 'Jazz as Discourse: A Contextualised Account of Locally-Composed Contemporary Jazz (Durban 1994–1995)'. Unpublished MMus thesis, University of Natal.

Ramanna, Nishlyn. 2013. 'Shifting Fortunes: Jazz in (Post)apartheid South Africa'. *SAMUS: South African Music Studies* 33: 159–172.

Rasmussen, Lars. 2001. *Cape Town Jazz 1959–1963: The Photographs of Hardy Stockmann*, edited by Lars Rasmussen. Copenhagen: The Booktrader.

'State Theatre'. 2012. South African History Online. Accessed September 4, 2014. http://sahistory.org.za/places/state-theatre.

Szwed, John. 2005. *Crossovers: Essays on Race, Music, and American Culture*. Philadelphia: University of Pennsylvania Press.

Terreblanche, Sampie. 2002. *A History of Inequality in South Africa, 1652–2002*. Scottsville: University of Kwazulu-Natal Press.

Thram, Diane. 2013. 'Generations of Jazz at the Red Location Museum: An Exhibition Catalogue'. Grahamstown: ILAM.

von Eschen, Penny M. 2004. *Satchmo Blows up the World: Jazz Ambassadors Play the Cold War*. Cambridge, MA: Harvard University Press.

von Kotze, Astrid. 1988. *Organise and Act: The Natal Workers Theatre Movement, 1983–1987*. Durban: Culture and Working Life Publications, Department of Industrial Sociology, University of Natal.

Webb, Jen, Tony Schirato, and Geoff Danaher. 2002. *Understanding Bourdieu*. London and Thousand Oaks, CA: SAGE Publications.

Whyton, Tony. 2010. *Jazz Icons: Heroes, Myths and the Jazz Tradition*. Cambridge: Cambridge University Press.

'Youth and the National Liberation Struggle: The June 16 Soweto Youth Uprising'. 2015. South African History Online. Accessed January 30, 2015. www.sahistory.org. za/topic/june-16-soweto-youth-uprising?page=2.

PART VI
To the East

13

FROM THE 'SULTAN' TO THE *PERSIAN SIDE*

Jazz in Iran and Iranian Jazz since the 1920s[1]

G. J. Breyley

Jazz has long played a marginal but significant role in Iran's music and socio-cultural scenes. It has been linked variously with the country's relations with 'the West', especially the United States, notions of 'modernisation', visions of freedom, sociability through collaboration, identification with oppressed people internationally and a form of national or cultural expression through fusion with Iranian art and regional music.[2] With its turbulent modern history, intersected by a colonial dynamic, Iran presents distinctive problems in the analysis of its relationship with jazz. The country has experienced a succession of regimes with totalitarian tendencies, in that they have sought to exercise control over cultural practices, including music.[3] The reasons for these controls have varied with the agendas of the successive regimes and, while jazz has rarely been completely suppressed, the possibilities open to particular practitioners of jazz in Iran have been deeply affected by those various agendas. The understanding of jazz itself has been in flux since it first arrived in Iran, illustrating the complex heterogeneity of the relationship between the music and totalitarianism.

This chapter examines aspects of the history of jazz as it has been practised and imagined in Iranian contexts. It considers the effects of Iran's distinctive political and social conditions on the nature of its music and the careers of its jazz musicians. Building on the platform of Bruce Johnson's 'Introduction', in which he reviews the theorisation of the term 'totalitarian', I begin with his observation that the usefulness of the term 'might best be judged according to the presence of the aspiration and by this measure, the term has far broader and more heterogeneous application. Contemporary totalitarianism studies have largely shifted from the formal political structures in themselves, to the point of tension between them and everyday life.' The respective positions on the totalitarianism spectrum of the political structures that have characterised

Iran's various regimes since the 1920s have been much debated by citizens of those regimes and historians alike. This chapter is less concerned with defining the regimes' respective positions on that spectrum than with examining tensions between their political structures and the musical possibilities of differently positioned individuals and groups. As Johnson (Introduction) documents, 'for some, the totalitarian framework might be experienced in daily life as no more oppressive than in any democratic society regulated by law'. Indeed, for those in positions privileged by their particular political structures, daily life and musical possibilities might appear freer and more expansive. Even for those in more ambiguous positions, whether due to social class, ethnicity, temperament, musical taste or other reasons, potential elements of oppression might sometimes be countered by various cultural, economic or other factors. The history of jazz and jazz-related music in Iran is characterised by examples of such apparent paradoxes and possibilities shaped by political tensions. I begin with a broad historical overview of the contending forces that shaped Iran's history in the twentieth century, as a background against which later developments may be better understood.

In Iran, as elsewhere, the advent of jazz and 'modernity' coincided, and the notion of modernity has been central to the country's conflicts and popular debate over the last century. This was especially evident in the first regime examined below (1925 to 1953), when aspirations to modernity, as well as fearful responses to it, combined with a defensive form of nationalism to contribute to ideologically paradoxical forms of control – or attempts at control – over all aspects of cultural life. As Philip Morgan (2003: 192) suggests, this kind of development may be read as 'an alternative "modernity", not an alternative to "modernity"'. Iran's particular twentieth-century modernities often sought forms of predictability and standardisation, even as they claimed to offer 'freedom' and 'progress'. The course of modernity in Iran and the role of jazz within it also reflect a shift in the mid-twentieth century from the dominance of the United Kingdom and the Soviet Union to that of the United States in Iran's international relations and, to some extent, its popular culture. While Iran was not directly colonised, many Iranians saw its relationship with Britain in the early to mid-twentieth century as akin to colonisation and some viewed its relationship with the United States from the 1950s to the 1970s in a similar way.

Until 1979, Iran was ruled by a succession of dynasties, in which the reigning Shahs held political power and maintained what Homa Katouzian (2006: 2) calls 'a system of arbitrary rule'. Iran's 'modernity' in the early twentieth century entailed a constitutional revolution in 1906, which saw a constitutional monarchy established. However, relations between the 'unaccountable government and ungovernable society', as Katouzian (2006: 50) puts it, failed to improve. In 1921, a coup led to the establishment of Iran's last dynasty, the Pahlavi, in which Reza Shah ruled from 1925 to 1941 and his son Mohammad

Reza ruled from 1941 to 1979. For the purposes of this chapter, however, I will divide the Pahlavi dynasty into the two periods 1925 to 1953 and 1953 to 1979. More than the change from Reza Shah to Mohammad Reza Shah, it was the CIA-led, British-backed coup of 1953 (see Byrne 2013) that saw a shift in the direction of Iran's 'system of arbitrary rule' and its effects on the history of jazz. This was mainly due to the regime's newly close relationship with the United States after the coup and a new resentment of that relationship among some Iranian people. Finally, the third period I consider is that of the Islamic Republic of Iran, established in the wake of Iran's 1979 revolution and continuing to the present day. Among other things, this revolution sought to reverse the many consequences of the 1953 coup, including the nature of the country's relationship with the United States, which had, to some extent, shaped the development of Iranian jazz in the 1960s and 1970s.

In each of the three periods, Iran's leaders sought to exercise control over popular culture, including music. In all three, jazz was widely seen as a Western form, but the implications of this shifted with each regime. Each regime made use of claims to an 'alternative modernity', which was often represented in paradoxically nationalistic terms. In the first period, the regime tended to compare and equate Iran's 'culture' with that of Europe, while the regime of the second period looked primarily to the United States. After the 1979 revolution, the emphasis was on cultural independence and a revival of what some saw as lost 'Iranian' values.

From 1925 to 1953, the two Pahlavi Shahs sought to 'modernise' Iran by force, and criticism could meet with harsh retribution. Many people in Iran resented the unequal distribution of wealth and the perceived 'theft' of the nation's oil revenue by 'outsiders', especially Britain. Although its level of effectiveness was in flux, Iran was still a constitutional monarchy, and in 1951 Mohammad Mosaddeq became the country's first elected prime minister. Mosaddeq's programme of nationalisation of the Anglo-Iranian Oil Company contributed to his widespread popularity in Iran. However, it was also the main factor in the fears shared by the Shah and his Western allies that Mosaddeq could lead Iran towards communism or, rather, that Britain and the United States would no longer have access to the oil revenues on which their economies depended.

It was in this Cold War context that the 1953 coup took place, removing Mosaddeq from his position and reinforcing the Shah's supremacy (and, with it, Western access to Iran's oil revenues), thereby introducing a new fear, or counter-fear, of the United States' power among many Iranians. Mohammad Reza Shah's relationship with the United States after the coup entailed a shift in the nature of his control over cultural life. He officially welcomed much that was promoted by the US government and sought to suppress cultural activity that promoted revolutionary or left-wing agendas, along with any that was seen as 'backward'. In the case of jazz, this meant that some US citizens living in or visiting Iran had considerable freedom in their musical practices, while Iranians who sought to use jazz as an expression of dissent had little freedom and no official support. For example, as outlined below, the most prominent jazz musician in mainstream Iranian media was a US citizen, while an Iranian bazaar merchant who recorded a song that was read as revolutionary was imprisoned. Practitioners of music that was seen as promoting dissent faced possible arrest and, along with others captured by SAVAK (the Shah's notorious secret police), the possibility of torture or even execution. Here, jazz as a specific musical form was not suppressed, but any vocalist who sang lyrics that could be interpreted as offensive to the regime was at risk. Of course, the risk increased with the level of circulation of recordings and corresponding perceived influence on society. Unknown performers whose music was heard only in small clubs had less to fear than those who sought or attained commercial success. However, Iranians who remember the post-coup period and who were not supporters of the regime recall the vigilance that was necessary at any public gathering, as the secret police were unpredictable and the regime's control of the media prevented dissemination of information about SAVAK's activities. Jazz did not constitute a special case in this context, but rather played an ambiguous role. It was a musical form that pro-Shah Iranians could love as a representation of 'friendship' with the United States. Jazz was also an 'international' form that invited creative 'disobedience' and 'independent' communal activities and, as such, appealed to some leftist dissidents. Most of the popular music that was both commercially successful and perceived as dissenting was not jazz, but, like much popular music of the time, carried traces of jazz. Two significant examples are the folk-rock singer Farhad and pop singer Dariush.[4] As discussed below, many Iranians at this time made little distinction between the various genres of 'Westernised' popular music, referring to all of them as 'jazz'.

Opposition to Mohammad Reza Shah's regime culminated in the 1979 revolution, which was closely followed by the Iran–Iraq War (1980–1988). During the years of war and reconstruction, the Islamic Republic's opposition to Western and popular music, including jazz, was based on its leaders' readings of Islam, as well as the desire to reverse the effects of what many saw as cultural colonialism by the West before the revolution. In this context, jazz did not hold a conspicuous position among the many forms of music seen as Western. Indeed, some Iranians (to generalise, mostly leftist intellectuals, often from the middle and upper classes) continued to see jazz as a less commercial form of popular music, one associated with oppressed people, and therefore closer to the ideals of revolution and equality than other forms, such as dance pop, which had been the dominant musical form under the Shah (various interviews with the author, Iran, 2014–2015). Shortly before his death in 1989, the leader of the 1979 revolution, Ayatollah Khomeini, declared, in effect, that music should not be completely forbidden. Iranian art music was the first form (apart from revolutionary anthems) to reappear publicly, but in the 1990s the production of popular music was also officially reintroduced. Official controls on this music, including jazz, are concerned with its perceived effects on its performers and audiences, as well as its associations. It should not incite any kind of anti-Islamic feeling or action and it should not imitate the perceived sensibilities of the West. The jazz that has thrived in these conditions has often been fusion with explicitly Iranian forms of music such as art or regional music.

Elements of jazz-related forms began to enter Iran's popular music in the late 1920s, as certain dance fashions, mainly originating in the United States, became popular internationally. Ali Bakhtiari (2012: 15) dates this first influence at 1928, when the bands of Hossein Ostovar (1896–1986; one of Iran's earliest pianists, whose music is usually described as 'classical'), Mostafa Nooriani, Parviz Iranpoor, Moosa Maarofi (a *tar* virtuoso) and others began to experiment musically. At this time, jazz in the Western sense was not yet widely accepted by the middle and upper classes of any country, and, as Iran's regime sought to introduce and promote cultural practices drawn from Europe's upper social echelons, it did not promote jazz. However, the word 'jazz' entered the Persian language and began to be applied to all genres of 'Westernised' popular music in Iran. Politically, this was a relatively calm point in Iran's turbulent twentieth century. Throughout the century, Iran's popular culture was conditioned by its relations with other countries, which were, in turn, shaped by ideological, territorial and economic interests. This had consequences for the nature of totalitarian tendencies in twentieth-century Iran and therefore for the opportunities afforded to some jazz practitioners and not to others. The ideological interests of Iran's 'modernisation' and 'Westernisation' programmes, combined with the economic interests of Europe and the United States, saw jazz – as a genre of the 'lower classes' in the early twentieth century – disregarded by the official milieu. In the mid-twentieth century, those same interests saw certain forms of US jazz officially promoted.

In 1919, the Anglo-Iranian Agreement (or Anglo-Persian Treaty) had failed in the context of rising mistrust of British imperialism. Katouzian (2006: 121–122) summarises popular Iranian attitudes towards the major international powers of the time:

> They were no longer afraid of Russia, whose two successive revolutions they had greeted with unbounded relief and optimism . . . they had received the news of the fall of the Tsarist regime as well as the Bolshevik declarations of friendship and goodwill towards their country with unmitigated joy and satisfaction. They viewed France as a disinterested and friendly nation with which Iran had already developed a close cultural bond. They regarded America as an almost selfless power – 'the protector of world peace', as Iraj put it in a verse – helping the weak and the vanquished.[5]

Britain, on the other hand, was represented in the press, literature, song and verse as a greedy thief or, in Mohammad Reza Eshqi's verse (Salimi n.d.: 305–308), a cat and a fox:

> It is the story of cat and mouse, our pact with Britain,
> Once it catches the mouse, how would the cat let it go?
> Even if we be the lion, she is the fox of our time,
> The fox famously defeats the lion.

The subsequent 1921 coup, which eventually brought Reza Khan to power as the new Shah in 1925, came to be viewed by some in Iran as a British plot. The above attitudes towards Russia, France, the United States and Britain were sometimes reflected in attitudes towards music from those countries, including jazz. Elements of popular music from France and the United States, such as the paso doble, entered Iranian repertoires early in the twentieth century, while it would take decades for British popular music to find large audiences in Iran.

The totalitarian tendencies of Iran's Shahs were also reflected in their attempts to control all aspects of popular culture, including music. In the first decade of his rule, Reza Shah became increasingly dictatorial. However, Katouzian's (2006: 314–315) examples from 1928 and 1935 illustrate the level of intensification of cultural repression that developed in the Shah's second decade in power:

> In 1928, when a large number of ulama [Islamic authorities] gathered in Qom to protest against the implementation of the military conscription law, [Prime Minister] Hedayat, [Minister] Taimurtash, the Imam Jom'eh of Tehran and his brother Zahir al-Islam went and humoured them, thus avoiding a major crisis.[6]
>
> But seven years later when a religious congregation in Mashad protested at the Shah's compulsory order to the male population to wear the European bowler hat, the Shah ordered them to be ruthlessly suppressed . . .
>
> A few months later, all women were ordered to take their veils off without the right to wear a scarf, on pain of persecution and arrest. They were allowed only to wear expensive and exclusive European hats which had been imported for the purpose.

In this context, as elsewhere in the world, notions of modernity and tradition, West and East, imperialism and nationalism, were paradoxical, but central to popular debate. Jazz may have represented a form of modernity from 'the West', arriving in Iran along with other 'imperialist' imports. However, it may also have represented aspects of the traditions of the oppressed people of the United States, who shared a longing for freedom with the poor and oppressed people of Iran. In his analysis of Iran's relationship with 'the West', Darioush Ashouri (n.d.) employs Nietzsche's notion of *ressentiment* to suggest that contemporaneous problems lead to resentment of either the Other – that is, the West – or the past – that is, a perceived shameful or flawed national heritage (see Mansouri-Zeyni and Sami 2014: 49). In Iran's case, such feelings of resentment have been exploited by political and other powers to promote or denigrate certain forms of music, among other cultural products. For the reasons mentioned above, jazz had a more ambiguous status than many other forms of music in this imagined system of definable divisions between different groups of people and measurable corresponding moral values. Jazz could be denigrated as belonging to 'the Other' or promoted as part of Iran's 'modern' future.

By 1940, Reza Shah's contradictory but un-nuanced approach to the control of cultural practices was well established and feared. The recording industry already reflected the replacement of most traditional Iranian instruments with Western instruments, such as the violin, piano and clarinet, but the introduction of radio in 1940 would transform Iran's musical life again. Sasan Fatemi (Breyley and Fatemi 2016) suggests that the advent of radio may be viewed, at least symbolically, as marking the advent of popular music in Iran. Jazz remained a minor influence on this popular music, which comprised a diverse range of 'Western' and 'Eastern' styles and derivations. The new and developing Iranian popular music was broadcast from the early days of Iranian national radio, generating a range of responses. Reasons to dislike or disapprove of the new music broadcast on radio were as diverse as its many listeners, but Jane Lewisohn (2008: 81) summarises the most common: 'singers and musicians on the radio were largely imitating international music, performing songs and tunes that not only had nothing to do with authentic Persian music, but did not follow the norms of international music either'. Such concerns were expressed mainly among Iran's formally educated music listeners, but they reflected the paradoxes imposed on cultural life by the Shah's policies of Persian nationalism and pride, combined with his visions of modernisation and Westernisation.

Of course, these developments coincided with the Second World War, which brought Allied occupation and the forced abdication of Reza Shah in 1941.[7] His place was taken by his young son, Mohammad Reza, whose reign began with some compromise and concessions, but gradually followed his father's path into dictatorship and cultural control. In 1941, Britain occupied southern Iran, while the Soviet Union occupied the north. Brian Spooner (in Daneshvar 2001: xiv–xv) sets the context:

> From 1941 to 1945 Iran was reduced to the most abject state of dependence of its modern history – while still nominally retaining its own independent government under the young Shah. The occupying powers subordinated everything to the economic and political objectives of

> supplying the eastern front and winning the war, with disastrous results for Iran's small economy . . . Existing extremes of poverty were exacerbated, disease rates increased, and typhus became a chronic problem. Corruption, incompetence and arrogance characterized almost anyone in authority, in national and local government, the army and the police. The influence of the occupying powers had a Christian-religious extension in the south, and a communist-ideological extension in the north, both of which were socially disruptive . . .
>
> The demoralization is evident in the exploitation of any position of power . . . Socialist ideas provide hope for the young. Opium offers an option for the old.

The 1940s saw many popular struggles, especially for various forms of social equality, as well as new forms of contact with representations of 'the West'. Jazz – seen occasionally as having associations with socialist or similar ideas of social equality, and opium and other drugs, among other things – was sometimes broadcast on radio, occasionally played on gramophones and, as elsewhere in the world, was open to diverse interpretations and associations.[8] As elsewhere, it could be linked with notions of immorality and self-indulgence, with oppressed or intellectual classes and with African-American, Jewish or European ethnic groups.[9] As notions of respectability, class and race accompanied the increasingly broad range of music heard in Iran, listeners' attitudes towards jazz were shaped by their views on political developments. The jazz-related form that apparently appealed most to 'the respectable classes' was the crooning style exemplified by Bing Crosby and adopted by some emerging Iranian singers. Meanwhile, the most practised forms among the broader population were 6/8 dance tunes, with little relation to Western jazz.

After the war and subsequent difficult negotiations between Iran, the Allies and the United Nations over control of the oil industry, among other things, many Iranians' desire for independence – economic, political and cultural – was strong. The national mood comprised elements of relief, bitterness and persistent resentment. Louise Fawcett (2014: 395) observes the 'dismissive and derogatory' language used by representatives of those non-Iranians who were making decisions about Iran's postwar future:

> This was particularly true of Britain, which, according to one recent account, demonstrated a 'profound contempt for Persia and its people' [de Bellaigue 2012], but also to a lesser extent of the United States, which also had a tendency to 'look down' on Iran [Bill 1988, 15–16] . . . The British ambassador in Tehran, Reader Bullard, . . . [c]omparing the Iran of 1945 to Britain in 1800, . . . wrote that the Iranian electorate would 'use power wildly' if they got it; Iran's 'only hope' lay with the United States [Bullard 1945]. Words like 'wily' and 'crafty' were used to describe

> politicians . . . adjectives suggesting weakness and vacillation were popular, with 'giggly' used in reference to Qavam and 'weepy' to describe Mosaddeq . . . The Majlis [Iranian parliament], in turn, was ridiculed as 'absurd', and likened to a 'monkey-house'.

Popular Iranian responses to such attitudes had diverse implications for tastes in music. My fieldwork among older Iranians suggests that, for some, indignation led to a desire to demonstrate the glories of a 'noble' Iranian past and an attraction to Persian art music. For others, a similar indignation led to a fraternal empathy with the United States' black and other suppressed people and an attraction to jazz and related forms.

The Iranian authorities of the time displayed similarly mixed responses and preferences. In the late 1940s, the Iranian Gendarmerie and the Air Force set up short-lived radio stations that broadcast a range of Iranian and imported popular music. Radio ownership was still largely limited to the middle and upper classes, but was already influencing tastes. The recording industry also began to respond to the emerging taste for Westernised music. In 1948, a pioneer of Westernised popular music, Jamshid Sheibani, released recordings of songs with foxtrot, tango, waltz and rumba rhythms. He came from Iran's land-owning classes, which, according to Anthony Shay (2010), were typically open to all things European and tended to be non- or even anti-religious. Thus, Sheibani's work reflects a further reason, apart from those of the political left, for some Iranians' attraction to music with links to jazz.

The European country that arguably had the greatest, or most explicitly embraced, cultural influence on Iran's upper classes in the early twentieth century was France. Modern Persian language includes a range of French words. Perhaps reflecting this influence, Iranians called the Western-style drum kit 'jazz' at this time, presumably from the French *batterie du jazz*. Sasan Fatemi (personal communication, 2014) suggests this may explain the subsequent use of the term 'jazz' for nearly all Western and Westernised popular music – or all music that was performed with a drum kit rather than the various drums traditionally played with the hands in Iran. This diverse music known as 'jazz' became increasingly popular, especially among Iran's postwar middle-class youth.

In 1953, political upheaval intervened again in Iran's cultural life, with far-reaching consequences. The coup of 19 August 1953 (28 Mordad 1332 in the Iranian calendar), which overthrew Prime Minister Mosaddeq, left scars that, in Ali Rahnema's (2012: 661) words, 'resemble the traumas of a civil war'. Rahnema (2012: 661) continues:

> It divided Iranian society between the proponents of Mosaddeq who believed they were the defenders of righteousness, nationalism, anti-colonialism, the peoples' [*sic*] right to sovereignty and self-determination

306 G. J. Breyley

and his opponents who claimed they were the defenders of national sovereignty, firm believers in God, Shah and the motherland and that Mosaddeq's politics were seditious and harmful as they would embroil the country in turmoil, anarchy, republicanism and communism.

The CIA-led coup established a relationship with the United States that permeated all levels of cultural activity. US citizens worked not only in the oil industry, but also in education, media, the arts and many other sectors. These migrants to Iran mostly lived privileged lives and the authorities also catered to their cultural tastes. Naturally, this made them new objects of resentment for some Iranians. The Shah promoted commercial, Westernised popular music, in line with the regime's desire to represent itself as modern and 'equal' to 'the West'.

Clearly, the history surveyed above has been intersected by a great range of political and cultural cross-currents, to an extent not suffered by countries less ambiguously situated in the 'West/East' axis. Not surprisingly, then, the situation of a music as culturally ambiguous as jazz (music of US capitalist imperialism or of historically oppressed people?) is unusually ill-defined. I turn now to the case of the most commercially successful star from mid-century Iran to illustrate these ambiguities. Crooner Vigen (Derderian; 1929–2003) began his career in 1951 with performances in Tehran's upmarket cafés and nightclubs. Significantly, he would soon become known as the 'Sultan of Jazz' (although 'jazz' was used here in the Iranian pre-revolutionary sense, as explained above).

Although he would go on to have problems with the Shah's regime, Vigen's smooth version of pop appeared to suit its requirements, as well as those of his fans, in the 1950s. During the Second World War, Vigen and his family had moved to the Iranian province of Azerbaijan, which was then occupied by Soviet forces. Attracted to the music played by the Soviet soldiers, the young Vigen bought his first guitar from one of them. After the war, his family joined other Iranians who were migrating to the capital city, Tehran. Vigen recorded his song 'Mahtab' (Moonlight) in 1954; it was played on high rotation on national radio and became an instant and enduring hit. This was the first of more than 600 songs recorded by Vigen in his fifty-year career. Non-Iranians might not classify Vigen's music as jazz, but it was the most Westernised popular music in Iran in the postwar period. He was aptly compared with Elvis Presley, with whom he shared aspects of style, as well as the appropriation and popularisation of elements of 'the Other's' music. Vigen collaborated widely with Iran's leading popular female vocalists, such as Delkash, Elaheh and Pouran, and with various songwriters. Like Presley, he also appeared in popular films.

Vigen's career throws useful light on the situation of jazz in the post-revolutionary period. The performer known in Iran as the 'Sultan of Jazz' had

Jazz in Iran since the 1920s **307**

migrated to the United States in the early 1970s, but continued to visit and perform in Iran until the revolution. Thereafter, he, along with many other popular musicians, was effectively exiled because his music was unacceptable to the regime. This tells us a great deal about the complexity of the relationship between jazz and non-Western totalitarianism. Vigen's music was, in fact, a fusion of many Western and non-Western traditions, and much of it might today be marketed as 'world music'. The Western elements cannot be disentangled from the influence on popular music of the jazz tradition, including phrasing, rhythms, vocalisations and instrumentation, as well as presentation (stage demeanour, costume and album design). Vigen's performance style was clearly non-Western, but strongly imbued with Westernised pop, itself permeated by jazz-derived developments. A number of YouTube clips convey a sense of his aural and visual style and approach. See, for example, www.youtube. com/playlist?list=PL574C05183F026202, www.youtube.com/watch?v=gWPa ToXTB0Y and www.youtube.com/watch?v=UpuAeKWJTAI. The second track (starting at 3:18) in the final clip could certainly be classified as 'funk/jazz/fusion'. Although jazz aficionados would be most unlikely to refer to his music as jazz, Vigen's nickname led some observers to declare that the post-revolutionary Iranian regime was keen to suppress music that was – or at the very least significantly incorporated – 'jazz'.[10] This underscores the many complexities in the understanding of diasporic jazz and the difficulties of generalisation when discussing its relationship with totalitarianism.[11]

After the 1953 coup, it was not just music that was repressed. Political dissent was not tolerated in any cultural sphere. As in the Soviet Union, Iranian writers, filmmakers and other artists turned to poetic means of communicating metaphorical or ambiguous political meanings. Some writers of popular songs also used this method of indirect dissent – or at least sections of their audiences assumed that they were doing so. The first significant example of this concerns a 1955 pop song with jazz traces, performed by another crooner, Hassan Golnaraqi. He was a bazaar merchant who, unlike Vigen, did not become a star, but was known only for this one song, 'Ma-ra bebus' (Kiss Me; lyrics by Heidar Raqabi, music by Majid Vafadar; www.youtube.com/watch?v=wt2wfPKkm44). The song's lyrics begin, 'Kiss me, kiss me for the last time; God keep you, I am going to my fate'. Just two years after the coup and in the immediate wake of the execution of thirty members of Iran's Marxist Tudeh Party's military branch, these lyrics were read as the cry of a political prisoner before his execution. The song continues with a series of supposed revolutionary metaphors: 'I have to give up this bright morning because I have a blood pact with a brighter morning . . . I have to start fires in the mountains'. 'Kiss Me' became a huge hit, retaining its popularity over several decades, and was covered by many Iranian stars, including Vigen. Golnaraqi himself was briefly jailed for his seminal recording of the song and thereafter abandoned the music industry.

308 G. J. Breyley

While many Iranian songwriters and performers experimented with international styles in the 1950s, Iran's new relationship with the United States conditioned possibilities for commercial recording and performance. By the mid-1950s, jazz was playing such an important and popularly accepted role in the commercial music industries of the United States that political leaders accepted a proposal from Harlem's Adam Clayton Powell Jr. to fight the Cold War with 'jazz ambassadors' (see von Eschen 2004) or its 'secret sonic weapon', as Belair (1955: 1) puts it.[12] The first tour of countries the United States sought to deter from a feared path or popular attraction to communism was arranged for Powell's friend Dizzy Gillespie in 1956, and Gillespie's first show was in Iran's oil city Abadan. Duke Ellington, Benny Carter, Harry Edison and others followed (see Patrick *et al.* 2002: 308), attracting young Iranian fans as well as many foreigners who were working and living in Iran. Of course, these tours did not always achieve the propaganda goals of the US government. The complex political and social histories embedded in much American jazz, including those of ongoing inequality, sometimes resonated with audiences in other countries. In Iran, with its conventions of multivalence in poetry and song lyrics, some music fans were in the habit of reading for ambiguity. Musically, however, the jazz tours did influence some Iranian musicians – and Iran influenced some US musicians. Compositions such as Duke Ellington's and Billy Strayhorn's 'Isfahan' were apparently inspired by, or at least named for, impressions these musicians gained on their tours.

By 1956, sections of Iran's urban intellectual communities, among others, were expressing concerns about a perceived lack of appreciation for Persian art and traditional music. Many saw the emerging popular music as 'tainted' by Western, Arabic, Turkish and other influences, including jazz. These concerns led Davud Pirnia to establish what would become Iran's most popular music programme on national radio. He called the show *Golha* (Flowers) and sought to play music he saw as 'authentically Persian'. Of course, such an arguably impossible definition made his goal difficult, but he did succeed in promoting appreciation of certain new forms of Iranian music. The music played on *Golha* was not entirely free of influences from various non-Iranian forms. Indeed, as Fatemi (Breyley and Fatemi 2016: 105) explains, the new style, while considered classical or art music, was 'not unrelated to *motrebi* music, on one hand, and Western music, on the other'. *Motrebi* is Iran's traditional light urban form of music, played at festive events by musicians who, along with the music itself, were usually held in contempt by art musicians and society more generally, much as many of the United States' early jazz musicians and their music were disdained. As the new Iranian style was 'simpler and lighter' than Persian art music, continues Fatemi, it was intended for both 'the popular masses and "cultivated music lovers"', who began to change their tastes and could be compared, in this regard, with the 18th-century European aristocracy and its penchant for simplicity at the time of the *galant* style'. Fatemi sees this period as one of confusion – or embrace – between the categories of classical and popular in Iran, with

> the former approaching the latter by being simplified and popularized, and the latter confused with the former, firstly because it was still at the beginning of this path separating it from classical music and secondly because it exploited a recently classicized mesomusic [see Vega 1966], which it valorized, sometimes even more than the great genre of classical music, i.e. free-metered and improvised music.
>
> *(Breyley and Fatemi 2016: 105)*

Golha brought together soloists who improvised in the 'modern (light) style, lyricists and composers, proponents of the Westernized style that sought to harmonize and orchestrate the fixed-meter works of Iranian music (the school of Vaziri) and singers who were known for their radio songs' (Breyley and Fatemi 2016: 105). This combination no doubt had some influence on the jazz fusion styles that would emerge from Iran (see the example of Hengameh Akhavan and her post-revolutionary private students, below). *Golha* continued until 1979 and was, in some ways paradoxically, seen as part of the 'back to roots' movement that was a significant factor in the revolution.

The establishment of *Golha* in 1956 was followed by the advent of television in 1959. Varieties of jazz were shown on Iranian television, along with a range of entertainment from the United States. Perhaps most prominent, though, was the new Iranian pop music, with its fashionable, glamorous stars, such as Googoosh and Fereydun Farrokhzad. This Iranian music was seen primarily as Westernised, as indeed it was, but it also bore traces of influences from several other cultural contexts, including Turkish, Arabic, Indian, Latin American and Eastern European. As elsewhere, jazz had contributed to the nature of mainstream pop, but was primarily a form for minorities, including left-wing intellectuals. Tehran was home to various small clubs and cafés, including some frequented by artists and others who sought closer contact with members of both the Iranian working classes and the 'creative' side of the Western presence in Iran, which, from the 1960s, included those on 'the hippy trail'. In such venues and in private homes, elements of jazz mixed with other musical forms, such as beat and folk.

While it may have seemed to those in Iran who feared cultural colonialism and *gharbzadegi* ('Westoxication'; see Al-e Ahmad 1977) that musical traffic was all in one direction, from 'the West' to 'the East', many Western musicians looked to the East for inspiration and others were influenced by 'Eastern' styles, whether or not they sought them out. As Andy Simons (2011) notes, the 1960s saw African-American jazz performers take a particular interest in music from the Middle East and North Africa. G. S. Nikpour (2012: 66) also comments on the problems in 'the historical narrative' that is most commonly presented:

310 G. J. Breyley

> The success of this era of Iranian pop is viewed as the express result of a culturally liberal political atmosphere that allowed musicians to learn from British beat bands and American soul singers, and then apply what they had learned to a classical idiom. Like most pop music from that era, however, the story is neither so neat nor so linear.

Indeed, while some may imagine or even remember the 1960s and 1970s in Iran as 'liberal', there were real dangers for dissidents, especially those on the left. Songwriters, including those who wrote metaphorically or ambiguously, could face arrest if they were seen to be offending the Shah's regime or promoting revolutionary thought. Of course, the most popular style of the era was dance pop with romantic lyrics, and this was generally 'safe'. Nikpour (2012: 66) continues:

> Pop musicians in Iran were influenced by the lush Italian pop of the Ennio Morricone school (Googoosh in particular was taken by this influence), the beats and rhythms of Bollywood and Indian pop, the fuzz guitars of Turkish psych, and the nearly global appeal of the Beatles and the Rolling Stones among countless others . . . the story of Iranian pop music is not linear – from west to rest and then suddenly crushed – but rather, like the music itself, one dominated by too many melodies and countermelodies to be captured in full in any one document.

A prominent example of a Western musician who exchanged music and ideas with Iranians in the 1960s and 1970s, with countless melodic results, is that of jazz musician turned Iranian art music 'defender' Lloyd Miller. Television, along with Iran's special relationship with the United States, was central to Miller's rise to prominence.[13]

To appreciate the political and cultural context and significance of Miller's roles in Iranian jazz, it is helpful to consider his movements after he first arrived in the country in 1957. That year, Iran's government invited Miller's father to establish a business college in Tehran. The young Miller went unwillingly with his parents, as he had already begun a jazz career in the United States. In Tehran, he was initially excited by the discovery of the Iranian instruments *tar* and *zarb* when he heard them on the radio, but after a year saw few prospects for his desired jazz career: 'I . . . realized I couldn't get anywhere with jazz in Iran, although the American school had some girls I trained and there were some guys I played jazz with at a couple of parties and dances' (Nikzad 2013: 65). With the freedom of his social position and nationality, and with his concept of 'Oriental jazz', Miller set off for Paris, where he collaborated with jazz improviser Jef Gilson and, in the early 1960s, converted to Mormonism. Miller had been playing Iranian instruments at Parisian nightclubs, but when his conversion led him to give up his partying lifestyle, he sought out the

Iranian master Dariush Safvat, who was also living in the city, to learn Persian art music formally. After two years of intensive study with Safvat, Miller returned to the United States, where he 'brought the house down' – in his own words (Nikzad 2013: 65) – with his *santur* performances.

Miller (Nikzad 2013: 66) also claims to have created a successful meeting of jazz and Iranian music in his collaboration with Press Keys in the United States:

> I'd play this Iranian stuff with the Arab *oud* and Turkish clarinet and Vietnamese flat harp, and we'd play some jazz things with these instruments. So instead of trying to play jazz on them, or trying to play Persian music on Western instruments, he played his jazz trio, and I played those instruments . . . Not blended at all. They met, and went side by side.

Miller's emphasis on the non-blended nature of this collaboration reflects the general aversion to notions of fusion or 'contamination' that was shared by supporters of the *Golha* radio programme and, by the late 1960s, by the Centre for the Preservation and Propagation of Iranian Music in Tehran.

The Centre was established by Miller's master Safvat, who had returned to Tehran in the context of intensified concern about the Westernisation that the Shah's regime was imposing. When Miller was awarded a Fulbright scholarship in 1970, he moved back to Iran, where he promoted the Centre, organised both art music and jazz concerts, worked at the Iran–America Society, and later worked as a journalist, using Persian pseudonyms. As a non-Iranian and under his pseudonyms, he had more freedom in this work than his Iranian intellectual colleagues and friends, as he recalls:

> They [Miller's employers] wanted to promote the thinking that 'Iranian music was going down the tube, it's the fault of Westernization, it's all the fault of America and its crummy culture and let's get the Yankees outta here.' I didn't mean it that way, but all these guys were left-wing and loved me ragging on America, and how our music was destroying theirs. I wrote about how great Safvat was saving traditional music.
>
> *(Nikzad 2013: 67)*

Musically, too, Miller had considerable freedom in 1970s Iran, and his forms of jazz were supported by the regime. He was able to present his love of both jazz and Iranian, Afghan and Turkish music on a weekly prime-time television programme, using one of his journalist pseudonyms, Kurosh Ali Khan. The show was called 'Kurosh Ali Khan and Friends' and featured improvisatory performances, mostly by young, unknown artists, directed by Miller. An English-language Iranian entertainment magazine article about the programme, published in the 1970s, quotes 'Kurosh' as saying the music world in the

United States was 'riddled with union dictatorship, hoods, fakes and swindlers' (see *Jazz Scope* n.d.), reflecting a different political perspective again from that of the left-wing paper for which Miller had worked. In Tehran, Miller also directed a documentary series on jazz history, presented another television programme in English on Iranian arts and recorded an album, *Oriental Jazz*, which was released by the Iran–America Society.

Miller was the most prominent practitioner of jazz in Iran in the 1970s, but he is just one of many US citizens who recall the many privileges they enjoyed in the country. However, even with those privileges and the sheltered nature of many US citizens' lives in 1970s Iran, some also remember the ever-present SAVAK and the real dangers faced by dissidents and anyone caught expressing a subversive thought. For example, Christine Westberg (2015), a US diplomat's daughter, remembers her life in Iran in 1978:

> My engagement book for the year . . . reveals a manic lifestyle . . . Skiing, hiking, outings to the horse track, discotheques, hotel bars, clubs for the expats, the British Council library, lectures at the cultural institutes, Fellini and Scorsese films at the elite Farabi Film Club, world-class directors and movie stars at the Tehran Film Festival, bookstores everywhere, an arts and intellectual scene fuelled by cosmopolitan interchange as much as by oil wealth . . .
>
> The young Iranian artists, architects, radio and television producers I was meeting had been trained in Europe, the States and the Soviet Union, but invariably strove for aesthetic synthesis with Persia's rich and unique cultural traditions. Political discourse was part of the scene. It had a seriousness and urgency I would never find in the States. I recall blithely excoriating the Marxist vocabulary of young Iranians and westerners alike. When university students approached me at the Iran–America Society's coffee shop, however, I assumed they were agents of Savak, the secret police, attempting to entrap me in anti-Shah commentary. I took the escalating crackdown seriously, but my entire adolescence had been shadowed by Savak and the CIA, and I am ashamed that at the time it all seemed like business as usual. I do remember, now, that I had started avoiding the bazaar and university districts in fear of the chaotic demonstrations which could erupt so suddenly.

Aspiring jazz musicians in 1970s Iran lived with the fears recalled by Westberg.[14] Even Miller would have felt the force of those fears, but for Iranians on the left – which described a considerable proportion of young experimental musicians – there was none of the immunity or possibilities for escape that US citizens enjoyed. To some extent, the risks were unpredictable, as during the regimes before and after the period from 1953 to 1979. Some musicians, like Miller, may have enjoyed great freedom of expression in public contexts, while others could practise their music only in private.

Over the decades since he left Iran, Miller has continued to bring together jazz and Iranian music (see, for example, his 2010 album with the Heliocentrics). He distinguishes jazz from the forms of Western music that he maintains are 'the enemy' of Persian art music: 'The main enemy of the *radif* is modernization, Westernization, rock 'n' roll, junk music. People think it's cool to mix the *radif* in with modern stuff, but it doesn't mix.' From the distance of Salt Lake City in 2013, Miller continues: 'The mullahs are right: if we don't have enough sense to make good music, we should just not do it at all' (Nikzad 2013: 67). His musical biography has been shaped by the nature of political relations between Iran and the United States. While he and his work benefited from the pre-revolutionary regime and would not have been possible in at least the first decade after the revolution in Iran, he maintains his support for the views developed by his fellow musicians at the Centre for the Preservation and Propagation of Iranian Music in the 1970s. Most of those musicians supported the revolution at the time and continued to work in the Islamic Republic of Iran, established in 1979. A few of them were still performing and teaching there at the time of writing (2015), and they enjoy great respect, especially from the fusion musicians who are the most significant representatives of jazz-related music in contemporary Iran.

Jazz could not be publicly performed or commercially recorded in Iran between the 1979 revolution and the mid-1990s. Since the resumption of popular music production at that time, fusion has become one of the most fruitful genres within which Iran-based jazz musicians can work. The Islamic Republic has a complex system for approval of music performances and recording, involving submissions to several government committees (see Youssefzadeh 2000). While some musicians submit to this process, seeking to perform or record in the largest and best technological environments, others prefer to work independently, thus evading the control of the authorities. Still others submit selected, 'suitable' work to the official process, but perform and release other music independently. Government restrictions prevent solo female vocalists from performing in front of unrelated males at authorised public events, and song lyrics for public performance or commercial recording are controlled. However, there is a thriving music industry in Iran, with several record companies and regular, well-attended concerts. Some of the (male) Iran-based jazz musicians I interviewed in 2014 commented that, in their opinion, too much is made of Iranian government restrictions on music in the Western media. One observed that Iran's restrictions are simply determined by different concerns from those that limit the freedom of musicians in the West, where commercial considerations may circumscribe musicians' possibilities as much as political considerations do for those in Iran. Some forms of jazz are legally taught, performed and recorded in Iran, where the genre shares with Iranian art music the value of improvisation.

Despite Miller's comments and the pre-revolutionary fear of musical 'contamination', many of today's musicians enjoy experimenting with various

314 G. J. Breyley

forms of fusion. Many work collaboratively and some make use of the new possibilities facilitated by technological change. Peter Soleimanipour (b. 1968), one of Iran's most prolific composers, is a multi-instrumentalist who has moved between jazz, pop, Western and Iranian art music and fusion (see Soleimanipour n.d.). His work reflects the political conditions that shaped his childhood and youth. As a child, he absorbed the diverse music in his family's record collections. In the 1970s, middle-class families typically built up their collections from the broad range of imported and locally produced records that were available. After the revolution, when it became difficult (though not impossible) to obtain records and cassettes, many young Iranians were musically influenced by their parents' 1970s records. Soleimanipour began music lessons at six and, despite the extreme post-revolutionary and wartime conditions in the early 1980s, began to compose at fourteen. He was twenty when the Iran–Iraq War ended, and he combined composition with studies in the visual arts and work as a graphic designer. With his jazz sensibility, Soleimanipour is collaborative and works across several genres, from theatre and film to commercial videos. His Peter Soleimanipour Ensemble has featured a diverse range of musicians, from jazz and art to fusion and 'world music'. Improvisation is central to much of his work, as is his notion of 'musign', the combination of music and graphic design. Soleimanipour has worked in Iran with official authorisation since the 1990s and has recorded with the Tehran-based Hermes Records, a champion of 'modern Persian music' (Hermes Records n.d.), including fusion and jazz.

Another prolific jazz musician who is active in Iran is Hamzeh Yeganeh. Like Soleimanipour, he is collaboratively involved with various jazz and fusion or 'world music' projects, including the Naima Persian Jazz Band, Arin Keshishi's Project and Damahi, which describes its genre as fusion/world music. These projects combine conventional jazz instruments with, for example, the *oud* (an Arabic instrument), as played by guitarist Ebrahim Alavi. Yeganeh's childhood was also overshadowed by the Iran–Iraq War in the 1980s, but inside his home the soundscape included a great deal of 1970s Western rock, as he recalled in a Facebook message in 2015:

> My father used to listen to music a lot specially rock music so i have listened to many different artist in my childhood most of all progressive rock, my favorite bands were ELP [Emerson Lake and Palmer], Mike Oldfield, Jethrotull, Yes, the return to forever, crosby still Nash and young and . . . The truth is that i have not listen to any iranian music in my childhood maybe just in some parties and i didn't like it that much!

There was also some jazz in Yeganeh's father's collection, and it had a lasting impact on him. He remembers his response to Chick Corea as a child: 'I can't really describe what i felt about it, there was a sense of freedom and

Jazz in Iran since the 1920s **315**

strange music with dreamy harmonies and fantastic players.' Unlike the 1970s, when aspiring jazz musicians, including children, could look to Miller's television programmes, and other places, for guidance, Iran's political isolation in the 1980s, combined with the conditions of war and a post-revolutionary government, made individual musical development a private matter. The attitudes and tastes of parents were therefore arguably more influential than in Western countries, as the family home was the primary site of musical activity.

While Yeganeh remembers the soundscape of his family home in the 1980s, another Tehran-based jazz musician of the same generation, Farzad Milani (2015), recalls the sounds that dominated his world outside the home at that time:

> My generation's childhood was surrounded by religious sounds, a sorrowful line of oriental melody, with words about Prophets and Imams. It was being played everywhere, TV channels, squares, loud speakers, in the 'Muharram' & 'Ramezan' mourning, etc. This kind of tones has formed Iranians' public music taste, its footsteps could be traced in Iranian pop songs nowadays.

Like Yeganeh and many others, Milani himself had different possibilities in his home and made use of every opportunity: 'I had the opportunity to listen different kinds of music, thanks to cassette tapes and VHS recorders! It was of my serious attempts to find the chords in the songs by listening and replaying it by my mini 2octave keyboard.' The 'DIY' approach that grew out of the war years for Iran's largest generation (there was a baby boom in the 1980s, encouraged by the post-revolutionary government's wartime policies) and the dichotomy of private and public sounds arguably contributed to the nature of today's Iranian jazz fusion.

Yeganeh (2015), who experiments with the Baluchi dulcimer *benju* and other instruments, but is primarily a pianist and keyboardist, explains the role of government policies in his choice of instrument:

> I started to play piano so late when i was 17. i was interested in drums first but in that period of time [early 1990s] instrument like that was banned in iran and i used to use different things like bowls and pans as drums! The reason that i started to play piano was that my uncle was interested in jazz and tried to learn jazz piano and looked for different jazz resources like tapes in music sheets so i could use them too, other reason was Keith Emerson that was like a hero to me since my childhood and i had his photos and albums. i wanted to play jazz piano but there was no jazz pianist in Tehran so i started classical piano with Mr. Gagik Babayan.

316 G. J. Breyley

Yeganeh's reference to the ban on drums and 'instrument like that' in the 1980s and early 1990s perhaps reflects the longstanding view in Iran that the drum kit is a symbol of Western music. While this ban was in force long enough to affect the practices of Yeganeh's generation, it did not prevent the development of a jazz scene led by that same generation. When the teaching of music was officially reintroduced in the 1990s, young Iranians again made the most of their opportunities, combining the autodidactic practices they had developed with their lessons of formal instruction in art and regional music. Yeganeh (2015) explains:

> Actually my main methods of learning is listening to music and transcription. i used to play different tunes by ear and this helped me a lot, also playing classical piano helped me to develop my technics and sight reading, i also studied music composition in university and started playing Iranian instruments like Santur and Benju and became interested in Iranian folk music specially Balochi music [from south-eastern Iran] and then i started to fuse folk music with jazz and rock.

By the late 1990s, the government's music policies were focusing on allowing an alternative to Western music to develop in Iran, but one that did not offend Islamic law and sensibilities. Iran's authorities did not represent jazz or jazz fusion as a particular threat, as by this time more popular forms, such as dance pop, were viewed as more explicitly 'non-Islamic', but they did not actively promote jazz, either. It was apparently neither as 'safe' as Western art music nor as unambiguously 'Iranian' as domestic art and regional music.[15]

While official discourses revolved around what was Islamic and what was Iranian, many musicians interested in jazz developed different philosophical concerns. For example, Yeganeh's (2015) approach is more outward-looking, seeking new possibilities for cross-cultural communication, rather than fearing the perceived dangers of contact with the wider world:

> I have found commons in jazz and iranian folk music in terms of improvisations so i have the idea of giving form and harmony to folk music so it is comprehensive for all international jazz musicians and they can improvise in these forms and chord changes, i believe jazz music is an international language and means for different cultures to communicate but in an isolated country like Iran it might be seen as a protest to the political situations.

Yeganeh prefers not to elaborate on the possibilities of jazz being viewed as protest, perhaps reflecting the ambiguous position of the genre. Other jazz musicians in Iran have told me that their music is not intended as protest and when it is read as such, it can distract from its appreciation and contribute to unnecessary fears among the authorities. Milani (2015) recounts his interactions with the authorities as primarily procedural:

> 'Ershad' [the Ministry of Culture and Islamic Guidance] . . . is a governmental organization for supervising art/culture products/performances. Anything you want to be officially released (books, music albums, film DVDs) or live music, theatre, art galleries, etc. should take Ershad's permission. I haven't seen rejection for instrumental albums because of their genre, since it is not gonna be viral as vocal albums, unless it was among the unusual kinds of music from their point of view (like hard rock, heavy metal or rap). In my personal case, during my concert procedure I had been asked if my genre is 'rock' or not! Whereas live performance office had checked my entire songs and lyrics in advance. Most of Ershad's sensitivity is on lyrics and artist's background, they haven't had problem with me yet.

Iranian jazz musicians are just as concerned about popular taste as they are about government restrictions. Yeganeh (2015) laments the dominance of 'poor pop' and the perceived exclusion of more creative jazz musicians from mainstream media in Iran:

> You know music in iranian younger generations is so poor and one of the reason is the national TV of iran because they never show instruments and the music is always poor pop music. the individual musicians are not few but they never find their way into Tv and so they are not heard by too many people, if musicians like dr. Loyd miller could come to iran and had concerts and TV shows there was a great development in music attitude. I personally like dr. Loyd miller and his interest in iranian music however to me the style of his fusion music is not too great like today musicians like avishai cohen and tigran hamasiyan i think these guys and some others can be called the real middle eastern jazz musicians.

While Yeganeh's concerns are related to the nature of Iran's government and its control of media, variations on those concerns are shared by some music lovers in Western countries, where governments are not seen as having totalitarian tendencies. Again, this may be an example of commercial control sometimes having similar effects on popular tastes to those caused by political control.

Like Yeganeh, Milani likes only some of Miller's work (personal communication, 2014) and he is more open to technological and 'modern' experimentation than Miller. Milani has produced a range of original musical experiments in which he combines elements of Persian art music with jazz. As with Yeganeh, it was old records and personal experimentation that motivated him (Milani 2015):

I am a self-taught musician, all of my music and sound knowledge comes from personal research and practice. I was teenager when I got familiar with jazz, records of Louis Armstrong, B.B. King, Benny Goodman, etc. inspired me a lot, and jazz became my destiny. The chords were very exciting for me because it was completely challenging to recognize the notes and to replay them. I got more impressed when I discovered Azerbaijani piano player 'Aziza Mustafa Zadeh' and her father, who truly have mixed 'Mugam' [the modes of Azerbaijani art music] scales with jazz harmonies. Then I figured out 'Oriental-Jazz' is an up-to-date music genre in many countries with oriental music background. It would be deliberating when I think we have had 'Dr. Lloyd Miller' in 1970s in Iran! Anyway, these guys as well as many other musicians have been my casual music teachers.

Rather than comparing the position of jazz in Iran with that in the West, Milani (2015) makes comparisons with Iran's neighbour Armenia, where jazz is 'a widespread style of music'. By contrast, in Iran:

Mostly young people with intellectual/modern artistic tastes (sometimes pretensions!) are interested in it, many others just listen to pop or traditional songs. It would be logical because official radio and television doesn't broadcast these styles of music [jazz and other forms that are seen as 'intellectual'], so public are not familiar with it. However, I think there would be one way to attract public to jazz. There are many who are interested in pursuing the oriental melodies in the song, even if it's been accompanied with unusual chords and rhythms, I usually take this issue to account. Some of my songs has been played severally from radio on the basis of people's request.

Milani's experience suggests that Iran's authorities may be unwilling to promote the experimental and 'intellectual'. However, the reasons for this in the twenty-first century may have as much to do with populism as with the kind of strict control sought on 'Islamic' and anti-imperialist grounds in the 1980s.

Jazz musicians like Soleimanipour, Yeganeh and Milani have successfully negotiated the conditions imposed by Iran's government since 1979. It is much more challenging for female jazz vocalists to work in Iran, as they have few opportunities to perform solo in front of large audiences or to record commercially. Therefore, many emigrate: for example, in 2012 Tara Tiba moved from Iran to Perth, Australia, where she has been able to pursue her interest in the links between Iranian art music and jazz (see Tiba n.d.). She was trained in Persian classical singing in Iran by the pre-revolutionary vocalist Hengameh Akhavan, a star of the *Golha* style, and has drawn on this training to provide jazz vocals for two groups in Australia. The first of these is Daramad, with whom Tiba vocally improvised with ensemble members Kate Pass, Reza Mirzaei, Mark Cain, Saeed Danesh and Mike Zolker. Pass (2013: 38), a jazz double-bass player, explains something of the process of adapting Persian music for jazz performances:

> Jazz musicians are often accustomed to soloing over frequently changing harmonic progressions and outlining the chord changes, but this is an unfamiliar concept for classically trained Persian musicians. One improvisational technique used by Persian classical musicians is to use the melody as the basis for improvisation . . . Another technique is to keep the rhythm very loose and flowing over the top of the meter. A jazz musician may call this technique 'playing rubato over strict time'. For the Persian musician, this allows them to express a melody in the way poetry would be phrased.
>
> A third technique involves soloing diatonically over the mode, a technique some jazz musicians may derogatively refer to as 'blanketing'. A jazz musician will use techniques such as chromatisism, chord substitutions, intervallic playing, side-stepping, extended guidetones and approach notes to add colour to modal or diatonic tunes. For the classically trained Persian musician, it could be said that colour and interest within improvisation are achieved in the way the soloist phrases melodies and uses ornamentation to decorate certain notes within the mode.

Pass gained her insights through her collaboration with Tiba. Thus, Tiba's work in Australia has already influenced a small section of the Australian jazz community and has brought the improvisatory work of pre- and post-revolutionary Iran to new audiences, especially as she has performed new jazz versions of pieces her teacher Akhavan performed and recorded in Iran. This is one of many unintended consequences of the regulations imposed on musicians and singers in contemporary Iran.

Another female jazz vocalist, Golnar Shahyar, migrated from Iran to Vienna, where her work has gained a large following. Her trio Sehrang (Three Colours) features Mahan Mirarab on guitar and Shayan Fathi on drums and percussion. Sehrang's repertoire overlaps a little with that of Daramad, notably with the song 'Moseme Gol' (Season of Flowers), which Akhavan recorded in Iran (see Pass 2013: 32–35). Mirarab worked extensively in Iran before his 2008 move to Vienna, collaborating with Yeganeh and many other jazz and fusion musicians in Tehran. He began work on his *Persian Side of Jazz* project while still based in Iran, in 2006. This combines Iranian regional and art music with jazz and was finally recorded in Vienna in 2010 (Kamino Records).[16] Mirarab's initial jazz inspiration came from some Wes Montgomery cassettes he found as a teenager in the late 1990s. After transcribing some of Montgomery's pieces, he discovered Charlie Parker, John Coltrane, Bud Powell and Clifford Brown, among others. At the same time, he learned the *tar* and began to experiment. As he developed his jazz style, he chose the fretless guitar as an instrument capable of playing Iranian quartertones and one that, in his eyes, reflected Iranian identity. Mirarab also credits the Armenian pianist Vahag Hyrapetian with enlivening Iran's jazz scene through a workshop he gave in Tehran in 2003. The work of guests and migrants from Armenia and Ukraine, among other places, in Iran's contemporary music education sector reflects shifts in the country's international relations since the days of 'Kurosh Ali Khan' and the effects of these shifts on its musical life.

The history of jazz in Iran has been shaped by the country's century of radical shifts in political affiliation. During the period from 1925 to 1953, the term 'jazz' was applied to all popular music from the West. The regime of that period, seeking to demonstrate Iran's 'modernity', enforced some aspects of what it saw as Western popular culture, but did not promote jazz, perhaps because it did not view this form of music as 'sophisticated' or 'respectable', reflecting its particular vision of Iranian modernity. Similarly, from 1953 to 1979, the US-backed regime rarely promoted jazz unless it was performed, directed or produced by US citizens. And since 1979 the Islamic Republic's authorities have not promoted jazz, but they have allowed it to develop, albeit in a male-dominated form. This has had the unintended consequence of the export of Iranian female jazz talent around the world.[17]

Notes

1 I am grateful to Bruce Johnson for his patience and support, and to him and the anonymous referees for their helpful comments and suggestions. Thanks also to Farzad Milani, Hamzeh Yeganeh, Golnar Shahyar, Vedad Famourzadeh, Sasan Fatemi, Peter Soleimanipour and many others who generously shared their experiences and observations.

2 The generalised comments about attitudes towards music in this chapter are largely based on an aggregation of the observations people have shared with me in Iran. I have made eleven trips there since 2003, staying for periods ranging from one month to ten months at a time and spending time with musicians and their fans across all generations, social classes and musical genres.

3 Since the 1979 revolution, the authorities have seemed more concerned with the appearance of control than with actual or total control, resulting in a great dichotomy between public and private spheres. While control is evident in nearly all public spheres, many Iranians have been relatively free in the privacy of their homes, as illustrated by the biographies of today's young jazz musicians, who grew up after the revolution. As a friend of Christian Bromberger (1998) put it: 'Before the Revolution, I used to go out in order to party with friends and I did my praying at home. Now you do your prayers in the mosque and you do your partying at home.'

4 On Farhad, see Ghadiri and Moinzadeh (2011) and Breyley and Fatemi (2016). For examples of his music, see www.youtube.com/watch?v=R5eNaqX_g0o. On Dariush, see Hemmasi (2013) and Breyley and Fatemi (2016). For examples of his music, see www.youtube.com/watch?v=OpDXSyH9Ye4.

Jazz in Iran since the 1920s **321**

5 Katouzian refers to Iraj Mirza's poetry (Mahjub 1989: 125).
6 Abdolhossein Taimurtash (formerly Sardar Mo'azzam-e Khorasani) was a leading figure in Reza Shah's government, having supported his ascendancy, but in 1932 he fell from favour and joined other former allies of the Shah who did not survive his rejection.
7 British and Soviet troops moved into Iran in 1941; US troops followed in 1943.
8 On the perceived links between jazz and socialism and jazz and drugs, see Heining (2012), Hore (1993), Collier (1978) and Winick (1959–1960).
9 See, for example, Walker (2010), Merwin (2006), Tucker (2001) and Gendron (1993).
10 Contemporary Iranians continue the debate whether Vigen's music should be called 'jazz'. See, for example, comments on a YouTube clip of one of his major hits, 'Lalai' (Lullaby) (www.youtube.com/watch?v=VpB5Enr3iaI, accessed on 3 August 2015):

> Kadkhoda Ahvazi (5 months ago): 'this was not a jazz singer and he never sang even one jazz song [my translation from the Persian]'
> nasir delshaad (2 months ago): 'WHAT DIFFERENT DOSE'T MAKE, WEATHER HE WAS CLLED KING OF JAZ OR KIN G OF POP, HE WAS THE BEST IN HIS PROFFESION'
> challia25 (2 months ago): 'Sir, between pop and jazz it makes no difference, don't take it so seriously [my translation from the Persian]'

11 When I ask Iranians who remember the pre-revolutionary period and who continue to use the term 'jazz' in its pre-revolutionary sense who they consider to be leading figures in the genre, the names of the smooth romantic pop singer Aref Arefkia (see www.arefrecords.com and www.youtube.com/watch?v=GoV-Zb1cmJg, accessed on 17 March 2016) and funky innovator Zia Atabai (see www.youtube.com/watch?v=wVv5T_OapXc, www.youtube.com/watch?v=Ns95UalHMxY, www.youtube.com/watch?v=TSd3i3vOK8A and www.youtube.com/watch?v=FxxR7BV9zXU, all accessed on 17 March 2016), who adapted the rhythms of his southern Iranian region to mainstream dance pop, are frequently mentioned. On the other hand, some younger Iranians, who define 'jazz' in its narrower sense, have told me they believe it was a form of music for 'elites' in 1970s Iran.
12 See also Devlin (2015). A variation on this practice resumed in 2015, with US jazz performer Bob Belden and his group Animation playing at an official music festival in Iran (see Jazz Video Guy, 'Iran Digs Jazz – Miles Davis in Tehran?', www.youtube.com/watch?v=a8kI50ChUPY, accessed on 3 August 2015).
13 See 'JAZZ IN IRAN 3, Lloyd Miller on NIRTV in the 1970s', www.youtube.com/watch?v=2Brl_iPjXrM, and 'Khourosh Ali Khan: Jazz Fusion in Iran', www.youtube.com/watch?v=5Oegi6LlG90, both accessed on 3 August 2015.
14 Westberg's memories of the music she and her friends enjoyed in Iran in 1978 provide a glimpse of the popular culture of young middle- and upper-class Iranians and their Western friends at the time. She mentions Stevie Wonder, Jimi Hendrix, Led Zeppelin, John Travolta and Olivia Newton-John's duets from *Grease* and, from a decade earlier, the Serge Gainsbourg and Jane Birkin duet 'Je t'aime, moi non plus'. Records by these and other pop and rock artists remained in the collections of some Iranians after the 1979 revolution and often influenced the music of the next generation in the 1990s and beyond.
15 An example of the shift in official attitudes towards music from the Shah's period was recounted to me by a young man completing his compulsory military service in the Army's music section in 2015. At the barracks, he was pleased to be directed to an array of high-quality instruments from the Shah's era, which had been kept in storage for around twenty-five years after the revolution. The collection included a saxophone, a clarinet and a piano.

16 See a 2013 performance in Tehran at www.youtube.com/watch?v=6LKuL-EszXk, accessed on 3 August 2015.
17 For a diverse selection, see 'Iranian Jazz and Rock Fusion', www.youtube.com/playlist?list=PLCD46BBDEE71147A2, accessed on 4 August 2015.

References

Al-e Ahmad, Jalal. 1977. *Gharbzadegi* [Westoxication]. Tehran: Ravâq.

Ashouri, Darioush. N.d. *Hoshyari-e tarikhi: negareshi dar Qarbzadegi va mabani-ye nazari-ye an* [Historical Consciousness: A Look at Westoxication and its Theoretical Bases]. http://ashouri.malakut.org/archives/upload/2005/03/ashouri-gharbzadegi.pdf, accessed on 31 December 2014.

Bakhtiari, Ali. 2012. *Iran: RPM, A Selection of Iranian Vinyl Soundtrack Covers*, Vol. I. London: Magic of Persia.

Belair Jr., Felix. 1955. 'United States Has Secret Sonic Weapon – Jazz'. *New York Times*, 6 November.

Bill, James. 1988. *The Eagle and the Lion: The Tragedy of American–Iranian Relations*. New Haven, CT: Yale University Press.

Breyley, G. J. and Sasan Fatemi. 2016. *Iranian Music and Popular Entertainment: From Motrebi to Losanjelesi and Beyond*. London and New York: Routledge.

Bromberger, Christian. 1998. 'Sport as a Touchstone for Social Change: A Third Half for Iranian Football'. *Le Monde Diplomatique*, April. http://mondediplo.com/1998/04/04iran, accessed on 2 August 2015.

Bullard, Reader. 1945. F0371/45434, Message from Tehran to the Foreign Office, 21 August.

Byrne, Malcolm. 2013. 'CIA Admits It Was behind Iran's Coup'. *Foreign Policy*, 18 August. www.foreignpolicy.com/node/1430798?page=full, accessed on 20 August 2013.

Collier, James Lincoln. 1978. *The Making of Jazz: A Comprehensive History*. Boston, MA: Houghton Mifflin.

Daneshvar, Simin. 2001. *Savushun: A Novel about Modern Iran*. Translated by M. R. Ghanoonparvar, Introduction by Brian Spooner. Washington, DC: Mage.

de Bellaigue, Christopher. 2012. *Patriot of Persia: Muhammad Mossadegh and a Tragic Anglo-American Coup*. New York: HarperCollins.

Devlin, Paul. 2015. 'Jazz Autobiography and the Cold War.' *Popular Music and Society* 38 (2): 140–159.

Fawcett, Louise. 2014. 'Revisiting the Iranian Crisis of 1946: How Much More Do We Know?' *Iranian Studies* 47 (3): 379–399.

Gendron, Bernard. 1993. 'Moldy Figs and Modernists: Jazz at War (1942–1946)'. *Discourse* 15 (3): 130–157.

Ghadiri, Momene and Ahmad Moinzadeh. 2011. 'The Comparative Analysis of Two Songs by Farhad Mehrad: The View of New Historicism.' *Theory and Practice in Language Studies* 1 (4): 384–389.

Heining, Duncan. 2012. *Trad Dads, Dirty Boppers and Free Fusioneers: British Jazz, 1960–1975*. Sheffield: Equinox.

Hemmasi, Farzaneh. 2013. 'Intimating Dissent: Popular Song, Poetry, and Politics in Pre-Revolutionary Iran'. *Ethnomusicology* 57 (1): 57–87.

Hermes Records. N.d. www.hermesrecords.com/en/home, www.facebook.com/pages/Hermes-Records/134685946552301, both accessed on 31 December 2014.

Hore, Charlie. 1993. 'Jazz – a People's Music?' *International Socialism Journal* 61. http://pubs.socialistreviewindex.org.uk/isj61/hore.htm, accessed on 4 August 2015.

Jazz Scope. N.d. www.jazzscope.com/VI.html, accessed on 31 December 2014.

Katouzian, Homa. 2006. *State and Society in Iran: The Eclipse of the Qajars and the Emergence of the Pahlavis*. London and New York: I.B. Tauris.

Lewisohn, Jane. 2008. 'Flowers of Persian Song and Music: Davud Pirnia and the Genesis of the Golha Programs'. *Journal of Persianate Studies* 1: 79–101.

Mahjub, Mohammad Ja'far, ed. 1989. *Divan-e Kamel-e Iraj Mirza*, 6th edition. Los Angeles: Sherkat-e Ketab.

Mansouri-Zeyni, Sina and Sepideh Sami. 2014. 'The History of *Ressentiment* in Iran and the Emerging *Ressentiment*-less Mindset'. *Iranian Studies* 47 (1): 49–64.

Merwin, Ted. 2006. *In Their Own Image: New York Jews in Jazz Age Popular Culture*. New Brunswick, NJ: Rutgers University Press.

Milani, Farzad. N.d. www.farzadmilani.com, www.youtube.com/farzadmilani, www.reverbnation.com/farzadmilani, www.facebook.com/farzad.milani.music, all accessed on 31 December 2014.

Milani, Farzad. 2015. Emails to the author.

Miller, Lloyd. N.d. 'Lloyd Miller Music'. www.facebook.com/LloydMillerMusic, accessed on 31 December 2014.

Miller, Lloyd Clifton. 1999. *Music and Song in Persia: The Art of Avaz*. Surrey: Curzon Press.

Morgan, Philip. 2003. *Fascism in Europe, 1919–1945*. London: Routledge.

Nikpour, G. S. 2012. 'Not(e) from the Orient: On the Re-Packaging and Re-Selling of Persian Pop'. *B | ta'arof: A Magazine for Iranian Culture, Arts, & Histories* 1: 61–66.

Nikzad, Ramtin. 2013. 'Music Side by Side: An Interview with Lloyd Miller'. *B | ta'arof: A Magazine for Iranian Culture, Arts, & Histories* 2: 64–67.

Pass, Kate. 2013. 'A Transcultural Journey: Integrating Elements of Persian Classical Music with Jazz'. Bachelor of Music dissertation, West Australian Academy of Performing Arts.

Patrick, James S., Morroe Berger and Edward Berger. 2002. *Benny Carter: A Life in American Music*. Ann Arbor, MI: Scarecrow Press.

Rahnema, Ali. 2012. 'Overthrowing Mosaddeq in Iran: 28 Mordad/19 August 1953'. *Iranian Studies* 45 (5): 661–668.

Salimi, Ali Akbar, ed. N.d. *Kolliyat-e Mosavvar-e Eshqi*. Tehran: n.p.

Shay, Anthony. 2010. Interview with the author.

Simons, Andy. 2011. 'Middle Eastern and Indian Jazz: An Improvisational Journey'. *IAJRC* 44 (2). www.readperiodicals.com/201106/2345048631.html, accessed on 17 March 2016.

Soleimanipour, Peter. N.d. 'Music'. www.petiachio.com/music.html, accessed on 31 December 2014.

Tiba, Tara. N.d. www.taratiba.com, accessed on 31 December 2014.

Tucker, Sherrie. 2001. *Swing Shift: 'All-Girl' Bands of the 1940s*. Durham, NC: Duke University Press.

Vega, Carlos. 1966. 'Mesomusic: An Essay on the Music of the Masses'. *Ethnomusicology* 10 (1): 1–17.

von Eschen, Penny M. 2004. *Satchmo Blows up the World: Jazz Ambassadors Play the Cold War*. Cambridge, MA: Harvard University Press.

Walker, Katherine. 2010. 'Cut, Carved, and Served: Competitive Jamming in the 1930s and 1940s'. *Jazz Perspectives* 4 (2): 183–208.

Westberg, Christine. 2015. '1978: One Last Fling in Iran before the Revolution'. *Guardian*, 7 February.

Winick, Charles. 1959–1960. 'The Use of Drugs by Jazz Musicians'. *Social Problems* 7 (3): 240–253.

Yeganeh, Hamzeh. 2015. Facebook messages and emails to the author.

Youssefzadeh, Ameneh. 2000. 'The Situation of Music in Iran since the Revolution: The Role of Official Organizations'. *British Journal of Ethnomusicology* 9 (2): 44–48.

14

ON THE MARGINALITY OF CONTEMPORARY JAZZ IN CHINA

The Case of Beijing

Adiel Portugali

This article explores the marginal position of contemporary jazz in China by means of a detailed study of the jazz scene in Beijing up to 2013. It specifically examines the way contemporary jazz in the city interacts with the political, rebellious, social and economic environments in which it subsists, and the way this complex and dynamic interaction affects its marginality. The topic is negotiated through a dual perspective. The first draws on the scholarly historical literature to trace the process that led to the off-centre position and image of jazz in China. The second, an insider's perspective, exposes the way individual musicians who are active in the jazz scene in Beijing experience and interpret its marginal characteristics. This inner perspective is based on an empiric–qualitative fieldwork study, including in-depth interviews and conversations with members of Beijing's contemporary jazz scene, and participatory observations in jazz festivals, clubs, jam sessions, music academies and workshops (2006–2012). The findings of this study reveal that jazz in China is marginal not because it is politically active or dangerous, but rather because it is seen as politically passive, and does not serve the needs of the market or the Chinese state.

Introduction

Jazz in China emerged during the 1920s as a pioneering style amid a rising wave of popular music in Shanghai. Its imperialistic connotation, decadent image and controversial expansion during the late republican period (1930s–1940s) and its sudden disappearance and ban following the communist revolution (1949) are discussed in a few works on early popular music and culture in China, such as Jones (2001), Chen (2005, 2007) and Field (2009). The second appearance of jazz in China, which gave rise to what I refer to here as 'contemporary jazz', took place in Beijing during China's 'new era' (1976–1989). Since then, modern music in China has developed, expanded and split into different styles and directions. Jazz too has rambled down this path, and today it can be found in major cities like Beijing and Shanghai – the centres of jazz happenings in China in terms of venues, institutes, festivals, clubs and quantity of active musicians; in secondary jazz centres, such as Chengdu, Guangzhou and Hangzhou; and in 'peripheral' cities that host minor jazz activities, such as Kunming, Xiamen, Suzhou and Nanjing. In most of these places, however, jazz is a *marginal* scene, meaning that it exists off-centre from the national and local music industries, as it is performed and known by only small circles of musicians and fans, and sometimes merely by a few individuals. This chapter aims to explore some of the factors that have generated the marginality of contemporary jazz in China through a detailed study of the off-centre position and image of the jazz scene in Beijing. This topic has not yet gained explicit academic attention and the present study is a first step toward filling this lacuna.

Into the Margins

Studies on genres of classical and popular music that emerged in China after the Cultural Revolution (1966–1976) reveal that their development, position and image have been implicated in a range of political, social, economic and cultural factors. Some of them give particular emphasis to the role the Chinese state plays in affecting the popularity or marginality of these musical expressions, and to the way musical practices in China interact with, or react to, political conditions. Barbara Mittler, for example, clearly argues that in China 'all music is political' (Mittler 1997, 125). A similar argument is made by Sheila Melvin and Cai Jindong, who write: 'There is no such thing as art that is independent of politics in China – and there probably never will be' (Melvin and Cai 2004, 320). Indeed, a random glimpse of titles of related books and articles published mainly during the 1990s gives the impression that music in China is essentially implicated in politics: 'dangerous', 'forbidden', 'ideology', 'opposition', 'struggle', 'red' (see, for example, Kraus 1989; Jones 1992; Brace and Friedlander 1992; Rea 2006) and similar key words and connotations demonstrate that when it comes to (music in) China, politics really matters. However, further studies, such as Baranovitch (2003), Harris (2005), Wang (2007), Fung (2008), Komlosy (2008), De Kloet (2010) and Moskowitz (2010), observe contemporary music in China through multifaceted perspectives. They do negotiate the political, yet give emphasis to other social, cultural, gender, ethnic and economic factors as well. This, I believe, is China today. Similarly, jazz musicians in Beijing stress that the development, position and image of contemporary music in China are implicated in a wide range of interests and affects. In general, they specify three main objectives that correspond to musical practices in China: *political, rebellious* and *commercial*. Pianist Liang Heping (2010, interview with author), for example, explains that 'political music' corresponds to musical acts that mean to serve the regime (*wei zhengzhi fuwu yinyue*); 'rebellious music' corresponds to music that entails or generates ideas of criticism and revolt (*wei sixiang fanpan de yinyue*); and 'commercial music' refers to music that serves the needs of the market (*wei shangye fuwu yinyue*).

This chapter examines the marginality of contemporary jazz in China through a dual perspective. First, in line with studies on contemporary music in China it draws on the scholarly literature that charts the historical narrative and complex process that led to the off-centre position and image of the country's jazz. Then, by employing an insider's view, it exposes the way musicians and individuals engaged in the jazz scene in Beijing have personally and subjectively experienced and interpreted its marginal characteristics. The first – political – section of the article examines the way that the Chinese government makes use of (or ignores) jazz and other musical styles, acts and musicians as means to transmit its ideology and strengthen its legitimacy. The second – rebellious – section discusses musical expressions that convey ideas and feelings that stand in contrast to the ideology of the Chinese regime. Finally, the third – commercial – section examines musical styles, acts and musicians that interrelate with, or are economically exploited by, the music industry in China and the state. The chapter reveals how contemporary jazz in Beijing interacts with the political, social and economic environment in which it exists, and points to the way this complex and dynamic interaction has affected its marginal position. At this point, my argument is that while political, rebellious and economic factors have all explicitly stimulated the evolution of contemporary music in China, either in public or underground, they have marginalized its jazz and pushed it to the side. Sometimes, as shown in this study, this process has involved deliberate, active and direct actions, but sometimes it has happened at random, by passive and rather indirect means.

Is It Political?

The idea that music could be used as a powerful political tool existed in imperial China from antiquity, and was reinforced in modern times as well (Baranovitch 2003, 192–193; Mittler 1997, 38–41). In the course of the 1930s, for example, much of the production, distribution and perception of modern music in the Republic of China was politicized. This tendency was related to the general modernization process of China's politics, culture and arts, and specifically to the period's patriotic and anti-imperialist feelings that swept through China following the invasion and aggression of Japanese troops on the mainland (Jones 2001, 44). In those days of political chaos and of external and internal wars, the musical interest of Chinese officials and scholars became less intellectual and artistic, and more ideological and pragmatic. Rightist and leftist political and cultural movements alike classified certain types of music as 'good', 'correct' and 'beneficial' to their cause, and other types as 'bad', 'wrong' and 'vain'.[1] In both cases, those in positions of power sought to employ 'desirable' music and musicians as carriers of public opinion, on the one hand, and criticized 'undesirable' musical expressions, such as, jazz, on the other.

In the 1930s, the Nationalist Party (KMT)[2] and its associated New Life Movement (*xin shenghuo yundong*) drew their artistic inspiration from the political aesthetics and musical activity of the Nazi and other fascist regimes in Europe (Yang 2007, 4; Bergère 2009, 219; Jones 2001, 49–52, 113, 117–119). For example, they organized singing rallies to spread ideas of conservative modernization and total loyalty to their leader Jiang Jieshi (Chiang Kai-shek) and the nation, which were tastily spiced with anti-imperialist and anti-communist sentiments; thus, they propagated a 'sinified' form of modern totalitarianism, which Bergère aptly terms 'Confucian Fascism' (Bergère 2009, 219). Their agenda was also articulated by music scholars and composers, among them Xiao Youmei, Cai Yuanpei and Dai Cuilun. Xiao, for example, promoted his vision of a 'sonic regime' in which music was destined to propagate a political ideo-logy, control the nation and manipulate the spirits of its people. In his view, jazz was a 'good' example of a 'bad' and needless type of music. His musical vision was articulated in a series of lectures 'The Power of Music', which was recorded and broadcast on the Great China Wireless Broadcasting Station in November 1933, sponsored by the Shanghai Municipal Bureau of Education (Jones 2001, 46–52; Liu 2010, 189–191). At the other end of the political spectrum, the Chinese Communist Party (CCP)[3] and its associated Leftist New Music Movement (*zuoyi xin yinyue yundong*) were also inspired by the political aesthetics and musical practices of totalitarian regimes in Europe, and particularly by the Soviet Union's model of mass music, revolutionary songs, singing marches, rallies and competitions. Their musical agenda was articulated by leftist scholars and composers, such as Xian Xinghai, Lü Ji and Nie Er, who criticized popular music for its political passivity and association with capitalist, imperialist and underworld powers, and regarded jazz in particular as a 'yellow' (pornographic) type of music that stood for the immoral and decadent lifestyles of the bourgeois classes. Ironically, the methods and channels they employed for producing and distributing their 'mass music', such as radio, sound recordings and film, were similar to those of jazz and the popular music they so harshly condemned.

Shanghai was not only the centre of popular culture and music in China, but also the place where the first generation of Chinese leftist writers, filmmakers, composers and musicians emerged; and they too, as mentioned, acknowledged and utilized the new music and media culture to spread their ideology. Nie Er's 'March of the Volunteers' (*yinyongju jinxingqu*; lyrics by Tian Han), for example, which became the national anthem of the People's Republic of China, was originally composed in 1935 for a commercial film called *Children of the Storm.* The exemplary musical model of the Chinese communists took shape a few years later, in 1942, during the Yanan Forum on Art and Literature (*yanan wenyi zuotanhui*; see Hong 1994). In the closing speech of this forum, Mao Zedong declared that 'mass culture' must act as a weapon ('cultural army') at the revolutionary front, and thus literature, art and music were all destined to serve the mass – the *people* (workers, peasants, soldiers and petty bourgeoisie) – and China's revolutionary cause (Yang 2007, 4; Hong 1994, 92). This cultural theory came to dominate the political aesthetics and musical practices of communist China until the late 1970s and beyond (Jones 2001, 106; Baranovitch 2003, 193).

On 1 October 1949 Mao Zedong announced the establishment of the People's Republic of China (PRC), with Beijing as its capital. Shortly thereafter, nearly every aspect of China's popular culture, art and urban lifestyle was changed (Wasserstrom 2009, 77–78, 86), and its music industry was nationalized and reorganized accordingly, to serve the needs and disseminate the ideology of the new communist state. The consequence for cosmopolitan Shanghai and its bubbling jazz scene was immediate, and in a few years its legendary reputation as the 'Paris of the East' was no more than a memory (Abbas 2000, 776). The first editions of the *People's Music Journal* (*renmin yinyue*) criticized popular music in general and jazz in particular as immoral and debased practices. In February 1951, for example, Wu Yongyi published his article 'Comments on American Jazz' (*ping meiguo jueshi yinyue*) in the *People's Music Journal* 6–7 (see Yang 2007, 11), in which he condemned jazz as an unrefined, vulgar dance music, a symbol of immorality and an artefact of the hedonist capitalist class. Then, in June of that year, Liao Fushu published his article 'Criticism of American Music' (*chi meihuo yinyue*) in the *People's Music Journal* 8–10 (see ibid.), in which he denounced popular music as the art of a nation on the edge of collapse. The PRC's dependence on Soviet support, the outbreak of the Korean War (1950–1953), the recognition the United States gave to Jiang Jieshi's regime in Taiwan and the chilling atmosphere of the Cold War generated a general aversion to the West and the culture it represented. The particular paranoia toward the United States positioned jazz as a terrifying capitalist phenomenon that was capable of harming its listeners and poisoning their souls.[4] This view was articulated, for example, in Tong Changrong and Wang Ying's April 1958 article 'American Jazz' (*meiguo jueshi yinyue*) in the *People's Music Journal* 36 (see Yang 2007, 12), and in Lü Ji's speech 'Music in the Service of Workers, Peasants and Soldiers' (August 1960), which once again highlighted a clear line between 'desirable proletarian' music and 'undesirable capitalist' music.[5] 'No matter whether it is called new music or jazz,' Lü claimed, 'it is permeated with capitalist poison, [and thus] is a tool of imperialism.'[6]

In the mid-1960s China was about to be flooded by a tsunami of radical totalitarianism – the Cultural Revolution. In this turbulent period, Mao and

330 Adiel Portugali

his Red Guards[7] launched a brutal campaign for cultural 'purification' in which numerous intellectuals, teachers, writers, journalists, artists, musicians and political opponents were arrested and sent to labour camps in remote rural areas. In those days of horror, the only 'right' way to think, create and act was the way of Chairman Mao, as explicated in his 'Red Book'. Accordingly, all forms of urban literature and performing arts were forced to submit to the strict censorship of the state, which was conducted with revolutionary zeal by Mao's infamous wife, the former actress Jiang Qing. Jazz, of course, was banned. In fact, in the days of the Cultural Revolution, not only Western music but other 'non-revolutionary' and non-Maoist cultural forms were censored and banned, and the only love songs that could be heard were devoted to Mao and the party. Folk and traditional songs were modified and nationalized as well, and even the national anthem, 'March of the Volunteers', was condemned as insufficiently 'red', and thus replaced (albeit temporarily) with a version of a folk song titled 'The East is Red' (Yang 2007, 13; Mao 1991). In the 'free world' at this time, jazz expanded its styles from bop to bebop, from Latin to fusion and so on; but in China its sparks were concealed under a thick dark screen.

The end of the Cultural Revolution and China's new leadership and reforms after Mao's death in 1976 initiated a new phase in the history of the PRC. In 1978, the new leader, Deng Xiaoping, launched a 'four modernizations' plan for economic, ideological and cultural reform in agriculture, industry, science and technology, and the military, and a year later he introduced the 'open-door policy', which opened China's market to foreign enterprises, investment and trade. Deng realized that opening China's gates to the West would mean that ideas, information and by-products that were incompatible with the ideology of the Communist Party could infiltrate as well. None the less he was willing to take the risk. 'Open the windows, breathe the fresh air', he said, 'and at the same time fight the flies and insects' (Schell 1994, 357). What Deng did not mention, however, was that a few 'songbirds' might fly in as well, alongside the foreign capital, modernization, information and some irritating ideas. The subsequent political, economic, social, cultural and musical changes were enormous. New flows of culture and music, such as the *gangtai* pop songs from Hong Kong and Taiwan, and the disco, pop and rock from the West, penetrated into China, and by the late 1980s local genres and forms of popular music, such as Northwest Wind (*xibeifeng*), Prison Songs (*qiuge*) and Beijing Rock (*yaogun*), also began to emerge and then spread.

Jazz in the PRC also took its first steps around this time. Since the early 1980s, a number of young musicians in Beijing, among them Liu Yuan, Du Yinjiao, Liang Heping and Liu Xiaosong, began to teach themselves and practise jazz. At that time this was a far from simple or straightforward task. There were no teachers, institutes, clubs or music shops for jazz, so the main way to learn and absorb the genre was through personal contacts and interaction with foreigners and overseas Chinese who brought tape cassettes, video recordings and notation books into China. In addition, random jam sessions involving foreign (mainly amateur) musicians started in a few Beijing campuses, hotels and restaurants. Gradually, a few local musicians joined these activities and created a small jazz community.

The cultural easing and consequent musical development that followed Deng's reforms did not mean, however, that the CCP ended its involvement in the performing arts (Melvin and Cai 2004, 313). Official institutions and organizations, such as the Ministry of Culture, the media, the municipal authorities and official associations of musicians, remained the main promoters and sponsors of music education, production and distribution in China. In practice, the Chinese government maintained its control over theatres, orchestras, record labels and magazines, journals and publishing houses, TV channels, festivals and singing competitions, among other music events. For example, the China National Symphony Orchestra comes under the auspices of the Ministry of Culture, the China Philharmonic Orchestra comes under the State Administration of Radio, Film and Television, and the Beijing Symphony Orchestra comes under the Beijing Culture Bureau (Melvin and Cai 2004, 314). Moreover, many musicians, singers and composers were – and indeed still are – members of governmental work units (*danwei*), which have provided them with housing, medical care, musical instruments and salaries. These benefits are mostly basic, yet sufficient to assure economic stability and a secure life for the musicians and their families. This system, however, has entailed administrative and financial dependency in the sense that the musicians could find themselves used as tools for propagating the ideology and narratives of the regime (Melvin and Cai 2004, 314–315; Baranovitch 2003, 194). For example, Baranovitch has shown that music TV channels in China have been utilized since the late 1990s to promote the political ideology and principles of the CCP, such as patriotism, centralized control, sovereignty (for example, over Tibet, Xinjiang and Taiwan), modernization, productivity, a harmonious society and 'moral' citizenship (Baranovitch 2003, 207–213, 215). This demonstrates, on the one hand, that the Chinese government directs or manipulates its artists to conform to its ideology and maintain its hegemony over the nation, while, on the other, the musicians and musical styles that conform to the official ideology and principles of the state have better opportunities for sponsorship and promotion than others.

In this context, jazz has no chance. How could its small, marginal scene serve the regime? How might its musicians endorse the ideology of the state and transmit its principles through a genre that often has no lyrics?[8] In fact, until recently the Chinese authorities did not recognize, support or even show any particular interest in the activities of the local jazz scene in Beijing. Today, jazz in China is no longer taboo; but it does not seem to serve the government in any way.

According to bassist Huang Yong (2010, interview with author), the lack of governmental involvement in jazz activity is one of the main factors that marginalizes the scene in Beijing. The state funds academic programmes for classical, traditional and popular music, he says, but not for jazz. It sponsors and promotes acts, composers, musicians and singers of contemporary music, but not of jazz. It sends talented musicians to play throughout the country and abroad, to promulgate their music and represent China's musical developments, but jazz musicians are usually excluded. Huang believes that the position of Chinese jazz will change only when the government starts to recognize that it is a valuable form of art. None the less, he says the responsibility lies in the hands of the musicians themselves: 'We need to dig into our music, Chinese music, [but] we still need time. We need to be patient and create an innovative kind of music and present it to our government; but at this point, we don't have yet enough to show' (ibid.). The apparent passivity of the Chinese authorities towards jazz does not mean, however, that they are unaware of it. Huang claims that the authorities are fully aware of the scene, but they choose not to interfere. The government keeps 'one eye open, and one eye closed', he says (ibid.).

Is It Rebellious?

The spirit of protest and voices of political, social and individual discontent have rumbled in the PRC since the late 1970s. The people's cries against the Cultural Revolution in April 1976, the poems, 'manifesto' letters and notes posted on the 'Democratic Wall' in 1978, the student demonstrations against state corruption in December 1986 and January 1987, and their later calls for political modernization and change in May and June 1989 are all examples of opposition to the formal ideology of the state. The distrust, frustration, anger and hope that these and other rebellious acts expressed were also implicated in China's musical arena. The Northwest Wind, Prison Songs and Beijing Rock of the late 1980s, the punk, urban–folk and underground scenes of the 1990s and early 2000s, the recent avant-garde and experimental music scenes, and other sounds, voices and noises have demonstrated various levels of political, social and individual criticism.[9] In Chinese rock, for example, the spirit of protest is generally manifested through its lyrics, and by associated gestures, such as the musicians' and their fans' alternative fashions and haircuts, bohemian lifestyles and nonconformist social behaviour. In Chinese jazz, however, there are usually no lyrics or tune titles that have explicitly rebellious connotations, and the musicians' performances and styles are relatively mild, and definitely not subversive. Even so, oppositional feelings and ideas can also be transmitted through ambiguous metaphors, between verbal lines and by words that remain unsaid (Rea 2006, 373–386). This happens in Chinese rock and also in Chinese classical compositions. For example, Mittler reveals how responses to the traumatic incidents in Tiananmen Square (1989) were evident in the work (and criticism) of various composers, among them Qu Xiaosong, Liu Yuan,

Tan Dun and Zeng Xingkui (Mittler 1997, 118). 'The musical reactions to the massacre at Tiananmen', she writes, 'are no longer meant to negotiate the politics of the Chinese government, but rather, unarticulated as they may be, they are intended to condemn and negate contemporary government policies' (ibid., 116). Therefore, it was not only the Chinese government but also artists who employed music as (silent) propaganda for their cause. In jazz, however, this was not quite the case. According to Barmé (1999, 99), the incidents of 4 June 1989 signalled the end of a relatively tolerant period of cultural policy in China and a return to tighter ideological control. Like Chinese intellectuals and artists, musicians had to modify their political involvement and artistic approach. Indeed, after 1989, popular music in China – and rock in particular – became less political, prudently social and more personal. Baranovitch (2003, 44, 46–47) describes this change as a shift from 'idealization' to 'realization'.

So what about jazz? Did it participate in the resistance? Did it seek freedom? And was it also affected by the aftermath of 1989? According to Rea (1999, 131–132), the suppression of live rock drove frustrated rock musicians to focus on jazz instead, which was seen by the authorities as a less threatening musical expression. This was one of the main factors, he argues, that led to the sudden vogue for jazz in Beijing. This point, I believe, requires further investigation; however, it is clear that the decline of Chinese rock around the mid-1990s stood in contrast to the expansion of Chinese jazz in the same period. This could be related to the specific political role that different musical styles play in China, and thus to the reaction of the state to these forms.

According to Baranovitch, during the 1990s the CCP's reaction to political challenges became more aggressive and repressive than hitherto; in the domains of culture and society, however, more liberties were granted. It is often suggested, he notes, that liberties in non-political aspects of life were tolerated so that people would abstain from political activities (Baranovitch 2003, 268–269). Arguably, this also meant that musicians who were independent of state politics, and thus less overtly controlled or suppressed, could focus better on their artistic work. This context of mutual passivity or toleration between the CCP and non-political music in China seems relevant when it comes to jazz, especially in the contemporary scene in Beijing. Around the time of the 2008 Olympic Games, for example, many cultural events and festivals in the city were cancelled or postponed. Certain bars and music clubs were closed; art galleries were ordered to remove provocative works from their walls; Olympic slogans decorated the avenues; crowded eateries in the old *hutong* lanes folded up their outdoor stools; and the regular *waidiren* merchants on the corners were replaced by jolly volunteers. Beijing was 'cleansed'; everything was ready; and life in the city seemed to be on hold.[10] As for jazz, however, business continued as usual. Official permits for festivals and concerts were granted without delay,[11] visiting musicians arrived to play, and the city's jazz clubs kept on swinging – no more than usual, but also no less.

334 Adiel Portugali

The limited scale of Beijing's jazz scene does not frame it as a tangible threat to political or social instability; however, its ongoing association with Chinese rock and certain genres of experimental music may relocate it, as least potentially, in the 'political zone'. The rock and the jazz scenes in the city have always been interrelated and sometimes even coalescent. Since the 1980s, some prominent rock musicians, such as Cui Jian, Liang Heping, Liu Yuan and Ren Yuqing, have also been pioneers of Chinese jazz, and vice versa. Even today, some leading jazz musicians, such as Xia Jia, Liu Yue, Beibei and Gao Xing, play with famous rock singers and bands. Similar bonds can be found in the corridors of the city's music institutes. The Beijing Midi School of Music and the Beijing Contemporary Music Academy (CMA),[12] for example, are the two major institutes for the study of both rock and jazz in the capital. In the late 1990s they began to integrate jazz studies into their curricula, and since then they have acted as melting pots for hundreds of students and teachers from all over the country. In some cases, the distinction between jazz, rock, fusion, improvisation and other musical styles in Beijing are indistinct. Some musicians and bands, such as Xia Jia, Li Tieqiao, Dou Wei, Bu Yiding, Xiao He, Fei Jia and Liang Heping, often venture across their generic musical borders and search for new musical directions, syntheses and sounds. None the less, while Chinese rock is commonly associated with political, social or individual criticism, Chinese jazz is not. It is important to emphasize that this is not to say that it is disconnected from the political, social, economic and musical realities within China. It is axiomatic that no expressive form exists in a power vacuum, outside either culture or history. Rather, it means that the CCP regards jazz differently from the way it regards other genres of popular music: that is, neither as a tool for propaganda nor as a subversive act of potential threat.

The notions of freedom and improvisation that typify jazz can be thought to stand in contrast to the conventional behavioural codes and homogeneous ideology the CCP wishes to promote. If jazz 'speaks' without words, if it expresses artistic freedom and spontaneous creativity and conveys individuality, then it may well entail, even partly and indirectly, rebellious feelings and thoughts. As mentioned above, skilled composers can articulate personal, social and even political criticism within their music. Thus, all the more, skilled jazz musicians can express rebellious feelings and ideas through improvisation, unpredictably and in real time. Moreover, the delicate subtext of the notion of freedom in jazz can raise ideas and associations that oppose the bureaucratic nature of political systems that are inclined towards totalitarian control. In fact, a number of jazz musicians in Beijing indicate that there is a conflict between the state's efforts to create homogeneity and standardization and the musicians' personal desire for musical creativity, spontaneity and originality. For instance, according to Liang Heping (2010, interview with author), the authorities in China detest freedom, improvisation or any other kind of expression that stands beyond their control. Pianist Moreno Donadel (2010, interview with author) says that the uniformity that the Chinese state promotes affects the behaviour of its citizens from an early age, and thus eventually shapes the character of the society. But playing jazz, he claims, is about free and fearless individual expression and not about uniformity and mechanical regimentation. Interestingly, however, most of the jazz musicians I interviewed or played with in Beijing, and elsewhere in China, associate freedom with musical conditions or a personal state of mind, and neglect (at least in public) political and social matters.

When Fei Jia (2010, interview with author) plays his guitar, for example, he feels free. It is not a conscious articulated sense, he says, but a spontaneous reaction that appears within the music. For drummer Izumi Koga (2010, interview with author), freedom is an instinctive and experiential condition that detaches him from reality. When he reaches this state of mind, he feels as if he is looking at himself from above. Huang Yong (2010, interview with author) claims that there is no connection between politics and the way musicians in China play jazz, saying that he never experienced political pressure or restrictions, either as a festival producer or as a jazz musician. The ability (or inability) to compose jazz, improvise and play expressive solos, he argues, is related solely to the skills, experience and depth of the musician. When Huang improvises or plays a solo, for example, he does not think about censorship, democracy or ideology, but about harmony, melody, rhythm and groove – namely, about the music. The link between jazz, freedom and politics in China, he believes, is forced and artificial; thus, he directs such related criticism back to the journalists and scholars (mainly from the West) who attempt to associate Chinese jazz with political affairs. People from abroad should come to Beijing and see the situation with their own eyes, he says, and only then should they judge.

Is It Commercial?

The relationship between music, state and capital power in modern China has been repeatedly discussed in studies of Chinese contemporary (mainly popular) music. In general, it is shown that this triangular link entails various generic, cultural, regional and, naturally, economic and political factors and interests. From the text above, it may be understood that in China pop music, state ideology and capital power go hand in hand, just as rock music, rebellious spirit and originality seem to be linked. In fact, in many cases, these connections do indeed hold good. But what happens, for instance, when the needs of the market stand in contrast to the ideology of the regime, and vice versa?

In the early 1980s, for example, the spread and popularity of *gangtai* in the PRC was not consistent with the official cultural policy of the state; it was unofficially disseminated without either the permission or the prohibition of the CCP. These light and tender pop songs were among the earliest musical

336 Adiel Portugali

expressions to enter post-Maoist China from the outside world (see note 9), and thus they were a challenge to the cultural hegemony of the state. People no longer depended exclusively on state-controlled radio, television, films and official performances to view entertainment and art. The simple technology of tape cassettes and the relatively low costs involved in obtaining audio recordings opened alternative and unofficial channels for new music, knowledge and culture (Baranovitch 2003, 13). At times, the Ministry of Culture launched educational campaigns against 'spiritual pollution' and the spread of pop culture (for example, in 1983 and 1985) and updated its regulations relating to the production, sale and dissemination of music, which also affected other fields of the performing arts. For example, some works of Tan Dun, one of China's most celebrated composers, were temporarily banned (Melvin and Cai 2004, 414). However, these clampdowns did not prevent the expansion of *gangtai* and the rise of Chinese pop.

China's rapidly expanding free market and cultural exchange with the outside world led to the appearance of a new sector of private entrepreneurs (*getihu*) and thus to the emergence of informal entertainment industries, which included the reappearance of night-clubs and dance halls. These developments inspired musicians to play outside of their work units. Some left the *danwei* simply to earn extra money, while others did so to gain more artistic freedom (Baranovitch 2003, 13–18). Eventually, the influential power and profitability of pop songs and the growing music industry in China led the CCP to modify its stance and join the trend. In 1986 Chinese pop was officially legitimized when it was presented as one of the categories in an annual state-run CCTV singing competition (Baranovitch 2003, 18). Accordingly, since the mid-1980s the Chinese authorities have succeeded in exploiting popular music both politically and economically. This demonstrates, on the one hand, the recuperative power of the CCP, and, on the other, that the power of the market can trump official policy, even in China. In this context, apparently, jazz is not so relevant. The state-controlled and -directed music industry does not count the genre as either politically useful or potentially commercial.

In the course of the 1990s, China accelerated its gallop towards modernization, professionalism and economic development. The start of this 'post-socialist' phase is often linked to Deng Xiaoping's 'southern visit' in 1992 and his encouraging call for the nation to 'grow rich' and speed up China's reform. According to Baranovitch, the new free-market economy and interaction with the capitalist, democratic West weakened the state's control over China's society and culture, but the interests of the state and the interests of the market were not necessarily opposed to each other (Baranovitch 2003, 215, 234, 268). De Kloet argues that in the 1990s the CCP's policies were implicated in processes of commercialization and transnationalization, and '*the people* gradually turned into *consumer-citizens*' (De Kloet 2010, 168–169; original emphasis). Ironically, music was no longer made to 'serve the people' (*wei renmin fuwu*), as declared by Mao Zedong in Yanan in 1942, but to 'serve the people's money (RMB)' (*wei renminbi fuwu*) (Huang 2001, 2). The rapid economic growth came with further flows of information, technology, foreign capital and products, followed by rising waves of commercialism and consumerism. This was a turning point for China's music industry and popular culture as a whole, and a period of change and expansion for jazz in Beijing. The mass media and the music industry, and record labels from Hong Kong and Taiwan, steered the music culture in the urban centres. Imported, as well as fake, tapes and CDs, and the emergence of *dakou*[13] albums, flooded the burgeoning PRC market with new musical styles and tunes. The growing population in the metropolitan areas precipitated the emergence of new socio-economic groups that wished to distinguish their status and differentiate themselves from the mass. The '*dakou* generation' (De Kloet 2010, 19) of musicians and youth in Beijing found common ground, for example, in rock, metal, punk, folk, hip-hop and dance scenes, while other 'arty' and *nouveau riche* groups adapted jazz, which they felt was more sophisticated and high class (Shi 2010, interview with author; Liang 2010, interview with author; Rea 1999, 131).

In 1993 the first Beijing International Jazz Festival was launched (*beijing guoji jueshiyue jicui*; literally, Beijing International Jazz Series). The public interest in and positive reviews for the festival led its organizer to turn it into an annual event and over subsequent years local musicians participated as well. In this period the jazz scene in Beijing reached new peaks of musical quality and musician quantity. The festivals contributed to public awareness of jazz in the city and encouraged businessmen, musicians and fans to expand the scene in the public sphere: on the one hand, intimate and affordable venues, such as the CD Jazz Café, the Sanwei bookstore and the Keep in Touch Club were founded; on the other, concerts were also held in formal theatres and concert halls, such as the Beijing Concert Hall, the Forbidden City Concert Hall and the Haidian Theatre (Zhu 2010, interview with author; Shi 2010, interview with author; Liang 2010, interview with author).

However, despite the musical advances and the expansion of the scene, it appeared that jazz in Beijing still could not pay the bills. In 2001, the festival ceased, and jazz concerts in bars and clubs were not as frequent or as prominent as previously. Some musicians played in hotel lobbies instead, or joined pop and rock bands. Others left Beijing or abandoned their instruments. Below the surface, however, the spirit of jazz in the capital continued to brew and in the mid-2000s a new generation of music students and graduates started to step onto the city's stages. At that time, veteran musicians also began to organize new projects and a number of expatriate musicians joined the scene and contributed to its general progress. Suddenly, a fresh jazzy vibe drifted across the capital and its results were cheering. In 2005, a number of jazz musicians, among them Liu Yuan, Huang Yong, Kong Hongwei, Jin Hao and Xia Jia, formed a committee to organize a new jazz festival and bring jazz back to the

338 Adiel Portugali

capital. A year later, Huang founded the Nine Gates International Jazz Festival, which has since become the main annual jazz event in Beijing. In something of an echo of the path of Chinese jazz in the 1990s, the scene expanded, festivals were launched, new clubs opened – most notably Liu Yuan's East Shore Live Jazz Café, which became *the* centre of jazz activity in Beijing – jam sessions continued into the night and the quality of musicianship improved. Even so, once again, it appeared that jazz in Beijing was not profitable.

On a freezing yet sunny afternoon in winter 2010, sitting with Huang Yong in his office overlooking a pleasant courtyard near Xinjiekou Street, I asked him what had gone wrong. He replied:

> I've been putting on this festival for four years. In the first year, we sold 3,000 tickets and thought that in the following year things would improve. In the second year, we sold 4,000 tickets. In the third year, we still sold 4,000 tickets; and in the fourth year, again, 4,000. So now I know, with respect to jazz and modern music . . . there is no market. There is no business. So, now, we have to think what to do.
>
> *(Huang 2010, interview with author)*

Later, while sipping a cup of cheering brewed coffee, Huang tried to clarify why Beijing is in this situation. He explained that the devoted work of the musicians and the good vibes towards and growing awareness of jazz in the city are not reflected when it comes to business. He believes that the city's jazz crowd consists mainly of people who identify themselves with the 'art circle': they attend festivals and special events, but they do not support or care about the local scene. Liang Heping (2010, interview with author) notes that jazz in China will never reach the 'big mass' (*dazhong*). It does not serve the interests of the market, he says; it is not connected to capital forces or the mass media, and thus it subsists among a 'small mass' (*xiaozhong*). According to Moreno Donadel (2010, interview with author), jazz in Beijing is uneconomic because it demands deep concentration, thought and time. Many businessmen wish to gain prompt financial returns from the *nouveau riche*, he explains, so they try to attach an elitist image to jazz in Beijing and direct the scene towards trendy, luxurious clubs. But Donadel's experience has taught him that jazz invariably fails in such spaces; it needs to be hosted in music-oriented and affordable places.

This, however, leads to an inevitable question: why *should* jazz be popular and profitable in China? Izumi Koga (2010, interview with author) claims that the limited popularity of the genre in Beijing is explained by the fact that jazz is based on simplicity, not on superstars. At the same time, he notes that he is unconcerned that the scene might become commercial in the future. Furthermore, Fei Jia (2010, interview with author) believes that there is no contradiction between good music, popularity, money and fame. One should be realistic, he says, and find a balance between artistic and commercial musical practices. Drummer Yong Hengwu (2010, interview with author), however, argues that money and fame are not among the main goals of Beijing's jazz musicians. When they compose, form bands and work on new concerts or albums, he says, they know that they will never make a fortune. Rather, the main motivation for these musicians derives simply from their love of playing.

The marginal position of the jazz scene in Beijing makes life tough for its members and harms its reputation among potential young musicians. Some of the music teachers and musicians I interviewed for this study revealed that many Chinese students pick their field of specialization entirely on economic grounds.[14] As a result, the number of students who choose jazz is generally quite low. Moreover, according to the Midi School's founder and director Zhang Fan (2010, interview with author), even though there are only a few jazz graduates every year, the scene in Beijing is so small that most of these young musicians cannot find work and eventually cease to play. Moreno Donadel (2010, interview with author) explains that many of his students at CMA live under social and existential pressures. He stresses that some of them come from low socio-economic classes and cannot afford to play jazz because they have families to support. And Huang Yong (2010, interview with author) notes that even wealthy parents refuse to let their kids learn jazz. The escalating cost of living in Beijing, he says, makes it almost impossible to pursue a career in jazz, even for the veterans. According to Yong Hengwu (2010, interview with author), musicians' constant worrying about the market does not leave them much time or mental space to 'dig in' the inner layers of the music they play, with the result that their integrity and creativity are often distorted or eroded. The perpetual pursuit of cash and success, he argues, makes people dishonest, not only to each other, but also to themselves.

So What (Is It)?

The marginal position and image of jazz in Beijing is a consequence of a wide range of political, social, cultural, economic and musical factors. This is evident from academic works on contemporary music in China, and from the insiders' perspective of the capital's jazz musicians. The first two sections of this chapter explore a political context in which music can act as a conveyor of political ideology, or stand against it. In both cases, however, it appears that jazz is not seen as serving or entailing clear political interests; it is not used for state-sponsored political propaganda and it does not incorporate explicit subversive messages. Therefore, I suggest that rather than the political it is the *non-political* position of jazz in Beijing that causes its marginalization. The third section shows that it does not necessarily matter if jazz (or any other genre) is artistically valuable, politically correct or rebelliously shocking. What really matters is whether it is profitable. At present, jazz in Beijing is neither commercially significant nor profitable. In order to develop, gain popularity and become

340 Adiel Portugali

profitable, jazz musicians in Beijing have long sought governmental recognition and support for their activities. Paradoxically, though, in order to obtain this official recognition and support, they first need to develop their scene, gain popularity and be profitable.

The findings of this study may disappoint those who wish to observe music in China from a political perspective. Perhaps certain words and connotations sound more powerful, and appealingly exotic, when articulated under the red flag than they sound in the West. Yet, as Bruce Johnson suggests in his Afterword, these superficially disappointing findings might well be profoundly instructive for contemporary re-theorizations of the political dimensions of jazz. Furthermore, it appears that music genres in China that are not distinctively political, rebellious or economic are usually not particularly 'interesting'. In fact, since the 1990s, dozens of studies on genres of contemporary music in China have been published, but almost none has focused on jazz. It seems that music genres in China that do not gain political, economic and indeed academic attention are left off the map, hidden in the margins, as if they do not exist.

In sum, I suggest that jazz in China is marginal not because of tension and negotiation with political ideologies, but rather because it is not distinctively political, rebellious or commercial. In other words, Chinese jazz is marginalized not because it is politically active or dangerous, but because it is politically *passive* and does not serve the interests of the market and the state. The 'bottom-up' findings of this study remind us that individual views and perspectives should not be ignored in academic research. It exposes new angles for understanding the complex relationship Chinese people have with their state, as seen and experienced from within, and more specifically it reveals that the means and thoughts of jazz musicians in Beijing *might* be implicated in political, patriotic, rebellious and economic factors, but not necessarily. These jazz musicians compose, improvise, play solos and interact with other musicians from China and around the world. While following the music, they too can feel free, imagine stories, envision places and sense or 'hear' different colours that go beyond the range of gold, blue and red.

Notes

1 They did so, for example, by establishing and supporting (or neglecting) research associations and education centres, such as the Beijing University Research Group (1919), the Institute for the Promotion and Practice of Music at Beijing University (1921) and the Shanghai Conservatory of Music (1927), and professional volumes and journals, such as *Music Magazine* (*yinyue zazhi*); see Jones 2001, 36, 42–45; Melvin and Cai 2004, 106–111.

2 *Guomindang* (*Kuomintang*), founded in 1911 by Sun Yat-Sen and Song Jiaoren.

3 *Zhongguo gongchandang*, founded in 1921 by Chen Duxiu and Li Dazhao.

4 This is not to say, however, that jazz was the only or the main music form under attack. The criticism of the leftist scholars and the CCP (see examples below) was not specific but directed towards Western 'new' music as whole.

5 Their desired model of proletarian music was 'updated' and characterized during the mid–late 1950s, following the second major debate on mass culture (proletariat versus bourgeois) that took place among members of the CCP, and in accordance with Mao Zedong's criteria of socialist mass culture; see Hong 1994, 92–96.

6 Lü Ji's speech was presented at the Second Representatives' Conference of the Chinese Musicians' Association, as reported in *People's Music Journal*, July–August 1960; see Yang 2007, 9.

7 A social movement of Mao's young supporters who mobilized during the early stages of the Cultural Revolution; see Shai 1998; Clark 2008; Kraus 2012.

8 This is not to say that instrumental music cannot be or was not utilized by the state. On classical music that serves the regime, for example, see Mittler 1997, 78–116.

9 Apparently, the sweet and romantic *gangtai* songs of the late 1970s and early 1980s gained popularity due to a natural and indirect reaction to the repressive cultural policies of the Cultural Revolution; see Baranovitch 2003, 18; Brace and Friedlander 1992, 17.

10 In fact, these were among the most tranquil, silent and still days I experienced during my four years in Beijing.

11 According to the deputy general manager of the Forbidden City Concert Hall, Zhu Jing (2010, interview with author), the authorities' attitude to jazz in this period was generally positive and the procedures to obtain approvals for jazz events were similar to those for classical and traditional music. This does not mean that people in the Ministry of Culture Affairs are fond of jazz music, but rather that organizing jazz events in Beijing is a matter of bureaucratic process.

12 Both established in 1993.

13 The *dakou* ('cut') albums were discarded cassettes and CDs from the West that were smuggled into China and nicked ('*dakoued*') by a device to mark them as not for sale.

14 Donadel, Koga, Zhang and Shi (2010, interviews with author), among other interviewees in different cities around China.

References

Abbas, Ackbar. 2000. 'Cosmopolitan De-scriptions: Shanghai and Hong Kong'. *Public Culture* 12(3): 769–786.

Baranovitch, Nimrod. 2003. *China's New Voices: Popular Music, Ethnicity, Gender and Politics, 1978–1997*. Berkeley: University of California Press.

Barmé, Geremie. 1999. *In the Red: On Contemporary Chinese Culture*. New York: Columbia University Press.

Bergère, Marie-Claire. 2009. *Shanghai: China's Gateway to Modernity*. Stanford, CA: Stanford University Press.

Brace, Timothy L. and Paul Friedlander. 1992. 'Rock and Roll on the New Long March: Popular Music, Cultural Identity and Political Opposition in the People's Republic of China'. In *Rockin' the Boat: Mass Music and Mass Movements*. Ed. Rebee Garofalo. Boston, MA: South End Press: 115–128.

Chen, Szu-Wei. 2005. 'The Rise and Generic Features of Shanghai Popular Songs in the 1930s and 1940s'. *Popular Music* 24(1): 107–125.

Chen, Szu-Wei. 2007. 'The Music Industry and Popular Song in 1930s and 1940s Shanghai: A Historical and Stylistic Analysis'. Ph.D. dissertation, University of Stirling.

Clark, Paul. 2008. *The Chinese Cultural Revolution: A History*. Cambridge: Cambridge University Press.

De Kloet, Jeroen. 2010. *China with a Cut: Globalization, Urban Youth and Popular Music*. Amsterdam: Amsterdam University Press.

342 Adiel Portugali

Field, Andrew. 2009. *Shanghai's Dancing World: Cabaret Culture and Urban Politics, 1919–1954*. Hong Kong: The Chinese University Press.

Fung, Anthony Y. H. 2008. *Global Capital, Local Culture: Transnational Media Corporations in China*. New York: Peter Lang.

Harris, Rachel. 2005. 'Reggae on the Silk Road: The Globalization of Uyghur Pop'. *China Quarterly* 183: 627–643.

Hong, Junhao. 1994. 'Mao Zedong's Cultural Theory and China's Three Mass-Culture Debates: A Tentative Study of Culture, Society and Politics'. *Intercultural Communication Studies* 4(2): 86–104.

Huang, Hao. 2001. '*Yaogun Yinyue*: Rethinking Mainland Chinese Rock 'n' Roll'. *Popular Music* 21(1): 1–11.

Jones, Andrew F. 1992. *Like a Knife: Ideology and Genre in Contemporary Chinese Popular Music*. Ithaca, NY: Cornell University Press.

Jones, Andrew F. 2001. *Yellow Music: Media Culture and Colonial Modernity in the Chinese Jazz Age*. Durham, NC: Duke University Press.

Komlosy, Anouska. 2008. 'Yunnanese Sounds: Creativity and Alterity in the Dance and Music Scenes of Urban Yunnan'. *China: An International Journal* 6(1): 44–68.

Kraus, Curt R. 1989. *Pianos and Politics in China: Middle-Class Ambitions and the Struggle over Western Music*. New York: Oxford University Press.

Kraus, Curt R. 2012. *The Cultural Revolution: A Very Short Introduction*. New York: Oxford University Press.

Liu, Jingzhi. 2010. *A Critical History of New Music In China*. Hong Kong: Chinese University Press.

Mao, Yuran. 1991. 'Music under Mao: Its Background and Aftermath'. *Asian Music* 22(2): 97–125.

Melvin, Shelia and Jindong Cai. 2004. *Rhapsody in Red: How Western Classical Music Became Chinese*. New York: Algora Publishing.

Mittler, Barbara. 1997. *Dangerous Tunes: The Politics of Chinese Music in Hong Kong, Taiwan, and the People's Republic of China since 1949*. Wiesbaden: Harrassowitz Verlag.

Moskowitz, Marc L. 2010. *Cries of Joy, Songs of Sorrow: Chinese Pop Music and its Cultural Connotations*. Honolulu: University of Hawaii Press.

Rea, Dennis. 1999. 'The LAND Tour and the Rise of Jazz in China'. *CHIME Journal* 10: 129–138.

Rea, Dennis. 2006. *Live at the Forbidden City: Musical Encounters in China and Taiwan*. New York: iUniverse.

Rea, Dennis. 2013. 'Ambushed from All Sides: Rock Music as a Force for Change in China'. In *The Routledge History of Social Protest in Popular Music*. Ed. Jonathan C. Friedman. New York: Routledge: 373–386.

Shai, Aron. 1998. *Twentieth-Century China*. Tel Aviv: MOD Press (in Hebrew).

Schell, Orville. 1994. *Mandate of Heaven: China's Long March to the Twenty-first Century*. New York: Simon & Schuster.

Wang, Qian. 2007. 'The Crises of Chinese Rock in the Mid-1990s: Weakness in Form or Weakness in Content?' Ph.D. dissertation, University of Liverpool.

Wasserstrom, Jeffrey N. 2009. *Global Shanghai, 1850–2010: A History in Fragments*. New York: Routledge.

Yang, Honlun. 2007. 'Power, Politics and Musical Commemoration: Western Musical Figures in the People's Republic of China 1949–1964'. *Music and Politics* 1(2): 1–14.

Interviews with Author

Donadel, Moreno. 9 March 2010. Beijing (English).
Fei Jia. 9 February 2010. Beijing (Chinese).
Huang Yong. 9 February 2010. Beijing (Chinese).
Koga, Izumi. 20 March 2010. Beijing (English).
Liang Heping. 17 March 2010. Beijing (Chinese).
Shi, Simon. 12 February 2010. Beijing (Chinese).
Xia Jia. 31 March 2010. Beijing (Chinese and English).
Yong Hengwu (a.k.a. Beibei). 29 March 2010. Beijing (Chinese and English).
Zhang Fan. 19 March 2010. Beijing (English).
Zhu Jing. 11 March 2010. Beijing (English).

15

AFTERWORD

Conclusions

Bruce Johnson

Whitney Balliett famously described jazz as the sound of surprise. Not only surprise for the audiences; any jazz musician will recognise the experience of self-surprise, of heading home from a gig wondering, 'Where did that come from?' But this editing exercise has also been the sound of surprise for me. I wrote the Introduction as a component of the proposal about a year before the book came together. I began to draft this Afterword as the chapters, in at least early draft form, came in. The result is surprise – a combination of what the parameters might be expected to produce and what I simply had not foreseen at all.

Inevitably, many of the propositions in the Introduction are generally borne out in the foregoing articles: the importance of mass media, of the local politics and its relationship to the United States, the history of national identity, the economics of the entertainment industry, postcolonial dynamics, gender issues. Framing them all is the proposition that both jazz and totalitarianism emerged during – and are in significant ways emblematic of – the twentieth century, and together they embody its contradictions. One pulls towards freedom of expression, the other towards regulation and homogeneity. Of all music genres up to the appearance of rock in the mid-twentieth century, if any music carried a message that challenged that political vehicle of modernity – totalitarianism – it was jazz. And the ideal citizen of the totalitarian state recalls T. E. Lawrence's description of the soldier, who 'assigned his owner the twenty-four hours' use of his body; and sole conduct of his mind and passions' (Lawrence 2000, 551). All these at least according to their *mythos*, if not always effectively in their practice. When the two converged, they dramatised the central tensions of modernity, between the cult of individualism and the pressures of mass culture. To a greater extent than any other musical form, in the first half of

Afterword: Conclusions **345**

the twentieth century jazz was the Aeolian harp sounding the harmonies and discords of the complex winds of modernity. Similarly, wherever it manifested itself, the push towards totalitarianism was a major experiment in modernisation, an 'alternative modernity'.

Unsurprisingly however, in light of recent developments in both jazz historiography and the theorisation of totalitarianism, it becomes clear that the simplistic binary that pits heroic jazz in resistance against state oppression is deeply misleading. As a public event, the case of Charlie Haden (Chapter 10) appears to present a straightforward dichotomy of jazz as a protest against a repressive state. But the shared public gestures at the festival, initiated by 'outsiders' (the US musicians), do not reflect the internal complexities of the relationship between jazz and the regime. Rather, in the way that the 'classic' models of totalitarianism, written from the outside, simplify the actual conditions of life and the political dynamics that frame them under the regime, so too in this Portuguese narrative. As all the other case studies suggest, the picture is not so simple, and a range of other lines of force are also active in the way jazz and the regime negotiated, including the presence of colonial participants, internal local dynamics, ambiguous tensions between the state's political and cultural objectives, and the encounter between the agenda of the foreign musicians who had a well-intentioned but reductive view of the politics, and local conditions which were more multifaceted.

In the Introduction I discussed the protean character of both jazz and totalitarian regimes over time and place. From region to region, from nation to nation, and even within individual nations and micro-communities, the two categories are experienced and practised in ways that are ever-varying. If it is difficult to fix either of them individually, it is impossible to fix them in relation to each other. The foregoing studies, both individually and as a collection, document this fluidity. As such, they incontrovertibly dissolve the encrusted clichés in the popular jazz/totalitarianism dichotomy. The schematic opposition between jazz and state repression, the image of jazz as embodying freedom in the face of a monolithic totalitarian apparatus, remains a place to start, but it does not carry us very far into an understanding of the lived dynamics of that relationship.

There is no question that jazz was seen as some kind of threat to political totalism, and perhaps this is most aggressively disclosed physically. The fact that the music is so predominantly instrumental, bearing no explicit lexical messages, raises very provocative questions regarding the bio-politics of sound itself. The distinctive ability of sonic modalities to trouble power blocs has been studied (Johnson and Cloonan 2008), and in this volume Eato (Chapter 11) addresses the politics of the trope of silence in the confrontation between jazz and the state. But to date little work has been done on the distinctive phenomenology and physiology of sound in relation to jazz, its often hostile reception, and new theories of cognition that challenge the mind/body duality. Given arguments about the synergies between new cognitive theory and sonic experience (see, for example, Johnson 2015), and the ecstatic nature of much jazz dance, there seems to be a very promising line of enquiry here. Little attention is paid to the political and cognitive dimensions of jazz dance, especially since the music has sought its aesthetic validation in the cerebral, with explicit scorn for 'toe-tapping' music. It is as dance that jazz makes perhaps its most visible protest against a politics of repression. The power of dance is implied in the joke about why the Methodists object to sex: because it could lead to dancing. And few images more clearly summarised the threat to traditional values in the early twentieth century than that of the jazz-dancing woman (Johnson 2000, 59–76). In their discussions of jazz dance, of what could be called the relationship between the political body and the body politic, Iglesias and Roxo (Chapters 7 and 9) open the door to such enquiry: jazz as a dance, and the dance as an ultimate site of transgressive autonomy.

While this literal embodiment of jazz proclaims its powerful agency most directly, that agency also emerges in other forms of confrontation between jazz and the state, as argued in several of the essays in this collection (especially Chapters 1 and 7). Not only as a set of social practices, but simply as a way of imagining life, jazz set up alternatives that challenged repression by positing a balance between individualism and collectivity (see Chapters 8, 10 and 12). Even the conceptual stereotypes of 'the jazz life' played an important role in the counter-imaginary to totalitarianism. Much energy has recently been invested in debunking the jazz stereotype of the outsider – the defiant and often socially dysfunctional individualist. The cliché of the obsessively, self-damagingly driven performer persists in the jazz mythology as exemplified in the recent movie *Whiplash*. This jazz imaginary might be a romanticised fiction in relation to the actual 'jazz life', but it had the power to inspire behaviours, valorisations and political gestures in a feedback loop. The enduring complex operation of colour in jazz mythology illustrates the point (see, for example, Dueck 2014). Chapters 7 and 8 incidentally remind us of the role of the cliché of jazz musician as outsider and the extent to which individuals and groups perform to these mythologies, especially in the face of a repressive state. To dismiss, wholesale, such stereotypes as misleading screens concealing some assumed reality is to forget that the 'reality' is also, to a significant extent, shaped by the stereotype, that 'performance', in every sense, is also scripted by clichés. Jazz musicians are equally likely to 'perform' to stereotypes of argot and demeanour, without necessarily being in other respects hipster rebels; and in fact, as circumstances change, they can become 'rebels without a cause' (Chapter 4). The stereotype is still powerful in determining agency and identity. Indeed, in an interesting twist on the image of jazz as the gesture of freedom, confronted by repression it can itself begin to function as a new counter-imperium, an institutionalised canon and repertoire of gestures that constrain the freedoms the music supposedly fosters (Chapters 10 and 12).

Afterword: Conclusions **347**

If jazz can be both an agent and a register of change, this is partly because it has always been a chameleon, adapting to circumstances to powerful effect. In its relationship with the state it has shown itself to be capable of assuming very heterogeneous forms and syncretisms. Especially since reversing its momentum from fission to fusion from the 1960s, it does not sit in some pristine, static and stately privilege as a beacon of freedom in the landscape, but occupies many different spaces and valorisations, showing a degree of adaptability that again challenges the essentialist models that long underpinned jazz discourse. One outcome of the confrontation with totalitarian forces is therefore, ironically, a rich diversification of the music into new forms which do not just reflect the ideological context but help to shape it (Chapter 1), (re-)coalescing with adjacent forms, whether native or other imported traditions like the blues (Chapter 8). Jazz outside the United States is in the proper sense of the word fully *viable* – able to generate its own independent 'life forms' evolving out of local political and cultural dynamics relating to such issues as religion, colonialism and adjacent power blocs. As Eato demonstrates in Chapter 11, it is possible to identify some of these changes through musicological analysis. These local blooms include regionally generated networks, bypassing the US 'source', in generating not only distinctive performance practices and infrastructures but the aesthetic and critical discourses of jazz, very much shaped by the repressive local, regional and national politics that framed them. The mediating impact of the Hot Club de France exemplifies the point, providing a model for the music and its networks, but a distinctive regional jazz with no conspicuous specific US analogue (see Chapters 7–10).

This shape-changing was part of the processes that characterise all diasporic jazz in its negotiations, in this case with a putatively totalitarian rigidity. I emphasise 'putative' because the other party to the negotiation also found it expedient to make practical tactical adaptations as the regime recognised the need to come to some kind of accommodation with the 'alternative modernities' which twentieth-century media forced it to confront. Radio and recordings in particular created cultural traffic over global distances and which recognised no regional or political boundaries in the diffusion of the quintessential new music of modernity – jazz (see, for example, Chapter 11). The combination of the medium and the music disclosed the tensions between the objectives of the authorities who sought to deploy radio as an instrument of total control and the unintended consequences of opening this Pandora's box which broke down the borders so zealously patrolled by totalitarian regimes (see especially Chapter 1). Goebbels recognised this 'jazz dilemma', declaring: 'What the press was to the nineteenth century, radio will be to the twentieth' (cited Bergmeier and Lotz 1997, 6). Radio was a crucial medium in promoting the Nazi cause, but equally Goebbels realised its ambiguous effects, especially as a disseminator of jazz. Since the German people could not be quarantined from this degenerate music, he established a state-sponsored broadcasting swing outfit, Charlie and

His Orchestra, who played US melodies with new propaganda lyrics (ibid., especially 136–137). The apparently simple 'jazz/totalitarianism' binary was thus constantly intersected and complicated by mutual adaptations taking place within communities and nations, the different 'cultural spaces of action', as deployed so effectively by Reimann in her study of jazz in Sovietised Estonia (Chapter 3): within any single national community, there are many levels of social practice and agency, and indeed individuals can strategically operate on more than one of these at the same time.

Likewise, national borders meant nothing to electronic media; hence the oft-noted impact of Voice of America radio programmes (Chapters 2, 4, 5 and 6). But all power blocs cast shadows. O'Dair's study of Finland (Chapter 6) – never a totalitarian society – begins with this hypothesis, which is entirely reasonable, given that the general pattern in studies of diasporic jazz is to attribute so much authority to the 'shadow' of the United States, a country that is generally far more remote from the case study than the USSR. Likewise, studies of jazz behind the Iron Curtain are predicated on the same 'shadow', and that can be cast even where an adjacent country was not Sovietised. What emerges is the perhaps slightly dismaying disclosure that the influence of that totalitarian shadow is ambiguous. But this is by no means an insignificant finding, since it tests and adds to our assumptions about cross-cultural influences and the musical expression of national identity. It is clear that many Finnish jazz musicians chose, consciously or unconsciously, to explore approaches that were independent of the US models. The tendency has been to think of these approaches in terms of national identity, national folk forms. But that model of inward-turning nationalism is not enough, since identity is also shadowed, incontestably but indefinably, by external and adjacent power relations, and not only with the United States. The case of Karelia embodies the point. The region is both central in the formation of national identity, largely because of the light cast by the work of Lönnrot and his followers, but with a complex reverberation arising from the Soviet annexation of Viipuri/Vyborg in the wake of the Continuation War. It is a site of both light and shadow. Finnish jazz provides an instructive case study in the subtleties of the dynamics of cultural and political diaspora, of the dangers of, in the metaphor used by Aunesluoma, seeing such processes through a single 'keyhole' (quoted in Gilmour and Stephenson 2013, 214).

The 'keyholes' that give access to an understanding of the shifting relationships between jazz and the totalist state are in fact beyond counting. However rigidly ideology is articulated, it also has to accommodate economic, technological and cultural factors, as well as simple human unpredictability and/or cunning. In all of the studies in this collection the relationship between jazz and the authorities is characterised by adaptations according to changing local and international conditions. There is nothing especially new in this insight: witness Starr's pioneering study of jazz in the Soviet Union, published

Afterword: Conclusions **349**

over thirty years ago (Starr 1983). But while Starr's emphasis was on shifts in the state's position, in these studies we are reminded that it took two to tango, and that the jazz community itself made strategic adjustments in a subtle pas de deux with the state. This often involved subterfuge, but also some-times produced a *rapprochement* between the two parties, and musical syncretisms that became new jazz forms. Perhaps one of the most startling outcomes was that the practice recognised as jazz became part of the regime's culture, a stabilising principle (see Chapters 2 and 5). These studies have thus given added momentum to re-theorisations not only of totalitarianism that challenge further the traditional top-down model but also of jazz essentialism and purism.

Not only is each of those terms open to question; it appears that the longer the diasporic journey in cultural terms, the more the binary itself that frames this collection is challenged, suggesting that it may itself be a Western solip-sism. I want to take a little more space to consider this. Culturally and politi-cally, the two essays in the part titled 'To the East' consider the longest diasporic journey. Partly for this reason, the lessons they provide are at the same time more diffuse, yet potentially radical in the global exploration of the jazz/totalitarian dynamic. In both cases, the outlines of that dynamic are fainter, yet they open the most unexpected doors of exploration. Or, to change to the aural modality which I think is probably essential to those enquiries, they are sufficiently far from the noise of US-centric discourses for us to hear faint but important messages.

Gay Breyley's historical review of jazz in Iran (Chapter 13) underlines the evasiveness of jazz as a set of musical practices, sucking a wide range of Western popular music genres into the semiotics of the music. To accept the term 'jazz' as a geographical and historical constant would very clearly be to misunderstand something constitutive of the diasporic process. Of all musical forms, jazz has been the most pervasive vehicle in the global emergence of modernity from the early twentieth century. But if we are to form a useful understanding of that crucial role, it is more important to respect divergent views as to what comprises jazz than to set up a purist definition of what, musically, it comprises. And it appears from Breyley's study that the farther the music moves away from the 'source', the more instructively heterogeneous that understanding becomes, as the multiple 'Other' becomes homogenised, and the function of jazz as a distinct genre in the pre-modern/modern dynamic will be less evident. In the case of the Iranian performer Vigen, as set out by Breyley, there is a fine lesson in the chameleon identity of jazz, and also in the reciprocal construction of 'Otherness', and it is encrypted in the convergence of East and West in the key words of the phrase 'Sultan of Jazz'. To Western ears, Vigen's music generally sounds like what we would hear in a generically 'Eastern' restaurant; yet, to the ears of Iranians, it was so clearly Western as to be suppressed as such. And it is the word 'jazz' that finds itself at that instructively complex interface. The fact that 'jazz' as it is understood in Western discourses is barely recognisable

350 Bruce Johnson

in the Iranian case even though it is explicitly deployed again reminds us of how instructive that long diasporic journey can be.

Similarly, Portugali's overview of jazz in contemporary China (Chapter 14), which argues that jazz simply does not have sufficient political, ideological or economic loading for the state to care much about it any more. Portugali's survey of jazz in contemporary Beijing arrives at conclusions that he predicts some might find 'disappointing': that is, that the Chinese government simply has no ideological interest in jazz. Yet, it could well be that this apparently un-arresting conclusion is in fact highly provocative of further theorisations. I suggest that, as in the case of Breyley's arguments about Iran, Portugali's apparently undramatic conclusions open questions for further revelations about the totalitarian/jazz relationship, especially outside the West. That is: it is notable that this new relaxation about and virtual indifference towards jazz seem to coincide with communist China's entry into its capitalist phase. Prior to the 'open-door' policy introduced in 1979, jazz in China was constrained by an ideological framework. The new regime has encouraged free markets, a course that carries with it the ascendancy of profit-driven cultural policy: as Portugali writes about the contemporary jazz scene, 'What really matters . . . is whether it is profitable.' And even more provocative of further research: as a totalitarian state enters into the global capitalist economy, does this affect its attitudes to an art form which has been held to be the musical embodiment of the greatest exemplar of modern capitalism? These are very large and speculative questions, but Portugali's case study raises them, and suggests some extremely interesting lines for future, extended enquiry.

If the totalitarian complexion is changing, so is jazz itself. Other forms of lyric-driven popular music remain under official scrutiny in China. As an instrumental music, as Portugali points out, any political critique contained in jazz is indirect. But in any case, perhaps jazz itself, as now generally understood, and many 'jazz' musicians have simply lost some contrarian energy. It is worth briefly observing the controversy that surrounded Kenny G's visit to China in 2014, a year after the period covered by Portugali's study. There are obvious and highly instructive differences between the forces at work in the persecution of jazz musicians who understand the dissenting thrust of their activity in the Soviet Bloc or Nazi Germany, and the situation of the internationally and commercially highly successful Kenny G. The latter is massively popular in China, and it is relevant here that a substantial proportion of his exposure is reportedly through commercial 'Muzak' situations: 'One of his tunes, "Going Home", is played in shopping malls and train stations at closing time, and is even used as a ringtone or a doorbell chime' (Chan 2014). While in China, his 'offence' arose from stumbling across the Occupy Central protests, evidently while sight-seeing, among which he was photographed and posed for 'selfies'. Occupy Central – a campaign of civil disobedience seeking universal suffrage – was active in Hong Kong in 2013–2014. It chose as its occupation site the centre of Hong Kong's business district, and the most strident public opposition came from business groups and tycoons who focused on the damage the campaigners were doing to the international reputation of Hong Kong as a major financial centre (see, for example, Fox 2014). (A reasonable place to begin – and I stress 'begin' – an examination of the movement is at 'Occupy Central with Love and Peace' n.d.)

The controversy Kenny G generated bears comparison with the case of another US musician who visited a totalitarian regime and became implicated in local politics: that of Charlie Haden over forty years earlier in Portugal (see Chapter 10). Haden, a long-time activist for whom music was a political weapon, purposefully used a jazz forum to make a statement against the Portuguese regime. Kenny G was another US musician visiting a country under totalitarian control, and he appeared at a protest site. These similarities make the differences even more dramatic. When G came under fire from the Chinese authorities for allowing himself to be photographed with the protesters, he was quick to declare that he did not understand the dynamic, and dissociated himself explicitly from any political alignment, reportedly tweeting: 'I was not trying to defy government orders with my last post . . . I don't really know anything about the situation and my impromptu visit to the site was just part of an innocent walk around Hong Kong' and 'It's unfair that I am being used by anyone to say that I am showing support for the demonstrators. I am not supporting the demonstrators' (Chan 2014). What was controversial was not simply that he visited the protest site, but that he so quickly dissociated himself from it, prompting one of the protesters to declare, insightfully: 'It comes across as if you are protecting your own capitalistic income and your own brand . . . yet Hong Kong is fighting for its life . . . Very disappointing and cowardly of you to offer this pathetic clarity.' Indeed, it does not appear that the authorities paid any attention to the event as *jazz-specific*. G was criticised not because he was a jazz musician, but because was a celebrity – one of a number of 'stars' from various fields who attracted censure. It was reported that 'Chinese propaganda officials have ordered state-run media to erase any mentions of 47 celebrities who are believed to support the Hong Kong protests, including martial arts star Chow Yun Fat' (Chan 2014).

The confrontation here is centred on a performer whose celebrity is based on commercial success. (And, unlike the case of Haden, many have questioned that 'jazz' achievement has anything to do with G's celebrity, most notably jazz guitarist Pat Metheny (see 'Pat Metheny on Kenny G' 2008). Indeed, is it possible to hear anything in G's 'Going Home' of the distinctive energy that critics of jazz throughout the twentieth century found so musically and politically confrontational?) In this case, the celebrity performer was accidentally caught in the cross-fire between two political forces – the regime and the protesters – and then dissociated himself from both. This is a very different dynamic from other cases explored in this collection, and gives some momentum to the

352 Bruce Johnson

speculation that it is entangled with issues of public image, tourism and capitalism rather than just artistic freedom against totalitarianism. Perhaps there are lessons here for the whole theorisation of jazz and totalitarianism in the context of global capitalism.

This collection is predicated on an active relationship between jazz and totalitarianism, with the general tendency to characterise that relationship as starting from negotiated antipathy. But the further we travel, culturally and geographically, from the 'centre' of these discourses – the West and especially the United States – the more the jazz/totalitarianism binary itself appears to be a discursive construction of the West, a model imposed globally from an 'imperial' centre. The dynamic cannot always and everywhere be couched in such convenient terms. As well as forming a heterogeneous range of permutations, it can also form none. In Iran, the first term in the binary, 'jazz', dissolves into the larger category of Western pop music. Portugali's study suggests that the sound and semiotics of jazz have little independent political purchase in contemporary China; the purist neo-scholasticisms that have animated debates in the Euro–US bloc – traditional versus modern, bop versus Dixieland, authenticity versus commercialism – simply do not have any leverage for national communities to whom, it might be said, we Westerners 'all look alike'. The West becomes the homogenised Other, a valuable reminder of the boundaries of our own cultural horizon. This is by no means a meagre point, for it has a reflexive significance for the study of jazz in general. As one prone to such extravagant enthusiasms, I can say that sometimes we become so engrossed in a research field that we lose scholarly perspective and become little imperialists ourselves. As scholars it is salutary, even intellectually necessary for the integrity and good faith of our work, to be reminded that our dominions have boundaries, and to have them documented and defined.

At an international conference organised by the 'Rhythm Changes' project in Amsterdam in 2011 a panel of highly regarded US jazz scholars participated in an earnest discussion on the ramifications for the future of jazz of the debate centred on the work of Wynton Marsalis at the Lincoln Center, New York. Without compromising collegiality or *politesse*, one of the UK delegates amiably made the point from the floor that no one present who was not from the United States really cared about this local spat. The most encompassing lesson that emerges from this collection is that all of the many insights they provide about jazz could have emerged only from a study of its diasporic forms. It is not only the meaning of jazz as the anthem of early twentieth-century modernity that is a creation of its diaspora; even some of the most effective incubators of the music, like jazz clubs and the earliest historiographies, analyses and articulations of jazz aesthetics, are primarily diasporic institutions. Yet even this term, 'diasporic', needs to be deconstructed. It is taken from the movement of populations from their homelands, an exodus. Some of the durable elements of the narrative of jazz are challenged here, not least that of the jazz diaspora as

Afterword: Conclusions **353**

a relentless one-way traffic from a US centre where the music came fully formed, out to the rest of the world, a collection of discrete peripheries which passively receive an imprint compromised by some kind of local cultural clumsiness.

In a survey of the global jazz diaspora over a decade ago, I argued that the centre-to-peripheries model implied by the etymology of 'diaspora' is misleading and that perhaps we should think instead of a 'polyspora' (Johnson 2002). The global migration of jazz has become multi-directional, challenging the one-dimensional one-way traffic – US-to-the-world – model that explicitly and still implicitly underpins both the discourse and, in the residual 'New York apprenticeship', the practices of jazz history. Jazz clubs in Catalonia, Madrid and Valencia were modelled on a club in Barcelona, which in turn was inspired not by a US model, but by the Hot Club de France, as mentioned above. In Perth, Australia, there is a jazz scene developing with strong Iranian inflections, introduced by the expatriate Iranian performer Tara Tiba (see Chapter 13). The politics that drove so many African-American jazz musicians to Europe (especially France and Scandinavia), where they significantly fostered local jazz scenes, also drove musicians from other countries to foreign destinations where they contributed to a distinctive syncretism: Tiba in Australia and Golnar Shahyar in Vienna carried in their luggage both US jazz practices and their own Iranian traditions – one of the 'unintended consequences' of various forms of repression in their homeland. In the history of jazz and its diaspora, the centre is now nowhere – or everywhere – and the diaspora cannot be mapped as lines radiating in one direction from a source, a one-way journey for a message of freedom.

It is a polyspora, a tangle of routes and gaps, criss-crossing and often doubling back. Its encounters with regimes inclined towards totalitarianism were not simply confrontations between two rigid monolithic discourses, but negotiations that could produce mutual accommodations, wary cohabitation, regional alliances, strategically circling around and even learning something new from each other. If the 'voice of America' was jazz, it did not just talk; it also listened. And if, as the cliché goes, 'jazz speaks all languages', it does not say the same thing in all of them.

References

Bergmeier, Horst J. B. and Rainer E. Lotz. 1997. *Hitler's Airwaves: The Inside Story of Nazi Radio Broadcasting and Propaganda Swing*. New Haven, CT, and London: Yale University Press.

Chan, Wilfred. 2014. 'Jazz Musician Kenny G Angers China with Hong Kong Protest Visit'. CNN, 24 October. Available at: http://edition.cnn.com/2014/10/23/world/asia/hong-kong-kenny-g-protest/, accessed 31 July 2015.

Dueck, Byron. 2014. 'Standard, Advantage, and Race in British Discourse about Jazz'. In Jason Toynbee, Catherine Tackley and Mark Doffman (eds), *Black British Jazz: Routes, Ownership and Performance*. Farnham: Ashgate: 199–220.

Hu, Fox. 2014. 'Hong Kong Democracy Protest Plan Worries Foreign Businesses'. *Bloomberg Business*, 11 June. Available at: www.bloomberg.com/news/articles/2014-06-11/hong-kong-democracy-protest-plan-draws-ire-of-foreign-businesses, accessed 18 March 2016.

Gilmour, John and Jill Stephenson. 2013. *Hitler's Scandinavian Legacy*. London: Bloomsbury.

Johnson, Bruce. 2000. *The Inaudible Music: Jazz, Gender and Australian Modernity*. Sydney: Currency Press.

Johnson, Bruce. 2002. 'The Jazz Diaspora'. In Mervyn Cooke and David Horn (eds), *The Cambridge Companion to Jazz*. Cambridge: Cambridge University Press: 33–54.

Johnson, Bruce. 2015. 'Cognitive Ecology: Music, Gesture and Cognition'. In Jadey O'Ragan and Toby Wren (eds), *Communities, Places and Ecologies: Proceedings of the 2013 IASPM Conference*: 155–163. Available at: www.dropbox.com/s/p49943716julss0/Communities%2C%20Places%2C%20Ecologies%20IASPMANZ%20Final.pdf?dl=0, accessed 18 March 2016.

Johnson, Bruce and Martin Cloonan. 2008. *Dark Side of the Tune: Popular Music and Violence*. Aldershot: Ashgate.

Lawrence, T. E. 2000 [1926]. *Seven Pillars of Wisdom: A Triumph*. London: The Folio Society.

'Occupy Central with Love and Peace'. N.d. Wikipedia. Available at: https://en.wikipedia.org/wiki/Occupy_Central_with_Love_and_Peace, accessed 18 March 2016.

'Pat Metheny on Kenny G'. 2008. YouTube, 18 July. Available at: https://www.youtube.com/watch?v=X-mjt1ypiF8, accessed 31 July 2015.

Starr, S. Frederick. 1983. *Red and Hot: The Fate of Jazz in the Soviet Union 1917–1980*, New York and Oxford: Oxford University Press.

INDEX

Note: Page numbers followed by 'f' refer to figures, followed by 'n' refer to notes and followed by 't' refer to tables.

actor-centred model of culture 72–3, 87–9
Aebersold, J. 284
Aelita jazz café 57
Africa, a place of imagined homecoming for US black musicians 280
Agur, U. 83, 84, 85
apartheid as a form of totalitarianism 242–3, 244, 270 *see also* South Africa, apartheid
Applebaum, A. 2, 3, 5, 6, 8
Arendt, H. 2, 3, 5, 7, 8, 96, 139, 242
Armstrong, L. 43, 54, 128, 141, 209; in Africa 279–80; in Spain 179–80
Australia: development of jazz 11, 12, 14–15, 17; Tara Tiba working in 318–19
authoritarian regimes as distinct from totalitarian regimes 159, 174–5

Ballantine, C. 11, 13, 16, 17, 21, 241, 244, 246, 252, 253, 269, 271, 275–6, 282, 285, 287n
Baresel, A. 15
bebop: failure in Finland 142–3; in South Africa 252, 268, 283, 285
Berendt, J.E. 123–4

biopolitics 160; of early Francoism, jazz in 165–8; Francoism and 160–2; of sound 345–6
Blue Notes 247, 251, 252, 256
Boddy-Evans, A. 269
Bogard Brothers 243–4
boogie-woogie 157, 164, 166, 177, 178, 179
Bourdieu, P. 271, 272, 278
Bril, I. 62
Brodacki, K. 102, 106, 107, 108, 109
Brom, G. 117, 120

Caetano, M. 219, 224, 225
Calado, R. 222, 224, 235n, 236n
Camacho, H. 185
Campbell, M. 282, 283
Catholic Church: Concordata de 1940 with Estado Novo 200; condemnation of jazz and modern dance 165–6, 166f, 168; moral panic in Portugal 200–2
censorship: China 329, 330, 331, 336; Estonia 76–7, 81; Iran 313, 317; Italy 43–4; Poland 100, 101, 105; Portugal 206, 212, 213, 221, 224–5, 226; South Africa 268, 273; Spain 158, 163, 165, 181, 184, 187
CETRA 42–3

356 Index

Chandler, D. 269–70
Charlie and his Orchestra 21, 347–8
China, contemporary 17, 325–43,
  350–2; Beijing International Jazz
  Festival 337; censorship 329, 330,
  331, 336; commercial, music as
  335–9, 350–2; Cultural Revolution
  329–30; *dakou* generation 337; *danwei*
  membership 331, 336; first appearance
  of jazz 325–6; freedom and
  improvisation of jazz in contrast to
  state ideology 334–5; *gangtai* 330,
  335–6; jazz as dangerous and harmful
  under Mao Zedong 329; Kenny G.
  350–1; marginalization of jazz scene
  326–7, 331–2, 333–4, 336, 337–9,
  339–40; market for jazz 337–9; music
  education at Beijing music institutes
  334, 339; national anthem of PRC
  328–9, 330; Nine Gates International
  Jazz Festival 338; 'open door policy'
  330–1; *People's Music Journal* 329;
  political tool, music as a 326, 327–32;
  'post-socialist' phase 335–9;
  publications 329; rebellious, music as
  332–5; record labels 331, 337; rock
  and jazz scene in Beijing 333, 334;
  Shanghai 328, 329; technology,
  unofficial channels for new music
  through 336; television 331;
  Tiananmen Square, music's response
  to 332–3; toleration of non-political
  music 333–4; totalitarian regimes of
  Europe influencing music agenda 328;
  venues for jazz 337, 338
chord scale theory 284
Cikhart, J. 126
Clube Universitario de Jazz 212, 218,
  222–4, 233
colonial: connections and jazz 17;
  ideology in Portugal 200, 206, 208
commercial: dilemma of jazz for
  totalitarian state 17–18; music in
  China 335–9, 350–2
Composers' Union, Soviet Union 53–6
concentration camps 3, 5, 8
Conover, W. 22, 60, 109, 110, 112n,
  127
cultural fields 271, 272–4, 277–8
Cultural History 4
cultural praxis, jazz as 121–30
Czechoslovakia in 1950s and 1960s
  114–35; before 1948 115–16;

associations 127–8; cement plant
  amateur jazz band 118; clubs 127;
  co-operation between state and
  members of jazz scene 117–18, 121,
  124, 130; as cultural praxis under state
  socialism 121–30; drastic break of
  1968 114, 121; festivals 127, 128;
  foreign jazz musicians 128; 'Golden
  Age' 119–21; Gustav Brom's band
  117, 120; Karel Krautgartner's state
  jazz bands 119–20; Karel Vlach's band
  116–17; live entertainment 116, 117,
  118, 121, 128, 129f; political power
  and 116–21; publications 117, 122–4,
  125–6t; radio and television
  broadcasting 124, 126–7; recordings
  117, 120; secret service 128–30;
  socialist discourse on jazz 118;
  Socialist Realism and 118, 119, 122;
  state control of touring jazz bands 18;
  state-supported band of Stalinist era
  117; underground practices of Stalinist
  era 117–18; venues 116, 119, 127,
  128, 129f; youth and 115–16, 118,
  119, 120, 122, 128
Czechoslovakian Youth Union 128

dance, jazz *see* jazz dance
Davis, M. 144, 226, 250
D'Efak, G. 185
Delgado, H. 221
Devroop, C. 268, 271, 273, 274
diaspora, jazz 349–50, 352–3; adaptability
  of 347–9; early 10–18, 23; increasing
  homogenisation of 22; and notion of
  jazz as invader culture 274–80
Donner, H.O. 140, 142
Doružka, L. 9, 116, 117, 118, 120–1,
  122, 123, 127, 130
Drum magazine 246, 249, 275

ECM label 147, 149, 277
EIAR (Ente Italiano Audizioni
  Radiofoniche): established 34–5, 39;
  increasing Fascistization of broadcasts
  43–4; 'Volgarizziamo la Radio'
  campaign 32–3, 35–41
Electric Jive archive 247–8, 249f, 250
Ellington, D. 43, 142, 209, 234, 308
Empire Students' House 223–4
Estonia, late Stalinist 69–93; actor-
  centred model of culture 72–3, 87–9;
  allowed–forbidden paradigm of jazz

69–70; American jazz, changing views on 74, 75, 77; anti-jazz practices, 'manoeuvring' around 77, 80–1, 82; censorship 76–7, 81; dance reform 74–5, 80; 'Estonianizing' of English lyrics 82; four spaces of jazz world 72–3, 87–9; institutional affiliations for non-professional collectives 79, 80; Jazz Orchestra of Estonian State Philharmonic (JOESP) 75–8, 77f, 87; late Stalinism, defining 71–2; literature review 70–1; Mickeys (jazz orchestra) 78–82, 87–8, 89; public/private divide 72–3; radio listening 85–6; radios as amplifiers 86; radios, confiscation of 82, 85; relaying music over telephone 86; repertoire approval by state 77, 81; *Sirp ja Vasar* articles 74–5, 87; source pluralism 73; Soviet paradox 76, 89; sovietization, defining 72; Swing Club 82–7, 88, 89; tape recording of music 86; *Zhdanovshchina* and disappearance of jazz from public realm 75, 89

Faria, M. de 201
Ferro, A. 197, 198–200; as director of state broadcaster EN 202–3; *The Jazz-Band Age* 198–9; *Salazar – The Man and his Work* 200
film: censorship in Spain 163, 165; introduction of 19; Italian national company 36; music in Portugal 220; synergy with radio in Italy 36–7; a vehicle for jazz dissemination 10, 97–8, 162, 163, 275
Finland in totalitarian shadow 12, 136–54, 348; 1950s–1970s, jazz 140–7; 1980s to present, jazz 147–50; American jazz 143–4, 145, 146, 148; bebop's failure 142–3; beginnings of jazz 16, 137; ECM label 147; festivals 141, 144; Finlandization 137–40; 'good neighbourliness' 136, 139, 140, 142–4; insularity 144, 145, 149; international relationships 144, 147–8, 149; jazz education 144; jazz festival 144; jazz musicians 140–1, 142, 143, 146, 148; jazz recordings 140, 143, 146, 147; Karelia 146, 147, 150; links with Eastern Europe 149; mood of Finnish jazz 141; national folk traditions in jazz 146, 148; Nordic

context, locating jazz in 149; 'nu-jazz' scene and move away from melancholia 148–9; radio broadcasts 143; refracted totalitarianism of 139, 140; relationship with Nazi Germany 137–8, 139, 145, 146–7; rock music 144, 146, 148; self-censorship 140; totalitarian shadow of Soviet Union 138–40, 141–4, 147; Treaty of Friendship, Co-operation and Mutual Assistance with the Soviet Union 141–2
folk music traditions and assimilation of jazz 13, 146, 148, 184–5
Foucault, M. 160, 161
France: attitudes to black jazz musicians 11, 16; development of jazz 10, 11, 13, 14; Hot Club de France 179, 206, 207, 347, 353
Friedrich, C.J. 2
Frumkin, B. 62
Futurist movement influencing diffusion of jazz in Italy 36–7

gangtai 335–6
Geertz, C. 4
gender, jazz and power relations 16–17
genre rebellion in music 271
Germany, Nazi: attitudes to black jazz musicians 11, 15; ban on music from US 20; Charlie and his Orchestra 21, 347–8; departure of jazz musicians 19, 20; development of jazz 9, 11, 12, 13, 15; Finland's relationship with 137–8, 139, 145, 146–7; hostility to jazz 18–19, 20–1; jazz at interface of ideology and popular culture 9, 10; jazz dilemma 21; radio 19, 347–8; state-controlled swing groups 21
ghoema 284–5
Gillespie, D. 308
Golha radio show, Iran 308–9
Golnaraqi, Hassan 307
Gómez-Figueroa 164
Goodman, Benny 58, 77, 209
Gorodinksi, V. 122, 125

Haavisto, J. 12, 16, 137, 138, 141, 142–3, 144, 146
Haden, C. 226–31, 345; arrest report 228–31; similarities with Kenny G. 351

358 Index

Hamm, C. 243, 244, 251, 252, 253, 255, 256, 268, 273
Hampton, L. 164, 181
Harvard Project 4
hegemony 269–70
Hightower, D. 182
Hitler, A. 7, 20, 98, 105, 138
Hot Club, Barcelona 162, 179, 181, 182, 188n, 207
Hot Club de France 179, 206, 207, 347, 353
Hot Club radio show, Portugal 205–6
Hot Clube de Portugal 210, 210f, 211–12, 211f, 220–1
Huang Yong 331, 335, 337, 338, 339
Huntley, I.B. 247, 250, 252
Huskisson, Y. 254, 255, 256

Ibrahim, A. 276, 281
improvisation: early jazz 12–13, 15; theory 284–5
instrumentation in jazz, early diasporic 12
International Cascais Jazz Festivals (1971–73) 226–33; Haden's arrest report 228–31; Haden's political protest at first 226–31; pamphlet at third 231–3, 232f
invader culture, jazz as 274–80
Iran 297–324, 349–50; Allied occupation 303–4; ambiguity of jazz 302–3, 306; beginnings of jazz 301; censorship 313, 317; Centre for the Preservation and Propagation of Iranian Music 311, 313; coup of 1953 and impact on cultural activity 299–300, 305–6, 307, 308; Crooner Vigen 306–7, 349; Dariush Safvat 311; dichotomy of public and private music in 1980s 315; discourse on Islamic and Iranian music 316; dissidents, dangers for 310, 312; drums, ban on 315, 316; exclusion of creative jazz from mainstream media 317, 318; Farzad Milani 315, 317–18; female jazz vocalists 313, 318–19; French post-war influences 305; *Golha* radio show 308–9; Golnar Shahyar 319; Hamzeh Yeganeh 314–16; Hassan Golnaraqi 307; Jamshid Sheibani 305; jazz contributing to mainstream pop 309; jazz fusion 309, 310–20; jazz in Armenia and 318,

320; Lloyd Miller 310–13, 317; Mahan Mirarab 319–20; Ministry of Culture and Islamic Guidance 317; modernities 298, 299; Mohammad Mosaddeq 299, 305–6; Mohammad Reza Shah 298–300, 303–4; *Motrebi* 308–9; music education, reintroduction of 316; musical influences growing up in 1980s 314–15; opposition to jazz 17; Otherness of jazz 303, 306, 349; Peter Soleimanipour 314; radio 303, 305, 308–9, 318; recording industry 303, 305; regime's failure to promote jazz 301, 306, 316, 318, 320; *ressentiment* in relationship with West 303; revolution, music following 300–1, 313–14; Reza Shah, dictatorial rule of 298–9, 302–3, 312; SAVAK (secret police) 300, 312; Tara Tiba and work in Australia 318–19; television 309, 317, 318; term 'jazz' applied to all genres of Western popular music 301, 305; US musicians touring 308; US relations with 298, 299–300, 301, 302, 304, 305, 306, 308, 312; venues for jazz 309; Western music, changing attitudes to 301–2, 304–5; Western 'tainting' of traditional music 308–9, 311, 313
isolation of individual 96
Italy, Fascist 31–49; Allied control of radio stations 44; American performers 37, 43; arrival of jazz 31–3; censorship 43–4; CETRA and production of Italian music 42–3; classical music, dictatorship's preference for 37–9, 41; competing viewpoints on jazz music 32–3, 42–3, 44; EIAR radio station established 34–5, 39; Futurist movement influencing diffusion of jazz 36–7; 'Industrial Model' of radio broadcasting 33–5; 'Italian way' of jazz 31, 37, 41, 42–4; radio, access to 35, 39, 41, 42; radio as a propaganda device 31, 34, 39, 41, 44; radio broadcasts, radical Fascistization of 43–4; 'radio-orchestras' 41, 43; radio technology 42; *Radiocorriere* 41, 42, 43; *Radiorario* 35, 37–8, 39, 41; record industry 36; SIP 35; synergy of radio, cinema and record industry 35–6; URI (Unione Radiofonica Italiana)

34, 36, 37, 39; 'Volgarizziamo la Radio' campaign 32–3, 35–41

Jamaican reggae 276
jazz: /totalitarian binary 345, 349, 352; adaptability to rigidity of totalitarianism 347–9; alignment with anti-totalitarianism 20–1; ambiguity as music of both American capitalism and oppressed African-Americans 9–10, 117, 151n, 231, 300, 302, 306; American–negroid association 15–16; defining 52; early diasporic 10–18, 349–50, 352–3; gender and 16–17; hostility of totalitarian states to 'contaminating' elements of 43, 101, 102, 103, 105, 109, 165, 177; improvisation, early 12–13, 15; increasing homogenisation of diasporic 22; instrumentation 12; internationalisation after Second World War 22; life as counter-imaginary to totalitarianism 346; modernity, music of 14–18, 186, 349; modernity, tensions at intersection of totalitarianism and jazz 23, 344–5; moral panic 15; musical migrations 17; political dynamics, local 16–18, 19–20; profile of early local performers 11–12; 'resistance' music of young in 1930s 19–20; resistant to totalitarian control 9, 345–6; during Second World War 20–2; as sound of freedom 9, 95, 111, 213, 234, 334; a threat to cultural gatekeepers 16–18; understanding 10–24; Wall Street Crash and end of initial phase 18–19
jazz cafés, Moscow 56–8
jazz dance 13–14; Catholic condemnation in Spain 165–8, 166f; concerns in Portugal 197–202; Estonia state reform of 80; Polish discussion on problems of light music and 107–8; a protest against political repression 346; Spain 162–6, 167–8, 169
jazz festivals: China 337, 338; Czechoslovakia 127, 128; Finland 141, 144; International Cascais Jazz Festivals (1971–73), Portugal 226–33; Moscow 58 61; Portugal 210, 212, 221, 222, 226–33; South Africa

286–7; Soviet Union 58–61; Spain 182, 183f
jazz improvisation theory 284–5
Jazz Orchestra of Estonian State Philharmonic (JOESP) 75–8, 77f, 87

Kajanová, Y. 115, 116, 119, 120, 122, 127, 130
Karmo, H. 82–3, 83–4, 85, 86
Katouzian, H. 298, 301–2
Kenny G. 350–1; similarities with Haden 351
Khrushchev, N. 51, 58, 59, 142
Kolakowski, L. 99, 104
Kombuis, K. 242
Kowal, R. 105
Kozyrev, J.P. 61, 62
Krautgartner, K. 117, 119
Krutob, H. 82, 83, 84, 85, 86
Kubik, G. 104, 290n
Kukko, S. 146

Lavery, J. 138, 139, 140, 142, 143, 144, 145, 147, 148, 151n
Linz, J.J. 2, 3, 4, 5, 7, 8, 9, 24, 159, 174, 175, 187n
Lloyd, C. 57, 60, 61, 128, 234
Loop, U. 84–5, 91n

Martin, D.-C. 276
Mascagni, P. 38–9
Matuszkiewicz, J.D. 106, 107, 110
May, B. 179
Mickeys (jazz group) 78–82, 87–8, 89
migration of jazz players 17; from Germany 19, 20; from Iran 318–19; from South Africa 246, 251, 256, 289n
Milani, F. 315, 317–18
Miller, G. 10, 21, 162
Miller, L. 310–13, 317
Mirarab, M. 319–20
modernity: jazz and totalitarianism representing tensions of 23, 344–5; jazz as music of 14–18, 186, 349; totalitarianism a phenomenon of 8–10
Mohammad Reza Shah 298–300, 303–4
Molodëzhnoe jazz café 56, 57, 58, 60
Moody, B. 120
Moradiellos, E. 175, 177, 178, 180, 181
moral panics 15, 200–1
Mosaddeq, M. 299, 305–6
Motrebi 308–9

360 Index

Mussolini, B. 8, 34, 36, 442; radio as a propaganda device 31, 34, 39, 41, 44

Naissoo, U. 83
Natal Playhouse, Durban 273
Navarro, V. 175
Nikpour, G.S. 309, 310
Nikzad, R. 310, 311, 313
Nogara 202

Os Excentricos do Ritmo (Rhythm Eccentrics) 203–4, 206, 208
Otherness of jazz 18, 23, 286, 303, 306, 349

Paakkunainen, P. 141, 146, 148
Peterson, B. 281
Poland, Stalinist 94–113; arts as an instrument of ideological struggle 103–4; censorship 100, 101, 105; Cold War ideology, complying with 94, 101, 102; Composers Convention 1949 and condemnation of jazz 101–3; defining Stalinist totalitarianism 95–6; development of new socialist intelligentsia 99–100; economy, centralization of 104–5; everyday life for jazz artists 105–10; history of jazz in 97–9; image of jazzmen 104, 108; institutionalization of jazz 97, 98, 99, 101, 104, 108–9; jazz goes underground 105–7; lifting ban on jazz music 108–9; myth of jazz as 'anti-system' 94–5, 104, 108, 110; period of Stalinist totalitarianism in Poland 96–7; political repression as a result of jazz participation 111; problems of light and dance music 107–8; radio listening 109–10; Socialist Realism and Stalinism 99–104, 110–11; state hostility to jazz 102, 103, 105, 109; unions and associations for musicians 101; YMCA clubs 105, 106
Polednák, I. 117, 118, 122, 123, 125, 127
Portugal, dictatorship 193–217; Anglo-American influences 198, 205, 208–12, 213, 220; Catholic Church and reactions to modern dance 200–2; censorship under Caetano 224–5, 226; censorship under Salazar 206, 212, 213, 221; Clube Universitario de Jazz 212, 218, 222–4, 233; colonial ideology of Estado Novo 200, 206, 208; colonial wars 219, 224, 225; colonial wars, protests over 226–33, 234; 'democratic mirage' 221–2; electoral fraud 221, 225; Empire Students' House 223–4, 233; EN broadcasting 202–3, 204, 205, 206; fascist type bottom-up organizations 196; Ferro's publications 198–200; film music 220; FNAT 196, 197, 203; foreign jazz musicians 209, 211–12, 234; Haden's political protest 226–31, 345; Hot Club radio show 205–6; Hot Clube de Portugal 210, 210f, 211–12, 211f, 220–1; Iberian Pact 204–5; International Cascais Jazz Festivals 226–33; jazz as an instrument of resistance 194–5, 226–33; jazz bands 198, 202, 203–4, 205, 206, 208; jazz festivals 210, 212, 221, 222, 226–33; *JAZZ* magazine 222–3; joins Marshall Plan 208, 210; Lisbon jazz scene in post-war era 220–2; Marcellism (1968–74) 224–6; mixing of local and African-American popular music 198; modern dance and dance music 198, 199, 200–2; National Union political party 196; Os Excentricos do Ritmo (Rhythm Eccentrics) 203–4, 206, 208; pamphlet distributed at Cascais jazz festival 231–3, 232f; Política do Espírito (Politics of the Spirit) 197; political constitution of 1933 196; post-war relations with US and Western democracies 208–9, 219–20; presidential election 1958 221; private events, jazz at 204; propaganda machine 194, 195–7, 213; publications 198–200, 222–3, 224; radicalization of student movements 225–6; RARET radio station 208–9; RCP radio station 206; 'real' jazz, Villas-Bonas and promotion of 205–8; recordings 198, 202, 206; Second World War and regime's shift in policy 204–5; state's reactions to jazz and modern dance 197–202; support for independence movement in colonies 223, 224; Swing 203, 204, 205, 213; US State Department involvement with cultural events 209–11

Index **361**

public/private divide of totalitarianism
72–3

radio 19, 347; access to, Italy 35, 39, 41,
42; Cold War propaganda from US
22, 60, 109, 127, 143, 151n, 348; in
Czechoslovakia 124, 126–7; EIAR,
Italy 32–3, 34–5, 35–41, 39, 43–4; in
Estonia 82, 85–6; in Finland 82; in
Germany 19, 347–8; *Gohla* radio
show, Iran 308–9; Hot Club radio
show, Portugal 205–6; 'Industrial
Model' of radio broadcasting, Italy
33–5; in Iran 303, 305, 308–9, 318;
listening, Poland 109–10; -orchestras,
Italy 41, 43; as a propaganda device,
Italy 31, 34, 39, 41, 44; radical
Fascistization of broadcasts, Italy 43–4;
Radio Bantu, South Africa 243,
251–6; RARET, Portugal 208–9;
RCP, Portugal 206; SABC
transcription archive 255–6; synergy
of radio, cinema and record industry,
Italy 35–6; technology, Italy 42; URI
(Unione Radiofonica Italiana) 34, 36,
37, 39; Voice of America 22, 60, 109,
127, 143, 151n, 348; 'Volgarizziamo
la Radio' campaign 32–3, 35–41;
Western impact behind Iron Curtian
127
Radiocorriere 41, 42, 43
Radiorario 35, 37–8, 39, 41
record labels: CETRA 42–3; in China
331, 337; ECM 147, 149, 277
resistance, jazz as music of 9, 19–20,
345–6; in China 332–5; myth in
Poland 94–5, 104, 108, 110; in
Portugal 194–5, 226–33; in South
Africa 281–5; in Spain 157, 158, 169
ressentiment 303
Reza Shah 298–9, 302–3, 312
Roberts, D. 2, 4, 5, 7, 8, 23, 176
rock music: blues influences in Spain
183–4, 186–7; Finnish jazz from
1950s to 1970s 144, 146, 148; and
jazz fusion in South Africa 243–4,
277; and jazz scene in Beijing 333,
334
Romantiki jazz café 56, 58
Rychkov, B. 62

Safvat, D. 311
Salazar – The Man and his Work 200

Salazar, A. de Oliveira 195, 208,
219, 224; relationship with Ferro
200
San Juan Evangelista College Dormitory
185
Sapozhnin, O. 76, 77
Sapozhnin, V. 76, 77, 78, 90n
Saulskii, J. 50, 63
saxophone 12, 80–1, 88, 117
Shahyar, G. 319
Sheibani, J. 305
Siniaia Ptitsa jazz café 57–8
Škvorecký, J. 20, 114, 115, 116, 123,
125, 126, 128, 130
Slim, M. 182
Socialist Realism: in Czechoslovakia
118, 119, 122; in Poland 99–104,
110–11
Sokorski, W. 94, 100–1, 102–3
Soleimanipour, P. 314
source pluralism 71, 73
South Africa, apartheid 241–66, 268–93;
Abdullah Ibrahim 276, 281; apartheid
as a form of totalitarianism 242–3,
244, 270; Bantu Education Act 1953
269; Bantu-Jazz 255; bebop 252, 268,
283, 285; black women in early jazz
groups 17; Blue Notes 247, 251, 252,
256; Bogard Brothers 243–4;
censorship 268, 273; contradictions to
Hamm's thesis on SABC and modern
jazz 252–6, 256–60; cultural fields
271, 272–4, 277–8; cultural hegemony
269–70; dance music 243, 255, 275–6;
diasporic currents and flows of jazz
274–80; diversity of jazz 243, 255;
Drum magazine 246, 249, 275; ECM
label 277; *Electric Jive* archive 247–8,
249f, 250; emulation of Hollywood
culture 275; exodus of musicians 246,
251, 256, 289n; films 275; formation
of republic 244; genre rebellion in
music 271; *ghoema* 284–5; Huskisson's
claims for Radio Bantu 255–6;
'invader culture', deconstructing view
of jazz as an 274–80; Jamaican reggae
practitioners 276; jazz festivals 286–7;
jazz improvisation theory 284–5; local
practice, jazz musicians drawing on
13, 250–1, 275–8; Louis Armstrong
visits Africa 279–80; mediation of jazz
in magnetic formats 278; music
education 282–5, 285–6; Natal

362 Index

Playhouse, Durban 273; Natives Land Act 1913 270; political context 242–4; Radio Bantu 243, 251–6; recording activity 247–51; recordings, inaccessibility of 247; resistance and jazz 281–5; rock and jazz fusion 243–4, 277; SABC archive of transcript recordings 255–6; Second World War and impact on jazz 21; state privileging of Western arts 285; State Theatre, Pretoria 272–3; Technikon Pretoria 282, 285, 286; townships, sharing of jazz in 250, 273, 282; uMsenge case study 256–60; 'universe of belief' 278; University of Natal 282, 285; urban black aspirations and jazz 16; US black music cultural links with 250, 279–80; venues for jazz 246, 254, 273, 282; Western arts, state privileging of 269, 272–4, 285

Soviet Union 50–66; American jazz musicians playing in 57; ban on saxophone 12; blurred boundaries between jazz scene and official organizers 56; Composers' Union discussion of jazz in 1962 53–6; continuing appeal of American jazz 57, 59–60; difficulties in defining totalitarianism and jazz 51–3; dilemma of how to control jazz 17–18, 50, 55–6, 60, 62–3, 139; early jazz in 52; efforts to develop Soviet jazz in contrast to US jazz 50, 52, 56, 60, 63; endless changes in policy on jazz 9–10, 142; integration of jazz into official cultural discourse 59–60; jazz at interface of ideology and popular culture 9–10; jazz cafés in Moscow 56–8; jazz education 61–2; jazz festivals in Moscow 58–61; jazz musicians 57, 58, 60; KGB infiltration of jazz scene 58; Khrushchev's attack on jazz 59; music agenda influence on China's 'mass music' 328; paradoxical nature of society 76, 89; propaganda, notion of 54; remuneration for jazz café musicians 58; totalitarian shadow over Finland 138–40, 141–4, 147; US jazz in favour in Second World War 21; Willis Conover visits Moscow 60–1

Spain, Francoist: African-American culture inspiring avant-garde movement 180; Afro-Cuban and Latin American music and dances 167; American cinema a vehicle for jazz dissemination 163; American jazz musicians performing in 164, 179–80, 181, 182; arrival of 'real' blues 178–81; authoritarian dictatorship 159–60, 174–5; biopolitics and Francoism 160–2; biopolitics of early Francoism, jazz in 165–8; black American music, official attitudes to 165, 168, 176–7, 181, 186; blues expansion during late Francoism 181–5; blues festivals 182, 183f; blues in post-war era 177–8; blues-related bands 183–4; boogie-woogie 157, 164, 166, 177, 178, 179; Broonzy May's concert 179; Catholic church condemnation of jazz and modern dance 165–8, 166f; censorship 158, 163, 165, 181, 184, 187; changing audience for blues 186–7; Civil War, jazz during 162; concerns about purity of Spanish 'race' 165; dance and popular music, jazz as 162–6, 169; dance halls 162, 163, 167–8; economic development and cultural liberalization policies 181–2; escapism of swing and boogie-woogie 177, 178; folk music movement in overt political opposition 184–5; Hilario Camacho 185; Hot Club, Barcelona 162, 179, 181, 182, 188n, 207; *The House of the Rising Sun* 183; identification with fascism 157, 165; Jamboree 182; jazz clubs 178–9, 181, 182, 185; Louis Armstrong visits 179–80; modernization process, blues plays an important role in 186; music in new articulation of Spanish identity 157–8; post-war climate of friendly relations with US 158, 180–1, 186; publications with conflicting discourses on jazz and black music 177–8; recordings 167, 178, 184–5; rock and pop, blues influence on 183–4, 186–7; San Juan Evangelista College Dormitory 185; self-censorship 184; singer–songwriters and appropriation of the blues 185; Sister Rosetta Tharpe 180; subversive role of jazz 157, 158, 169; swing 157, 162, 163–4, 167, 177, 178; Whisky Jazz Club, Madrid 182; youth socialization 161–2

Spooner, B. 303–4

Stalinist totalitarianism, defining 95–6

Starr, S.F. 10, 11, 12, 14, 15, 17, 21, 52, 55, 117, 139, 142, 143, 147, 165, 348–9

State Theatre, Pretoria 272–3

stereotype of jazz outsider 104, 346

Swidler, Ann 73

swing: in Germany 21; in Portugal 203, 204, 205, 213; in Spain 157, 162, 163–4, 167, 177, 178

Swing Club, Estonia 82–7, 88, 89

Technikon Pretoria 282, 285, 286

television: in China 331; in Czechoslovakia 127; in Iran 309, 317, 318

terror 3, 139

Tharpe, Sister Rosetta 180

The House of the Rising Sun 183

The Jazz-Band Age 198–9

Tiba, T. 318–19

totalism 7, 242

totalitarianism 109; /jazz binary 345, 349, 352; adaptability of jazz to rigidity of 347–9; apartheid as a form of 242–3, 244, 270; Arendt's analysis 3, 5, 7; constants in discourse on 7; contemporary studies 5–7; defining Stalinist 95–6; as distinct from authoritarianism 159, 174–5; Friedrich's list of structural features 2–3; hostility to 'contaminating' elements of jazz 43, 101, 102, 103, 105, 109, 165, 177; jazz aligns with anti- 20–1; jazz as counter-imaginary to 346; and jazz representing tensions of modernity 23, 344–5; jazz resistant to total control of 9, 345–6; limitations of top-down model of 3–5; as phenomenon of modernity 8–10; public/private divide 72–3; refracted 139, 140; and terror 3, 139; understanding of 2–10, 51; widening definition 5–7

Treufeldt, U. 79, 80, 81, 82

Truhlár, A. 115, 123, 126, 127, 128

Tsfasman, A. 50, 52, 54, 55, 59, 62, 63

uMsenge case study 256–60

United States: ambiguous position of jazz 9–10, 116, 151n, 231, 300, 302, 306; critique of centre-to-peripheries model of jazz 353; cultural links of black music with Africa 279–80; Estonian views on American jazz 74, 75, 77; expansion of hegemony after Second World War 22; Finland, American jazz in 143–4, 145, 146, 148; government sponsoring of jazz tours and events abroad 22, 128, 151n, 181, 209–11, 234; jazz as a cultural weapon 22, 151n; jazz musicians touring abroad 37, 43, 57, 60–1, 144, 151n, 164, 179–80, 181, 182; Portugal, jazz influences in 198, 205, 208–12, 213, 220; Portuguese post-war relations with 208–9, 219–20; radio for Cold War propaganda purposes 22, 60, 109, 127, 143, 151n, 348; relations with Iran 298, 299–300, 301, 302, 304, 305, 306, 308, 312; Soviet effort to develop jazz in contrast to jazz from 50, 52, 56, 60, 63; Soviet Union, continuing appeal of American jazz to 57, 59–60; Spanish official attitudes to American jazz 165, 168, 176–7, 181, 186; Spanish post-war relations 158, 180–1, 186; troops in Europe 21, 32, 44, 74, 180–1, 184, 205; Voice of America 22, 60, 109, 127, 143, 151n, 348

'universe of belief' 278

University of Natal 282, 285

van Heerden, A. 284–5

Velebný, K. 123, 126, 127

Ventosa, J. 187

venues for jazz 13–14; in China 337, 338; Clube Universitario de Jazz, Portugal 212, 218, 222–4, 233; in Czechoslovakia 116, 119, 127, 128, 129f; Hot Club, Barcelona 162, 179, 181, 182, 188n, 207; Hot Club de France 179, 206, 207, 347, 353; Hot Clube de Portugal 210, 210f, 211–12, 211f, 220–1; in Iran 309; Moscow jazz cafés 56–8; in South Africa 246, 254, 273, 282; in Spain 162, 178–9, 181, 182, 185; YMCA clubs, Poland 105, 106

364 Index

Vesala, E. 141, 145, 146, 147, 148, 149
Vigen, C. 306–7, 349
Villas-Boas, L.: founding of Hot Clube de Portugal 220–1; Hot Club radio show 205–6; move away from commercial jazz to real jazz 205–8; organizer of International Cascais Jazz Festivals 226
Vlach, K. 116–17
Vogel, E.T. 116, 127
Voice of America 22, 60, 109, 127, 143, 151n, 348

'Volgarizziamo la Radio' ('Radio to the People') campaign 32–3, 35–41

Ward, C. 71–2
Wein, G. 210–11
Westberg, C. 312
Whisky Jazz Club, Madrid 182
women: fear of jazz and modern 16–17, 166–7; jazz vocalists emigrate from Iran 318–19; swing in Spain and 163–4

Yeganeh, H. 314–16